The Genealogical Directory

with
British Local History

2000

Edited & Compiled
by
Robert Blatchford and Geoffrey Heslop

Editorial

This is the fourth edition of the Genealogical Services Directory. It sees a major expansion into Local History sources and Societies because family history is inextricably linked with local history. This expansion has been made in association with The British Association for Local History.

Again we have tried to make this book the essential and prime source of information for Family and Local Historians, Genealogists and Researchers. To do this the listings have been increased again and provide about 5000 essential addresses for the reader. Some of the new listings have been incorporated following suggestions from readers in previous years.

Nearly every organisation listed in this edition has been contacted and asked to confirm that our information is correct with reply paid envelopes for reply. We are grateful to those organisations who took the time to reply but we must express disappointment that there were some who did not.

The listings have as far as possible continued to take account of the counties as they were prior to 1974. However it is now twenty five years since that reorganisation. There was further reorganisation in 1996. We have reached the stage where some new local unitary authorities and other organisations wish to be included in the lists in their own right.

We hope you, the reader, continues to find this book useful and a ready source of information. We have listened to our readers' suggestions and have included new additional information. If you have suggestions for the inclusion of further sources in future editions please let us know as we are always happy to receive them. We have been asked again if we would include the listings of researchers' individual interests and our reply has to be the same each time that this area is adequately catered for in the Genealogical Research Directory each year.

This edition has many new articles from prominent researchers, historians and genealogists which adds enormously to the Directory and we gratefully acknowledge their contibutions. The breadth of topics will hopefully enable each reader to find items of interest to them.

Robert Blatchford & Geoffery Heslop

Contents

7　　Three Generations of Ladies - Three Changes of Surname
9　　A Respectable Trade?
13　　I Never Thought of That! - Useful tips from the Miss Marple of Family History
17　　Borderlanders
21　　The Civilian Roll of Honour
23　　Paupers or Pensioner - an introduction to the new Poor Law 1834 - 1929
25　　Caring for Your Family Records
27　　The Conservation & Restoration of Family Documents
31　　Genetics & Genealogy
33　　British Education Records
37　　Illustrate Your Family History
41　　Maps - an Essential Aid for Family & Local Historians
45　　Miscellaneous Sources for Family & Local History
53　　Gretna Green Marriages
55　　Palaeography for Family Historians
182　　Hearth Tax Returns

Military History

167　　Family History at The Imperial War Museum
171　　Soldiers Died in the Great War
173　　Register of Man Fallen at Gallipoli 1915 - 1916
174　　National Inventory of War Memorials
175　　The Commonwealth War Graves Commission
177　　Why DO People Visit Battlefields ...?

235　　Local History Section in association with the BALH
237　　Family History & Local History - You can't have one without the other
238　　Brave New World
239　　Metting the Ancestors
240　　Dead Language
241　　The Tingle Factor
242　　BBC History 2000
　　　　plus Local History Listings

Listings

Family History Societies　　212
Superintendent Registrars　　257
Archives & Record Offices　　271
Museums & Military Museums　　294
Libraries　　319
LDS Family History Centres　　343
Cemeteries & Crematoria　　345

plus Articles about

100	The Suffolk Record Office
119	Glamorgan Family History Society
115	Estate Records at The National Library of Wales
131	The Family History Scene in Aberdeen - and beyond
137	Maritime Dundee
149	State library of New South Wales, Australia
153	New Zealand - treasures await...
157	Using Local Directories in Western Canada
189	Genealogy Software
191	Internet Genealogy
213	Hillingdon Family History Society
271	Clothing the Bones - Future Access to Minor Records
274	The Central Index of Decrees Absolute
291	The Land Registry
294	Beamish - The Development of an Open Air Museum
319	Libraries & Genealogical Research
322	Let's get FAMILIA!
342	*Rhyming Relations* - Genealogy in Verse

Regular Features

Starting Your Family History	**77**
The Chapman Codes	**59**
The Public Record Office	**63**
The Family Record Centre	**67**
The National Library of Wales	**11**
The National Archives of Scotland	**123**
The General Register Office for Scotland	**125**
The National Archives of Ireland	**140**
The Irish Genealogical Project	**141**
Dublin City Archives	**143**
The Public Record Office of Northern Ireland	**146**
Probate Records	**338**

tracing the birth parents of adopted persons in England and Wales

federation of FAMILY HISTORY SOCIETIES

research services: a code of practice for family historians

federation of FAMILY HISTORY SOCIETIES

the strays clearing house and the national strays index

federation of FAMILY HISTORY SOCIETIES

in search of your soldier ancestors

federation of FAMILY HISTORY SOCIETIES

you and your record office: a code of practice for family historians using county record offices

federation of FAMILY HISTORY SOCIETIES

new to family history: can we help?

federation of FAMILY HISTORY SOCIETIES

For Information contact The Federation of Family History Societies,
The Benson Room, Birmingham and Midland Institute, Margaret Street, Birmingham B3 3BS.
For Publications (*over 150 titles now in stock*) price list and catalogue available on application from Federation of Family History Publications, 2-4 Killer Street, Ramsbottom, Bury, Lancs BL0 9BZ, Telephone: 01706 824254.
Email at: admin@ffhs.org.uk or at: info@ffhs.org.uk

Three generations of ladies - three changes of surname ...

The Cover Photographs for The Genealogical Services Directory 2000

The photographs on the cover are of my mother, her mother, and her mother!

Three generations of ladies - three changes of surname and thus a challenge to any family history enthusiast who is not merely pursuing one particular name.

Sarah STOCKDALE was baptised on 28th January 1849 at Norton (Malton) North

Yorkshire, England. She was the youngest of six children of Simeon and Sarah Stockdale. He was described as a wheelwright/ Joiner in the 1851 census. I believe Sarah went 'into service' because on 4th October 1875 she married George Atkinson at Doncaster and their address was CARR HOUSE, - a one time small mansion and later fever hospital. George was a joiner. They moved to York and produced six children. Having studied books on costume and hairstyles I think this photograph must have been taken about 1870. It is the only picture we have of Sarah who died shortly after the birth of her last child.

Grandmas love to tell you about their lives.....

Martha Stockdale ATKINSON was born on 20th December 1884 at York and was the

fourth of six children. She became a children's nurse and met her husband Thomas Arthur JACKSON when she was employed in Whitby, North Yorkshire.

"He saw this pretty young nursemaid, pushing a pram down the pier and fell in love with her." They married in Whitby on 5th June 1910 and raised five children. Thomas Arthur Jackson was a hairdresser and had businesses variously at Whitby, Stokesley, Harrogate and Great Ayton. Martha led an active life. She loved sport and excelled at tennis. Martha assisted her husband in his business and became a great grandmother. She died in her 90th year.

Dorothy JACKSON was the second eldest child of Martha and Thomas Arthur. She was born on 9th January 1913 at Whitby and became a hairdresser.
She married John James TURNER in Stokesley, North Yorkshire and then had one daughter. Dorothy is now a great grandmother.

I still have many sources of research to tap into for details about Sarah and Martha. Dorothy is now in her 87th year and is therefore a wonderful primary source of information - not only with regard to her own life but those of her parents, siblings, aunts and uncles and the times they have lived through. Even she did not realise that Martha's middle name "STOCKDALE" had been her grandmother's maiden name.

Do not be discouraged from pursuing the female lines on your family trees. Grandmas love to tell you about their lives and 'listening now' could save you hours of sometimes fruitless searching.

Elizabeth Blatchford

The UK's Big Telephone Number Change 2000
New area codes and local numbers for six places
From now, you can use the new area codes with the new local numbers to make a national call. To call new local numbers, you must also use the new area code until 22nd April 2000. After this date you will be able to use the new eight figure local call number without the area code.

City	Existing Area Code:	New Code & Number:
Coventry	01203 XXXXXX	(024) 76XX XXXX
Cardiff	01222 XXXXXX	(029) 20XX XXXX
Southampton	01703 XXXXXX	(023) 80XX XXXX
Portsmouth	01705 XXX XXX	(023) 92XX XXXX
London	0171 XXX XXXX	(020) 7XXX XXXX
London	0181 XXX XXXX	(020) 8XXX XXXX
Local Call	0345 XXXXXX	0845 7XXXXXX

Northern Ireland
Antrim

Place	Existing	New	Place	Existing	New
Ballycastle	012657 XXXXX	(028) 207X XXXX	Londonderry	01504 2XXXXX	(028) 712X XXXX
Ballymena	01266 3XXXXX	(028) 253X XXXX	Londonderry	01504 3XXXXX	(028) 713X XXXX
Ballymena	01266 4XXXXX	(028) 254X XXXX	Londonderry	01504 4XXXXX	(028) 714X XXXX
Ballymena	01266 6XXXXX	(028) 256X XXXX	Londonderry	01504 6XXXXX	(028) 716X XXXX
Ballymena	01266 8XXXXX	(028) 258X XXXX	Londonderry	01504 8XXXXX	(028) 718X XXXX
Ballymena	01266 XXXXX	(028) 256X XXXX	Limavady	015047 XXXXX	(028) 777X XXXX
Ballymoney	012656 XXXXX	(028) 276X XXXX	Magherafelt	01648 2XXXXX	(028) 792X XXXX
Kilrea	012665 XXXXX	(028) 295X XXXX	Magherafelt	01648 3XXXXX	(028) 793X XXXX
Larne	01574 XXXXXX	(028) 28XX XXXX	Magherafelt	01648 4XXXXX	(028) 794X XXXX
Martinstown	012667 XXXXX	(028) 217X XXXX	Magherafelt	01648 5XXXXX	(028) 795X XXXX

Armagh

Place	Existing	New	Place	Existing	New
			Magherafelt	01648 XXXXX	(028) 796X XXXX
Armagh	01861 XXXXXX	(028) 37XX XXXX	**Fermanagh**		
Belfast	01693 XXXXX	(028) 302X XXXX	Enniskillen	01365 3XXXXX	(028) 663X XXXX
Newry	01693 2XXXXX	(028) 302X XXXX	Enniskillen	01365 4XXXXX	(028) 664X XXXX
Newry	01693 3XXXXX	(028) 303X XXXX	Kesh	013656 XXXXX	(028) 686X XXXX
Newry	01693 6XXXXX	(028) 306X XXXX	Lisnaskea	013657 XXXXX	(028) 677X XXXX
Portadown	01762 XXXXXX	(028) 38XX XXXX	**Down**		

Belfast

Place	Existing	New	Place	Existing	New
			Banbridge	018206 XXXXX	(028) 406X XXXX
Antrim	01849 XXXXXX	(028) 94XX XXXX	Downpatrick	01396 5XXXXX	(028) 445X XXXX
Bangor	01247 2XXXXX	(028) 912X XXXX	Downpatrick	01396 6XXXXX	(028) 446X XXXX
Bangor	01247 4XXXXX	(028) 914X XXXX	Downpatrick	01396 8XXXXX	(028) 448X XXXX
Bangor	01247 5XXXXX	(028) 915X XXXX	Kircubbin	012477 XXXXX	(028) 427X XXXX
Bangor	01247 8XXXXX	(028) 918X XXXX	Newcastle	013967 XXXXX	(028) 437X XXXX
Ballyclare	01960 XXXXXX	(028) 93XX XXXX	Rostrevor	016937 XXXXX	(028) 417X XXXX
Belfast City	01232 XXXXXX	(028) 90XX XXXX	**Tyrone**		
Lisburn	01846 XXXXXX	(028) 92XX XXXX	Ballygawley	016625 XXXXX	(028) 855X XXXX
Saintfield	01238 XXXXXX	(028) 97XX XXXX	Carrickmore	016627 XXXXX	(028) 807X XXXX

Londonderry

Place	Existing	New	Place	Existing	New
			Cookstown	016487 XXXXX	(028) 867X XXXX
Coleraine	01265 2XXXXX	(028) 702X XXXX	Dungannon	01868 XXXXX	(028) 87XX XXXX
Coleraine	01265 3XXXXX	(028) 703X XXXX	Fivemiletown	013655 XXXXX	(028) 895X XXXX
Coleraine	01265 4XXXXX	(028) 704X XXXX	Newtownstewart	016626 XXXXX	(028) 816X XXXX
Coleraine	01265 5XXXXX	(028) 705X XXXX	Omagh	01662 2XXXXX	(028) 822X XXXX
Coleraine	01265 8XXXXX	(028) 708X XXXX	Omagh	01662 4XXXXX	(028) 824X XXXX
Coleraine	01265 XXXXX	(028) 703X XXXX	Omagh	01662 8XXXXX	(028) 828X XXXX

Email and Internet or Web Addresses
Email and Web addresses shown in this book have been notified to us by the Organisation or advertiser.
Unlike a normal postal address these addresses are subject to change, sometimes fairly frequently, especially since the introduction of Free Internet Service Providers (e.g. Freeserve).
In the case of businesses Email forwarding and Website transfer are usually provided by links to the original address. This does not always happen and the only solution is to use the various search engines
available on the internet.
Many of the Browsers and Search engines will accept an address beginning
with either http:// or www.

A Respectable Trade? Bristol & Transatlantic Slavery
Sue Giles
Bristol Museums & Art Gallery

On 6 March 1999, the City Museum & Art Gallery in Bristol opened a new temporary exhibition. It was the biggest and the most sensitive exhibition the museum had done for many years, and no one was sure what the reaction would be. The subject was Bristol's role in the slave trade of the 18th century, a subject everyone knew about (or thought they did) but which the City never officially acknowledged.

The exhibition was the culmination of a programme designed to redress this problem. What caused this change in the official attitude to the slave trade? It started with the Festival of the Sea in 1996, a four-day celebration of Bristol's maritime history which surrounded the launch of the replica of John Cabot's Mathew. This was a commercial festival, not run by the City although with its full support. For a festival dedicated to maritime history, set in the historic harbour of Bristol, the Festival was strangely quiet on the subject of the slave trade. It was there in the Festival events, but not prominent. This caused some disquiet and resentment.

The following year, Bristol City Council organised the quincentennial celebrations of Cabot's voyage to Newfoundland. It was hoped that this would be an inclusive event, unlike the Festival of the Sea, and local groups were encouraged to take part. Two groups were not interested: artists and the black community. Some perceived Cabot's voyage as the beginning of colonisation and exploitation, and Cabot as the man who set the slave trade in motion. The Council decided to address the issue, and established a working group to look at how the City could acknowledge its slaving history. The Bristol Slave Trade Action Group included City Councillors, Council officers, individuals and representatives of local black organisations. The Group established a series of aims, including a small display in The Georgian House (to set this period house in the context of its builder, a rich sugar plantation owner and sugar trader), a trail around sites in the centre of the city connected with the slave trade, a major temporary exhibition and a permanent gallery.

'A Respectable Trade?' was the major temporary exhibition. The Museum established a community advisory group, both

RUN away the 7th Inſtant, from Capt. Tho. Eaton, of the Prince William, a NEGRO MAN, named *Minge*, of a good black Complexion, ſmooth Face; wears a black Wig; had on two ſhort blue Waiſtcoats, and brown Breeches; about 5 Foot 5 Inches high, his Legs a little bent, his upper Teeth ſcagg'd and broken, has a *Cut* on his *Right Wriſt*, which ſtands up in a Bunch. He ſpeaks pretty good Engliſh; has been in and out of this City about eight Years. Whoever will deliver the ſaid Black into the Poſſeſſion of his Maſter, Capt. Eaton aforeſaid, ſhall have a Guinea Reward.

N. B. All Perſons are hereby forbid entertaining the ſaid Black at their Peril: And if he will return to his Duty, he will be kindly received, and have his Oſſences pardoned.

Advertisement for a runaway slave
From Felix Farley's Bristol Journal
15th November 1746

self-selected via public meetings and invited, and an academic advisory group to work with the exhibition team. This was the first time that the staff had worked with outside advisers on such a big project. It was a steep learning curve, given the timescale and the importance of the project, but it could not have happened without the advisers. Their input allowed us to avoid many errors and pitfalls, not least in the language used.

One of the aims of the exhibition was to try and humanise the story. It is very easy to look at the slave trade in terms of slaves and owners, without ever seeing them as people. We were telling the story of Bristol, so we were able to look at individual slave traders, captains, sailors, brass makers (a major trade item), African slave traders and enslaved Africans. We had portraits of some of the Bristolians involved, like the sugar merchant John Pinney and the brass manufacturer Thomas Hale. We had the will of Edward Mapham, a sailor, written before he joined a slaving voyage, and the account of the voyages of several Bristol ships. We

At the *EXCHANGE* COFFEE-HOUSE, On SATURDAY the 9th of *Auguſt*, at Twelve o'Clock,

25 Puncheons of very Fine R U M,
Juſt imported from JAMAICA.

One Puncheon in a Lot——Samples to be ſeen at the Offices of
W. GAYNER, and R. LANCASHIRE, *Brokers*.

To be Sold,

A Negroe Boy, about ten Years old,
He has had the SMALL-POX.

For Particulars enquire at the *Printing-Office* in *Small-Street*.

ALL Perſons who have any Demands on the ESTATE of the late WILLIAM THOMAS, at the Lamb and Lark, in *Keynſham*, in the County of *Somerſet*, are deſir'd to bring in their reſpective Bills immediately, as the Widow is going to leave off Buſineſs:——And all Perſons indebted to the ſaid Eſtate, are deſired to pay the ſame forthwith to the ſaid Widow THOMAS.

Advertisement for a sale of a slave
from Felix Farley's Bristol Journal
2nd August 1760

had the letter from a West African slave trader, Duke Ephraim, berating his trading partner James Rogers of Bristol for the fact that his captain had kidnapped two of the Duke's men and taken them as slaves. We took the famous plan of a ship's slave deck packed with slaves, and put over the slaves' bodies their own accounts of how they were enslaved. We borrowed portraits and objects from the descendants of the slave-trading Henry Bright and slave-owning James Tobin, and had the spoken words, through headphones, of slave owners, the agents in Antigua of slave trader Isaac Hobhouse and Abolitionists like John Wesley.

The enslaved Africans, the 'cargo' of the trade, were never as well documented as the white traders involved in slavery. In Bristol we have the famous grave of an African slave, one Scipio Africanus (a good Classical name) who died in 1720 aged 18. We borrowed a portrait of an African who may, but equally may not, be Olaudah Equiano, the slave who bought his own freedom and campaigned for the Abolition movement. There are references to many African slaves and freemen in Bristol: some came here when their owners returned home from their sugar plantations and brought one or two of their house slaves with them, others were bought at a discount by the ships' officers as a perk of their job. The church registers for births, marriages and deaths often qualify entries with a comment like 'a black woman'. There are advertisements in the local papers for runaway slaves, but only two for the sale of a slave. Most sales would be by private agreement.

There are many myths about the slave trade in Bristol. The most repeated is that slaves were brought in to the docks, kept in Redcliffe Caves and sold by public auction on Blackboy Hill. The fact that there is no evidence for auctions in the city, that Blackboy Hill was not so named until the 19th century, that all the shipping records show that the vast majority of the slaves bought in Africa were taken direct to the Americas and sold there (assuming they survived the Middle Passage across the Atlantic), that there was no profit in selling slaves here and taking them to the plantations, and no demand for African labour here in Britain, cannot change the myths.

Page from the accounts book of the *Africa* showing the equal shares of the 8 owners in the outset costs of £5692.16s.0d

The slave trade was risky but profitable. In the early years, in the late 17th and early 18th centuries, people speak of 100% profits on a voyage, although there is little documentary evidence to support such claims. But perhaps 50% was possible: that could represent £2000 profit on an outlay of £4,000. Multiply the figures by anything between 50 and 80 to get an idea of the equivalent values today, and you see why merchants were willing to take the risks involved in the trade. In 1723, the *Joseph and Anna*, owned by Abraham Hooke & Co, sailed for West Africa. She brought 260 Africans to Montserrat to be sold by Nathaniel Webb, co-owner of the voyage. It was reported that the ship had made a 'golden voyage which hath very much enrichen'd the former owners.' Other ships might not be so profitable: the *Marlborough* was lost in 1752 to a revolt of the slaves on board, the *Bristol* was taken as a prize by the French in 1758 during the Seven Years War, the *Phoenix* sank off the coast of Calabar in 1782, with the loss of 430 slaves and 22 of the crew. James Rogers, the biggest but least efficient Bristol slave trader, went bankrupt in 1793.

Until 1698, trade with Africa was reserved, by Royal charter, to the Royal African Company, a company of London merchants. The merchants in provincial ports campaigned long and hard to have this monopoly lifted, and in 1698 the trade was opened to all. Bristol, as the second port in the country after London, had been involved in the lobby against the RAC through the local merchants, organised as the Society of Merchant Venturers. Early in 1698, the *Beginning*, the first

Bristol ship to trade legally in African slaves, left Bristol for Africa and delivered a cargo of slaves to Jamaica. There is evidence for Bristol merchants breaking the London monopoly from the 1670s.

The Great Circuit or triangular trade worked by carrying full cargoes on each leg of the voyage: manufactured goods to Africa for trade, slaves from Africa to the Americas, and slave-produced goods, like sugar, tobacco, rum, indigo, rice and cotton, from the plantations back to the home port. Each leg of the voyage, in ideal circumstances, made a profit for the owners. Another of the aims of the exhibition was to show how the slave trade spread out into the city and beyond. It was not just the merchants who were involved: the people who worked in the brass industry, and the coal miners who supplied the brass works, and the carpenters who built and repaired ships, and the bakers who supplied bread, and those employed in the sugar refining industry and manufacturers further afield in Manchester, Birmingham, London, were all involved, knowingly or unknowingly. Most of the labourers in the industries supplying the slave trade would have no ethical stance on their work, and most would not be able to afford the luxury of an ethical position. The idea in the exhibition was not to spread the blame for the slave trade across the whole population of 18th century Bristol, but to show how the trade underpinned so much of the life of the city.

Headstone erected over the grave of Scipio Africanus, in Henbury churchyard, a few miles outside Bristol

A great deal was invested in a slaving voyage. The return was also large. Bristol merchants sent out some 2,108 slaving ventures between 1698 and 1807, the period of legal trading. The majority came home safely and profitably. Those profits, about 9% of the outset costs by the end of the 18th century, were shared amongst the owners. The results are to be seen in and around Bristol: fine town buildings, banks, country estates, the railway infrastructure and the canal system. Slave traders and sugar merchants had money to invest, and that money helped the industrial revolution. It can be argued how much this wealth contributed directly to the industrial revolution, but it certainly helped the growth of capitalism and commercial institutions which facilitated industrialisation. When Abolition came in British

STANSFIELD & Cᵒˢ
Super-Fine Tobacco,
Castle-Street BRISTOL

Trade card for a tobacconist showing African slaves in tobacco leaf costume territories in 1833, it was not due just to humanitarian feeling, but also to the realisation that slavery was not an economic method of production and the offer of substantial compensation for slave owners.

The exhibition was extremely successful: 161,000 visitors came to see it, it generated a lot of publicity locally, nationally and internationally, and produced over 2,000 comments from visitors on the comments board. We have had a huge number of enquiries arising from it, and a few fascinating discoveries. The most interesting was a local woman who contacted us: her great great grandfather was a runaway slave who had escaped from an American plantation via the Underground Railway, and ended up living in Bristol.

He married a local woman, and one of their daughters married an Irishman. African people have been living in Britain since the days of the Roman invasion, Queen Elizabeth decided there were too many and ordered them out of England, many more came during the period of the transatlantic slave trade, when it was fashionable to have a black servant. Like the runaway slave, many married into the local population, and many British people would be surprised to find that they have black ancestry.

The exhibition closed in September 1999, but a modified version is set to open in April 2000 in the Bristol Industrial Museum. A permanent gallery will be included in the future Museum of Bristol.

Further Reading

Peter Fryer *Staying Power: A History of Black People in Britain*, Pluto Press 1985
Donald Jones *Bristol's Sugar trade and Refining Industry*, Bristol Historical Association 1996
Pip Jones and Rita Youseph *The Black Population of Bristol in the Eighteenth Century*, Bristol Historical Association 1994
C M McInnes Brisol and the Slave Trade in *Bristol in the Eighteenth Century* edited by Patrick McGrath, David & Charles 1972
Peter Marshall *The Anti Slave Trade Movement in Bristol*, Bristol Historical Association 1996
Kenneth Morgan *Bristol and the Atlantic Economy in the Eighteenth Century*, Cambridge University Press 1993
Richard Pares *A West India Fortune*, Longmans 1950
David Richardson *Bristol, Africa & the Eighteenth Century Slave Trade to America* (4 vols), Bristol Record Society Publications 1986- 1996
David Richardson *The Bristol Slave traders, a Collective Portrait*, Bristol Historical Association 1996

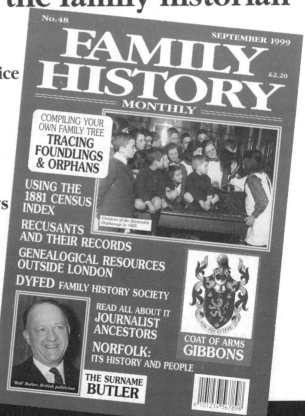

I NEVER THOUGHT OF THAT ! Useful tips from the Miss Marple of Family History

Anne Batchelor

Have you just slammed into your first genealogical brick wall? Or perhaps you have been banging your head on one for months — or even years? Worry not —we all have experience of this frustrating aspect of family research. Take heart! The longer you have been battering away at your own particular wall, the more wonderful and indescribably thrilling is the moment when all is revealed. It is a cross between winning the Lottery and scaling Everest! Here are a few thoughts and ideas to encourage you.

Become a Detective

Think like Sherlock Holmes. Perhaps the person you are seeking so desperately never existed. For about five years John Buckley had been seeking his own father's birth registration. He knew his father's name — John Arthur Dennis Buckley — , his birth date and details of his career in the Hussars and his work at Tetley's Brewery. John looked after the old man in his later years, yet the birth of John Arthur Dennis Buckley seemed never to have been registered.

Together John and I sought the answer to the puzzle for a further two years. We tried all the usual sources, including his Army record, whose date of birth tallied with that which John knew, and Tetley's pension records —the same date. We tried to find medical records, driving licence records even Romany records, for Buckley proved to be a common Romany name.

As there was no J.A.D.Buckley on the St. Cath's index of births, we listed all the John Buckleys, Arthur Buckleys and Dennis Buckleys — hundreds of them —but which might be our man? John's father never spoke about his parents nor any brothers or sisters. "Strange!" I thought. Nor did he speak about life anywhere but Leeds — though John seemed to remember him once saying, "When I was a boy in Hove ————" but again and when questioned, the old man had clammed up. None of the boys we had found on the St. Cath's index was registered at Hove or anywhere near it. To add to our confusion, J.A.D.Buckley did not always use his full name. On his marriage certificate he was Arthur Buckley, on his son's birth certificate John Arthur Dennis Buckley, and on the back of a photograph of himself in uniform (found in his wallet after his death) was written," From Dennis, with love."

I spent hours pondering the reason for these discrepancies in his name, trying to think like Sherlock Holmes. Perhaps he was one of twins — John Arthur and Dennis. Perhaps he was an adopted child, born John Arthur Dennis and adopted by a Buckley family? Perhaps he was the illegitimate child of a Miss Dennis who later married a Mr. Buckley? This way madness lies! I followed up all of these, and got nowhere. Eventually John decided to abandon the search, but like a dog with a bone I would not let go! In the old man's wallet was just one other photograph. It showed a wedding group — groom (not J.A.D.B.) in WWI uniform, a young bride, two sets of parents, some friends and, at the front, a group of children including a little girl with her arm around a dog.

Remembering the remark the old man had made about Hove, I decided to send a copy to the local Hove newspaper. Not knowing their name or address, I simply wrote on the envelope, "THE EDITOR, THE LARGEST LOCAL NEWSPAPER IN HOVE, HOVE, SUSSEX." I put

a 1st class stamp on to show that I meant business, and no return address on the back. I knew that it would be a nuisance for the Royal Mail to have to open it, read it and return it. They would find it easier and quicker to deliver it as requested! With the photograph went a cry for help. "Does anyone recognise this picture?" After all, any group photograph is usually reprinted for all the people in it. Someone out there must recognise our picture.

Eventually came the response we had longed for, in the form of a letter from a lady whose mother was the little girl holding the dog. It was the wedding of a Percy Bayford, she told us. "And I can tell you why you can't find the birth registration of John Arthur Dennis Buckley — he was not really John Arthur Dennis Buckley at all. He was William Norris Bayford! When his beloved brother Percy "joined up", the under—aged William joined up, too, changing his name so that his father would not be able to find him and bring him back home." A similar non—existent person was James Kelly, who on applying for work in the Civil Service declared on oath that — "I am the Joseph Theophilus Batchelor named on the enclosed baptism record." So you would never find this chap on the St. Cath's index under K for Kelly, but under B for Batchelor! No wonder family historians tear their hair out in frustration!.

Take Every Piece of Genealogical Information with a Large Piece of Salt

"Your great—grandma, Eliza Foskett, came from Luton where they made straw hats," said my Uncle Fred. No she didn't! I discovered that she was a Berkhamsted straw—plaiter who sold her plait at Hitchen market to the Luton straw hat makers.

"We are descended from the Duke of Wellington," a family historian was told. The poor man eagerly researched his family only to discover that a recent ancestor kept a pub — the Duke of Wellington!

"We came from Scotland, according to the census," said one lady. Yes, but it was Scotland near Harrogate, Yorkshire. There is also a Botany Bay south of Potters Bar, Herts. Think what confusion that could cause!

"A member of our family shot her lover on the steps of the Stock Exchange," a friend of mine was told. The newspapers, however, revealed that he was a member of the Stock Exchange, and she stabbed him outside the Post Office!

This family history research is like a mad game of Chinese Whispers, so proceed with caution!

Don't feel guilty

Sometimes a family historian will confess to me, with a guilty air, that they have wasted time going off down some irrelevant sideroad because it was so interesting. Don't worry! Your research is valid, whatever your reason for doing it, and there is no rule which says you can't waste time. Just enjoy it!

My own weakness in that area is odd names. I just can't resist recording Marfity Snipt (not a lady out of a Dickens story but a girl who worked in the scullery of the Earl of Dorset); Gertie Giggle and her brothers Nathan, Herbert and Rufus who all died as babies; Anastasia Galilee, a rag sorter; dear old Happy Nappy Stork from an East Yorkshire register, and perhaps my favourite, Mr. Holroyd from

Castleford Gas Works, who christened his children Zerah, Ziha, Zeuriah, Zelha, Zillah, Zibiah — and Joe! Whenever we record these names, for whatever reason, then that person is, for a moment, remembered and not lost in the mists of time. That to me is good enough reason to "waste time" on them.

Be Prepared
When researching, always take an extra pair of reading glasses, just in case. Mind you, that is not always foolproof. I once sat down at a reader in Luton and the lense fell out of my spectacles. Smugly I put on my spare pair, switched on — and the bulb blew!

When visiting your roots, take not one but two cameras. On my first visit to Chesham, seeking my Batchelor roots, my whole film turned out black and blank —apart from the last two pictures, taken from my flat window to use up the film! Now I never go without a back—up second camera. The small throw—away ones are ideal.

Tips for Your Trips
Visiting the place where your ancestors lived is magic — it is real time—travel. I can recommend calling at the local post—office and pub, commenting on the weather and saying, "It's much colder / hotter / wetter than in Leeds." "You're from Leeds?" they respond. "What are you doing here? On holiday?" It works like a charm, poor souls, and you then have a captive audience whom you can question about anyone of your name still in the area.

When calling at the local church, note the list of flower ladies or sidesmen on the notice—board. You might find one of your people still around. Then sign the visitors' book, adding "Researching the Bloggs family." Red ink makes your entry stand out! Always get in touch with the churchwarden rather than the vicar. Vicars tend to be newcomers to an area. Churchwardens are usually born and bred there, and know all the local gossip. As a last resort you could send a small donation for flowers for the church in memory of your ancestors, asking that it be mentioned in the notices on Sunday. You never know, the name might ring a bell for one of the parishoners. Never miss a trick, as my mother would say.

Advertise!
The more people you tell about your research, the more success you will have. Use Teletext's Lost Touch and Service Pals on Channel 4, or similar contact services. Through Teletext I found my mother a cousin she had never met and three little girls she was nanny to in 1933. Service Pals brought me a man who was a few yards behind my uncle when he was killed by a landmine in Italy in 1944.

Remember it was a newspaper that helped me solve the mystery of John Arthur Dennis Buckley? Don't send an advertisement to the Personal column — it costs money and few people read it. Instead write to the Editor, and ask him to use your cry for help as a news item. That is free! It is useful to develop a grovelling style of letter—writing for these moments. I recommend the Batchelor approach — "Dear Sir or Madam, I know you must be awfully busy, and

letters like mine must be a great nuisance, but I would be so very grateful if you could possibly find the time, when you are not too busy 'It works a treat!

The British Legion magazine has a contact section, and through it I found an ex—landgirl who knew my late uncle in 1943. She was able to give me a lovely word—picture of him. The elderly person's magazine,"Yours", has a similar page. Through it I found a "girl", now in her eighties, who was at the Godfrey Walker Waifs and Strays Home in York with my mother in 1921. I was then able to arrange a meeting for the two elderly "girls". Such a happy day! Remember, family research does not have to take you back hundreds of years to be fascinating. The recent past, too, has its delights.

Use your Imagination
Have you lost your Richard Nelson? Perhaps when he gave his details to the Parish Clerk or census man he had a very bad cold, or adenoids. He might have been recorded as Dellson. Try holding your nose and saying your family name out loud. It might give you an idea to try.

Lost your Thomas Snellson? Try Thomas Nelson. Can't find James Snowball? Try James Noble. Remember, many names were recorded as heard. Want a cheap way of advertising your missing person? You don't need the Internet. I made a label from a cornflake packet and a safety pin — "HELP! EDWARD HERBERT TREVOR JUKES aged 88. DO YOU KNOW HIM ?" I wore it pinned to my bosom at the London Family History Fair. A lady from the Middlesex stall mentioned it to her friend when she got home and BINGO! She knew him!

Seeking a family memorial or grave but don't know which church? Photocopy an eye—catching appeal for help and send it to local libraries and churches, for their noticeboards, to newspapers (for publication), to CROs — even pubs in the area might display one for you. Saturation bombing pays off. The more people you tell, the more likely your success.

Learn to think sideways. Look for school and college records. You can get wonderful stories from some school log books, and career details from university records. Try occupational lists, such as railwaymen or cordwainers, as well as military records, street directories and newspaper archives. The latter will contain reports of accidents, weddings,school nativity plays, trials and inquests —in fact a detailed picture of life in your ancestor's area. There is a wealth of wonderful information out there, just waiting for you. Think how your family lived, and use your imagination to track down their records and put flesh on their bones.

Above all - Enjoy Yourself!
Don't get worried or agitated if your research is frustrating. Think positive! You are doing valuable social research, whatever the problems. If it were too easy, at the push of a button, where would be the thrill of the long—sought discovery? It is the friutless hours —weeks — years which give you that moment of elation when you cry, ' Yes! At last! Gotcha! ' So have fun. Happy hunting —and enjoy!

Anne Batchelor was born in Leeds following a period with the Leeds Library service she trained as a teacher. For the next 30 years Anne taught in local Secondary Schools. Following early retirement in 1987 she began to pursue her new interest in family history. She made a film with the BBC about her family research for the "Timewatch" series. She teaches Family History and is a regular broadcaster on local radio and Radio 4. She is in great demand as a speaker around the country. She has written three books and is now working on her fourth.

"A Batchelor's Delight" published by Highgate Publication (Beverley) Ltd in 1990 ISBN 0-948929-40-5 Price £5.85
"My Gallant Hussar" published by Highgate Publication (Beverley) Ltd in 1993 ISBN 0-948929-79-0 Price £4.50
    - both are out of print but available through Inter Library Loan
"My Name is Frances" published by Highgate Publication (Beverley) Ltd in 1998 ISBN 0-948929-45-6
    £8.95 + £1.00 p & p. Available from the Author - Anne Batchelor, 34 Barncroft Heights, Leeds LS14 1HP

BORDERLANDERS
Gabriel Alington

A story is told of a wealthy landowner who for many years allowed his tenant farmers to graze their stock on the pasture of the neighbouring estate. When the estate changed hands the new owner protested; the sheep and cattle must be removed. There was no response. He protested again; he did so repeatedly. His well-established neighbour refused to comply, encouraging his farmers, militant by now, to encroach more widely and obtrusively. Eventually the newcomer instructed his servants to plant hundreds of candles in the long ditch bordering the estate, which, when lit after dark, appeared as a great line of people overlooking the disputed land. What else could it be but a mighty force of soldiers ready to attack?

The tenant farmers with their families fled in alarm so that their landlord was forced to concede defeat. The stock was withdrawn from the trespassed land.

The story is true. It happened seven centuries ago. The estate in question belonged to the diocese of Hereford, or so it was claimed though in fact the boundary at that time was indefinite. The new landlord was the recently appointed bishop, Thomas Cantilupe, a lawyer and efficient administrator; his long-standing neighbour was Peter Corbet, one of the powerful Marcher barons, who owned extensive lands along the borders of Wales.

The Corbets, like a number of other families, the Harleys, Verduns, de Lacys, de Clares, still live and farm in that part of the country. Yet though deep-rooted - after almost a millenium - exceptionally so - with family trees set out with enviable certainty, historically they were the intruders, the outcomers.

Roughly two hundred years earlier these families had been part of the Norman conquest, invaders seizing and occupying land, building strongholds, digging themselves in. They needed to; they were hardly welcome, either by the English, the Anglo Saxons, or when they reached the west, by the Welsh, the Celtic people who inhabited the mountainous country beyond.

It was the fiery Welshmen who, far more than the English, refused to take this invasion lying down, who put up the fiercest opposition and who, long after the English had accepted their Norman overlords, continued to rebel. Indeed, even after 1282, when Edward I, defeating Llywelyn ap Gryffud, the last of the Welsh princes, took the whole principality under his control, the rebels kept up their guerilla type attacks. Emerging from the hills they would carry out raids on castles, villages and monasteries, plundering and killing ruthlessly. Early in the 15th century, during the reign of Henry IV, Owain Glyndwr succeeded in uniting the Welsh into an organised force. The threat of an uprising brought new life to Hereford Castle, which since 1282 had been allowed to fall into disrepair and which was then hastily refortifed. The work was justified; the castle was attacked. But soon afterwards, in 1416, Owain Glyndwr disappeared, literally, mysteriously. The Welsh rebellion lost momentum; it died away.

Hereford Castle, the earliest to be mentioned in the Anglo Saxon Chronicle, was built before the conquest by Ralph, Count of Vexin, a nephew of Edward the Confessor. When, in about 1055, Ralph, reputedly an arrogant and overbearing character, was soundly defeated by the combined forces of the English and French, the castle was destroyed, the city

The tenant farmers with their families fled in alarm ...

wrecked and burned. Soon after the conquest the castle was rebuilt by William I's great henchman, William FitzOsbern. FitzOsbern, who was Earl of Hereford, was a powerful and effective administrator. In only five years - he was killed in Flanders in 1071 - he strengthened the defences along the Welsh border with a chain of castles; Clifford, Longtown, Kilpeck and many more. He also redesigned and expanded the city, building a new settlement and market place to the norh of the old Saxon defences, the area now called High Town, to encourage trade.

After FitzOsbern's death, his son, Roger, was involved in a plot to depose the king. The plot failed but the FitzOsbern estates including Hereford Castle were taken over by the crown.

Another of FitzOsbern's key strongholds, Wigmore Castle, some 20 miles to the north of Hereford, was granted to Ralph de Mortimer. The Mortimers, also of Norman origin, were soon to become one of the most powerful families not only in the borderlands but in the whole of England. During the Barons' War Roger Mortimer, a leading supporter of Simon de Montfort, was instrumental in organising Prince Edward's escape from Hereford Castle, where he was imprisoned. The Prince, at that stage on de Montfort's side, took refuge in Wigmore Castle.

In the early 14th century, another Roger Mortimer, the first Earl of March, became involved with Queen Isabella, the French wife of Edward II. Together they plotted to get rid of the King. In 1326 Roger, imprisoned in the Tower for armed rebellion, managed to escape to France where Isabella was waiting. With a small force of men they landed in England, captured the King and eventually had him murdered in Berkeley Castle. For four years Roger and the Queen, openly lovers, ruled the country. And then in 1330 Edward III ascended the throne; Roger was arrested and hanged at Tyburn.

A century later, when the 5th earl of March died without an heir, his estates went to his nephew the Duke of York, one of the leading players in the Wars of the Roses. Richard was killed at the Battle of Wakefield but a few weeks later his 19 year old son, the future Edward IV, met the Lancastrians at Mortimer's Cross near Leominster. After a long and bloody battle, Edward was victorious. The battle is commemorated on a large stone outside the Monument Inn on the edge of the village of Kingsland.

Another king who left a significant imprint on the landscape of the region lived many centuries earlier during the time known as the Dark Ages, the period between the Roman occupation and the Norman invasion, when Anglo-Saxon England was divided into seven autonimous kingdoms each with its own government and king. The Marches were part of Mercia, the most powerful kingdom, a vast area stretching from East Anglia to Wales. The Welsh, mainly Celts driven out by Saxon tribes who had swept across most of the region in the 5th century, were generally hostile, constantly mounting cross border attacks, devastating property, plundering stock. To counter this and to define his border, Offa, the 8th century king of Mercia, organised the building of a dyke, an earthbank roughly 238 kilometres long that stretched from Prestatyn in north Wales to Sedbury in Gloucestershire. Alongside the dyke, which took between

ten and twelve years to construct, was a ditch roughly two metres deep. Although twelve centuries later most of the dyke has disappeared long stretches can still be traced - and walked; most of the dyke is marked with footpath signs. And here and there, notably near the village church at Lyonshall, you find not only the ditch but a definite earthbank. Such discoveries bring the past to life.

Offa's kingship was flawed by his involvement in the murder of Ethelbert, the young king of East Anglia, who is said to have been buried in the original Hereford Cathedral.

For by that time Christianity was spreading throughout England, churches were built, monasteries founded. One of the most beautiful in the region must be Dore Abbey, the church belonging to the Cistercian monastery in the Golden Valley, a beautiful part of west Herefordshire.

The monastery was founded in the spring of 1147 and through the years that followed the abbey and the monastery buildings grew in size and prosperity. By the time it was completed the Abbey was more cathedral than church with an immensely long nave and square ended altar, both requirements of the Cistercian order. The Abbey overall was roughly 80 metres long with either a tower or pointed spire. Research has revealed that the outer walls were almost certainly limewashed so that, vast and impressive in its green valley, the entire building was gleaming white.

It was John Scudamore's great grandson ....

But we cannot be sure for in 1537, with the Dissolution of the Monasteries, Dore was closed down. The land and titles were granted to John Scudamore of Holme Lacy who, at the sale of goods which took place afterwards, bought most of the building materials from the Abbey, the refectory, the chapter house. the dormitory, all the iron, glass, timber , all that was worth having, for what, even then, was a derisory sum. The once beautiful Abbey, desecrated and abandoned, lay open to thieves, to wind and rain.

It was John Scudamore's great grandson, Viscount Scudamore, also John, who in 1632 began the restoration of the Abbey. Or rather part of it. The nave and all the surrounding buildings were no more than crumbling ruins so he concentrated on the eastern arm of the buding, constructing a new wall at the western end. John Scudamore and his wife Elizabeth, were friends of Archbishop William Laud, who often came to stay and may well have given advice on some aspects of the restoration. It was probably due to Laud's influence that stained glass was set into the east window, a highly controversial decision at that time. Laud, a generation older, was a father figure to the Scudamores helping them to come to terms with the deaths of five of their infant children. And it was probably Laud who intimted to John Scudamore that his ownership of what had once been church land, therefore God's land, was a sin, so that John cme to believe that losing his infants was divine punishment. The rebuilding of Dore Abbey was, therefore, an act of expiation.

The restoration, undertaken by the finest craftsmen, was superbly done, and at considerable expense. When on John Scudamore's birthday in 1634, the reconsecration took place, he must have felt justly proud. Perhaps he also felt forgiven. The Scudamore family have a long history in the region. During the Civil War Barnabas Scudamore fought bravely for the Royalists at Hereford. Today their name is also associated with horse racing.

Another distinguished family deep roots in the Marches are

the Harleys, who have lived at Brampton Bryan in south Shropshire since the Conquest. Brampton Bryan castle, the ruins of which are in the middle of the village, was one of the chain of border strongholds built by the Normans. There is a saying that between Brampton Bryan and Aberystwyth you can only walk on Harley land.

One particularly colourful Harley was Lady Brilliana, who was born about 1600 at the Brill in the Netherlands, where her father was lieutenant governor. Having married Sir Robert Harley, Brilliana settled at Brampton Bryan castle and provided him with numerous children. She was deeply religious and distinctly puritanical, indeed outspokenly so and during the Civil War she made no secret of her Parliamentarian sympathies though the Marches were staunchly Royalist. As a result in 1643 Brampton Bryan Castle was beseiged for six weeks by Royalist troops led by Sir William Lingen. Lady Brilliana was a celebrated letter writer. She wrote copiously to her friends and as they grew up to her many children, long, descriptive letters which give a vivid picture of her life. More than two hundred of her lettes are preserved at Brampton Bryan by the present Harleys.

The late Christopher Harley had a great knowledge and love of trees, so much so the he was known as 'Trees' Harley. Another long established Marcher family also much involved with trees and plants are the Banks of Hergest, who are descendants of the famous botanist, Sir Joseph Banks.

In 1768 Joseph Banks, aged 25, set sail from Plymouth with Captain James Cook in the Endeavour. During their three year voyage right round the world, they spent many months Australia and New Zealand, where Banks discovered many previously unknown species of animals and plants. He catalogued all he found and, though due to conditions, he was unable to bring back many specimens, he did manage to introduce a number of new plants into Europe. The genus of trees and shrubs (about 50 species) known as Banksia, are named after him. Returning from a second expedition with Cook in the Resolution, he was widely acclaimed, knighted and made President of the Royal Society, a post he held from 1778 for 42 years. Which must be some kind of a record.

It was in about 1814 that Richard Banks, having married a Miss Davies from Herefordshire, moved to the small town of Kington in the north of the county. At first they lived in Bridge Street at the bottom of the town but in 1840 his son, Richard William Banks, inherited Ridgebourne, a fine house set on high ground close to Hergest Ridge. It was Richard William's son, Wiliam Hartland Banks, who in 1896, created Hergest Gardens. The acres of skilfully landscaped gardens have become well known for they are filled with a great variety of unusual trees and shrubs, many first introduced by Joseph Banks.

The present generation, Laurence and Elizabeth Banks, open the gardens to the public and to wander round, along walks and arbours, is endlessly delightful and interesting.

And sometimes through the trees you catch sight of the countryside beyond, the farmland stretching to the distant hills. If you stand a moment and look at it, an unhurried look so that you take it in, so that it gets to you, then perhaps you will be able to appreciate the words of some one who knew the Marches well.

It was Sir Edward Elgar, who, while he was composing his Introduction and Allegro, described his music as inspired by 'my sweet borderlands'.

Family Tree Services

30 Eastfield Road :Peterborough : Cambs. : PE1 4AN
Tel & Fax : 01733 890458

9.30 am to 3 p.m. & 4.30 p.m. to 7 p.m. Monday to Thursday
& 9.30 am to 3 p.m. Fridays:
All other times answer phone / fax

GRO : Certificate you supply full reference (AS GIVEN IN THE INDEX)	£8.50
Certificate with full date & details	£9.00
Certificate including up to 3 year search	£10.00
Certificate including up to 5 year search	£13.50
Certificate including up to 10 year search	£18.50
Refund if unsuccessful UK or Airmail	£6.50
Census FULL PRO film number, folio, page, Surname (e.g. RG 11/2020 f.12 p 2 Smith)	£3.00
Census known address includes photo copy (road or street number)	£5.00
Street search includes copy (no number)	£6.00
Small village search includes copy	£7.50
Township search includes copy	£8.50
Additional copies of census returns at same time	£0.70
1881 CENSUS INDEX first two sheets per surname / county	£4.50
Additional copies at 70p per frame(at same time)	£0.70 by airmail 80p
Wills up to 5 year search	£8.50
Pre 1858 PCC up to 5 year search	£10.00

a £5.00 refund if no document found

Airmail unless a price is stated, please add 50p to the price.

International Genealogical Index print - outs(a A4 sheet)	20p
RootSeeker print - outs	30p
GRO index surname extractions B,D & M print - outs	45p

USED Microfiche readers	collect from	£35.00
Hand Held readers	including UK P&P	£11.00
Briefcase second user	collect from	£100.00
Microfilm reader		POA

For a FREE Booklet detailing ALL our services telephone or fax.

The Commonwealth War Graves Commission Civilian Roll of Honour
Peter Francis Commonwealth War Graves Commission

In 1938, the Imperial, now Commonwealth, War Graves Commission unveiled the Australian Memorial at Villers-Bretonneux. It was the last of the Great War memorials to be completed from the war that was to end all wars and yet within a year the Second World War had started and the Commission was called upon to prepare for a new harvest of death. This second catastrophe of the twentieth century was a very different conflict to the one that had taken place only twenty or so years previously. The war was one of quick movement - the German Blitzkrieg sweeping all before it and forcing the Commission to temporarily relinquish control of the cemeteries and memorials in occupied Europe.

With the conquest of mainland Europe complete, Hitler's forces concentrated their efforts on the invasion of the United Kingdom. In order to invade, Germany had first to achieve total air superiority and so began the Battle of Britain and the large-scale bombing of airfields, factories and later in an attempt to smash the morale of the British people, cities. Distinctions between soldiers and non-combatants were non-existent. The phrase Total War was coined to represent the fact that civilian populations as well as front line troops were now considered targets.

On 7 September 1940 the first major air raid on a British city was carried out by the Luftwaffe. The Commission's founder, Fabian Ware, witnessed first hand the deaths of women, children, firemen and air-raid wardens. This new and horrifying war was impacting on communities like never before. Surely, he reasoned, each casualty deserved a fitting commemoration? Soon London itself was a target of the Blitz. Ware decided to act and wrote to the Prime Minister, Winston Churchill, on 18 September, urging the commemoration of those civilians killed by enemy action. In his words, "The deliberate slaughter of civilians was creating a new category of normal war casualties. Theirs should be counted an equal sacrifice".

Churchill, who had so successfully argued for the Commission's principle of equality of treatment for the war dead while Chairman of the Commission during the parliamentary debates on commemoration of the early 1920s, had no objection. In fact, he believed that civilian deaths might well outnumber military casualties - fortunately, he was not proved correct.

In January 1941, the Commission began to keep records of all civilian deaths caused by enemy action and its Royal Charters were adjusted to give it the necessary powers to do so. The biggest single obstacle to this task was obtaining the names and addresses of those killed. The information provided by the authorities, like the Registrar General, was not always complete and often did not include the addresses of next of kin. In February 1941, to encourage a greater flow of information and further publicise the commemoration of civilians, Ware decided to make a tour of the hard-hit areas. During his tour he enlisted the help of mayors and local authorities and the information provided to the Commission greatly improved. In November 1941, he made a further appeal on national radio and in the press for help and the records began to take shape - the Commission already had over 18,000 individuals recorded.

However, Ware was not satisfied with the mere recording of names at the Commission's headquarters. As the Commission would have no responsibility for the graves of civilians, Ware suggested to the Dean of Westminster in January 1942 that the names should be inscribed on a Roll of Honour which might be placed in the Warrior's Chapel of the Abbey. "The symbolic significance of ...the admission of these civilian dead to the adjacency and companionship with the Unknown Soldier would...give a right inspiration." The Dean readily agreed.

In December 1942 the first typed lists, leather bound in three volumes, were deposited for safekeeping at Westminster. The volumes were not put on display until after the war because it was believed that if the extent of civilian casualties were known, it might damage the morale of the nation. It was not until 1956 that the completed volumes of the Civilian Roll of Honour were handed to the Dean of Westminster by the Duke of Gloucester. Today, there are six volumes with over 66,000 names recorded. In a fitting tribute to those commemorated, the books are still on display to the public at the Abbey. A new page of the Civilian Roll of Honour is turned every day and so unfolds 66,000 tragic stories - the sudden death of a pensioner aged one hundred or of an infant a few hours old, of 163 people killed in an instant when a V2 rocket fell on Woolworth's at New Cross, and of the 1,500 dead of Malta.

What information does the Civilian Roll of Honour have? The casualty details available include the person's name, age, date of death, last known address and the particulars of the next of kin. The entries are structured along the lines of the old Borough system and then alphabetically by surname. Just one moving example reads: Betty Francis, Civilian War Dead. Died 9 April 1941, Aged 2. Daughter of Emily and the late Tom Francis of Clevedon Road, Balsall Heath. County Borough of Birmingham. The civilian records, like the military records, are still updated to this day. Amendments made on the computerised system are later added to the leather bound volumes at the Abbey twice a year by a member of the Commissionís records department. In this way, that 'equal sacrifice' is preserved for future generations.

For the family historian, all of this information is available from the Commission's enquiries department in Maidenhead and the Debt of Honour Register at www.cwgc.org The Civilian Roll of Honour is a highly moving tribute not only to the many innocents who had their lives brutally cut short by war but to the bravery of services like the Fire Brigade and Ambulance crews who risked their lives to save others. The Commonwealth War Graves Commission keeps faith with them all, ensuring that

Their Name Liveth For Evermore.

Paupers or Pensioner
- an introduction to the New Poor Law, 1834-1929
Simon Fowler

By the 1830s it was clear that the old system of poor relief, which had its origins in the reign of Elizabeth I was breaking down. It could not cope with the unemployment created by the rapid growth in the population taking place as the result of the industrial revolution or the economic dislocation caused first by the Napoleonic Wars and then by peacetime conditions which followed. At the same time an almost universal belief arose amongst the middle classes that the poor should be self-sufficient where ever possible. Samuel Smiles, the greatest exponent of self-help (the phrase comes from a title of one of this books) argued that 'any class of men that lives from hand to mouth will ever be an inferior class. They will necessarily remain, impotent and helpless, hanging onto the skirts of society, the sport of time and season.'

The Poor Law Amendment Act, 1834 set up some 636 Poor Law Unions throughout England and Wales under elected boards of guardians. Each Union had to establish a workhouse wherein the poor of the parish would reside. Workhouses would house the poor of the community, either those who could not work - the senile and bastard children -or those who would not - vagrants and the so-called "able-bodied poor". In return for basic board and lodging inmates were set to work, where ever possible, breaking stones and picking oakum (that is unpicking tarred rope). Conditions in the workhouse were designed to be a deterrent encouraging the poor to fend for themselves rather than become a burden on the rates. Those who refused to enter the workhouse would loose their right to assistance. The conditions inside the house would be such as to deter all but the most desperate.

Conditions in the workhouse were designed to be a deterrent .....

By the end of the 1830s most parishes had been combined into unions and had established a local workhouse. This was achieved relatively peacefully in southern England, but in the industrial areas of the north, and rural East Anglia, there were considerable protests. Richard Oastler, a well known radical, for example wrote in the Northern Star in March 1838 that:

> The real object of [the New Poor Law]...is to lower wages and punish poverty as a crime. Remember also that children and parents are lying frequently in the same Bastille without seeing one another or knowing the other's fate.

Where the new system was peacefully set up the benefits, to the taxpayer at least, was immediately apparent. The Poor Law Guardians of Richmond, Surrey wrote in a petition to Parliament in 1841 that they had:

> No hesitation in stating it is the result of their experience in this union, that it has been eminently beneficial as a means of reclaiming many of the labouring classes from indolent and vicious habits, encouraging industry and forethought and restoring that independence of character which the old Poor Law was rapidly destroying.

The poor law and workhouses in particular soon got the reputation, which haunts them even today, of being cruel and heartless places. During the 1840s, there were a number of scandals about conditions in workhouses which rather reinforced this view. The worst of which was at Andover. Conditions at the local workhouse were so bad that the paupers were reduced to eat the marrow from the bones for sustenance they were supposed to be crushing. In the official enquiry one witness reported on the behaviour of the inmates of the house:

> They said that when they found... a fresh bone, one that appeared a little moist, that were almost ready to fight over it, and that the man who was fortunate to get it was obliged to hide it that he might eat it when he was alone.

Despite the Act of 1834, and circulars from Whitehall in 1841 and 1869, the old system of out-relief, that is paying pensions to paupers outside the workhouse, continued. In 1849, out of a total of just under 1,100,000 some 960,00 paupers (88%) were relieved outside the workhouse. The reasons were simple. Out-relief cost less and was more humane. In Richmond the guardians estimated they spent 3s 11d on each inmate of the house in 1861. The average out-relief payment was 2s 6d per week. As most paupers receiving out-relief were elderly they could expect to be cared for by relations and friends, thus further saving an expense of nursing.

The workhouses were set up to house the able-bodied' poor who theorists argued need the constant reminder of the workhouse as an incentive to find work. Yet by the end of the nineteenth century the number and type of paupers had changed totally. The numbers of paupers were now very small, less than 3% of the population, compared with 6% and more at the height of the mid-Victorian slump.

The reason for the change is simple. Most workers experienced a rise in their living standards between 1850 and 1900. Real wages nearly doubled, although wages were still often pitiably low. This was coupled with a slight decline in the price of commodities and housing. For the first time most workers could now afford to save for periods of unemployment with friendly societies, the Post Office Saving Bank, or the insurance company.

This was coupled with a deep and abiding fear amongst the working classes, nay hatred, of the workhouse and the humiliation it reputedly meted out daily to the paupers by the authorities. They sought assistance from neighbours, friends, and sometimes charities. The stigma, for example, against pauper funerals was so great that Mrs Pember Reeve found in 1912, in Lambeth, that they would go to great lengths to avoid it.

> The pauper funeral carries with the pauperisation of the father of the child - a humiliation which adds disgrace to the natural grief of the parents. More than that they declare that the pauper family is wanting in dignity and in respect to their dead. One woman expressed the feeling of many more when she said she would soon have the dust-cart call for the body of her child than 'that there Black Maria'.

Over the sixty years between the end of the great mid-Victorian slump and the outbreak of the First World War the role of the workhouse and the poor law guardians changed. Gone, except at times of crisis, were the able-bodied paupers.

Workhouses increasingly became the refuge of outcasts

from society. Paupers now overwhelmingly consisted of the elderly, orphans, nursing mothers with bastard children, and the insane. A survey in 1897 found that a third of old people over seventy were helped in some way by the poor law authorities. Conditions for the elderly in particularly varied. One observer found that in Chelmsford the old people were, after 1901, allowed to walk in the garden to 5pm, but they still had to go to bed by 7pm, and garden seats were not provided until 1905. In Bradford, however, the position was rather different aged paupers were provided with separate day rooms equipped with armchairs, cushions, curtains, and coloured tablecloths.

Despite fears that any softening of the regime would encourage people to seek relief the poor law slowly changed to meet the new needs. Whitehall cautiously encouraged these changes. Guardians became increasingly responsive to the needs of the workhouse inmates. This was helped first by the election of women as guardians and secondly by the election of working class people in a few areas who were determined to improve conditions. Guardians were particularly aware of the need to educate children in their care and many unions set up successful schemes to foster orphans. By the standards of the day workhouse schools were generally better than other ones locally. Pupils were trained in practical trades, as well as the bible, to ensure that they could be independent. Boys were apprenticed and girls went into service as soon as practicable so as not to remain a burden to the ratepayers a minute longer than necessary.

the old people were, after 1901, allowed to walk in the garden to 5pm, but they still had to go to bed by 7pm

For most paupers food and drink was of crucial importance and was the source of constant grumbling and occasional complaint. The Poor Law Commissioners in Whitehall (and their successors) laid down dietaries which workhouses had to follow, although there some local discretion was permitted. The diet was filling but dull, but it was probably better than what the poorest of the working class ate outside the workhouse. For example, the recommended diet in 1869 was that able bodied paupers had for breakfast 7 ounces of bread, and 1.5 pints of porridge. At Christmas and national celebrations - such as Queen Victorian's Diamond Jubilee - inmates of the house might be treated to roast beef. Whether they were allowed a glass of beer with their Christmas meal was often a matter of great debate locally with advocates of temperance strongly against this little luxury.

Despite these changes the poor law seemed increasingly outdated by the beginning of the twentieth century. The government set up a royal commission in November1905 to investigate the matter and it make recommendations for its reform. When the Commission finally reported in 1909 it was split. Both reports however recommended the abolition of the Boards of Guardians and the workhouse and the assumption of their work by local government. However it wasn't until 1930 however that the system was finally dismantled.

Most workhouse buildings became hospitals; indeed a few still remain in use, but they have largely been demolished. The National Trust is restoring a working at Southwell near Nottingham to its full Victorian rigour which will a fascinating if grim place to visit when it opens to the public.

The Records
It can be difficult to identify pauper ancestors. Sometimes the information is given on death or birth certificates or on a census entry. Occasionally a family legend may suggest that a ancestor spent their declining years in the workhouse. Most records are held at county record offices. The survival of records is a bit patchy, but you should be able to find something about a pauper ancestor. Jeremy Gibson and Colin Rogers, Poor Law Union Records (4 vols., Federation of Family History Societies, 1994) is the essential guide to the history and records. Amongst the most important series of records are:
• Admission and discharge registers to the workhouse. They record the names and ages of everybody admitted and discharged, with the reason for discharge.
• Creed registers, giving religion of each applicant together with other personal details.
• Minute books of Boards of Guardians, together with committee books, record almost every decision made about the running of the Union. The fates of individual paupers are often described. Detailed accounts of Guardians' meetings usually appear in local newspapers.
• Outdoor relief order books recording applicant, amount and the period the relief was to be paid for.
• Published lists of accounts and indoor and outdoor paupers relieved. They may give other information, such as lists of pauper children sent to Canada.
• Registers of births, baptisms, burials and deaths in the workhouse.
The Public Record Office also has many records relating to the poor law. The most important series is correspondence between local unions and Whitehall (MH 12) although there is very little about individual paupers. Inmates in poor law asylums and schools may be listed in MH 17 and MH 27 respectively. The asylums and schools were mainly in the London area. The records run from the mid-1840s up until 1910. Paupers of course are also listed in census returns which are at the Family Records Centre, although frustratingly initials are often given instead of full names.

Conclusion
If your elderly ancestor suddenly disappears and you suspect he hasn't died or if a great-great aunt has a bastard child then it might be worth checking the poor law records to see whether they spent any time in the workhouse. The records can be very detailed, but are surprisingly little used by family historians.
Simon Fowler *is archivist at the Society of Genealogist and a well known lecturer and writer on family history subjects.*

Census Returns
A Census has been taken every 10 years since 1801 except in 1941 during the Second World War.
The census returns for 1801, 1811, 1821, 1831 were not preserved. However there are some areas where returns for these years have been found. The first census that is useful to researchers is the one taken in 1841.
The Census returns were taken on:

| 1841 | 7th June 1841 | 1851 | 30th March 1851 | 1861 | 7th April 1861 |
| 1871 | 2nd April 1871 | 1881 | 3rd April 1881 | 1891 | 5th April 1891 |

These census returns can be consulted. They were subject to public closure for 100 years because of the sensitive personal information they contained. At the present time the 1901 census is subject to that closure until 2nd January 2002.

Caring For Your Family Records

Susan Flood - Collections Manager, Hertfordshire Archives and Local Studies

If you are researching your family history you will find that after a time you build up a large collection of documents and records - photographs, original birth, marriage or death certificates, newspaper cuttings - perhaps even an apprenticeship indenture, a school report, a family bible or some title deeds to a property once owned by the family. This article will set out some simple steps that you can take to ensure that these items, very precious to your family history, are preserved for future generations. There are also some definite reminders about what not to do!

Loose papers:
Any documents which are handed down in families may well have suffered from the effects of poor storage conditions in the past and could come to you folded and creased, dirty and torn around the edges.

The first thing to do is to flatten items out very carefully taking care not to lose any pieces that may be torn or detached. Ensure that any small fragments are wrapped up together for safe keeping. These can be re-attached very easily by a skilled conservator.

Remove any paper clips or pins that might have been used in the past – although this could be difficult if they have rusted. Take care not to tear the document further. Plastic paper clips can be substituted if absolutely necessary.

If any kind of sticky tape has been attached to the documents this may have turned brown with age which looks very unsightly. To remove this however is a job for a specialist conservator and even then some brown staining may well remain. The lesson is very clear – don't put any kind of pressure sensitive tape (for example sellotape or 3M) anywhere near a precious document.

Any surface dust can be removed with a soft brush.

Parchment:
If you have a bundle of title deeds, particularly dating from over 100 years ago, you will find that the majority of them will have been written on parchment. Parchment is made from the skin of sheep and has been used as a writing material since early times. It is very resilient and can be subjected to the most extreme conditions before it even appears to suffer damage. However insect pests and mice love it, and small holes and frayed edges can often be the evidence of their interest in your documents in the past. Sometimes bundles of title deeds can include paper documents as well. It is perfectly acceptable to keep these together. Provided you give them a clean and stable environment there is every reason to expect that your parchment documents to survive well into the next millennium. Any items which feel particularly limp and fragile should be referred to a professional conservator.

Volumes:
Any bound volume much loved by a family such as its bible will have suffered from the ordinary wear and tear of everyday use – loose bindings and pages with stained corners. Particular use of one page or section may result in that part becoming detached from the rest of the volume. It is best not to try to 'mend' torn or detached pages yourself by using any kind of sticky tape. A skilled conservator can remedy these defects very easily and quickly. Only volumes in particularly bad condition would require a complete rebinding. If a leather binding is a little dry, but otherwise sound, a leather dressing can be lightly applied with a soft cloth (this can be purchased from art shops). The use of acid free tissue for wrapping will ensure that the spine will be kept free of dust.

Photographs:
Of all the items you may have collected, photographs are the most prone to damage and are the most difficult even for professional conservators to repair. It is not advisable to bundle them together in envelopes as they can damage each other and begin to curl. Fit them into a good quality photograph album using corner mounts. Don't mount photographs facing or touching each other. If you already have a family album where this has happened interleave the pages with 'silversafe tissue'. The pages of the album should be stiff enough so that on turning the pages the photographs themselves are not allowed to bend or flex. Never use adhesive of any kind and definitely not those modern PVC albums with pockets or flaps you place over the pictures.

An alternative to an album is to use individual plastic wallets. There is a plastic manufactured by modern suppliers like Nicholas Hunter Ltd of Unit 8, Oxford Business Centre, Osney Lane, Oxford OX1 1TB which can be used to store old photographs totally safely. However if you have only one or two photographs this may not be a cost effective option. Find out if there is a Photographic Club or Society in your area who will be able to offer you advice. It may be worthwhile for a group of members together to purchase a stock of plastic wallets and silversafe tissue.

Many good photographic firms will copy images for you and make a modern negative if you are unable to do this yourself. Always store the negatives separately in suitable made to measure envelopes (paper is best). If you are lucky enough to have any glass negatives wrap these individually and store in sturdy boxes made for the purpose. Sadly it is the colour photographs of the 1960s and 70s which may well have faded beyond recognition – black and white images (unless extremely early in date) are surprisingly durable. The golden rule is always to handle old photographs wearing unbleached cotton gloves. These can be purchased cheaply at good hardware stores.

Storage:
Keeping items flat with a cover for protection against dust is vital. Acid free tissue can be purchased at W H Smith relatively inexpensively for wrapping items individually. If you have access to no other material a plain brown manila envelope or good quality brown paper will do the job very well. As a precaution it is best to cut the sticky bit off the flap of the envelope. If you wish to write on the outside of the package a description of its contents use a pencil (not a biro). Most importantly – never use plastic bags or plastic wallets or folders to store original documents. Don't use string to tie a bundle together as over time this can eat into the edges of the documents. It is much safer to use a soft ribbon or cotton tape. The less documents are folded the better, although large parchment items may always have been folded so keeping them that way will do them no more harm.

Having protected your documents keep them in a cool, dry

*some simple steps...
you can take
to ensure....
items ....
are preserved for
future generations.*

place – certainly not in the shed or garage or loft because these places may suffer from extremes of temperature and humidity at different times of the year. They also harbour pests which may wish to make a hearty meal of your documents! Good ventilation is vital – you must never store documents wrapped tightly in plastic or in a sealed container.

Don't be afraid to use a modern photocopier to make a working copy of an item provided the document is not too large to fit on top of the machine safely. This is not harmful if done only once. Your original can then be stored away. Newspaper cuttings are especially vulnerable, so make a copy as quickly as you can. The chemicals used in the production of newspapers will over time cause discolouration and make the item very weak and prone to damage if handled too often.

If you have copied and protected your original documents

by following the steps above you will ensure that no further damage will occur. Good storage will provide stable conditions for their preservation. However some documents may already have considerable damage which can be reversed by a skilled conservator. Your local Record Office conservator should be able to recommend someone to help you. Some offices do offer a private service to the public or the following firms will provide estimates for work at no charge:

RILEY DUNN & WILSON Ltd, Glasgow Road, Falkirk, Scotland, FK1 4HP (Tel 01324 621591) or Red Doles Lane, Huddersfield, HD2 1YE (Tel 01484 534323);

CEDRIC CHIVERS Ltd
9A/B Aldermoor Way, Longwell Green, Bristol BS30 7DA (Tel 0117 935 2617)

DERRY, St Ervan Road, Wilford, Nottingham, NG11 7AZ

THE CONSERVATION AND RESTORATION OF FAMILY DOCUMENTS
Richard Reeve - R-Craft Conservation and Restoration

In 1994 I set up a small business specialising in the conservation and restoration of books and documents. Having previously worked as an archive conservator for my local record office, I became aware of a lack of this type of expertise being available in the private sector. I therefore decided to give it a whirl myself. Since then the business has grown, with the majority of customers being institutions such as record offices, museums, libraries, universities etc. However I also receive a surprising number of enquiries from members of the public. These tend to be for the restoration of family documents. Most families have material handed down to them from relatives, which is very often in a state of disrepair and therefore requires specialist treatment in order to be preserved and enjoyed by generations to come.

Typical items sent for restoration include family bibles, scrapbooks, photograph albums, letters, old deeds etc. Most documents suffer from similar types of damage which broadly speaking falls into three categories. Firstly, in-built damage caused by chemically unstable materials being used in the manufacture of documents. Secondly, damage caused by the environment to which the object has been exposed, and thirdly, general wear and tear caused by us (human beings).

This article discusses the three main causes of damage found in old documents, and gives suggestions as to their future preservation and safe-keeping. In addition, it goes on to give a brief insight into the fascinating world of document conservation and restoration.

Hand-made paper is an extremely stable and long-lasting material. Indeed documents produced from this material, given the correct storage conditions, will last for many centuries. This all changed however during the industrial revolution, with the papermaking process becoming increasingly mechanised. During this period, harmful chemicals such as chlorine and aluminium sulphate were added to the paper pulp. Later, the traditional cotton, linen or jute fibres were replaced with highly acidic ground wood as the main ingredient of the paper making pulp. All in all, the quality of paper deteriorated, with the product becoming inherently weak and unstable. The same is also true of leather and board. As the amount of chemicals being used in their manufacture increased, so the quality went down. Unfortunately the majority of family documents I come across are relatively modern and therefore produced on unstable materials. Consequently, over the years paper becomes yellowed and brittle, leather dries out and crumbles and boards break.

> **Most families have material handed down .... which is very often in a state of disrepair**

The environment in which a document is kept also has a great effect on its life span. In days gone by the air was heavily polluted from factories which churned out harmful gases into the atmosphere. This polluted air found its way into buildings and inevitably took its toll on documents, with paper becoming yet more acidic as a result. These days the air is much cleaner, although there are still potentially harmful factors to be considered when storing documents. Prolonged exposure to ultra-violet light is very damaging. The light acts as a catalyst in speeding up chemical reactions already taking place within the paper. This effect can clearly be seen on old newspapers where the outer sheets and edges having been exposed to light are yellowed, yet inside where light has not entered, the paper is unharmed.

Extremes of temperature and humidity are also harmful. If the temperature and humidity are too high insects are attracted which thrive on the animal glue used in old bindings. In addition, the outbreak of mould is likely. This eats its way through the paper, reducing it to dust. If the humidity is too low, paper will become brittle and fracture.

It is only in recent years that any thought has been given to preserving the past. Our ancestors must have discarded many items that today would be highly treasured. Those that do survive are quite often in poor condition due to ill treatment. Pages are torn and dog-eared and impregnated with dirt and grease from years of mishandling, whilst outer covers have become scuffed and worn.

In many cases some attempt has been made at repairing this damage. More often than not this has involved the application of copious amounts of sellotape. This causes irreparable damage to the document as the adhesive used on the tape gradually seeps into the paper producing yellowish brown stains that cannot be removed. It is understandable that this kind of amateur handy work has taken place. The repairs were carried out with good intention, using sellotape, this being the only repair method known to them. Indeed if it were not for these repairs having been carried out, the documents may have been lost forever.

Much can be done to prolong the life of a document without the need for hands-on treatment. This falls into the category of passive conservation. As mentioned earlier, environmental conditions can greatly affect a document's life span. The British Standard recommended temperature range for the storage of documents is 55 to 65 degrees fahrenheit, with a relative humidity of between 55 and 65 %. It is likely that most people's houses will fall outside of this range, as we prefer a warmer environment in which to live. However, some improvement can be made by not heating the room during winter months in which books and documents are stored. In addition, a de-humidifier can be used to lower the relative humidity, as this tends to be too high when the weather is cold. During the summer it is probable that temperature levels will go above 65 degrees. This we must accept as an unavoidable factor, unless of course you have an air conditioning system, in which case a constant temperature and humidity level may be achieved all year round.

Light should be kept to as low a level as possible. This can be achieved by simply storing material in a drawer or cupboard. Never allow direct sunlight to fall on your documents, as this will considerably shorten their life span. Try not to look at your material too often, and certainly avoid photocopying. This process involves high exposure to ultra-violet light and is therefore extremely harmful.

When consulting your documents, try to stop dirt and grease from your hands soiling the surface of the paper. Always wash your hands prior to handling or ideally wear cotton gloves. If you wish to attach sheets to one another, use brass paper clips rather than the steel variety. These will not cause rust spots on the surface of the paper.

Encapsulation of documents in conservation standard polyester sleeves is an excellent way of storing material. The polyester gives support to the contents and offers protection against soiling.

It is always best to leave the hands-on repair of documents to a qualified conservator. Having said this however, some people will no doubt want to attempt to repair documents themselves. This should be limited to relatively simple treatments such as surface cleaning and the repair of minor tears etc. If you wish to have a go, rather than reaching for the roll of sellotape, please try to follow these basic instructions.

Surface dirt may be removed using a plastic eraser. These are readily available from stationers, and can be extremely effective. You should only proceed if the document is reasonably robust and able to withstand the friction caused by the eraser. Work from the centre of a sheet moving out towards the edges. There will always be a tendency for the paper to tear, so proceed with caution. If the document is too weak to withstand this type of cleaning, a certain amount of dirt can be removed using a cotton wool pad. If the paper is in an extremely fragile state, a soft-haired brush should be used. Very often you must accept that not all of the dirt can be removed, for to do so could cause further damage to the document.

Tears in paper should be repaired using strips of very fine tissue. This can be purchased from specialist conservation suppliers, or you may find something suitable in your local hobby or craft shop. The tissue is laid over damaged areas and marked to shape with a lightly dampened artist's brush or draughtsman's pen. The pen should contain water rather than ink. Once wetted the tissue is easily torn to shape. The tearing process produces a fibrous edge to the tissue, which blends in well when applied to the document. The prepared strips of tissue are affixed using a starch-based adhesive. Flour and water paste will suffice, however you may choose to use a more pure adhesive available from specialist retailers. Avoid ready-made adhesives such as wallpaper paste, as this contains fungicides and other impurities, which in the long term may cause further damage to your material. Sparingly brush the paste onto the tissue and lay it over the area to be repaired. Lightly blot away excess moisture then place non stick sheets such as greaseproof paper either side of the document and leave to dry under a light weight.

If carried out with care, the repairs once dry, will be barely visible, and certainly will not cause any further damage to the paper to which they are applied. In addition the tissue can easily be removed, by simply damping and peeling it away from the surface of the paper, leaving the document completely unharmed. This is important, as in the future it is possible that superior repair methods to those currently used will be developed. We may therefore at some point wish to update previous conservation work, and it is for this reason that all treatments carried out should be fully reversible.

There is a great deal more that could be said on the subject of conservation and restoration, but it's not a skill that can be learnt from simply reading a text. My own knowledge has been gained through many years' experience of working in this field, with the necessary skills being gradually acquired. However, I do hope this article will be food for thought, and has given you some guidance for the future care of your family documents. After all, we are merely temporary custodians of the aforesaid and as such have a responsibility to do the best we can to preserve them for those who take on the role after us.

WWW: www.r-craft.co.uk
Email: richard@r-craft.co.uk

GENETICS AND GENEALOGY
RICHARD C. F. BAKER, PhD FHG
The Institute of Heraldic and Genealogical Studies

Inherited diseases have, perhaps, been brought into prominence by the twentieth-century success of sanitation and hygiene in virtually eradicating infectious diseases such as tuberculosis, cholera, typhoid and dysentery. Now, the big killers are heart disease, stroke and cancer. Environment and diet are certainly important contributors, but it is also recognised that genetic factors are very influential, too. Each year, about one hundred diseases are newly recognised as having a genetic component — which emphasises the importance of genealogists and family historians maintaining records of the causes of death of their forebears.

The application of genealogical research techniques to studies in inherited diseases is nothing new. The Institute of Heraldic and Genealogical Studies has been conducting a charitable research project for the past fifteen years, this arising from earlier pioneering studies on the familial inheritance of Huntington's chorea and retinoblastoma.

Ethical considerations mean that we may only conduct research into those families which medical teams ask us to investigate; normally, these will have exhibited a clear pattern of familial inheritance of the propensity to a specific condition. Familial patterns of inheritance suggest strongly that these inherited traits are due to a mutation or mutations of the genetic material.

The employment of genealogists by geneticists has two principal objectives. The first is to trace the defect back, perhaps through five or six generations; working forward from this point enables us to identify numerous individual descendants who may have inherited the defective gene. Not only can they be screened for the abnormality, but those who test positive can be treated whilst the condition is still at a pre-clinical stage, thereby enhancing the prognosis for successful treatment. Counselling at this early stage can also be beneficial.

The second thread of research is to attempt to link separate families, exhibiting the same condition, to a common progenitor. In our work on early-onset hereditary Alzheimer's Disease we were able to prove the descent of two affected families from a common progenitor — one John Smith (and they don't come much more common than that!) who was born in 1825. Today's descendants inherited less than 3% of their genetic material from John Smith, thereby enabling molecular biologists to concentrate their efforts to map the site of the gene; this, in turn, could facilitate the development of gene therapy to combat this particularly debilitating disease.

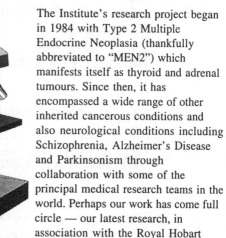

The Institute's research project began in 1984 with Type 2 Multiple Endocrine Neoplasia (thankfully abbreviated to "MEN2") which manifests itself as thyroid and adrenal tumours. Since then, it has encompassed a wide range of other inherited cancerous conditions and also neurological conditions including Schizophrenia, Alzheimer's Disease and Parkinsonism through collaboration with some of the principal medical research teams in the world. Perhaps our work has come full circle — our latest research, in association with the Royal Hobart Hospital, is on a family exhibiting Type 1 Multiple Endocrine Neoplasia (MEN1), which appears to have been introduced into the southern hemisphere by one poor unfortunate transportee who arrived in Van Diemen's Land in 1844.

We are indebted to those who have given financial support to this research; without their generosity, none of this would have been possible. We are also indebted to our team of selfless, dedicated volunteer searchers who have donated many hours of their leisure time to research that is sometimes fruitless and often frustrating, but ultimately satisfying. Every reader who wishes to contribute to this vitally important research should contact the author.

Essential Books by Colin R Chapman

Tracing Your British Ancestors - £4

Pre-1841 Censuses & Population Listings in the British Isles - £5

Marriage Laws, Rites, Records & Customs - £5.50

The Growth of British Education & Its Records - £5

Ecclesiastical Courts, Officials & Records - £5

(Sin, Sex & Probate)
How Heavy, How Much & How Long - £5

Books on Tracing Ancestors in Bedfordshire, Rutland and
Northamptonshire also available at £4.50 each

Add 75p per title for postage and packing

6 Holywell Road, Dursley, Glos., GL11 5RS, England

British Education Records
Colin R Chapman

Helpful sources
Education records can provide helpful information on names, ages, backgrounds and performances of pupils and students, on teachers and instructors, and on schools, colleges, universities and other educational establishments. Some surviving British education records begin in the 1200s, others were written only yesterday. They, therefore, cover a wider time period than parish registers, manorial documents or wills.

Yet many family historians incorrectly believe that their ancestors never went to school, let alone university, thinking their families were too poor or had the wrong background. Hopefully this article will change that belief. Some records include details of school and college buildings and fund-raising activities. Reports from inspectors on teachers and students appear in certain classes of records, while others incorporate information on significant local and national events, including the weather when it affected attendance numbers.

Some education records are difficult to locate and many are lost but those that have survived merit better usage by family historians

Universal education
Throughout the country from earliest times religious and secular charities alike offered free or subsidised education. From 1406 parents were entitled to send their children to any school in the realm. Nevertheless, only a century ago most youngsters left school when extremely young to contribute towards the family income. They had no chance of practising basic literacy skills except when signing a marriage register or witnessing a will - often making a rather shaky mark, having forgotten even how to hold a quill firmly. The more fortunate returned to their learning in later years guided by a compassionate clergyman or squire's lady, or perhaps at an adult Sunday School or a Mechanics' Institute.

Apprenticeships
Apprenticeships offered boys and girls opportunities to learn a craft or trade with a skilled master or mistress. Education, in addition to skills training, should have been provided for children formally bound by an indenture (agreement) until the age of 21 (boys until 24 before 1778). Normally the agreement was made between the master or mistress and the child's father, both signing the indenture.

> ..many family historians incorrectly believe that their ancestors never went to school ...

Parish churchwardens were able to arrange apprenticeships for orphans and illegitimate children, providing them with a skill to support themselves without draining the parochial, or poor law union, finances. Apprenticeship records are mostly in County Record Offices (CROs), those of poor children usually filed with Poor Law documents - but be aware that many CROs index all education records under "schools". Some CROs have printed catalogues such as the *Conspectus of State Education Records*, published by the Bedfordshire and Luton Archives. Children apprenticed through a city guild or livery company will be found in their records, generally in city archives.

Universities
Boys who stayed on at school until their teens had an opportunity to attend university, or for those wishing to be taught Common Law, to one of the four Inns of Court, having spent a year or so at one of the Inns of Chancery. Until the late 19th Century many believed that girls had no desire for higher education; London University first admitted girls for degrees in 1878, Oxford in 1920 and Cambridge in 1923, although ladies' colleges were founded at Cambridge from 1869 for honours examination candidates. Oxford and Cambridge were the only two universities in England and Wales until 1836 when London University was founded. In mediaeval times, a boy could enter university at the age of 14 but he had to remain loyal to the Established Church. Before the mid-16th Century Reformation, this meant that only Roman Catholics could attend university, and after that time only Anglicans could attend. Roman Catholics and other Nonconformists had to find higher education elsewhere until the 20th Century. Roman Catholic seminaries for English and Welsh students were opened on Continental Europe; their records have been published and indexed by the Catholic Record Society. The records of other university students are discussed below.

Education providers
Education was sponsored and provided by religious bodies, the ancient guilds and fraternities, charities supported by various groups, army and naval establishments, individual merchants, factory owners and philanthropists. Immediately following the Reformation all children could be taught legally only by Anglican teachers licensed by an Anglican bishop. From 1779 Nonconformists were permitted to open their own schools and academies. References to teachers' licences, not essential after 1869, are in diocesan registers, now in CROs and similar archives.

Some establishments offered accommodation and boarding facilities; in the early days this was regarded as providing hospitality, and so these places were termed hospitality or hospital schools. Some of these schools provided coloured coats and other garments, gaining names such as Blue and Yellow Coat schools. In 1698 the Society for the Promotion of Christian Knowledge (SPCK), with links to the Anglican Church, was one of the first bodies to open a Charity School. Other Charity Schools were linked to a town or even small parish charity, usually endowed by a local benefactor. From

Around the world for free
with *Local History Magaz_ine*

How? Because all subscribers can place up to 50 words <u>free</u> in the magazine's Noticeboard, which also appears on our World Wide Web site, at no extra cost. Each issue contains the latest news, the best articles and more book and periodical reviews than anywhere else. All of which makes for the best local history magazine you can buy.

FOR YOUR FREE SAMPLE COPY, contact us by post, phone, fax or e-mail, mentioning *The Genealogical Services Directory*. Or visit our website on www.local-history.co.uk to get a flavour of what's in the latest issue.

The Local History Press Ltd
3 Devonshire Promenade, Lenton, Nottingham NG7 2DS.
Telephone: 0115 9706473 — Fax: 0115 9424857.
E-mail: editors@local-history.co.uk.

1730 in Wales, travelling teachers regularly visiting groups of adult and young pupils in any convenient local building (the Circulating School system) acted as Charity Schools.

Military schools provided schooling for soldiers and sailors and their families and for some civilians within the forces. Some units and regiments had their own teachers. The army and naval colleges at Sandhurst and Greenwich (earlier at Portsmouth) also provided education, mostly for potential officers.

Borstals and Reformatories, known also as Certified Industrial Schools and Day Industrial Schools, were built from the early 1800s by organisations and individuals for juveniles in need of care and support. Reformatory ships were moored off Cardiff, Devonport, Dundee, Gravesend, Helensburgh, Hull, Liverpool and Purfleet. In 1933, most similar establishments still operating were renamed Approved Schools. The youngsters were educated and trained in a skill to help them to obtain a job and so keep out of further trouble; in many cases the records have been deposited in county archives.

Which School or University?
Local street and trade directories usually give school addresses with names of the head teachers in their area. From the late 19th Century a variety of specialist directories and school year books included names of governors and teachers, mini histories, and the occasional illustration of a school in both public and private sectors. Your local library can advise you where old editions of street directories and educational year books are held.

Surviving census returns from 1801 to 1891 give locations of schools and, for residential schools, names of teachers and pupils. Local histories usually include details on schools in the area, while some schools have their own comprehensive histories. The local studies library, or the county or similar archives, should be able to advise you on the whereabouts of copies of these.

Universities published similar books on the location and histories of their colleges. Addresses of all current higher educational establishments around the world, some established several hundred years ago, with names of their principal officers, professors and the subjects they teach, may be found in the *World of Learning*, published annually by Europa.

School and University Records
Details on mediaeval Cathedral schools, and on Monastery, Abbey, Chantry, Song or Almonry schools, and records of their teachers and pupils are in *The Growth of British Education and Its Records*, (see Bibliography). Many Grammar Schools were established and endowed by Henry VIII, Edward VI and a number of wealthy merchants in the mid-1500s, subsidising school fees from their investments. Some were re-endowments of even older schools. Not a few became Public Schools, still open today, with records stretching back to their foundation. The Society of Genealogists' Library holds a most comprehensive collection of published school registers and histories.

Records of small schools in towns and villages are less easy to locate, and unfortunately many have perished. However,

the county archives, local studies library or even the local education offices, may hold records of local schools. Some old registers are occasionally retained at schools still open today. Some school registers and other records are held in the archives of the charity or religious denomination that sponsored the educational facilities originally.

Oxford and Cambridge University records stretch back to the 1200s; those of the Inns of Court and Chancery from the 1400s. During the 1800s other higher educational institutions were set up and began offering courses in engineering and science. Most of these are now independent universities, although originally their students sat external examinations from the University of London and, if successful, were awarded degrees from there. Lists of names of students and staff have been published and indexed in *alumni* or similar books, although the individual colleges and Inns generally have more details on individuals. The best-known series are *Alumni Oxoniensis* (for Oxford), covering 1500 to 1886 in eight volumes and *Alumni Cantabrigiensis* (for Cambridge), to 1900, in four volumes, held by most large reference libraries. Many universities and Inns of Court have published very similar works So, having found your ancestor in an *alumni* book, write to discover if the original records hold further information for you.

School Registers and OtherRecords
Most of the Grammar and Public Schools and Universities published "registers" (as such printed books are usually termed); but these are really collections of biographies (albeit extremely brief) of former students. In some cases notes on later careers, names of spouses and even death dates are incorporated.

Among a school's working registers were normally an Admissions Register, noting the pupil's date of admission, date of birth (and occasionally baptism, if a Church School); normally the name and address of the father is recorded with, sometimes, his occupation. Some Admissions Registers also record the name of a pupil's previous school (if any) and the date of departure to another school, place of higher education, apprenticeship or work. Separate Attendance Registers were used to record daily attendance, or illness or truancy causing non-attendance. Several schools produced annual Class Lists with names of the teacher and pupils; some schools printed these. From the 1890s many schools took photographs of classes and sports teams or of every pupil on a panoramic picture.

Issuing School Magazines every term began in the mid-1800s with essays and poems by the pupils, reports on important events, academic and sporting achievements and biographical notes on certain pupils and teachers. Sketches and drawings were used as illustrations until the 1920s, when photographs, perhaps of your ancestors, began to appear. North American schools tended to publish Year Books, rather than the more frequent British school magazines.

Log Books were maintained by many schools, following an Act of Parliament in 1861, recording day-to-day life at the school.
Financial support, thus teachers' pay, depended upon pupils'

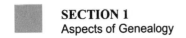
attendance figures and examination results, and the Log Book entries were used to justify attendance numbers. Accordingly, log book entries coincidentally portray vivid pictures of life in the local community and at the school. Children helped in the fields in rural areas, creating entries such as "harvest not yet over, attendance poor", "Queen Victoria's Jubilee, school closed" and so on. Other entries refer to children misbehaving and their punishments (though these were sometimes entered in a separate Punishment Book), visits from a school governor or inspector, school or class outings, notes on changes in teaching staff, and reactions to alterations to timetables and lessons.

Examination and Assessment Books were used at a number of schools to record students' achievements. Honours Books were sometimes used to specifically record above-average educational performance, leadership qualities or appointments of prefects or monitors.

Rolls of Honour were quite separate books, or sometimes painted panels in the school hall, produced at many schools to commemorate former pupils who served during conflicts such as World Wars 1914-18 and 1939-45. In many instances a Roll gives a former student's regiment or vessel which may enable you to pursue further lines of research.

Student-based Education Records
Text books, primers and readers and old examination papers, provide examples of the subjects your ancestors were taught and to which level. Most students were given termly or annual reports of progress (for their parents or guardians) and rewards for educational achievements in the form of certificates, medallions, plaques and trophies. Apprentices demonstrated competence by producing a model or test piece. In the late 1800s and early 1900s many schools awarded medals for regular and punctual attendance, often engraved with the student's name. Pupils of certain ages leaving school between 1876 to 1918 were issued with School Leaving Certificates (often called Labour Certificates) by the local Education Authority or Board. These stated the pupil's name, address, date of birth and minimum attendance record at a named school.

Rewards could be for proficiency in a sport or hobby - the best arranged stamp collection, a beautifully embroidered tray-cloth or quality solo singing. On returning home some prizes were pushed to the back of a cupboard, others were lovingly polished every week and are still retained within the family. Sadly most of these student-based records have disappeared over the years; but you may be able to find some surviving items in the homes of your older relatives.

Other related records
Minutes of meetings of School Governors, Trustees and Managers are likely to include names of subscribers, information on teachers, with notes on appointment dates, salaries and performance or termination of service, but normally there are few references to pupils. Such records may be in the relevant CRO. The Public Record Office (PRO) has records on national educational policy and on elementary and secondary schools, technical and further education, special education services and on teachers, but virtually no records of pupils; see the Information Leaflets 77, 78, 79 and 80, on the PRO website <http://www.pro.gov.uk>.

School Inspectors, whether appointed by the government or diocesan or denominational authorities, prepared regular reports for their respective bodies on secular, Church, Jewish, Nonconformist and Catholic schools. Pupils are mentioned on occasions, as are some teachers, but these reports, held nowadays at the relevant head offices, mostly refer to general standards.

Local newspapers often reported Speech Days, sporting and social events and sometimes examination results at the schools in their area. Prize winners may be mentioned, with details on who presented the awards; photographs are included only on a regular basis only from the 1930s. Outstanding events, or events involving a national celebrity or a celebrity's child, are likely to appear in national newspapers. Local newspapers are often held in CROs or local studies collections in libraries; local and national newspapers are held in the British Library, Newspaper Library.

Bibliography
Chapman, Colin R. *The Growth of British Education and its Records*. Lochin Publishing. 2nd edition. 1992, reprinted 1996.
Chapman, Colin R. *Basic Facts About Education Records*. FFHS. 1999.
[Europa]. *The World of Learning*. Europa. (An annual publication.)
Jacobs, Phyllis M, Dr. *Registers of the Universities, Colleges and Schools of Great Britain and Ireland*. Athlone Press. 1964.
Some Useful Addresses
Society of Genealogists, 14 Charterhouse Buildings, London EC1M 7BA.
Public Record Office, Ruskin Avenue, Kew, Surrey, TW9 4DU.
British Library Newspaper Library, Colindale Avenue, London NW9 5HE.

ILLUSTRATE YOUR FAMILY HISTORY
Yvonne K.L. Coldron

In the early days of photography people bored their friends and relatives with their holiday 'snaps', then family events were captured on Cine film, followed in recent years by Camcorders. Is it now Family Trees that are shown off to a yawning audience? If you are going to show off the results of your research the least you can do is make it as interesting as possible. One way of doing th's is to illustrate your Family History.

It is said that a picture is worth a thousand words, in which case just think how much writing you can save if you illustrate your Family History! Are your files full of notes, family record sheets, trees, certificates, I.G.I. sheets, etc.? If so, consider how dull it will be when your descendants look at your files when you are dead - words, words and more words, and they may just decide not to keep them!

> a picture is worth a thousand words, ...just think how much writing you can save if you illustrate your Family History

So where do you start? The following will, I hope, give you some ideas, but I am sure it is not fully comprehensive. However, once you start thinking about 'illustration' I am sure the possibilities are endless.

Probably the most obvious and readily available items are photographs. Ask around all the members of your family to see what photographs and other items they have hidden away. If they are reluctant to part with photographs ask to borrow them. You can then have them copied for your files and return the originals to the lender. Family events will obviously be the main photographs, but consider using photographs of Schools, houses, places of work and perhaps personal items such as medals.

Have you, or your relatives, any of the following tucked away in lofts and attics?

Apprenticeship Indentures; Baptism Cards; Identity cards; Invitations - weddings, or perhaps to Buckingham Palace for Tea with the Queen. In Memorium cards or photographs of graves. It is possible to obtain photographs of Military graves from the Commonwealth War Graves Commission - see their advert elsewhere in this Directory. Membership certificates of Societies and Clubs; Old passports; Maps - street maps or in the case of a village a map showing its location in the County; Newspaper pictures of events - such as a medal presentation; Sporting pictures - individual or team, often found in local papers; Sunday School cards etc., etc., etc.

Most of the above are family items but when you have exhausted all your family contacts you need not give up

because you can start looking for old picture postcards. Picture postcards first became available in Great Britain in 1894, however most of the ones you will find today (at sensible prices!) date from 1902. The subjects depicted are diverse but the ones of most interest to the family historian will be street scenes and Churches. Street scenes may show the house or cottage where your ancestor lived, or the shop they owned, the Pub they ran, the windmill they worked, or the Manor House where they worked. You may find the ship an ancestor sailed on or the railway station where someone worked. Any card may be used as an example even if it does not show something directly related to your ancestor - what about scenes of hop-picking in Kent when you know that your ancestors owned a hop farm? What about a hospital where your ancestor worked? As I said, the possibilities are endless.

With Churches you may be lucky enough to find interior and exterior views of the Churches where your ancestors were baptised, married and buried. You may even find a view of the very Font where a baptism took place! The exterior view may show the grave where your ancestors are buried. Sometimes village churches include street scenes that could show an ancestor's cottage.

Postcard collecting is a major hobby (like family history!) and there are many Postcard Fairs up and down the country. Postcard collectors have a magazine - Picture Postcard Monthly (see details at the end) - each month it carries a three month calendar of forthcoming Postcard Fairs. The major event each year is the Picture Postcard Show held at the Royal Horticultural Hall in London (yes, where the Society of Genealogists have been holding a Family History Fair in May each year, so the location is well known to thousands of family historians). The Picture Postcard Show in 2000 will be held from Wednesday 30th., August to Saturday 2nd., September and there will be millions of postcards for sale! Well worth a visit. The Picture Postcard Show is run by the Postcard Traders Association. Details of members can be found on the Internet at www.postcard.co.uk - some members run their own Postcard Fairs and some may also operate a postal approvals services.

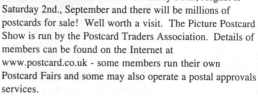

Family Tree Magazine and Practical Family History (see details elsewhere in this Directory) carry adverts for "Family History Fairs" held in various parts of the country, at which a postcard dealer may have a stand. Many of the major Family History Fairs, such as York and Preston, which are annual events, or Leicester and Weston-Super-Mare, which are biennial, have postcard stands. Open Days and Fairs run by Family History Societies or Groups of Societies, sometimes have a stand run by a postcard dealer. (See the Events Diary in this Directory.)

I must confess a vested interest in postcards! I run Picture Past, which is a service dealing only with old picture postcards of churches in England. It is a postal service, details of which will be found in my advert elsewhere in this Directory, but I also have stands at many of the Family History events I have mentioned. Picture Past was started ten years ago purely for Family Historians - I just happen to be potty about churches.

I have not mentioned the cost of postcards for two reasons. Firstly, because prices vary so much due to age and condition, secondly, because whilst you may find the font you want for around 75p., and feel thrilled with that, someone else may be quite happy paying £20 for a street scene that shows their grandparents' cottage.

A picture postcard may be the only way of obtaining a picture of a church or building for your Family History. Many churches were bombed during W.W.II and were either demolished or rebuilt in a different way. Those that survived the war have frequently been demolished by planners in the name of 'progress', for road building or widening, or to build supermarkets and car parks. Sometimes the churches were closed as the congregations dwindled and are looked after by the Redundant Churches Fund. Others are still there but are no longer used for worship, having become bookshops, craft centres, restaurants or meeting halls.

When putting your postcards, photographs, or other items, into your Family History files you should use photo-corners. It is not a good idea to stick things with glue, you cannot move things around when you make further finds, but worse than that you ruin and devalue them. Remember to identify your items so that they do not need to be taken out to have their backs examined, constant handling causes damage.

Whilst on the subject of identifying things, I wonder how many of you have photographs without any identification on them stored away in boxes and albums. A job to do on a dark winter night - get out all your photographs and add names, places and dates. A soft pencil and a light touch are essential! YOU may know it's Auntie Fanny on the beach at Blackpool but does anyone else?

Another file you could consider starting is one on you and your family and descendants, adding pictures etc., lurking in the above mentioned boxes and albums. It makes a pleasant change from dealing with your ancestors - we seem to forget that one day WE will be the ancestors!

Earlier I mentioned approvals service for postcards. Some postcard dealers are happy to provide a postal approvals service for people unable to attend postcard fairs, however many dealers are not prepared to send approvals overseas. You will find some dealers on the Postcard Traders Association list and further addresses can be found in the classified advertisements in Picture Postcard Monthly.

Picture Postcard Monthly can be obtained at Postcard Fairs or on subscription from Reflections of a Bygone Age, 15 Debdale Lane, Keyworth, Nottingham, NG12 5HT.
Tel : 0115 937 4079. e- mail: reflections @ argonet.co.uk
www.postcard.co.uk/ppm

Happy hunting!

Post Codes
To find out the
Royal Mail Post Code
for a UK address.
Telephone: 0345 111222
To find out a UK post code by the internet.
www.postcodes.royalmail.co.uk
Type in the address on the search page and the post code will be provided.
Another website is **www.afd.co.uk**

The Institute of Heraldic
and
Genealogical Studies

The Institute of Heraldic and Genealogical Studies is a charitable educational trust that was established in Canterbury, Kent in 1961 to promote the study of the history and structure of the family. To fulfil this aim a series of day, residential, evening and correspondence courses are run throughout the year for the benefit of family historians and genealogists. The courses range from those suitable for complete beginners to the subject, to those aimed at individuals wishing to pursue genealogical research as an income earning profession.

The day and residential courses offered in 2000 are —

The Commonwealth Gap	Residential Course	**10-12 March**
Introduction to Family History	Day School	**8 April**
The Professional Approach	Day School	**13 May**
Nonconformity	Day School	**24 June**
Tracing Your Family History	Residential Course	**24-28 July**
Tracing Your Family History	Residential Course	**7-11 August**
The Parish Chest	Day School	**14 October**
House History	Residential Course	**17-19 November**

Accommodation for the residential courses is provided at one of the historic hotels in the delightful medieval city of Canterbury, close to the Institute's comprehensive library.

The Institute also runs a pair of linked evening courses that encompass the whole of its syllabus required for qualification in genealogical research. These two courses, Introducing Genealogy (28 weeks) and Practical Genealogy (30 weeks) are both held each year in central London at the London School of Economics. One of the courses is also offered at Canterbury. These lead to graded assessments and examinations for certificates and diploma.

Introducing Genealogy	28 week evening course at the LSE	**25 September**
Practical Genealogy	30 week evening course at the LSE	**25 September**
Introducing Genealogy	28 week evening course at IHGS	**28 September**

For those students not able to study in Canterbury or London, the Institute runs a very popular correspondence course that is accredited by the Open and Distance Learning Quality Council. This is composed of a series of 24 in-depth assignments, each requiring written answers to questions on the particular topic. Individual tutorial guidance is given. The course is also open to students from abroad with an interest in British genealogical research and takes two or three years to complete, studying on a parttime basis.

Full details of the courses can be obtained from the Registrar on receipt of a large SAE.
Please send your enquiry to IHGS, 79-82 Northgate, Canterbury, Kent, CT 1 1BA
Tel 01227 768664   Fax 01227 765617
registrar@ihgs.ac.uk   http://www.ihgs.ac.uk/

Maps – an essential aid for Family and Local Historians
Alan Godfrey

Names are the crucial element in genealogy: surnames, maiden names, Christian names of course, but another name is invariably close at hand, the place name. The places where our ancestors were born and died, and perhaps were married, but also – and these may be both more elusive and more interesting – the places where they lived, worked, loved and laughed. And for any understanding of these places, and therefore for any understanding of the way our forebears spent their lives, there is no alternative to a good map.

For anybody whose ancestors lived in Britain or Ireland, at least in the 19th and 20th centuries, a good map will more often than not mean the Ordnance Survey. Other countries had their own surveys, of course, normally referred to as the cadastral maps, sometimes printed, sometimes in manuscript, including beautifully detailed maps for the Austro-Hungarian Empire, and the more populist large scale plans prepared for many Belgian towns by Monsieur Popp. It is with Britain and Ireland that these brief notes are concerned.

Most great surveys grew out of two basic requirements, and this is reflected in their names: Ordnance, implying a military connection, and cadastral, referring to taxation and hence the need to measure the land. In Britain the military rôle was paramount in the early days, and the early work on the Ordnance Survey, first in Scotland after the Jacobite rebellion of 1745-6, later on the South Coast of England as the Napoleonic Wars brought the threat of invasion. The Ordnance Survey *per se* was effectively founded in 1791 and its first maps, of Kent, were published in 1801. These Kent sheets were privately printed but thereafter the Ordnance Survey decided to do all the work themselves, forming a Corps of Royal Military Surveyors and Draughtsmen in 1805. Early work concentrated on southern England, and it would be 1870 before all of England and Wales, let alone Scotland, was covered.

This early mapping was at the scale of one inch to the mile, which was to be Britain's best known topographical scale until the 1970s, when it was replaced by the 1:50,000 series. Although a relatively small scale it is of immense use to genealogists in showing the country – and the countryside in particular – in reasonable detail, with all the roads, railways and canals and a good measure of other features, from churches and windmills to pubs and woodland. Most serious genealogists will, I guess, have access to a current 1:50,000 Landranger map of an area where they are doing extensive research, but at least one older one-inch map would provide a useful insight into the past. The maps of around 1870 have been reprinted by David & Charles and we ourselves are currently reprinting some slightly later than that. For the 20th century secondhand maps can sometimes be obtained; it is not necessary to go back that many years to find maps of interest. In many ways the best maps of all are the early '7th Series' maps of the 1950s, which have the benefit of great clarity of style while also showing areas just before many railways and collieries had been abandoned and ring roads, industrial estates and suburban sprawl had taken over.

Although invaluable for genealogical (and indeed almost every form of historical) research, the small scale maps can beg more questions than they answer. They show the town but not the street name. However, in Ireland a better solution was early on the scene, for in 1824 the decision was taken to provide a large scale survey of that island, encouraged by an urgent need to assess rates and taxes more efficiently. Because Ireland is a largely rural land the six inch map has proved ideal over the years and many major libraries will have sets, possibly bound, of the early six-inch maps of their county. Work started from the north and in the Ulster counties the Ordnance Survey gave an enormous bonus: the Parish Memoirs. The name came from the term 'Aide-Memoire' and these volumes, which accompanied the maps, gave statistical information, topographical descriptions and items of social interest . They were produced through the 1830s until the government withdrew funding at the end of the decade. These memoirs are therefore available in great detail for the counties of Londonderry and Antrim (but not Belfast), and in a less complete form for Armagh, Cavan, Down, Fermanagh and Tyrone. As a social commentary they are unrivalled since the Domesday Book. A random dip into one volume finds the parish of Clogher, in Tyrone, where we are told that "the people seem to pay very little regard to comfort or cleanliness, either in their person or their habitations. Their food is potatoes and oaten bread, sometimes varied with stirabout or flummery. They seldom get fresh meat, but salt beef and pork dried are used on particular occasions of festivity. The fuel is turf at all times, but in some parts it is rather scarce. The dress of the people is, except on Sundays and holidays, very slovenly". There follow detailed break-downs of the religious make-up of the parish, the occupations, the buildings, townlands, agriculture and so on. They are a treasure trove of information, and happily have been transcribed and reprinted (in hardback and paperback) by the Institute of Irish Studies at Queens University, Belfast. If you have ancestors from the northern counties, make sure you have the relevant volumes! The maps, alas, may be more difficult to get hold of.

In England, meanwhile, large scale mapping was left to – often inaccurate – private surveys. This was in contrast to several European countries where detailed cadastral maps were produced for taxation use, albeit usually in manuscript form only. Nevertheless, it was clear that in many cases taxation was not seen as the sole use for these maps, and at a conference in Brussels in 1858 it was remarked that "nous ne voulons pas que le cadastre soit seulement un instrument fiscal; nous voulons que sa mission soit élevée:nous voulons que le cadastre soit l'inventaire de la propriété foncière du pays, le grand livre où chaque propriétaire puisse trouver les titres de sa propriété". Most continental maps were essentially property maps (though there were also some beautiful maps of miliary establishments) and this would be regarded as the primary purpose for a similar survey in Britain. From 1842 onwards Lancashire, Yorkshire and several Scottish counties were surveyed at the six inch scale. From the 1850s, however, it was decided that a larger scale was required and this would be at 1:2,500, the first significant step towards metrication and a nod towards European practice. However, this scale also had the advantages of being roughly 25 inches to the mile (25.344 inches to be precise) while one square inch was almost precisely one acre. Work on this survey started in 1853-4 – Ayrshire, Dumfriesshire, Durham, Linlithgowshire, Northumberland, Peeblesshire and the Plymouth area of

Devon were among the first areas to be surveyed – and the country was essentially covered by 1896. Mountain and moorland, not surprisingly, was never covered at this scale; some maps, especially along the coast, are notable for their emptiness in any case!

This 1:2,500 or 25" survey is invaluable to genealogists and it is with these maps that we concentrate most of our own publication programme. The maps are true plans, rather than maps: that is, they do not distort the width of roads or other major features, and even railway lines are shown to scale. (During the 'Railway Mania' many OS surveyors went to work for the railways, and railway surveys were always of a very high standard; the Ordnance Survey was normally willing to accept these surveys, the only privately prepared surveys they regarded as to a sufficiently reliable standard.) Early maps were accompanied by Books of Reference but unlike the Parish Memoirs for Ireland, these are of little or no interest to genealogists, including only acreages and land use. The maps, however, have great detail and show individual houses along with factories, mills, pubs, railway tracks, and so on, together with many natural features. It is possible, therefore, to find the house where an ancestor lived, see the tram tracks that took him to work, the factory or mill where he spent the day, the public house where he spent his pay packet, and perhaps the police station where he spent the night!

These maps do have two disadvantages which users should be aware of. Firstly, the earliest maps at this scale were published on a parish basis and an adjacent parish would be left blank. As a result, several maps might be needed to cover one very small area. This practice was later discontinued and maps were published on a more manageable county basis; users should therefore try to get hold of the later printings wherever possible. More seriously, the maps were only revised every 20 or 30 years – sometimes longer, over a hundred years in the case of much of the Isle of Man! – so clearly some houses will have been built and demolished between revisions and never appeared on a map at all. To give a few examples: County Durham was surveyed between 1854-7, revised 1894-7 and again 1912-19, followed by a further but incomplete revision 1937-42. Wiltshire, by contrast, did not receive its first 1:2500 survey until 1873-85, was revised in 1898-1900 and again 1921-4, with a partial revision 1936-43. In Wigtownshire the pattern was different again, with a first survey, but only at 6" (or 1:10,560) in 1843-7, and no 1:2500 survey until 1892-5, with a revision in 1906-7. (After the Second World War maps were revised onto the National Grid, often at 1:1250 scale, but this is, I think, of less interest for the present article. The Ordnance Survey over the last 50 years is, as they say, another story.)

The 1:2,500 survey is of the greatest interest to genealogists but for those studying relatives in the larger towns there is a bonus in the form of the town plans. Progress on these was made more urgent by the various epidemics, notably of cholera, in and about the 1840s, which culminated in the Public Health Act of 1848. However, the first town plans predate this Act, and from the early 1840s the Ordnance Survey was mapping towns of more than 4,000 population, plus county towns, at a scale of 1:1056 or 5 feet to the mile. By the 1850s even this scale was regarded as too small for sanitary engineers, and maps were produced at 1:500 or 1:528, or around 10 feet to the mile. The earliest maps in these series – and the Lancashire

towns are especially well covered – have an extraordinary wealth of detail, even including the interiors of some public buildings, such as churches, theatres, railway stations and (until security considerations came to the fore) prisons. With sanitation a prime consideration some of the early 1:528 plans even showed individual outdoor privies. The coverage varied greatly across the country – London, for instance, was only surveyed at the 5' scale, and then not until the 1870s – but anybody studying relatives from the northern cities should certainly try to examine these maps if possible. We have reprinted a few ourselves, principally of central Manchester in the 1840s – reducing them down to a yard to the mile – but perhaps none are as attractive as the lovely early map of Dublin, the so-called 'Castle Sheet'.

However, it is to the 25" or 1:2500 maps that the genealogist will normally return. For those wishing to study them the County Record Office will normally be the starting point, although the quality and completeness of collections varies greatly. The maps are also large – around 40" by 30" – and awkward to handle, so it is not normally possible to examine more than two or three maps at a time. Bear in mind, too, that the maps cover only small areas, one and a half square miles in the case of the 25" maps, considerably less than this with the town plans. Problems with storage makes owning them far from easy, even if you can find secondhand copies to start with.

We ourselves have reprinted well over a thousand of these maps, and are issuing new titles all the time. To make them more manageable we reduce them in scale, to approximately 15" to the mile, and we also commission a historical introduction for the reverse. Wherever possible, we also include extracts from contemporary directories, a feature that has always been popular (although only one reader has complained to us that "it was a pity we had to waste space by putting a map on the back of the directory"!) I hope our maps provide good value.

Obviously we concentrate on the towns, and especially blocks of towns; our series has proved especially successful in conurbations such as London, the Black Country and South Yorkshire where readers can examine several maps together and get a broad social picture, something that is not possible with the cumbersome originals, especially within the confines of a library. Of course, some genealogists only want to see the actual house where their ancestor lived, but I always find that rather sad; the maps have so much else to offer, and close examination of all the minutiae brings the real journey back into time.

But however hard we work we can never reprint all the maps. Their number is truly legion, especially when we consider that most sheets are available in several different editions. A quick calculation shows that Durham, scarcely one of our largest counties and one with significant moorland left uncovered at the larger scales, had over seven hundred 1:2500 plans. Indeed, in the 1st Edition the number was still higher, as the maps were issued on a parish base, so that two or more sheets might be necessary to cover one map area! When we realise that the earliest editions were hand-coloured we can only sit back and wonder at the Herculean grandeur of the task.

Miscellaneous Sources for Family and Local History
Doreen Hopwood

A keen awareness of relevant sources is vital if you want to carry out successful and comprehensive research into the history of your family. Gone are the days (I hope!) when "doing a family tree" meant that you simply acquired a chart of names and dates and very little about the kinds of lives your ancestors lived. Family, local and social history are all inextricably linked - our forebears have played their part in global events, whether as a soldier in the trenches of the Somme, or as one of the politicians responsible for making the decision to go to war. The transition of England from a rural economy into an industrial nation depended heavily on our "ag labs" who had to exchange their country skills for urban ones.

There is a large range of sources available which can be used either on their own or to complement the most widely-used material - the GRO Indexes, census returns, the IGI and parish registers. As well as helping you to take your familys' history further back, they will enable you to "put the flesh on the bones" and give you an insight into the society in which your ancestors lived. This list of sources is by no means exhaustive, but covers those which you should be able to access without too much difficulty. Most are deposited in main reference libraries or county record offices and you may already have some of them at home (such as grave papers, school reports, obituaries, military service medals and photographs).

> There is a large range of sources available which can be used either on their own or to complement the most widely-used material -

Records of Voters - Electoral Registers and Poll Books
Electoral registers have been compiled annually since 1832, and their forerunners were the BURGESS or FREEMANS ROLLS. However, until the latter half of the nineteenth century these are of limited use as only about one in every three men was entitled to vote in local or parliamentary elections. It wasn't until 1928 that the franchise was extended to include all residents over the age of 21 and no registers were compiled during the First and Second World Wars. Absent Voters lists were published in 1918 and 1919 and can be particularly helpful in tracing a surviving serviceman as his service details (including his regiment/ship, rank and number) are given. Modern registers can be used to ascertain when people moved from a given address, died or reached the age of majority. As they are arranged by street - cadestrally - you need to know an address in order to utilise this resource. Not all authorities have kept voting lists for every year since 1832, but surviving records are usually deposited in the main library of a large town or in the County Record Office. POLL BOOKS generally cover the period up to 1872 - the year when the Secret Ballot Act was passed. They include the name of the elector, his residence (and also his qualifying address - where his property was situated), his occupation and how he voted. These are useful for social and local history as well - giving an insight into the political hierarchy of the area. Many poll books were printed after the election and so may survive in several locations. As with many of the sources mentioned, there is a guide published by the Federation of Family History Societies listing where to find surviving records.

Town and County Directories
The first directory for London appeared in the 17th century and then more or less annually, with county and major town directories being published from the late 18th century. They were designed to provide commercial travellers and potential customers with names and addresses of professional people and tradesmen in the area - a sort of forerunner of the telephone "Yellow Pages" directories. As well as giving details of commerce and trade, these directories - which became more comprehensive as the years progressed - include a general description of each place covered, communications (stagecoaches and carriers, and later, railways), churches, institutions and inns. From about 1850, most directories contain the following sections:
Street Index - a list of tradesmen and householders, arranged alphabetically by street and often give a reference to a map incorporated in the directory.
Court Section - a list of the residential addressses of wealthier inhabitants, local dignitaries and officials. Later this became the Private Residents Section and by the early 20th century includes most householders.
Commercial Section - an alphabetical list of businesses and individual tradesmen, arranged by name and giving the business address.
Trades Section - an alphabetical list of trades and professions. In areas where a particular trade is predominant - such as the gun trade in Birmingham - it is listed under sub-headings, according to specific tasks.
An individual may appear in more than section, and in these cases, it should be possible to obtain a residential address. Directories are especially useful in finding an address close to a census date, pinpointing a move or the sale of a business. They are also interesting as a means of identifying changes in the structure of an area and the types of work available. By the 1970s, telephone directories were doing almost the same job as the commercial directories, and publication ceased.

Wills and Letters of Administration
Prior to 1858, wills were proved in the ecclesiastical courts and the place of probate depended on a number of factors - the residence of the testator, where his property was situated and its value. In many cases, this would be the Bishops' Consistory Court, and surviving wills can generally be found in the county record office. However if the testator left property in more than one diocese, the will would have been proved at either the Prerogative Court of Canterbury (PCC) or the Prerogative Court of York.(PCY). All PCC wills and those proved during the Commonwealth (1649-1660) are held at the Public Record Office, and those for York are at the Borthwick Institute. During the period 1530-1750, it is common to find an Inventory of all the deceased persons' moveable goods. On the order of the court, this was made by appraisers, (3 or 4 local men) who drew up a list furniture, clothes, tools, household goods, and, where applicable, farm stock and their approximate values. Surviving inventories provide an excellent insight into the status and lifestyle of an ancestor and these documents can be found in the same repository as the wills themselves - and they are often name-indexed. Since 1858, wills have been proved at the Principal Probate Registry (formerly Somerset House) or at a District Probate Registry. Where a person dies without making a will - intestate - letters of administration are granted, usually to the next of kin, and these do not contain as much information as a will. Annual indexes - calendars - of all wills and letters of administration proved in England and Wales (generally known as "Wills and Admons") have been published since 1858. These are arranged alphabetically by surname of the deceased person

and entries appear in the index for the year in which probate was granted, which is not necessarily the same as the year of death.. The entry includes the name, occupation, address, place and date of death of the deceased, the name(s) of the executor(s)/executrix(es)/administrator(s), value of the estate and the date and place of probate. The latter is essential if you wish to purchase a copy of the document. Many District Probate Registries have deposited wills and admons proved at that office more than fifty years ago at either the county record office or main reference library, where they can be consulted. Indexes to wills and admons that are less than fifty years old can generally be examined at the District Probate Registry Office. Various taxes have been imposed on estates and the Death Duty Registers from 1796 -1894 (at the PRO), used in conjunction with the wills and admons, provide supplementary information about the beneficiaries, such as names of individuals and their relationship to the deceased.

Photographs
We are probably as guilty as our ancestors of not recording "who,where and when" on our family photographs, so getting into the habit of doing just that will be appreciated by generations to come! Whilst photographs of our relatives show us what they looked like and their social status, many large libraries have collections of photographs depicting local scenes over the last hundred years or so. These can be especially valuable where the church at which your ancestors married has been demolished or in "redevelopment /improvement areas" where their homes disappeared. Photographs of the same area over a specific time span show just how (or in some cases, how little) the landscape has changed. Whilst you may not be able to find a photograph of the actual house in which your family lived, you will probably find one like it, and photographs of churches, pubs , schools and places of entertainment survive in large numbers. If you have an undated family photograph, try costume books to identify the period by the style of clothes and hair, and if the name and address of the photographers' studio is shown, a search of relevant trade directories will enable you pinpoint the date more accurately . Military men can be identified by their badges and insignia by reference to books on uniforms and medals.

Newspapers and Periodicals
The first national daily newspapers, The Times, was published in 1785 as the Daily Universal Register, changing its name some three years later, and microfilm copies, along with its quarterly indexes, can generally be found in main reference libraries. As well as obituaries, notices of birth, death and marriage, the index includes bankruptcies, knighthoods and criminal and civil court cases. London newspapers originated in the early 17th century, whilst the Norwich Post first appeared in 1701 and by 1800 there were about 100 provincial papers - mostly published weekly. Many more appeared in the 1850s when stamp duties were abolished and they started to include more local news. Whilst local newspapers can be a great boon to the family and local historian, their greatest drawback is that they are rarely indexed. However, reading the newspapers of the areas where our ancestors lived gives us a wider picture of their lives - even to the advertisements for local shops and businesses! Modern newspapers are especially useful in respect of the "Births, Deaths and Marriages" announcements as they can help us to locate the funeral details once a death certificate has been obtained. Once families have moved away from an area, announcements

are often published in the newspapers of their former home town. The London Gazette was first published under the name of the Oxford Gazette in 1665 and continues today as the information sheet of the government, detailing court announcements, appointments in the armed forces and clergy, grants of peerage, naturalisations, awards of medals, changes of name and bankruptcy/liquidation notices. The Gentleman's Magazine was published between 1731 and 1868 and also contains similar information to the London Gazette, but may include biographies of "ordinary" people if they lived to a great old age or were involved in a newsworthy event.

Maps
The earliest useful maps for family and local historians are the county maps which started to appear in the reign of Elizabeth I, and since then a wide range of maps has been produced, many of which enable us to learn more about the areas in which our ancestors lived and worked. Specialised maps showing parishes and civil registration districts are invaluable research aids and transport maps detailing railways and canals are helpful in tracing ancestors who worked in these industries, as well as for tracing migratory forebears. Town plans can be traced back to the eighteenth century and whilst they are useful in showing the development of urban areas, and when streets first appear, their degrees of detail - and accuracy - varies. Tithe maps and awards were mostly produced in the 1840s and are particularly helpful for rural areas - they cover about two-thirds of all English and Welsh parishes- and came about as a result of the Tithe Commutation Act of 1836, which converted payment for rent in the form of tithes (one-tenth of the lands' produce) into a cash sum. Three copies were produced and can be found at the PRO with others at CROs or main libraries. An apportionment register was produced for each tithe award, giving details of the land owner, occupier, state of land and (sometimes) its valuation. Ordnance Survey maps have been produced in different series since 1801 and the first edition consisted of 110 sheets covering the whole of England and Wales at a scale of one inch to the mile. For the family and local historian, the series produced at 25 inches to the mile is most informative, as they show roads accurately, and schools, churches, factories and other buildings are named. In the 1890s maps of large towns were produced at a scale of 126 inches to the mile and these are particularly useful in conjunction with census returns as they show the location of back-to-back houses and named properties. Maps can be found in local studies departments of libraries, CROs and many have been reprinted and are available to purchase.

Educations Records - Schools, Colleges and Universities
Elementary education became compulsory in England and Wales as a result of Forsters Education Act of 1870, but not all school records have survived. The first step is to ascertain the school which your ancestor attended. The maps mentioned above or commercial directories will give addresses of local schools, and the Victoria County History series may be helpful in detailing when schools were opened (and closed). It was not uncommon for books to be given as prizes for good attendance as well as achievements, and if you have these in your possession, the bookplate usually shows the name of the pupil, the school and the date of the award. Similarly, school leaving certificates and reports can be helpful. Public and grammar schools usually retain their own records, whilst those of the Local Education schools/colleges can generally be found in CROs or in at the Education Department of the relevant

*useful maps ....
are the
county maps
which started
to appear
in the reign
of Elizabeth I,*

MARCORRIE
Hotel

**20 Falmouth Road
Truro   TR1 2HX
England**

Open all Year

Centrally situated in the Cathedral City of Truro in a delightful Victorian and Edwardian street only five minutes walk to the Cathedral and City Centre.

The Marcorrie Hotel is a small family run establishment; personal service and assistance is always to hand. The centuries of Cornish family tradition and hospitality are yours to saviour during a leisurely stay. In Springtime and early Summer the nearby famous Cornish gardens are yours to explore and admire.

The Marcorrie Hotel plays host to many family history researchers
including organised tours
from the North America and Australasia.

The fifth return trip to the Hotel of the
Australian/Cornish Family History Group in 1999
was an overwhelming success.

Whether you be an individual, family or organised group a welcome awaits you
at the Marcorrie Hotel.

Telephone, write or fax for details of our tariff and further information
on what we have to offer for family historian researchers.

Payment:
All Major Credit Cards accepted.
Cheques with valid Bankers Card.
Travellers Cheques or Cash accepted.

Telephone: 01872 277374

Fax: 01872 241666

Web: www.cornwall.net/marcorrie

council. School logs books - the day to day diary - are the most likely records to have survived, but unless your ancestor was very good (or very bad!), no mention will probably be made of him/her in these. Admission registers usually show the date of admission, name, address and date of birth of the child, with the name of his/her father/guardian. Colleges - especially those specialising in certain subjects - publish lists of awards gained by their students and every university has a list of its graduates (alumni). Those of Oxford and Cambridge have been published up to about 1900 and contain biographical details of their graduates.

Occupational Records

Each of the professions publish annual lists of their members - the Medical Directory/Register, the Law List and Crockford's Clerical Directory for example- and these are readily accessible in major libraries. Military sources have been discussed elsewhere in this publication, and records can be found at the PRO(Kew). The Army, Navy and Air Force Lists can also be found in main libraries, but they include the officer class only. Records of trade unions and contemporary accounts of working life in factories also help us to gain an insight into the types of work our ancestors did and many large organisations, such as the Post Office maintain their own archives of employees. Company records and trades catalogues may survive, but in many cases these do not include staff records. Apprenticeship records prior to 1834 may be found amongst the parish records if a child was apprenticed by the parish or with the Poor Law records after that date, and they detail the terms of the apprenticeship, its dates, and outcome. Lists/indexes of masters and apprentices can usually be found in CROs.

Cokayne, Debrett, Walford, Burke

The above have all published guides to the peerage, baronetcy, landed gentry and county families on a regular basis. The volumes show the lineage of each family along with coats of arms. If the person you are researching worked for one of these families, it is possible to obtain an overview of their daily life as many biographies have been published. and surviving estate papers may contain details of staff.

Quarter Sessions Records

Justices of the Peace met four times a year and the records of these courts up to the latter part of the nineteenth century contain administrative records as well as judicial ones. Few are indexed, but some of the material included in this resource , usually to be found in CROs or city/borough archives, can be of particular interest to the family and local historian. These include victualler's licences, calendars of prisoners, lists of jurors, oaths of allegiance, lists of recusants and tax returns.

Poor Law Records

From Elizabethan times it was the responsibility of the parish to levy a poor rate in order to relieve the poor of the parish. Strenuous efforts were made to keep the rate down and ensure that payments were only made to those who were eligible. Surviving rates books include names of both those paying the rate and those in receipt of relief. Prior to the passing of the Poor Law Amendment Act in 1834, records are usually found amongst the parish records, and after that date, with the Poor Law Union records as responsibility was then passed to the Boards of Guardians. Overseers were keen to remove paupers back to their parish of origin and a huge amount of paperwork was generated in the forms of settlement certificates, removal orders and bastardy examinations and bonds.

Cemetery Records and Monumental Inscriptions

If an ancestor was buried in a family grave, there may be grave papers held by a member of the family. These detail the names of all persons buried in the grave and the dates of burial. Alternatively funeral cards may be held giving burial details, and once the grave has been located, the superintendent of the cemetery can provide names and dates of interment. If you are trying to find the burial place of an ancestor, try the local churches with burial grounds or directories give the addresses of municipal cemeteries. There may have been an obituary or announcement in the local press giving details of the funeral, and the Federation of Family History Societies has an ongoing project to record all legible monumental inscriptions in church burial grounds. They are usually published by local family history societies and are name-indexed.

There are numerous additional "miscellaneous" sources available to the family and local historian - some of which may be of particular help with your own research. Because family history is not a discrete subject, be prepared to explore sources that are not directly associated with genealogy - and in doing so you will certainly be able to "put the flesh on the bones" of your ancestors.

Family Archive CDs

Family History: Notable British Families, 1600s-1900s

A collection of authoritative works on British genealogy, this Family Archive contains images of the pages of eleven volumes of pedigrees and lineage records by the British publishing house Burke's Peerage. This Family Archive was produced in collaboration with the Genealogical Publishing Company and references more than 539,000 individuals. Burke's pedigrees are easy to read, easy to follow, and easy to understand. In general, each genealogical study begins with a brief biographical sketch followed by a wealth of detail about that person's lineage. Often, you'll learn details of:

- ▶ Education
- ▶ Service
- ▶ Occupation
- ▶ Honours
- ▶ Family members
- ▶ Places of birth, residence & death
- ▶ Descriptions of coats-of-arms

This Family Archive includes the best reference work ever published on British heraldry, The General Armoury of England, Scotland, Ireland, and Wales, as well as other volumes of high quality and value.

£27 (CD No. 367)

International Land Records: Irish Flax Growers, 1796

Irish Flax Growers

In 1796, the Irish Linen Board published a list of nearly 60,000 individuals who received awards for planting between one and five acres of flax. Individuals who planted one acre were awarded four spinning-wheels, and those growing five acres were awarded a loom. The "Flax Grower's List," reproduced in this Family Archive, is an extremely useful genealogical record since virtually no Irish census of the nineteenth century has survived. Find an ancestor among the individuals listed and you will be able to determine his full name and the parish and county in which he grew flax. With the information listed, you may be able to compensate for the lack of genealogical records available for Ireland at this time. If you are one of the nearly 70 million individuals worldwide with Irish heritage dating to the 18th century, this CD can be an invaluable resource. This Family Archive CD was produced in collaboration with Heritage World and the Genealogical Publishing Company.

Please note: This CD cannot be used with Family Tree Maker for Power Macintosh.

£20 (CD No. 271)

Genealogical Records: Loyalists in the American Revolution

Loyalists

in the
AMERICAN
REVOLUTION

Loyalists were American colonists who retained allegiance to the British Crown. Also known as "Tories," Loyalists were estimated to have made up one-third of colonial America's population. The thirteen volumes of records included in this Family Archive CD comprise some of the most useful works ever published on Revolutionary War Loyalists, and contain records for more than 87,000 individuals. Originally published by the Genealogical Publishing Company, these volumes include biographies, compensation applications, land records, military diaries, muster rolls, orderly books, and pension applications. While the majority of the records reference colonies where the Loyalist cause was the strongest (e.g., Georgia, the Carolinas, New York, and Pennsylvania), this Family Archive also includes individuals from Florida, Great Britain, Louisiana, Massachusetts, Maryland, Mississippi, New Brunswick, New Jersey, Nova Scotia, Ontario, and Virginia.

£20 (CD No. 144)

Naturalisation Records: Philadelphia, 1789–1880

PHILADELPHIA
NATURALIZATION

RECORDS

With information on more than 113,000 immigrants from nearly 100 countries, this Family Archive CD will be a great resource for researchers whose families settled in the mid-Atlantic region, especially Eastern Pennsylvania. It lists information on the naturalisation of individuals who applied for citizenship through the Philadelphia court system between 1789 and 1880. Information compiled in this CD was originally edited by P. William Filby and produced as a book called Philadelphia Naturalisation Records. Most of the records list an individual's name, any alternate spellings or interpretations of that name, that individual's country of former allegiance, as well as the date and location he or she filed a declaration of intention and oath of allegiance. This Family Archive was produced in collaboration with Gale Research.

£27 (CD No. 258)

Family Archive CDs

International Records: English Settlers in Barbados, 1637–1800

Throughout most of the 17th and 18th centuries, a continuous flow of British settlers left Barbados for virtually every point along the Atlantic seaboard. As a result, many early American families can trace their origins in the New World first to Barbados. This Family Archive CD contains images of pages from six volumes originally published by the Genealogical Publishing Company: Barbados Records: Baptisms 1637–1800; Barbados Records: Marriages 1643–1800, Volumes I and II; and Barbados Records: Wills 1639–1725, Volumes I–III. Approximately 200,000 individuals are referenced in these source records. Each record includes vital information about the corresponding baptism, marriage, or probate record.

£27 (CD No 22)

Irish Immigrants to North America, 1803–1871

This Family Archive CD contains images of the pages of twelve volumes of compiled passenger lists. It was produced in collaboration with the Genealogical Publishing Company and lists approximately 46,000 Irish passengers who arrived in the United States and Canada primarily in the nineteenth century. For each individual listed in this CD, you will generally find the following information: name and age, arrival date, and occupation. For your searching convenience, Broderbund has provided an electronic name index.

£27 (CD No. 257)

Germans to America, 1875–1888

The first fully-searchable version of an invaluable resource, this Family Archives CD contains information on approximately 1.5 million immigrants who arrived in the United States between 1875 and 1888. Edited by Ira A. Glazier and P. William Filby, and published by Scholarly Resources, Inc., the print version of Germans to America was the first extensive, indexed source of German surname immigrants. This Family Archive CD contains the information taken from Volumes 32 through Volume 56 of the Germans to America series. It covers the high point of German immigration to America (the years 1880 through 1885); during that period 797,900 Germans immigrated to America. Most of the records list an immigrants age, gender, occupation, village or town of origin and destination, plus the name of the ship, and the date of arrival.

£40 (CD No. 356)

Passenger and Immigration Lists Index, 1538–1940

Updated in 1999, this Family Archive CD contains listings of nearly 3 million individuals who arrived in United States ports between 1538 and 1940. Originally compiled by P. William Filby, these records can provide valuable family history information to those with immigrant ancestors. This data was collected from published passenger lists, naturalisation records, church records, family and local histories, as well as voter and land registrations, and is the most complete source of immigration information available on CD, especially for the early years of this time period. For each individual listed, you will find the following information: name and age; year and place of immigration; names of family members with whom they travelled; full source information; and source code of immigration record. Depending on the original source, you may also learn the name of the ship on which the individual arrived, ports and dates of departure and arrival, occupation, religion, places of origin and residence, and naturalisation date.

£40 (CD No. 354)

Passenger and Immigration Lists Index, 1538–1940 *1999 Supplement*

Do you already own the original Passenger and Immigration Lists CD No. 354 published in 1998? Now you can access the 245,880 new names added this year at a special price. Since this is such a significant resource, with names constantly being added, annual updates to the Index are anticipated.

£13 (CD No. 590)

Passenger and Immigration Lists: Boston, 1821–1850

This Family Archive CD contains alphabetical listings of approximately 161,000 individuals who arrived at the port of Boston from foreign ports between 1821 and 1850. For each individual listed, you will find the following information: name and age, gender, arrival date, country of origin, and occupation. With the information provided, you should be able to establish a very complete record for your ancestor. For each record, you will also learn where to find a microfilm copy of the original passenger list. By researching with this microfilm, you may be able to determine the name of the ship on which an ancestor sailed and the location in which he wished to settle.

£27 (CD No. 256)

GRETNA GREEN MARRIAGES
Cecil R. Humphery-Smith, FSA
Principal of The Institute of Heraldic and Genealogical Studies

There were a fair number of centres in villages along the border country between England and Scotland where enterprising local individuals were prepared to celebrate and register marriages under the Law of Scotland. These were marital unions by consent and cohabitation in the presence of a witness, which is all that the Law required. Most of these "marriage priests" set up their booths or had their "offices" in the vicinity of the toll bars on the principal roads between the two kingdoms. The ecclesiastical history of Scotland contributed to their existence as, later, did Lord Hardwicke's Marriage Act of 1753 which did not run north of the border. Couples came from far afield, often pursued by angry parents and guardians, to establish their matrimonial rights through these clandestine ministers. Effectively brought to an end by Lord Brougham's Marriage Act of *1856,* it was not until 1939 that marriage by mutual consent of the parties concerned was abolished. Nonetheless, the romance continues to this day, and "marriages" are still performed at Gretna Green, whether or not there was a smithy and an anvil in the old days!

these "marriage priests" set up their booths or had their "offices" in the vicinity of the toll bars

The village of Gretna stood between Lamberton and Springfield Tolls. It was not until 1825 that Gritney or Gretna Hall was converted into an hotel and marriage shop for eloping couples. William "Auld Watty" Coulthard had been one of the first of the "priests" and taught Joseph Pasley, who, on a pint of Scottish brandy (whisky was "a woman's drink") a day, lasted until he was 82. He died in 1814 but, already, his apprentices in the trade, Robert Elliot and David Lang, were in business; they were aided by stagecoach proprietors, Wilson and Fairbairn, who would arrange for the couples and their parties to be brought to the shops.

During a trial in London, at which Lang was a witness in a matrimonial dispute, a judge called him a "forger of marriages" and named him "Mr Blacksmith"; so began the legend upon which tourism has since subsisted. Lang's rival in trade, Tom Little, an incomer from Cumberland, took advantage and put up the sign of the "Blacksmith's Shop" by his house in Springfield. When all was *officially* over, Lord Neave wrote a song about the Gretna Green marriages which neatly sums up the whole farce:

"... suppose that Jocky and Jenny say 'we two are husband and wife', the witnesses needn 't be many, they 're instantly buckled for life."

Of course, the practice, however romantic, in the event, gave way to desertion, neglect, bigamy and legalised rape.

There are more than a dozen collections of border marriage records in several repositories. One of the largest is the Lang Collection, currently being indexed and held at the Institute of Heraldic and Genealogical Studies in Canterbury, from whom details of the several sources may be obtained. Miss Meliora C. Fowle Smith wrote under the pseudonym of "Claverhouse" a splendid account of *Irregular Border Marriages* in 1934, and an article "Irregular Border Marriages" by G. S. Crighton appeared in *The Genealogists' Magazine* Vol. 20, No. 8, pp. 208, 264-266. D. J. Steel deals with such irregular marriages in Vol. XII of *The National Index of Parish Registers, Sources for Scottish Genealogy and Family History* (1970), pp. 97-107, and in Vol. I, *General Sources of Births, Marriages and Deaths before 1837(1968,* third impression 1976), pp. 315-317. Vol. 18, No. 151 (1997) of *Family History* pp. 247-259 deals with "The Gretna Green Marriage Records".

CORNWALL
FAMILY
HISTORY
SOCIETY

LOST
YOUR
GRANDAD

... your GREAT-grandad, or even your GREAT-GREAT-grandad?

For anyone researching their family roots or local history, the Cornwall Family History Society is indispensable.

- **free help and advice** - members are always on duty during opening hours to offer assistance and to point you in the right direction

- **GRO index** - births, marriages and deaths for all England and Wales from July, 1837. A quarterly alphabetical Index.

- **census returns** - from 1851 to 1891 for Cornwall with several being alphabetical. That of 1881 covers the whole of England and Wales, alphabetical by County.

- **the International Genealogical Index** - covering most of the world, this renowned index lists millions of baptisms and marriages

- **marriages** - most marriages for Cornwall between C16th and 1837 are indexed alphabetically by Husband and by Wife

- **burials and monumental inscriptions** - the burial registers for Cornwall have been transcribed and indexed from 1813 to 1837. The monumental inscriptions for most burial grounds have been recorded and indexed

The Society also holds family pedigrees, old photographs and postcards, parish histories, ships passenger lists etc., etc., and many of the records are available on computer.

For further details contact:
The Secretary, Cornwall Family History Society, 5 Victoria Square,
Truro, Cornwall, TR1 2RS   Tel: 01872 264044
Email: Secretary@cfhs.demon.co.uk

Palaeography for Family Historians
Marc Morris

Over the last few years, access to historical records has improved beyond measure. Archives and libraries are now more willing to cater for family historians and even provide leaflets designed specially for them. In the foreseeable future, computer technology, which has made finding records so much easier, may be widely used to publish original documents. Even as I write, Microsoft is digitising the entire Vatican archive and releasing it on the web.

However, getting hold of the records is only the first step and, having found our documents, we need to interpret them. Problems tend to occur when we delve into records from the 18th century and beyond. During this period, even basic administrative documents, like parish registers, didn't follow a standard format and the quality of record keeping depended heavily on the scribe or parish clerk. The deeper we dig, the more rarefied our sources will become, and the more likely we are to encounter manuscripts written in scripts that range from the unfamiliar to the indecipherable.

Some people think that original manuscripts dating from before the 19th century will be far too difficult and time-consuming to read. However, many others love using records that are centuries old because physical contact with these documents heightens their sense of the past. They may also discover information which the compiler of a printed edition felt was unnecessary to include. Of course, researchers consulting material that hasn't been transcribed or published have no choice but to rely on the original sources.

Unfortunately, the ability to read old manuscripts won't develop overnight and, as with most skills, proficiency only comes with practice. However, observing these basic points will save time and effort when tackling documents written in unfamiliar scripts. Firstly, before you even start looking for a document, you should read up about the source and the kind of information you expect it to contain. This may seem unnecessary with straightforward records like parish registers, but it will save you valuable time if you're using more complex sources like death duty records. For example, many legal and administrative documents have standard introductory and concluding paragraphs. A will, for instance, may contain in its opening sentences a number of stock religious sentiments expressing the author's humility and conveying his soul to God. With a little advance preparation you will be able to identify a document's various parts, and decide which sections you need to decipher and which you can afford to ignore. The Public Record Office produces an excellent range of well-written and concise guides covering the more popular classes of documents used by family historians. These books will also prepare you for the many unfamiliar terms and abbreviations that you might otherwise have skipped or puzzled over for hours.

Sooner or later the task of deciphering old manuscripts boils down to our ability to recognise the forms of individual letters. The fact that we can understand manuscript and printed documents produced today is due to our familiarity with the shape of both whole words and individual letters, which, in turn, enables us to skim documents for the information we're looking for. When approaching unfamiliar scripts, these skills have to be re-learned.

There are several books on the market that contain crib sheets featuring individual letter shapes from scripts that date back as far as the 16th century. Examples include Lionel Munby's *Reading Tudor and Stewart Handwriting*, which introduces you to earlier alphabets, while Eve McLaughlin's *Reading Old Handwriting* focuses on later styles. Don't waste too much time trying to commit tables of letter forms to memory, however. Instead, choose a set of records and then start working on them right away. It's a good idea to begin on fairly straightforward documents that include lots of similar entries — pre-19th century parish registers would be a good source to cut your teeth on. Once you feel more confident with these simple records, you can tackle more complex documents written in the same hand.

the ability to read old manuscripts won't develop overnight .... proficiency only comes with practice

When you begin deciphering a document, approach the task as you would a crossword puzzle. Proceed one letter at a time, transcribing the words, or parts of words, that you recognise and then work out the rest of the text based on what you already know. For example, you might use the unusual letter forms in common names and phrases to help you unravel more arcane words or misspellings. If you get really stuck, try counting the number of vertical strokes within a particular word. Palaeographers call these strokes 'minims', for the sole reason that the word 'minim' itself contains ten such strokes. If, for instance, you encountered (but were unable to make out) the word 'union', you would nevertheless probably be able to discern that there was an 'o' towards the end of the word, and that the final letter was 'n'. However, the first part of the word might prove more of a problem, especially if the scribe failed to dot the 'i'. However, once you establish that the start of the word contains five minims, you should then experiment with various alternatives — 'm', 'n', 'l' and 'u' — until the most plausible reading of the text presents itself.

The biggest problem that beginners are likely to encounter are abbreviations. If you're unlucky, you might be faced with a text littered with semi-formed words, or even seemingly meaningless strings of letters with marks or dashes above them. The abbreviations you find in records produced during the 16th, 17th and 18th centuries developed from a system of shorthand that grew up in the later medieval period. During the 12th and 13th centuries, there was a remarkable rise in the number of manuscripts produced, as religious and secular authorities came to rely more on written proofs and less on visual and oral evidence. Papal and royal chanceries (writing offices) poured forth thousands of documents, while various universities were founded to train scholars. An expansion in the legal profession, which provided employment for countless notaries and clerks, took place, while paper was introduced as a cheap alternative to parchment at about the same time.

As a result of these changes, handwriting itself began to alter. The highly ornate letter forms that we associate with the medieval period were, in fact, confined to expensive decorated books and bibles. Working documents, on the other hand, needed to be produced as quickly as possible, using simple letter forms and numerous abbreviations. Hundreds of symbols were devised by scribes and, over the centuries, these abbreviations became highly standardised — they had to be, if the content of any message was to be properly understood by its recipient.

Many of these symbols were used until fairly recently. Notaries, scribes, parsons and parish clerks — anyone whose work involved writing on a regular basis — continued to employ this standard form of shorthand. However, as time went by, the more rarefied abbreviations fell by the wayside, until only a handful of the most common ones were left. This process was accelerated as more and more documents were produced in English, since the original symbols had been introduced when Latin was the only universal written language.

The abbreviations you come across fall into two categories. They will either be suspensions, where only the end of a word (sometimes just the final letter) has been omitted, or they will be contractions, where letters within the word have been left out. Generally, a line above the last letter of a word indicates that a final 'm' has been omitted ('m' is a very common ending in lots of Latin words). Sometimes you will find what looks like a small '2' written above the end of a word. This was a symbol devised during the Carolingian period to signify that the 'ur' ending of a Latin word had been dropped and, occasionally, it was used by clerks writing in English. For example, 'saviour' might be written 'savio2'. In later documents, suspensions were indicated by a dash, or an apostrophe, at the end of a word. Generally speaking, in such cases the word is so obvious that it can be readily understood from its context. If someone's place of birth was recorded as Lond', it's clear that he was a native of London.

Contractions may be more difficult to decipher, but there are relatively few of these in later documents. Undoubtedly, the most common form of contraction you'll encounter are the prefixes *pre-*, *pro-* and *per-*. Latin scribes would simply use the single letter 'p', with a horizontal line at varying positions on or above the stem, in place of these prefixes. If the line was marked at the top, then the symbol stood for the letters 'pre-'. If it extended backwards from the centre, at the same level as the bottom of the bow of the 'p', it signified 'pro-'. Finally, if the line crossed the descender of the 'p', this denoted the prefixes 'per-' or 'par-'. These Latin abbreviations were also employed by clerks writing in English and you may find the word 'parish' written using the symbol for 'per'. Similarly, I have seen the word 'proper' written using both the 'pro-' and 'per-' abbreviations together.

A final tip is to get into the habit of transcribing documents so that it's clear where you have extended any abbreviations in the original. Palaeographers do this by placing the expanded part of the word between round brackets. For instance, if the word 'proper' had been abbreviated in the way I've described above, it would be transcribed as 'p(ro)p(er)'. Another device that's worth using is to indicate words you're not sure about by placing them between 'daggers' or obeli, to give them their formal title. For example, if you've transcribed a name as Matthew — although you think it might be Martin — you should write it as †Matthew†. By employing these conventions, you'll be able to make any necessary revisions when you return to your notes later, perhaps with fresh evidence that suggests alternative readings.

Further Reading:
Reading Tudor and Stuart Handwriting, Lionel Munby (1988)
Reading Old Handwriting, Eve McLaughlin (1987)
For more information about the growth of literacy, see *M.T. Clanchy's From Memory to Written Record* (1993), while Michelle Brown's *A Guide to Western Historical Scripts from Antiquity to 1600* (1990) examines the history and development of various scripts.

Marc Morris is studying for a D. Phil. in History at Oxford University, and was formerly Assistant Editor, *Family History Monthly*.

❀❀❀❀❀❀❀❀❀❀❀❀❀❀❀❀❀

SOME QUESTIONS FOR FAMILY HISTORIANS

Did your ancestors come from several different parts of the British Isles?
Is the place where your ancestors lived a long way away from where you live now?
Would it help your research to have ready access to the largest collection of parish register copies, tombstone inscriptions and census indexes in the Commonwealth?
Would it help to borrow microform copies of parish registers to use at, or near, your home and at your convenience?
Are there gaps in you knowledge or expertise which you would like to fill?
- the reading of old handwriting, army, naval, nonconformist, Scottish, Irish or Welsh sources?

Have you ever hit a brick wall in your research and need of some help and advice from some-one more experienced?
Do you need help and advice on using computers, genealogical software or the Internet?
Would it help to browse in the best-stocked specialist family history bookshop in the country?

The Society of Genealogists is the one-stop resource for family historians in the British Isles. We have a unique collection of research material - where records of your Irish, Welsh, Dorset or Yorkshire ancestors are only a few paces away from those in London. We offer a range of progressive skills courses to help you in your research & record-keeping, and a programme of lectures and courses to broaden your understanding of the lives our ancestors led. The Society of Genealogists is a registered charity and its facilities are open to all - on payment of current fees.

If you have answered yes to any of the questions above and have a serious interest in family and social history, you should become a member of the Society.

Members are entitled to free access to the library (with some borrowing privileges); a 20% discount on all Society publications, lectures and courses and Genealogists Magazine free every three months. All for just £30 a year.

For more information visit our web site
www.sog.org.uk
or contact
The Society of Genealogists
14 Charterhouse Buildings, Goswell Road
London EC1M 7BA
Tel: 020 7251 8799

TREE TOPS FREE FAMILY TREE & WE'LL MEET AGAIN Services on Sky TV

Mary Kearns Trace, Calgary, Alberta T2E 6E7 traces@cadvision.com

Best described by Carol as "a hobby that has got out a little out of hand," the weekly television FAMILY TREE QUERY service began in October 1995. In March 1996, due to demand, an extra service called "WE'LL MEET AGAIN" was commenced. These services are run on a completely VOLUNTARY basis and both keep Carol very busy. ANYONE, anywhere in the world, with British or European interests, can advertise on these pages. It is not necessary to subscribe to Sky TV to participate.

Family Tree Query Service:
It is estimated that over 5000 queries from all over the world have been on Sky TV since it began. It's no great surprise as it's completely FREE. There are no catches involved. Every Monday new queries appear on page number 268 (digital 468) of SKY NEWS TEXT. Queries (messages) stay on screen for a week.

We'll Meet Again Query Service:
This service addresses the needs of people organising reunions (Armed Services, Schools etc) and is also used for people looking for missing living family members. As expected, it is not as heavily used as the Family Tree Service but it becomes very popular near Armistice Day and prior to special anniversaries. This service can be viewed on page 267 (digital 467) of SKY NEWS TEXT.

Submitting Queries:
The only limitation on submissions is the number of words in the query. The maximum is 40 words, including submitter's name and address (e-mail or snail mail) &/or fax/telephone number. Bear in mind that these messages are broadcast throughout the UK & Ireland as well as many parts of Europe and messages circulate world-wide. Some people may not be willing to telephone or fax from such long distances and many do not have e-mail. It is best to include a postal address as well.

Queries may be submitted by e-mail or letter. CAPITAL LETTERS are requested for the surname(s) being researched (so no errors are made) as well as for the name and address of the submitter. Submit as many queries as you likes at one time but be advised they will NOT all appear on the same week. Only E-mail submissions are acknowledged. It is regretted that neither telephone calls or faxes can be returned due to cost. There is no financial backing whatsoever for this service. Donations are gratefully received and are used solely for maintenance of the service. Send your queries (messages) to:

TREE TOPS, P.O. Box 116, Swindon, Wilts SN3 2SX UK
Tel/Fax: 01793-538730
PLEASE no calls between 10pm - 9am UK time
e-mail: tree.tops@virgin.net
Website: http://freespace.virgin.net/tree.tops/

To best serve the needs of persons who do not have access to SKY NEWS TEXT a Tree Tops Genealogical Journal was commenced. This Journal is only available by e-mail (for a small charge) at the 1st of each month. A query may have to be shortened to fit on the screen, however full text of the query is provided in the e-mail journal. Only 1998 and 1999 e-mail journals are still available. Please state your country of residence when enquiring about the Journal.

FREE SURNAME SEARCHES
These are available for queries submitted between 1995 and 1998 and queries can be provided for small charge.

The success of Tree Tops, which offers a willingness to help others find their ancestors and friends, is apparent by the number of people who use the service regularly, to great effect, and the fact that it received a credit in the recent Granada TV series "Find A Fortune." It's success is due to a lot of hard work on Carol's part. However, she wishes to acknowledge the generous assistance, support and guidance provided by two very good "genealogy friends," Pat Wilson and Mary Trace, both experienced genealogists and indexers. Their help has been invaluable.
Pat Wilson (of Tuffley, Gloucester) operates the Wiltshire Index Service: Burials, Wills & 1871 Census (http://www.wis.mcmail.com) and is also the agent for
1) The Ring: Wiltshire Marriages
http://freespace.virgin.net/tree.tops/mring/ring.htm
2) Wiltshire 1851 Census Productions
http://www.wis.mcmail.com/wil51cen.htm

Mary Trace (of Calgary, Alberta, Canada) operates **Traces From Your Past** (http://www.cadvision.com/traces). This home page is the gateway to Genealogy Alberta (indexes for 1891 Alberta Census & various southern Alberta references); Canadian Immigration Finding Aids; and British Strays in Canada index (starting Jan 2000). She functions as Carol's jack of all trades' and webmaster, thus adding a little international flavour.

Somewhere amidst the work involved to prepare and manage the TREE TOPS SERVICES Carol has found time to work on other projects of benefit to family historians. She maintains growing indexes of obituaries and accidents & inquests for Wiltshire as well as a small collection of surname indexes for monumental inscriptions for Glamorgan, Wales and Cheshire. Some information has been published. Many of these indexes appear on her Website. Other indexes in the pipeline include Birthday Memories and In Memoriams.

A New FREE Search Service has been commenced for OBITUARIES, 1992-1999, from the Swindon Evening Advertiser Newspaper (Wiltshire).
Contact Carol at tree.tops@virgin.net.
Original copies (on hand) of over 12,000 obituaries have been indexed. The FREE search will provide the full names of the people bearing your requested surname. Maiden names have also been indexed. PLEASE, do not dismiss this index because of the years of death. Many reached a great age and were born in the late 1890s - early 1900s. Many who are listed died outside the Wiltshire area.

Further information from the obituaries is available for a small charge and will consist of (where given) date & place of death, age, where buried and name of spouse if already deceased. NO information will be given on people who are still living. PLEASE - ONE SURNAME enquiry per e-mail!

Carol's willingness to help others with their family history has resulted in her collecting many friends and contacts across the globe. Her unique TREE TOPS query services are invaluable to researchers but they need to be more widely publicised. You can help Carol by passing on this service information to others. It is only with your support that this FREE Family Tree advertising service can survive.

Carol looks forward to receiving your query & asks you mention the Genealogical Services Directory when you contact her.

TRACE YOUR BRITISH ANCESTORS

through our expert personal service

You will receive:

- a bound report complete with all documents acquired during our search
- swift and reliable results
- thorough and accurate research
- all the convenience of a professional service.

Our network of trained researchers covers the whole of the United Kingdom and is ready to start working for you immediately.

Write for a free brochure to the address below, or telephone 01344 872409,   fax 01344 875265 or Email windsor.ancestry@btconnect.com

Windsor Ancestry Research
**(GS/01) Bridge House, 18 Brokenhurst Road,
SOUTH ASCOT, Berkshire SL5 9DL, UK**

County & Country Codes (Pre 1974 counties)

These codes are used to avoid confusion in the use of abbreviations for countries and counties.
Created by Dr Colin Chapman they are universally recognised and should always be used.

England		Wales		Ireland (Eire)			
England	**ENG**	**Wales**	**WLS**	**Ireland** (Eire)	**IRL**	Latvia	**LAT**
All Counties	**ALL**	Anglesey	**AGY**	Antrim	**ANT**	Liechtenstein	**LIE**
Bedfordshire	**BDF**	Brecknockshire	**BRE**	Armagh	**ARM**	Lithguania	**LIT**
Berkshire	**BRK**	Caernarvonshire	**CAE**	Carlow	**CAR**	Luxembourg	**LUX**
Buckinghamshire	**BKM**	Cardiganshire	**CGN**	Cavan	**CAV**	Netherlands	**NL**
Cambridgeshire	**CAM**	Carmarthenshire	**CMN**	Clare	**CLA**	New Zealand	**NZ**
Cheshire	**CHS**	Denbighshire	**DEN**	Cork	**COR**	Norway	**NOR**
Cornwall	**CON**	Flintshire	**FLN**	Donegal	**DON**	Papua New Guinea	**PNG**
Cumberland	**CUL**	Glamorgan		Down	**DOW**	Poland	**POL**
Derbyshire	**DBY**	**GLA**		Dublin	**DUB**	Rep South Africa	**RSA**
Devonshire	**DEV**	Merionethshire	**MER**	Fermanagh	**FER**	Romania	**RO**
Dorsetshire	**DOR**	Monmouthshire	**MON**	Galway	**GAL**	Russia	**RUS**
Durham	**DUR**	Montgomershire	**MGY**	Kerry	**KER**	Slovakia	**SLK**
Essex	**ESS**	Pembrokeshire	**PEM**	Kildare	**KID**	Slovinia	**SLO**
Gloucestershire	**GLS**	Radnorshire	**RAD**	Kilkenny	**KIK**	Spain (Espagne)	**ESP**
Hampshire	**HAM**			Leitrim	**LEI**	Sweden	**SWE**
Herefordshire	**HEF**	**Scotland SCT**		Leix(Queens)	**LEX**	Switzerland	**CH**
Hertfordshire	**HRT**	Aberdeenshire	**ABD**	Limerick	**LIM**	Ukraine	**UKR**
Huntingdonshire	**HUN**	Angus	**ANS**	Londonderry	**LDY**	United Kingdom	**UK**
Kent	**KEN**	Argyllshire	**ARL**	Longford	**LOG**	United States	**USA**
Lancashire	**LAN**	Ayrshire	**AYR**	Louth	**LOU**	USSR	**SU**
Leicestershire	**LEI**	Banffshire	**BAN**	Mayo	**MAY**	Yugoslavia	**YU**
Lincolnshire	**LIN**	Berwickshire	**BEW**	Meath	**MEA**		
London (city)	**LND**	Bute	**BUT**	Monaghan	**MOG**		
Middlesex	**MDX**	Caithness-shire	**CAI**	Offaly(Kings)	**OFF**		
Norfolk	**NFK**	Clackmannanshire	**CLK**	Roscommon	**ROS**	**Australia**	**AUS**
Northamptonshire	**NTH**	Dumfriesshire	**DFS**	Sligo	**SLI**	Aus Capital Territory	**ACT**
Northumberland	**NBL**	Dunbartonshire	**DNB**	Tipperary	**TIP**	New South Wales	**NSW**
Nottinghamshire	**NTT**	East Lothian	**ELN**	Tyrone	**TYR**	Northern Territory	**NT**
Oxfordshire	**OXF**	Fifeshire	**FIF**	Waterford	**WAT**	Queensland	**QLD**
Rutland	**RUT**	Forfarshire	**ANS**	Westmeath	**WEM**	South Australia	**SA**
Shropshire	**SAL**	Invernessshire	**INV**	Wexford	**WEX**	Tasmania	**TAS**
Somerset	**SOM**	Kincardineshire	**KCD**	Wicklow	**WIC**	Victoria	**VIC**
Staffordshire	**STS**	Kinrossshire	**KRS**			Western Australia	**WA**
Suffolk	**SFK**	Kirkcudbrightshire	**KKD**				
Surrey	**SRY**	Lanarkshire	**LKS**	Austria	**OES**	**Canada**	**CAN**
Sussex	**SSX**	Midlothian **MLN**		Belarus	**BRS**	Alberta	**ALB**
Warwickshire	**WAR**	Moray	**MOR**	Belgium	**BEL**	British Columbia	**BC**
Westmorland	**WES**	Nairnshire	**NAI**	Croatia	**CRO**	Manitoba	**MAN**
Wiltshire	**WIL**	Orkney Isles	**OKI**	Czechoslovakia	**CS**	New Brunswick	**NB**
Worcestershire	**WOR**	Peebleshire	**PEE**	Czech Republic	**CZR**	Newfoundland	**NFD**
Yorkshire	**YKS**	Perthshire	**PER**	Denmark	**DEN**	North West Terr	**NWT**
YKS E Riding	**ERY**	Reffrewshire	**RFW**	Estonia	**EST**	Nova Scotia	**NS**
YKS N Riding	**NRY**	Ross & cromarty	**ROC**	Finland	**FIN**	Ontario	**ONT**
YKS W Riding	**WRY**	Roxburghshire	**ROX**	France	**FRA**	Prince Edward Islands	**PEI**
		Selkirkshire	**SEL**	Germany (1991)	**BRD**	Quebec	**QUE**
		Shetland Isles	**SHI**	German Old Emp	**GER**	Saskatchewan	**SAS**
Channel Islands	**CHI**	Stirlingshire	**STI**	Greece	**GR**	Yukon Territory	**YUK**
Alderney	**ALD**	Sutherland	**SUT**	Hungary	**HU**		
Guernsey	**GSY**	West Lothian	**WLN**	Italy	**ITL**		
Jersey	**JSY**	Wigtownshire	**WIG**				
Sark	**SRK**						
Isle of Man	**IOM**						
Isle of Wight	**IOW**						

Lochin Publishing, 6 Holywell Road, Dursley GL11 5RS England

Achievements (Established 1961)
To throw light on your ancestry, Coats of Arms, Family & House histories. See Advert on Page 60

Centre for Heraldic & Genealogical Research and Artwork, 79 - 82 Northgate, Canterbury, Kent, CT1 1BAGSD
Tel No: 01227-462618;   Fax No: 01227-765617
Email: achievements@achievements.co.uk.
Web site: www.achievements.co.uk

Ancestors of Dover Ltd
National and international research carried out by a team of local expert record agents directed by professional genealogists. See Advert on Page 60

The Chapel, Belgrave Road, Dover, Kent, CT17 9QYGSD
Tel No: 0800-1066-1066   Fax No: 01304-201102
Email: enquiries@ancestor.demon.co.uk
Web site: www.ancestors.co.uk

Ancestral Locations
Family histories researched throughout the UK by experienced genealogist. Special Introductory Research Package £250. See Advert on Page 60

9 Edgebury, Woolavington, Bridgwater, Somerset, TA7 8ES
Tel No: 01278-685255;   Fax No: 01278-685255
Email: lesleyt@ancestorsuk.com
Web site: www.ancestorsuk.com

Back to Roots Family History Service
Back to Roots offers a complete & comprehensive service to Family Historians. Well established research company which also sells books and other aids. See Advert on Page 198/199

16 Arrowsmith Dr., Stonehouse, Gloucestershire, GL10 2QR
Tel No: 01453-821300   Fax No: 01453-821300
Email: mike@backtoroots.co.uk
Web site: www.backtoroots.co.uk

Brewster International
Ancestral and missing persons research including adoption adoption related investigations. Research at all London Archives, etc. See Advert on Page Inside Front Cover

12 Avery Gardens, Ilford, Essex, IG2 6UJ, England.
Tel No: 0208-550-0333;   Fax No: 0208-550-7766
Email: brewsterint@cs.com
Web site: www.missing-people-found.com

Debrett Ancestry Research Limited
Meticulous, professional research in Britain, North America and Austalasia. UK house histories also undertaken. Free information pack available. See Advert on Pages 46, 76, 90

Dept GSD, PO Box 7, New Alresford, Hants. SO24 9EN
Tel No: (0)1962-732676;   Fax No: (0)1962-734040
Email: enquiry@debrettancestry.demon.co.uk
Web site: www.debrettancestry.demon.co.uk

Ian J Hilder, BA(Hons)
All records searched anywhere in the UK. All Sussex and London archives searched. Abstracts and translations arranged. See Advert on Page 76

23A Grantham Bank, Barcombe Cross, Lewes BN8 5DJ
Tel No: 01273-400604   Email: HilderGen@aol.com.

Link Investigations
Private and commercial investigations. Name tracing covering the UK. Missing friend and family. Plus many other investigative services. See Advert on Page 160

22 Swan Mill Gardens, Dorking, Surrey, RH4 1PN
Tel No: 01306-880707;   Fax No: 01306-888077
Email: info@linkinvestigations.co.uk
Web site: www.linkinvestigations.co.uk

People Search Tracing Services
Missing persons and living relatives traced in the UK. Current electoral registers searched by name. Friendly, personal service. Plus other specialist research. See Advert on Page 62

30A Bedford Place, Southampton, SO15 2DG
Tel No: 02380-562243;   Fax No: 02380-562243
Email: info@people-search.co.uk
Web site: www.people-search.co.uk

Patrick Yarnold Research
Genealogist & Record Agent. Research countrywide for 19th & 20th Centuries. Earlier periods research in London, Berkshire, Hampshire and Surrey. See Advert on Page 72

93 The Street, Puttenham, Guildford, Surrey, GU3 1AT
Tel No: 01483-810564

Pinhorns, Genealogists
Family, local and architectural history research throughout the UK. See Advert on Page 62

85 Etnam street, Leominster. HR6 8AE

U.K. Searches
Instant telephone search of the Electoral rolls for England, Scotland, Wales and also Ireland. See Advert on Page 62

Helouan, Merchant St, Bognor Regis, W. Sussex, PO21 1QH
Tel No: 01243-842444   Fax No: 01243-841418
Email: hac@abel.co.uk
Web site: www.uksearches.com

UK Tracing Services
Tracing service specialists in finding missing friends, family and beneficiaries, living in the UK. No find, no fee usually available. See Advert on Page 74

11 Woodfield Ave., Bredbury, Stockport, Ches., SK6 1DB
Email: tracer@talk21.com

Windsor Ancestry Research
An expert service covering the whole of the British Isles to discover and document your personal family history promptly and on affordable terms. See Advert on Page 58

Bridge Hse, 18 Brockenhurst Rd, Sth Ascot, Berks SL5 9DL
Tel No: 01344-872409;   Fax No: 01344-875265
Email: windsor.ancestry@btconnect.com

The Public Record Office
John Wood, Reader Information Services Department

The Public Record Office is the national archives of England Wales and the United Kingdom. The PRO, as it is popularly known amongst its users, is based at Kew in south west London. It houses one of the most definitive archive collections in the world representing the events and people of the past millennium. The records stored on 167 km of shelving at Kew were created in the course of government and dispensing of justice. Although the PRO is recognised as a major international research institution in fact around 80% of the visitors use the records for family history or local history research. This is not surprising when you delve into the records, for although the government wouldn't have a file solely dedicated to you, your ancestors or your community it will come as no shock to find that somewhere in the mountain of paper there is something to fill out your search. After all nearly 65,000 visitors a year are using the facilities to do just that. From the ex serviceman looking for the missing details in the exploits of his unit or ship during the second world war, the woman searching for details of exactly when their cousin sailed away to America or to the classroom researching the coming of the Railway to their town, all are visiting the PRO as the definitive source of such information.

Starting your research?
Although ultimately your research trail should lead you to the PRO or it's sister organisation, the Family Records Centre, for those new to family or local history research the PRO is not usually the best place to start. This is because the records held here were not formed with the future researcher in mind - the government kept records for the purpose of administering the country - not histories of individuals or communities. It is always best to try local sources before research in any record office. A good starting point is your local library. They often stock books dedicated to local history as well as a range of books designed to help beginners get started in family history research. They also may have access to back editions of local newspapers and these can be invaluable to researchers. Other overlooked sources are local studies centres and the resources of the local family history society, many of which feature in this publication. There are also monthly magazines dedicated to family history and local history research that are available from any good news outlet. Last but not least word of mouth is often a good starting point, older members of the community or relatives are particularly useful in that regard.

Why the PRO ?
After the initial groundwork has been done the question arises of where to go next?. The modern answer is often the Internet. The PRO's website is geared up to the needs of family and local historians. Not only does the website on http://www.pro.gov.uk/ allow you access to nearly two hundred the 'easy search' information leaflets providing practical information on how to research individual topics but the PRO has also made its catalogue available on the website. The website also has links to other sites of interest to the research community. For areas of popular research the first stop on the PRO website are the research information leaflets. They run through the diverse range of the material available at the PRO from subjects as varied as Apprenticeships, Coastguards, Soldiers discharge papers, Immigration, and Railway staff records through to Shipwrecks, Bankruptcy and Court records. These leaflets, also available onsite at Kew, are easily downloaded. Once read they give pointers into which areas of the PRO catalogue to browse either over the website or in the reading rooms. Although you cannot access the original documents on the website the online catalogue allows you to make a 'keyword' search so that you can readily see the range of files available before you make a visit to Kew. There is a full 'help' facility on the catalogue browser.

There is also the PRO information line on 020 8392 5200, staffed during Office hours, to provide general research information on the material available. Once you have discovered the wealth of material that is available then all that remains is for you to make arrangements for your visit.

Opening hours
The PRO is open 6 days a week generally throughout the year but the Office does close on bank and public holiday weekends as well as the annual stocktaking week - usually in December. The daily opening times vary slightly between 9 and 10 am. The Office closes at 5pm each day except Tuesdays and Thursdays when it is open until 7pm. You can write in for a general opening times leaflet if your library or family or local history society doesn't have one. Before setting off check the website or telephone the information line for up to date information. As well as confirming the opening times the information line is also a good source for travel tips to make your journey to the Office easier.

All roads lead to Kew
The PRO is easy to get to by either public transport or by road. The Office is 200 yards level walk from Kew Gardens station which is served by both the District underground line as well as the Silverlink Metro rail service. Kew Bridge station is only half a mile away. Local bus services run nearby. As the PRO is situate next to the A406 South Circular road, one of the main London road arteries, road access to all the main London motorways is good. Free parking is available on site. Many family history and local history groups run regular coach trips to the PRO. They are always booked in advance. They are a useful way of sharing the cost of travel as well as sharing those all important research tips. Details of the nearest Society to you are found elsewhere in this book. There is limited parking for coaches and they need to be booked

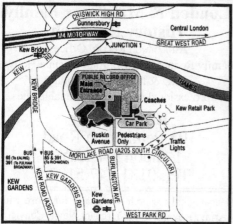

well in advance. To request a coach party booking simply telephone the information line or email coach-bookings@pro.gov.uk

What can I expect?

Admission to the PRO is free and, other than for coach parties and large groups, no advance booking is required. You will need to obtain a readers ticket on arrival. To do so you will need to bring means of identification such as a passport, driving licence or national identification card. If you are unsure whether you have the right means of identification then the information line will put you right beforehand. Once registered you will usually be given a short induction and tour by staff to help you familiarise with the research trail in the PRO. Features of the induction are practical instruction on how to use the document ordering system and how to use the self service system in the microfilm reading room. The PRO has a policy of microfilming heavily used records, often those most popular with family history researchers. These are all available in the microfilm reading room. In the other reading rooms there are always staff on hand to help you make the most of your research and to advise on the different avenues that you can follow. Please remember that for the preservation of the files and documents there are strict rules as to what you can take into the reading rooms. For example, pencils, note books and laptop computers are allowed, but pens, erasers and foodstuffs are strictly out of bounds. Access for the disabled is good with a lift to all floors. There are a wide range of facilities on site. There is an extensive range of document copying facilities. The ground floor shop is a goldmine of useful books and other publications with many titles dedicated to family history or local history topics. The shop also has a mail order service, details on the website. The restaurant is a focal point for friends and strangers to meet up and pass on research tips - as well as having lunch. The PRO gardens and the lakes make for a pleasant interlude.

Into the new Millennium

In late spring the new Museum and Visitor centre will open on the ground floor. This will feature live document displays as well as graphic representations displaying key events form the nations history. Although at the time of going to press the displays are not finalised it is expected that the Magna Carta, Guy Fawkes confession, Shakespeare's will, the abdication of Edward VIII and Nelson's logbook from the Victory will all make an appearance at some stage in unique collection.

The PRO is also a participant in the River Thames based 'String of Pearls' series of events to be staged throughout 2000. With open days, exhibitions and guest lectures throughout the year there is something for everyone. Full details of all the events can be obtained form the PRO website or by telephoning the events team on 020 8392 5323.

World War 1 experience

World War 1 was a defining point in history. The PRO has a wealth of original material that together with the census records and births marriages and deaths indexes available at the Family Records Centre form a valuable source for family and community historians. Throughout the year a series of exhibitions, workshops and talks both onsite and around the country will focus on the ongoing programme of releasing the surviving service records of the period and matching them to records with a local significance that together make the World War 1 experience.

Outreach

The PRO has an extensive outreach programme. Members of staff regularly present talks, lectures and workshops throughout the country dedicated to aspects of Family or Local history. The Office attends major family history fairs across the country where staff are on hand to provide practical advice. Details of the appearance schedule can be found on the website and are covered in the monthly family history magazines.

Essential contacts and information

The Public Record Office
Kew, Richmond, Surrey
TW9 4DU, United Kingdom

website: http://www.pro.gov.uk/
Information Line: 020 8392 5200 Fax: 020 8392 5286
email: enquiry@pro.gov.uk
events: 020 8392 5323 bookshop: 020 8392 5266
Coach Party bookings: 020 8392 5200 or email: coach-bookings@pro.gov.uk

The
Family Records
Centre

John Wood
Reader Information Services, Public Record Office
A service provided by the Public Record Office and the Office for National Statistics

Main Holdings
• Indexes of births marriages and deaths for England and Wales since 1837
• Indexes of legal adoptions in England and Wales since 1927
• Indexes of births, marriages and deaths of some British citizens abroad since 1796, including deaths in the two World Wars
• Census returns for England and Wales 1841- 1891
• Prerogative Court of Canterbury wills and administrations 1383 - 1858
• Death Duty Registers 1796 -1858 and indexes 1796 - 1903
• Many non-conformist registers 1567 - 1858

Other Resources at the Centre

FamilySearch
CD-ROMs compiled by the Church of Jesus Christ of Latter Day Saints (LDS) containing:
• International Genealogical Index (IGI) for Britain, Ireland and other countries (IGI for Britain and Ireland is also available at the FRC on microfiche)
• Ancestral Search (family trees donated by researchers)

• Scottish Church Records from the late 1500's to mainly 1854 but with some as late as 1900

• USA Social Security Death Index and Military Index
No fee is charged to use the above but there is a time limit of one hour per customer to use the CD-ROM version

1881 Census Index
CD-ROMs containing an index of surnames from the 1881 Census covering England, Wales, Scotland, Isle of Man and the Channel Islands (Also available at the FRC on microfiche but not including Scotland)
No fee is charged to use the above but there is a time limit of one hour per customer to use the CD-ROM version

Public Record Office (PRO) Catalogue
On-line link to the PRO catalogue at Kew

Scottish Link
On-line link to the General Register Office in Edinburgh. The link comprises:
• Indexes to statutory registers of births marriages and deaths in Scotland since 1855
•Scottish parish registers from 1553 to 1854
• Index to divorces in Scotland since 1984
Booking is essential. There is a maximum time limit of two hours searching per customer per day and a fee of £4 per half hour is charged. For further information and booking telephone 020 7533 6438

Northern Ireland Birth Index
• Computerised index of births recorded in Northern Ireland from 1922 to 1993
There is no charge to use this facility

Electoral Registers
The latest version available of Electoral Registers for England and Wales, Scotland and Northern Ireland. Archive versions are not available. A charge is made for business customers but not for personal enquirers

Copying Facilities
Copies of certified certificates of births, marriages and deaths relating to entries in the indexes for England and Wales can be ordered and collected or posted to you after four working days . There is a charge of £6.50 per certificate. A next day priority service is available at the charge of £22.50

Pages from the census for England and Wales 1841 to 1891, and PCC wills and administrations can be copied for a small charge at the time of visiting the FRC, either on a self service basis or by asking staff to carry out the work at a slightly increased charge. Rechargeable copy cards may be purchased if customers intend to do a large amount of copying over time.
A photocopier is also available for use by customers.

Refreshment Area
A refreshment area is provided on the lower ground floor with vending machines dispensing sandwiches, rolls, crisps, confectionery etc as well as hot and cold drinks.
A place to eat is provided for customers who have brought their own food.
There are a large number of outlets in the vicinity of the FRC which provide drinks, snacks and meals

Directions to the FRC
There is a map at Angel underground station on the main concourse which features the FRC. There is a similar map at Farringdon station.
Bus routes 19, 38 and 341 run very close to the FRC: visitors should ask for Tysoe Street or Finsbury Town Hall
There are commercial car parks in Bowling Green Lane and Skinner Street as well as a limited number of parking meters in the surrounding streets

Groups Visiting the FRC
We welcome visits from family history societies and other organisations but we do need to know in advance when you are coming. Please arrange your visit by telephoning 020 8392 5300. Coach drivers should be asked to drop passengers in Rosebery Avenue

Disabled Users
There is reserved parking at the FRC for visitors with disabilities but spaces must be booked in advance of your visit. Please telephone 020 7533 6460

Opening Hours
FRC opening times are as follows:

Monday, Wednesday and Friday	0900 - 1700
Tuesday	1000 - 1900
Thursday	1000 - 1900
Saturday	0930 - 1700

We are closed on Sundays and Bank & Public Holidays as well as the Saturdays at Christmas and Easter

For further information about
The Family Records Centre
Telephone 020 8392 5300
Internet http://www.pro.gov.uk

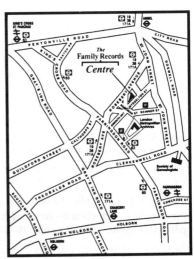

Society of Genealogists

14 Charterhouse Buildings, Goswell Road, London EC1M 7BA
Telephone: 020 7251 8799 Fax: 020 7250 1800 Email: info@sog.org.uk

Objects – The Society exists to promote,encourage and foster the study, science and knowledge of genealogy. It is a registered charity (No. 233701) and a Limited Company (No. 115703).

Membership – Members have access to the Society's Library without payment and, subject to certain exceptions, may borrow material from the Library. They also receive the *Genealogists' Magazine* quarterly free of charge. members are eligible for election as Fellows of the Society.

Applications for Membership – are welcome from all those with an interest in genealogy and family history. New members have to pay an entrance fee of £7.50 and their first subscription – which, for those paying by direct debit, is currently set at £30 per annum. New members not paying by direct debit pay £33. New members pay pro rata from the beginning of the month in which they apply but those applying after 30 June must pay to the end of the next calendar year. Renewal subscriptions are due on 1 January. UK tax payers are encouraged to pay under a deed of covenant. Direct debit and covenant forms are available on request.

Non-Members – may use the Library on payment: £3.00 for an hour; £8.00 for 4 hours and £12.00 for a day.

The Library – is unique in the British Isles with a large collection of family histories, civil registration andcensus material and the widest collection of Parish Register copies in the country (over 9,000). They are arranged with local histories, poll books and directories, other topographical material and the publications of county records and archaeological societies. Sections relate to the professions, schools and universities, the services, religious denominations, the peerage and heraldry and on English persons living abroad, in the Commonwealth and USA. Boyd's Marriage Index covers some 2,600 parish registers with nearly seven million names: a general Card Index contains some three million references: there are about 6,000 rolls of microfilm (including Scottish civil registration indexes) and the International Genealogical Index on both CD Rom (FamilySearch with over 200 million names) and fiche.

Opening Hours – the Library is open from 10.00am to 6.00pm on Tuesdays, Fridays and Saturdays and from 10.00am to 8.00pm on Wednesdays and Thursdays. It is closed on Mondays, Bank Holidays and, (for stocktaking), during the week which includes the first Monday in February.
– the Bookshop is open when the Library is open and also on Mondays (except the first in February and bank Holidays) from 10.00am to 5.00pm. The Bookshop is open to non-members and sells a wide range of books, fiched material and computer software – much by mail order. Details may be had on request.

Courses, Lectures and Visits – take place throughout the year. They are open to non-members but members receive a 20% discount. Details may be had on request.

Payments – may be made by MasterCard, Visa, Delta and Switch and the Bookshop accepts book tokens.

Computers – the Society runs a range of lectures and courses on the application of IT to genealogical research and publishes a quarterly periodical Computers in Genealogy at an annual cost of £8.00 for members and £10.00 for non-members.

Internet – please visit our web site http://www.sog.org.uk/ for up to date details.

SOCIETY OF GENEALOGISTS

Registered Charity No. 233701 Registered Company No. 115703

the FAMILY HISTORY fair

May 6th & 7th 2000
Saturday 10.00am – 6.00pm   Sunday 10.00am – 4.00pm

Royal Horticultural Society
New Hall and Conference Centre, Greycoat Street, Westminster, London, SW1
Day admission £6.00 at the door Advance tickets (before April 14th) **£4.00** with ssae from:

Society of Genealogists
14 Charterhouse Buildings, Goswell Road, London EC1M 7BA
Telephone: 020 7253 5235   Fax: 020 7250 1800

Email: sales@sog.org.uk
Visit our website at www.sog.org.uk

"Stockdale, Stockdill, Stogdale: Alan de Stokdale 1332 SRCu; William de Stokdale 1379 PTY. From Stockdale (Yorks, Cumb)."

A Dictionary of English Surnames, by P H Reaney & R M Wilson.

STOCKDALE/STOCKDILL is a North of England surname, principally from Yorkshire, deriving from places called Stockdale, the root name. The society is open to anyone of the name, or recognised variant, and to anyone with Stockdale/dill ancestry or who is interested in researching the origins and history of the surname.

Stockdale variants include: Stockdill, Stogdale, Stogdill, Stockdell, Stogdell, Stockdle, Stockdall, Stocksdale, Stocksdill, Stogsdale and Stogsdill.

Web site:- http://ourworld.compuserve.com/homepages/roystock
Secretary/Journal Editor: Roy Stockdill, 6 First Avenue, Garston, Watford, Herts WD2 6PZ. E-mail: roystock@compuserve.com

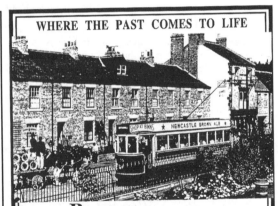

FEDERATION PUBLICATIONS

Books for Family Historians written by Family Historians

♦ Well over 100 titles commissioned by the Federation of Family History Societies and produced at attractive prices, plus a selection of titles from other publishers.

♦ A range of basic and introductory texts with detailed guidance on most aspects of family history research.

♦ Gibson Guides giving explicit advice on the precise whereabouts of major record sources.

♦ Stuart Raymond's extensive listings of published family history reference material at national and local level

Most titles are available from your local family history society and by post from:-

Federation Publications, 2-4, Killer Street, Ramsbottom, Bury, Lancs, BL0 9BZ

For further information consult our website; http://www.ffhs.org.uk/pubs/

Ancestor Detective
All research by experienced professional - 100% commitment guaranteed. Specialist in East and City of London, Middlesex and Essex, but all enquiries welcome. See Advert on Page 72

139B Fencepiece Road, Hainhault, Ilford, Essex, IG6 2LE
Tel/Fax No: +44(0)208-500-6330
Email: gsmith50@tesco.net

Ancestral Research by Paul Lister
Family history research undertaken at very reasonable and competitive rates. See Advert on Page 72

4 Sergison Road, Haywards Heath, West Sussex, RH16 1HS
Tel No: 01444-453880   Email: piggleston@aol.com.
Web Site: members.aol.com/piggleston/ancestralresearch/

Brewster International
Research at PRO, Family Records Centre, etc and all London Archives. Family Records Centre only 35 mins from our office. See Advert on Page Inside Front Cover

12 Avery Gardens, Ilford, Essex, IG2 6UJ
Tel No: 0208-550-0333   Fax No: 0208-550-7766.
Email: 106422.164@compuserve.com.
Web Site: www.missing-people-found.com

Brian Walker
Research service for all records in the PRO Kew at Kew, including Army, Navy, RAF, Convicts, Metropolitan Police, Irish Constabulary, etc. See Advert on Page 76

78 St James's Avenue, Hampton Hill, Middlesex, TW12 1HN
Email: brianwalker1@compuserve.com.

Canterbury Research Services
Research in Kent and London Archives. Probate and intestacy searches. Palaeography and Latin translations. See Advert on Page 72

71 Island Wall, Whitstable, Kent, CT5 1EL
Tel No: 01227-275931

Carolynn Boucher
Family history research in Herts and London including parish records, certs, wills, census, etc. See Advert on Page 72

1 Ivinghoe Close, Chiltern Park, St Albans, Herts. AL4 9JR
Tel No: 01727-833664
Email: carolynn.boucher@tesco.net

Family History Shop & Library
Ancestral research and records obtained service undertaken by experienced researcher. See Advert on Page 94

24d Magdalen Street, Norwich, NR3 1HU
Tel No: 01603-621152
Email: jenlibrary@aol.com
Web Site: www.jenlibrary.u-net.com/

Family Tree Services
Printouts from the IGI, General record search & supply, Rootseeker service. For a free booklet detailing all FTS services telephone or fax. See Advert on Page 20, 52

30 Eastfield Road, Peterborough, Cambridgeshire, PE1 4AN
Tel No: 01733-890458   Fax No: 01733-890458.

Gendocs
Genealogical, Missing Beneficiaries, Lost Family and Friends, House Histories researched at all London Archives. See Advert on Page 74

19 Mortar Pit Road, Northampton, NN3 5BL
Tel No: 01604-413025   Fax No: 01604-784281
Email: john@j-e-infotech.freeserve.co.uk
Web Site: www.gendocs.demon.co

Grandpa Staten's Family History Services
Full family history provided including searches and certificates obtained. See Advert on Page 46

37 Widgery Road, Exeter, Devon, EX4 8AX
Tel No: 01392-207259; 0771-902104
Email: staten@one-name.org

Ian J Hilder, BA(Hons)
All Sussex and London archives searched inc PRO, Census, Certificates, Wills, etc. Abstracts and translations arranged. See Advert on Page 76

23A Grantham Bank, Barcombe Cross, Lewes BN8 5DJ
Tel No: 01273-400604
Email: HilderGen@aol.com

Janice O'Brien, B.Ed.
Research undertaken by experienced researcher at the India Office Collections for reasonable fees. Plus general research in all the London Archives. See Advert on Page 74

11 Ravenscar, Bayham Street, London, NW1 0BS
Tel No: 0171-388-0452

John Dagger
Genealogical research especially for those with Army, Navy, Convicts and British India ancestors. See Advert on Page 66

Oak House, Horsmorden, Tonbridge, Kent TN12 8LP
Tel No: 01892-722272   Fax No: 01892-722671
Email: j.dagger@btinternet.com

Link Line Ancestral Research
Research Service for all records in the PRO, Kew and at all major London Repositories. Military, Naval, Railway and Criminal Records.   See Advert on Page 72

16 Collingtree, Luton, Bedfordshire, LU2 8HN
Tel No: 01582-614280   Fax No: 01582-614280
Email: iwaller@cableol.co.uk

Patrick Yarnold Research
Genealogist & Record Agent. Research undertaken in London, Berks, Hants and Surrey. See Advert on Page 72

93 The Street, Puttenham, Guildford, Surrey, GU3 1AT
Tel No: 01483-810564

Paul Blake
Genealogical, historical and picture research undertaken by AGRA Member. Specialist in Royal Navy, Military, British India and London research. See Advert on Page 64

18 Rosevine Road, West Wimbledon, London, SW20 8RB
Tel No: 0181-946-6395   Fax No: 0181-946-6395
Email: paulblakeexx@compuserve.com
Web Site: ourworld.compuserve.com/homepages/paulblakexx

Peter F Gardner
For researching all subjects at the PRO including Army, Navy, etc., plus all other London Archives and Society of Genealogists sources. See Advert on Page 64

Malt Cottage, Petworth Road, Witley, Godalming GU8 5LZ
Tel No: 01428-685529 Fax No: 01428-684450
Email: pfg@dial.pipex.com

Red Cat Research
Genealogical and associated research at PRO and Family Records Centre plus research at London's many newspaper, map, picture and local archives. See Ad on Page 74

25 Lakeside Road, London, W14 0DX
Tel No: 0171-603-0295; 020-7603-0295

Roots Family History Service
Lancashire, Manchester and National research. Civil indexes for Scotland, Ireland and England. Parish Records, Census, etc. See Advert on Page 94

372 Bury New Road, Whitefield, Manchester, M45 7SY
Tel No: 0161-796-7130
Email: stoutroots@aol.com

Rosie Taylor
Research at the Family Records Centre, First Avenue House (wills), PRO Kew, plus all other London Archives including the National Newspaper Library. See Advert on Page 66

103A Pemberton Road, London, N4 1AY
Tel No: 0181-347-5107

Southern Counties Ancestry
GRO Indexes, Census Returns, IGI, Wills & Admons, Parish Registers and many other sources reliably searched at reasonable rates. See Advert on Page 88

St Michaels, 2 Church Rd, Polegate, East Sussex, BN26 5BX
Tel No: 01323-488885
Email: drb.sammyd.demon.co.uk
Web Site: www.sammyd.demon.co.uk

Sydney G Smith
Genealogical searches undertaken by AGRA Member throughout London and Kent including the Family Records Centre and PRO. See Advert on Page 66

59 Friar Road, Orpington, Kent, BR5 2BW
Tel No: 01689-832800
Email: ss.famhist@virgin.net.

Sylvia Hunt-Whitaker Research Service
For comprehensive research in all London and Essex repositories. Reasonable rates. Send SAE or 2 IRCs for details. See Advert on Page 86

245 Ashingdon Road, Rochford, Essex, SS4 1RS
Tel No: 01702-540627
Email: sylviahunt.whitaker@btinternet.com (plus also) stella.whitaker@btinternet.com

Tree of Discovery
Specialising in record searches and research in London and the South East. See Advert on Page 74

3 Waterlock Cottages, Canterbury Rd, Wingham CT3 1BH
Tel No: 01227-720271

Victor Longhorn
Genealogical and other research undertaken by Record Agent in Genealogy Cert (IHGS). See Advert on Page 80

53 Theydon Ave, Woburn Sands, Milton Keynes, MK17 8PN
Tel No: 01908-582660
Email: victor.longhorn@btinternet.com

Welsh Ancestors
Research undertaken in Wales plus regular visits to the National Library of Wales and the Public Record Office in Kew. Overseas enquiries welcome. See Advert on Page 116

Tel No: 01446-733969 Fax No: 01446-733969.
Email: 113053,2231@compuserve.com

LONDON ARCHIVES (BARNET)

Hertfordshire Archives & Local Studies
HALS offers a Family History Centre with a wide range of resources on offer and a paid research service for those unable to visit the Centre in person. See Advert on Page 91

County Hall, Pegs Lane, Hertford, Hertfordshire, SG13 8EJ
Tel No: 01992-555105 Fax No: 01992-555113.
Email: hals@hertscc.gov.uk.
Web Site: www.hertslib.hertscc.gov.uk

A Basic Guide to Starting Your Family History

Some flash of inspiration! A visit to an historic building! Something a relative says to you! An article in a newspaper

or magazine! Anyone of these can suddenly bring about a desire to know more about your family. Where do you begin?

Firstly. It is most important to assemble all the information you can about your family from relatives, old family records. Details of the approximate date of birth, occupation and religion, marriage and births of family members and their place of origin should be collected.

There is no easy route to discovering your ancestors. It involves patience, luck and in some cases perseverance. Do not be put off. It is a great deal of fun. The more you discover the more you will want to know about your ancestors. There is some small cost to this fascinating hobby but the rewards will be great. Where your ancestors have moved around from area to area you will have a ready excuse to holiday in many places both at home and abroad - if some of your ancestors emigrated. There is nothing more satisfying that visiting a town, finding out about the historic events that took place some two hundred years previously and realising that an ancestor of yours may have been a witness or perhaps even took part!

You will make new friends and discover new relatives. They will provide an insight and perhaps some knowledge of the family background. It is also, in many cases, a stimulus for your new relatives. They will become interested in the family and eventually send you information for your Family History.

Perhaps the first thing is to join your local Family History Society. Is there one in your area? Well by consulting this Directory you will see whether there is one in your area. The hobby is a growth area and there are new Societies always starting up.

There are many benefits to joining a local Family History

Society, the annual subscriptions to which are modest. Also visit your nearest Family History Centre of the Genealogical Society of Utah, part of the Church of Jesus Christ of Latter-day Saints, which may hold much relevant material.

A good starting point for the beginner is to consult a copy of the International Genealogical Index. It is available for consultation at Family History Centres of the Church of Latter Day Saints, The Mormons, at most large public libraries. Family History Societies usually have a copy for their members to consult. The I.G.I. contains about 80 million records of baptisms and marriages from 1538-1875, taken from thousands of British parish registers and the majority of the non-parochial registers at the Public Record Office.

Many societies sell directories of surnames being researched. Similar indexes of names and copies of pedigrees already researched can sometimes be found in record offices and public libraries. Many of the names being researched worldwide are listed in the Genealogical Research Directory (1200+ pages) edited by Keith Johnson and Malcolm R Sainty and published annually, (further details from Mrs E Simpson, 2 Stella Grove, Tollerton,

Nottingham NGI2 4EY - please see their advertisement) and the British Isles Genealogical Register (The Big R) published on microfiche by The Federation of Family History Societies in 1997 and obtainable from most Family History Societies. By the time you read this Big R 2000 will be under way and will be published in the year 2000.

A Family History Society usually publishes a journal several times a year (the readership of which is worldwide in the majority of cases) and gives members the opportunity to register particular surnames. The cost of the Journal is usually included in the membership fee. As well as a Journal the Society usually meets every month with guest speakers covering items of interest and hints on how to do your own research. The Society may have access to indexes of monumental inscriptions from churchyards and burial grounds as well as census indexes and indexes of parish records of births, marriages and deaths.

You must have an exact location to have any chance of tracing an ancestor. However,the more uncommon the surname, the easier searches can be, and some idea of the number of people bearing a certain surname and their distribution can be obtained by looking at local telephone directories.

The Guild of One-Name Studies has over one thousand members who are researching particular surnames in depth; they record every occurrence of that name in a particular area, many of them nationally and internationally.

What records are there and where are they available? The main sources and record repositories for the British Isles, including Ireland, are listed in this Directory. An initial letter to them will usually tell you what records and sources they have in their possession.

In England and Wales the Civil Registration of Births, Marriages and deaths has been compulsory since 1837. The indexes of Civil Registration can be examined at The Family Records Centre, London (Certificate enquiries Tel: 020 7233 9233), or at a local Register Office. Local libraries and Record Offices may have copies of the indexes on microfilm or microfiche. Additionally a birth or marriage might be located in the International Genealogical Index or a marriage might be found in Boyd's

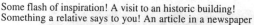

Marriage Index. There is no national index of burials for the period prior to 1837 but the Federation of Family History Societies has commenced a national project involving local Societies to fill this gap.

Copy certificates for Births, Marriages, Deaths Certificates of all registered births, marriages and deaths since 1837 are obtainable by post from The General Register Office, Smedley Hydro, Southport, Merseyside PR8 2HH or the Superintendent Registrar for the area where the event was registered.

A birth certificate gives date and place where the event occurred, the child's forename(s), as well as the name and occupation of the father, the name and maiden surname of the mother with her usual residence if the birth took place elsewhere, and the name and address of the informant for the registration. A marriage certificate gives the names and usually the ages of the marrying couple, their addresses and occupations, the names and occupations of their fathers, the date and place of marriage, and the names of the witnesses.

A death certificate records name(s), date, place, age, cause

IF YOU WANT TO START TRACING YOUR FAMILY TREE

THEN YOU NEED

practical FAMILY HISTORY

Practical Family History is especially formulated for the less experienced family historian.
It embraces a wide range of subjects and in an informative, yet simple style, shows how best to get the most out of available sources.

For more information please contact

Armstrong Boon Marriott Publishing

61 Great Whyte, Ramsey, Huntingdon Cambridgeshire PE17 1HL
Phone 01487 814050 Fax 01487 711361
www.family-tree.co.uk

of death, occupation of the deceased, residence if different from the place of death, and the name and address of the informant for registration. It does not show place of birth or parentage. After 1968 more details had to be recorded on the certificate.

Births, marriages and deaths are listed in separate indexes. Birth certificate details give sufficient information to help find the marriage of parents, and the marriage certificate usually gives clues for the births of the marrying couple as well as the fathers of each. Access is only to the quarterly indexes and no information is available except in the form of a certificate. There are separate indexes to the births, marriages and deaths of British Subjects returned by Consuls abroad (from 1809), in the Army (from 1761), and at sea (from 1837). The public search room is open Monday-Friday 0830-1630. If you are writing from abroad always enclose three international reply coupons. Microfilm copies

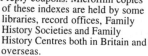

of these indexes are held by some libraries, record offices, Family History Societies and Family History Centres both in Britain and overseas.

Census Returns
A census of the population has taken place every 10 years; from 1851 onwards the Census Returns give names, ages, relationships to head of household, occupations and places of birth. The census for 1841 does not give place of birth or exact age. Censuses before 1841 survive only in numerical statistics. From 1851 the return completed by an occupier of a house or residence had to include all people resident at that address on the census night.

A complete set of microfilms of the Returns 1841-1891 is currently available at The Family Records Centre, 1 Myddelton Street, London EC1R 1UW. Telephone : 0171 392 5300. Many County Record Offices and Public Libraries hold sets for their own counties or areas.

To aid the location of specific families at known addresses, street indexes are available for most large towns that have a population of over 40.000. Surname indexes have been compiled by Family History Societies of which the 1851 census has been universally done.

The 1881 census has been the centre of a national indexing project which was completed in 1996. All of the county indexes have now been published and many local Family History Societies and some Libraries have purchased full copies for all the counties. Therefore the place and approximate date of birth of any person whose name and address has been obtained from records of civil registration should be found in these returns, thus leading one to the appropriate Parish Registers for pre - 1837 information. In 1999 the whole of the 1881 Census was published on CD-Rom and is available for purchase from The Church of Latter Day Saints for a cost of about £30.00.

In certain circumstances and on payment of a fee information may be supplied to a researcher from the 1901 census. This will comprise only the age and place of birth of a named individual at a precise address and the application must be supported by written authorisation from a direct descendant of the person whose details are requested. Applications in such cases should be sent to General Register Office, Office of Population, Censuses and Population Surveys, 10 Kingsway, London

WC2B 6JP. No information can be supplied from census returns after 1901.

Parish Registers and Bishops Transcripts
The most valuable source of information before 1837 is the registers of the 14,000 parish churches throughout England and Wales which recorded baptisms, marriages and burials; and, the Bishops' Transcripts of the parish registers - the yearly copies sent by the parishes to their bishops. Some go back as far as 1538 and most are deposited in the appropriate county record office, which may also hold modern copies with indexes. Again Family History Societies may have undertaken to transcribe and index the Parish Registers for their area.

Some of the registers of baptisms and burials of non-conformist congregations before 1837 may be inspected at

the Public Record Office. Registers not deposited may still be with the congregation, in the appropriate county record office, or at the headquarters of the body concerned. Between 1754 and 1837 the marriages of all non-conformists, other than Quakers and Jews, had to take place in a Church of

England Church. Many County Record Offices and Libraries have microfilms of the Registers for their counties.

Many people were married by licence, obtained from the Bishop of the Diocese, his Surrogate, or the Archbishop of the Province. The allegations upon which these licences were granted often give valuable information about the parties. They are usually deposited in the county record office. Those issued through the Faculty Office and Vicar General of the Archbishop of Canterbury are now in Lambeth Palace Library, London SE1 7JU, and those for the Diocese of London are at the Guildhall Library. The majority of those for Yorkshire are held at the Borthwick Institute.

Wills
The will of a deceased relative or potential relative may provide a great deal of important information about the family and the maker of the will. Copies of all wills proved in England and Wales since 1858 may be obtained from the Probate Service. See the article later in this Directory. Before 1858 wills were for the most part proved in the Archdeaconry or Peculiar Court having

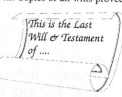

This is the Last Will & Testament of ....

jurisdiction over the area where the deceased died or held property. If he held property in more than one jurisdiction the will was generally proved in the Prerogative Courts of Canterbury(PCC) or York(PCY). Where the deceased held property in more than one Archdeaconry of the same diocese his will went to the Diocesan Consistory Court. The PCC Wills (1383 - 1857) are at The Public Record Office and there are printed indexes covering the years 1383-1700 and 1750-1800. For subsequent years there are manuscript indexes for each year to 1857. Those for York commence in 1389.

This article has been updated and repeated for the benefit of those readers who need initial advice on starting research into family history. It is also a useful aid for those more experienced in research as a revision aid when needed.

BEDFORDSHIRE

BUCKINGHAMSHIRE, HERTFORDSHIRE
HUNTINGDONSHIRE

Family and Local History Research
undertaken by

Member

**Mr Colin N. Davison
66 Sudeley Walk, Bedford.
Bedfordshire MK41 8JH
England
Tel: 01234-364956**

All enquiries welcome

VICTOR LONGHORN

Record Agent in Genealogy Cert. (IHGS)

Genealogical and other Historical
Research Undertaken
in

Bedfordshire

Buckinghamshire, Hertfordshire,
Northamptonshire,
and the Main London Repositories.

MEMBER

*53 Theydon Ave,
Woburn Sands,
Milton Keynes.
MK17 8PN.*

*Telephone. 01908 582660
e-mail: victor.longhorn@btinternet.com*

BMSGH

THE BIRMINGHAM AND MIDLAND SOCIETY
(STAFFORDSHIRE   WARWICKSHIRE   WORCESTERSHIRE)
FOR GENEALOGY AND HERALDRY
(The BMSGH)

The BMSGH covers the three counties, was founded in 1963 and has 5000 Members. Membership includes a quarterly journal, publications, a library and regular meetings at branches in Birmingham, Burton-on-Trent, Stoke-on-Trent, Wolverhampton, Kenilworth, Bromsgrove, Stourbridge, Worcester and London.

For further details contact

MR M BRITTAIN,
111 Kenilworth Court, Coventry CV3 6JD

Or consult our web site: www.bmsgh.org

Registered as a Charity No. 505916-R

BEDFORDSHIRE

See also: Ancestral Research - Comprehensive on Page 61

Colin Davison Family History Research
Family and local history research service provided by AGRA member. All enquiries welcome. Full range of archival documents examined. See Advert on Page 80 opposite

66 Sudeley Walk, Putnoe, Bedford, Bedfordshire, MK41 8JH
Tel No: 01234-364956

Victor Longhorn
Genealogical and other research undertaken by Record Agent in Genealogy Cert (IHGS)See Advert on Page 80 opposite

53 Theydon Ave, Woburn Sands, Milton Keynes, MK17 8PN
Tel No: 01908-582660
Email: victor.longhorn@btinternet.com

BERKSHIRE

See also: Ancestral Research - Comprehensive on Page 61

Patrick Yarnold Research
Genealogist & Record Agent. Research Countrywide for 19th & 20th Centuries. Earlier periods research undertaken in London, Berks, Hants and Surrey. See Advert on Page 72

93 The Street, Puttenham, Guildford, Surrey, GU3 1AT
Tel No: 01483-810564

Southern Counties Ancestry
GRO Indexes, Census Returns, IGI, Wills & Admons, Parish Registers and many other sources reliably searched at reasonable rates. See Advert on Page 88

St Michaels, 2 Church Rd, Polegate, East Sussex, BN26 5BX
Tel No: 01323-488885
Email: drb.sammyd.demon.co.uk
Web Site: www.sammyd.demon.co.uk

BIRMINGHAM

See also: Ancestral Research - Comprehensive on Page 61

John S Griffiths
27 years experience in all aspects of genealogical and related research. Black Country and surrounding counties. National Library of Wales collections. See Advert on Page 96

30 Coniston Road, Erdington, Birmingham, B23 6HJ
Tel No: 0121-384-3928

Vanessa Morgan
Research undertaken from one name searches to complete family histories. Also offers location photography service at competitive rates. See Advert on Page 88

33 Plymouth Road, Redditch, Worcestershire, B97 4PX
Tel No: 01527-62472   Fax No:01527-457176.
Email: Vanessa@snackbox.freeserve.co.uk

BRISTOL

See also: Ancestral Research - Comprehensive on Page 61

Hidden Heritage
A research service into any and all records in glorious Gloucestershire, Bristol and surrounding counties. No task is too small or too large. See Advert on Page 87

11 Old Cheltenham Road, Longlevens, Gloucester, GL2 0AS
Tel No: 01452-503831   Fax No:01452-503831
Email: ejack@gloster.demon.co.uk
Web Site: www.gloster.demon.co.uk

Robert J Haines, BSc
Genealogical research by experienced researcher. Reliable service at reasonable rates. Send SAE/IRC for details. See Advert on Page 89

25 Lynch Road, Berkeley, Gloucestershire, GL13 9TA
Tel No: 01453-810052

BUCKINGHAMSHIRE

See also: Ancestral Research - Comprehensive on Page 61

Colin Davison Family History Research
Family and local history research service provided by AGRA member. All enquiries welcome. Full range of archival documents examined. See Advert on Page 80

66 Sudeley Walk, Putnoe, Bedford, Bedfordshire, MK41 8JH
Tel No: 01234-364956

Kathleen Wilshaw, BA
Family and local history research. Professional and friendly service by experienced researcher at reasonable rates. All enquiries welcome. See Advert on Page 96

The Shieling, Duns Tew, Oxfordshire, OX6 4JS
Tel No: 01869-340364
Email: kwilshaw@compuserve.com

Victor Longhorn
Genealogical and other research undertaken by Record Agent in Genealogy Cert (IHGS)See Advert on Page 80

53 Theydon Ave, Woburn Sands, Milton Keynes, MK17 8PN
Tel No: 01908-582660
Email: victor.longhorn@btinternet.com

CAMBRIDGESHIRE

See also: Ancestral Research - Comprehensive on Page 61

East Anglian Village Research
EAVR are specialists at tracing ancestry in the rural communities of Eastern England, including the English origins of emigrant families. See Advert on Page 86

1 Ivy Cotts, Long Rd West, Dedham, Colchester, CO7 6EL
Tel No: 01206-322213
Email: eavr@btinternet.com
Web Site: www.btinternet.com/~p.w.w/eavr.htm

THE HISTORY OF YOUR FAMILY

Have you ever thought about tracing YOUR ancestry?

Do you know where to begin?

Did you know that there is an Organisation that can show you the way?

Family history researching is an absorbing and inexpensive pastime.

For a free information pack giving further details including meetings in your area please contact:

The Secretary,
Cleveland, Nth Yorkshire & South Durham F.H.S.
1 Oxgang Close
REDCAR
Cleveland
TS10 4ND

(please include a large SAE or stamp)

How far back do you think you can trace YOUR ancestry? as far back as 1538?

BUCKINGHAMSHIRE
FAMILY HISTORY SOCIETY

Founded 1976
Registered charity 290335

http://www.bucksfhs.org.uk

Publications include:
marriages, wills, census, monumental inscriptions
and name indexes from a variety of sources

For a list send sae to:
Mr Alan Dell FSG, 3, Swallow Lane, Stoke Mandeville, Aylesbury,
Buckinghamshire. HP22 5UW

A marriage database complete for the whole of
Buckinghamshire from 1558-1837

Details from Mrs Lesley Williams, 20 Southcourt Avenue, Linslade,
Leighton Buzzard, Bedfordshire. LU7 7QD

A complete transcript of the 1851 census for the County

Details from Miss Shirley Nicholls, 'Faircross', Hare Lane, Little Kingshill,
Great Missenden, Buckinghamshire. HPI6 0EF

Other databases - Baptisms, Burials and Wills

Meetings held monthly on Saturdays in Aylesbury and
group meetings held in Bourne End and Bletchley are open to non-members

ANNUAL OPEN DAY

All the society's facilities available for research also guest societies and
commercial stands.
Saturday July 22nd 2000, 10 a.m. - 4 p.m.
at Aylesbury Grammar School, Walton Road, Aylesbury

Membership Secretary

Mr John Bartlett, 19A, Station Road, Stoke Mandeville, Aylesbury,
Buckinghamshire. HP22 5UL
Please send sae for membership form

CHESHIRE

See also: Ancestral Research - Comprehensive on Page 61

John S Griffiths
27 years experience in all aspects of genealogical and related research. Black Country and surrounding counties. National Library of Wales collections. See Advert on Page 96

30 Coniston Road, Erdington, Birmingham, B23 6HJ
Tel No: 0121-384-3928

Paperchase Genealogical & Research Services
Research and/or full genealogical service by a qualified genealogist and AGRA Member with over 25 years experience. See Advert on Page 98

5 Glebe Close, Blythe Bridge, Stoke on Trent, ST11 9JN
Tel No: 01782-394147   Fax No:01782-394147.
Email: elderton@one-name.org.
Web Site: www.ukancestors.com

Staffordshire Knot Research
Research carried out in Staffordshire and surrounding counties. £5 per hour. Parish Registers; Census; Estate Records; etc. See Advert on Page 98

36 Whalley Ave, Penkhull, Stoke on Trent ST4 5NE
Tel No: 01782-25231
Email: pcotton@netcentral.co.uk *or*
        annfurber@haywood751.freeserve.co.uk

CORNWALL

See also: Ancestral Research - Comprehensive on Page 61

Southern Counties Ancestry
GRO Indexes, Census Returns, IGI, Wills & Admons, Parish Registers and many other sources reliably searched at reasonable rates. See Advert on Page 88

St Michaels, 2 Church Rd, Polegate, East Sussex, BN26 5BX
Tel No: 01323-488885
Email: drb.sammyd.demon.co.uk
Web Site: www.sammyd.demon.co.uk

Tony Shopland - Ancestral Research
See under "Dorset" in adjacent column.

CUMBRIA

See also: Ancestral Research - Comprehensive on Page 61

Sydney G Smith
Compiler of the Westmorland and North Lancs Index (1700-1837) contact for details. See Advert on Page 66

59 Friar Road, Orpington, Kent, BR5 2BW
Tel No: 01689-832800   Email: ss.famhist@virgin.net.

DERBYSHIRE

See also: Ancestral Research - Comprehensive on Page 61

John S Griffiths
See under "Derbyshire" in adjacent column.

Looking Back
Thorough family history research by experienced researchers. £6 per hour. See Advert on Page 96

5 Bishop's Close, Keyworth, Nottingham, NG12 5LS
Tel No: 0115-937-6759
Email: lookingback@fhist.freeserve.co.uk

Staffordshire Knot Research
See under "Derbyshire" in adjacent column.

Victoria Walker
Family history research, adoption searches, access to parish registers, IGI, wills, monumental inscriptions, census returns, etc. Location photographs. See Advert on Page 84

11 Belper Lane, Belper, Derbyshire, DE56 2UG
Tel No: 01773-826025
Email: vaw@belper.jireh.co.uk

DEVON

See also: Ancestral Research - Comprehensive on Page 61

Grandpa Staten's Family History Services
Comprehensive service for family historians including PRO searches, GRO certificates, wills, etc., obtained. See Advert on Page 46

37 Widgery Road, Exeter, Devon, EX4 8AX
Tel No: 01392-207259; 0771-902104.
Email: staten@one-name.org.

Southern Counties Ancestry
See under "Cornwall" in adjacent column.

Tony Shopland - Ancestral Research
See under "Cornwall" in adjacent column.

DORSET

See also: Ancestral Research - Comprehensive on Page 61

Tony Shopland - Ancestral Research
Experienced Researcher to undertake assignments in Devon, Somerset, Dorset & Cornwall. See Advert on Page 84

22 Joslin Road, Honiton, Devon, EX14 8RH
Tel No: 01404-45686   Fax No:01404-45686.
Email: Tony@Shopland.freeserve.co.uk

DURHAM

See also: **Ancestral Research - Comprehensive on Page 61**

Geoff Nicholson
Genealogical research by AGRA member of many years experience with unrivalled knowledge of the region. 'Native Guide' and 'pedigree services'. See Advert on Page 102

57 Manor Park, Concord, Washington, Tyne & Wear, NE37 2BU
Tel No: 0191-417-9546
Email: geoff@genic.demon.co.uk
Web Site: www.genic.demon.co.uk/index.html

Neil Richardson
Family history research, friendly service and expert advice. Microfiche available on Master Mariners & Ship Owners, North East Ports. See Advert on Page 102

12 Banbury Way, South Beach Estate, Blyth, Northumberland, NE24 3TY   Tel No: 01670-353605
Email: k.richardson@ukonline.co.uk
Web Site: www.ukonline.co.uk/northumweb/index.htm

Original Indexes
Well known microfiche publishers of Indexes to parish registers and other historical records also offer a genealogical research service. See Advert on Page 102

113 East View, Wideopen, Tyne and Wear, NE13 6EF
Tel No: 0191-236-6416
Email: fiche@original-indexes.demon.co.uk
Web Site: www.original-indexes@demon.co.uk/index.htm

ESSEX

See also: **Ancestral Research - Comprehensive on Page 61**

Ancestor Detective
All research by experienced professional - 100% commitment guaranteed. Specialist in East and City of London, Middlesex and Essex, but all enquiries welcome. See Advert on Page 72

139B Fencepiece Road, Hainhault, Ilford, Essex, IG6 2LE
Tel No: +44(0)208-500-6330   Fax No:+44(0)208-500-6330.
Email: gsmith50@tesco.net.

East Anglian Village Research
EAVR are specialists at tracing ancestry in the rural communities of Eastern England, including the English origins of emigrant families. See Advert on Page 86

1 Ivy Cotts, Long Rd West, Dedham, Colchester, CO7 6EL
Tel No: 01206-322213   Email: eavr@btinternet.com
Web Site: www.btinternet.com/~p.w.w/eavr.htm

Essex Record Office
A professional research service by post for all with Essex connections, using the extensive genealogical resources of the Essex Record Office. See Advert on Page 86

Wef 1/1/2000 Wharf Road, Chelmsford CM2 6YT
Tel No: 01245-244644   Fax No:01245-244655
Email: ero.search@essexcc.gov.uk.
Web Site: www.essexcc.gov.uk

Sylvia Hunt-Whitaker Research Service
For comprehensive research in all London and Essex repositories. Reasonable rates. Send SAE or 2 IRCs for details. See Advert on Page 86

245 Ashingdon Road, Rochford, Essex, SS4 1RS
Tel No: 01702-540627
Email: sylviahunt.whitaker@btinternet.com
stella.whitaker@btinternet.com

Tree of Discovery
Specialising in record searches and research in London and the South East. See Advert on Page 74

3 Waterlock Cottages, Canterbury Rd, Wingham, Kent, CT3 1BH
Tel No: 01227-720271

GLOUCESTERSHIRE

See also: **Ancestral Research - Comprehensive on Page 61**

Ancestral Trails
For the provision of a comprehensive professional research service and also offers a photographic history service to bring alive ancestry places of origin. See Advert on Page 88

Copper Beeches, Colesbourne, Gloucestershire, GL53 9NS
Tel No: 01242-870297
Email: pamb@freenet.co.uk

Gwen Kingsley, BA(Hons)
Genealogical research undertaken by experienced researcher. Friendly, efficient service. See Advert on Page 16

'Lyndon', Queen Street, Kingswinford, West Mids, DY6 7AQ
Tel No: 01384-293514   Fax No:01384-826516.
Email: Kingsley@cableinet.co.uk
Web Site: www.wkweb5.cableinet.co.uk/kingsley/

Herefordshire Family History Research
All record types researched from 1538 onwards for Herefordshire, Worcs and Glos. Hereford Diocese Probate records a speciality. See Advert on Page 16

17 Whitefriars Road, Hereford, HR2 7XE
Tel No: 01432-341270
Email: eleanor.harris@which.net.
Web Site: www.homepages.which.net/~eleanor.harris

GLOUCESTERSHIRE (Cont.)

Jennifer Day
Experienced researcher offers efficient, friendly service. All Enquiries welcome. See Advert on Page 98

Lantern Cottage, Rhodyate, Blagdon, N. Somerset BS40 7TP
Tel No: 01761-462426

GLOUCESTERSHIRE & BRISTOL

Family History Research
20 years experience
Reasonable Rates
SAE/IRC to

Robert J Haines B.Sc.
25 Lynch Road
Berkeley
Gloucestershire
GL13 9TA
Tel: 01453 810052

Southern Counties Ancestry
GRO Indexes, Census Returns, IGI, Wills & Admons, Parish Registers and many other sources reliably searched at reasonable rates. See Advert on Page 88

St Michaels, 2 Church Rd, Polegate, East Sussex, BN26 5BX
Tel No: 01323-488885   Email: drb.sammyd.demon.co.uk
Web Site: www.sammyd.demon.co.uk

Vanessa Morgan
Research undertaken from one name searches to complete family histories. Also offers location photography service at competitive rates. See Advert on Page 88

33 Plymouth Road, Redditch, Worcestershire, B97 4PX
Tel No: 01527-62472   Fax No:01527-457176.
Email: Vanessa@snackbox.freeserve.co.uk

HAMPSHIRE AND ISLE OF WIGHT

See also: Ancestral Research - Comprehensive on Page 61

Ancestral Research by Paul Lister
Family history research undertaken at very reasonable and competitive rates. See Advert on Page 72

4 Sergison Road, Haywards Heath, West Sussex, RH16 1HS
Tel No: 01444-453880
Email: piggleston@aol.com
Web Site: members.aol.com/piggleston/ancestralresearch

Patrick Yarnold Research
Research countrywide for 19th & 20th Centuries. Earlier period research undertaken in London, Berkshire, Hampshire and Surrey. See Advert on Page 72

93 The Street, Puttenham, Guildford, Surrey, GU3 1AT
Tel No: 01483-810564

Southern Counties Ancestry
GRO Indexes, Census Returns, IGI, Wills & Admons, Parish Registers and many other sources reliably searched at reasonable rates. See Advert on Page 88

St Michaels, 2 Church Rd, Polegate, East Sussex, BN26 5BX
Tel No: 01323-488885
Email: drb.sammyd.demon.co.uk
Web Site: www.sammyd.demon.co.uk

HEREFORDSHIRE

See also: Ancestral Research - Comprehensive on Page 61

Gwen Kingsley, BA(Hons)
Genealogical research undertaken by experienced researcher. Friendly, efficient service. See Advert on Page 16

'Lyndon', Queen Street, Kingswinford, West Mids, DY6 7AQ
Tel No: 01384-293514   Fax No:01384-826516.
Email: Kingsley@cableinet.co.uk
Web Site: www.wkweb5.cableinet.co.uk/kingsley/

Herefordshire Family History Research
All record types researched from 1538 for Herefordshire, Worcs and Glos. Hereford Diocese Probate records a speciality. Local professional service. See Ad on Page 16

17 Whitefriars Road, Hereford, HR2 7XE
Tel No: 01432-341270
Email: eleanor.harris@which.net.
Web Site: www.homepages.which.net/~eleanor.harris

Hidden Heritage
A research service into any and all records in glorious Gloucestershire, Bristol and the surrounding counties. No task is too small or too large. See Advert on Page 87

11 Old Cheltenham Road, Longlevens, Gloucester, GL2 0AS
Tel No: 01452-503831   Fax No:01452-503831.
Email: ejack@gloster.demon.co.uk
Web Site: www.gloster.demon.co.uk

John S Griffiths
All aspects of genealogical and related historical research. Black Country and surrounding county records. National Library of Wales collections. See Advert on Page 96

30 Coniston Road, Erdington, Birmingham B23 6HJ
Tel No: 0121-384-3928

Pinhorns, Genealogists
Family, local and architectural history research throughout the UK. See Advert on Page 62

85 Etnam Street, Leominster. HR6 8AE

HERTFORDSHIRE

See also: Ancestral Research - Comprehensive on Page 61

Colin Davison Family History Research
Family and local history research service provided by AGRA member. All enquiries welcome. Full range of archival documents examined. See Advert on Page 80

66 Sudeley Walk, Putnoe, Bedford, Bedfordshire, MK41 8JH
Tel No: 01234-364956

East Anglian Village Research
EAVR are specialists at tracing ancestry in the rural communities of Eastern England, including the English origins of emigrant families. See Advert on Page 86

1 Ivy Cotts, Long Road West, Dedham, Colchester, CO7 6EL
Tel No: 01206-322213   Email: eavr@btinternet.com
Web Site: www.btinternet.com/~p.w.w/eavr.htm

Mrs Carolynn Boucher
Comprehensive family history research in Hertfordshire and London including parish records, certificates, wills, census, etc. See Advert on Page 72

1 Ivinghoe Close, Chiltern Park, St Albans, Herts, AL4 9JR
Tel No: 01727-833664   Email: carolynn.boucher@tesco.net

HERTFORDSHIRE (Cont.)

Victor Longhorn
Genealogical and other research undertaken by Record Agent in Genealogy Cert (IHGS)See Advert on Page 80

53 Theydon Ave, Woburn Sands, Milton Keynes, MK17 8PN
Tel No: 01908-582660
Email: victor.longhorn@btinternet.com

HULL

HUNTINGDONSHIRE

See also: Ancestral Research - Comprehensive on Page 61

Colin Davison Family History Research
Family and local history research service provided by AGRA member. All enquiries welcome. Full range of archival documents examined. See Advert on Page 80

66 Sudeley Walk, Putnoe, Bedford, Bedfordshire, MK41 8JH
Tel No: 01234-364956

KENT

See also: Ancestral Research - Comprehensive on Page 61

Ancestral Research by Paul Lister
Family history research undertaken at very reasonable and competitive rates. See Advert on Page 72

4 Sergison Road, Haywards Heath, West Sussex, RH16 1HS
Tel No: 01444-453880   Email: piggleston@aol.com
Web Site: members.aol.com/piggleston/ancestralresearch

Canterbury Research Services
Research in London Archives and also Kent. East Kent Burials Index 1813 - 1841. Probate and intestacy searches. Palaeography and Latin translations. See Advert on Page 72

71 Island Wall, Whitstable, Kent, CT5 1EL
Tel No: 01227-275931

Centre for Kentish Studies
Family and local history research by the Staff of Kent County Archives Service available at Maidstone, Canterbury and at Dover. See Display on page opposite.

East Anglian Village Research
EAVR are specialists at tracing ancestry in the rural communities of Eastern England, including the English origins of emigrant families. See Advert on Page 86

1 Ivy Cotts, Long Rd West, Dedham, Colchester, CO7 6EL
Tel No: 01206-322213   Email: eavr@btinternet.com
Web Site: www.btinternet.com/~p.w.w/eavr.htm

John Dagger
Genealogical research by Kent based researcher, especially for those with Army, Navy, Convicts and British India ancestors. See Advert on Page 66

Oak House, Horsmorden, Tonbridge, Kent TN12 8LP
Tel No: 01892-722272   Fax No: 01892-722671
Email: j.dagger@btinternet.com

Maggi Young
Family History Research service provided by qualified researcher in East Kent. All sources covered.
See Advert on Page 92

Park View, Ninn Lane, Great Chart, Kent, TN23 3DB
Tel No: 01233-626455; 07979-232828.
Email: maggi_young@wecnet.co.uk

Southern Counties Ancestry
GRO Indexes, Census Returns, IGI, Wills & Admons, Parish Registers and many other sources reliably searched at reasonable rates. See Advert on Page 88

St Michaels, 2 Church Rd, Polegate, East Sussex, BN26 5BX
Tel No: 01323-488885   Email: drb.sammyd.demon.co.uk
Web Site: www.sammyd.demon.co.uk

Sydney G Smith
Research by AGRA Member for Kent. Compiler of West Kent Marriage Index (1538-1812).   See Advert on Page 66

59 Friar Road, Orpington, Kent, BR5 2BW
Tel No: 01689-832800   Email: ss.famhist@virgin.net

Tree of Discovery
Specialising in record searches and research in London and the South East. See Advert on Page 74

3 Waterlock Cotts, Canterbury Rd, Wingham, Kent, CT3 1BH
Tel No: 01227-720271

LANCASHIRE and MANCHESTER

See also: Ancestral Research - Comprehensive on Page 61

Chris E Makepeace Local History Consultancy
Specialist in history of the Manchester and surrounding area. For all aspects of historical research, talks and lectures. Stockist of Godfrey OS maps. See Advert on Page 92

5 Hilton Road, Disley, Cheshire, SK12 2JU
Tel No: 01663-763346

Jane Hamby, LHG
Genealogical research undertaken by experienced genealogist at reasonable rates. All enquiries welcome. Contact for further information. See Advert on Page 94

22 St Michaels Road, Preston, Lancashire, PR1 6LY
Tel No: 01772-881873

Lancashire Record Office and Local Studies Library
Repository for records relating to Lancashire including the Lancashire Local Studies Collection. Display Advert gives details of opening and closed weeks – Advert on Page 273

Bow Lane, Preston, Lancashire, PR1 2RE
Tel No: 01772-264021   Fax No:01772-264149.
Email: Lancs.Record@treas.lancscc.gov.uk.
Web Site: www.lancashire.com/lcc/edu/ro/index.htm

Roots Family History Service
Lancashire, Manchester and National research. Civil indexes for Scotland, Ireland and England. Parish Records, Census, etc. See Advert on Page 94

372 Bury New Road, Whitefield, Manchester, M45 7SY
Tel No: 0161-796-7130
Email: stoutroots@aol.com

Sydney G Smith
Compiler of Westmorland and North Lancs Index (1700-1837). See Advert on Page 66

59 Friar Road, Orpington, Kent, BR5 2BW
Tel No: 01689-832800   Email: ss.famhist@virgin.net

LEICESTERSHIRE

See also: Ancestral Research - Comprehensive on Page 61

John S Griffiths
Genealogical and related historical research for the Black Country and surrounding counties. See Advert on Page 96

30 Coniston Road, Erdington, Birmingham, B23 6HJ
Tel No: 0121-384-3928

Looking Back
Thorough family history research by experienced researchers. £6 per hour. See Advert on Page 96

5 Bishop's Close, Keyworth, Nottingham, NG12 5LS
Tel No: 0115-937-6759
Email: lookingback@fhist.freeserve.co.uk

Leicestershire & Rutland

- Family & Local History Research
- Reasonable Rates
- SAE to:

Josephine Pegg
81 Rowan Street
Leicester LE3 9GP
Tel: +44(0)116 253 1882

RESEARCH SERVICE

Whatever your research interest we are here to help.
For details of services
and charges contact:
Mrs Pat Grundy BA(Hons)
The Record Office for
Leicestershire, Leicester & Rutland
Long Street, Wigston Magna Leicester LE18 2AH
Tel: 0116 257 1080

LEICESTERSHIRE GENEALOGICAL RESEARCH SERVICE

LINCOLNSHIRE

See also: Ancestral Research - Comprehensive on Page 61

Looking Back
Thorough family history research by experienced researchers. £6 per hour. See Advert on Page 96

5 Bishop's Close, Keyworth, Nottingham, NG12 5LS
Tel No: 0115-937-6759
Email: lookingback@fhist.freeserve.co.uk

MIDDLESEX

See also: Ancestral Research - Comprehensive on Page 61

Ancestor Detective
All research by experienced professional - 100% commitment guaranteed. Specialist in East and City of London, Middlesex and Essex, but all enquiries welcome. See Advert on Page 72

139B Fencepiece Road, Hainhault, Ilford, Essex, IG6 2LE
Tel No: +44(0)208-500-6330   Fax No:+44(0)208-500-6330
Email: gsmith50@tesco.net.

Hertfordshire Archives & Local Studies
HALS offers a Family History Centre with a wide range of resources on offer and a paid research service for those unable to visit the Centre in person. See Advert on Page 91

County Hall, Pegs Lane, Hertford, Hertfordshire, SG13 8EJ
Tel No: 01992-555105   Fax No:01992-555113.
Email: hals@hertscc.gov.uk.
Web Site: hertslib.hertscc.gov.uk

NORFOLK

See also: Ancestral Research - Comprehensive on Page 61

Family History Shop & Library
For publications relating to Norfolk and Suffolk genealogical research plus an ancestral research service by an experienced researcher - contact for details. See Advert on Page 94

24d Magdalen Street, Norwich, NR3 1HU
Tel No: 01603-621152
Email: jenlibrary@aol.com
Web Site: www.jenlibrary.u-net.com/

Gill Blanchard, BA, MA, PGCE (PCE)
Genealogical Researcher - Norfolk area. Courses for beginners in Family History also available: days; weekends and/or evenings. Contact for details. See Advert on Page 94

1 Whitwell Street, Reepham, Norwich, Norfolk, NR10 4RA
Tel No: 01603-872367
Email: gblanchard@whitwellresearch.demon.co.uk

NORTHAMPTONSHIRE

See also: Ancestral Research - Comprehensive on Page 61

Gendocs
Genealogical, Missing Beneficiaries, Lost Family and Friends, House Histories researched. Records search and supply from all London Archives. See Advert on Page 74

19 Mortar Pit Road, Northampton, NN3 5BL
Tel No: 01604-413025   Fax No:01604-784281.
Email: john@j-e-infotech.freeserve.co.uk
Web Site: www.gendocs.demon.co.uk

Northamptonshire continued ......

NORTHAMPTONSHIRE (cont)

John S Griffiths
27 years experience in ancestral research. All aspects of genealogical and related historical research. Black Country and surrounding county records. See Advert on Page 96

30 Coniston Road, Erdington, Birmingham B23 6HJ
Tel No: 0121-384-3928

Sue Comont Research Services
Research undertaken in all types of records held at Nothamptonshire Record Office, also G.R.O. indexes searched and certificates obtained. See Advert on Page 96

26 St Margaret's Avenue, Rushden, Northants. NN10 9YH
Tel No: 01933-312876
Email: sue.comont@tesco.net.

Victor Longhorn
Genealogical and other research undertaken by Record Agent in Genealogy Cert (IHGS). See Advert on Page 80

53 Theydon Ave, Woburn Sands, Milton Keynes, MK17 8PN
Tel No: 01908-582660
Email: victor.longhorn@btinternet.com

NORTHUMBERLAND

See also: Ancestral Research - Comprehensive on Page 61

Geoff Nicholson
Genealogical research by AGRA member of many years experience with unrivalled knowledge of the region. 'Native Guide' and 'pedigree' services. See Advert on Page 102

57 Manor Park, Concord, Washington, Tyne & Wear, NE37 2BU
Tel No: 0191-417-9546
Email: geoff@genic.demon.co.uk
Web Site: www.genic.demon.co.uk/index.html

Neil Richardson
Family history research, friendly service and expert advice. Microfiche available on Master Mariners & Ship Owners, North East ports. See Advert on Page 102

12 Banbury Way, South Beach Estate, Blyth, Northumberland, NE24 3TY
Tel No: 01670-353605
Email: k.richardson@ukonline.co.uk
Web Site: www.ukonline.co.uk/northumweb/index.htm

Original Indexes
Microfiche publishers of a range of publications relating to family and local history including many indexes, which also offer a genealogical research service. See Advert Page 102

113 East View, Wideopen, Tyne and Wear, NE13 6EF
Tel No: 0191-236-6416
Email: fiche@original-indexes.demon.co.uk
Web Site: www.original-indexes@demon.co.uk/index.htm

NOTTINGHAMSHIRE

See also: Ancestral Research - Comprehensive on Page 61

Ancestors in Nottinghamshire
Family history research by an experienced researcher. Comprehensive reports. Friendly, efficient service only £5 per hour. All enquiries welcome. See Advert on Page 96

37 Castlefields, The Meadows, Nottingham, NG2 1HN
Tel No: 0115-840-9701

John S Griffiths
27 years experience in ancestral research. All aspects of genealogical and related historical research. Black Country and surrounding county records. See Advert on Page 96

30 Coniston Road, Erdington, Birmingham B23 6HJ
Tel No: 0121-384-3928

Looking Back
Thorough family history research by experienced researchers. £6 per hour. See Advert on Page 96

5 Bishop's Close, Keyworth, Nottingham NG12 5LS
Tel No: 0115-937-6759
Email: lookingback@fhist.freeserve.co.uk

Victoria Walker
Family history research, adoption searches, access to parish registers, IGI, wills, monumental inscriptions, census returns, etc. Location photographs. See Advert on Page 84

11 Belper Lane, Belper, Derbyshire DE56 2UG
Tel No: 01773-826025
Email: vaw@belper.jireh.co.uk

OXFORDSHIRE

See also: Ancestral Research - Comprehensive on Page 61

John S Griffiths
27 years experience in ancestral research. All aspects of genealogical and related historical research. Black Country and surrounding county records. See Advert on Page 96

30 Coniston Road, Erdington, Birmingham B23 6HJ
Tel No: 0121-384-3928

Kathleen Wilshaw, BA
Family and local history research. Professional and friendly service by experienced researcher at reasonable rates. All enquiries welcome. See Advert on Page 96

The Shieling, Duns Tew, Oxfordshire, OX6 4JS
Tel No: 01869-340364
Email: kwilshaw@compuserve.com

Mrs Hilary Clare, MA(Oxon)
All genealogical and historical research undertaken by experienced history graduate with Latin, palaeography and archives training. See Advert on Page 96

Blunsdon, Faringdon Road, Abingdon, OX14 1BQ
Tel No: 01235-525898   Email: hilary.clare@cwcom.net

SHROPSHIRE

See also: **Ancestral Research - Comprehensive on Page 61**

Gwen Kingsley, BA(Hons)
Genealogical research undertaken by experienced researcher. Friendly, efficient service. See Advert on Page 16

'Lyndon', Queen St., Kingswinford, West Mids. DY6 7AQ
Tel No: 01384-293514   Fax No:01384-826516.
Email: Kingsley@cableinet.co.uk
Web Site: www.wkweb5.cableinet.co.uk/kingsley/

Herefordshire Family History Research
All record types researched for Herefordshire, Worcs and Glos. Hereford Diocese Probate records which includes South Shropshire are a speciality. See Advert on Page 16

17 Whitefriars Road, Hereford, HR2 7XE
Tel No: 01432-341270
Email: eleanor.harris@which.net.
Web Site: www.homepages.which.net/~eleanor.harris

John S Griffiths
27 years experience in ancestral research. All aspects of genealogical and related historical research. Black Country and surrounding county records. National Library of Wales collections. Welsh Non Conformity. See Advert on Page 96

30 Coniston Road, Erdington, Birmingham, West Midlands, B23 6HJ
Tel No: 0121-384-3928

Mrs Sue Cleaves, BSc, ALA
Family and local history research by experienced researcher. All enquiries welcome. Contact for further information. See Advert on Page 98

3 Gilbert Close, Newport, Shropshire, TF10 7UU
Tel No: 01952-812060   Fax No:01952-812060.

Paperchase Genealogical & Research Services
Research/ full genealogical service by a qualified genealogist and AGRA Member with over 25 years experience including computerised reporting if required. See Advert on Page 98

5 Glebe Close, Blythe Bridge, Stoke on Trent ST11 9JN
Tel No: 01782-394147   Fax No:01782-394147.
Email: elderton@one-name.org.
Web Site: www.ukancestors.com

Staffordshire Knot Research
Research carried out in Staffordshire and surrounding counties. £5 per hour. Parish Registers; Census; Estate Records; etc. See Advert on Page 98

36 Whalley Ave, Penkhull, Stoke on Trent ST4 5NE
Tel No: 01782-25231
Email: pcotton@netcentral.co.uk *or*
        annfurber@haywood751.freeserve.co.uk

SOMERSET

See also: **Ancestral Research - Comprehensive on Page 61**

Ancestral Locations
Family histories researched throughout the UK by Somerset based experienced genealogist. Also professional location photography. See Advert on Page 60

9 Edgebury, Woolavington, Bridgwater, Somerset, TA7 8ES
Tel No: 01278-685255   Fax No:01278-685255.
Email: lesleyt@ancestorsuk.com
Web Site: www.amcestorsuk.com

Jennifer Day
Experienced researcher offers efficient, friendly service. All Enquiries welcome. See Advert on Page 98

Lantern Cottage, Rhodyate, Blagdon, North Somerset, BS40 7TP
Tel No: 01761-462426

Southern Counties Ancestry
GRO Indexes, Census Returns, IGI, Wills & Admons, Parish Registers and many other sources reliably searched at reasonable rates. See Advert on Page 88

St Michaels, 2 Church Rd, Polegate, East Sussex, BN26 5BX
Tel No: 01323-488885
Email: drb.sammyd.demon.co.uk
Web Site: www.sammyd.demon.co.uk

Tony Shopland - Ancestral Research
Experienced Researcher to undertake assignments in Devon, Somerset, Dorset & Cornwall. See Advert on Page 84

22 Joslin Road, Honiton, Devon, EX14 8RH
Tel No: 01404-45686   Fax No:01404-45686.
Email: Tony@Shopland.freeserve.co.uk
Ancestral Research

STAFFORDSHIRE

See also: **Ancestral Research - Comprehensive on Page 61**

Gwen Kingsley, BA(Hons)
Genealogical research undertaken by experienced researcher. Friendly, efficient service. See Advert on Page 16

'Lyndon', Queen St, Kingswinford, West Mids, DY6 7AQ
Tel No: 01384-293514   Fax No:01384-826516.
Email: Kingsley@cableinet.co.uk
Web Site: www.wkweb5.cableinet.co.uk/kingsley/

John S Griffiths
All genealogical and related historical research. Black Country and surrounding counties. See Advert on Page 96

30 Coniston Road, Erdington, Birmingham B23 6HJ
Tel No: 0121-384-3928

Staffordshire continued ....

The Suffolk Record Office
Gwyn Thomas - Senior Archivist

In Suffolk the County Council's archive and local studies service is delivered through Record Offices in the three largest towns, Bury St Edmunds, Ipswich and Lowestoft. In terms of their catchment areas Bury covers west Suffolk and Ipswich east, with the exception of the Waveney district, which is the responsibility of Lowestoft. The three offices have different histories but they are all part of the same service, with the same objectives, and the systems in use within them are all broadly similar. We are part of the County Council's Libraries and Heritage department which places particular emphasis on a high quality of service to our customers; and family historians represent about 63% of our customer base.

The basic family history sources are delivered in microform. Each office holds microform copies of all the Suffolk parish registers from the beginning usually down to 1900. The censuses of 1851, 1881 and 1891 for the whole county are available in each office while 1841, 1861 and 1871 are held for each office's catchment area. In addition each office has the CD-ROM version of the 1881 UK census. All offices have the Suffolk section of Boyd's marriage index and the 1994 edition of the IGI for the whole of the UK, (Bury also has the IGI for Australia, New Zealand, Canada and the eastern United States). In order to assist our readers to use their time with us most profitably, all the microform sources are on open access and are available on a self-help basis. There are, across the three offices, 46 microfilm and microfiche readers and four self-service reader/printers. Despite being the busiest county archive service in the country we do not insist on bookings for readers (or for places in the more traditional searchrooms), at Bury or Lowestoft, although booking machines is advisable at Ipswich.

Turning to original archive sources, all the offices hold for their areas extensive collections of the kind family historians find most useful; the records of probate courts, ecclesiastical and civil parishes, boroughs and other local authorities, manors, chapels, schools, charities and societies, and Public Records, particularly those of Coroners, Quarter and Petty Sessions and Hospitals. There are good collections of family and estate records for those whose ancestors worked for the 'big house' and at Bury the Suffolk Regiment archive is one of the heaviest-used collections.

Full details of our holdings of the main genealogical sources and the finding aids to them can be found in the *Guide to Genealogical Sources*. This is being published in parts; each part is available separately or the whole can be bought for a discount. Some parts of the *Guide* are still in preparation: to see what is currently available have a look at our web site (address below).

Suffolk Record Office though is not just about documents. Since 1976 the archive service in Suffolk has been merged with the county's Local Studies reference stock, so that manuscript and printed sources for the area are combined under one roof (or strictly speaking three roofs), with obvious benefits for the researcher. In addition to books and pamphlets, for Suffolk and surrounding counties, the Local Studies collections are strong in newspapers (nearly all of which are on microfilm), press cuttings and sales particulars. Two parts of the collection are worth highlighting. At Bury the Cullum collection (formerly the private library of a local gentry family) includes hundreds of books on genealogy, heraldry, topography and local history, not just for Suffolk but for the whole country. As a result it contains many printed parish registers for London and Yorkshire, printed visitations for most of England and a good range of eighteenth century county histories. At Ipswich the library of the Suffolk Family History Society is situated in the Record Office. The Office and the Society enjoy excellent mutually-supportive relations and the Society's library, with its large collection of register and MI transcripts which complement those on the Local Studies shelves, is available for use by Record Office customers.

All the Local Studies stock is currently being added to the County Library's electronic catalogue which is accessible over the World Wide Web at http://libcat.suffolkcc.gov.uk/. And speaking of the Web, each office provides free Internet access for its users.

Admission to the Record Offices and use of the manuscript, printed and microform sources is of course free. Bury and Ipswich are open Monday to Saturday, 9.00-5.00. Lowestoft is open as follows: Monday. Wednesday and Friday 9.15-5.30, Tuesday 9.15-6.00, Saturday 9.15-5.00. Photocopying and self-service print-out from microform are available at prices ranging from 40p to 60p. Microfiche copies of most Suffolk parish registers can be purchased at £2.00 per fiche plus a handling charge of £5.00.

The other service for which a charge is made is our postal research service. If you cannot easily get to Suffolk, or if you have a specific enquiry for which a visit would not be worth while, we can carry out the research for you. This service is not limited to family history and can extend to translation and transcription. The cost is £20.00 an hour for research and £30.00 for translation or transcription.

There is much more information about the research service and all our other services on our web site, which is under constant revision. The site includes details of recent accessions, order forms for the research service, the *Guide*, parish maps of Suffolk and the duplifiche parish register service, and a selection of images of documents to whet the appetite of potential researchers. You can find it at http://www.suffolkcc.gov.uk/libraries_and_heritage/sro/ To contact us direct the offices are at:

77 Raingate St, Bury St Edmunds, IP33 2 AR
Tel: 01284 352352 Fax: 01284 352355
Email: bury.ro@libher.suffolkcc.gov.uk
Gatacre Rd, Ipswich, IP1 2LQ
Tel: 01473 584541 Fax: 01473 584533
Email: ipswich.ro@libher.suffolkcc.gov.uk
Central Library, Clapham Rd. Lowestoft NR32 1DR
Tel: 01502 405357 Fax: 01502 405350
Email: lowestoft.ro@libher.suffolkcc.gov.uk

STAFFORDSHIRE (Cont.)

Mrs Sue Cleaves, BSc, ALA
Family and local history research by experienced researcher. All enquiries welcome. See Advert on Page 98

3 Gilbert Close, Newport, Shropshire, TF10 7UU
Tel No: 01952-812060   Fax No:01952-812060.

Paperchase Genealogical & Research Services
Research/ full genealogical service by a qualified genealogist. Computerised reporting if required. See Advert on Page 98

5 Glebe Close, Blythe Bridge, Stoke on Trent ST11 9JN
Tel No: 01782-394147   Fax No:01782-394147.
Email: elderton@one-name.org.
Web Site: www.ukancestors.com

Staffordshire and Stoke on Trent Archive Service
For research into all Staffordshire records including parish and non-conformist registers, census and electoral registers. See Advert on Page 98

Staffs Record Office, Eastgate Street, Stafford ST16 2LZ
Tel No: 01785-278379   Fax No:01785-278384.
Email: staffordshire.record.office@staffordshire.gov.uk.
Web Site: www.staffordshire.gov.uk

Staffordshire Knot Research
Research carried out in Staffordshire and surrounding counties. See Advert on Page 98

36 Whalley Ave, Penkhull, Stoke on Trent ST4 5NE
Tel No: 01782-25231
Email: pcotton@netcentral.co.uk or
         annfurber@haywood751.freeserve.co.uk

Vanessa Morgan
Research undertaken from one name searches to complete family histories. Also offers location photography service at competitive rates. See Advert on Page 88

33 Plymouth Road, Redditch, Worcestershire, B97 4PX
Tel No: 01527-62472   Fax No:01527-457176.
Email: Vanessa@snackbox.freeserve.co.uk

SUFFOLK

See also: Ancestral Research - Comprehensive on Page 61

East Anglian Village Research
EAVR are specialists at tracing ancestry in the rural communities of Eastern England. See Advert on Page 86

1 Ivy Cottages, Long Rd West, Dedham, Colchester, CO7 6EL
Tel No: 01206-322213
Email: eavr@btinternet.com
Web Site: www.btinternet.com/~p.w.w/eavr.htm

Family History Shop & Library
Publications relating to Norfolk and Suffolk and genealogical research experienced researcher. See Advert on Page 94

24d Magdalen Street, Norwich, NR3 1HU
Tel No: 01603-621152   Email: jenlibrary@aol.com
Web Site: www.jenlibrary.u-net.com/

SURREY

See also: Ancestral Research - Comprehensive on Page 61

Ancestral Research by Paul Lister
Family history research undertaken at very reasonable and competitive rates. See Advert on Page 72

4 Sergison Road, Haywards Heath, West Sussex, RH16 1HS
Tel No: 01444-453880
Email: piggleston@aol.com
Web Site: members.aol.com/piggleston/ancestralresearch

Patrick Yarnold Research
Genealogist & Record Agent. Research countrywide 19th & 20th Centuries. Earlier periods research undertaken for London, Berks, Hants and Surrey. See Advert on Page 72

93 The Street, Puttenham, Guildford, Surrey, GU3 1AT
Tel No: 01483-810564

Southern Counties Ancestry
GRO Indexes, Census Returns, IGI, Wills & Admons, Parish Registers and many other sources reliably searched at reasonable rates. See Advert on Page 88

St Michaels, 2 Church Rd, Polegate, East Sussex, BN26 5BX
Tel No: 01323-488885
Email: drb.sammyd.demon.co.uk
Web Site: www.sammyd.demon.co.uk

SUSSEX

See also: Ancestral Research - Comprehensive on Page 61

Ancestral Research by Paul Lister
Family history research undertaken at very reasonable and competitive rates. See Advert on Page 72

4 Sergison Road, Haywards Heath, West Sussex, RH16 1HS
Tel No: 01444-453880   Email: piggleston@aol.com
Web Site: members.aol.com/piggleston/ancestralresearch

Ian J Hilder, BA(Hons)
Sussex and London archives searched plus a photography service in Sussex. See Advert on Page 76

23A Grantham Bank, Barcombe Cross, Lewes, Sussex, BN8 5DJ
Tel No: 01273-400604   Email: HilderGen@aol.com

Southern Counties Ancestry
Reliable research in all sources e.g. GRO Indexes, Census Returns, Parish Registers, etc. See Advert on Page 88

St Michaels, 2 Church Rd, Polegate, East Sussex, BN26 5BX
Tel No: 01323-488885
Email: drb.sammyd.demon.co.uk
Web Site: www.sammyd.demon.co.uk

Tree of Discovery
Specialising in record searches and research in London and the South East. See Advert on Page 74

3 Waterlock Cottages, Canterbury Rd, Wingham, Kent, CT3 1BH
Tel No: 01227-720271

TYNE & WEAR

See also: Ancestral Research - Comprehensive on Page 61

Geoff Nicholson
Genealogical research by AGRA member of many years experience. See Advert on Page 102

57 Manor Park, Concord, Washington, Tyne & Wear, NE37 2BU
Tel No: 0191-417-9546
Email: geoff@genic.demon.co.uk
Web Site: www.genic.demon.co.uk/index.html

Neil Richardson
Friendly, family history research. Microfiche available on Master Mariners & Ship Owners. See Advert on Page 102

12 Banbury Way, South Beach Estate, Blyth NE24 3TY
Tel No: 01670-353605
Email: k.richardson@ukonline.co.uk
Web Site: www.ukonline.co.uk/northumweb/index.htm

Original Indexes
Genealogical research service by well known publishers of microfiche indexes. See Advert on Page 102

113 East View, Wideopen, Tyne and Wear, NE13 6EF
Tel No: 0191-236-6416
Email: fiche@original-indexes.demon.co.uk
Web Site: www.original-indexes@demon.co.uk/index.htm

WARWICKSHIRE

See also: Ancestral Research - Comprehensive on Page 61

Ancestral Trails
For the provision of a professional research service including pedigree charts, wills, newspapers, military and court records. Also a photographic history service. See Advert on Page 88

Copper Beeches, Colesbourne, Gloucestershire, GL53 9NS
Tel No: 01242-870297
Email: pamb@freenet.co.uk

Gwen Kingsley, BA(Hons)
Genealogical research undertaken by experienced researcher. Friendly, efficient service. See Advert on Page 16

'Lyndon', Queen St, Kingswinford, West Mids, DY6 7AQ
Tel No: 01384-293514   Fax No:01384-826516.
Email: Kingsley@cableinet.co.uk
Web Site: www.wkweb5.cableinet.co.uk/kingsley/

John S Griffiths
27 years experience in ancestral research. All aspects of genealogical and related historical research. Black Country and surrounding county records. See Advert on Page 96

30 Coniston Road, Erdington, Birmingham B23 6HJ
Tel No: 0121-384-3928

Kathleen Wilshaw, BA
Family and local history research. Professional and friendly service by experienced researcher at reasonable rates. All enquiries welcome. See Advert on Page 96

The Shieling, Duns Tew, Oxfordshire, OX6 4JS
Tel No: 01869-340364
Email: kwilshaw@compuserve.com

Vanessa Morgan
Research undertaken from one name searches to complete family histories. Also offers location photography service at competitive rates. See Advert on Page 88

33 Plymouth Road, Redditch, Worcestershire, B97 4PX
Tel No: 01527-62472   Fax No:01527-457176.
Email: Vanessa@snackbox.freeserve.co.uk

WESTMORLAND

See also: Ancestral Research - Comprehensive on Page 61

Sydney G Smith
Genealogical Researcher for Kent and London including the Family Records Centre. Also compiler of the Westmorland and North Lancs Index (1700-1837). See Advert on Page 66

59 Friar Road, Orpington, Kent, BR5 2BW
Tel No: 01689-832800
Email: ss.famhist@virgin.net

WILTSHIRE

See also: Ancestral Research - Comprehensive on Page 61

Southern Counties Ancestry
GRO Indexes, Census Returns, IGI, Wills & Admons, Parish Registers and many other sources reliably searched at reasonable rates. See Advert on Page 88

St Michaels, 2 Church Rd, Polegate, East Sussex, BN26 5BX
Tel No: 01323-488885
Email: drb.sammyd.demon.co.uk
Web Site: www.sammyd.demon.co.uk

Wiltshire Archaeological & Natural History Society
Unique Wiltshire material for the family historian, including pedigrees, maps, photos, postcards, etc. Photocopying and research facilities available. See Advert on Page 104

WANHS Library, 41 Long Street, Devizes, Wilts, SN10 5JH
Tel No: 01380-727369   Fax No:01380-722150.

WORCESTERSHIRE

See also: Ancestral Research - Comprehensive on Page 61

Ancestral Trails
Professional research service including pedigree charts, wills, newspapers, military records. A photographic history service brings alive ancestry places of origin. See Advert on Page 88

Copper Beeches, Colesbourne, Gloucestershire, GL53 9NS
Tel No: 01242-870297
Email: pamb@freenet.co.uk

Gwen Kingsley, BA(Hons)
Genealogical research undertaken by experienced researcher. Friendly, efficient service. See Advert on Page 16

'Lyndon', Queen St, Kingswinford, West Mids, DY6 7AQ
Tel No: 01384-293514   Fax No:01384-826516.
Email: Kingsley@cableinet.co.uk
Web Site: www.wkweb5.cableinet.co.uk/kingsley/

Herefordshire Family History Research
All record researched from 1538 onwards for Herefordshire, Worcestershire and Gloucestershire. Hereford Diocese Probate records a speciality. See Advert on Page 16

17 Whitefriars Road, Hereford, HR2 7XE
Tel No: 01432-341270
Email: eleanor.harris@which.net.
Web Site: www.homepages.which.net/~eleanor.harris

Hidden Heritage
A research service into any and all records in glorious Gloucestershire, Bristol and the surrounding counties. No task is too small or too large. See Advert on Page 87

11 Old Cheltenham Road, Longlevens, Gloucester, GL2 0AS
Tel No: 01452-503831   Fax No:01452-503831.
Email: ejack@gloster.demon.co.uk
Web Site: www.gloster.demon.co.uk

WORCESTERSHIRE continued

John S Griffiths
27 years experience in ancestral research. All aspects of genealogical and related historical research. Black Country and surrounding county records. See Advert on Page 96

30 Coniston Road, Erdington, Birmingham B23 6HJ
Tel No: 0121-384-3928

Vanessa Morgan
Research undertaken from one name searches to complete family histories. Also offers location photography service at competitive rates. See Advert on Page 88

33 Plymouth Road, Redditch, Worcestershire, B97 4PX
Tel No: 01527-62472   Fax No:01527-457176.
Email: Vanessa@snackbox.freeserve.co.uk

YORKSHIRE

See also: Ancestral Research - Comprehensive on Page 61

York Minster Library Databank
Library containing half a million entries on Yorkshire people before 1600. Search fees £10.   See Advert on Page 104

York Minster Library, Dean's Park, York,
Tel No: 01904-625308

Looking for Ancestors in Bradford?

BRADFORD FAMILY HISTORY SOCIETY

Secretary: Mr Dennis Flaxington, 2 Leaventhorpe Grove, Thornton, Bradford, West Yorks. BD13 3BN
The Society's Web site is at   http://www.genuki org.uk/big/eng/YKS/bfhs/

Founded in 1982 to further the interest of family history research, the Society now has over 600 members in the U.K. Australia, North America, New Zealand and Europe. Not all members have Bradford ancestors but all have an interest in family history. Those able to attend the evening meetings benefit from talks, visits and the opportunity to discuss their research problems and successes with other members. Family history publications may be purchased from our bookstall and borrowed from our library.

An expenses-only, limited research facility, provided by volunteers working in their spare time, is available for those members unable to make a personal visit to some local libraries and archives. Requests for help and details of Members' Interests are published in the quarterly newsletter 'The Bok-Kin which is distributed free to all members.

The Society has the 1881 Census for all English counties and a postal search service is available.

Should you decide to join the Bradford Family History Society not only will your personal family research benefit but you will also have the opportunity to assist in the current project work.

SOCIETY PUBLICATIONS

The following Society publications are available from Ms Pat Barrow, 37 Churchfields, Fagley. Bradford. West Yorkshire BD2 33N, from whom details can be obtained.

Surname Index Series

This series contains alphabetical lists of SURNAMES and the FOLIOS (or PAGES in the case of Bradford 1841) in which they can be found

- The 1841 Census for Bradford Surname index
- The 1861 Census for Bradford Surname Index
- The 1871 Census for Bradford, Surname Index
- The 1891 Census for Bradford Surname Index
- The 1841 & '51, 1861 & '71, and 1891 Censuses for Bingley, Surname Index

Parish Register Transcription Indexes

- The Name Index to Bradford Parish Church Burials 1681 - 1837

This transcription includes SURNAME, FORENAMES, AGE, RELATIONSHIP TO OTHERS, OCCUPATION, ABODE and DATE OF BURIAL. AGE was not often put in the registers before standardised registers were introduced in 1813, whereas after 1812 it was included but RELATIONSHIP TO OTHERS was not. The only information not transcribed is the clergyman performing the ceremony.

- Indexes On microfiche of the Thornton Bell Chapel registers:
  Baptisms 1731-1785, marriages 1732-1751 and burials 1731-1787.

Other Publications

"Where to find Recorded Monumental Inscriptions (Yorks.)", published 1998 by the North East Group of Family History Societies, of which Bradford F.H.S. is a member.

Doncaster & District
Family History Society

The Society meets on the 3rd Thursday of each month (except August)
7.00 p.m. for 7.30 p.m.
Doncaster Central Library, Waterdale

PUBLICATIONS -
A5 Books

Burial Indexes - taken from *commencement* of parish registers to at least 1900 for many of the parishes within the Archdeaconry of Doncaster.

1851 Census Index & Marriage Indexes - for all parishes covered by the Society.

MICROFICHE

Cemetery Registers - for Bentley with Arksey, Conisbrough, Mexborough (New), Mexborough (Old) & Doncaster Hyde Park.

Monumental Inscriptions - All churches & churchyards within the Archdeaconry of Doncaster & Doncaster Hyde Park Cemetery.

1891 Census - A complete transcription of most parishes covered by the Society.

Doncaster Health Authority Death Registers - for deaths which occurred in Doncaster from 1875 to 1928

Name Search & Printout Service - on various records covering Doncaster & District:
1851 Census Master Index, 1881 Census Index, 1891 Census full transcription), 1871 Census (for Doncaster only), Surname Index on MIs in all the churches & churchyards in the Archdeaconry of Doncaster, Bawtry & Doncaster Cemetery MIs, & Vital Records Index for the British Isles.
Send SAE for leaflet on services & charges.

MILLENNIUM FAMILY HISTORY DAY

Saturday 28th October 2000
9.45am to 4.15pm

at
Yorkshire Residential School for the Deaf, Leger Way, Doncaster
"I am England" - The life and times of Queen Elizabeth 1st by Lizzie Jones

Society resources and various databases available during early morning, coffee breaks and lunch time.

- Ample Free Parking
- Disabled Facilities
- Optional Lunch
- Further details and leaflets for any of the above from:-

Mrs June Staniforth, 125 The Grove, Wheatley Hills, Doncaster DN2 5SN   Tel: 01302 367257
Website: http://www.doncasterfhs.freeserve.co.uk

Keighley and District Family History Society

**Hon Secretary: Mrs S Daynes,
2 The Hallows, Shann Park, Keighley
West Yorkshire BD20 6HY**

Meetings held on first Monday of each month (excluding bank holidays, then second Monday) at 7pm for 7.30pm at Trinity Church, Spencer Street, Keighley.

PUBLICATIONS FOR SALE INCLUDE:-
Monumental Inscriptions, Utley Cemetery Vols 1 to 6; Keighley News Marriages Indexes and Deaths Indexes 1862 to 1901; 1851 Census index for Broughton, Carleton, Elslack, Lothersdale, & Stirton with Thorlby; Kildwick Baptisms 1572 to 1622 (published) and 1622 to 1778 (coming soon). Prices £3 to £6 each incl p&p.

**Further details on publications from:-
Mrs J Wood, High Wheathead Farm,
Exley Head, Keighley.
West Yorks. BD22 6NB**

WHARFEDALE ANCESTORS?
Then join:-
**THE WHARFEDALE
FAMILY HISTORY GROUP**

Covering the parishes of Addingham, Adel, Arncliffe, Arthington, Baildon, Bolton Abbey, Burley in Wharfedale, Burnsall, Conistone, Denton, Fewston, Guiseley, Harewood, Hebden, Horsforth, Hubberholme, Ilkley, Kettlewell, Leathley, Linton in Craven, Menston Otley, Pool, Rawdon, Rylstone, Stainburn, Weeton, Weston, Yeadon,

Meetings held at Burley in Wharfedale & Grassington

Quarterly Journal, Bookstall & Library, wide range of research aids, Publishing programme of transcripts & indexes

Membership £7 per annum (£9 Overseas)

**Membership secretary:-
Gerald Lawson, 47 Hall Park Avenue,
Horsforth, Leeds. LS18 5LR**

Full list of publications available
(including local history material) from:-

**Stanley Merridew, 206 Moseley Wood Gardens,
Cookridge, Leeds. LS16 7JE**

Wakefield and District Family History Society

We cover the Metropolitan District of Wakefield, which includes the parishes of Ackworth, Badsworth, Castleford, Crofton, Darrington, Featherstone, Ferry Fryston, Hemsworth, Horbury, Knottingley, Normanton, Ossett, Pontefract, Sandal Magna, South Kirkby, Wakefield, Warmfield, West Bretton, Wooley, Wragby and parts of the parishes of Dewsbury, Felkirk, Royston and Thornhill

The Society meets on the first Saturday of each month (except August) from 10am at St Michaels Church Parish Rooms, Westgate End, Wakefield.

Publications
1851 Census Index in 40 volumes
1813 – 1837 Marriage Index in 28 volumes
Towns and Villages – Parish Index
Tradepeople and Craftsmen in 1834 in 3 volumes
A search-and-print service for the 1851 census master index is available

For further details about the Society contact the Membership Secretary
Mrs Eileen Piper, 46 Ledger Lane, Outwood, Wakefield. WF1 2PH
(SAE please)

Website
http://www.homepage.virgin.net/wakefield.fhs

e-mail
wakefield.fhs@virgin.net

STEPPING STONES

Trade Directories on CD - £11.99 + p&p

City Centre only Directories £7.99 + p&p

Pigot's 1822 Northumberland
Pigot's 1834 Durham
Slater's 1848 Northumberland
Kelly's 1872 East Riding Post Office Directory
Kelly's 1872 North & East Riding
Kelly's 1897 North Riding Street & Trade
Kelly's 1897 East Riding
Kelly's 1897 Hull Street Directory
Kelly's 1897 York Street + York Inns
       + Photos Circa 1860 +

1897 North & East Riding Court & Commercial
Kelly's 1919 Cornwall
1902 Scarborough, Filey, Whitby & Villages
Principal Cities Trade Directory
Newcastle l3th-l4th Journal
Illustrated Yorkshire Churches
Wales 1829-30 Trade Directory
Sheffield City Centre 1822
Middlesborough City Centre 1897

We have a forthcoming list of CD's which will be available throughout the year, please ring us to see if we have your area and we will contact you when it is available!

We also have scanned images of coloured city centre Maps circa 1860s from £4.00 each to add to your Family album.

Contact us at:
3 George Hudson Street YORK YO1 6JL
01904 652666 or Fax 01904 656333
Email judd©mjudson.freeserve.co.uk

Over 5000 Church postcards in stock
From £1.50 each ring for details

Web Page www.stepping-stones.co.uk

YORKSHIRE ARCHAEOLOGICAL SOCIETY

Family History Section

Can we help you with your
Family History in Yorkshire?

Our thriving Society was founded in 1973

Over 1800 Members Worldwide

Members have use of our extensive Library
Quarterly journal
Helpful Publications by post or at meetings
Printout service available from the 1881 Census Index
and International Genealogical Index
Meetings held monthly

http://www.users.globalnet.co.uk/~gdl/yasfhs.htm

Details from: Miss L. Raistrick, Hon. Sec.
Claremont, 23 Clarendon Road, Leeds, LS2 9NZ

Registered Charity No 224083

RIPON HISTORICAL SOCIETY
and
Ripon, Harrogate & District Family History Group

Secretary:
Mrs W A Symington
18 Aspin Drive
Knaresborough HG5 8HH

Publications include:
Yorkshire Hearth Tax Lists
Index of Wills & Administrations for area
Ripon Parish Registers
Historical Sources for District
1851 Census Index
Monumental Inscriptions on M/fiche
Plus others

For further details about membership and
publications of the Society send sae to the
Secretary at above address.

THE
City of York & District

FAMILY • HISTORY • SOCIETY

The Society meets on the 1st Wednesday of each month (excluding August)
The Priory Street Centre, York
at 7.00.p.m. for 7.30.p.m.

❋ ❋ ❋ ❋ ❋ ❋ ❋ ❋

If your ancestors came from York and District they may be in our Indexes

Publications on Microfiche

YORK **Parish Registers** St Martins, Coney Street Holy Trinity, King's Court Holy Trinity, Goodramgate St Giles Copmanthorpe St Mary's Bishophill Junior		*NEW* **POLL BOOK** for the City of York **1820**
NEW *1851 CENSUS* *YORK AREA* Ask for details of Parishes		*ROLL of HONOUR* NORTH EASTERN RAILWAY 1914 - 1918 *NEW*
York Marriage Index Part 1 : 1701 - 1750 Part 2 : 1751 - 1800 Part 3 : 1801 - 1837	**Burial Index** **Yorkshire** **North Riding** 1813 - 1837	**York Burial Index** 1813 - 1837 [Three Parts]
Memorial Inscriptions *NEW* **Sutton on the Forest**	**York Cemetery Memorial Inscriptions** ALL SECTIONS NOW COMPLETED *NEW* after 25 years work *NEW* Ask for a Name Search, or details of Sections	

For further details about the indexes, the Society or membership please write to
The Secretary
Mrs Carol Mennell
4 Orchard Close, Dringhouses, York, YO24 2NX, England
enclosing a Stamped Addressed Envelope or TWO International Reply Coupons

Look at our website at www.yorkfamilyhistory.org.uk

LLYFRGELL GENEDLAETHOL CYMRU
PRIF LYFRGELL YMCHWIL CYMRU

THE NATIONAL LIBRARY OF WALES
WALES' PREMIER RESEARCH LIBRARY
Penglais, Aberystwyth, Ceredigion, SY23 3BU ☎ 44(0)1970 632800

HOFFECH CHI GAEL HELP
I HEL EICH ACHAU?
GOFYNNWCH AM FFURFLEN Y
GWASANAETH CHWILOTA

DO YOU NEED A HELPING HAND
TO TRACE YOUR FAMILY TREE?
ASK FOR DETAILS OF THE
LIBRARY'S SEARCH SERVICE

'Even the common people retain their genealogy, and can not only readily recount the names of their grandfathers and great-grandfather, but even refer back to the 6th or 7th generation, or beyond them ...'

The Description of Wales Giraldus Cambrensis
(Gerald the Welshman) 1194

GLAMORGAN FAMILY HISTORY SOCIETY

reg. charity 1059537

PUBLICATIONS

All publications are available on Microfiche, many have also been produced in Booklet form

Publications in BOOKLETS & MICROFICHES contain identical information

PARISH REGISTERS: *Transcription and index (over 100)*   **MIs:** *over 230 available*

ೞ⁊ꙮ

MICROFICHES ONLY

MIMI - *Master Index of Monumental Inscriptions (90,000 names)*
GLAMORGAN MARRIAGE INDEX - *a pre-1837 index of Brides & Grooms*
1841 & 1851 CENSUS of GLAMORGAN

Name Index & As Enumerated, published in sets, to cover the whole of the old county

ೞ⁊ꙮೞ⁊ꙮೞ⁊ꙮ

Send SAE for price lists:

FICHE Mrs M.Baird, Dyfed House, Glenside Court, Ty Gwyn Road, CARDIFF, CF23 5JS
BOOKLETS Mrs R.Knight, 6 St.Margaret's Crescent, Roath, CARDIFF, CF23 5AU

Leaflet from: Membership Sec., 11 Cherrydown Close, Thornhill, CARDIFF, CF14 9DJ
or via Web Site **http://hometown.aol.com/gfhsoc**

Llyfrgell Genedlaethol Cymru
The National Library of Wales
Eirionedd A. Baskerville
Head of Readers' Services - Department of Manuscripts and Records

An interest in family history is part of the Welsh psyche. According to the Laws of Hywel Dda, it was necessary to know one's relatives to the ninth remove, and Giraldus Cambrensis on his crusading tour of Wales in 1188 noted that the humblest person was able to recite from memory his family tree, going back six or seven generations.

The National Library of Wales is the premier centre for family history research in Wales, holding as it does abundant records covering the whole of Wales. Its three main Departments all have something different to offer. The Department of Printed Books holds electoral lists, newspapers and directories, while the Department of Pictures and Maps has plans, sale catalogues, and tithe maps and schedules. However, the most important Department from the point of view of genealogical research is the Department of Manuscripts and Records, which holds a whole range of useful resources.

The Department has microform copies of the returns for the whole of Wales for each of the ten-yearly censuses 1841-91, and microfiche copies of the index to the 1881 census for the English counties as well as those for Wales. In addition, some of the returns have been transcribed and indexed by enthusiastic individuals and societies who have kindly made them available to the Library's users.

Civil registration of births, marriages and deaths was introduced in England and Wales on 1 July 1837, and microfiche copies of the General Register Office's indexes of the registration records from 1837 to 1992 are available for searching free of charge at the National Library. The Library does not issue certificates, but a search of the indexes can be undertaken for a fee.

Before the introduction of civil registration, the `rites of passage' were noted in parish registers, following the order of 5 September 1538 that a register of every baptism, marriage and burial in every parish should be kept. However, the earliest surviving registers for most Welsh parishes do not commence until after 1660, although starting dates vary greatly. Parish registers held at the National Library are available on microfilm to readers. The Library also holds transcript copies of some parish registers, which have been kindly donated by the compilers. In addition, the 1988 edition of the International Genealogical Index, while far from complete, can prove a useful starting point for tracing the parish in which a baptism or marriage was registered.

Although the ravages of weather and rodents, inept vicars and disrespectful parishioners have resulted in the disappearance of many original parish registers, the bishops transcripts (annual returns submitted by Anglican parish clergy to the bishops containing copies of all the entries recorded in their parish registers during the preceding twelve months), often come to the rescue of the family historian. Transcripts were ordered to be sent annually

from 1597 onwards, but there are no transcripts before 1661 in the records of the Church inhales deposited in the Library. Even after this date there are many gaps in the returns, only a few transcripts before 1723 being extant for parishes in the diocese of Llandaff, and hardly any for the eighteenth century for parishes in the archdeaconries of Cardigan and St David's.

The transcripts cease at dates varying from parish to parish during the middle of the nineteenth century, although there are a few examples from the early twentieth century from some parishes. Transcripts of marriage entries normally cease with the introduction of civil registration in 1837. The transcripts held by the Library are listed in schedules available in the Department of Manuscripts and Records. At present the original transcripts are available to readers, but the task of preparing microfiche copies is underway.

Marriage bonds and allegations are the next most important class of Anglican Church record of use to the genealogist. These documents were executed in order to obtain a licence to marry without having banns called publicly in Church on three Sundays before the solemnisation of the marriage. Generally speaking, these records cover the eighteenth and nineteenth centuries and the first three decades of the twentieth century. The amount and nature of the information varies with the type of document, and are particularly valuable when the approximate date of a marriage is known but not its venue. The pre-1837 bonds and allegations in the Library have been indexed and may be searched on computer in the Department's Catalogue room. Also available for the diocese of St David's are registers of marriage licences, mainly for the nineteenth century.

Another class of records of paramount interest to the genealogist is wills and administrations, and those which before the introduction of Civil Probate on 11 January 1858 were proved in the Welsh ecclesiastical courts, have been deposited in the Library. Roughly speaking, the covering dates of the surviving probate records of each of the consistory courts are: Bangor, 1635-1858; Brecon, 1543-1858; Chester (Welsh Wills), 1557-1858; Hawarden, 1554-1858; Llandaff, 1568-1857; St Asaph, 1565-1857; St David's, 1556-1858. These wills have also been indexed and may be searched on computer.

For the period after 1858 the Library has custody of register copy wills from five registries, covering all but one (Montgomeryshire) of the Welsh counties, and a full microfiche set of the annual index of all wills and administrations granted in England and Wales (the Calendar of Grants), from 1858 to 1972.

Despite the fact that they are much less comprehensive than the records of the Anglican Church in Wales, Nonconformist records are an important source of information for genealogists. Many registers of dissenting congregations were deposited with the Registrar-General after the Civil Registration Act of 1836, and the Library has microfilm copies of these. A few registers of that period which never found their way to London and some other later registers are now deposited at the Library.

Other nonconformist records of genealogical value at the Library include manuscript lists of members and contribution books of individual chapels, printed annual reports, usually including lists of members and their contributions, which have been produced by many chapels since about 1880, and denominational periodicals, which often contain notices of births, marriages and deaths.

Records of the Court of Great Sessions of Wales, the most important legal and administrative body between the Act of Union and its abolition in 1830, may also prove useful for genealogical purposes. Occasionally challenge pedigrees were filed in connection with certain actions, and other documents of considerable value are depositions, which often state the age of the deponent, jury lists and coroners' inquests.

Whereas the official Quarter Sessions records for the county of Cardigan, held by the Library comprise little more than the order books from 1739, there are also some related materials among the archives of landed estates or solicitors' firms, for example a few sessional rolls and land tax records 1780-1839 from Cardiganshire, some land tax records (the most useful class of records for the genealogist) for Montgomeryshire and Breconshire, order books 1647-75 and rolls, 1643-99 for Denbighshire, and sessions records from Montgomeryshire.

Local government at a level between county and parish was practically non-existent before the formation of Poor Law Unions under the Poor Law Amendment Act 1834 Most Poor Law Union records are now deposited at the appropriate county record office, but there are some records at the Library, mainly from Montgomeryshire. Civil parish records are also mainly held by the appropriate county record office, although the Library holds vestry books and other parochial records for many parishes for which parish registers have been deposited.

The manorial records held by the Library are mainly to be found with the estate records and listed with them They are most comprehensive for Montgomeryshire (mainly the Powis Castle and Wynnstay estate records), with substantial holdings for Glamorgan and Monmouthshire also (mainly the Badminton, Bute and Tredegar estate records). It should be noted that in many parts of Wales the manorial system never really took root.

The Library has recently prepared a manorial database for Wales in conjunction with HMC available to readers on the Internet http://www2.hmc.gov.uk/Welsh_Manorial_Documents_Register.htm.

Most of the estate records and personal papers held by the Department of Manuscripts and Records are detailed in typescript schedules. The estate records contain title deeds, rentals, account books, correspondence, etc. Rentals may prove particularly useful in indicating a death or change of residence when a name disappears from a series of rentals.

The Department holds many manuscript pedigrees. These vary from descents of nobility, compiled in the later Middle Ages and copied time and again with additions by later genealogists, to charts which are the work of amateurs of modern times who have given copies of their compilations to the Library. For searchers particularly interested in the pedigrees of gentry families there are several important printed works available.

There is a general card index to most of the typescript schedules of the collections in the Department of Manuscripts and Records, and probably the most useful for the family historian are the sections devoted to wills, marriage settlements, inquisitions post mortem, and pedigrees. The index to the general collections of manuscripts (NLW MSS) may also be of use to genealogists. In addition, a basic inventory of the contents of the Library's Annual Report up to 1996 is available on-line in the Catalogue room.

For further information on sources for family history research at the National Library of Wales, it is worth consulting the Department of Manuscripts and Records' pages at the Library's web site at: http://www.llgc.org.uk/

Estate and Related Records at the National Library of Wales
Eirionedd A. Baskerville
Head of Readers' Services - Department of Manuscripts and Records

When information available in parish registers, bishop's transcripts and wills has been exhausted, genealogical researchers should turn their attention to the records of the manor and the estate. From the medieval period to the beginning of the twentieth century, large landed estates owned by the aristocracy and gentry were a prominent feature of the Welsh countryside, and much of the population lived and worked as tenants on these estates. Estate records are, therefore, an important source of information on tracing the history of an area and its inhabitants.

Records drawn up in the administration of an estate, such as rentals, surveys, title deeds (leases, mortgages, etc.) may enable you to discover names of owners and occupiers over several centuries. While the muniments of many large landed estates are likely to include good series of rentals and accumulations of title deeds, not all Welsh estates will be represented by long series of manorial records. The manorial system never came to full development in the counties of the medieval Principality, in west Wales, but the Marcher lordships generated a wealth of manorial records. However, notable amongst the series of manorial records held by the National Library of Wales are those for north Wales in the archives of the Chirk Castle and Wynnstay estates, and for mid-Wales in the Powis Castle archives. Amongst those of Badminton are manorial records for Chepstow, from 1568, Monmouth, from 1416, Porthgaseg, from 1262, Raglan, from 1364, Treleck, from 1508, and Usk, from 1517, while Bute includes manorials records from the fourteenth century for many manors in cos. Glamorgan and Monmouth, and Tredegar contains records of many Monmouthshire manors, those of the manor of Brecon and others in co. Brecon. A manorial database for Wales can be found on http://www.hmc.gov.uk/nra/nra.htm.

In general terms, amongst the manorial documents are found the Court Leet rolls which give the names of the manorial officers and local jurors and details of cases brought to court, e.g. the scouring of ditches, straying of cattle and cases of assault, theft or trespass. Court Baron rolls deal with tenancy matters and property disputes, while extents and surveys contain descriptions of boundaries, valuations and names of tenants, their holdings and rents paid. Custumals contain names of all the tenants with details of the land which they held and particulars of rents, labour services and payments owed to the lord, while bailiffs' accounts list the income from rents and fines and expenditure on ploughing, repairs and replacing implements, and the names of incoming and outgoing tenants can be found in admittances and surrenders.

It must be remembered that not all estates were secular - prior to the dissolution of the monasteries in 1536 the Church was a powerful landowner. The Library's Wynnstay archive contains a group of early charters of Strata Marcella abbey, while the Margam Abbey group of records in the Penrice and Margam collection is one of the fullest surviving British monastic archives. Crosswood

Deeds and Documents 1184 is a translation of a charter of Rhys, Prince of Wales, and his sons, Griffith, Rhys and Meredith, granting and confirming to the abbot of Strata Florida all the lands previously granted by the said prince and then held by the said abbey.

References to the acquisition of monastic estates by secular landowners can be found throughout the estate records held by the National Library, as shown in the following example from the schedule to the Crosswood collection:

1659-60 Mar 10 Indenture (counterpart) being a grant from John Vaughan of Trowscoed, co. Card. esq to Morgan Herbert of Havodychtrid, co. Card. esq of the tenement called *Dol-dologe* in the parish of Gwnnus and in the grange of Cwmystwith, co. Cardigan, being late parcel of the possessions of the dissolved monastery of Strata Florida, but reserving to the grantor the minerals thereunder, a perpetual yearly rent of £5 and suit at Pyran Mill

The records of the Welsh Church Commission held at the National Library of Wales also prove a fruitful field for researchers. Surveys were undertaken in the early 1940s, and contain much information on the history of manors: rentals, surveys, disputes over manorial rights, and especially foreshore rights around Bangor, going back to the 16th and 17th centuries. They also contain some tithe records which could provide valuable cross-references to the tithe material held in the Department of Pictures and Maps. The Church in Wales schedules give reference to relevant records such as glebe terriers, surveys not only of glebe land but also of all buildings, including parsonages and church cottages.

The amount of land, and hence power and patronage, held by an estate in a parish or parishes was of supreme importance in determining the whole character of parishes. Title deeds will usually give a history of landowning and landholding, that is the acquisition of properties, the takeover of one estate by another, sometimes by purchase but usually through marriage. Lewis Owen (d. 1691) was responsible for the first substantial addition to the Peniarth estate, co. Merioneth, by marriage. In 1653 he married Jane, daughter of Richard Lloyd of Esclusham, Denbighshire, who eventually brought with her the Gelli Iorwerth estate in the parishes of Trawsfynydd and Llanddwywe. A further example is found in the Tredegar Papers:

109/9 1633, March 26
1 William Morgan of Therrowe, co. Brecon, esq;
2 Sir William Morgan of Tredegar, co. Mon., knight, and Thomas Morgan of Machen, esq., eldest son of the said Sir William Morgan, and Roweland Morgan, gent., another son of the said Sir William Morgan

Settlement made before the marriage of the said William Morgan and Elizabeth Morgan, one of the daughters of the said Sir William Morgan, and in consideration of sixteen pounds paid to the said William Morgan, touching the

See Also: *Section 2A Research - Comprehensive*
Most of the Researchers listed in that Section also
undertake research in Wales.

John S Griffiths
27 years experience. All aspects of genealogical and
related research. National Library of Wales collections.
Welsh Non Conformity. See Advert on Page 96

30 Coniston Road, Erdington, Birmingham B23 6HJ
Tel No: 0121-384-3928

Newport Reference Library Research Service
See next Page 118

GLAMORGAN & GWENT

Family history research
in and about
Glamorgan and Gwent
by
experienced, locally based,
researcher.

Nicholas J Davey
27 Soberton Avenue, Heath,
Cardiff. CF14 3NJ
Tel: 02920-211431
Email: ndavey@baynet.co.uk

Welsh Ancestors
Glamorgan and Monmouthshire
Census, I.G.I.
Births, Marriages & Deaths
Register of Electors,
Parish Registers, Wills

Fast reliable service

Phone/Fax: **01446 733969**
Email: **113053,2231@compuserve.com**

CARW
Consultant Ancestral Research Wales

Family History Research undertaken in
County and National Archives/Libraries
A comprehensive and reliable service.
20 years experience.
Welsh ancestry a speciality,
also mariners and railway employees.
International clientele.

All enquiries welcome.

**Dewi W. Thomas
4 Rhodfa Anwyl
Rhuddlan
Denbighshire
LL18 2SQ**

☎ **01745 591372**
email: DThomas715@aol.com

Welsh Ancestry

Mariners

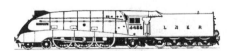

Railway Employees

lordship of Keinsham *alias* Neither Keinsham with its appurtances in cos. Hereford and Radnor; the divided third part of the lordship of Lliswen with its appurtances in co. Brecon; the capital messuage called *Therrowe* with its appurtenances in the parishes of Glasbury and Lliswen, co. Brecon; other messuages and lands in the parishes of Lliswen; a messuage and lands called *the Gare* in the parishes of Glasbury, Lliswen, and Llandevalty, co. Brecon; lands, being parcel of the demesnes of the lordship of Brecon, called *Heneuske* in the parish of Llavayes *alias* Llanvary, *the Greene* in the same parish, *the Lake* in the parish of St John's; other lands in the parish of St John's including those called *Pedebagh, Henny, Plucklocke, St John's land*; lands called *Tyr y Piscoidwr* in Glintawy in the parish of Divynocke; lands at Tallemere, parcel of the lordship of Brecon; lands in the parish of Llanham Wokgh (sic); messuages and lands called *Tir blaen Carrand* and *Tir dan y Graig* in the parish of Vaynor; properties in the parish of Penderin; and messuages and lands called *Tyr Carne y Crochan, Tir Pant y Lloyne, Tir pulch y gelynen, Tyr Blaen Neath, Tir Aber Llia(?), tyr Kay yr Hendre, Tir Lloyn Bedo, Tir Nant David Croyn, Tir Maes David Gwyn, Tir Inys Willy* and *Tyr bulch Ryweddedw'th, all in the parish of Istradvelty, co. Brecon.*

Generally called conveyances but also known by various technical names, (e.g. feoffment, bargain and sales; leases and releases; final concords, and common recoveries), title deeds give the name, abode and occupation of parties with relationships, names of witnesses, details of seals in early deeds, recital of earlier deeds affecting the property, names of farms and houses and references to all kinds of property - mills, chapels, schools and fisheries - together with foreshore rights. They are valuable sources of information for the growth and decline of the estate, the history of a particular house of farm, the distribution of local trades, the origins of schools or chapels, and family history.

However, estates are not only of relevance to rural communities; there were great urban landlords. It is a sobering thought that perhaps half the population of Wales today live within what was once the boundaries of the Bute and Tredegar estates in Monmouthshire and Glamorgan. By studying the rentals of these two estates you can virtually see before your very eyes the green fields being turned into streets. The same is true, to a lesser extent, of Aberystwyth (in the Crosswood, Nanteos and Gogerddan estates). Estates also held mineral deposits, and much of the early industrial history of Wales is to be found in the archives of landed families - Bute and Tredegar with coal and iron, Nanteos and Wynnstay with lead mines, the Chirk Castle archives with the early iron and coal industries of north east Wales, whilst the early industry of the Swansea area is reflected in the Badminton archives and the beginnings of its copper industry in the Vivian archives.

Estate accounts provide a wealth of information on the income of domestic and farm labourers. Servants, whether domestic or labourers were the most transient of the community, moving from household to household and from parish to parish, as is amply borne out by evidence in the estate accounts of the high turnover of staff.

Under estate management are found surveys which contain descriptions of land and buildings, names of tenants, fields and the rents payable and valuations, with details of land use and state of cultivation and content of buildings. In an age lacking precise statistics, the chief economic indicator of a rural society's fortune within estate archives are the rentals which give the names of tenants, their holdings, acreage and rents paid; they reflect periods of agricultural depression and boom. A study of the rentals of the Gogerddan estate, co. Cards., in 1756 and 1757, where little is noted in the column `cash received' but where there are numerous entries in the arrears column, reveals that farmers were struggling in those years owing to disastrous harvests. However, the rental for the same estate in 1810, in the middle of the Napoleonic War, when demand for livestock and corn was exceptionally high, shows that cash received is equivalent to the rent demanded, apart from one entry of arrears of £3.

Estate ledgers include accounts and wages books containing details of indoor and outdoor labour, wages paid and the prices of goods and provisions. Household management records of the housekeeper or butler, including ledgers, bills and vouchers, accounts of servants' wages, provisions and domestic utensils and cellar books, are valuable sources of information for family life; education of children; changing trends in food; furniture, clothing and household goods; employment of servants; and prices, wages and costs of goods and provisions. In addition, family papers often contain pedigrees and genealogical notes.

In 1870 a list was published of estates which were either over 3000 acres in extent or carried an annual rental of over £3000 per annum. The Library holds records of 54 such estates totalling roughly about three-quarters of a million acres. If we add to this the archives of about 600 smaller estates then the figure must be nearly a million acres. Such a vast class of records is bound to contain information of immense value to the local historian.

Outstanding among the National Library of Wales' archives of landed families are those of Badminton, which contain records of the Welsh estates of the dukes of Beaufort, earlier of the earls of Worcester and William Herbert, first earl of Pembroke. These include records for the Breconshire lordships of Crickhowell, from 1382, and Tretower, from 1532, ministers' accounts for Monmouthshire lordships from 1387 and records of the Seignory of Gower and Kilvey from 1366 and for the borough and manor of Swansea, 1657-1835, deeds for the 13th cent. and industrial records for the 16th cent. Brogyntyn contains estate records and family correspondence, 14th-20th cent., of the families of Owen of Brogyntyn, Wynne of Clenennau, Glyn and Ystumcegid, Maurice of Clenennau, Vaughan of Corsygedol, Longueville, Godolphin and Owen of Glasynys and Ormsby-Gore, barons Harlech, and others, whose estates lay mainly in cos Caernarfon, Flint, Merioneth, Montgomery and Salop. Chirk Castle was, from 1595, the estate of the Myddelton family, and the collection holds estate and family records relating mainly to co. Denbigh, while the Wynnstay Archive includes many legal manuscripts of 16th and 17th century, election papers, and manorial records.

A related category of archives is that which derives from

solicitors' offices. Solicitors were often the election agents for the landed gentry, and records from the offices of Longueville & Co. of Oswestry, solicitors for many prominent north Wales families, Eaton Evans & Williams of Haverfordwest, and D. T. M. Jones of Carmarthen are notable examples.

Although the Land tax was introduced in 1692, few records have survived before 1780 when copies of the assessments began to be filed by the Clerk of the Peace. Land tax assessments contain the names of the owner and the occupier of the property, a description of the property (not always given and then often vague, e.g. 'house and land'), and details of the sum assessed. As well as the records of central government taxation, parochial rate assessment (church rate, poor rate, highway rate, etc.) also give details of occupiers of a property. You will be lucky, however, in Wales, to find a complete series of rate assessment books for a particular parish, even during the second half of the 19th c. It is much easier to trace the history of a property if it formed part of a large estate.

A study of Quarter Sessions records can also prove rewarding. Most of these records have long since been transferred from the National Library of Wales to local County Record Offices. What remains at the Library is a quantity of stray records, often embedded in the archives of landed families (for example, the early Denbighshire Quarter Sessions records among the Chirk Castle archives) and a number of small deposits, including some of the few surviving Cardiganshire records. Amongst these are lists of freeholders to serve on juries.

The twentieth century has seen the demise or fragmentation of many landed estates in Wales, and the Library's Department of Pictures and Maps holds numerous sale catalogues which give details of the properties - farms, cottages, implements, etc.,- which were on sale. Thus, the documents relating to the life of an estate, from its birth, through its periods of growth occasioned by the accession of other properties or from mineral and industrial wealth, to its decline and final demise, can provide an invaluable source of information to the local and family historian who is prepared to delve into its records.

GLAMORGAN
FAMILY HISTORY SOCIETY
(Registered Charity no 1059537)

Glamorgan FHS celebrated its 25th anniversary in 1999. Initially, the Society was known as the Heraldic & Genealogical Society of Wales, but later changed its name to the South Wales Family History Society. When Dyfed and Gwent formed separate county groups, the Society assumed the title by which it is known today.

The first meetings were held in Cardiff, but following the formation of branches in Bridgend and Swansea in 1983, the original nucleus at Cardiff became the Cardiff Branch. Since then, three more branches have been formed at Merthyr Tydfil, Aberdare and Pontypridd to accommodate the growing numbers of enthusiasts involved in the compulsive task of tracing their ancestors. The six branches form a corporate group rather than totally unrelated entities. They are linked by the Executive Committee and work together in various ways including the Society's annual Open Day, and the many projects.

Glamorgan FHS encourages research into genealogy and allied subjects, especially those relating to the old county of Glamorgan. Many members are actively involved with work on local records, particularly those in danger of being lost through damage, decay or modern development. Even members with little time to spare take part in these various projects. The many skills shared by the helpers cover the transcription of Parish Register entries and Memorial Inscriptions in church and chapel yards, gathering information offered by local libraries and record offices, entering these on computer, and then checking the results prior to final indexing and publication. Projects completed so far include the Glamorgan Marriage Index, an alphabetical list of over 60,000 names of Brides & Grooms married in the county before 1837; Census Returns for 1841 and 1851 for the whole county fully transcribed and indexed; MIMI - Master Index of Monumental Inscriptions - containing 90,000 names. Also available are indexed registers for over 100 Parishes and the MIs for 230 graveyards.

All six Branches of the Glamorgan FHS hold monthly meetings, where members share experiences, sort out problems, exchange information and enjoy the guest speakers whose topics cover Family History research and records, and the many complementary sources of interest such as Local History, Customs, Notable Inhabitants etc. Beginners' Nights are always included in each year's Programme. A Society Journal, published quarterly, is distributed free to all members. There is a Search Service available, and each Branch has a bookstall and library

Our annual Open Day is held in July. Each Branch in turn, organises this at a venue in their section of the county. Help and advice on Family History is available, with each Branch offering their expertise on their own particular area. Fiches, booklets, local history books are on sale and many other groups and societies, both local ones and those outside the county, are present. All facets of the now widespread help and information facilities we offer are there -you name it, we've got it - on paper, in booklet form, on fiches, on computer, via the Internet. Glamorgan FHS is a member of the Federation of Family History Societies, joins with other Welsh societies for twice-yearly meetings of the Welsh Association of Family History Societies, and is part of the SW Group (covering South Wales and West of England societies) which holds a biennial Family History Fair at Weston super Mare - next one scheduled for summer 2001. The London Group, composed of members from Glamorgan. Dyfed, Powys and Gwynedd, holds quarterly meetings at the SoG, and anyone visiting London is welcome to attend.

Tracing ancestors has a certain excitement and fascination. Genealogy in its simplest form constructs the Family Tree which contains the names and the dates; Family History adds the detail. These discoveries - noting where the families lived, their occupations and activities, what they ate and what they wore - can bring the past vividly to life, and we gain a greater insight into the day-to-day existence of our forebears. It is rather like detective work, unravelling clues, casting aside red herrings, and the most unlikely family will have a skeleton in one of its cupboards ! The main problem always is - how to make a start. This is where all Family History Societies come to the aid of those just starting out on their Ancestral Hunt, by offering beginners guidance and expert advice.

Glamorgan FHS is a friendly and active group and is always pleased to welcome new members. Annual subscription rates, due January 1st, are : Ordinary UK: £7.50 Family/Institution:£10.00 Pensioner/student UK: £6.00 Overseas: £10.00 Europe & BFPO pay UK rates For Membership and general enquiries please contact: Mrs S.Mackay, 11 Cherrydown Close, Thornhill, Cardiff, CFI4 9DJ e-mail: sue. mackay@virgin. net Web-site at http:/hometown.aol.com/gfhsoc
Now that we have celebrated our first quarter century, we look forward eagerly to the Society's next 25 years.

Cymdeithas Hanes Teuluoedd DYFED Family History Society

Incorporating the Counties of Carmarthenshire, Cardiganshire and Pembrokeshire

Member of the Federation of Family History Societies
and the Association of Family History Societies of Wales

Registered Charity No. 513347

Llwydd/President: The Right Revd. D. Huw Jones
Bishop of St Davids

The Society was formed in 1982 to help those who are researching their families in these counties. The land that was Dyfed in the time of the Welsh Princes.

Over 1000 members are at present researching families who lived in the three counties and those who migrated to other parts of Wales and beyond. Members queries and success stories appear in the journal which is sent to members three times each year.

Branches meet in Cardigan, Carmarthen, Haverfordwest, Llanelli and Llandovery
- and with other Welsh societies we support a branch that meets in London.

For a list of publications on microfiche, write, enclosing a stamped addressed envelope, to:-
Mr P. W. Gibby, 40 Bunkers Hill, Milford Haven, Pembrokeshire, SA73 1AG
or visit our Internet Website at:-
www.westwales.co.uk/dfhs/dfhs.htm

A membership application form can be printed from this website and sent to:_
Mr John James, 38 Brynmelyn Avenue, Llanelli, Carms, SA15 3RT

Membership forms are available also from:-
Mr John Jarman, 32 New Zealand Street, Llanelli, Carms SA15 3EN

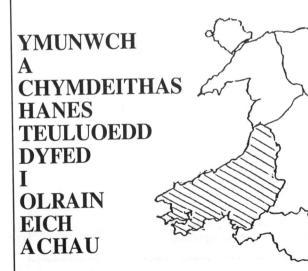

**YMUNWCH
A
CHYMDEITHAS
HANES
TEULUOEDD
DYFED
I
OLRAIN
EICH
ACHAU**

**JOIN
DYFED
FAMILY
HISTORY
SOCIETY
-
AND
TRACE
YOUR
ROOTS**

The Scottish Genealogy Society

Library & Family History Centre

Researching your ancestors in Scotland?

Make THE SCOTTISH GENEALOGY SOCIETY your first port of call. Situated in the heart of Edinburgh's Old Town, its Library and Family History Centre is a treasure trove of books, manuscripts, CDs, microfilm and microfiche to help you unlock the mysteries of your ancestors.

The Library has a large collection of graveyard inscriptions, family histories, maps, and many books on family and social history for sale. It's also within walking distance of New Register House, The National Archives of Scotland and The National and Central Lending Libraries.

The Library and Family History Centre is open during the following times:

TUESDAY	10.30AM - 5.30PM
WEDNESDAY	10.30AM - 8.30PM
THURSDAY	10.30AM - 5.30PM
SATURDAY	10.00AM - 5.00PM

THE SCOTTISH GENEALOGY SOCIETY

15 Victoria Terrace, Edinburgh, EH1 2JL.
Tel & Fax: 0131 220 3677. E-mail: scotgensoc@sol.co.uk
Internet Web Page: http://www.sol.co.uk/s/scotgensoc/

The NATIONAL ARCHIVES of SCOTLAND

David J Brown Head of Reader Services

Formerly known as the Scottish Record Office, the National Archives of Scotland (NAS) hold one of the most varied collections of records in Britain. Occupying some 57 kilometres of shelving, the records date from the 12th century to the present day. They include the formal records of pre- and post-Union government, the law courts, the public registers of deeds and sasines (land transfers), the records of the Church of Scotland as well as those of some other denominations, estate papers of landed families, a large collection of maps and plans, the Scottish railway archives, and the records of a variety of businesses, charitable institutions and public bodies.

Two books, both by Cecil Sinclair, give much fuller information about these and other records. They are: *Tracing Your Scottish Ancestors. A Guide to Ancestry Research in the Scottish Record Office* (Stationery Office, 1997, price £9.99) and *Tracing Scottish Local History* (Stationery Office, 1994, £7.95). Both enable family historians to assess likely sources of information before they visit us, so as to make the best use of their time in our search rooms.

Before visiting the National Archives, it is advisable to start investigating Scottish ancestry in the records held by the General Register Office for Scotland. Hopefully these should provide a skeleton tree, to be fleshed out from the records held by us. As most readers of this *Directory* will know, the GRO(S) is located at New Register House, Edinburgh EH1 3YT. This is next door to our main building, HM General Register House. Both are at the east end of Princes Street. The GRO(S) holds old parish registers of the Church of Scotland (up to 1854), statutory registers of births, marriages and deaths (from 1855) and census returns (from 1841- open up to 1891).

For family historians, the most popular NAS records are the registers of wills and testaments, dating from the 16th century to the 1970s. To search for a testament you need to have an idea of the date of death and - for wills recorded before 1876 - a place of residence. There are good indexes for the years to 1823, organised by locality. From 1876 to 1959 there is a detailed annual index covering all Scotland. Indexes for other periods are less satisfactory. NAS has just embarked as a partner in a major project, the Scottish Archive Network. Financed principally by the Heritage Lottery Fund, partly by NAS itself and partly by the Genealogical Society of Utah, one object of the Network is to generate digital images of all the testaments for the years before 1876 and produce a union index for them. Each image will be linked electronically to its index entry, enabling readers to gain almost instant access to any testament. The index will also be freely available on the Internet. The imaging process will take some time, and the original testaments will be progressively withdrawn from public access over the years 1999-2001. They will be replaced by substitutes, either microfilms or digitally generated photocopies. Consequently readers intending to visit are advised to contact us to confirm whether particular records are available.

Perhaps the second most popular class of records is the **Register of Sasines**, beginning in 1617 and recording the transfer of lands and houses, together with transactions in which land was used to secure loans. Sasines contain

information or clues about the individuals and families involved in these transactions, although they do not mention tenants. There are good indexes for the years after 1781, but before that the indexes are less straightforward and searching may have to be done using minute books. The Royal burghs kept a separate series of their own for urban property transactions.

The **Retours** (or **Services of Heirs**) deal with the inheritance of land. Although they deal only with landowners, a small proportion of the population, they can be a valuable resource. They run from 1530 until modern times, although they are of declining importance after 1868. When a vassal of the Crown died, his heir had to prove his right to inherit his ancestor's lands by obtaining an inquest by jury which delivered a return ('retour') to Chancery. The procedure could similarly be used by people who were not Crown vassals in order to provide evidence of their right to inherit land. Until 1847 the record was kept in Latin and the published indexes for the years before 1700 (the *Inquisitionum ad Capellam Regis Retornatarum Abbreviatio*) are also in Latin. Retours are very stylised documents, however, and a researcher will need only a minimum of instruction to understand their contents. The indexes from 1700 are in English.

The **church records** held by NAS are often consulted by family historians who have been unsuccessful in tracing an ancestor in the Old Parish Registers held by the GRO(S). These records, although catalogued, are not indexed. In consequence the most profitable searches tend to be those where a family has an association with a particular denomination and parish. The largest bodies of these records are those for the kirk sessions of the Church of Scotland (minute books, communion rolls, etc) and those for the other presbyterian churches which broke away from the Church of Scotland in the years after 1733, and which subsequently reunited with it. The collection is large, but not complete. Another group of church records meriting special mention is that of the Roman Catholic Church. These consist of bound sets of photocopies of Scottish Parish registers, particularly of baptisms and marriages. The earliest of these dates from the 18th century, but in most parishes they do not start until the 19th century.

The NAS operates two search rooms in Edinburgh. One, the Historical Search Room at General Register House, Princes Street, EH1 3YY, is used mainly by family historians. The other, at West Register House, Charlotte Square, may hold relevant material and is the principal store both for judicial records and for our plans collection. Please telephone well before any visit to check which search room is most appropriate for your work and to ask about any arrangements for consulting out-housed records. You should also make sure that your visit does not coincide with public holidays. The NAS has its annual stocktaking in November and the Historical Search Room is closed for the first two full weeks in that month, the West Search Room for the third.

Enquiries:
Telephone 0131 535 1334 E-mail: research@nas.gov.uk

The NATIONAL
ARCHIVES
of SCOTLAND

REFURBISHMENT OF HM GENERAL REGISTER HOUSE

Preparations are underway for the next stage of the refurbishment of HM General Register House. This will comprise: the replacement of the present antiquated electrical system, including a major enhancement of the supply to the Historical Search Room; the replacement of the heating system made necessary by, among other things, the severance of the link with the former New St Andrew's House; and the installation of air-conditioning to selected parts of the building.

Because the heating system is involved, it will be necessary to carry on works outside the heating period, i.e. during the summer months of next year, and it will be impossible to avoid disruption to reader services during that time. It is intended that the following arrangements will be made:

- For the two weeks from Monday 1 May to Friday 12 May 2000 inclusive, the Historical Search Room and all its attendant facilities will be closed to the public. This will be offset by the abandonment of the normal stocktaking period during the first two weeks of November.
- For the four weeks after that, i.e. from Monday 15 May to Friday 9 June 2000 inclusive, the Historical Search Room will remain closed, but it is hoped that a limited service to readers will be provided in what is currently the Electronic Search Room in the Robertson Wing.
- Throughout the summer, certain classes of records, yet to be determined, may for a time be unavailable to readers.
- For a period yet to be determined, reprographic facilities may have to be restricted.
- The Legal Search Room is not directly affected by these provisions, but the movement of material for copying between the Search Room and the Reprographic Section may from time to time be disrupted, with consequent delays.

We apologise to readers for the inconvenience these arrangements may cause, but hope that they will have patience with us as we seek to bring the fabric of this historic building up to the standard it deserves. Further information can be obtained by contacting Historical Search Room staff on 0131-535-1334 or by e-mailing: research@nas.gov.uk

Patrick Cadell
Keeper of the Records of Scotland

GENERAL REGISTER OFFICE FOR SCOTLAND
New Register House, Edinburgh EH1 3YT, Scotland, UK
Tel: 0131 334 0380 Fax: 0131 314 4400
Email: nrh.gros@gtnet.gov.uk

New Register House

New Register House is at the east end of Edinburgh's Princes Street, directly opposite the Balmoral Hotel, a few minutes' walk from the main Waverley railway station, the bus station and the airport bus stop. There is no space for car parking or for baggage storage. If informed in advance we can make arrangements for customers with disabilities.

Opening hours 09:00 to 16:30 Mondays to Fridays (except some Scottish public holidays)
We have 100 places available for self-service searching. Booking is free but there is a statutory fee for access.
For further information please phone 0131 314 4433.

If you would like us to search in our records for a specific event and sell you an extract (an officially certified copy of an entry) please post or fax details to the above address. A 24-hour priority service is available.

To find out more about our records and services see our Web-site at
http://www.open.gov.uk/gros/groshome.htm

GENERAL REGISTER OFFICE
FOR SCOTLAND

Registration of births, deaths and marriages in Scotland

Registration of baptisms and proclamations of marriage was first enacted in Scotland by a Council of the Scottish clergy in 1551. The earliest recorded event - a baptism of 27 December 1553 - can be found in the register of baptisms and banns for Errol in Perthshire. Following the Reformation registration of births, deaths and marriages became the responsibility of the ministers and session clerks of the Church of Scotland. Standards of record-keeping varied greatly from parish to parish, however, and even from year to year. This together with evidence of the deterioration and loss of register volumes through neglect led to calls for the introduction of a compulsory and comprehensive civil registration system for Scotland. This came into being on 1 January 1855 with the establishment of the General Register Office for Scotland headed by the Registrar General and the setting up of 1027 registration districts. In 1999 registration districts number 340.

Records in the custody of the Registrar General
The main series of vital events records of interest to genealogists are held by the Registrar General at New Register House in Edinburgh. They are as follows:

Old Parish Registers (1553-1854): the 3500
surviving register volumes ("OPRs") compiled by the Church of Scotland session clerks were transferred to the custody of the Registrar General after 1855. They record the births and baptisms; proclamations of banns and marriages; and deaths and burials for 900 Scottish parishes. They are far from complete, however, and most entries contain relatively little information. Microfilm copies of these records are available world-wide and there are computerised and microfiche indexes to baptisms and marriages. A project to index the death and burial entries got under way in 1997 and is still ongoing.

Register of Neglected Entries (1801-1854): this
register was compiled by the Registrar General and consists of births, deaths and marriages proved to have occurred in Scotland between 1801 and 1854 but which had not been recorded in the OPRs. These entries are found at the end of the appropriate parish register entries and are included in the all-Scotland computerised indexes.

Statutory registers of births, deaths and
marriages (from 1855): these registers are compiled by district registrars. They are despatched by the district examiners to New Register House at the end of each calendar year ready for the creation of all-Scotland computerised indexes. Microfiche copies of the register pages are available in the New Register House search rooms.

Adopted children register (from 1930): persons
adopted under orders made by the Scottish courts. The earliest entry is for a birth in October 1909.

Register of divorces (from 1984): records the names
of the parties, the date and place of marriage, the date and place of divorce and details of any order made by the court regarding financial provision or custody of children. Prior to May 1984 a divorce would be recorded in the RCE (formerly the Register of Corrected Entries now The Register of Corrections,Etc.) and a cross-reference would be added to the marriage entry.

Births, deaths and marriages occurring outside Scotland (The Minor Records): these relate to persons who are or were usually resident in Scotland.
Marine Register of Births and Deaths (from 1855)
Air Register (from 1848)
Service Records (from 1881)
War Registers (from 1899) for the Boer War (1899-1902) and the two World Wars
Consular returns (from 1914)
High Commissioners' returns (from 1964)
Foreign Marriages (from 1947)
Register of births, deaths and marriages in foreign countries (1860-1965)

Census records (from 1841): the enumerators' transcript books of the decennial census of the population of Scotland. They record the name, age, marital state, occupation and birthplace of every member of a household present on census night. Census records are closed for 100 years and only the schedules for the 1841 to 1891 Censuses are open to the public. The 1901 Census records should be open to the public in January 2002.

Searching at New Register House
New Register House was opened in 1861 as a purpose-built repository for Scotland's civil registration records. Today it provides 100 search places and is open to the public from 09:00 to 16:30, Monday to Friday. Access to the indexes requires payment of a statutory fee but this also allows self-service access to microform copies of all the open records. The fee can be for a day, a week, four weeks, a quarter or a year. There are discount arrangements and a limited number of seats can be booked in advance. There is also provision for group evening visits.

Indexes to the statutory records (including overseas events), OPR baptism and marriage entries, the 1881 and 1891 Censuses are available on computer. There is self-service access to the statutory register pages on microfiche and the OPR and Census records on roll microfilm. It is also possible to order official extracts of any entry.

Online Access to the New Register House Indexes
The all-Scotland computerised indexes can also be accessed from local registration offices which have links to the New Register House system. Some local registration offices have taken this one step further: they provide search room facilities with access to microfiche copies of the statutory registers for their area. It is therefore possible to search the indexes from Shetland to Dumfries. From April 1997 the joint Office for National Statistics and Public Record Office Family Records Centre in London has provided online access too - the "Scottish link"; and from April 1998 the indexes to the records over 100 years old have been available for searching on the Internet, at a statutory fee.
To find out more see the GRO(S) website at
http://www.open.gov.uk/gros/groshome.htm.

THE SCOTS ORIGINS INTERNET SERVICE
General Register Office for Scotland

Scots Origins is the GRO(S)'s fully searchable database of historical indexes on the World Wide Web and has been running since 6 April 1998. It is maintained on behalf of the department by OMS Services Ltd and provides access to the indexes to birth and marriage records over 100 years old and death records over 75 years old. To avoid raising concerns about browsing among records relating to living persons, indexes to entries 100 years old or less for births and marriages and 75 years old or less for deaths are not available on the Internet.

The Indexes
Origins provides access to indexes of Scottish birth and marriage records from 1553 to 1898 and death records from 1855 to 1923. There is no all-Scotland index to the pre-1855 death and burial entries. All-Scotland indexes to the 1881 and 1891 census returns are also available permitting access to some 25 million index entries. An additional year of historical index data will be added to the database at the beginning of each year, so 1899 birth and marriage and 1924 death data will become available in 2000.

Searching
New users can look at a demonstration version and refer to a detailed online guide to searching the indexes before they actually log on. They are then invited to register with the database and give name, postal address and credit-card details over a secure link to the Origins server. The complex security software has the approval of one of Britain's largest retail banks, the National Westminster, and authorisation is in real-time taking approximately 10 seconds. Card details are not stored and are transferred via an encrypted channel. Following authorisation by the bank that issued the card the server debits the card account with the £6 fee and gives the user a credit worth 30 pages to be viewed within a 24 hour period (allowing a customer to log off and on the Internet as required via a designated user code and password).

Those familiar with the New Register House system will find that *Origins* is slightly different in several respects. Searches can be made across the database, that is, for OPR, statutory and census indexes; for a given year plus or minus up to five years; for all or just one type of event; on more than one name; and narrowed down to a particular district name. Tables of registration district and parish names are available online with links to Scottish and British maps. A Soundex option can be used to search for similar-sounding names an important point as the spelling of names can vary considerably (Mac changing to Mc and so on) particularly in the OPRs .

The search form is easy to use being similar to those of web search-engines with check-boxes and blank data-entry fields. Search terms can be in upper or lower case and can include the standard wild-card characters '*' and '?'. The results of a search are initially displayed as an on screen summary of the number of 'hits' found on the database and the number of pages (comprising a minimum of one and a maximum of 15 entries) it would take to display them all. It is then possible either to download the pages to refine the search.

Once downloaded a page can be stored as a file on the user's computer (for viewing off-line or printing at a later date) or it can be consulted again gratis on the *Origins* database as often as required during the same session. The hits are displayed in a colour -coded table - there is an explanatory key at the bottom of the screen - with columns for event, sex, age, date (in the statutory index this is the year but in the OPR index the date in full), surname, first name, parents' or spouse's name (depending on event type) and the district or parish. A miscellaneous column gives the parents or spouse and OPR microfilm frame number where appropriate. Microfilm copies of the OPR and open census records can be consulted at libraries and Mormon family history centres world-wide.

Ordering Extracts
Alongside each index entry is a button which can be selected to order the full register extract direct from the database. There is a charge of £10 per document which includes postage. Online helptext provides full details of what is contained in the different types of register extract backed up by images of sample pages from the statutory, OPR and census records. Orders are processed by staff at GRO(S) in Edinburgh who send out the paper documents by ordinary post, aiming at a response within 15 working days.

Future developments
Looking further ahead it is likely that developments in scanning and Internet technology will allow access not just to indexes text, but to images of the actual records themselves - a huge task for the department but a logical extension to the policy of providing wider access to the historical records in its care.

SCOTS ORIGINS can be accessed at
http://www.origins.net.

The GRO(S) product for genealogists
In Scotland, the statutory responsibility for registration of births, deaths and marriages, and the provision of public access to the permanent registers thus created, lies with the Registrar General for Scotland.

Originally the registers, and the alphabetical indexes to them, were all on paper. This format meant they could be consulted by only a handful of customers at a time. In the early 1990s all the records were finally liberated from this physical constraint. The 50 million statutory index entries were keyed as text - a huge but one-off task. They are now held entirely in electronic form and may readily be searched by computer. The statutory register pages, the old parish register pages and the open census records were filmed, and are now all held in microform (either jacketed microfiche or roll microfilm).

Searching in New Register House, and from other locations
The modern formats in which the records are now held allow us to make them available at the 100 search places we provide in our 1861 listed building, New Register House, located at the east end of Princes Street in Edinburgh. This number of search places has been sufficient in recent years to meet demand on all but a few peak days in summer, but searchers should book in advance if possible. All of our 100 search places have access to our computer indexes on easy-to-use search terminals. Customers do their own searching, but our staff are always on hand to assist first-time users.

Because our index material is therefore in very active daily use, we and our search-room customers, many of them professional genealogists, frequently bring to light simple errors or mis-interpretations of the records of the past. Because we have the original paper documents located in the same building, we are often in a position to correct the computerised indexes, which are therefore being continually improved and made more reliable.

With on-line access to computerised indexes, and the possibility of replicating microform sets of pages, unlimited expansion of our searching service is possible without providing more search places in New Register House. Searching the full set of indexes from 1553 to 1998 can now be undertaken remotely, by visiting one of a number of local authority registration-service sites in Scotland (Glasgow, Aberdeen, Dundee, Inverness, Shetland) and at the Family Records Centre in London. The historical indexes 1553-1898 can be accessed from anywhere in the world by visiting http://www.origins.net, the *Scots Origins* website, where on a pay-per-view basis customers can view a sub-set of the indexes held in New Register House. This pioneering application of electronic commerce was a world first in the genealogy field.

Our website and others

Scots Origins is the official GRO(S) searching site and permits users to access index entries to the historical records held in New Register House in Edinburgh. The site at present contains over 25 million index entries (a) to the registers of births/baptisms, deaths/burials and marriages for the years 1553 to 1898, and (b) to the census of Scotland for the year 1891.

The indexes on the Internet are currently restricted to entries over 100 years old since these are the ones most valued by genealogists. The 100 year limit avoids raising concerns about casual browsing among the records of living persons, even though these are in fact in the public domain. By 2000 we plan to reduce the restriction on death registers to 75 years, enabling Internet users to access Scottish death information up to the year 1923. We welcome the development of other websites containing genealogical information with a Scottish content. These sites all help to increase interest in Scottish historical records, already a rapidly expanding field. As a Government department entrusted with the permanent conservation and care of many of these irreplaceable original records we are committed to the wider dissemination of the information they contain.

We are concerned to ensure that only accurate information is provided about the 'vital events' that our predecessors recorded for permanent preservation. We have therefore reservations about certain material on the Internet, for we are aware that some sites purporting to offer details of Scottish records in fact derived their information by interpreting elderly microfilms made in the 1950s and 1960s from our original paper documents. While much of the information will obviously be the same as we hold, inevitably there will be discrepancies. Our own process of continual amendment and updating (highlighted above) makes us confident that the accuracy of the information we hold on computer is greater than on other sites, whose source material may on occasion be open to question.

We strongly recommend that people who are serious about tracing their Scottish ancestry should ensure that they go straight to the most accurate information, or that they should verify any information they might have obtained elsewhere. On the Internet this can be done only through the official *Scots Origins* site.

Local searching still has advantages

The on-site product in New Register House is different from the on-line product. A customer searching in the indexes from a seat in New Register House buys a package which includes immediate self-service access, without further payment, to the complete range of microform records. Searchers can take their own notes, and need not buy official paper extracts to get at all the data held. A customer searching on-line from say Glasgow, will be able in that office to inspect a wide, but not complete, range of microform records for the west of Scotland. A customer searching on-line from London or California has no access at present to images of the records, and will need to order a full official extract of any register entry they want to see, after which GRO(S) will post out the paper extract certificate.

Genealogy and Tourism

One of the characteristics of genealogy as an interest is that it is an open-ended quest - and therein lies its fascination for many people. The customer in California searching for the answer to a specific question about their ancestry *may* find it by searching on-line and never leave San Diego. However, they are much more likely in the course of doing so to turn up several interesting possibilities they hadn't been aware of before, not all of which can be properly explored just by sitting at home and mail-ordering certificates. If this interest is maintained, the idea of a trip to Scotland may germinate. A visit to the towns, villages or crofting lands identified in family research adds colour and vibrancy to the work of the genealogist. We have never been of the view that the extension of searching among Scotland's genealogical records by Internet will have anything other than a net positive effect on Scotland's visitor totals!

Another characteristic of genealogy relevant to tourism is that customers do not get the opportunity to choose the geographical areas their ancestors lived in. Each area will have something to offer to some potential visitor. If an ancestor of yours lived all their life in Dalbeattie, you're not going to find traces of them in Dundee - or Shetland. Areas are not in direct competition for genealogical visitors, as they might be for other visitors looking for scenery or climate. Genealogical interests can therefore afford to be co-operative, and we are looking at ways of improving co-operation with central and local government bodies and tourist interests.

The Next Century

We envisage further developments for Scotland's five centuries of genealogical records. In summer 1999 we began a pilot project to scan as digital images all the returns of the 1891 census of Scotland and to link them to the indexes for these records, already keyed as electronic text. The next step is likely to be full digital imaging of *all* the records at present held in microform, a not inconsiderable task, but one which would enable immediate electronic service delivery and reduce the need for posting paper certificates to customers.

Articles and information supplied by
The General Register Office for Scotland

The Family History Scene in Aberdeen - and Beyond
Jean Shirer

A word association game. Scotland? - tartan, whisky, castles, oil, Burns, the Bruce, Wallace, haggis, Bonnie Prince Charlie and (depending on holiday locations) midges. NE Scotland? well, castles, whisky,oil, Balmoral on Royal Deeside, family names of Cordon, Fraser, Forbes and Buchan, fishing, farming, no mIdges. Aberdeen? - er, oil ... and to the properly discerning few The Family History Shop - for information on farming, fishing, castles, tartan and names, names, names (no midges) and much else as background to the interest that absorbs us all.

The Family History Shop is owned and managed by the Aberdeen and NE Scotland Family History Society which was formally constituted in June 1978. At that time, it was only the second society outside Edinburgh in existence - the other being Glasgow and West of Scotland. Previously, the Scottish Genealogy Society (SGS) established in the early 1950s and based in Edinburgh had been the only focus for family history/genealogy in Scotland. And now? Well, there are nearly twenty societies from Shetland to Dumfries and Galloway, all members of the Scottish Association of Family History Societies (SAFHS) and all supporting, encouraging and developing in whatever ways possible an interest in family history in their local areas.

The Aberdeen Society is one of the few to own premises. Our first Shop was opened in 1987 and very quickly proved inadequate for the visitors and backroom workers. We welcomed the chance in 1992 to move a few doors down the same street and now own what were adjacent shops, one serves as our sales outlet and Research Centre and the other is used for office/storage. The premises are joined at basement level for the Reference Library and additional research facilities. The Centre is staffed 51/2 days and 2 evenings per week by a rota of volunteers. It is thanks to all volunteers front of Shop and back that we have twice now received a "Highly Commended" certificate from the Aberdeen and Grampian Tourist Board in the annual "Come to Aberdeen" scheme of awards.

The facilities at the Research Centre are available free to members ; non-members are charged £3.00 per hour after some basic (free) advice. All income is ploughed back into the Society for purchase of equipment, book, fiche, film, CD—ROM - anything relevant to NE Scotland local history, family history and research aids; IGI, OPRs, census for the North East, St Catherine's Indexes to births, Marriages and Deaths and much more. A computer gives researchers access to the collection of CD-ROMs built up over the last

few years. The-range of material held in the Library and for research is described in our Information Booklet sent to all applying for membership. On joining the Society individuals are asked to complete a Record of Ancestors chart which is then indexed. An annual alphabetical printout of interests is produced for consultation in the Centre; each entry states name being researched, location and membership number and the appropriate chart may then be consulted (all are kept in numerical order) to establish relevance to individual research. This arrangement replaces the more usual printed Directory of Members' Interests. A limited amount of research (for members only) is undertaken by the Research Team for reimbursement of expenses - the assistance provided depends on the availability of local volunteers at the time; and we emphasise that we do not compile complete family trees.

Members received a quarterly Journal, an annual List of Members, a Publications for Sale List and may sumbit 4 research queries per year to the Journal free of charge; non-members are charged for each query (£1.00). Regular meetings are held in Aberdeen from September to June; branches in Glasgow and Elgin arrange their own syllabus.

Each Scottish Society has a publishing programme and the main interest is in Monumental Inscriptions and Census Indexes. Our own publications certainly feature MTs (nearly 50 booklets) and census (1851 for Banffshire); but in the North East we are particularly fortunate to have still available the results of the Poll Tax of 1695. This was a Scottish tax, supposedly levied on every person over the age of sixteen not a beggar. Our facsimile reprints and indexes are based on the transcription and publication, in two volumes, by the Gentlemen of the County in 1844. Once we have completed publication of the indexes (about the year 2005!) we may well move on to census material — there is growing collection of indexes for 1841—1871 in the Society Library. One indexing project recently completed is Deaths recorded at Aberdeen Royal Infirmary 1743—1897 (in 4 volumes); one aspect of current work is based on the Poor Relief Registers 1845-1930 of the NE as kept by the parochial boards/parish councils.

To encourage members to put pen to paper (how often is it said "I just need a bit more information THEN I'll write up my family history"?) we introduced our Bruce Henderson Award in memory of a much esteemed chairman who died in 1988. Entries must have particular relevance to the North

East; the winner of this annual award has his/her entry published and is presented with a number copies and engraved momento of the occasion. To date we have had as winning entries family histories, parish, farm and village histories, church records transcribed and family letters annotated — not great "best sellers" but a gentle encouragement to produce something of worth and share research. When the family historian dies where do all the notes, charts and trees end up? At least with this award research of local interest is preserved in the relevant area and , with legal deposit copies, in the national libraries. All our titles are, of course, for sale in the Shop together with those from all the other Scottish Societies and SAFHS, and some from FFHS, GOONS and the Society of Genealogists.

If you are starting research into Scottish ancestry, however, a word of warning concerning your reading material. Beware the title of a book where the area is not mentioned - look for "Scots" or "Scottish" otherwise you will learn a great deal about research in England and Wales which might just be useful sometime (the way folks moved around!) but not if you are a beginner. And there are differences in researching north and south of that border! The important one is that civil registration in Scotland started on 1st January 1855 — not 1837 as for England and Wales — and, dare I say it, the certificates contain more information. The main source of information pre-1855 is the Old Parish Registers: the records of the Church of Scotland. i.e. the established Presbyterian post-Reformation (1560) Church. There was much upheaval in the Church of Scotland during the 18th and 19th centuries - your ancestor may have been a member of one of the breakaway churches, be an Episcopalian, a Roman Catholic or a Quaker. Use the index to the OPRs and the IGI with care and GOLDEN RULE NUMBER 1: always check the original material. The following books are useful for details of the various religious demoninations in a parish and when

their churches were established: The First (or Old) Statistical Account of Scotland (1790s), The Second (or New) Statistical Account (1840s) and the Ordnance Gazetteer of Scotland (1880s/1890s).

Also, we don't have County Record Offices in Scotland. We rely on the National Archives of Scotland (NAS) in Edinburgh and local government Archive Offices, Libraries, Institutions and Family History Societies. In fact the address of some Scottish Societies (East Ayrshire, Lothians, Troon & District, Highland and Lanarkshire) is "c/o" the local library or school where research facilities may have been made available. There's a lot of co-operation and goodwill around up here! Leaflets are usually available from Libraries and Archives about their resources for Family History and useful guides to local sources of information for FH have been produced by the Societies for Fife, Dumfries & Galloway, Aberdeen & NE, Shetland (for pre-1855 parish sources), Troon & District (for Ayrshire) and Glasgow & West Scotland (for Strathclyde).

Under the direction of SAFHS, Scottish Societies are currently working on the National Burial Project to record the death/burial entries in the OPRs (the index prepared by the Mormon Church records births, baptisms, proclamations and marriages). Many of the individuals involved with this cut their teeth on national projects with transcribing the 1881 census. Does any other interest have such an input of unpaid labour?!

Such national and local activity go a long way to answering those standard questions: How do I start? What is available to help me? Where do I find information? We try, in Aberdeen, to give the answers, advice and assistance with a smile - with over 3000 visitors a year to our Shop/Research Centre we like to think we're getting something right.

Please, come and visit us if you're ever up this way.

Aberdeen & NE Scotland Family History Society
164 King St., Aberdeen
Tel: 01224—646323; Fax 01224—639096
Email: anesfhsrsc.co.uk Website:http://www.rsc.co.uk/anesfhs

Membership rates: a £2.00 joining fee should be added to the following
One person £10.00   Institutional £10.00
Family (2 named persons at one address) £14.00
We accept cheques in local currency for Australia, New Zealand, Canada and USA
Publications for Sale List available on receipt of A5. (6"x9") stamped addressed envelope (31p.)

Suggested reading for Scottish Research
Exploring Scottish History. M Cox
My Ain Folk. Holton and Winch
Scottish Roots. A Jones
Tracing Scottish Ancestry. R Bigwood
Tracing your Scottish Ancestors in the Scottish Record Office. C Sinclair
Tracing you Scottish Ancestry. K B Cory

The Genealogy of Archives
Iain Flett Dundee City Archives

Family historians and local historians are familiar with using archives in their search for genealogy; the swathe cut by the last Local Government Reorganisation in 1996[1] means that archivists already are having to use the skills of genealogists to work out the labyrinthine trail of the survival and location of official fonds, or original records.

Broadly speaking, Scottish local government until the major reorganisation of 1975[2] consisted of a rich collection of burghs, many originating from the 12th century, all with their own heritage and records, all proudly guarded by their Town Clerks, and of a range of shires or counties, which were well documented after the eighteenth century. In 1975 the alien concept of 'regionalisation' was imposed on the country, riding roughshod over a practical evolution of 800 years of administration, when even the four major cities were reduced to district council (housing, libraries and parks) status.

The only authorities to escape with all-purpose responsibility, with associated heritage and record keeping were the Island Authorities of Orkney, Shetland and the Western Isles. In theory this would logically have been followed by a blanket imposition of regional archive centres, possibly on the French model, but thankfully, as it turned out, the record keeping provisions of the 1973 Act were left so permissive and elastic as to allow local arrangements. Thus the City of Dundee District Council looked after the records of Tayside Regional Council, and Strathclyde Regional Council looked after the records of the City of Glasgow District Council, while within Aberdeen there co-existed, with some duplication, the separate repositories of Grampian Regional Council and of the City of Aberdeen District Council.

The reorganisation of 1996 returned all-purpose responsibility to the four Cities of Edinburgh, Glasgow, Edinburgh and Dundee, and gave all-purpose status to recognisable, if not historically accurate, county areas. Most important of all, in record-keeping terms, the Act not only gave local government record offices in Scotland the legitimacy that England and Wales had enjoyed since 1974[3], but in fact gave the Keeper of the Records of Scotland powers to lay down standards of record keeping, record collection, and access that will now statutorily have to be developed by every single local government authority in Scotland.

If only this structure is allowed to exist for more than 21 years, then there is real hope of a comprehensive and integrated local record service, with integrated finding aids and a common high standard of service, but ironically the imminent arrival of another tier of government, in the form of the revitalised Scottish Parliament, very probably heralds yet another reorganisation.

For the time being it may therefore be useful to provide a quick Cook's (or more appropriately, Macbrayne's) tour by former Regional and Islands Authorities, to summarise current provision, and gaps being filled.[4] The regional councils have now all been disbanded, together with their geographical postal descriptions, but for the purpose of this exercise they can provide a rough guide to archival births, deaths, marriages, divorces and adoptions. The established archival theory of transmission would prefer that archives should be at the sharp record creating end, such as the old Town Clerk's Department, now known by a plethora of 'Yes-Minister-speak' such as those of Corporate Affairs, Executive or Administration.

However, in practice many archives can be found in museums or libraries services, who now face the unaccustomed additional heavy statutory burden of records management. Records Management is the complete genealogy of record keeping from the cradle to the grave, which brings an awesome responsibility of dealing with tonnes and tonnes of traditional records and megabytes of electronic information. If you are intending to use their services, please assume that advance booking will be necessary for all offices.

Family historians unused to Scottish records should bear in mind that a different and separate administrative and church history has led to different and separate record series. The established church in Scotland is the Presbyterian Church of Scotland, which means that other churches, including the Scottish Episcopal Church are not established. Civil registration began in Scotland in 1855, and amid great debate about the legality of this action at the time, the Registrar General collected together all the Church of Scotland (but not including the Free Church) registers of baptisms, marriages and funerals up to that date. These Old Parochial Records (known as the OPR's) are held centrally in New Register House, Edinburgh, although microfilms of the baptisms and marriages are widely available throughout libraries, archives and family history societies in Scotland. A good internet guide to family history sources and locations has been written by Vivienne S Dunstan [5].

The Historical Search Room, Scottish Record Office, HM General Register House, Edinburgh EH1 3YY, will be pleased to help locate any records of non-established churches that are known to be in the care of local government repositories and the Scottish Record Office. The Scottish Record Office, unlike the Public Record Office in Kew, has centrally collected a wide range of church records, including the non-OPR elements of the Church of Scotland, and has copied series such as some Roman Catholic church records. Records held in the Scottish Record Office are available for inspection free of charge, whereas records in New Register House are liable to

production charges. Dundee City Archives and Dumfries & Galloway Archives both have flourishing Friends organisations, which are proving invaluable in enriching the collections through voluntary work. Such voluntary labour (directed so as not to weaken the establishment of professional archive posts), and application to external funding such as Lottery and the EEC, will hopefully strengthen the Scottish local archives network into becoming an enviable resource in European terms.

SHETLAND ISLANDS COUNCIL
Shetland Archives, 44 King Harald Street, Lerwick ZE1 0EQ. Continuation of previous service.
ORKNEY ISLANDS COUNCIL
Orkney Archives, The Orkney Library, Laing Street, Kirkwall KW15 1NW. Continuation of previous service.
WESTERN ISLES COUNCIL
Western Isles Council, Council Offices, Sandwick Road, Stornoway HS1 2BW is developing an archive service.
HIGHLAND REGIONAL COUNCIL
Highland Council Archive, The Library, Farraline Park, Inverness IV1 1NH. Continuation of previous service, with future planned expansion to deal with records management.
North Highland Archive, Wick Library, Sinclair Terrace, Wick KW1 5AB. Built with EEC assistance, this successful area office may herald a pragmatic strategy of dealing with local heritage in a vast rural sparsely populated area
GRAMPIAN REGIONAL COUNCIL
Aberdeenshire Council Archives. Broadly the records inherited from Grampian Regional Council. At the moment being managed by Aberdeen City Archives. Aberdeen City Archives, Town House, Broad Street, Aberdeen AB10 1AQ. Continuation of City of Aberdeen District Council, who are now also managing Aberdeenshire Archives.
Moray Council Archives, Grant Lodge, Cooper Park, Elgin IV30 1HS. Former Moray District Archives at Forres are being restructured, but records can be produced by prior appointment.
CENTRAL REGIONAL COUNCIL
Stirling Council Archives Services, Unit 6, Burghmuir Industrial Estate, Stirling FK7 7PY. Continuation of Central Regional Council Archives Department, but Falkirk and Clackmannan records have mostly been transferred to appropriate authorities.
Falkirk Council Archives, Falkirk Museum, Callendar House, Callendar Park, Falkirk FK1 1YR. Continuation of Falkirk District Archives, with appropriate transfers from Stirling Archives.
Clackmannanshire Council Archives, 26-28 Drysdale Street, Alloa FK10 1JL. New service set up with transfers from Stirling Archives.
TAYSIDE REGIONAL COUNCIL
Dundee City Archives, 21 City Square, Dundee DD1 3BY. Continuation of City of Dundee District Council Archive Centre, which managed the records of Tayside Regional Council, but Perth & Kinross and Angus/Forfarshire records have been transferred to appropriate authorities. First local government Friends organisation in Scotland, followed by Dumfries & Galloway.
Angus Archives, Montrose Library, 214 High Street, Montrose DD10 8PH. Continuation of Angus District Archives, with transfers from Dundee City Archives.
Perth & Kinross Council Archive, A.K.BELL Library, 2-8 York Place, Perth PH2 8EP. Continuation of Perth & Kinross District Council Archives, with transfers from Dundee City Archives.
FIFE REGIONAL COUNCIL
Fife Council, Fife House, North Street, Glenrothes KY7 5LT is developing an archive service. Consultant's report being considered. Alison Baillie, Team Leader, General Services, can locate records within the Council.
STRATHCLYDE REGIONAL COUNCIL
Glasgow City Archives, Mitchell Library, North Street, Glasgow G3 7DN. Continuation of Strathclyde Regional Archives and its predecessor Glasgow City Archives Office, but many records are being transferred to appropriate offices.
Argyll & Bute Council Archives, Manse Brae, Lochgilphead PA31 8QU. Continuation of Argyll & Bute District Archives, with transfers from Glasgow City Archives.
West Dunbartonshire Council, Council Offices, Garshake Road, Dumbarton G82 3PU is developing an archive service.
East Dunbartonshire Council, Tom Johnston House, Civic Way, Kirkintilloch G66 4TJ, is developing an archive service.
Inverclyde Council, Municipal Buildings, Greenock PA15 1LY, is developing an archive service.
Renfrewshire Council, The Robertson Centre, 16 Glasgow Road, Paisley PA1 3QG, is developing an archive service.
East Renfrewshire Council, Council Offices, Eastwood Park, Rouken Glen Road, Glasgow G46 6UG is developing an archive service.
North Lanarkshire Archive, 10 Kelvin Road, Lenziemill, Cumbernauld G67 2BA.
Includes geographical area of historical Dunbartonshire and Stirlingshire, and inherited records of Cumbernauld New Town.
South Lanarkshire Archives and Information Management Service, Records Management Unit, 30 Hawbank Road, College Milton, East Kilbride G74 5EX.
Includes geographical area of historical Lanarkshire proper, and inherited records of East Kilbride Development Corporation, local district councils and burghs.
Ayrshire Archives is a joint service being developed between North Ayrshire Council, East Ayrshire Council and South Ayrshire Council, whereby the Archivist has intellectual control over the various sites in the area. North Ayrshire Council inherited the records management centre of Irvine Development Corporation, and is developing its historical collections. East Ayrshire Council is developing a modern record centre at Kilmarnock. South Ayrshire is providing the headquarters of the service at Ayrshire Archives Centre, Craigie Estate, Ayr KA8 0SS, in a newly adapted building, which vies with Falkirk in being near to excellent catering facilities.
LOTHIAN REGIONAL COUNCIL
City of Edinburgh Council Archives, City Chambers, High Street, Edinburgh EH1 1YJ, is a continuation of the City of Edinburgh District Council Archives, who have inherited the records of Lothian Regional Council.

West Lothian Council Archives, Rutherford Square, Bellsquarry, Livingston EH54 9BU has inherited the modern records of Livingston New Town, and is now collecting historical material.
Midlothian Council Archives, Library Headquarters, 2 Clerk Street, Loanhead EH20 9DR, inherited the modern records of Midlothian District Council, and co-operates with the Local Studies section in preserving historical records.
East Lothian Council, Council Buildings, Haddington EH41 3HA, is developing an archive service.

DUMFRIES AND GALLOWAY REGION
Dumfries and Galloway Archive Centre, 33 Burns Street, Dumfries DG1 2PS, is a continuation of the Dumfries Archive Centre, which has merged with Dumfries and Galloway Libraries to provide a council-wide service and is exploring Heritage Lottery funding for an archive centre in Sanquhar. At the moment has the only Friends organisation in Scotland apart from Dundee City.

BORDERS REGION
Scottish Borders Archive and Local History Centre, St Mary's Mill, Selkirk TD7 5EW, is a continuation of the former Borders service. Can locate records in dispersed centres.

(1) The Local Government etc. (Scotland) Act 1994 c.39

(2) The Local Government (Scotland) Act 1973 c.65

(3) The Local Government Act 1972

(4) For those of you with access to a computer linked to the Internet, or to a public library with Internet facilities, the following sites will give you more up to date and detailed information; the Historical Manuscripts Commission list all Scottish sites with manuscripts on <http://www.hmc.gov.uk/nra/locresult.asp?lctry=Scotland>, and archivists themselves run an information site on <http://www.archivesinfo.net/uksites. html>. Both sites have useful links to related topics on history and genealogy.

(5) <http://www-theory.dcs.st-and.ac.uk/~mnd/genuki/intro.html>

This article by Iain Flett is based on an earlier version which appeared in
Scottish Archives (Volume 4 1998)
published by The Scottish Records Association

Maritime Dundee
Iain Flett - Dundee City Archives

The earliest document in Dundee City Archives relating to the city's maritime past is itself a red herring, for it is an infrared photograph of a charter copied onto the parchment rolls of King John of England, for the year 1199, in the Public Record Office at Kew. Historians have had to look at the copy in London because the Dundee original, addressed to the burgesses of Earl David [of Huntington], has vanished. Measuring probably only about 30 x 10 cm., it would either have been taken, together with other early burgh documents, as booty for ransom during the Wars of Independence by the invading English forces, or simply burnt during the siege of the town. Robert I of Scotland (The Bruce) eventually had to issue a Confirmation of Dundee's burgh privileges in 1327 because no official documents before that time could be found. However, this scrap of evidence from 1199 tells us a great deal about Dundee as a maritime centre. It granted merchants from Dundee freedom from tolls in English ports except London, and was what we would today call a bulk trading agreement. It would have cost a lot of money to persuade the ungenerous King John (remember his temper at Runnymcde?) to consider such a grant, and to pay his court officials to negotiate, draft and draw up the parchment. The Dundee merchants would have had to be wealthy enough to make this investment, and to have had enough large seagoing ships by 1199 to make this negotiation worthwhile. So although Dundee celebrated its Octocentenary in 1991 to commemorate 800 years of documented recognition of burgh status, it must in fact have had ships and a trading base for a good part of the twelfth century. It would have been fascinating to have known who exactly the 'burgesses of Earl David' were, but we have to remember that in the twelfth century European government still relied on oral testimony and oral traditions, and that detailed written records outside of royal government in Scotland were scarce and unusual.

The former District Council of Dundee, prior to Scottish local government reorganisation in 1996, had much satisfaction in advising Estonian local government on quality control in its developing food industry after its liberation from the Eastern bloc. Officials from both sides were delighted to be reminded that this was a relationship which was not new, but which had developed in the Middle Ages and was only interrupted by The Great War in 1914. The surviving records of the burgh from this period are full of references to Dundee's trade with the Baltic and north Europe. In the Town Clerk's Notaries records for 1521, there is a rough copy of a birth brieve addressed to Cracow in the kingdom of Poland to confirm that the merchants Adam and David Mores were the sons, gotten in lawful matrimony, of the 'umqhile' or deceased Alexander Mores. The original, on parchment and written in Latin, would have acted as a letter of introduction and passport for their

trading activity. Another entry in the same commonplace book for 1527 shows what rates of exchange in gold coin Nicholas Cant would pay at Leith or by his factor in Copenhagen. An interesting illumination when it is considered that in 1527 payment in gold, whatever the coinage, was as universal as the impending introduction of the Euro 472 years later. It can also be seen that by the 16th century there was a wealth of documentary detail about burgh and merchant families and their trading activities, but a wealth of such abundance that national and local publishing societies have just uncovered the tip of the genealogical iceberg. The iceberg can be melted, but intending researchers should bear in mind that Scots handwriting, with its French influences, was substantially different from English contemporary script, and that Scottish notaries public, like modern lawyers, were busy men whose writing descended into idiosyncratic scribbles and short cuts when under pressure. Entries could be in Latin or colloquial phonetic Scots (c) be prepared for phlegmatic phrases like 'quharuntil' for whereunto or 'quhairfour' for wherefore.

Brisk trading led to traffic jams; one entry in the burgh court books of 1560 was headed 'anent lyeing at the schoir', otherwise an instruction to skippers to park their vessels tidily by the bulwarks so as to not cause obstruction to other traffic and damage to the wooden pierwork. The resulting fine, under the pain of 10 Scots, for those who disobeyed or who parked carelessly, would burn a hefty hole in any merchant's pocket.

This was the golden age of trading in Dundee, when the burgh was second only to Edinburgh in wealth and importance, and when Glasgow was a small cathedral town. The sacking by Cromwell's General Monck in 1651 changed all that forever. The men of military age in the town were literally decimated and all wealth was plundered, although it was rumoured that the Roundheads' ill gotten booty foundered at the bar of the Tay, where it may still lurk as a siren, like the Tobermory galleon treasure, to lure salvage adventurers.

The Dutch engineer Slezer provided the first reliable historical illustrations of Dundee in 1692, probably using the camera obscura technique. This was the modern equivalent of a pin hole camera, in the form of a blacked out tent in which a drawing table was illuminated by a mirror image. Slezer's view from the East showed a quiet view of the harbour. It took a long time for trade and shipping to recover, although even by the 1670's there were indications that the traditional resilience of the burgh against adversity was shining through. An entry in the Lockit Book for 16 March 1676 showed that John Marr, mariner, had been granted an honorary burgessship 'gratis' or free. This would be our present day equivalent of the Freedom of the City, and this was in recognition of the charting of the North Sea that Marr had carried out as a merchant skipper in his own time. His work was deeply appreciated by skippers beyond Dundee, who found his tireless attention to detail made their hazardous voyages much safer.

The prize exhibit of Dundee Museums, the brass Portuguese Astrolabe of 1555, is one of the finest examples of a navigational instrument to have survived in Europe, and has been copied by the maritime museum in Portugal. The manuscripts in the City Archives have helped to establish that it came to the town through trading links. Rediscovered in the 1950's, wrapped in paper at the bottom of a tea chest by the late James Boyd, Curator of Dundee Museum, the only clue about its provenance was the owner's stamp, `Andrew Smeaton'. Some clever detective work twenty years later by Veronica Hartwich, now herself head of the Scottish Maritime Museum at Irvine, established that Andrew Smeaton had been made a burgess, or freeman, on 17 September 1670, and that he was a man in a hurry. The entry in the Town's 'Lockit Buik' (Locked Book) showed that while the rest of the merchants on that day got their freedom through inheritance or marriage, Andrew Smeaton paid cash down, and his entry was scribbled at the end of the meeting, as though he had just strode in through the door with his seaboots on and placed his bag of gold on the council table. A later entry in the Shipping Register seven years later showed what Andrew made his money out of; 'Andro Smetton, maister of the ship called the Unitie, of Dundee, loaded with salt from Rotchelle...' This tells us that Andrew was trading in French waters, and that he bought the astrolabe when it was already 120 years old, when it would still have been highly regarded as a working, sturdy and reliable instrument. Many Scottish burghs, together with their crafts and guilds, have 'Lockit Buiks' which identify merchants and skippers, and whether they bought into the town as strangers. If they gained their 'freedom' by inheritance, the Lockit Buiks can provide a swift genealogical route through the spouse's family. The wife's family activity need not be related to that of the husband; it is possible to see a rising Dundee merchant gaining his 'freedom' through his wife who could be the daughter of a burgess 'baxter' (baker) or 'maltman' (brewer).

Maritime trade could not have survived without the harbour, and there are many documents relating to this, ranging from the royal grants of rights from 1327 onwards, to the entries in the burgh court books in the 16th century, and to the formation of a separate administration in the form of the Dundee Harbour Commissioners in the 19th century. Pressure for harbour reform was shown by a test legal case in 1813, when the Town Council was sued for negligence in allowing an Aberdeen galliot to run onto quay repairs. This could be compared to feverish activity two years later, when the letter books of the new Harbour Commissioners show that they were pressing their consulting engineer, one Thomas Telford Esq., then working at Inverness, to concentrate on the Dundee harbour works and beat the weather. By 1838, James Leslie, also famous for his civil engineering in the local waterworks, was building further harbour extensions, and the meticulous coloured drawings

of lock gates and machinery are works of art in themselves, and almost give a three dimensional feel to this early Victorian development.

Local firms, such as the Dundee, Perth & London Shipping Company, were instrumental in using the facilities of the harbour and in developing the technology of the steam engine to improve reliability and profitability. Indeed it was a tribute to that firm's tenacity and flexibility that as the 'DP&L' it still thrives on charter travel and factoring. The records of this business range from the minute books commissioning elegant sailing vessels of 1826 for the London trip, to the chilling insurance photographs of the devastation to the DP&L Thames terminal after the blitz in the Second World War. Dundee City Archives, like many other maritime repositories, are constantly asked for crew and passenger lists of travellers who sailed on the vessels, but unfortunately the survival of such lists was the exception rather than the rule. Busy shipping companies were under the same financial pressure as modern travel companies. Annual accounts and records of plant and machinery had to be kept for accounting purposes; crew and passenger records were too voluminous to be kept for any length of time, and there were no financial reasons to do so.

Dundee, with its Victorian nickname of 'Juteopolis' was a world leader not only in processing jute but in making the machinery to process the jute, and now, alas, it is a fading memory that Dundee also made the vessels and the engines that transported it. Shipyards like Gourlays, Stephens, and the Caledon turned out an impressive array of general and specialised ships that travelled all over the world. Outline ship plans, usually called 'general arrangements', from Gourlays and the Caledon showed river paddle steamers for South America, gunboats for Turkey and 'Fifies' (car and passenger ferries) for the Tay. Photographs show gleaming engine rooms in publicity shots, which were probably kept as proudly gleaming in use as they were on trials. The financial pressures on shipbuilding firms were the same as shipping firms, with the result that while the voltage details of vessels built in the 1920s are fairly easy to establish, it is difficult to identify the men who built a vessel unless the trade union records survive.

Alas for Dundee, the final chapter in jute production has closed, and the excellent theme park facilities in Verdant Works, the working textile mill of Dundee Industrial Heritage, now show textile work as past history. There now seems a possibility that maritime activity may be heading in the same direction, with the possibility that the Frigate Unicorn of 1824 and the RRS Discovery of 1901 may be joined by a harbour development that would convert the Victoria Dock into a maritime theme park. However, it must be hoped that the timeless nature of the Tay and the sea, which gave birth to Dundee, will continue to bring it visitors, trade and new horizons, and, in its wake, many more maritime records.

See Also: *Section 2A   Research - Comprehensive*
Most of the Researchers listed in that Section also undertake research in Scotland.

Caroline Gerard
Family history research throughout the wealth of Scottish Records. All work from minor to major. Friendly, enthusiastic service. See Advert on Page 126

6 Belford Mews, Dean Village, Edinburgh, EH4 3BT
Email: caroline.gerard@btinternet.com.

David G C Burns, ASGRA, Ancestral Researcher
Tracing family history in Scottish Records: Searches for relatives; Typed report and chart. Over 30 years experience. Lecturer in Genealogy. See Advert on Page 126

16/7 Craigmount Hill, Edinburgh, EH4 8HW, Scotland
Tel No: 0131-339-6959

Dundee City Council - Genealogy Unit
Special unit providing a customised research facility and/or service covering records for the Dundee and Angus areas. Research service available. See Advert on Page 134

89 Commercial Street, Dundee, DD1 2AF, Scotland. Tel No: 01382-435222   Fax No:01382-435224.
Email: registrars@dundeecity.gov.uk.
Web Site: www.dundeecity.gov.uk/dcchtml/sservices/genealogy

Elizabeth Mortimer, MA, ASGRA
Professional genealogist specialising in ancestry and living relative searches throughout Scotland including National Archives of Scotland. See Advert on Page 128

Kilcombe, St Thomas's Well, Stirling, FK7 9PR, Scotland.
Tel No: 01786-463470   Fax No:01786-463470.
Email: elizabeth.mortimer@lineone.net

John Adams
HIGHLANDER or LOWLANDER, RICH or POOR, your Scottish ancestry can be pursued by an experienced researcher. See Advert on Page 126

8 North Gardner Street, Glasgow, G11 5BT, Scotland.
Tel No: 0141-334-1021
Email: jadams@primex.co.uk.

Leslie Hodgson
Scottish family history searches using the records in New Register House, the National Archives of Scotland and the National Library of Scotland.   See Advert on Page 126

5 St Stephen Place, Edinburgh, EH3 5AJ, Scotland
Tel No: 0131-225-2723

Root-Finder
Genealogical research in the Statutory Indices, Old Parish Registers, Census Returns for Scotland and also in the National Archives of Scotland.   See Advert on Page 136

10 Garden Terrace, Falkirk, FK1 1RL, Scotland
Email: jean.gibb@clara.co.uk

Rosemary Philip, BA(Hons), CSFHS (Stirling)
Family and local history research in statutory registers, Old Parish Registers, census returns, wills, sasines, church records and many more.   See Advert on Page 128

15 Beresford Gardens, Edinburgh, EH5 3ER, Scotland
Tel No: 0131-552-8021

Scots Ancestry Research Society
Research undertaken in Scottish records by experienced team of researchers. Set up in 1945 and formerly of 29b Albany Street, Edinburgh. See Advert on Page 130

134 Thornhill Road, Falkirk, FK2 7AZ, Scotland
Tel No: 01324-622429
Email: scotsanc@aol.com.
Web Site: http://www.royalmile.com/scotsancestry

Scots-Heritage of Auchterarder
Professional research in Archives in many parts of Scotland. Historical background a speciality. See Advert on Page 128

31 Beechtree Place, Auchterarder, Perthshire, PH3 1JQ, Scotland. Tel No: 01764-664998   Fax No:01764-664998.
Email: norman@scots-heritage.co.uk.
Web Site: http://www.scots-heritage.co.uk

Susan Miller, BSc, ASGRA
Family History research from Statutory, Census and Old Parish Registers. Searches in Glasgow City Archives and other local sources. See Advert on Page 130

36 Branziert Road North, Killearn, Glasgow, G63 9RF
Tel No: 01360-550633

WESTERN ISLES

CO LEIS THU? Research Centre
Genealogical resource and research service for the Western Isles of Scotland. Books and publications on local history available. See Advert on Page 122

The Old School House, Northton (Taobh Tuath), Isle of Harris, HS3 3JA, Scotland. Tel No: 01859-520258   Fax No:01859-520258.
Email: 113143.1710@compuserve.com.
Web Site: http://www.hebrides.com./org/genealogy

The National Archives
Bishop Street Dublin 8
Ireland
Tel. 4072 300 FAX 4072 333
Established in 1986 is an amalgamation of the older
Public Record Office of Ireland
(est.1867 in the Four Courts, Dublin) & the State Paper Office (est.1702 in Dublin Castle).
It is the state repository for the census returns of 1901 and 1911
(and earlier nineteenth century census, where extant);
for all wills and grants, for the Records of the Church of Ireland.

It also holds the Tithe Applotment Books, and Griffith's Primary Valuation - both for the nineteenth
century. It holds extensive information on those sentenced to transportation,
those who participated in rebellions, and those who participated
in nineteenth century central and local administration.
The National Archives is open Monday - Friday from 10.00.a.m. to 5.00.p.m.

The National Archives of Ireland
Aideen M Ireland

The National Archives comprises the holdings of the former Public Record Office of Ireland and of the State Paper Office. The combined holdings date from medieval times to the present day.

The holdings comprise the records of the former Chief Secretary's Office in Dublin Castle, including papers relating to the Rebellion of 1798, the Fenian movement of the 1860s, and crimes and convictions throughout the nineteenth century. The Transportation Records are of particular importance to Australians whose ancestors were transported from Ireland to Australia as convicts in the period 1788 to 1868. Microfilms and a computerised index of the most important records relating to transportation have been deposited in the Australian National Library in Canberra and copies of the microfilms are available at state libraries throughout Australia. Record collections include those relating to the employment of Resident magistrates and other local government officials. There are also excellent prison records.

The national Archives collections also comprise the records of the former Public Record Office of Ireland. This office suffered in 1922 during the Civil War and many of the records were destroyed. However, in many cases there are copies, transcripts, précis and indexes of this material. Many other records of genealogical and historical interest have been acquired since 1922.

Among other records which are available in the National Archives are the census returns of 1901 and 1911 (and nineteenth century census returns for the decades 1821 - 1851, if extant), which list all persons living in Ireland on the nights on which the census were compiled. There are also some eighteenth century census collections.

For the nineteenth century Griffith's Primary Valuation of Ireland of 1846 - 1863 lists all immediate house and land occupiers except those living in tenements. This is a return of the head of the family only. The Tithe Applotment Books of 1823 - 1837 list all those holding over one acre of (agricultural) land who were obliged to pay a tithe for the maintenance of the local Church of Ireland clergyman. This also is a return of the head of the family only. The Tithe Applotment Books are least satisfactory for urban areas. The census returns and the records of the Primary Valuation and of the Tithe Applotment are available in microform and there are comprehensive finding aids.

Wills, grants of probate, grants of administration, and schedules of assets survive for the twentieth century and are available for consultation if older than twenty years. Many of the records also survive for the nineteenth century and earlier - either in copy or precis form. Much of the testamentary material has been abstracted by professional genealogists in the period before 1922 or by the Commissioners for Charitable Donations and Bequests and is available for research. Some Inland Revenue returns of wills, grants of probate and grants of administration survive for the first half of the nineteenth century. The testamentary collection is a particularly rich and important source for genealogists. There are comprehensive finding aids to all these testamentary collections.

Records for the Church of Ireland survive in original, copy or extract form. The records in local custody have, in many instances, been copied on microfilm and are also available for research. There is a comprehensive finding-aid to all known surviving records.

Many other collections will also be of interest to the genealogist. These include the records of the National School system up to modern times (especially regarding the employment of National School teachers), admission registers to workhouses (where they survive), estate collections (including leases and tenants' agreements), Voters' registers (where they survive) and the records of local administration in Ireland throughout the nineteenth century.

The National Archives is open to the public, Monday to Friday from 10.00 a.m. to 5.00 p.m. Documents are not produced after 4.30 p.m. However, the reading room does not close over lunchtime. The office is closed for periods at Christmas and Easter and on Public Holidays. Staff are always available in the reading room to give advice and help researchers. There are comprehensive finding aids in the Reading Room and printed leaflets, which are updated regularly, are available to assist the researcher.

Bishop Street is easily accessible on foot from both St Stephen's Green and St Patrick's Cathedral.

From O'Connell Street via Trinity College - O'Connell Street O'Connell Bridge, Westmorland Street College Green (passing the Front Gate of Trinity College on your left, Grafton Street, St Stephen's Green West, Cuffe Street Kevin Street Lower, Bride Street Bishop Street (West end).

From the Four Courts via St Patrick's Cathedral - Inns Quay, O'Donovan Rossa Bridge, Winetavern Street (passing under the arch of Christ Church),Nicholas Street, Patrick Street (passing St Patrick's Cathedral on your left) Kevin Street Upper, Bishop Street (West end).

From the National Library and Genealogical Office -

Kildare Street, St Stephen's Green North, St Stephen's Green West, Cuffe Street, Kevin Street Lower, Bride Street, Bishop Street (West end).

From the General Register Office -
Either Lombard Street East, Pearse Street, College Street and get the number 83 or 155 bus. - **Or**, Lombard Street East, Westland Row, Lincoln Place, Leinster Street, Kildare Street and continue walking as from the National Library.

The best bus routes from the City Centre to Bishop Street are the number 83 to Kimmage and the number 155 to Greenhills Get of at the stop on Redmond's Hill cross the road at the next traffic lights, walk along Kevin Street Lower, turn right onto Bride Street and almost immediately again onto Bishop Street and cross the street . The National Archives is the building in front of you as you cross Bishop Street.

The Irish Genealogical Project

Kathleen Neill, AUGRA (Hon. Life Mem.) & IGCO (RG) Executive Director AUGRA

Genealogy in Ireland has changed in the last few years. This is a brief guide to available sources. Compulsory civil registration of births, deaths and Roman Catholic marriages did not begin in Ireland until 1864 (non Catholic marriages had been registered by law since 1845). Prior to these dates all such events were voluntarily recorded in local parish church records (the condition and accuracy of which depended entirely upon the interest of the clergyman in office at the time). As very few of these parish records were indexed, this meant that if you wanted to find vital records for an individual you needed to know where their family lived, and worshipped, at the time of his/her birth and you needed to know the name of the town, village or parish. Even the name of the county alone was not normally sufficient as it covered a large administrative area - the equivalent of a State in the USA Many people did not have that information and found that their attempts to trace their family was halted before it began.

The Irish Genealogical Project, sponsored by the International Fund for Ireland and by other central and local government departments in the north and south of Ireland is to make genealogical information in Ireland more readily available. Computer indexing centres have been, and are being, set up throughout the country and some of the established independent genealogists and genealogical organisations have received grant aid to enable them to computer index their holdings. The index will guide the inquirer to the relevant centre or Genealogical Organisation. The index will contain the person's name, date, type of record (i.e. baptismal record, birth certificate, marriage record, obituary notice, gravestone inscription, etc.), county of origin and the name of the Centre or Genealogical Organisation.

When fully developed, the Irish Genealogical Project will prove to be the most important development ever in Irish genealogy. Irish Genealogy Limited, is to oversee the development of the project and its standards. The Company is a partnership between Centres,some government bodies, tourist boards, training agencies, record repositories and The Association of Professional Genealogists in Ireland (APGI), c/o 2 Kildare Street, Dublin 2, Irish Republic, and Association of Ulster Genealogists and Record Agents (AUGRA), c/o Glen Cottage, Glenmachan Road, Belfast BT4 2NP. Irish Genealogy Limited, ESB Complex, Parnell Avenue, Harold's Cross, Dublin 12, Irish Republic. It should be remembered that some computer indexing had started before the project was started. The indexing started with Roman Catholic Church records, then the church registers of other denominations. It will take between three and seven years to complete the project. A list of the Centres and their progress is as follows:

Co.Antrim / Co Down	Ulster Historical Foundation, 12 College Square East, Belfast BT1 6DA, Has completed the Catholic parishes of Belfast.
Co.Armagh	Armagh Records Centre, Ara Coeli, Armagh BT61 7QY, Northern Ireland. Has computerised the Catholic records for the Diocese of Armagh which also includes parts of Co.'s Tyrone, Louth & Down. These records can be accessed through: Armagh Ancestry, 42 English Street, Armagh, Co. Armagh.
Co.Carlow	No Centre has yet been designated
Co.Cavan	Cavan Heritage & Genealogy Centre, c/o Cavan County Library, Cavan, Ireland. Almost all County Catholic Church Records & Griffith's Valuation & Tithes.
Co.Clare	The Clare Genealogy Centre, Corofin. Co. Clare, Irish Republic. Complete indexing of all county church records as well as some other major sources.
Co.Cork North	Mallow Heritage Centre, 27-28 Bank Place, Mallow, Co. Cork, Irish Republic. Complete indexing of most of the Catholic records for north Cork and substantial proportion of the Church of Ireland records for that county.
Co.Donegal	Donegal Genealogical Committee, Letterkenny, Co. Donegal; Ramelton Heritage Project, The Old Meeting House, Ramelton, Co. Donegal. Indexed almost all the county Presbyterian Church records and the Catholic records for the Inishowen peninsula as well as most of the rest of the county.
Co.Down	see Antrim and Armagh.
Co.Dublin North	The Fingall Heritage Centre, The Carnegie Library, Swords, Co. Dublin, Irish Republic. Centre has indexed a substantial number of the Catholic records.
Dublin City	Dublin Heritage Group, Clondalkin Library, Clondalkin, Co. Dublin, Irish

	Republic. Indexed church records for west Dublin and some Dublin city records.
Co.Dublin South	Dun Laoghaire Heritage Centre, Moran Park House, Dun Laoghaire, Co.Dublin Complete Index - Dun Laoghaire Catholic church records, work continues for other parishes.
Co.Fermanagh	Irish World, 26 Market Square, Dungannon, Co. Tyrone, Northern Ireland.
Co.Tyrone	Computerising Griffith's Valuation, Tithe Books and gravestone inscriptions in Co.Tyrone. Gravestone inscriptions for more than 300 graveyards (N.I.)
Co.Galway East	Woodford Heritage Centre, Main Street, Woodford, Co. Galway, Irish Republic.Over 50 of the Catholic records for Co. Galway - indexed and some of the Church of Ireland for Galway East.
Co.Galway West	Co. Galway Family History Society, 34 Upper Abbeygate Street, Galway, Co. Galway. The Society has indexed over 50 of the Catholic records for west Galway.
Co.Kerry	No centre designated as yet.
Co.Kildare	Kildare Genealogical Committee, County Library, Newbridge, Co. Kildare. Have indexed around half the Catholic records for the county.
Co.Kilkenny	Kilkenny Archaeological Society, Rothe House, Kilkenny, Co. Kilkenny. Over 50 of the county Catholic church records indexed and a some Church of Ireland records and a large number of gravestone inscriptions for the county.
Co.Laois / Co.Offaly	Family History Research Centre, Charleville Road, Tullamore, Co. Offaly Have completed over 75 of all county church records. This centre also holds a large number of other sources and is very active in local history.
Co.Leitrim	**Leitrim Heritage Centre**, County Library, Ballinamore, Co. Leitrim. This centre has completed all the church records for the county as well as Griffith's Valuation, Tithe Books and other sources.
Co.Limerick	Limerick Archives, The Granery, Michael Street, Limerick. All church records for the county are now indexed along with a wide range of other sources.
Co.Longford	Longford Genealogical Centre, c/o VEC, Battery Road, Longford. Has indexed over 50 of the Catholic church records for the county on cards.
Co.Louth	see Meath.
Co.Londonderry	Inner City Trust, Genealogy Centre, 8 Bishop Street, Londonderry BT48 6PW, N Ireland. Complete indexing of well over half the Catholic church records, Griffith's Valuation, Tithe Books, emigration records, the 1831 census,a number of Presbyterian church records for the county as well as emigration records for the port of Londonderry.
Co.Mayo Mayo North	North Family History Research Centre, The Boreen, Crossmolina, Co. Mayo. Completed indexing of virtually all the church records for the county.
Co.Mayo South	Family History Centre, Town Hall, Ballinrobe, Co. Mayo,. Completed almost all Catholic and Church of Ireland records for the county this centre also has a large collection of indexed school rolls.
Co.Meath / Co Louth	Meath Heritage Centre, Trim, Co. Meath. Has completed most of the surviving Church of Ireland records and around 50 of the Catholic records for Co. Meath and some for Co. Louth.
Co.Monaghan	Monaghan Ancestral Research centre, 6 Tully, Monaghan. Around 50 of the total church records for the county and a wide variety of other sources have now been indexed
Co.Offaly	see Laois.
Co.Roscommon	Roscommon Heritage & Genealogical Centre, Strokestown, Co. Roscommon. Has virtually completed the indexing of the Catholic church records and a large proportion of those of the Church of Ireland for the county.
Co.Sligo	Sligo Heritage & Genealogical Centre, Stephen's Street, Sligo, Co. Sligo. Complete indexing of all church records and almost all gravestone inscriptions for the county.
Co.Tipperary North	Nenagh District Heritage Society, Governor's House, Nenagh, Co. Tipperary. More than 50 of the Catholic and Church of Ireland records completed.
Co.Tipperary South	Boru Boru Heritage Centre, Cashel, Co. Tipperary. Access to the Catholic Church records for the Diocese is limited by the Bishop.Holds a wide range of other indexed sources, including civil records.
Co.Tyrone	see Fermanagh.
Co.Waterford	Waterford Heritage Survey Ltd, St. John's College, Waterford, Co.Waterford, Indexed almost all of the parishes in the Diocese of Waterford and Lismore.
Co.Westmeath	Dun ni Si Heritage Centre, Moate, Co. Westmeath. Have completed some Catholic and Church of Ireland records. The centre is in its early stages.
Co.Wexford	Tagoat Community Council, Tagoat, Rosslare, Co. Wexford, Irish Republic. Has completed more than 50 of the Catholic records for the county.
Co.Wicklow	Wicklow Heritage Centre, Court House, Wicklow, Co. Wicklow,. Almost all the Catholic church records for the county indexed.

DUBLIN CITY ARCHIVES

Dublin City Archives comprise the historic records of the municipal government of Dublin from the twelfth century to the present. The City Archives contain a significant number of medieval documents, including two important bound manuscripts written on vellum: the White Book of Dublin (also known as the *'Liber Albus'* and the Chain Book of Dublin. The City Archives also include a series of Assembly Rolls, written on parchment, which record the minutes of the Dublin City Assembly (a forerunner of today's City Council) from 1447 to 1841. The Assembly Rolls, together with the White Book and Chain Book, were transcribed and translated by Sir John T. and Lady Gilbert and published as *Calendar of Ancient Records of Dublin* (19 vols, Dublin, 1889-1944).

In addition to these published materials, the Dublin City Archives contain a wealth of records which have not been published and are available for research. These records include City Council and committee minutes, account books, correspondence, reports, court records, charity petitions, title deeds, maps and plans, photographs and drawings, all of which document the development of Dublin over eight centuries. The Archives hold the magnificent series of 102 charters granted to the city by successive English monarchs. The earliest was issued by King Henry II in 1171/2, giving the men of Bristol the right to live in the city of Dublin. Later charters contain grants to Dublin of rights, privileges and property, and taken together they form the basis of municipal law in Ireland.

THE ANCIENT FREEDOM OF DUBLIN

The Dublin City Archives holds lists of citizens who received the Freedom of Dublin between 1468 and 1918. It is possible to trace several generations of old Dublin families through these lists, which are a useful source for genealogical research. The ancient Freedom of Dublin was instituted at the time of the Norman Invasion in the late 12th century, Holders of the Freedom were known as "Free Citizens" and were entitled to significant trading privileges and the right to vote in municipal and parliamentary elections . Admission to the Freedom of Dublin was granted by the Dublin City Assembly at the great feasts of Christmas, Easter, Midsummer and Michaelmas. In order to qualify for the Freedom, it was usually necessary to have been born within the city boundaries, or "franchises", and to be a member of one of the Trade Guilds of Dublin. Members of "the Irish Nation" were excluded, but in practice many people with Irish surnames succeeded in obtaining the Freedom. Under the Penal Laws, Roman Catholics were excluded from the Freedom of Dublin from 1691 until 1793. There were six main categories of admission:

1.Admission by Service was granted to those who completed an apprenticeship in one of the Trade Guilds of Dublin.

2. Admission by Birth was granted to sons, and sometimes daughters, of Free Citizens. Several generations of one family could hold the Freedom of Dublin.

3. Admission by Marriage was granted to sons-in-law of Free Citizens.

4. Admission by Fine was confined to prosperous professional men who were required to pay a substantial sum of money into the city treasury. Sometimes the Fine consisted of the presentation of a pair of gloves to the Lady Mayoress.

5. Admission by Grace Especial also known as Special Grace was the equivalent of the modern Honorary Freedom, and was reserved for dignitaries and for craftsmen who were not in a trade guild.

6. Admission by an Act of Parliament to "Encourage Protestant Strangers to Settle in Ireland" was granted to French Huguenots and Quakers from England.

Lists of those admitted to the ancient Freedom of Dublin survive for the period 1225-1250, 1468-1512 and 1575-1918. These lists may be consulted at Dublin Corporation Archives, City Hall, Dublin 2. A computerised index to the lists is being prepared by the Dublin Heritage Group. The lists are of interest to students of social and economic history and are also important for genealogical research.

HONORARY FREEDOM OF THE CITY OF DUBLIN

The Honorary Freedom of Dublin was instituted under the Municipal Privileges Act, 1876 and is presently conferred under the provisions of the Local Government Act 1991. The founder of the Home Rule Party, Isaac Butt, was the first person to receive the Honorary Freedom of Dublin. Other illustrious recipients include Charles Stewart Parnell, George Bernard Shaw, John Count McCormack and John Fitzgerald Kennedy, President of the United States of America. In recent years, it has been conferred on Pope John Paul II;Mother Teresa of Calcutta; the world champion cyclist Stephen Roche; and the former President of Ireland, Dr. Patrick Hillery. Nelson Mandela received the Freedom in 1988, whilst still a political prisoner. It has also been conferred on Jack Charlton, manager of the Republic of Ireland football team; & Bill Clinton, President U.S.A.

WIDE STREETS COMMISSION

The Wide Streets Commission was established in 1757 to develop wide and convenient streets through the city of Dublin. Among its other achievements, thc Commission built Parliament St., Westmoreland St. and D'Olier St. as well as Carlisle Bridge (now O'Connell Bridge). The minute books, maps, title deeds and architecttral drawings produced for the Commission before it was abolished in 1849 are all held in the Dublin City Archives. These important records tell the story of the lay-out and development of much of Georgian Dublin.

MANSION HOUSE FUND FOR RELIEF OF DISTRESS

Ireland was beset by harvest failure during the 1870's and in 1880 famine threatened the country. To prevent this, the Mansion House Fund was set up to collect money from Irish emigrants all over the world. The records of the Fund are held in the Dublin City Archives and are important for local history because they contain reports from 800 local committees which distributed relief in every county in Ireland. Records of other relief committees are also available for inspection.

RECORDS OF URBAN DISTRICT COUNCILS

The areas of Rathmines and Rathgar and of Pembroke each had their own local government until 1930, and their records are preserved in the Dublin City Archives, describing the development of these suburbs from the mid 19th century. The records of the Howth Urban District Council are' also available, from 1318 to 1940.

Dublin City Archives are housed in the City Assembly House (beside the Powerscourt Town House Centre) where a Reading Room is provided for members of the public who wish to consult the Archives. An advance appointment is essential. Some records, because of their antiquity or fragile condition, may be withdrawn for conservation treatment and may not always be available for research.The City Archives are for reference and research and may not be borrowed; access to the storage area is not permitted. The Archivist will be pleased to answer any queries relating to the records. Photocopying, photography and microfilm services are provided as appropriate. The Archivist can advise on costs and conditions of copyright.

Dublin City Archives, City Assembly House,
58 South William Street, Dublin 2.
Tel: (01) 677 5877 Fax: (01) 677 954 Opening Hours:
Monday-Friday, 10.00- 13.00; 14.15- 17.00

See Also: *Section 2A   Research - Comprehensive*
Most of the Researchers listed in that Section also undertake research in Ireland

HERITAGE WORLD

- Discover the path to your Irish roots -
Heritage World, Ireland's foremost genealogy research company, caters for all family history requirements. We offer a comprehensive, efficient service covering all Ireland, and a full range of heritage products including family coats of arms, keyrings, name scrolls, personalised notepaper and publications on aspects of Irish culture. Our recently published a CD-ROM Index to Griffith's Valuation of Ireland, is an invaluable guide to everyone seeking information on their Irish ancestry. For a brochure and full details of all our services and products, please contact us by mail, telephone, fax or e-mail. We shall be happy to assist you discover the path to your Irish roots.

Heritage World Family History Services
26 Market Square, Dungannon, Co. Tyrone,
Northern Ireland BT70 1AB.
Tel. 01868-724187; Fax. 01868-752141
Email: irishwld@iol.ie Web: http://www.iol.ie./irishworld

HISTORICAL RESEARCH IRELAND

Full Family History Research including births, marriages and deaths.
Also Census 1901 - 1911

Contact
Patrick Hogan
92 Bishopswater, Wexford, Ireland
Telephone: 353 534 5976
Email: hri@gofree.indigo.ie

Irish Roots
Family History Magazine

For the past eight years, this quarterly glossy magazine has been the essential guide for all those tracing Irish ancestors. Features on genealogy, heraldry and history form the bulk of its content. News from the world of Irish genealogy keeps readers abreast of all new developments. *Irish Roots* circulates in Ireland, UK, USA, Australia and Canada. It's easier to find your Irish roots if you read *Irish Roots*

ANNUAL SUBSCRIPTION (4 ISSUES BY MAIL)
IRELAND & UK: £8.00; USA: US$20;
AUSTRALIA: A$28; CANADA: CAN$28;
REST OF WORLD: £14 (SURFACE), £16 (AIR)
PAYMENT MAY BE MADE BY PERSONAL CHEQUE, CREDIT CARD, INTL MONEY ORDER OR CASH.
DETAILS & PAYMENTS TO:
BELGRAVE PUBLICATIONS, BELGRAVE AVENUE, CORK, IRELAND; EMAIL: irishrts@iol.ie

If you should need printing or presentation services, perhaps an interactive family history on CD Rom, or complex heraldic illustration on your hand crafted family tree, maybe you're not sure and need some advice, call us and we will be happy to discuss...

~Digital

Printers of the
Genealogical Services Directory 2000

Providing all the services you may require in visual media...

~from Leaflets to Books

~from one to FULL colour print

~Display & Exhibition Stands

~CD & Multi Media Presentations

~Animated Graphics

~Traditional Calligraphy

Tel: 07041 428220 (*BT Lo-Call rate*)
Visit our website:
www.awpdigital.co.uk

Public Record Office
of Northern Ireland

66 Balmoral Avenue, Belfast, BT9 6NY

Tel. 01232 255905 Fax.01232 255 999

E-mail: proni@nics.gov.uk   Website http://proni.nics.gov.uk/index.htm

The Public Record Office of Northern Ireland was established in 1923, against the background of the partition of Ireland and the extensive destruction by fire of the Public Record Office, Dublin, in 1922. This has resulted in the common belief that most of the records have been lost and that PRONI holds no pre-1922 material. This could not be further from the truth.

Whilst the archives destroyed included records of 1,006 parishes throughout Ireland, records of over 1000 churches of all denominations have survived and are held in PRONI. Indeed, the records of over 60 Church of Ireland parishes date from the eighteenth century. The first Deputy Keeper, Dr D.A. Chart, who had been on the staff in Dublin, was well acquainted with the records which had been lost. Duplicates, copies and abstracts were assembled as substitutes for many of the destroyed documents, through application to other repositories, government departments, private collections, solicitors' offices and individuals who had worked with the originals. Appeals were also made to many of the landed families for estate records and family papers, with the result that PRONI is now the main source of genealogical records in Northern Ireland.

What distinguishes PRONI from other archival institutions in the British Isles is its unique combination of private and official records. It is at one and the same time, Public Record Office, Manuscripts Department of a National Library, and County Record Office for each of the six counties of Northern Ireland. From the records of central government to those of small local authorities; from archives of major linen companies to the records of street corner groceries, all are gathered together, preserved and made available in one building. Today we have almost 53 shelf kilometres of records, a wealth of historical and genealogical material relating largely, but not exclusively to Northern Ireland with records dating from the middle ages to the present day. We are essentially, however, a repository for modern records, with the greater volume of the material dating from the late eighteenth century to the present day. The range of records increases markedly in the nineteenth century with greater government involvement in the economy and society. The records of the Boards of Guardians (the workhouses) and those of the national schools are two such archives. More national school records survive (and are held in PRONI) than for the rest of Ireland.

Visiting PRONI Last year (1997/98) we had over 16,000 visitors, (many from overseas) 60% of whom came to trace their family tree. Admission to the office is free, no appointment is necessary. All you need to provide is proof of identity such as a driving licence.

New readers are greeted upon arrival by a member of the Search Room staff; who will guide them through the initial stages of their visit. Whilst our staff cannot carry out research, we understand that a first visit to a record office can be a daunting experience, and this orientation is appreciated by many. In addition to a series of family and local history leaflets (which are available on the PRONI website also) a touch screen interactive video is sited in the waiting area, providing information on all aspects of our service. If you are unsure of what material may be most useful for your search, a few minutes looking at the video may save those precious hours.

Group Visits We can arrange for visiting groups to receive an introduction to the office from an experienced member of Reader Services staff. Advance notice is required.

Publications A full list of PRONI publications is available on request and from the website. These may be ordered by post. Over the past number of years we have published a series of Guides to PRONI Sources on particular themes and geographical areas (e.g. *Church Records, Landed Estates, Education, Women's History, Guides to Co. Armagh, Fermanagh and Monaghan. A Guide to Sources for Co. Tyrone* is available for consultation in the Public Search Room. Other county guides are currently in production.

Making Copies of Records PRONI provides a comprehensive copying service to the public. Many of the records can be photocopied for private study, although suitability for copying is dependent on the age, condition and size of the document. You should note that the reproduction of documents, or quotations from any of them, in any publication, may be a violation of copyright. Requests for permission to publish must be made, in writing, to the Reader Services Section. A same-day service is available only for limited numbers of copies and with requests received before 11. 00. am. This is not available for maps as they are copied off-site.

New Facilities Computerised ordering of documents is now fully operational and the terminals in the search room should be used to order most documents except wills and land registry records, for which manual dockets must be used. Church microfilms and 1901 census records should also be ordered with manual dockets. Up to five orders for documents can be placed at one time.

Recently, PRONI opened a new self-service microfilm reading room which, in addition to church records, now includes the 1901 Census of Ireland for the six counties of N Northern Ireland. More spacious than our previous microfilm area, a greater number of readers can now use this already popular facility.

A reference library is now open to the public between 2-4 pm daily. This resource is particularly useful for local history researchers, with many works of 19th century local historians available for consultation.

Soon to be introduced is an updated version of the geographical index in touch screen format, giving references to documents for every parish and townland in Northern Ireland.

Opening hours   PRONI is open to the public on weekdays between 9.15 am and 4.45 pm. On Thursdays it is open until 8.45 pm. Documents may be ordered up to 4.15 pm, extended to 8.15 pm on Thursdays. The Office closes to the public each year for 2 weeks in late November/early December during which vital stocktaking operations are

carried out.
Refreshments A restaurant facility is open daily from 10 am - 3.45 pm.
How to find us By a Malone or Balmoral bus (Citybus Nos. 71 or 59) both of which leave from adjacent stops in Donegall Square East, Belfast. Alighting at Balmoral Avenue it is only a short walk to PRONI. Balmoral Station (Northern Ireland Railways) is also close at hand.
Car Parking Limited car parking facilities are available in car parks at the front of the building. Cars may also be

parked locally, although visitors are reminded that Balmoral Avenue is a I clearway before 9.30 am and after 4.30 pm.

Research PRONI regrets that it is unable to carry out research for private individuals. A list of commercial researchers active in this area is available on the PRONI website or from the Public Search Room.

National School Records in the Public Record Office of Northern Ireland
Heather Stanley

One of the most useful series of records held in PRONI are those of the National Schools. Founded by the Irish Chief Secretary, Edward George Stanley, Earl of Derby, the Irish System of National Education came into being in 1831. Originally non-denominational in concept, some 2,500 schools were built with the aid of the Commissioners of National Education and local trustees between 1832 and 1870. Records of over 1,500 such schools, for the north of Ireland, have survived and are available for consultation in PRONI. The majority of the records date from the last quarter of the 19th century to the 1920's, with the earliest registers dating from the mid 1850's.

It is important to note that the successors of the national schools, the public elementary schools which were set up by the newly established Government of Northern Ireland, retained their original registers which often cover both pre- and post-Partition periods. Therefore registers for schools established long before Partition (i.e. pre-1922) are available in PRONI.

The value of this material for the genealogist cannot be over-estimated. In many cases the school registers provide sufficient information - name and date of birth or age at entry of each pupil, occupation and address of parents, religion, details of attendance and academic progress - for the material to be regarded as surrogate census returns for the period 1861-91, no Irish census records having survived for this period. A copy of an entry in a school register has long been accepted in Northern Ireland as proof of date of birth for pension purposes. This is a firm testimony to the administrative accuracy of this material.

In some schools conscientious record keepers recorded details of the previous school attended. This may permit the researcher to trace the geographical origins of nomadic' families, useful during recognised periods of migration to urban areas. As Belfast was the most rapidly growing industrial city in the British Isles during the second half of the 19th century, many families would have moved to the city attracted by the availability of work. Details of a previous school in this case would give a clue to the rural origins of the family.

The main series of original national school registers are available at PRONI reference **SCH 1-1583.** However registers can be located elsewhere. Under the Poor Law Act of 1838, a system of workhouses was established. Many of these had schools attached which received aid from the National Education Board. In 1846 there were 99 such schools and PRONI holds some of the registers under the reference **BG.** Other national schools developed out of estate schools, good examples being those established by the Drapers' Company in Co. Londonderry and those under the patronage of the Antrim family in the Glenarm area in Co. Antrim.

In addition to the wealth of material contained in the

registers, Inspector's Observation Books (also referenced at SCH) have survived for many schools. Whilst these volumes do not give names of individual pupils they paint a colourful local picture of school life in the late 19th and early 20th centuries. Indeed some of the comments made by inspectors lend the lie to the stereotypical view held of education at this time, that of tidy children sitting in orderly rows, reciting arithmetic tables. Teachers appear to have suffered from similar problems of discipline as today, as one observation made by a District Inspector in November 1900 bears out:

Order should be more strictly observed. The pupils run about the room and leave their belongings in the desks. The School should be so organised that every pupil will be usefully employed throughout the day. Some were idle during portions of the time of my visit.

In October 1899 another bemoaned the fact that:
Only 10 pupils were present by 10 o'clock. Pupils were arriving at irregular intervals until 10:55

More earthy problems were raised by an Inspector in 1906:
The floor would be the better of a scrubbing. The pits of the out offices (lavatories) *want emptying and the seats should be kept dry -they were wet today. Some deodorising material should be used.*

Finally, an Inspector in 1897 came to a rather harsh conclusion:
Striking improvement has been effected in this School during the year and particular attention has been paid to style, order and explanation of subject matter. If the result is not successful the teacher is in no way to blame for the deficiency, which may be explained partly by irregular attendance and - to some extent - by abnormal dullness on the part of the pupils.

They certainly believed in plain speaking in some areas!

For those researchers interested in tracing a teacher at a particular school, rather than a pupil, the initial grant -aid application to the Commissioners of National Education (PRONI reference ED/I) may be a useful source of information, as grants were awarded for teacher's salaries. Subsequent applications were made for assistant teachers and work-mistresses. Registers of correspondence, between the schools and the Commissioners of Education (ED/6) should also be consulted. These records list all previous teachers as well as those currently in post. However, the researcher will need to have some knowledge of the geographical area in which his forebear may have taught, as a complete list of teachers is not available.

National School records have been a relatively untapped source of genealogical information. It is well worth taking note of this source, as information contained within school registers has enabled researchers to close gaps in their family history when other sources, such as church records, have failed to deliver.

AUSTRALIAN
Genealogical Resources

Books - Charts - Maps - Computing - Microfiche - Video & Audio

The largest range of Australian genealogical resources
Plus a wide selection from many other countries including the British Isles

BOOK CATALOGUE
- AUSTRALIA—genealogy, reference, exploration, convicts & early settlement, social & general history, ethnic history, religious history, local history, biography, diaries, journals.
- GENERAL—photography, handwriting, writing & publishing, oral history, computers & more.
- BRITAIN • IRELAND • SCOTLAND • WALES—genealogy, reference, history, etc.
- OTHER COUNTRIES—Europe, Canada, Germany, Jewish ancestry, Italy, NZ, US & more.
- HERALDRY • NAMES • BIOGRAPHY • JOURNALS • FAMILY HISTORIES (Australia & overseas)
- MARITIME HISTORY • MILITARY HISTORY—mainly Australian reference works.

STATIONERY CATALOGUE—charts, record systems, archival storage products.

MAP CATALOGUE—Australia, Britain, Ireland, Scotland & Wales, Germany & other countries
 —maps, atlases & gazetteers, old map reproductions, parish maps.

COMPUTER CATALOGUE
- GENEALOGY SOFTWARE for PC & MAC: •Brothers Keeper • Family Origins • Family Tree Maker • Generations • Legacy •The Master Genealogist •Relatively Yours • Reunion and others.
- OTHER RESOURCES & SOFTWARE: BDM indexes for most Australian states, other Australian, British & Irish records, multimedia historical reference titles, mapping and other records—other useful software.

Check our many microfiche & CD-ROM/disk resources for UK

MICROFICHE CATALOGUE—Australia, Britain, Ireland, Scotland, NZ, other countries—shipping, newspaper, cemetery, probate, naturalisation and other records & indexes, electoral rolls, directories (hundreds for British Isles), out of print histories and more.

VIDEO & AUDIO CATALOGUE—Australian history over the last 100 years.

For the most up to date and complete listing of products available visit our web site

Gould Books Online

our entire catalogue of 7500 titles online
latest additions ● regular specials ● classified ads

http://www.gould.com.au

OR ASK FOR OUR PRINTED CATALOGUE
A$5 posted (Payment by Visa & Mastercard)

GOULD BOOKS
Family & Local History Supplies

PO Box 126, Gumeracha, South Australia, 5233
Telephone: (08) 8389 1611   International +61 8 8389 1611
Fax: (08) 8389 1599   International +61 8 8389 1599
Email: gould@adelaide.on.net   Internet: http://www.gould.com.au

Family History Resources –
State Library of New South Wales, Australia
Kathi Spinks (Librarian, State Reference Library)
and
Mark Hildebrand (Dixson Librarian)

The State Library of New South Wales consists of two major research collections : the
State Reference Library and the Mitchell and Dixson Libraries which make up the Australian Research Collections.

Address:
State Library of New South Wales, Macquarie Street, Sydney 2000 Australia Phone: 61 2 9273 1414 Fax: 61 2 9 273 1255

Opening hours: The State Reference Library is open on weekdays between 9am and 9pm, weekends 11am to 5pm. The Mitchell Library is open on weekdays between 9am to 9pm and on Saturday between 11am to 5pm. It is closed on Sundays.

Services
The Family History Service in the State Reference Library is where people should begin their family history research in the State Library. It is staffed by librarians and holds a large collection of useful material, both Australian and International.

The Mitchell Library is based on the collection of David Scott Mitchell (1836-1907) Australia's first and greatest collector of Australian historical materials. The Dixson Library was the private collection of Sir William Dixson (1870-1952) Both collections are useful for fleshing out family history and include the largest collection of Australiana in the world as well as coins, manuscripts, medals, stamps and pictures.

Clients can place an information request via the State Library of New South Wale's web page at **http://www.slnsw.gov.au/request/yrreq.htm.** Should clients need more time-consuming research done for them then they should be advised to employ a researcher. The Library has developed a list of researchers available on our web site at **http://www.slnsw.gov.au/request/profres.htm**

Catalogues
Material in the pictures and manuscripts collections of the Mitchell Library and Dixson Library catalogued since 1992 is now available on the PICMAN database which is available on our web site at
http://www.slnsw.gov.au/picman/welcome.htm
The computer catalogue can be searched through the State Library's web site at
http://www.slnsw.gov.au/cat/welcome.htm

Major Australian resources:
Births, Deaths and Marriages
The Family History Service holds indexes to births, deaths and marriages for NSW and the other Australian states on CD ROM and on microfiche. These are indexes only, you need to write to the appropriate registry in each state to order the full certificate.

We hold pre 1856 church records for New South Wales on microfilm, which are part of the Archives Office Kit of New South Wales. Civil registration commenced in NSW in 1856 and before 1856 there are no official certificates, only church records or parish registers which cover baptisms, burials and marriages.

Electoral rolls
We hold NSW electoral rolls from 1859 to the present day. We hold some early electoral rolls for other Australian states and all electoral rolls for other states from 1990 onwards. Before 1990 names in electoral rolls are arranged by electorate and subdivision, so it is necessary to know the suburb where a person lived. From 1990 onwards names are listed in alphabetical order by state. To check for the electorate before 1900 the Family History Service has a card index for New South Wales divisions and for post 1900 electorates for the whole of Australia, you need to check the Commonwealth of Australia electoral redistribution maps.

Archives Office of NSW Genealogical Research Kit
In 1988 the Archives Office of New South Wales (now known as the State Records New South Wales) made available their most popular records - the Archives Office of NSW Genealogical Research Kit. This Kit includes passenger lists and indexes for New South Wales between 1826-1900, which include Victoria and Brisbane until 1851 and 1859 respectively before they became separate colonies and also convict indents, which list convicts who arrived on transports to New South Wales and Van Diemens Land (Tasmania) between 1788-1842. The State Library of New South Wales also holds passenger arrivals and indexes for other states.

Sands directories for New South Wales
The Library holds a number of postal directories, mainly for New South Wales, and some for other states, which list people alphabetically, and by street, suburb and by trade. The most popular postal directory is Sands directory for NSW, which we hold on microfiche from 1858-1932

Telephone directories
The Family History Service holds Sydney telephone directories between 1889 - 1985 and New South Wales country directories between 1915 - 1985 on microfiche. Later years for New South Wales are held in book form in the Mitchell Library. Incomplete series are held for other Australian states.

Newspapers
The State Library of New South Wales collects and keeps an extensive collection of local newspapers published in New South Wales. Various indexes to newspapers such as to the Sydney Gazette, 1803-1829 and the Australian, 1824-1842 are held.

Major international genealogical resources available include: International Genealogical Index (IGI): St. Catherine's House Index (England & Wales) : Tithe Applotment Books (Ireland)

The Irish Transportation Records on CD ROM was a bicentennial gift from the Government and people of Ireland to the Government and people of Australia. It contains an index to the names of over 20,000 men and women who were sentenced to transportation or death between 1788-1868. We have the full records on microfilm. These contain information such as name, age, place, date of trial, crime and may include the name of ship and sentence, and petitions of prisoners pleading for clemency.

Internet
Internet access is available in both the State Reference

THE
GENEALOGICAL SOCIETY
OF
VICTORIA INC.

AUSTRALIAN FAMILY HISTORY
RESEARCH PROFESSIONALS

Over 250 million names on fiche, CD-ROM, BDM indexes,

Parish, census and cemetery records; 18,000 books;

On-site consultants for helpful assistance

On Line Catalogue of Resources

Distributors and suppliers of

The Genealogical Services Directory

for Australasia

contact for details and /or bulk orders.

Located at
Ancestor House, 179 Queen Street, Melbourne, 3000, Australia

Tel: +61 3 9670 7033 Fax: +61 3 9670 4490
Email: GSV@alphalink.com.av
http://www.alphalink.com.au

Library and Mitchell Library. We have bookmarked some popular and useful sites.

Mitchell Library:
Maps
The Mitchell Library holds an extensive collection of Australian maps: sheet maps (including parish maps and subdivision plans), charts, series sheets, aerial photographs and atlases. The emphasis is on Australia but overseas maps are also included.

Manuscripts
The manuscripts collections of the Mitchell and Dixson Libraries include unpublished personal papers, diaries and journals eg. some describe the experiences of settlement in the colonies or voyages by ship, company records, records of organisations, family trees, family bibles, transcriptions of governors despatches. Some of these records are frequently used for family history such as the records of the Benevolent Society.

Pictures
The Mitchell and Dixson Libaries also hold very large collections of documentary pictures in all media such as oils, watercolour, prints, drawings and photographs. You can search under the name of a ship, residence, locality/place, person or topic.

The Australian Joint Copying Project (AJCP)
The AJCP is a very useful research tool and historical records relating to Australia, New Zealand and the Pacific held in the Public Record Office, London, and other British libraries and archives. The bulk of the records copied are from the Public Record Office, London and comprise the archives of the departments of central government (eg. Colonial Office, Home Office, War Office, Admiralty etc).

Other Resources:
Mitchell Library holds copies of convict trials in London's Central Criminal Court (the Old Bailey) between 1776-1870.

The Mitchell Library is recognised as one of the worlds largest repositories of information by, for and about Aboriginal people. A pathfinder is available called "Black routes through the library: a guide to aboriginal family and local history resources relating to NSW" which identify the main resources for aboriginal family history in one easy to read guide.

NSW Colonial secretary 1788 to 1825 Index to papers
Historical Records of Australia and the Havard Index to these
Church Registers on microfilm

New Zealand

Elizabeth Parkes

Grinz DipFH(Prof)
Member Aagra, Grinz &Apg

Specialist in New Zealand Genealogy and Family History

I will bring your personal heritage to life by searching for your Kiwi ancestors and other relatives in a wide variety of resources. Discover the truth or otherwise of family stories or legends. Discover what happened to your relatives who emigrated to New Zealand. Discover relatives you didn't
know you had.

Missing Persons

Estate beneficiaries, long-lost relatives and friends identified and traced throughout New Zealand. if required, I will make contact on your behalf

211 Vanguard St,
Nelson,
New Zealand 7001

tel/fax: +64 3 548 9243
email: eparkes@ts.co.nz
http://genealogyNZ.co.nz

I find people ~ dead or alive

NEW ZEALAND treasures await...

Elizabeth K. Parkes, GrinzDipFH(Prof.)

A former British colony, the south sea isles of New Zealand contain material of value not only to descendants of people who emigrated there, but of possible value to those not descended from immigrants too. This article attempts to describe just some of those records and the positioning of family happenings against historical events. The majority of my comments are largely about the European population in New Zealand rather than the indigenous Maori population.

It is arguable whether the settling of New Zealand by Europeans was done in an orderly fashion but it is indisputable that New Zealand contains rich, varied and accessible records. The great majority of European settlers to New Zealand went to better themselves. Land, work and freedom from rigid class systems were powerful enticement. It is tempting to believe that because a record is available for one end of the country it will be available for the other. This is not necessarily so and it is important that all comments in this article be viewed with that proviso in mind.

Records begin ... when the first missionaries began their work ... in 1814

Earliest Records

Records begin from when the first missionaries began their work in the Bay of Islands in 1814. The first settlers arrived in the 1830s and the type of record available widens. In addition to possible personal records kept by individuals, e.g. family bibles, diaries, journals, letters, newspaper cuttings and etc., passenger records come into play, as do baptisms, marriages and burials.

In 1848 births and deaths began to be officially recorded. Until 1842 New Zealand was under the New South Wales government and wills of New Zealanders may be found there. Coroners' Inquests are available from 1845 onwards up to fifty years ago.

Mobile Populations

The mistake if often made of thinking the population of the 19th century was static. Many family historians have discovered this is not so.

Even "problem" forebears can be investigated. A person might have left any point in Europe, Scandinavia or even Russia and travelled, for instance, to London, lived there for a while and departed for New Zealand leaving behind a wife and children to commence a new life. The records mentioned in this article not only have the potential to identify such a person but to provide additional information about them.

Where the fate of a seafaring relative is unknown, it could be that he ended his days in New Zealand. If the name and approximate year of a voyage of a British registered ship is known during the period searches can be made for the ship's papers. Depending on time period these papers include crew agreements in which seamen's ages and places of origin are likely to be shown. These are held at Public Record Office, Kew and Maritime Museum, Memorial University of Newfoundland, Canada. Records differ depending on time period and not all records survive.

The discovery of gold in 1856 what is now called Golden Bay saw the first rush of goldminers to New Zealand followed by greater goldrushes to other places soon after. This influx of mostly men was from Australia, Europe and California. The goldrushes are an historical event against

which to investigate the possible movements of otherwise unaccounted for relatives.

The same applies to the land wars which occurred in the 1860s and 1870s and involved British troops. Copies of their records are available in New Zealand but persons in Britain may best access them at the Public Record Office, Kew.

Immediately before and after the two world wars saw huge influxes of immigrants from Europe including Britain, to New Zealand. The Armed Forces files of New Zealand service personnel are available.

By and large, passenger lists from 1911 onwards are not indexed so these would not be the first record to attempt to access to prove a relative's presence in New Zealand after this time. Directories, electoral rolls, marriages and deaths are better options.

Births, Deaths and Marriages

Post-1875 births contain parents' ages, places of birth, date and place of marriage and the mother's maiden surname. The Adult Adoption Information Act 1985 permits only adoptees and their natural parents access to adoption records and pre-adoption birth registrations. Post-1875 deaths contain, among other things, parents' names including mother's maiden surname, when and where buried, place of birth and length of residence in New Zealand, place of marriage, age at marriage and spouse's name including females' maiden surnames, and sex and number of living issue. From 1880 onwards marriages contain, among other things, the parties' ages and places of birth, usual residence, present residence, parents' names including mothers' maiden surnames, and fathers' occupations. From 1857 notices of intention to marry will contain the name and relationship of the person providing permission for a minor to marry. Not available in the marriage document, this is an additional detail available only in Notices. And in the case of a pre 1880 marriage when parents' names are not in marriage registrations, this is particularly valuable and can provide that vital clue for identifying the family in their place of overseas origin.

Naturalisation

From 1843 'aliens' could apply for naturalisation. The contents of naturalisation papers varies but almost always provide place of origin and age or date of birth; sometimes their original name and their Anglicised name. Naturalisation papers are very useful for finding out about non-UK ancestors.

Land Records

The dream of owning their own land came true for many settlers. Land Information offices throughout New Zealand are the main repositories for land records. Strange as it may seem to Kiwis today, until the passing of the Land Transfer (Compulsory Registration of Titles) Act 1924 it was not compulsory for land documents to be registered. Nevertheless most were registered and are searchable. Hand-written copies or photocopies may be obtained depending on the format of the original documentation. Land documents help paint a fuller picture of forebears' lives. The changing values of land may be seen. A landowner's will registered over land in the form a Transmission may be the only surviving copy of that person's will.

Photographs
Nothing quite matches seeing one's ancestors' features for the first time. Enterprising settlers included photographers. As towns sprang up, so did photography businesses. A directory is available which describes and locates extant collections and indicates the subject of each collection and whether or not prints are available. The Nelson Provincial Museum, Nelson holds the largest collection of historic photographs in the southern hemisphere. Numbering 1.2 million mostly portrait negatives taken in Nelson city and environs, the collection dates from 1856 to circa 1980. Prints are obtainable.

Clearly, photograph collections are of interest to persons whose ancestors were in New Zealand but family historians living outside New Zealand whose g.g.grandparents emigrated together with some of their children should also be interested. A person living in the UK or elsewhere and descended from one of the children who did not emigrate, could have a photograph of their g.g.grandparents in New Zealand just waiting to be discovered. Photographs of businesses, street scenes, public events and panoramic views are also common and a family's environment as it was when they were alive, may be seen.

Probate Files
No restrictions exist to accessing probate files throughout New Zealand. Copies may be obtained not only of the will in a probate file but of the accompanying affidavits as well for no additional fee. Containing less information but nevertheless potentially useful, are letters of administration where a person died intestate.

Schools
One thing of importance to New Zealand settlers was the setting up of a free education system for all. Prior to 1852 education was largely left to the churches or to private enterprise. In 1852 the provincial governments took control.

School records of most use to family historians are admissions registers. While the extent of their details varies, the child's birthdate, parent's name and address, and the child's previous school (if any) and subsequent destination (another school, work, home or etc.) are usually recorded.

Electoral Rolls
Having one of the first women in the world to vote in your family is something to celebrate especially when considering that it is usually more difficult to find out about women than men. In 1893 New Zealand became the first country to grant universal suffrage to women. While many women entered their occupation as 'domestic duties' or similar, a surprising number gave occupations indicating their involvement in business. Electoral rolls are available from 1858 up to the present day.

Directories
Personal, business and postal directories abound. Many are all-New Zealand-inclusive and are therefore useful finding aids. The first directories were published in 1842. Personal and trade directories faded in the late 1950s with the proliferation of telephone directories.

Censuses
The greatest disappointment in New Zealand records is the lack of censuses as successive governments have failed to preserve census records. Yet a few censuses have survived! If you are lucky enough to have relatives in New Plymouth, Auckland or Nelson in the 1840s you may be able to find information about them not available elsewhere. Those three places all have censuses taken in 1845 but Nelson has a census taken in 1849 and this is by far the most valuable. It contains details of all persons in households (but the name of only the head of each household), births deaths and marriages that have occurred in each household, educational standard of each person, occupation of householder, family's religious denomination, country of origin, number of persons employed on site, structure of buildings, kinds and numbers of animals, types and acreage of crops, and sometimes comments about the state of the roads and bridges (usually the dire need of!) and the need or otherwise of schools.

Some censuses of portions of the Maori population have survived and these are especially valuable because, generally, there are fewer records for the Maori population than for the New Zealand European population.

Conclusion
A pot pourri of possibilities awaits anyone with New Zealand connections. Preserving its comparatively short European history is of vital importance to many New Zealanders and copying and indexing original records is ongoing. Few restrictions exist to accessing records and its possible to build full and colourful pictures of New Zealand ancestors and their historical environment.

Elizabeth Parkes
is a full-time qualified professional genealogist who searches for people's ancestry and for missing living people. She says her slogan "I find people ~ dead or alive" very neatly sums up what she does.

Reach over 60,000 North American Family Researchers through *Family Chronicle*

Family Chronicle is America's most popular genealogical magazine and is filled with articles from the world's best genealogy writers.

America's top genealogy software, book and CD publishers, genealogy services companies and genealogists advertise regularly in *Family Chronicle* to reach this affluent market. If you want to reach the huge North American genealogy market you can do so very affordably with *Family Chronicle.*

Prices of Small Ads (Payable in US Dollars)

40 word Classified	**$15**
Research Cards (2$^{1/4}$" x 1")	**$25**
Marketplace (2$^{1/4}$" x 3 $^{1/8}$")	**$55**
Rapid Research - Single Spot Colour (2$^{1/2}$" x 2")	**$75**
FC library - Full Colour (2$^{1/2}$" x 2$^{3/8}$")	**$100**

Call Victoria Pratt at (416) 491-3699 ext.114 for full details on small space advertising programs or Ron Wild at (416) 491-3699 ext.115 for details on large space (display) advertisements or fax (416) 419-3996, e-mail *ronwild@familychronicle.com* or write

Family Chronicle, PO Box 1201, Lewiston NY, 14092 USA

Visit us on the web at *www.familychronicle.com*

Interlink Bookshop
● GENEALOGICAL SERVICES ●

Interlink was founded in 1988
by **Sherry Irvine,**
the lecturer and author of
Your English Ancestry and *Your Scottish Ancestry*
and co-author of *Going to Ireland.*

We have a superb selection
of books and maps for English, Irish,
Scottish and Welsh research.

We're online at
www.pacificcoast.net/~ibgs

3840A Cadboro Bay Road, Victoria, B.C., Canada V8N 4G2

Phone (250) 477-2708   Fax (250) 658-3947

Credit card orders: Call 1 (800) 747-4877

Debrett Ancestry Research Limited
Meticulous, professional research in Britain, North
America and Austalasia. UK house histories also
undertaken. Free information pack available.
See Advert on Pages 46, 76, 90

Dept GSD, PO Box 7, New Alresford,
Hampshire. England SO24 9EN

Tel No: (0)1962-732676;   Fax No: (0)1962-734040
Email: enquiry@debrettancestry.demon.co.uk
Web site: www.debrettancestry.demon.co.uk

Joanne Harvey CGRS
AMERICAN CENSUS
for 1790 through 1850 and for 1900 & 1920 is
INDEXED!
Let me find your people.
Please send one international reply coupon with
initial enquiry to cover return postage
2420 Newport Drive
Lansing, Michigan, 48906 3541 USA

Ancestors of Dover Ltd
National and international research carried out by a
team of local expert record agents directed by
professional genealogists. See Advert on Page 60

The Chapel, Belgrave Road, Dover, Kent,
England CT17 9QYGSD

Tel No: 0800-1066-1066   Fax No: 01304-201102
Email: enquiries@ancestor.demon.co.uk
Web site: www.ancestors.co.uk

Currer Briggs Genealogical Index
Private index from multiple sources including wills,
court records, Port Books, some Dutch notarial
records 1550 -1700 and a large collection of Virginia
and New England records. See Advert on Page 14

3 High Street, Sutton-in-the-Isle, Ely,
Cambridgeshire, England. CB6 2RB
Tel No: 01353-777079   Fax No:01353-777079.

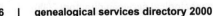

Using Local Directories in Western Canadian Research
Dave Obee

The 20th century witnessed a dramatic transformation in the four provinces that make up Western Canada. There was a tremendous migration to the area, from other parts of Canada as well as from the United States, Great Britain, and scores of other countries.

As a relatively young area, the printed sources of interest to genealogists are also quite young. And that poses a problem, considering the restrictions placed on the release of crucial documents such as census microfilms. The most recent Canadian census open to the public dates from 1901 - too early for many researchers working on the West. The area that is now home to about seven million people was covered in 1901 by a mere 15 microfilms. There are, however, alternative sources of information that may be used in the absence of census records. They are not as comprehensive as census returns - but they can still help plug gaps in a family history. One example is the voters' list. At the municipal level, these are available for many communities in British Columbia, Manitoba, Alberta and Saskatchewan. Lists from federal elections since 1935 are available from the National Archives in Ottawa.

Another example is the local directory. These were released more often than lists of voters, and often contained more detail. They are also readily available, for researchers who know where to look. The first directories in Western Canada were published in Victoria in 1860 - seven years before Canadian Confederation, and 11 years before British Columbia joined the new country. The first directories on the Prairies were published in Winnipeg 16 years after the Victoria ones. By the turn of the century, the West was seeing the first stages of its sharp increase in population - and local directories, by then commonplace, helped record this change.

The major companies publishing directories kept expanding in the first half of the 20th century, adding editions and serving more and more areas. It was a golden time for directories, before the big cities got too big to cover, before people moved so readily, and before the Internet took away much of the need for the publication. While women were rarely mentioned in the earliest directories, they were generally included in listings published in the middle of the 20th century. Directories on microfiche and microfilm may be found in the public libraries in most cities in Western Canada, as well as in university and college libraries and in provincial archives. In most cases, they may be ordered through inter-library loan. For directories on microfilm or microfiche, there are five basic sources:

•The Peel Collection, based on A Bibliography of the Prairie Provinces to 1953, by Bruce Braden Peel. Most of the printed matter listed by Peel has been gathered on microfiche by the National Library of Canada in Ottawa.
•The Canadian Institute for Historical Microreproductions (CIHM) collection includes thousands of microfiche, representing virtually everything published in Canada prior to 1900. This includes most of the local directories to 1900.
•The Vancouver City Archives has copied 50 directories on

50 rolls of 16-millimetre microfilm.
•The University of British Columbia in Vancouver has done the most extensive work with microfilming B.C. directories. It has produced a series on 35-millimetre microfilm.
•The Glenbow Archives, in Calgary, Alberta has filmed a variety of directories not found in other collections. They are on 35-millimetre microfilm. To make the most of research in directories, some basic rules apply:
•Determine the time period and location where the person is likely to be found. Then look in the directories for several different years.
•Watch for other people living at that address. Look for children at the home of their parents, then trace them after they move to their own homes if possible. It's possible to estimate birth years and marriage years, which in turn will speed searches in other records.
•Watch for the disappearance of a wife, which could indicate that she has died. If the name of the wife changes, it could be a clue that the wife has died and the husband has remarried.
•If a woman you're tracing is in the directory one year but gone the next, check the reverse section, where people are listed by street address, for the second year. Find out the surname of the people living at the house where she had been. It's possible she married and took her new husband's name, but stayed in the same house.
•If the name you're looking for is not of British origin, check for variations in spellings. It appears many of the people hired by the directory companies weren't familiar with German names, French names, or names from many other countries.
•In large cities, use a map to find the location of the residence, as well as nearby churches and schools. This will help you narrow your search for parish registers and school records.
•Use the house address to start a search for land records. You'll probably need the full legal description to get access to these records, but the address is the first place to start.
•Check the names of the neighbours, using the street portion of the directory. It's remarkable how often people lived close to their relatives or in-laws. You can also determine, based on occupations, the general social standing of the area.
•Remember that the years given on the directories may not be the actual year the information was collected. Bracket your searches - by checking the year before and the year after the one you would expect to find the person.
•Remember also that business people were almost always listed, but labourers rarely were included in the early directories.
•And always be aware that the people giving information were under no legal obligation to tell the truth.

Dave Obee is a partner in Interink Bookshop and Genealogical Services in Victoria, B.C. He has compiled three finding aids for genealogists, including Western Canadian Directories on Microfiche and Microfilm.

Interlink Genealogical Bookshop
http://www.pacificcoast.net/~ibgs
Western Canada's only genealogy store

The Regional Archives System of the National Archives
United States of America

You don't have to go to Washington, D.C., to visit the National Archives. The National Archives has regional archives in or near Boston, New York, Philadelphia, Atlanta, Chicago, Kansas City, Fort Worth, Denver, Los Angeles, San Francisco, Seattle, and Anchorage. They are national resources in local settings.

In 1969 the Archivist of the United States established a regional archives system to make regionally-created, historically valuable Federal records more accessible to the public. Each regional archives in the system has historical records from Federal courts and from regional offices of Federal agencies in the geographic areas each serves.

Records
Records preserved at regional archives (except Pittsfield) document Federal Government policies and programs at the local and regional level. They are kept because of their permanent historical, fiscal, and legal value, and their importance to the continuing work of the U.S. Government.

Record content varies from region to region. As a rule, each regional archives accessions records from field offices of Federal agencies located in the area it serves. Records unique to a single region include:
Government of American Samoa, 1899-1965, at the Pacific Sierra Region;
Tennessee Valley Authority, at the Southeast Region;
Alaska Railroad, 1894-1969, at the Alaska Region;
U.S. Commission for the U.S. Science Exhibit at the Seattle World's Fair,
1956-1963,at the Pacific Northwest Region.

Because certain Federal field activities are normally performed in all regions, many records accessioned by several regional archives arc similar. Records common to several regions are from the District Courts of the United States, the Bureau of Indian Affairs, Bureau of Customs, and Office of the Chief of Engineers.

Before using original records, every researcher must obtain a researcher identification card. An applicant must show identification that includes a photograph, such as a driver's licence, school or business identification, or passport, and complete a short form giving name, address, telephone number, and brief description of the proposed research topic. A researcher ID card, valid for two years and renewable, is then issued. It must be presented during each research visit.

Microfilm Publications
The regional archives have extensive holdings of National Archives microfilm publications, which reproduce with introductions and annotations some of the most frequently requested records in National Archives custody. They contain basic documentation for the study of pre-Federal and early Federal history, U.S. diplomacy, immigration, Indian affairs, the land and other natural resources, and war and military service. Of special interest are Federal population censuses for all states, 1790 to 1920.

Guides to Regional Holdings
Guides to regional archive' records and microfilm publications are available free of charge. Requests for these two separate publications should be addressed to individual regional archives. Titles Titles by region, for example, *Guide to Records in the National Archives - New England Region* or *Microfilm Publications in the National Archive- Great Lakes Region*.

Public Programs
Public programs supplement regional archives research and archival services. Each regional archives gives tours of its facility; presents workshops on archival research, genealogy, or related subjects; hosts exhibits; and plans other special programs to commemorate historical events. Such programs are often coordinated with colleges and universities, historical societies, genealogical groups, museums, and other archives.

Volunteers & Gift Fund
Each regional archives has a volunteer program and a gift fund. Volunteers have opportunities to learn about archives by assisting staff in various aspects of archival work. The gift fund permits purchases, not otherwise possible, of microfilm and reference materials which facilitate research.

Agency Services
The regional archives provide access to the historical records that an agency previously transferred to a regional archives, and assist agencies with historical programs, exhibits, and commemorations. In cooperation with other offices of the National Archives and Records Administration, the regional archives assist field offices of Federal agencies in identifying valuable historical records for transfer to NARA.

Hours
The regional archives are open for research weekdays, except Federal holidays, from 8.00. A.M. to 4.00 P.M. Contact individual regional archives for information on additional research hours.

The United States of America Library of Congress
Reference Services & Facilities of The Local History & Genealogy Reading Room

The Local History and Genealogy (LH&G) Reading Room is on the ground floor of the Thomas Jefferson Building, Room LJ G42 and is open 8:30 A.M. to 9:30 P.M.- Monday, Wednesday & Thursday; 8:30 A.M. to 5 P.M., Tuesday, Friday & Saturday. It is closed on all federal holidays.

Volumes from the Library's general collections may used in the Reading Room. In addition to these works, there are some 10,000 indexes, guides, and other reference works available in the Reading Room. Most special catalogues and indexes are arranged by family name.

The reference collection and catalogues are intended primarily to facilitate research in U.S. rather than foreign local history and genealogy. Research in foreign genealogy or local history should begin in the Thomas Jefferson Building, at the Computer Catalogue Centre and the Main Card Catalogue. Check appropriate subject headings, e.g., Germany-Genealogy; Heraldry-Poland; Registers of Births, etc, Dublin, to learn what material is available at the Library.

Reference staff are available to assist readers identify publications that relate to the subjects of their research, chiefly by explaining how to use the indexes and catalogues in the room. A Reader Registration Card is required to use the Library's reading rooms. Readers must present identification which includes a photograph and current address, such as a driver's licence, or passport. This card may be obtained at the Reader Registration Station, Room LJ 640.

The staff of the Library of Congress cannot undertake research in family history or heraldry. Some assistance may be obtained from the Board for Certification of Genealogists, P. O. Box 14291, Washington, DC 20044 (http://www .genealogy .org/-bcg/). Another source is the The Genealogical Helper, a periodical published bimonthly by the Everton Publishers, Inc. P.O. Box 368, Logan, Utah 84321, which generally carries as annual features a "Directory of Genealogical Societies, Libraries, Periodicals and Professionals" in the United States and abroad, and a "Directory of Genealogists" in the United States, including amateurs as well as professionals. Names of professional genealogists can also be obtained from the advertisements of their services carried in many genealogical periodicals. A convenient list of these periodicals appears in Ulrich's International Periodicals Directory, a standard reference work available in many libraries.

A complete transcript of the Family Name Index in the LH&G Reading Room, as of December 1971, was published in two volumes in 1972 by the Magna Carta Book Company. Entitled Genealogies in the Library of Congress, a Bibliography, and edited by Marion J. Kaminkow, it lists over 20,000 genealogies, including many in foreign languages. One volume supplements, issued in 1977 and 1987 list works added to the Library's collections from January; 1972 to June 1986. An additional supplement entitled Genealogies Catalogued by the Library of Congress since 1986 was issued by the Library in 1992. These works are available in many public libraries.

United States Local Histories in the Library of Congress, a Bibliography, also edited by Marion J. Kaminkow and published by the Magna Carta Book Company in 1975, lists in five volumes some 90,000 works, arranged according to the Library's classification for U.S. local history, which is primarily geographical (regional, subdivided by state and further subdivided by period, county, and city). Many of the works listed in the bibliography provide information on early settlers, the establishment of government, churches, schools, industry and trade, and biographical sketches of community leaders. This compendium also may be available in large libraries.

Inquiries for information on ship passenger lists and on census, land, naturalisation, and military service records should be directed to the National Archives, Washington, D.C. 20408 (http ://www.nara.gov/).

The Library does not permit its books on genealogy, heraldry, and U.S. local and state history to circulate on interlibrary loan. However, material in microform for which the Library holds the master negative is available for loan (or purchase). Since the Library has microfilmed most of its books relating to United States genealogy published from 1876-1900, a significant part of the genealogical collection is available for loan. Consult a local reference library about borrowing microfilmed material.

The Library; does not have copies of genealogies for sale. Dealers in books, including out-of-print materials, may be able to assist in securing copies of publications. It also may be possible to purchase photocopies of out of print items. Detailed suggestions are given in a circular entitled "Out-of-Print Materials and Reprinted Publications," available free from Library of Congress, National Reference Service, Washington, D.C. 20540-4720.

The Library's Photoduplication Service routinely supplies photocopies of items located in the Library collections if there are no copyright restrictions. The Library of Congress, Photoduplication Service, Washington, D.C. 2054-4570.

The Library of Congress provides many resources and services via the Internet, all are described or available from the Library's homepage at http ://lcweb.loc,gov. The Home page (http ://lcweb.loc.gov/rr/genealogy) provides general information about the reading room (hours; location; requirements for reader registration; information about tours; descriptions of the collections; details for presenting gift books to the Library; the full-text of the reading room's bibliographies and guides; and links to other Internet sources on local history and genealogy.) Both the Library's and the Local History and Genealogy Reading Room's homepages provide access to the Library's online catalogue. While the Library is beginning to offer some digital versions of books in the collections, no genealogies are included and only a few local histories have been digitised. To search for genealogies on the Library's online catalogue, use the search term "Family" after the name of the family, e.g. Hill Family.

ADOPTION

Brewster International
Adoption Related - Specialists in searching for birth parents and adopted children plus searches for missing friends and relatives.   See Advert on Page Inside Front Cover

12 Avery Gardens, Ilford, Essex, IG2 6UJ
Tel No: 0208-550-0333   Fax No:0208-550-7766
Email: 106422.164@compuserve.com
Web Site: http://www.missing-people-found.com

Victoria Walker
Family history research, adoption searches, access to parish registers, IGI, wills, monumental inscriptions, census returns, etc. Location photographs. See Advert on Page 84

11 Belper Lane, Belper, Derbyshire, DE56 2UG
Tel No: 01773-826025
Email: vaw@belper.jireh.co.uk

BRITISH INDIA ANCESTRY

See Also: *Sec. 2B   Research - London & National Archives*
The PRO holds records concerning British India matters and many of the Researchers listed in that Section undertake research into this subject

Link Line Ancestral Research
Research Service for all records in the PRO Kew and at all major London Repositories including research on the British in India.   See Advert on Page 72

16 Collingtree, Luton, Bedfordshire, LU2 8HN
Tel No: 01582-614280   Fax No:01582-614280
Email: iwaller@cableol.co.uk

Janice O'Brien, B.Ed.
Ancestors in British India? Your research undertaken by experienced researcher of the India Office Collections for reasonable fees.   See Advert on Page 74

11 Ravenscar, Bayham Street, London, NW1 0BS
Tel No: 0171-388-0452

John Dagger
Genealogical research by AGRA Member, especially for those with Army, Navy, Convict, and British India (civil, military) ancestors.   See Advert on Page 66

Oak House, Horsmonden, Tonbridge. Kent TN12 8LP
Tel No: 01892-722272   Fax No: 01892-722671
Email: j.dagger@btinternet.com

Paul Blake
Genealogical, historical and picture research undertaken by AGRA Member. Specialist in Royal Navy, Military, British India and London research. See Advert on Page 64

18 Rosevine Road, West Wimbledon, London, SW20 8RB
Tel No: 0181-946-6395   Fax No:0181-946-6395
Email: paulblakeexx@compuserve.com
Web Site:
ourworld.compuserve.com/homepages/paulblakexx/research

CLOTHING RESEARCH

CONVICTS & CRIMINALS

See Also: *Sec. 2B   Research - London & National Archives*
The PRO holds records concerning convicts and criminals and many of the Researchers listed in that Section undertake research into this subject.

Brian Walker
See under British India in adjacent column.

John Dagger
See under British India in adjacent column.

Link Line Ancestral Research
See under British India in adjacent column.

Murder Files
This firm has information on thousands of murders that have taken place in the UK from 1700 onwards and can assist enquiries relating to these matters. See Advert on Page 46

'Marienau', Brimley Road, Bovey Tracy, Devon, TQ13 9DH
Tel No: 01626-833487   Fax No:01626-835797
Email: ukmurders@bigfoot.com
Web Site: http://www.bigfoot.com/~ukmurders

EMIGRATION RELATED

CUSTOMS, EXCISE & POLICE

See Also: *Sec. 2B Research - London & National Archives*
The PRO holds records relating to Customs, Excise, the
Metropolitan Police and many of the Researchers listed in
that Section undertake research into these subjects.

Brian Walker
Research service for all records in the PRO Kew at Kew,
including Customs, Excise, Convicts, Metropolitan Police
and Irish Constabulary. See Advert on Page 76

78 St James's Avenue, Hampton Hill, Middlesex, TW12 1HN
Email: brianwalker1@compuserve.com

John Dagger
Genealogical research by AGRA Member, especially for
those with Army, Navy, Convict, and British India (civil,
military) ancestors. See Advert on Page 66

Oak House, Horsmonden, Tonbridge. Kent TN12 8LP
Tel No: 01892-722272 Fax No: 01892-722671
Email: j.dagger@btinternet.com

Peter F Gardner
For researching all subjects at the Public Record Office and
other London Archives including Coastguard and
Metropolitan Police. See Advert on Page 64

Malt Cottage, Petworth Rd, Witley, Godalming, GU8 5LZ
Tel No: 01428-685529 Fax No:01428-684450
Email: pfg@dial.pipex.com

MARINERS/SEAMEN/NAVAL

See Also: *Sec. 2B Research - London & National Archives*
The PRO holds records concerning Naval matters and many
of the Researchers listed in that Section also undertake
research into this subject.

Brian Walker
Research service for all records in the PRO Kew at Kew,
including Navy, Royal Marines, Coastguards, Merchant
Navy, Customs, Excise, etc. See Advert on Page 76

78 St James's Avenue, Hampton Hill, Middlesex, TW12 1HN
Email: brianwalker1@compuserve.com

MARINERS/SEAMEN/NAVAL (continued)

CARW
Family history research undertaken in county and national
archives. Welsh ancestry a speciality, also mariners and
railway employees. See Advert on Page 116

4 Rhodfa Anwyl, Rhuddlan, Denbighshire, LL18 2SQ,
Wales. Tel No: 01745-591372 Fax No:
Email: DThomas715@aol.com

Peter F Gardner
For researching all subjects at the Public Record Office
including Royal and Merchant Navy, Royal Marines,
Coastguard. See Advert on Page 64

Malt Cottage, Petworth Road, Witley, Godalming, GU8 5LZ
Tel No: 01428-685529 Fax No:01428-684450
Email: pfg@dial.pipex.com

Red Cat Research
Genealogical and associated research including naval (Royal
& Merchant) and London's many newspapers, map, picture
and local archives. See Advert on Page 74

25 Lakeside Road, London, W14 0DX
Tel No: 0171-603-0295; 020-7603-0295

MILITARY RELATED RESEARCH

See next Section which is wholly devoted to matters concerning Military Research and related subjects.

MURDER FILES

Murder Files
For assistance with research on thousands of murders in the UK from 1700 onwards. See Advert on Page 46

'Marienau', Brimley Road, Bovey Tracy, Devon, TQ13 9DH
Tel No: 01626-833487   Fax No:01626-835797
Email: ukmurders@bigfoot.com
Web Site: http://www.bigfoot.com/~ukmurders

NEWSPAPER LIBRARY ARCHIVES

Audrey Collins BA - Genealogist & Record Agent
Research in the Family Records Centre, PRO and other London Record Offices. Specialist in research at the Newspaper Library.

20 Illmington Road, Harrow, HA3 0NH
Tel: 0181-933-6208   Email: audrey@kenaud.dircon.co.uk
Web Site: http://www.kenaud.dircon.co.uk

Colin Dale Researches (GSD)
For research at the Colindale Newspaper Library for possible information about ancestors and other information in the newspapers at the Library. See Advert on Page 160

1 Furham Field, Pinner, Middlesex, HA5 4DX
Tel No: 0181-428-4577

Paul Blake
Genealogical, historical and picture research undertaken by AGRA Member. All London research including research at the Newspaper Library. See Advert on Page 64

18 Rosevine Road, West Wimbledon, London, SW20 8RB
Tel No: 0181-946-6395   Fax No:0181-946-6395
Email: paulblakeexx@compuserve.com
Web: ourworld.compuserve.com/homepages/paulblakexx/research

Red Cat Research
Genealogical and associated research especially at London's many newspapers, map, picture and local archives. See Advert on Page 74

25 Lakeside Road, London, W14 0DX
Tel No: 0171-603-0295; 020-7603-0295

Rosie Taylor
Research at the Family Records Centre, First Avenue House (wills), PRO Kew, and London's many archives, plus the National Newspaper Library. See Advert on Page 66

103A Pemberton Road, London, N4 1AY
Tel No: 0181-347-5107

The Name Shop
Suppliers of copy newspapers for specific dates from times gone by. See Advert on Page 18

Unit 28, Parade Shops, St Marys Pl., Shrewsbury SY1 1DL
Tel No: 01743-270220   Fax No: 01952-410689
Email: gary.huston@cableinet.co.uk
Web Site: http://www.family-name.co.uk/history

RAILWAYS & RAILWAY EMPLOYEES

CARW
Family history research undertaken in county and national archives. Welsh ancestry a speciality, also mariners and railway employees. See Advert on Page 116

4 Rhodfa Anwyl, Rhuddlan, Denbighshire, LL18 2SQ, Wales. Tel No: 01745-591372   Fax No:
Email: DThomas715@aol.com

Link Line Ancestral Research
Research Service for all records in the PRO Kew and at all major London Repositories including research in Railway Records. See Advert on Page 72

16 Collingtree, Luton, Bedfordshire, LU2 8HN
Tel No: 01582-614280   Fax No:01582-614280
Email: iwaller@cableol.co.uk

SPECIALIST RECORDS & INDEXES (Research)

Currer Briggs Genealogical Index
Private index from multiple sources including wills, court records, Port Books, some Dutch notarial records 1550 -1700 and a large collection of Virginia and New England records. See Advert on Page 14

3 High Street, Sutton-in-the-Isle, Ely, Cambs. CB6 2RB
Tel No: 01353-777079   Fax No:01353-777079

I.G.I. - Printouts & Rootseeker Index
Family Tree Services
Printouts from the IGI & Rootseeker Index searches. Free booklet detailing all services. See Advert on Page 20, 52

30 Eastfield Road, Peterborough, Cambridgeshire, PE1 4AN
Tel No: 01733-890458   Fax No:01733-890458

Lost Ancestors? - Try Monumental Inscriptions
We have thousands of names from monumental inscriptions in many counties, small fees for searching our indexes for entries. See Advert on Page 44

65 Sarratt Avenue, Hemel Hempstead, Herts. HP2 7JF
Email: Patrick.Gainstratton@btinternet.com.

Gendocs - Victorian London Research Aids
Material relating to London Churches, Pubs, Inns & Taverns, London street Index, Police Divisions, Lodging Houses, and more. See Advert on Page 74

19 Mortar Pit Road, Northampton, NN3 5BL
Tel No: 01604-413025   Fax No:01604-784281
Email: john@j-e-infotech.freeserve.co.uk
Web Site: http://www.gendocs.demon.co.uk

Gone for a Soldier

re-tracing THEIR steps

CARTE POSTALE

Correspondance

Expertly Guided Tours to the Western Front from only £165*
Battlefield & History Tours - Worldwide

For your copy of our 2000 Brochure
FREEPHONE 0800 731 1914

* Special visits to War Graves are possible on most of our longer tours.

Holts Tours Limited
Golden Key Building. 15 Market Street, Sandwich, Kent CT13 9DA
Telephone: +44 (0) 1304 612248 Facsimile: +44 (0) 1304 614930
E-mail: info@holts.co.uk Internet: battletours.co.uk

See Also: Sec. 2B Research - London & National Archives The PRO holds records concerning military related archives and many of the Researchers listed in that Section are able to undertake research into this subject.

Brian Walker
Research service for all records in the PRO Kew, including Army, Navy, RAF, Royal Marines. See Advert on Page 76

78 St James's Avenue, Hampton Hill, Middlesex, TW12 1HN
Email: brianwalker1@compuserve.com

John Dagger
Genealogical research by AGRA Member, especially for Army, Navy, etc, ancestors. See Advert on Page 66

Oak House, Horsmonden, Tonbridge. Kent TN12 8LP
Tel No: 01892-722272   Fax No: 01892-722671
Email: j.dagger@btinternet.com

Link Line Ancestral Research
Research Service in all major London Repositories for all records including Military, etc See Advert on Page 72

16 Collingtree, Luton, Bedfordshire, LU2 8HN
Tel No: 01582-614280   Fax No:01582-614280
Email: iwaller@cableol.co.uk

Peter F Gardner
For researching all subjects at the PRO and including Army, Navy, and Coastguard. See Advert on Page 64

Malt Cottage, Petworth Road, Witley, Godalming, GU8 5LZ
Tel No: 01428-685529   Fax No:01428-684450
Email: pfg@dial.pipex.com

Red Cat Research
Genealogical and associated research including military, naval, Air Force records. See Advert on Page 74

25 Lakeside Road, London, W14 0DX
Tel No: 0171-603-0295; 020-7603-0295

War Research Society
Soldiers died searches by our own research team. Graves and memorials photographed. See Advert on Page 166

27 Courtway Avenue, Maypole, Birmingham, B14 4PP
Tel No: 0121-430-5348   Fax No:0121-436-7401
Email: battletour@aol.com
Web Site: http://www.battlefieldtours.co.uk

Paul Blake
Research by specialist in Royal Navy, Military, British India and London research. See Advert on Page 64

18 Rosevine Road, West Wimbledon, London, SW20 8RB
Tel No: 0181-946-6395   Fax No:0181-946-6395
Email: paulblakeexx@compuserve.com
Web: ourworld.compuserve.com/homepages/paulblakexx/research

Sunset Militaria
All Military Research undertaken and also holder of Sunset Military Index covering service personnel and civilian medal winners of all periods. See Advert on Page 176

Dinedor Cross, Herefordshire, HR2 6PF
Tel No: 01432-870420   Fax No:01432-870309
Email: sunsetmilitaria@btinternet.com

Family History
at
The Department of Printed Books
Imperial War Museum

The Imperial War Museum was formed in 1917 to record the part played by the British and Imperial forces in the First World War. It was officially opened by King George V at Crystal Palace in 1920, but moved to its present home at Lambeth Road in South London, the former Bethlem Mental Hospital ñ or Bedlam ñ in 1936. When the second major war of the century began in 1939 the Museum's remit was extended to include this. It was later extended again to include all post-1945 conflict. Today, it is actively seeking materials illustrating the actions in Bosnia and Kosovo.

The Museum has also grown in size and now has several outstations; Duxford, a former Royal Air Force station near Cambridge; HMS Belfast, a Second World War cruiser anchored opposite Tower Bridge on the Thames; Churchill's Cabinet War Rooms beneath Whitehall; and the projected Imperial War Museum North, a progressively-designed gallery scheduled to open in the Manchester area in 2002. None of these outstations has reference facilities open to the public, but each has a unique insight and experience to offer the interested visitor. The main Museum building in London however, remains the focal point for archival access and can be a real treasure trove for the family historian.

From the beginning, the Museum has not just been interested in the fighting man at the front, either on land, sea or air. In an age of total war Britain has seen involvement at all levels. From the Museum's earliest days a Women's Work Subcommittee was established to record the experiences of women in the First World War - whether in the services, working in a medical capacity or in munitions factories, driving ambulances and buses, or pounding the beat in the police force. Rationing and air raids, conscription and conscientious objection, evacuation and internment, are all well covered at the Imperial War Museum. A visit to the Trench or Blitz Experiences can be educational in its own right, but it can also be enlarged upon by a look behind the scenes.

There are seven different reference departments - Art, Documents, Exhibits and Firearms, Film and Video, Photographs, Printed Books and Sound - within the Museum. Of these, the Department of Printed Books (the reference library) is the most usual starting point for those pursuing their family history. Well over 100,000 books together with many periodicals, maps and ephemeral collections are maintained here. It is important to note, however, that individual service records and official documentation collated by the War Office, Admiralty and Air Ministry are not held by the Imperial War Museum. The family historian will need to be in possession of some basic facts before they can take advantage of our collections. If details of service are unknown then this information needs to be obtained from elsewhere - usually the Public Record Office or the Ministry of Defence. The Department of Printed Books does, however, hold a large collection of printed and published materials, which can help flesh out the bare facts surrounding an individual's career. Once details of the relevant battalion, ship or squadron are known we can advise on available published sources. For those genealogists at the beginning of their enquiries, we are happy to provide more detailed guidance on the probable availability and location of official documentation. We have recently produced four guides for the layperson with no detailed knowledge of the Royal Navy, the Army, the Royal Air Force, and the Merchant Marine. (These can be purchased direct from the Museum, although at the time of going to press final publication details and price had yet to be determined.)

To put the Museum's collections in context, visitors should be aware that we only cover the period from 1914 onwards. For information on British units and campaigns before this date it would be more appropriate to visit the National Army Museum in Chelsea, the National Maritime Museum at Greenwich, or the Royal Naval Museum at Portsmouth. Details of pre-1914 military service are held at the Public Record Office, Kew.

Sadly, it is usually the case that if an individual died in service then you are likely to find out more about him than if he survived. If the serviceman died but details of his unit are unknown, the best initial source is generally the Commonwealth War Graves Commission at Maidenhead (see the entry elsewhere in this Directory). The Commission has created a database, entitled Debt of Honour, from the huge collection of original ledgers covering fatalities in both world wars ñ including civilian deaths in the Second World War ñ and this can now be accessed directly from their website or via the link from our own website. This database makes the search by name easier than it has ever been. A CD-ROM version of this is likely to be available sometime in 2000, and a copy will be located in the Department of Printed Books reading room. In the meantime, there is an interactive version of the database commemorating the dead of the First World War available for personal visitors in one of the Museum's exhibition galleries. A set of grave and memorial registers for both wars published by the Commission is available for consultation in the reading room. The registers are divided up by cemetery or memorial and contain useful information about the cemeteries, including a map. They may also provide further clues, for example, details of medical facilities in the locality, which may relate to relatives who died of wounds or disease. These registers are often studied by those seeking to record all the men from one particular unit who died, or by people who are trying to research the names on a war memorial.

Another digitised source that has made searching for Army unit information much simpler is the CD-ROM version of Soldiers Died in the Great War, 1914-19. The original eighty-volume work was published by HMSO in 1920, and reprinted in association with the Imperial War Museum in 1989. However, being arranged by regiment and then alphabetically within each battalion, it was essential to know the individual's regiment before full use could be made of the publication. The information supplied is quite brief but helpful in confirming details of the individual's unit and date of death. The entry includes the regimental number and rank, place of birth, place of enlistment, rough cause of death (such as killed in action, died of wounds or died of natural causes) and theatre of death. If the soldier was awarded any gallantry medals these will also be indicated as will a former regiment and regimental number. There is also a companion volume called Officers Died in the Great War, 1914-19, although this is even less detailed. Copies of both the original volumes and the commercially published CD-ROM are available for consultation in the public reading room. A more recently published reference work by S D and J B Jarvis, the multi-volume Cross of Sacrifice, is also readily accessible to our readers. These are very useful as they provide brief details of death

combined with a reference to the Commonwealth War Graves Commission register so that details can be cross-referred. The different volumes cover Army officers as well as members of the Royal Air Force, Royal Navy and Merchant Navy.

One potentially useful unpublished source held by Printed Books is a copy of the War Office roll of honour for members of the British Army, listed by regiment, who died during the Second World War. The Public Record Office also has a copy. A multi-volume published version of this is currently being commercially produced by Promenade Publications.

Many individual rolls of honour were produced after both world wars, and these can be extremely useful to the family historian. Printed Books has an extensive collection covering schools, colleges, professional bodies, churches, companies, societies and other organisations. There are more of these for the First World War than the Second, but it is always worth checking. Local histories of towns and villages often include personal details. Interest in local war memorials has been partially stimulated by the work of the National Inventory of War Memorials, which is based at the Museum. [It should be noted that the NIWM does not record individual names inscribed on the memorial on their database, but much information is noted in supplementary files.] We are always grateful to be notified about any new publications arising from this growth in local interest, or to be put in contact with local history enthusiasts who may have knowledge of war memorials that have been moved or destroyed.

For the relative tracing events surrounding a death on active service, one of the most useful general sources is the British official history. In fact, the Department of Printed Books has reprinted all the First World War volumes, covering war on land, sea and air, and a selection from the Second World War (particularly events on land in Europe), in an attempt to make this valuable resource more widely available. The First World War official histories contain particularly useful sketch maps, which can then be supplemented by more detailed trench maps. Generally, if the date of death or service details are known, it is possible to build a very detailed picture of how and where the serviceman died ñ sometimes to the very trench - from the available published unit histories for individual divisions, regiments, ships and squadrons.

Basic information on officers can usually be supplied by the Army, Navy and Air Force Lists. The Department also has a good collection of material relating to the Commonwealth. For example, there is a complete run of the Indian Army List from 1914 to 1947, we have published nominal rolls for most of the original Canadian Expeditionary Force units of the First World War, and also a microfiche nominal roll of First World War members of the Australian Imperial Force. In addition to complete sets of all the official history volumes produced by the different nationalities, there are large numbers of unit histories relating to both our Allies and our opponents, including an excellent collection of First World War German regimental histories, and an extensive number of titles on the American Forces.

Another strength of the Department of Printed Books' collection, is the quantity and quality of the large numbers of service and prisoner of war periodicals among its holdings. Regimental journals can be very informative, giving a valuable taste of service life - especially in the inter-war and post-war years. Coverage may include sports days, births, marriages, deaths, staff movements, exercises and trooping abroad. Old Comrades Associations also produce newsletters and magazines although, sadly, these are dwindling. Traditionally, these have been a good way of establishing contacts with possible informants or of tapping very specific expertise.

These publications are complemented by material held in some of the other collecting archives. The Department of Printed Books shares a reading room facility with the Department of Documents making it is easy to consult both department's holdings on the same day. The latter's unique collection of unpublished diaries, letters, and memoirs is essentially of a personal nature and may contain unexpected references unavailable elsewhere. There are a number of items such as Changi Internment Camp Register and the Milag Nord Register (a Second World War prison camp for captured merchant seamen in Germany) which list the names and provide additional details. If you are able to locate a collection written by an individual who served in the same unit as your relative, this can prove extremely helpful for background information. This may also be true of the personal accounts recorded by our Sound Archive and the contemporary miles of film stored by the Film and Video Archive. At the very least they will provide a more human personal context to your research.

The Photograph Archive may be able to produce an official unit photograph from their collection of six million prints. However, the Archive does not contain pictures of every single serviceman, and it is probably very unlikely that you will be able to positively identify your relative (although many individuals have been 'definitively' identified and claimed - sometimes by several different families). Portraits of named individuals tend to be those of higher rank or those who have won the highest awards for gallantry. Even so, these pictures do form a visual record which may prove useful, and to find a picture of a ship in which a relative served, or a hospital where they worked, can be very rewarding. [Please note that neither staff in the Photograph Archive nor in Printed Books are able to identify photographs sent in by researchers. We do have a large collection of reference books on badges, uniforms, buttons and medals and we are happy to recommend titles that may be of assistance.] This summary of our collection and its fellow departments will, we hope, encourage you to make an appointment to use them. The military side has, necessarily, been stressed. However, we are also proud of the social, economic and political content of the library, and of our coverage of other conflicts that the public may not expect, from the Spanish Civil War to unrest in Algeria, Chad and Indonesia. We have probably the largest public collection of war literature and poetry in the United Kingdom, and a fine and unusual collection of ephemeral items. All this material is available for public consultation by prior appointment.

Department of Printed Books Imperial War Museum, Lambeth Road, London SE1 6HZ
Tel: 020 74165342 (general enquiries) Fax: 020 74165246
Email: books@iwm.org.uk
Museum website: http//:www.iwm.org.uk
Opening hours: Monday to Saturday, from 10am-5pm (appointment necessary)
Nearest underground station: Lambeth North (Bakerloo) or Elephant and Castle (Bakerloo and Northern Lines) Nearest main-line station: Waterloo
Catalogue of Printed Books reprint publications available upon request.
For further details of the four booklets on tracing servicemen's careers please telephone us on 020 74165346

Soldiers Died in the Great War 1914-1919

Now published on CD-ROM

There can hardly have been a family in Britain which was not touched in some way by the tragedy of the First World War, the "Great War for Civilisation". Great Britain, alone among the major European nations, went to war in 1914 with an army based on voluntary enlistment, numbering just over 247,000 at the outset with 486,000 Reserves and Territorials. By November 1918 almost a further 5,000,000 had enlisted, over half of them volunteers. For the first time since Napoleon, Britain had become a nation in arms and, in January 1916, for the first time in the country's history, conscription was introduced. The war developed into one of attrition as the allies strove to break through the formidable enemy defences, and by the end casualties on both sides were on a scale hitherto unparalleled.

In 1921 81 volumes embracing every regiment and corps of the British Army were published listing approximately 635,000 Soldiers and 37,000 Officers who died in the war, and it is this immense undertaking which is now published by The Naval & Military Press on one fully-relational database **CD-ROM**.

Ordering Details:

Order Number
CD1

**Price:
£220·00**
US$330·00

VAT, where applicable,
(UK and EC member
states) £38·50

plus p&p £2.50/$4.00

Soldiers Died in the Great War

Search Criteria

SORT	Surname : LUKE
Browse View	Rank : Private(s)
Print Results	

New Search
Officers Died
HOME PAGE

Sort Order : Surname, Christian Name(s)

Regiment or Corps	King's (Liverpool Regiment)	
Battalion/etc.	19th Battalion.	
Surname	LUKE	
Christian Name(s)	Alexander Frederick	Initials A F
Born	Dunoon, Argyll	
Enlisted	Glasgow	
Residence	Dunoon	
Died Date	22/03/18	Rank PRIVATE
Died How	Killed in action	
Theatre of War	France & Flanders	Number 57428
Supplementary Notes	FORMERLY 1136, LOWLAND DIVISIONAL CYCLIST COMPANY.	

First Record | Previous | 3 of 51 | Next | Last Record

Screen from Soldiers Died CD-ROM showing a typical search result

---

Published by The Naval & Military Press
Tel: 01435 830111   Fax: 01435 830623
Order Dept, PO Box 61, Dallington, Heathfield, East Sussex TN21 9ZS

Website: http://www.great-war-casualties.com   email: order.dept@naval-military-press.co.uk

Soldiers Died in the Great War. Perhaps one was a relative!

How to get even more from your CD-ROM. This CD is for searching. And not just for names.
Geoff Bridger

Several decades ago I started researching civil and military genealogy, my father sparking my penchant for the Great War. I soon learnt that no lists of names ever compiled are 100% accurate or complete. The International Genealogical Index [IGI] is notorious for its mistakes. The census returns are incomplete. The Family Record Centre's birth, death and marriage records have errors and omissions. There are names in *Soldiers Died...* that are not in the Commonwealth War Graves Commission (CWGC) records and, of course, the reverse applies. The Medal Index Cards [MIC] at the Public Record Office have limitations. However each of these sources is invaluable as an aid to locating a more definitive solution. In short, if you want to be efficient at research, verify your sources against, where possible, original documents. So it is with *Soldiers Died....*

The CD-ROM is a word for word copy of the original 1921 War Office edition. The clerks who prepared its 81 volumes were overworked, tired, poorly paid and probably bored silly by the time they had transcribed over 703,000 tatty hand-written index cards. They were human. They made mistakes. Nevertheless whatever the errors the result was, and still is, an indispensable tool for every military researcher. The information is not duplicated by the CWGC. Their records contain very different details and are equally fallible. Let us however examine *Soldiers Died....*

As well as being involved in the production of *Soldiers Died in the Great War* (and *Officers Died...*) onto CD-ROM I am probably one of its heaviest users. For years I searched the printed edition looking for elusive casualties. It was easy to find a man if you knew the name under which he served and also had a good idea of his unit. If the regiment was known it was fairly quick to check its thirty or so battalions. That assumes the ready availability of the appropriate hard copy of *Soldiers Died...* or, as in my case, a set on microfilm. The drawback there, of course, was threading the correct film each time you wanted to use it and then squinting at the ever degrading image that flickered back from my ancient viewer. Times, they are a-changing - and fast.

"What can I achieve by using *Soldiers Died...* on CD-ROM that cannot be achieved by using the printed version?" Please read this article and judge for yourself.
"But surely it is not too difficult to look up a name or two in the books." *It is, and those 81 books cost a fortune and also occupy two yards of shelf space.*   .
"Are not genealogists and military researchers patient folk - do I need it?" *Yes, they are, but to expand your research you certainly do need it.*
"It must need an expensive computer and lots of training." *Any basic 'off the shelf' computer with a CD ROM drive will run the CD.* I am no computer buff. Basically I hate computers and much prefer books but this product is so easy to use. No instruction books are required - just the ability to type with one finger and lots of imagination as to what you are going to ask of it. Let us examine some examples of what can be achieved.

If you are British then you probably had ancestors who fought in the First World War. Most joined the army, and tragically, about one in five who fought did not return. Did a member of your family die for his country? Before departing for war, and whilst their uniform was still pristine, most soldiers had their picture taken to send to family and sweethearts. Perhaps there is one in your album but you are

unsure of his identity. Very often there are hidden clues that can be interpreted and a name discovered. The photographs doubled as postcards and often contained simple messages although rarely signed with a full name. An abbreviated Christian name is more usual. Do not despair however. The cards have common features. The photography was invariably excellent and consequently the cap badge identifiable. It was probably taken locally soon after he enlisted and donned his uniform. Most cards advertise the photographer's name and address. He will have had brisk business from local recruits. In most cases you will now have at least a regiment, Christian name and town. Try *Soldiers Died...* using 'Regiment', 'Christian Names' and 'Enlisted' and if, as was so often the tragic case, the young man was killed, you will be hopefully have a clue to his identity.

Seeking a name or two is usually easy but it is most time consuming to abstract all of one name from the books. You would have to check each volume (remember there are 81 of them) maybe thirty or so times just to collate one family name. And it is so easy to miss one. With the CD-ROM just type in the chosen name and a complete list appears very quickly. A great boon for one name studies folk. One can sometimes locate that lost relation for the first time! It is simple to attribute unusually named Memorial plaques. The results of a chosen search can be displayed in many orders ranging from alphabetical, to date of death, regimental, place born, home town, serial number, etc

Soon however the real beauty of the application becomes apparent. Its versatility is almost limitless and is only circumscribed by the user's imagination and aptitude. If you are unsure of the correct spelling of the name, or want variations of it, then by entering a 'wild-card' symbol you can get even incomplete names to be revealed. Not sure if the man is Bridger or Bridges. By entering Bridge? both are listed. Want more variations of Bridger - then enter Bridge* and get Bridge, Bridgeford, Bridgehouse, Bridgeland, Bridgeman, Bridgemert, Bridgen as well as Bridger and Bridges. All sorts of tricks can be played with combinations of 'wild-cards' which can be used in front of or even in the middle of a name.

Six years ago I wrote the book *Valiant Hearts Of Ringmer* which chronicles the lives and deaths of those on the Ringmer War Memorial. It was probably the first of its type to add an illustrated biography to the stark names that appear on a war memorial. It was well received and I regularly give talks nationally on the techniques of the extensive research used to compile it. How I wish I could have had a computerised version of *Soldiers Died...* when I first started. I still shudder at the memory of going through countless battalions on microfilm looking for those elusive names. And what about the names missed off the memorial? Who were they? Today it is so much easier. By entering the chosen town or village in the fields 'born' 'enlisted' or 'residence', lists of people from that place appear almost immediately. For example if you want to know which dead soldiers had been born in York - just ask. Very soon they will be listed in whatever order you chose. It is then simple to compare that list, which can be printed, with the war memorial. Similarly the process can be repeated for enlistment or home. Whilst *Soldiers Died...* will not find every casualty, it does not include sailors for example, it will certainly greatly aid research into those brave men and women commemorated on the local war memorial.

Field Service Post Cards only permitted the sender to delete unwanted stock phrases and then add a signature and date. If anything else was written the card was normally destroyed. One example which escaped censorship includes the serial number 43461. It does not show a unit. The signature is 'B. Burrows'. *Soldiers Died...* lists two possible 'B Burrows' and both called Benjamin. But only one has the serial number G/43461. We are now fairly confident that it was Private Benjamin Burrows 1/Middlesex Regiment, sadly killed in action on 23/10/1918, who signed that field postcard two years earlier.

Ever had a photograph of a war memorial with no indication of its location? I have. The photography is of such a high standard that the names of the fallen are clearly visible with a magnifying glass. For years it sat in the 'unknown' category until I spent a few minutes checking those names to ascertain a common place of birth, enlistment or residence. I started with unusual names and often had only very few hits. Sometimes none - that man could have been in the navy! It did not take long however before the same town kept coming up. After further tests to eliminate coincidence I telephoned a friend who lived locally and he soon confirmed my theory. I now know my war memorial postcard comes from Pendleton, Lancs.

Another postcard has apparently even less to go on. The printed title reads, 'Cooden Camp, Bexhill-on-Sea.' The picture shows a tented army camp with men in civilian clothes standing in line. It is just signed, 'your loving boy H'. The message is however headed '362 C. Company Cooden'. Cooden is in Sussex and, from local papers we learn that the Southdown Battalions of the Royal Sussex Regiment trained there from September 1914 to July 1915. All their serial numbers, at that time, were prefixed with 'SD'. A search was made of *Soldiers Died...* in which the initial 'H' was entered together with serial number 'SD/362'. The only hit obtained (with and without the prefix) was for Harold Sloman, 11/Royal Sussex Regiment who died of wounds on 27/7/1916. From other previously unattributable personal details on the card it is now obvious that the writer has been correctly identified. The serial numbers of soldiers during the First World War were rarely unique. Each Regiment used a consecutive numbering system and so there were many duplications although the addition of several different prefixes reduced this somewhat. We cannot therefore be 100% certain that a particular serial number referred to one individual without corroborating evidence. It would have been wrong to assume that '362 C. Company' was indeed Harold Sloman without the other signs.

I have a photograph which depicts a battlefield burial in a flooded shell crater. One of the wooden crosses has barely readable writing on it. With a good magnifying glass I could just make out the rank (Spr), parts of a serial number, the odd letter from the name, and, on the next line which was a little clearer, '475 F-- Coy RE'. The words killed in action were visible but the date was blurred. I chose Royal Engineers in the Regiment field and then entered '475' in 'Supplementary Notes'. If those numbers are anywhere in that field its automatic wild-card will find them. Royal Engineer Companies are shown in 'Supplementary Notes' which also often includes previous service and other useful information. Lastly I entered as much of the serial number as was discernible and placed the wild-card '?' where digits were unreadable. The search took a few minutes and came up with only one candidate, Sapper 496113 A E. Callaway 475 Field Company Royal Engineers who was killed in action on 16/8/1917. His body was evidently recovered from his original watery grave and re-interred in New Irish Farm Cemetery, St Jean-les-Ypres, Belgium.

The Colonel of Duke of Lancaster's Own Yeomanry gave endorsed handkerchiefs as Christmas presents in 1914. One is inscribed 'J P Biddle 3619' He did not appear in the Cavalry volume of *Soldiers Died* when I searched it long ago and I assumed he had survived the war. With the CD it is so easy to type in the name and check every one that appears. The list included Private 46463 James Pearson Biddle who had died of his wounds with 11th Battalion Manchester Regiment on 29/9/1918. Why am I so sure it is the right man? Well, the Supplementary Notes field tells us that he was, 'formerly 3619, D.L.O Yeomanry'. Case proved.

Many years ago I purchased a piece of trench art from an elderly man who said it came from the family in Brighton. It is in the form of a peaked cap made from a shell case. It is dedicated to 'Bert' who was killed in action 22nd August 1918 and includes 'The Queens' badge. Bert was a very common name and a shortened form of, among others, Albert, Hubert, Herbert, Bertram and of course just plain Bert. Not an easy task to trace this item! There were however only a few possibilities when a combination of the date, regiment and killed in action, (as opposed to other means of dying), were added into the selection criteria. The search narrowed it down to five choices and in the end I attributed it to Herbert Sach 1/24th London Battalion The Queen's Royal West Surrey Regiment, who was born in Brighton.

My new book on the Battle of Neuve Chapelle should soon be published. It was vital to my research to learn how many soldiers were actually killed in that battle for the contemporary sources varied widely. It was no good just entering the parameter dates of 10th to 13th March 1915 in *Soldiers Died...* for men also perished during that time well away from Neuve Chapelle. I decided to ascertain for myself the daily casualties for each fighting unit and the analysis of those figures proved fascinating. Each regimental history seemed to claim that their men had suffered more than other battalions involved. At last the truth could be discovered. It was not quite as simple though as might be supposed. Not all units reported their casualties at the same time. For example, 2/Middlesex which suffered appallingly in the initial assault, only recorded seven fatalities for that first day. They did not catch up and report the true figures until 14th March, and it is for that date that they are attributed, but by then they had actually ceased fighting. Like many computer products, *Soldiers Died...* on CD-ROM is a fantastic aid to research but you do still need to include in the recipe a 'Mark 1 Eyeball' and a modicum of common sense.

The possibilities are almost endless for genealogists and anybody wishing to remember those brave people who died in the 1914-18 War. It is amazing how many men and women, for it is not just men who are listed, bear the name you are researching. For the first time you can find out details of those who died in the Great War from your chosen town. There are many more examples I could illustrate but alas space does not permit. It is fair to say however that *Soldiers Died...* is a research tool that I find utterly indispensable to my work as both a military and family historian. And I am sure that once you try it you will be equally convinced.

Soldiers Died 1914-19 CD-ROM is available directly from the Naval & Military Press, PO Box 61, Dallington, Heathfield, East Sussex, TN21 9JS. Tel: 01435 830111. A full preview is available at www.great-war-casualties.com They are now working in conjunction with the Public Record Office to produce a similar CD-ROM for World War Two casualties.

Register of Men Fallen at Gallipoli 1915-16

Gallipoli, April 1915 - January 1916:

Before dawn on the morning of April 25, 1915, a combined force of British, Australian, New Zealand, Indian and French forces carried out an amphibious assault on the Gallipoli Peninsula. The goal of the assault was to secure the Dardanelles, the strait, which separates European Turkey from Asian Turkey and connects the Aegean Sea to the Sea of Marmara. The success of this operation would have forced the surrender of Turkey, allowing the British to better assist Russia in its fight against Germany in the east. Two assaults earlier in the year - one by sea and the other by a small force of Royal Marines - had failed to achieve any success. They had, however, alerted the Turks to the aims of the British and allowed them to prepare an almost impenetrable defence.

The assault took place in two sectors located 12 miles apart. British and French troops landed at Helles to the north, and Australian and New Zealand troops (along with the Ceylon Planters Rifles and units of the Royal Marines) landed to the south. The invaders called this southern sector Anzac, after the Australian-New Zealand Army Corps (ANZAC) to which many of the troops belonged. Elements of the all-Jewish Zion Mule Corps also landed in both sectors.

The assault failed to achieve nearly all of its objectives, and what was supposed to have been a quick victory against the Turkish defenders turned into a long and costly land and sea campaign. The failure of several major assaults against the Turks between April and July 1915 resulted in landings in a new sector in August. The opening of the Suvla sector, which bordered Anzac immediately to the north, coincided with a major effort by the Australians and New Zealanders (along with Indians and British troops which had been secretly landed in the area) to break out of their sector and thus link up with the troops at Suvla. This in turn coincided with a major diversionary assault in the Helles sector (the Battle of Krithia Vineyard).

Like the earlier battles, those of August were costly yet unsuccessful. From then on the campaign devolved into a campaign of trench warfare, the monotony occasionally broken by small raids against the enemy. In September 1915 the Newfoundland Regiment, the final Dominion to send troops to Gallipoli, landed and began suffering casualties.

By the time the last troops were evacuated from Gallipoli on the night of January 8/9, 1916, 34,000 British and Dominion troops, and several thousand French and French colonial troops, had lost their lives. Nobody will ever know how many men died as a result of their Gallipoli service after they left the Peninsula, but the number must be considerable. The shame of it all is that the men who sent them to their deaths did so knowing that they had virtually no chance of success.

About the Register

For the past 10 years I have been working diligently to commemorate each of the 34,000 British and Dominion servicemen who died at Gallipoli. I am also including those men who died as a result of wounds and illness sustained at Gallipoli after they left the Peninsula, those who died in Turkish prisoner of war camps and two nurses of the Canadian Army Medical Corps who died while treating casualties at Mudros on the Greek island of Lemnos.

My goal is to include as much information as I possibly can about each person. I am also trying to locate photographs of each man and first hand accounts of their deaths. I am trying to include the following details about each person:

Name; Date and place of birth; Service number and Service Unit and or Regiment; Date and place of enlistment; Names of parents (to include mothers maiden name, father's occupation and address in 1915); Name of spouse (to include maiden name, date and place of marriage and address in 1915); Names and birth dates of children; Education; Occupation; Date and place of death: Circumstances of death: Place of burial; Location of photograph (even if I cannot reproduce it)
Personal details and anecdotes (physical description, personality, interests, aspirations and interesting experiences)

Using a variety of sources I am trying to put together as complete a picture of each person as is possible. These include regimental histories, casualty rolls, printed rolls of honour and commemorative books, cemetery registers, unit and personal diaries, letters, and newspaper reports and obituaries.

Additionally, I am relying on the help of genealogists all over the world for information about family members. As a genealogist myself, the value of the information which only people like us think to preserve about our families is quite clear to me. While the main intention is to commemorate the people who fell at - and as a result of - Gallipoli my secondary goal is to create an educational tool, which will be useful for the novice. Too often historians make the mistake of assuming that their audience knows just as much about their subject as they do, an assumption which is all too often incorrect.

Thus, in an effort to make my register useful and understandable to everyone, an introductory section will be included which will briefly explain life on the Gallipoli Peninsula, diet (poor diet resulted in the deaths of hundreds of men due to dysentery), the evacuation and treatment of casualties, burials, etc. A glossary will also be added which will explain the location and naming of the major and minor geographical features at Gallipoli including, where possible, the colourfully named trenches.

Over the last four years I have proven 12 Gallipoli deaths and 2 burials to the Commonwealth War Graves Commission (at the time of writing, I am building a case for 9 more deaths). I have also corrected numerous errors in the records of the Commission, resulting in changes to cemetery and memorial registers, memorials and gravestones. As a result, the Commission has requested a completed copy of my register so that it might update and correct it's records.

I would like to personally appeal to everyone with ancestors who died at Gallipoli; people with diaries, letters and photographs in their possession; and anyone with an interest in local men who died at Gallipoli for help. Without your help, this register can never hope to be the memorial it is intended to be.

Gallipoli Campaign 1915 - 1916 Biographical Index

Patrick Gariépy, 3966 Robin Avenue, Eugene, Oregon 97402, U.S.A.

e-mail: patrick@efn.org

The National Inventory of War Memorials

Based at and administered by the Imperial War Museum, this national survey was initiated in 1989 with the aim of surveying all of Britain's estimated 54,000 war memorials. Although full time office staff are employed to organise field work and collate the information as it arrives, all the field work itself is carried out by enthusiastic volunteers from a wide variety of backgrounds. We would welcome the assistance of further volunteers if they felt able to lend us their time, energy and expertise.

The work would involve liaising with existing NIWM fieldworkers and, in some cases, local Co-ordinators. We encourage volunteers to have their names added to our list of field workers, as we have found this to be the most effective means of taking full advantage of people's valuable time and minimising the risk of duplication.

The survey is nearing completion, with just under two years remaining of the current National Heritage Memorial Fund grant, but a recent audit of the collection has identified the following areas of England and Wales which urgently require additional field work in order to ensure their completion. In particular, local Co-ordinators are still required for Northern Wales and Cornwall. In Scotland a comprehensive survey under the guidance of an independent Co-ordinator is nearing completion. In Northern Ireland a comprehensive survey has been initiated by the Western Front Association. Details of Co-ordinators are given below:

England

Tyne and Wear
Janet Brown, Bilsdale, Ulgham, Northumberland
Tel:01670 790465
North-West England
(Greater Manchester and Lancashire)
STEPHEN LOWE 130 Gawsworth Rd, Macclesfield,
Cheshire SK11 8UQ Tel:(01625) 424 921
The Midlands (West Midlands and Warwickshire)
Gillian Ellis 42 Tyndale Crescent, Great Barr,
Birmingham B43 7NP
The South East
(Kent, Essex and East/West Sussex)
Paul Rason 1 South Drive, Orpington, Kent BR6
9NG Tel: 01689 855 061

Lincolnshire
John Chester, 8 Laburnam Grove, Spalding
Lincolnshire PE11 2LX
Gloucestershire
Mrs P Utechin The Lodge, Headington House, Old
Headington, Oxford OX3 9HU
Greater London
Co-ordinator: Hilary Wheeler 17 Bath House, Bath
Terrace, London SE1 6PU
Hertfordshire
Roger Bardell 1 Nathans Close, Welwyn
Herts AL6 9QB
Cornwall
Co-ordinator: To be confirmed

Most other English counties have broadly been very well surveyed. However, we do have a list of around forty administrative districts which require work to bring them up to the standard of the rest of their counties. So, if you would like to help but are not based in any of the above areas please contact us anyway, as you may find that you can still help.

Wales
Northern Wales
Co-ordinator: To be confirmed
Southern Wales
David Hughes 23 St Teilos Way, Caerphilly
South Wales CF83 1FA

Scotland
Tony Martin Birch Grove, Harviestoun Rd, Dollar,
Clackmannanshire FK14 7PT
Northern Ireland
Jim Heyburn 56 Orpen Rd, Finaghy
Belfast BT10 0BQ

If you feel you could help in any way or would just like to find out more details, we would really like to hear from you. Please contact either the Project Co-ordinator, Nick Hewitt, or one of the Project Assistants, Jane Armer and Lorraine Knight, at:

The National Inventory of War Memorials
Imperial War Museum
Lambeth Road, London SE1 6HZ
Tel: (0171) 416 5353/5281 Fax: (0171) 416 5379 E-mail: memorials@iwm.org.uk

The Commonwealth War Graves Commission
Peter Francis Commonwealth War Graves Commission

The Commonwealth War Graves Commission, was established by Royal Charter of 21 May 1917, the provisions of which were amended and extended by a Supplemental Charter of 8 June 1964. Its duties are to mark and maintain the graves of the forces of the Commonwealth who died during two world wars, to build and maintain memorials to the dead whose graves are unknown, and to keep records and registers. The cost is shared by the partner governments - those of Australia, Canada, India, New Zealand, South Africa and the United Kingdom - in proportions based upon the numbers of their graves.

The Commission is responsible for 1.7 million commemorations, with war graves at over 23,000 locations and in some 150 countries. The work is founded upon the principles that each of the dead should be commemorated individually by name either on the headstone on the grave or by an inscription on a memorial; that each of the headstones and memorials should be permanent; that the headstones should be uniform; and that no distinction should be made on account of military or civil rank, race or creed.

Today, the Commission's major concern is the maintenance of those graves, cemeteries and memorials, to the highest standards, in the face of exposure to the elements and the passage of time - to ensure that "Their Name Liveth For Evermore". In addition to the day to day horticultural and structural maintenance of the cemeteries and memorials, an enquiry service is on offer to the public, whereby the commemorative details for any Commonwealth casualty who died during either of the two world wars can be provided. Based at the Commission's headquarters in Maidenhead, the records call centre answers over 40,000 enquiries a year. Commemorative information for Commonwealth civilians killed by military action in the Second World War is also available on a Roll of Honour numbering over 66,000 names.

Originally, casualty data was stored on card indexes in over 3,000 drawers. After the First World War, details were compiled into some 1,500 cemetery registers. All enquiries were handled by a wholly manual process until 1995. The work was carried out, as it had been for decades, by dedicated, knowledgeable staff, using large ledgers. The ledgers are organised by country, name of cemetery and alphabetically by surname. To overcome the challenge of an enquirer only knowing a casualty's surname and not the place of burial, there are large volumes of alphabetical lists, cross-referenced by code numbers to the appropriate cemetery register. In late autumn 1995 the Commission's vast resource of information was computerised, allowing for a more efficient service to be offered to the public. The information for each entry was broken down into searchable 'fields' - For example, Surname, Age, Regiment, Cemetery Name, Date of Death etc.

Not only do the computerised records allow for better access to the casualty details and place of commemoration, it also allows the operator to trace single casualties more quickly, from less information, and offer services like casualty-listing reports. This has become increasingly important as the value of the database for educational purposes is recognised and enquiries become more complex. Some of the most popular criteria for casualty listings include a same surname search, a regimental search and a home town search. It is even possible to trace, for example, how many Captains were killed on the first day of the Battle of the Somme.

In line with this public access policy, the Commission took the initiative to use the Internet to further promote access to the records. In November 1998, to coincide with the eightieth anniversary of the Armistice that brought to an end the First World War, the Debt of Honour Register was launched. The Register, a search by surname database, is available to the public via the Commission's web site at www.cwgc.org. The database provides known details of the casualty as well as the name of the cemetery or memorial, directions on how to find it and the exact plot, row, grave or memorial panel reference to enable the enquirer to locate the place of burial or commemoration should they make a pilgrimage to the cemetery or memorial. A second page on the web site prints the casualty details in the form of a commemorative certificate for the enquirer.

The launch of the Debt of Honour Register on the Internet has been an incredible success. After the launch, the site was overwhelmed, receiving on average 600,000 'hits' a week until April 1999 from all over the world. This has now levelled off to a more manageable 200,000 'hits' a week. The Register has widened public knowledge and interest in commemoration, reunited families with the records of their long-fallen loved ones, assisted the historian, researcher and the student and most importantly, proved a highly effective way of keeping the names of those the Commission commemorates alive in the hearts and minds of a new generation.

The Commission's horticultural and structural maintenance of the cemeteries and memorials around the world ensures the memory of those who died during the two world wars endures. With the launch of the Debt of Honour Register, names once kept alive only in stone are now readily available to be carried in the hearts and minds of a new generation. This is a vital part of ensuring the perpetuity of the Commission's commemoration so that people will contact the Commission, visit the cemeteries and memorials, remember, ensure that "Their Name Liveth for Evermore".

Further Information
The Commission welcomes enquiries from the public. Please supply the Commission's enquiries department with as much information as possible. This will enhance the chances of a positive trace. A full list of the Commission's services and publications on offer to the public is available from:

The Records & Enquiries Section
The Commonwealth War Graves Commission
2 Marlow Road, Maidenhead Berkshire SL6 7DX UK
Tel: 01628 634221 Fax: 01628 771208
E-mail: cwgc@dial.pipex.com Web Site: www.cwgc.org

WHY *DO* PEOPLE VISIT BATTLEFIELDS.....?
Maureen Silver

Since, as a company, we have been in the business of taking people to battlefields for over 23 years now, we might be expected to give a neat answer to this question. Not so, however. Reasons are as varied as the people that travel with us, and the range of interest never diminishes. Despite the fact that our repertoire of battlefield and historical sites is extensive and diverse – our 2000 brochure offers just short of sixty different options - we are constantly researching new venues. Our current champion traveller, Robert Walter, has just completed his hundredth tour with us. It's his ilk that keeps us on our toes.

For some of our travellers their selection of tour is eclectic, perhaps in an attempt to assimilate a grasp of history never quite achieved at school. Lists of dates never were conducive to inspiring a passionate interest; but put any battle thoroughly into the context of its time and a vivid history lesson emerges. It is not just a case of what happened at this battle but also why did this battle happen, and what happened afterwards. History is like a piece of spaghetti. You can tackle it in the middle, but to fully appreciate it you must nibble both backwards and forwards.

But whilst some of our travellers use battles to gain a general perspective of history, others specialise. We have, for example, a committed group that follows joyfully in the footsteps of Napoleon, ever attempting to better understand that charismatic Emperor, empathising with his bold victories, debating his disastrous defeats, and eating wonderful meals in the process. Others are more committed to Wellington. There are those who are mediaevalists, always keen to hone their skills on the long-bow. We have 1st and 2nd World War buffs, who, having perhaps taken on board an overall picture, then extend their knowledge in depth. Others, again, go further afield and combine a general interest in military history with the opportunity to visiting an exotic and beautiful location – Kwa-Zululand for Rorke's Drift and Isandlwana, for example, or Nepal to meet Gurkha veterans, shake the hand of a Gurkha VC and trek gently into the foothills of the Himalayas under the protection of Gurkha guides.

Undoubtedly some of our travellers come with us on a personal voyage of rediscovery. It takes an

... travellers come ... on a personal voyage of rediscovery. It takes an enormous degree of courage ... for any veteran to return to the scene of action

enormous degree of courage, I think, for any veteran to return to the scene of action. Not only can painful memories emerge, but even a sense of nostalgia, of lost youth. I was privileged to be on a coach of American veterans on the 50th anniversary of the D Day landings back in 1994. They were an amazing group of men, buoyed up by each other's company, wise-cracking and joking, joyfully returning the waves of the French people in the little villages that we went through. The only thing that seemed to disconcert them was the rumour that they were to be greeted by the local French Mayor and kissed on both cheeks. They cheerfully admitted that, outside of their own field of operation they had had very little idea of the general battle strategy of June 1944. They had been a small part of a jigsaw, largely ignorant of the overall picture. "So *that's* who those guys were, over to the right of us," one of them said as the overall story was told.

When we actually reached the beaches, however, the mood changed. Only one of them – the quietest on the coach - had actually been in the first wave that hit Omaha on 6th June 1944 at 6.30am. Standing there on the beach he spoke softly about what happened to him. His job had been to come ashore with a radio operator and confirm the positions of the German guns. He and the radio operator had cross-trained, so that in the event of one of them `not making it' they could each do the other's job. In the event, however, they were separated in the chaos of the landing and the radio lost. There was nothing he could do, our quiet American told us, but throw his lot in with the other troops in their painful attempts to get through the German defences into the hinterland. But the slopes up from the beach were mined. "So one guy would go," he said, "as far as he could get – you understand what I'm saying here. And they'd run a white tape up to where he got to, and the next guy would go." Nothing, before or since, has for me ever evoked more clearly what it must have been like to go into battle than those words softly spoken on a beach still wet with the receding tide.

For some people it is not so much a personal journey as a sense of group identity that prompts a battlefield visit. Some simply follow their own regiment. Others are inspired by a strong interest in local history. Few stories are more poignant that those of the `Pals' Battalions of the 1st World War. In an effort to raise the 100,000 men per month that he estimated he would need to fight this war, Kitchener actively encouraged local town groups to form their own battalions. No doubt it was good for morale; with the local solicitor as your officer and surrounded by your mates you could go off to war with a strong feeling of comradeship. But when the casualty lists for a single battle started coming in, the impact on a local community in terms of diminution of the male population was devastating, and the effects became part of local folklore. Thousands of our recent ancestors lie side by side by locality in France and Belgium, representing that innocent seeming population of pre-First World War Britain. We are always extremely proud to organise special trips for groups interested in their own local history to pay tribute to their own Pals' Battalion.

And more and more, as the number of people who can actually remember being in action inevitably diminishes, there is a sense of not wanting to allow living memory to fade into history. Nowhere is this more evident than with the 1st and 2nd World Wars. The phenomenal growth of research into family history means that more and more people are saying to us "I've just discovered that my dad fought at........." or "I believe my great uncle is buried at...."

Incidentally, sometimes the process works the other way. Rather than research prompting a battlefield visit, the visit aids research. We recently took Margaret and Jeffrey Blakeborough on a tour which included a visit to Thiepval Memorial. Jeffrey is extremely keen on researching his family history but I imagine that was a low priority in his mind when we arrived at Thiepval. This Memorial to the Missing of the Somme is a sombre edifice, dominating the battlefield and carrying on its walls the names of 73,412 men who have no known grave. To his amazement Jeffrey found two Blakeboroughs named, hitherto unknown to him, but coming, he said, from the right area. It had given him a whole new line of inquiry and it was clear that he was eager to follow it up as soon as he got home.

One of the things we pride ourselves on is including as many `special visits' as our itinerary will feasibly allow. On a recent tour, which was actually to follow in the footsteps of the Soldier Poets, one of our travellers had mentioned when he booked that his father had received the MC at a place called Flers during the Battle of the Somme. "He never talked about it," he said, almost reproachfully, over the phone. "He was only nineteen. I don't suppose you know where this Flers place is, do you? Nothing to do with poetry, of course". Yes, we knew where Flers was, it is close by Delville Wood, and a bit of digging in the regimental history established pretty accurately where young 2nd Lt Mark Jopling had helped rally a foundering attack and steady his men. A little lane ran pretty much along where his trench had been, and given that the countryside was looking particularly beautiful and not at all like the lunar landscape of 1916, it was easy to imagine what he had been looking at and even a little of what he might have been feeling. His son stood where he had stood, eyeing the objective of the attack – the little village of Flers hardly a stone's throw away - and trying to look nonchalant. "I'm incredibly moved," was all he finally said.

In my experience `special visits' are always incredibly moving, not necessarily easy to cope with and very precious. A couple of years ago a lady booked to come on a 1st WW tour with her husband. With her booking form she included, rather tentatively, a request for a special visit. Her mother's older brother, she had just discovered, had been killed in the Battle of Arras in April 1917, aged 18, and was buried somewhere called Tank Cemetery. If it wouldn't be too much trouble could we possibly....? Tank Cemetery is tiny, just south of Arras, flanked on one side by a field of maize, with a view over the gently sloping battlefield. Along its back wall is a mass grave of 64 Cameronians, buried in a line. This lady's uncle, however, had been with the 2nd/5th Gloucesters, a regiment well represented here. Once we had located where the headstone was we asked her whether she and her husband wanted to visit the grave on their own, should the rest of us stay on the coach, or would she prefer it if we joined her. "Oh, I don't mind who comes," she said. "It's not as if I knew him....the more the merrier, really,,,.." Inside the cemetery she approached the gravestone diffidently. She laid a simple poppy wreath and stood back, looking confused, as though confronting a stranger. And then her face suddenly cleared. "Hello," she said softly. "I never met you, you know. But I have now."

Maureen Silver is a part-time guide with Holts Battlefield and History Tours, specialising in The Soldier Poets of the 1st World War

Aberdeen & North East Scotland Family History Society
Publications mail order service for members/non-members. Range of titles available. Send 31p for publications list or visit the Society's Web Site. See Advert on Page 134
164 King Street, Aberdeen, AB24 5BD, Scotland
Tel No: 01224-646323   Fax No: 01224-639096
Email: anesfhs@rsc.co.uk Web Site: www.rsc.co.uk/anesfhs

Back to Roots Family History Service
A well established research company which also sells a wide range of books, recording aids and computer software always at very competitive prices. See Advert on Page 198/199
16 Arrowsmith Drive, Stonehouse, Glos. GL10 2QR
Tel No: 01453-821300   Fax No: 01453-821300
Email: mike@backtoroots.co.uk
Web Site: www.backtoroots.co.uk

British Association for Local History
The BALH has an extensive catalogue of books and other publications relating to matters relevant to local and family historians available for sale. See Advert on Page 235/236
PO Box 1576, 24 Lower Street, Harnham, Salisbury, SP2 8EY
Tel No: 01722-332158 Fax No: 017722-413242
Email: mail@balh.co.uk or info@balh.co.uk
Web Site: www.balh.co.uk/

Broderbund Software Ltd
In addition to producing Family Tree Maker computer program Broderbund also publish a wealth of research material CD-ROM and the WWW. Sees Pages 50 & 200
Tilgate Forest Business Park, Elm Park Court, Brighton Road, Crawley, West Sussex, RH11 9BP,
Tel No: 01293-651300   Fax No: 01293-651301
www.familytreemaker.com

Chapel Books
Books for family and local historians. See Page 118
Chapel Cottage, Llanishen, Chepstow, NP16 6QT, Wales
Tel No: 01600-860055   Fax No: 01600-860100

Chris E Makepeace Local History Consultancy
Stockist of Godfrey Edition of OS maps for the North and Midlands and many other publications relevant to family history research, etc. See Advert on Page 92
5 Hilton Road, Disley, Cheshire, SK12 2JU
Tel No: 01663-763346

Don Steel: Family History Enterprises
Supplier of books, maps, charts & forms relating to family local history research. Send for catalogue. Extensive range of all material available. See Advert on Page 42
'Brooking', Jarvis Lane, East Brent, Highbridge
Somerset, TA9 4HS   Tel No: 01278-760535

Family and Local History Book Club
Book Club operated by Don Steel Family History Enterprises devoted to the supply of family and local history publications at advantageous terms. See Entry Above.

Family History Bookshop - Institute of Heraldic and Genealogical Studies
For all your reference needs contact the Family History Bookshop operated by the Institute of Heraldic and Genealogical Studies. See Advert on Page 39
Northgate, Canterbury, Kent CT1 1BAGSD
Tel No: 01227-768664   Fax No: 01227-765617

Family History Shop & Library
For a variety of directories and listings relating to Norfolk and Suffolk plus a range of books on genealogical and family history research. See Advert on Page 94
24d Magdalen Street, Norwich, NR3 1HU
Tel No: 01603-621152   Email: jenlibrary@aol.com
Web Site: www.jenlibrary.u-net.com/

Family Trees - A Manual by Marie Lynskey
A detailed guide on the preparation and presentation of family trees by an accomplished and experienced presenter of material in display formats. See Advert on Page 40
109 Nutcroft Grove, Fetcham, Surrey, KT22 9LD,
Tel No: 01372-372334   Fax No: 01372-372334
Email: ml@clara.net   Web Site: http://www.ml.clara.net

Family Tree Magazine Booksales
In addition to being a premier monthly magazine Family Tree also has a booksales operation which has an extensive range of titles available. See Advert on Page 30
61 Great Whyte, Ramsey, Huntington, Cambridgeshire, PE17 1HL
Tel No: 01487-814050   Fax No: 01487-711361
Email: family-tree-magazine@mcmail.com
Web Site: www.family-tree.co.uk

Federation of Family History Societies Bookshop
The Federation through its Bookshop service is a major publisher and distributor of genealogical publications and research material. See Advert on Page 4
The Benson Room, Birmingham & Midland Institute,
Margaret Street, Birmingham, B3 3BS
Tel No: 070-41-492032 Fax No: 01564-703100
Email: admin@ffhs.org.uk   Web Site: www.ffhs.org.uk

Federation of Family History Societies (Publications) Ltd
Publishers for FFHS. See Advert on Page 71
2 - 4 Killer Street, Ramsbottom, Bury, Lancashire, BL0 9BZ
Web Site: www.ffhs.org.uk/pubs/

Genealogical Society of Victoria
Society with full range of for family history researchers and also a major distributor of genealogical publications for all Australia. See Advert on Page 150
Ancestor House, 179 Queen Street, Melbourne 3000, Victoria, Australia
Tel No: +61-03-9670-7033 Fax No: +61-03-9670-4490
Email: gsv@alphalink.com.au
Web Site: www.alphalink.com.au/~gsv/

Genealogical Research Directory
From the Library of Australian History
The GRD is the largest surnames queries listing published annually in book form. Published since 1981, the Directory is distributed in May each year. See Advert on Page Inside Back Cover
UK Distribution:
2 Stella Grove, Tollerton, Nottingham NG12 4EY
Tel No: 0115-937-2287 0115-937-7018.
Web Site: www.ozemail.com.au/~grdxxx

genealogyPro
Internet shop selling family history publications and services via a dedicated internet sales site. See Advert on Page 203
76 Tartan Drive, Nepaen, Ontario, K2J 3K3, Canada
Email: jholwell@genealogypro.com
Web Site: www.genealogy.com

GENfair
Internet shop selling the publications, books etc of Family History Societies and other suppliers. See Page 193
9 Fairstone Hill, Oadby, Leicester, LE2 5RL
Tel No: 0116-271-3494   Email: info@genfair.com
Web Site: www.genfair.com

Gould Books
Major distributor of genealogical resources for Australia researchers including books, CD-ROMs, publications, plans and maps, and computing aids. See Advert on Page 148
PO Box 126, Gumeracha, South Australia, 5233, Australia
Tel No: +61-8-8389-1611   Fax No: 08-8389-1599
Email: gould@adelaide.on.net Web Site: www.gould.com.au

Heritage World Family History Services
Supplier of local history information; heritage type products, books, other publications, etc. Member of the Irish Family History Foundation. See Advert on Page 145
The Heritage Centre, 26 Market Street, Dungannon, Co Tyrone, BT70 1AB, Northern Ireland
Tel No: 01868-724187 Fax No: 01868-752141
Email: irishwld@iol.ie   Web Site: www.iol.ie./irishworld

Interlink Bookshop & Genealogical Services
Genealogical services bookshop serving Western Canada. Extensive range of books, CD-ROMS and fiche, relating to the UK, Canada, and Europe. See Advert on Page 156
3840A Cadboro Bay Rd, Victoria, B.C., V8N 4G2, Canada
Tel No: (250)-477-2708 Fax No: (250)-658-3947
Email: ibgs@pacificcoast.net.
Web Site: www.pacificcoast.net/~ibgs

Kingfisher Free International Booksearch (GSD)
Booksearch any title/author/subject. No Obligation
See Advert on Page 26/187
6 Ash Grove, Skegby, Sutton in Ashfield, Notts. NG17 3FH
Tel No: 01623-552530 Fax No: 01623-552530
Email: malc.kbs@argonet.co.uk.
Web Site: www.argonet.co.uk/users/malc.kbs

Learning Company (UK) Ltd
Publisher of the 'Ultimate Family Tree' computer genealogy program the Learning Company Inc publishes and markets a family of premium software brands that educate across every age from young children to adults. See Pages 188, 192
Tilgate Forest Business Park, Elm Park Court, Brighton Road, Crawley, West Sussex, RH11 9BP,
Tel No: 01293-651300 Fax No: 01293-651301.
Email: jcielecki@mindscape.com.
Web Site: http://www.learningco.com

Local History Publications
Non-profit making publisher reprinting antiquarian local histories, church guides, etc, as well as selling contemporary local history publications. See Advert on Page 44
316 Green Lane, Streatham, London, SW16 3AS
Tel No: 0181-677-9562

Lochin Publications
Publishing and publications sales business of the respected author on family history and genealogical matters - Colin R. Chapman. See Advert on Page 32.
6 Holywell Road, Dursley, Gloucestershire GL11 5RS
Tel No: 01453-547531

Naval & Military Press
Publishers/distributors of an extensive range of material on naval and military matters. See Advert on Page 170
PO Box 61, Dallington, Heathfield, East Sussex, TN21 9ZS
Tel No: 01435-830111 Fax No: 01435-830623
Email: order.dept@naval-military-press.co.uk.
Web Site: www.naval-military-press.co.uk

People Search Tracing Services - Search Pack
Researchers offer "The People Search Pack" - a handbook on tracing in the UK plus other specialist research. See Page 62
30A Bedford Place, Southampton, SO15 2DG,
Tel No: 02380-562243   Fax No: 02380-562243
Email: info@people-search.co.uk.
Web Site: http://www.people-search.co.uk

Pinhorns
Genealogical Researchers with a range of books and specialist publications available for sale
85 Etnam Street, Leominster, Herefordshire, HR6 8AE
Tel No: 01874-610200 Fax No: 01874-610200

S A & M J Raymond
Genealogical Bibliographers & Publishers of a number of guides to the extensive range of published material that is available to Genealogists. See Advert on Page 44
PO Box 35, Exeter, Devon, EX4 5EF Tel: 01392-252193

S & N Genealogy Supplies
Major UK distributor of family tree computer software also supplies computers and other genealogical research aids including books and publications. See Advert on Page 2
Greenacres, Salisbury Rd, Chilmark, Salisbury, Wilts. SP3 5AH
Tel No: 01722-716121 Fax No: 01722-716160.
Email: 100064.737@compuserve.com.
Web Site: http://www.genealogy.demon.co.uk

Scottish Families Histories
Reference work on Scottish Families by J P S Ferguson, available from the National Library of Scotland booksales department. See Advert on Page 130
Nat Library of Scotland, George IV Bridge, Edinburgh, EH1 1EW
Tel No: 0131-226-4531 Fax No: 0131-622-4803.
Email: enquiries@nls.uk   Web Site: http://www.nls.uk

Society of Genealogists - Bookstore
In addition to other services on offer the Society also operates a major bookstore which has one of the most extensive range of publications on the subject. See Advert on Page 56, 69, 70
14 Charterhouse Buildings, Goswell Rd., London, EC1M 7BA
Tel No: 020-7251-8799

Sutton Publishing
Major publisher of books relating to genealogical and local history matters plus titles on military, aviation, transport, archaeology and many other subjects. See Page 360
Phoenix Mill, Thrupp, Stroud, Gloucestershire, GL5 2BU
Tel No: 01453-731114 Fax No: 01453-731117
Email: sales@sutton-publishing.co.uk

Tree Tops
Internet and media publicity via Sky TV News features and teletext listings provided for genealogists. See Page 54, 57
PO Box 116, Swindon, Wiltshire, SN3 2SX
Tel No: 01793-538730 Fax No: 01793-538730
Email: tree.tops@virgin.net.
Web Site: http://freespace.virgin.net/tree.tops/

OTHER SUPPLIERS OF PUBLISHED MATERIAL

Most Family and Local History Societies and many other Organisations and Businesses referred to in this Directory listed below have publications for sale both of a general nature and specific to their areas. Refer to their individual adverts for details of publications available - the page number of the relevant advert is shown in brackets after each entry.

ENGLAND

BIRMINGHAM
Birmingham & Midland Society for Genealogy & Heraldry (80)

BUCKINGHAMSHIRE
Buckinghamshire Family History Society (83)
Chess Valley Archealogical & Historical Society (90)
Hillingdon Family History Society (212)

CHESHIRE
Bob Dobson Books (94)
North Cheshire Family History Society (84)
Northern Writers Advisory Services (84)

CLEVELAND
Cleveland Family History Society (82)
Kingpin (102)
Printability Publishing Ltd (102)

CORNWALL
Cornwall Family History Society (54)

CUMBRIA
Cumbria Family History Society (84)
Northern Writers Advisory Services (84)

DURHAM, TYNE & WEAR, NORTHUMBERLAND
Cleveland Family History Society (82)
Kingpin (102)
Neil Richardson (102)
Original Indexes (102)

EAST MIDLANDS
East Midlands Ancestor (52)

GLOUCESTERSHIRE
Gloucestershire Family History Society (88)

HERTFORDSHIRE
Hertfordshire Family & Population History Society (90)

ISLE OF MAN
Isle of Man Family History Society (90)

LANCASHIRE
Bob Dobson Books (94)
Northern Writers Advisory Services (84)
Cumbria Family History Society (84)

LINCOLNSHIRE
Lincolnshire Family History Society (94)

LONDON
Gendocs (74)
Trueflare Ltd (75)

NORFOLK
Family History Shop & Library (94)

STAFFORDSHIRE
Birmingham & Midland Society for Genealogy & Heraldry (80)

SUFFOLK
Family History Shop & Library (94)

SUSSEX
Sussex Family History Group (212)

WARWICKSHIRE
Birmingham & Midland Society for Genealogy & Heraldry (80)

WESTMORLAND
Cumbria Family History Society (84)

WILTSHIRE
Wiltshire Archaeological & Natural History Society (104)
Wiltshire Index Service (104)

WORCESTERSHIRE
Birmingham & Midland Society for Genealogy & Heraldry (80)

YORKSHIRE
Bob Dobson Books (94)
Yorkshire Archaeological Society (109)

YORKSHIRE - SOUTH
Doncaster & District Family History Society (107)

YORKSHIRE - WEST
Bradford Family History Society (106)
Keighley & District Family History Society (108)
Wharfedale Family History Group (108)

YORKSHIRE - NORTH
City of York & District Family History Society (110)
Cleveland Family History Society (82)
Ripon Historical Society & Ripon, Harrogate & District (109)
Wharfedale Family History Group (108)

WALES

Chapel Books (118)
Dyfed Family History Society (120)
Glamorgan Family History Society (112)
Merthyr Tydfil Historical Society (114)
Powys Family History Society (112)

SCOTLAND

Aberdeen & North East Scotland Family History Society (134)
Glasgow & West of Scotland Family History Society (130)
Leopard Magazine (122)

IRELAND

Flyleaf Press (144)
Heritage World Family History Services (145)
Irish Roots (145)

Hearth Tax Returns
Nesta Evans

The hearth tax was collected throughout England and Wales from 1662 to 1689. Like the early 16th century subsidies, this tax is an excellent source for regional studies of topics such as wealth. It makes available lists of inhabitants, and the size of the houses they occupied, village by village across England and Wales. Of course, they have to be used with care, because different lists vary widely in their inclusion of, for instance, the exempt poor. Despite this, Christopher Husbands has pointed out the potential of the hearth tax returns 'to provide a general framework for the socio-economic history of the later 17th century'. With the exercise of due caution, these documents can be used to study population, the incidence of poverty, regional variations in housing, local industry, tax evasion, and other subjects. They are also ideal for finding lost ancestors, since they can pin down which parish registers are worth searching, and the number of hearths, and thus house size which gives some sort of indication of status.

In England and Wales the hearth tax was levied from 1662 to 1689. Its records are mainly to be found in the Public Record Office in class E179, but for some counties, such as Kent, the enrolled Quarter Sessions copy has survived and these are housed in County Record Offices. The essential guide to the whereabouts and condition of these documents, and the existence of published returns is *The Hearth Tax and other later Stuart Tax Lists and the Association Oath Rolls,* compiled by Jeremy Gibson, 2nd edition, 1996. This costs *£4.50* plus p&p, and can be obtained from the compiler at Harts Cottage, Church Hanborough, Witney, Oxon 0X8 8AB or the Federation of Family History Publications Ltd, 2-4 Killer Street, Ramsbottom, Bury, Lancs BL0 9BZ.

Roehampton Institute, London, together with the British Record Society and County Record Societies has embarked on a project to publish at least one hearth tax, and preferably one from the 1660s and another from the 1670s, for every English and Welsh county, which does not already have published returns.

The first two volumes, for which publication is expected in 1999-2000, will be the returns for Cambridgeshire Michaelmas 1664 and Kent Lady Day 1664. The transcriptions have been completed and the introductions are being written for County Durham, and work is advancing rapidly in Northumberland, Norfolk, Huntingdonshire, Lancashire, Lincolnshire, Westmoreland, Essex, Oxfordshire, Northamptonshire and Warwickshire. Each will have a full scholarly introduction together with maps and tables, and indexes of surnames and places.

They are also ideal for finding lost ancestors

This item originally appeared in Local History News

The Phillimore Lecture 2000
Saturday, 3rd June 2000
Stationers Hall, London
will be delivered by
Professor Margaret Spufford
based on her work with
Hearth Tax Returns

Colin Dale Researches (GSD)
For research at the Colindale Newspaper Library for possible information about ancestors and other required material in newspapers. See Advert on Page 160

1 Furham Field, Pinner, Middlesex, HA5 4DX
Tel No: 0181-428-4577

Computers in Genealogy
A quarterly periodical published by the Society of Genealogists available to members and also non-members. See Advert on Page 56, 69, 70.

14 Charterhouse Buildings, Goswell Rd, London, EC1M 7BA
Tel No: 020-7251-8799

Current Archaeology
Leading British archaeological magazine bridging the gap between the amateur and the professional.

9 Nassington Road, London NW3 2TX
Tel No: 0171-435-7517   Fax No: 0171-916-2405
Email: editor@archaeology.co.uk
Web Site: www.archaeology.co.uk

East Midlands Ancestor
'East Midlands Ancestor' is quarterly periodical from the Publisher of 'Finding East Midlands Ancestors' 152 page book.   See Advert on Page 52

9 Slatebrook Close, Groby, Leicester LE6 0EE
Email: pfisher@globalnet.co.uk.

Family Chronicle Magazine
Premier family history magazine published in Canada and distributed world-wide. Covers a wide range of genealogical matters. Available on subscription. See Advert on Page 155

Canada - 10 Gateway Boulevard, #490, North York, Ontario, M3C 3T4 Canada
Tel No:1-888-FAMCHRO (326-2476) - (1-888-326-2476)
Email: magazine@familychronicle.com
Web site: www.familychronicle.com

Family History
Journal of the Institute of Heraldic and Genealogical Studies. See Advert on Page 39

79 - 82 Northgate, Canterbury, Kent, CT1 1BAGSD
Tel No: 01227-768664   Fax No: 01227-765617
Email: ihgs@ihgs.ac.uk   Web Site: www.ihgs.ac.uk

Family History Monthly
A premier monthly family history magazine published in the UK for all family historians and genealogists wherever they may be.   See Advert on Page 12

45 St Mary's Road, Ealing, London W5 5RQ
Tel No: 0181-579-1082   Fax No: 0181-566-0529.

Family Tree Magazine
Published by A B M Publishing the ever popular Family Tree Magazine contains information and articles for all involved in family history research. See Advert on Page 30

61 Great Whyte, Ramsey, Huntington, Cambs. PE17 1HL,
Tel No: 01487-814050 Fax No: 01487-711361
Email: family-tree-magazine@mcmail.com
Web Site: www.family-tree.co.uk,

History Today Magazine
Magazine devoted to a wide range of matters historical. Available from newsagents and on subscription.

20 Old Compton Road, London, W1V 5PE
Tel No: 0171-534-8000
Email: n.martin@historytoday.com
Web Site: www.historytoday.com

Irish Roots
A quarterly genealogy, history, Irish Culture magazine which provides essential information for those engaged in Irish Family History research.   See Advert on Page 145

Belgrave Avenue, Cork, Ireland
Tel No: 021-50-0067   Fax No: 021-50-0067
Email: irishrts@iol.ie
Web Site: www.iol.ie/~irishrts/

Kingpin (North Easterner Magazine)
Magazine for those with an interest in North East England. See Advert on Page 102

21 Meldon Way, Winlaton, Tyne and Wear NE21 6HJ
Tel No: 0191-414-0503
Email: michael@north-easterner.freeserve.co.uk
Web Site: www.north-easterner.freeserve.co.uk

Leopard Magazine
Quality Magazine dedicated to the interests of the North East of Scotland. Regular features on news, history, culture and the arts.   See Advert on Page 122

Waverley Unit, Wellheads Pl., Dyce, Aberdeen AB21 7GB
Tel No: 01224-770101   Fax No: 01224-722166
Email: d.pyper@leopardmag.co.uk.

Local History Magazine
Independent national subscription magazine published 6 times per annum with news, articles, reviews and a FREE Noticeboard for all subscribers. See Advert on Page 34

Local History Press Limited, 3 Devonshire Promenade, Lenton, Nottingham NG7 2DS
Tel No: 0115-9706473   Fax No: 0115-9424857
Email: editors@local-history.co.uk
Web Site: http://www.local-history.co.uk

Local History News
A topical magazine published by the British Association for Local History. See Advert on Page 34
PO BOX 1576, 24 Lower St., Harnham, Salisbury, SP2 8EY
Tel No: 01722-332158   Fax No: 017722-413242
Email: mail@balh.co.uk or info@balh.co.uk
Web Site: www.balh.co.uk/local_history_news.htm

Newspaper Service by the Name Shop
The Name Shop producers of framed displays of Coats of Arms & detailing name histories also supplies copies of past newspapers for dates required. See Advert on Page 18

Unit 28, Parade Shops, St Marys Place, Shrewsbury SY1 1DL
Tel: 01743-270220   Fax No: 01952-410689
Email: gary.huston@cableinet.co.uk
Web Site: Web Site: http://www.family-name.co.uk/history

MAGAZINES, PERIODICALS & NEWSPAPERS (Cont)

Newspapers Research Service by Paul Blake
Genealogical, historical, newspaper and picture research
undertaken by AGRA Member. See Advert on Page 64

18 Rosevine Road, West Wimbledon, London SW20 8RB,
Tel No: 0181-946-6395   Fax No: 0181-946-6395
Email: paulblakeexx@compuserve.com
Web Site:
http://ourworld.compuserve.com/homepages/paulblakexx

Practical Family History
A magazine especially formulated for the beginner and less
experienced family historian by the publishers of Family Tree
Magazine. See Advert on Page 78

61 Great Whyte, Ramsey, Huntington, Cambs. PE17 1HL,
Tel No: 01487-814050 Fax No: 01487-711361
Email: family-tree-magazine@mcmail.com
Web Site: www.family-tree.co.uk,

The Local Historian
A quarterly journal published by the British Association for
Local History. See Advert on Page 235, 236

PO BOX 1576, 24 Lower St., Harnham, Salisbury, SP2 8EY
Tel No: 01722-332158   Fax No: 017722-413242
Email: mail@balh.co.uk or info@balh.co.uk
Web Site: www.balh.co.uk/local_historian.htm

Ulster Origins
Magazine provided by specialists in genealogical, historical
and cultural research within Northern Ireland.

Stranagard, Desertmartin, County Londonderry BT45 5LP
Northern Ireland
Tel No: 01648-300540   Fax No: 01648-300540
Email: ulor@hotmail.com

POSTCARDS

Picture Past
A specialist service devoted to supplying old postcards
depicting churches of the time - extensive range - send for
details of availability. See Advert on Page 14.

47 Manor House Park, Codsall, Staffordshire. WV8 1ES

PLANS & MAPS

Alan Godfrey Maps
Publishers of reprints of large scale Ordnance Survey maps
mainly from the late 19th and early 20th centuries for towns
and cities across the British Isles. See Advert on Page 40

12 The Off Quay Building, Foundry Lane, Newcastle upon
Tyne, NE6 1LH
Tel No: 0191-276-1155   Fax No: 0191-265-9800   Web
Site: http://www.alangodfreymaps.co.uk

Chris E Makepeace Local History Consultancy
Specialist in history of the Manchester and surrounding area.
Stockist of Godfrey Edition of OS maps for the North and
Midlands.   See Advert on Page 92

5 Hilton Road, Disley, Cheshire, SK12 2JU
Tel No: 01663-763346

PLANS & MAPS (Cont)

Don Steel: Family History Enterprises
Supplier of books, maps & charts relevant to genealogical
and local history research. Send for catalogue. Extensive
range of all material available. See Advert on Page 42

'Brooking', Jarvis Lane, East Brent, Highbridge, Somerset,
TA9 4HS
Tel No: 01278-760535

Gould Books
Major distributor of genealogical resources for Australia
researchers including books, CD-ROMs, publications, plans
and maps, and computing aids.   See Advert on Page 148

PO Box 126, Gumeracha, South Australia, 5233, Australia.
Tel No: +61-8-8389-1611   Fax No: 08-8389-1599
Email: gould@adelaide.on.net
Web Site: www.gould.com.au

MM Publications
Specialist publisher of Directories, Military Lists, and other
useful guides - on microfiche. Maps of Counties and Town
Plans (paper) available also. See Advert on Page 22

White Cottage, The Street, Lidgate, Near Newmarket,
Suffolk, CB8 9PP
Email: michael@mmpublications.softnet.co.uk.
Web Site: www.mmpublications.co.uk

Stepping Stones
Supplier s of Trade, Street and Commercial Directories on
CD-ROM. Also supplies old coloured maps of town centres,
etc. See Advert on Page 109

3 George Hudson Street, York, YO1 6JL
Tel No: 01904-652666   Fax No: 01904-656333
Email: jud@mjudson.freeserve.co.uk
Web Site: www.stepping-stones.co.uk

British Census and National Index - 1881

The Church also distributes the 1881 British Census and National Index on a set of CD-ROMs' and these are available for viewing at many locations including the Family History Centres and numerous public libraries and is available for purchase from the Church's Distribution Centre.

399 Garretts Green Lane, Birmingham, B33 0HU
Tel No: 0121-784-9555   Web Site: www.lds.org

British Directories on Microfiche

British Directories on microfiche covers all counties of England, Wales, Scotland and Ireland. Send SAE for catalogue. See Advert on Page 44

Lyndon, Queen St., Kingswinford, West Mids. DY6 7AQ,
Tel No: 01384-293514   Fax No: 01384-826516
Email: Kingsley@cableinet.co.uk
Web Site: www.wkweb5.cableinet.co.uk/kingsley/

British Families Index

A fast growing index of genealogists' interests run by Don Steel Family History Enterprises. Contact the organisers for further information.

'Brooking', Jarvis Lane, East Brent, Highbridge
Somerset, TA9 4HS   Tel No: 01278-760535

Convicts & Criminals Indexes by Stuart Tamblin

Indexes to a variety of personal names found in documents in the custody of the PRO, mainly criminals and military subjects in the 19th & 20th centuries. See Advert on Page 22

14 Copper Leaf Close, Moulton, Northampton, NN3 7HS
Email: fhindexes@genfair.com
Web Site: www.genfair.com/fhindexes/

County Directories, etc by MM Publications

County Directories, Military Lists, and other useful guides - on microfiche. Prices from only £1.50. Send SAE (A5) or visit web site for details. See Advert on Page 22

The White Cottage, The Street, Lidgate, Near Newmarket, Suffolk, CB8 9PP
Email: michael@mmpublications.softnet.co.uk.
Web site: www.mmpublications.co.uk

Family Tree Magazine - Readers Research Listings

Each issue of the Family Tree Magazine features listings of lines of research on which subscribers are seeking assitance. See Advert on Page 30

61 Great Whyte, Ramsey, Huntington, Cambs. PE17 1HL
Tel No: 01487-814050   Fax No: 01487-711361
Email: family-tree-magazine@mcmail.com
Web Site: www.family-tree.co.uk

Genealogical Research Directory - World-wide reference

The GRD is the largest surnames queries listing published annually in bookform. Distributed in May. Published since 1981. Also on CD-ROM 1990/1998. See Advert on Page Inside Back Cover

British Isles Distribution:
2 Stella Grove, Tollerton, Nottingham NG12 4EY
Tel No: 0115-937-2287   0115-937-7018
Web Site: www.ozemail.com.au/~grdxxx

Gypsies & Rural Life - Cottage Books

Leading supplier of out of print books on rural life, work history and Gypsies. Send for free catalogues. Postal only. Wants lists welcome.   See Advert on Page 160·

Gelsmore, Coleorton, Leicestershire, LE67 8HQ

International Genealogical Index (I.G.I.)

The International Genealogical Index (known as the I.G.I.) is produced by The Church of Jesus Christ of Latter Day Saints. The Index is unique in its scope offering an initial source of information for researchers world-wide. It is available for viewing on line on the Internet and in microfiche form and CD-ROM at many different locations especially the Family History Centres usually located at the local Church premises (UK Centres listed at a later Section in this Directory).

Web Site: www.lds.org

I.G.I. Records Copies by Family Tree Services

Printouts from the IGI, General record search & supply, Rootseeker, plus new and second-hand microfiche readers supplied. See Adverts on Pages 20 & 52

30 Eastfield Road, Peterborough, Cambs. PE1 4AN
Tel No: 01733-890458   Fax No: 01733-890458

Mariners/Seamen from NE England - Neil Richardson

Microfiche available on Master Mariners & Ship Owners, Newcastle, North and South Shields, Seaton Sluice, Blyth and Sunderland.   See Advert on Page 102

12 Banbury Way, South Beach Estate, Blyth,
Northumberland, NE24 3TY   Tel No: 01670-353605
Email: k.richardson@ukonline.co.uk
Web Site: www.ukonline.co.uk/northumweb/index.htm

Military History Indexes by Stuart Tamblin

See earlier item in this Section - "Convicts & Criminals Indexes by Stuart Tamblin"

Military Lists on Microfiche by MM Publications

See earlier item in this Section - "County Directories, etc by MM Publications"

Military Publications by Naval & Military Press

Publishers and distributors of an extensive range of material relating to naval and military matters of interest to military, local and family historians.   See Advert on Page 170

PO Box 61, Dallington, Heathfield, East Sussex, TN21 9ZS
Tel No: 01435-830111   Fax No: 01435-830623
Email: order.dept@naval-military-press.co.uk
Web Site: http://www.naval-military-press.co.uk
Web Site: http://www.great-war-casualties.com

Murder Files

Information on thousands of murders that have taken place in the UK from 1700 onwards and can assist general enquiries, family historians, writers, etc.   See Advert on Page 46

'Marienau', Brimley Road, Bovey Tracy, Devon, TQ13 9DH
Tel No: 01626-833487   Fax No: 01626-835797
Email: ukmurders@bigfoot.com
Web Site: www.bigfoot.com/~ukmurders

River Thames Boatmen Indexes

Trueflare Ltd supply copies - in microfiche format - of the River Thames Licensed Watermen & Lightermen Bindings Index showing.   See Advert on Page 75

19 Bellevue Road, Bexleyheath, Kent DA6 8ND
Tel No: 0181-303-7000
Email: RJCIndex@aol.com.

South African (Boer) War 1899 - 1902

Service records of over 1,700 women of the British Empire. Military and civilian nurses, lay women, civilian volunteers. M-I-D and RRC Rolls. See Advert on Page 165

54a Towai Street, St Heliers, Auckland, 1005, New Zealand.
Tel No: (09)-575-8572
Email: smgray@ihug.co.nz.

Trade & Street Directories by Stepping Stones

Trade Directories on CD. Also covering Street, Commercial and Court Directories. Easy to use - no software to install. See Advert on Page 109

3 George Hudson Street, York, YO1 6JL
Tel No: 01904-652666   Fax No: 01904-656333
Email: jud@mjudson.freeserve.co.uk
Web Site: www.stepping-stones.co.uk

Trade & Street Directories - Original Indexes

Regional and National Indexes for Historians available on microfiche covering matters such as Street Direcories, indexes to parish registers, etc. See Advert on Page 102

113 East View, Wideopen, Tyne and Wear, NE13 6EF
Tel No: 0191-236-6416
Email: fiche@original-indexes.demon.co.uk
Web Site: www.original-indexes@demon.co.uk/index.htm

Victorian London Research Guides

Gendocs publish and distribute a series of Research Aids to Victorian London subjects such as Churches, Pubs, Inns & Taverns, Lodging Houses, and more.See Advert on Page 74

19 Mortar Pit Road, Northampton, NN3 5BL
Tel No: 01604-413025   Fax No: 01604-784281
Email: john@j-e-infotech.freeserve.co.uk
Web Site: http://www.gendocs.demon.co.uk

ACCOMMODATION

Cornwall - Marcorrie Hotel
Small family run Hotel with comfortable facilities, ideally situated for family history researchers visiting Cornwall. See Advert on Page 48
20 Falmouth Road, Truro, Cornwall, TR1 2HX
Tel No: 01872-277274   Fax No: 01872-241666
Web Site: www.cornwall.net/marcorrie

London - Foreign Missions Club
Christian guesthouse, approx 2 miles from the Family Records Centre & Society of Genealogists. On a private road near the West End and the City. See Advert on Page 66
26 Aberdeen Park, Highbury, London, N5 2BJ
Tel No: 0171-226-2663   Fax No: 0171-704-1853
Email: FMC_GH@compuserve.com
Web Site: www.foreignmissionsclub.co.uk

Yorkshire - Upper Carr Chalet & Touring Park
Well appointed site for caravanning family history researchers having its own genealogical resources library facility. See Advert on Page 354
Upper Carr Lane, Malton Rd, Pickering. N. Yorks YO18 7JP
Tel No: 01751-473115   Fax No: 01751-475325
Email: green@uppercarr.demon.co.uk
Web Site: www.uppercarr.demon.co.uk

ARMORIAL & HERALDRY

Achievements (Established 1961)
To throw light on your ancestry, Coats of Arms, Family & House histories. See Advert on Page 60
Centre for Heraldic & Genealogical Research and Artwork,
79 - 82 Northgate, Canterbury, Kent, CT1 1BA (GSD)
Tel No: 01227-462618   Fax No: 01227-765617
Email: achievements@achievements.co.uk
Web Site: www.achievements.co.uk

Fine Detail Art
Family crests and mottoes. See Advert on Page 186
3 The Avenue, Churchdown, Gloucester, GL3 2HB
Tel No: 01452-713057   Fax No: 01452-715031
Email: fine.detail.art@keldale.com
Web site: www.keldale.com/finedetailart

Institute of Heraldic & Genealogical Studies
Established academic institution offering facilities and support for anyone involved in genealogy and heraldry or research these subjects. See Advert on Page 39
79 - 82 Northgate, Canterbury, Kent, CT1 1BAGSD
Tel No: 01227-768664   Fax No: 01227-765617
Email: ihgs@ihgs.ac.uk   Web Site: www.ihgs.ac.uk

Marie Lynskey
Family trees, coats of arms, scrolls, certificates, maps, poems on vellum, parchment, etc.   See Advert on Page 40
109 Nutcroft Grove, Fetcham, Surrey, KT22 9LD
Tel No: 01372-372334   Fax No: 01372-372334
Email: ml@clara.net   Web Site: http://www.ml.clara.net

Name Shop
Framed displays depicting Coats of Arms & detailing name histories, beautifully produced for you and your ancestors to treasure. See Advert on Page 18
Unit 28, Parade Shops, St Marys Pl., Shrewsbury SY1 1DL
Tel: 01743-270220   Fax No: 01952-410689
Email: gary.huston@cableinet.co.uk
Web Site: www.family-name.co.uk/history

BOOKBINDING/DOCUMENT CONSERVATION

British Records Association
The BRA brings together everyone interested in archives: owners, custodians and users. It publishes, informs, lobbies and plays an active part in the work of preserving records. See Advert on Page 26
40 Northampton Road, London, EC1R 0HB
Tel No: 0171-833-0428   Fax No: 0171-833-0416

R-CRAFT Bookbinding and Restoration/Conservation
Family bibles, parchment deeds, paper documents, maps and plans, wax seals, whatever your requirements for restoration. See Advert on Page 29
7 Tammy Hall Street,Wakefield, West Yorkshire, WF1 2SX
Tel No: 01924-210052   Fax No: 01924-210052
Email: richard@r-craft.co.uk
Web Site: www.r-craft.co.uk

Ultimate Family Tree Deluxe UK Version is the ultimate genealogy program for compiling your family history.

Ultimate Family Tree Deluxe (UK Version) £39.99

Record all your family's details including census and medical records, with step-by-step help and then produce beautiful journals, reports, photo albums, including your own photos, newspaper cuttings, marriage certificates and more which can be handed down from generation to generation.

KEY FEATURES:
- Multilingual Records Requester - an invaluable database of worldwide addresses and telephone numbers of vital records offices, their fees, requirements etc. which automatically generates pre-addressed letters in 13 languages.
- UK specific events and sources
- Revised UK historical timelines
- UK Tutorial - provides in depth tutorials of where to get further information on different record types within the UK.

— Exclusive members-only genealogy web-site and access to thousands of online sources.
- Largest selection of charts and reports
- Family photos can be included in the reports
- Input data from and export data to any GEDCOM compatible software
- Prints journals with beautiful borders, coloured backgrounds, title page, table of contents, credits page, index and endnotes in either English, French or German.
- Exclusive Passenger lists of emigrants arriving in the US from 1820-1830 never before published on CD ROM. Features 173,000 names spread out among different countries.

Ultimate Family Tree Deluxe (Version 3.0) COMING SOON! £44.99

The Easy Way to Create Your Family Tree
Easy Step-By-Step Instructions
- Quick entry Wizards make entering data a breeze.
- In-depth tutorials help you find your ancestors records.
- Beginning and advanced editing modes let you tailor the program to suit your needs.
- Source templates show you how to properly document your information.

Find Your Family
- Ultimate Family Search Report – tells you where to find more information on your family.
- Free professional search ñ choose from 1 of 10 databases totalling over one billion names.
- Multi-Language Records requester – instantly creates letters requesting records in 13 languages.
- Easily share and exchange information with you friends and family.

Print Beautiful reports
- Easily create hundreds of reports, including attractive family trees.
- Personalise your printouts with your own photographs and scanned documents or choose from hundreds of images,

maps and photos.
- Print a complete family book in English, French or German. Program automatically creates a narrative from the information you enter.
- Automatically print out mailing lists, calendars and historical timelines.
- Make a beautiful scrapbook and multimedia slide show.

What's New in Version 3.0?
Ancestor Box Chart that shows ancestors for any given individual.
Ancestor/Descendant Box Chart displays a person's ancestors and descendants together on one family tree.
Heredity Statistics Report allows users to easily analyse family data for a better understanding of family dynamics, including medical history.
Ultimate Family Search searches the Internet and hundreds of CD ROM resources for users family information
Private Text for sharing information easily and without the worry of divulging confidential information
Global Find and Replace allows for making changes to data base information quickly and easily.

Genealogy Software
Nigel Bayley BA MBCS

The wide range of different genealogy programs makes it a daunting task to choose a program to hold your valuable family data. There are a lot of runners in the race for "Best genealogy program" so to help you select a winner I am going to describe the different and unique strengths of the most popular programs. As with many areas there are "Horses for Courses" and choosing the most suitable program is dependant on your requirements.

Generations Deluxe and Grande Suite

It has many unique strengths in the area of customising charts and reports. It is the only package that allows you to drag elements of your family tree

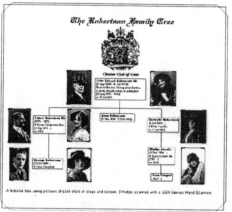

around and place pictures anywhere on the chart; it even allows you to combine charts by copying a descendant chart and adding it to an ancestor chart. The reporting feature will start your Wordprocessor up automatically and create the reports in it allowing you to add trees and photographs. It's easy to learn and comes with a comprehensive manual sample files and a freely distributable player program so you can give your relatives a special copy of your research.

With one hundred note areas of ten pages, unlimited events, facts and flags per person, it will store all the data you will normally come across. A UK SETUP CD is available when purchasing the program from S&N which will give you Birth, Baptism, Education, Occupation, Marriage, Death and Burial all on the main screen. This is far more than the other leading programs provide. It also gives you UK events which provide a context to the lives of your ancestors especially on timeline charts. This gives a line

showing the lifespan of each of your relatives plotted against time.

Genealogy for Windows

This is one of the few UK authored programs available, it's main advantage is the use of a research database that links in to the genealogy program. Extensive notes can be linked externally linked and your own favourite Wordprocessor can be used to edit them. It also has the unique feature of being able to draw charts in a form suitable for use by geneticists. The passing of a condition from generation to generation may be tracked and the person marked as a carrier, unaffected or affected.

Family Tree Maker

This has been a best selling program for many years and has added new features with each new version. It is unique in that it allows you to add any fact to a chart

to give anything from a very brief outline to an extensive and detailed chart. Version 7 will now create Maps locating your ancestors, All-in-One Charts, hourglass chart with both ancestors and descendants on the same tree and also has the option of fan or circular charts. It comes with the largest name index given away with any genealogy product and has £180 worth of research CDS included in the Deluxe edition. It is also easy to learn and comes with a thick reference manual.

Family Origins

If you require good search facilities, books and web publishing then Family Origins is an excellent choice. With no limit to the amount of people or the number of events that can be recorded and with a six condition search with any event selectable for searching, it is ideal for large amounts of data. The International Genealogical Index has millions of peoples details

taken from Parish records which can be searched and put onto floppy disc. The LDS Church can provide you with the results of a search for a surname on a floppy disc and Family Origins is the ideal tool to handle these large amounts of information.
The latest version has photo wallcharts, web publishing and a wide range of charts and reports

TMG

The Master Genealogist has long been regarded as the ultimate research program. It has the ability to record all your research information without omission. You might have several dates of birth from different sources such as Census (accuracy 5 years), gravestone, family bible or baptism. If these conflict it can be difficult to choose one. In TMG you don't have to choose they all can be included along with a surety value saying how reliable you think a date is.

TMG can also take a huge amount of data, external WP documents and high res photographs can be linked to a person or the same information can be kept in the TMG file. In some programs files can grow to be hundreds of megabytes but in TMG you can prevent this with the choice of linking large items externally.

Legacy

This recently released program brings down the cost of the more sophisticated research programs. It is like TMG in that you can have surety values and store a large amount of information. The search system allows you to use a Query by Example or a three condition search with logic. The duplicate search and merge facility in Legacy is both powerful and comprehensive. If you are taking information from several sources this could prove an invaluable tool. Unusually for a product in this price range it comes with a paper manual.

Ultimate Family Tree

With UK census events this US package has been redesigned for the UK market. It is another program

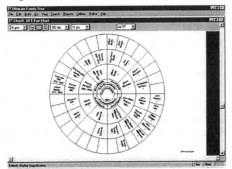

suited for research and has the unusual feature of providing circular charts of various types including 1/4, Ω or full circle.

Family Heritage

This package was originally written by a team of programmers from Corel, famous for Corel Draw. It can produce a large range of charts which can include photographic backgrounds. The program comes complete with photo retouching software, surname derivations, coats of arms and several research CDS.

WinGenea

This is one of the few shareware programs that draws a chart in a similar dropline style to that used by most books on English Genealogy. It draws them with the

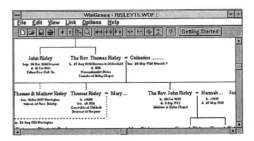

Husband's details, equals symbol, Wife's details with lines descending from the equals symbol to their offspring. The chart can be manipulated by dragging on names and the lines will follow. Up to three charts can be stored in each of·your files and they are not restricted to ancestor or descendant.

Brothers Keeper

The most popular shareware program in both DOS and Windows has kept it's position because of the wide range of reports and charts it allows

Summary

When choosing a program it is important to bear in mind what you require in terms of charting, reporting and recording. The wide range of programs available for Windows 95/98 should ensure you can find a program to help you avoid being buried in paperwork.

S&N can help you with advice on a suitable program to meet your needs. S&N also publish a book "Computer Aided Genealogy" which covers the use of a computer in family history and compares the many programs available, it also includes demos of them on a free CD. Phone 01722 716121 for their free catalogue or to buy the book at £5.95.

INTERNET GENEALOGY
Roy Stockdill

A SOMEWHAT curious statistic caught my eye the other day in one of the various Internet genealogical mailing lists to which I belong. Apparently, genealogy is the second most popular feature on the Internet, lagging only behind - pornography!

Whether this fascinating juxtaposition of interests says anything about family historians is something on which I would not like to speculate. But, joking aside, there can be no doubt that the Internet phenomenon has spawned an incredible boom in interest in genealogy and family history. It has also produced an enormous outpouring of information and exchange of data that genealogists of earlier generations would have been barely able to comprehend.

Not all of it, in my view, is entirely beneficial, but I will come to that later.

First, those of you who know nothing of Internet genealogy, and are novices even to computers, are probably asking: "What is it all about?" Well, there are three principal areas in which using the Internet can expand your genealogical contacts and knowledge immensely...

.... genealogy is the second most popular feature on the Internet

1. E-MAIL. For me, this has proved a tremendous boon, enabling me to keep in regular touch with members of the Stockdill Family History Society in the UK, America, Canada and Australia at the press of a computer key. When I arranged our first-ever Reunion in Yorkshire in 1997 I was virtually in daily contact with a cousin in Washington DC who was organising the visit of 16 of my American relatives. Once upon a time, this would have involved lengthy delays while we waited for conventional "snail mail" letters to pass between us, or costly international phone calls. But via e-mail we could exchange information about hotel bookings, flight times, the Reunion itinerary and a host of other details, send a message and get an answer back within an hour or so and all for the price of a local phone call.

My Canadian cousins are now in the throes of arranging our next Reunion in British Columbia in May 2000 and, naturally, all the arrangements are being made by e-mail in a 3-way link- up between Canada, America and Britain. When gathering material for my family journal, or for the Journal of One-Name Studies, I also find it very handy indeed to receive articles and pictures via e-mail, enabling me just to pull them straight off the computer and into a page for editing.

2. MAILING LISTS and NEWSGROUPS. These comprise a sort of "mini conference" of like-minded people who share common interests. If you subscribe to a mailing list you can exchange messages, chat, information, advice and just general gossip about family history with other genealogists around the world. There are many Internet groups devoted to a particular country. One of the major ones is called GENBRIT, which is for anyone researching their British ancestry. However, there are a large number of mailing lists that are more specialised. There is a group dedicated to every county in Britain, for instance, and lists devoted to researching in every State of the USA. Plus, there are lists for those with specialised research interests, such as gypsy, Huguenot and Quaker ancestry, and a vast number dedicated to individual surnames. These range in size from having several thousand members to only a few dozen. Organisations like the Society of Genealogists and the Guild of One-Name Studies have their own lists restricted to members only. ROOTSWEB, the US-based organisation which runs many of the genealogical lists, operates over 10,000 different groups. If you belong to a mailing list, you can choose to receive messages in one of two forms either individually or altogether in one long digest. Personally, I prefer the digest mode, since you can download the whole lot at once, scan the headings and skip over those subjects you are not interested in.

By taking part in these debates with other family historians around the world, you can add to your store of knowledge and experience, for however much you think you may know about the subject, there is always someone who can give you a new insight into an aspect or problem of genealogy. The real bonus comes when you make contact with a new-found cousin who is researching one of the same family lines as you. This has happened to me once when I noticed on the YORKSGEN mailing list, a group dedicated to researching in Yorkshire, a message from a lady in Australia seeking information on the name BRACEWELL. I responded and it transpired we shared a common ancestor in the Yorkshire Dales, my gt-gt-grandfather Richard Braccwell, and that we seemed to be third cousins. It doesn't often happen, mind you, but it's nice when it does!

Beware, though, the whole thing can become addictive! I belong to half a dozen lists and wading through the several digests a day that some of them put out can become quite time-consuming. By the way, many people may be afraid of venturing into the big wide world of the Internet because they are under the mistaken impression that it costs a fortune in phone bills. This is not the case, provided you use it wisely. One thing you do NOT do is to send or read messages while you are online. You write all your e-mails or newsgroup messages offline, then send them in one operation which should take only seconds. Likewise, you download all your messages and mailing list digests in one fell swoop, then read them offline, so that the telephone clock is not ticking away.

3. The WORLD WIDE WEB. This is where the greatest explosion of all in Internet Genealogy has taken place. There are literally tens of thousands of sites devoted to family history, the vast majority of them run by individuals but many also operated by FH societies. Cyndi's List, one of the most famous of all genealogy websites run by Cyndi Howells in America, has links to more than 41,000 other family history sites throughout the world at **http://www.cindislist.com**

Another important site is that for GENUKI, the virtual library for genealogical information on the British Isles. By accessing these pages at **http://genuki.org.uk** you can go to any county in the UK and find sites for most of the family history societies, plus a vast amount of data from published records and indexes. And, of course, everyone has by now heard of the FamilySearch website, operated by the Church of Jesus Christ of Latter Day Saints at **http://www.familysearch.org**

Here, you will find indexes of hundreds of millions of dead people, including the IGI, and links to the websites of many others who have published their pedigrees and family

Family Tree Companion – Only £14.99

Ultimate Family Tree Companion UK Version is the ultimate genealogy program for getting you started on compiling your family history. It is compatible with all other genealogy programs on the market.

KEY FEATURES:
- **Multilingual Records Requester** - an invaluable database of worldwide addresses and telephone numbers of vital records offices, their fees, requirements etc. which automatically generates pre-addressed letters in 13 languages.

- **UK Tutorial** - provides in depth tutorials of where to get further information on different record types within the UK.
- Exclusive Passenger lists of emigrants arriving in the US from 1820-1830 never before published on CD ROM. Features the first recorded records for this port, with 173,000 names spread out among different countries.

- **Compatible with any genealogy title on the market.**
- Can be used as a companion, stand alone product to researching your family history, as well as a companion product to all other genealogy titles. Features the exclusive Passenger List, never published before on CD ROM.

System Requirements 486DX / 33 MHz or higher, 16MB RAM Windows 95 or higher, 70 MB Free hard disk space, Double speed CD-ROM drive (4 speed recommended), SVGA video card supporting 640x480, 256 colours, Windows compatible sound card Windows compatible mouse. OPTIONAL: 14.4K bps Modem or faster recommended Windows compatible printer TWAIN compatible scanner

Softkey Family Tree – Only £9.99

If you're a budding genealogist or simply want to know more about your family's history, Softkey's Family Tree will help you enjoy this fascinating hobby. It can analyse statistics, let you focus on individual family members and if course print out a wide variety of trees.

FEATURES:
Choose from a variety of tree styles with flexible layout options
Add photographs, clipart and sound clips
Take a snapshot of your tree to use in other Windows applications
Analyse statistics, search records or use the perpetual calendar
Conforms to GEDCOM, the international standard format

System requirements IBM Compatible PC with 386SX or higher, Windows® 3.1 or higher, 4MB RAM, 4MB disk space

Softkey Family Origins – Only £9.99

Introducing the best way to preserve your family's unique heritage. Simply enter names and dates and Family Origins does the rest ñ automatically linking family members and building a visual display of your family tree. It's never been easier to document your genealogy and bring your family's memories to life!

FEATURES:
Just fill in the blanks – it automatically links all entries for you
Print customised, full-colour wall charts, to-do-lists, reports and more.
Create a multimedia scrapbook with photographs
Use the date calculator to determine ages and the relationship calculator to determine the relationship between any two people
Import and export GEDCOM data (includes full LDS support)

System requirements Windows® 3.1/95/98, 386/33Mhz or better, 4MB RAM, 5-20 MB Hard Drive space (Depending on installation), Double-speed CD_ROM drive, mouse required

BUY ONLINE AT:
www.learning.co.uk
or mail order on
01664 481563

information on the Internet. Genealogy software packages, like Family Tree Maker, also provide links to websites where you can trawl through a huge quantity of information. My own modest little website has resulted in many enquiries about the Stockdill/Stockdale surname and society, and has even gained me a few new members among people who have come upon it by accident whilst browsing on the world wide web. There is no doubt that this snowball will just go on rolling and rolling and gathering pace. More and more information, data and genealogical indexes will gradually be available online, just waiting to be accessed by the ordinary family historian sitting at home in front of his/her computer. It all sounds wonderful news for the genealogist, and mostly it is. But is there a downside to this incredible explosion of family history on the Internet? In one sense, I believe - Yes, there is.

I don't want to appear too carping, but I can't help noticing that a whole new breed of family historian has surfaced on the Internet, comprising people who are not steeped or

... a whole new breed of family historian has surfaced on the Internet ...

trained in the more traditional techniques of research. The popular press may perhaps be partly to blame for this, for they have given the impression that with things like the FamilySearch website all you have to do is log on and, hey presto, you can have your family tree back to William the Conqueror in an afternoon! Most of us know this to be nonsense, of course, but, unfortunately, there are newcomers to genealogy out there who will believe it. I have noticed in some of the mailing lists to which I belong that questions are being asked which display ignorance of even the most basic facets of research, and that there are people who think that all they have to do is access a few websites and it will all be at their fingertips. The other potential danger is that a good deal of misinformation and downright inaccurate data is going to creep onto the Internet and become enshrined as gospel if we are not very careful. It is, therefore, incumbent upon experienced genealogists to constantly hammer home the message to newcomers that, wonderful tool though it is, everything discovered on the Internet MUST be checked and confirmed by going back to the original sources.

ROY STOCKDILL is the Editor of the Journal of One-Name Studies, official publication of the Guild of One-Name Studies website at **http://www.one-name.org**
He is also founder of the Stockdill Family History Society, dedicated to the surname Stockdale/Stockdill/Stogdale and other variants website at **http://ourworld.compuserve.com/homepages roystock**

Family History Software

New version 4.0

EMBLA ©
Family Treasures

COMPUTING

Back to Roots Family History Service
Back to Roots offers a complete & comprehensive service to Family Historians including vast stocks of computer software always at very competitive prices. Adverts on Pages 198/199

16 Arrowsmith Drive, Stonehouse, Glos, GL10 2QR
Tel No: 01453-821300   Fax No: 01453-821300
Email: mike@backtoroots.co.uk
Web Site: www.backtoroots.co.uk

Broderbund Software Ltd
Producer of the genealogy program; Family Tree Maker. Also publishers of genealogical research material on CD-ROM and the Web. See Adverts on Pages 50/51, 200/201

Tilgate Forest Business Park, Elm Park Court, Brighton Road, Crawley, West Sussex, RH11 9BP
Tel No: 01293-651300   Fax No: 01293-651301
Web Site: www.familytreemaker.com

Church of Jesus Christ of Latter Day Saints
Well known for its International Genealogical Index (the IGI) The Church also produces the 'Personal Ancestral File' (PAF) computer program for organising and managing genealogical information plus supplementary programs which enhance the basic program. Copies of the programs can often be done via the Family History Centres usually located at the Church premises (UK Centres listed later in the GSD) or from:-

LDS Church UK Distribution Centre
399 Garretts Green Lane, Birmingham. B33 0HU
Tel No: 0121-784-9555

LDS Church North America Distribution Center
Salt Lake Distribution Center, 1999 West 1700 South, Salt Lake City. Utah 84104 USA

David Walker Photography
Professional Black & White or Colour Photographic restoration service. Photographs and documents also transferred onto CD-ROM. See Advert on Page 207

PO Box 220, Barnsley, S75 3YG
Tel No: 01226-200788   Fax No: 01226-200788
Email: david@davidwalkerphotography.freeserve.co.uk
Web Site: www.davidwalkerphotography.freeserve.co.uk

Embla AS
Publishers of Embla Family Treasurer computer program available from genealogical computer supply outlets or the Internet. See Adverts on Pages 194/195
Rogaland Science Park,

PO Box 8034, Stavanger, 4068, Norway
Tel No: 0047-51-87-46-90   Fax No: 0047-51-87-46-91
Email: sales@wmbla.no   Web Site: www.embla.no/uk

Gendocs
Image scanning (documents, photographs, pictures, etc, and printed text converted to computer text file), CD-ROM recording, Internet Page Design. See Advert on Page 74

19 Mortar Pit Road, Northampton, NN3 5BL
Tel No: 01604-413025   Fax No: 01604-784281
Email: john@j-e-infotech.freeserve.co.uk
Web Site: www.gendocs.demon.co.uk

genealogyPro
An Internet shop site dedicated to the sales of family history publications and services for those wishing to purchase or sell via the Internet. See Advert on Page 203

76 Tartan Drive, Nepaen, Ontario, K2J 3K3, Canada
Email: jholwell@genealogypro.com
Web Site: www.genealogy.com

GENfair
GENfair is an Internet shop selling publications and services of Family History Societies and other suppliers of resources to family history researchers. See Advert on Page 193

9 Fairstone Hill, Oadby, Leicester, LE2 5RL
Tel No: 0116-271-3494
Email: info@genfair.com
Web Site: http://www.genfair.com

Gould Books
Major distributor of genealogical resources for Australia researchers including books, CD-ROMs, publications, plans and maps, and computing aids. See Advert on Page 148

PO Box 126, Gumeracha, South Australia, 5233, Australia
Tel No: +61-8-8389-1611   Fax No: 08-8389-1599
Email: gould@adelaide.on.net
Web Site: www.gould.com.au

Grandpa Staten's Family History Services
Computer drawn family trees. Full printing services, booklets, laminating, mounting, encapsulation. Photographic restoration service also offered. See Advert on Page 46

37 Widgery Road, Exeter, Devon, EX4 8AX
Tel No: 01392-207259; 0771-902104
Email: staten@one-name.org

Internet History Resources
History Document Service providing access from home to over 8000 pages of original historical documents for New South Wales 1850 - 1920. See Advert on Page 151

55 Dangar St., Armidale, New South Wales, 2350, Australia
Tel No: 02-6772-3987   Fax No: 02-6772-3987
Email: smcinnes@mail2.northnet.com.au or
amcinnes@northnet.com.au
Web Site: www.ihr.com.au

Learning Company (UK) Ltd
Publisher of the 'Ultimate Family Tree' computer genealogy program which gives access to the Ultimate Family Tree web site. See Advert on Page 188, 192
Tilgate Forest Business Park, Elm Park Court, Brighton Road, Crawley, West Sussex, RH11 9BP
Tel No: 01293-651300   Fax No: 01293-651301
Email: jcielecki@mindscape.com
Web Site: www.learningco.com

Leicester Microdata Bureau Ltd
Service to convert paper, drawings and datafiles to CD-ROM, Microfilm and/or DVD. C.O.L.D. See Advert on Page 28
87 Avenue Road Extension, Leicester, LE2 3EQ
Tel No: 0116-270-9749   Fax No: 0116-270-6298
Email: info@lmb-microdata.co.uk
Web Site: www.lmb-microdata.co.uk

Marathon Microfilming Ltd
Transfer of information to fiche or CD-Rom. Print-out service. Storage equipment. Servicing and spare parts for microfilm machinery. See Advert on Page 205
27/29 St Mary's Place, Kingsway, Southampton, SO14 3HY
Tel No: 023-80-220481   Fax No: 023-80-230452
Email: marathon_micro@yahoo.com.

S & N Genealogy Supplies
Premier distributor of family tree software. Also supplies computers and genealogical research aids including books and publications. See Advert on Page 2
Greenacres, Salisbury Road, Chilmark, Salisbury, SP3 5AH
Tel No: 01722-716121   Fax No: 01722-716160
Email: 100064.737@compuserve.com
Web Site: www.genealogy.demon.co.uk

Stepping Stones
Trade Directories on CD. Also supplies street, commercial and court directories. Easy to use. Old coloured city centre maps also available. See Advert on Page 109
3 George Hudson Street, York, YO1 6JL
Tel No: 01904-652666 Fax No: 01904-656333
Email: jud@mjudson.freeserve.co.uk
Web Site: http://www.stepping-stones.co.uk

COURSES, CONFERENCES & EDUCATION

BBC History 2000
History 2000 is a BBC Millennium Project to encourage audiences in the UK to find out more about history.
See Article and Advert on Pages 242

British Broadcasting Corporation, History 2000 Dept., White City, 201 Wood Lane, London W12 7TS
Web Site: www.bbc.co.uk/history

Chris E Makepeace Local History Consultancy
Specialist in history of the Manchester and surrounding area. For all aspects of historical research, talks and lectures.
See Advert on Page 92

5 Hilton Road, Disley, Cheshire, SK12 2JU
Tel No: 01663-763346

Don Steel: Family History Enterprises
Organiser of Week and Day courses on family and local history subjects at locations in Somerset, Wiltshire, Gloucestershire and Devon. See Advert on Page 42

'Brooking', Jarvis Lane, East Brent, Highbridge, Somerset, TA9 4HS   Tel No: 01278-760535

Elizabeth Mortimer, MA, ASGRA
Professional genealogist and lecturer specialising in ancestry and living relative searches throughout Scotland. Contact for further information. See Advert on Page 128

Kilcombe, St Thomas's Well, Stirling, FK7 9PR, Scotland
Tel No: 01786-463470   Fax No: 01786-463470
Email: elizabeth.mortimer@lineone.net

Gill Blanchard, BA, MA, PGCE (PCE)
Genealogical Researcher - Norfolk area. Courses for beginners in Family History also available: days; weekends and/or evenings. Contact for details. See Advert on Page 94

1 Whitwell Street, Reepham, Norwich, Norfolk, NR10 4RA
Tel No: 01603-872367
Email: gblanchard@whitwellresearch.demon.co.uk

Institute of Heraldic & Genealogical Studies
Academic institution offering facilities and support for those wishing to study for qualifications in genealogy and heraldry or research these subjects. See Advert on Page 39

79 - 82 Northgate, Canterbury, Kent, CT1 1BAGSD
Tel No: 01227-768664   Fax No: 01227-765617
Email: ihgs@ihgs.ac.uk   Web Site: www.ihgs.ac.uk

Mr David G C Burns, ASGRA, Ancestral Researcher
Researcher and Lecturer in Genealogy with over 30 years experience. Contact for details. See Advert on Page 126

16/7 Craigmount Hill, Edinburgh, EH4 8HW, Scotland
Tel No: 0131-339-6959

War Research Society
First and Second World War battlefield/pilgrimage tours. Expert Battlefield Tour Guides. See Advert on Page 166
27 Courtway Avenue, Maypole, Birmingham B14 4PP
Tel No: 0121-430-5348   Fax No: 0121-436-7401
Email: battletour@aol.com
Web Site: www.battlefieldtours.co.uk

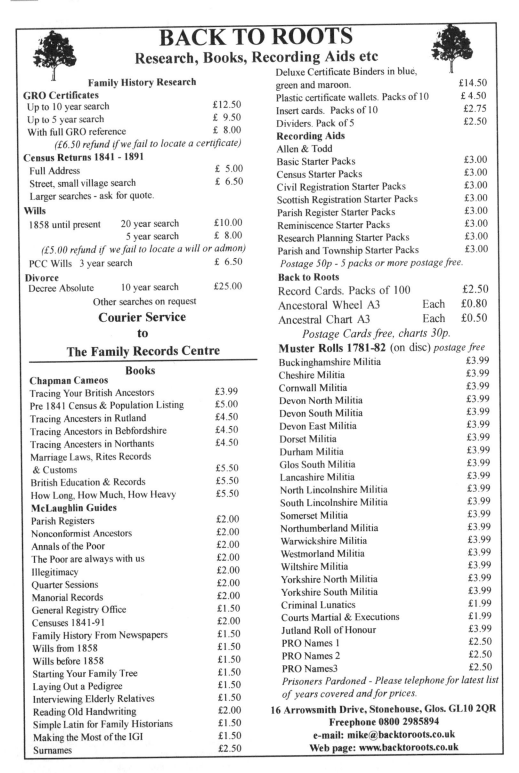

BACK TO ROOTS
Research, Books, Recording Aids etc

Family History Research

GRO Certificates

Up to 10 year search	£12.50
Up to 5 year search	£ 9.50
With full GRO reference	£ 8.00

(£6.50 refund if we fail to locate a certificate)

Census Returns 1841 - 1891

Full Address	£ 5.00
Street, small village search	£ 6.50
Larger searches - ask for quote.	

Wills

1858 until present	20 year search	£10.00
	5 year search	£ 8.00

(£5.00 refund if we fail to locate a will or admon)

PCC Wills 3 year search	£ 6.50

Divorce

Decree Absolute	10 year search	£25.00

Other searches on request

Courier Service
to
The Family Records Centre

Books

Chapman Cameos

Tracing Your British Ancestors	£3.99
Pre 1841 Census & Population Listing	£5.00
Tracing Ancesters in Rutland	£4.50
Tracing Ancesters in Bebfordshire	£4.50
Tracing Ancesters in Northants	£4.50
Marriage Laws, Rites Records & Customs	£5.50
British Education & Records	£5.50
How Long, How Much, How Heavy	£5.50

McLaughlin Guides

Parish Registers	£2.00
Nonconformist Ancestors	£2.00
Annals of the Poor	£2.00
The Poor are always with us	£2.00
Illegitimacy	£2.00
Quarter Sessions	£2.00
Manorial Records	£2.00
General Registry Office	£1.50
Censuses 1841-91	£2.00
Family History From Newspapers	£1.50
Wills from 1858	£1.50
Wills before 1858	£1.50
Starting Your Family Tree	£1.50
Laying Out a Pedigree	£1.50
Interviewing Elderly Relatives	£1.50
Reading Old Handwriting	£2.00
Simple Latin for Family Historians	£1.50
Making the Most of the IGI	£1.50
Surnames	£2.50

Deluxe Certificate Binders in blue, green and maroon.	£14.50
Plastic certificate wallets. Packs of 10	£ 4.50
Insert cards. Packs of 10	£2.75
Dividers. Pack of 5	£2.50

Recording Aids

Allen & Todd

Basic Starter Packs	£3.00
Census Starter Packs	£3.00
Civil Registration Starter Packs	£3.00
Scottish Registration Starter Packs	£3.00
Parish Register Starter Packs	£3.00
Reminiscence Starter Packs	£3.00
Research Planning Starter Packs	£3.00
Parish and Township Starter Packs	£3.00

Postage 50p - 5 packs or more postage free.

Back to Roots

Record Cards. Packs of 100		£2.50
Ancestoral Wheel A3	Each	£0.80
Ancestral Chart A3	Each	£0.50

Postage Cards free, charts 30p.

Muster Rolls 1781-82 (on disc) *postage free*

Buckinghamshire Militia	£3.99
Cheshire Militia	£3.99
Cornwall Militia	£3.99
Devon North Militia	£3.99
Devon South Militia	£3.99
Devon East Militia	£3.99
Dorset Militia	£3.99
Durham Militia	£3.99
Glos South Militia	£3.99
Lancashire Militia	£3.99
North Lincolnshire Militia	£3.99
South Lincolnshire Militia	£3.99
Somerset Militia	£3.99
Northumberland Militia	£3.99
Warwickshire Militia	£3.99
Westmorland Militia	£3.99
Wiltshire Militia	£3.99
Yorkshire North Militia	£3.99
Yorkshire South Militia	£3.99
Criminal Lunatics	£1.99
Courts Martial & Executions	£1.99
Jutland Roll of Honour	£3.99
PRO Names 1	£2.50
PRO Names 2	£2.50
PRO Names3	£2.50

Prisoners Pardoned - Please telephone for latest list of years covered and for prices.

16 Arrowsmith Drive, Stonehouse, Glos. GL10 2QR
Freephone 0800 2985894
e-mail: mike@backtoroots.co.uk
Web page: www.backtoroots.co.uk

BACK TO ROOTS
Computer Programs and Software

Family Tree Maker version 6 8CD's	£37.00
Family Tree Maker version 6 15 CD's	£46.50
Family Tree Maker version 7	£43.50
Family Tree Maker Upgrade version 7	£19.00
Generations Grande Suite version 6	£54.00
Generations Deluxe version 6	£38.00
Generations Deluxe version 5.2	£16.00
Ultimate Family Tree Deluxe (UK)	£36.00
Ultimate Family Tree (UK) basic	£15.50
Comptons Family Tree	£14.00
Europress Family Tree	£14.00
Softkey Family Tree	£ 8.50
LDS Companion	£16.00
Genmap Historical mapping system	£24.95
Birdie 32	£22.50
Wizard	£ 9.95
Northumberland & Durham Pigots Directory 1834	£20.00
Bucks Pigot Directory 1930	£20.00
Value of the pound	£ 6.50
Date Calculator	£ 6.50
1902 Street and Trade Directory for Scarborough, Filey & villages	£11.99
Kelly's 1872 Post Office Directory for the East Riding of Yorkshire	£11.99
Kelly's Street & Trade Directory of York, including York Inns with photos	£11.99
Principal Cities Trade Directory	£11.99
Kelly's 1919 Trade Directory of Cornwall	£11.99
Slaters 1848 Trade Directory of Northumberland	£11.99
Baines 1822 Trade Directory for West Riding of Yorkshire	£11.99
Kelly's 1897 Trade Directory for Hull & surrounding villages.	£11.99
Kelly's 1872 Directory of North & East Riding of Yorkshire	£11.99
Kelly's 1897 Street & Trade Directory for North Yorkshire	£11.99
Newcastle & Gateshead 13th & 14th Century Journal	£11.99
Pigots 1822 Trade Directory for Northumberland	£11.99
Pigots 1834 Trade Directory for Durham & surrounding villages	£11.99
Pigots Essex 1933-4	£11.99
Pigots N Wales 1828-9 S Wales 1830	£11.99

Postage £4.00 Family Tree Maker & Generations. All others postage free.

Pigots Cheshire 1829-9		£11.99
Sheffield Town Centre 1822		£11.99
Pigots Devonshire 1830		£11.99
Leeds 1853 Street Directory		£11.99
Kelly's 1897 Residents Directory for East Riding of Yorkshire		£11.99
Criminal Registers 1805-1816		
Somerset & Dorset	2400	£4.99
Devon & Cornwall	2732	£5.99
Wiltshire	1058	£2.99
Gloucestershire & Bristol	2417	£4.99
Wales & Monmouthshire	1252	£2.99
Oxfordshire & Berkshire	1438	£3.99
Northamptonshire, Leicestershire & Rutland	1450	£3.99
Buckinghamshire & Herefordshire	1327	£3.99
Bedfordshire, Cambridgeshire & Huntingdonshire	954	£2.99
Cumberland, Westmorland, Northumberland & Durham	1626	£2.99
Middlesex	1226	£2.99
Hampshire	2266	£4.99
Derbyshire, Nottinghamshire & Lincolnshire	2773	£5.99
Cheshire	1558	£3.99
Shropshire & Staffordshire	2446	£4.99
Herefordshire & Worc.	1736	£3.99
Warwickshire	2453	£4.99
Norfolk & Suffolk		£6.99
Essex		£5.99
Surrey		£6.99
Kent		£6.99
Sussex	1027	£2.99
Lancashire	8184	£12.99
Yorkshire	3595	£6.99
1817-1828		
Cornwall	1291	£2.99
Dorset	1482	£3.99
Bedfordshire	1165	£2.99
Devon	4826	£8.99
Bristol	2251	£4.99
Leicestershire	2251	£4.99
1829-1840		
Cornwall	2614	£4.99
Dorset	2546	£4.99

16 Arrowsmith Drive, Stonehouse, Glos. GL10 2QR
Freephone 0800 2985894
e-mail: mike@backtoroots.co.uk
Web page: www.backtoroots.co.uk

Family Tree Maker

Family Tree Maker Version 6.0
European Edition
Features:

All-in-One Tree
Exclusive to FTM v6.0, shows every member of the family file in one continuous tree.

The Vertical Ancestor Tree
Centres the primary individual at the bottom of the tree with ancestors branching upward in a 'V' shape

Tree Improvements
More background colours, highlight relationships between two individuals, show non-natural parental relationships

Background Pictures
Choose from a selection of 200 ClickArt™!images or use images from personal photos

Book Improvements
Add pictures, include photos in text items, insert page breaks, create custom index pages, reserve page numbers

Report & Research Improvements
● Soundex calculator (search by consonant sounds)
● Relationship Calculator
● Date & Time stamp
● Privatise information
● Letter requests & multiple language translations (English, Italian, German, Spanish Italian)
● Web search agents - search worldwide sites (& send you email when they find something)

Version 6 has more localised information than any previous version:
● Manual is localised
● Extra European CD
● European Publication - Internet Guide to sites containing UK information
● Inbox CDs contain European data as well as US data - marriage records, World Family Tree CDs

Available NOW! 9CD Set £39.99 or 16 CD Set £59.99

Still not convinced? Here are some experts' opinions about Family Tree Maker

"(Family Tree Maker)...has to be one of the easiest and most complete resources for building family trees."
ComputerActive July 99

"Family Tree Maker for Windows 95 and 98 is the world's best selling family tree program. It has many unusual features and is very good at handling facts, figures and notes"
Daily Telegraph April 99

"The types of information it will store is extraordinary..."
PC Advisor March 99

"Advanced research tools allow you to discover and preserve your family history more easily than you ever have before."
Windows Made Easy No.7 1999

WHICH VERSION IS RIGHT FOR YOU?	FTM 8-CD SET	FTM DELUXE 15-CD SET
Program Version	6.0	6.0
FamilyFinder Index – 3 CDs (200 million names)	✔	✔
Social Security Death Index – 2 CDs	✔	✔
U.S./International Marriage Records Index (1560 to 1900s) – 1 CD	✔	✔
Birth Records: US/Europe (900-1800) – 1 CD	✔	✔
Military Records: US Soldiers (1784-1811) – 1CD		✔
Family Histories Mid-Atlantic Genealogies – 1 CD		✔
Local & Family Histories: New England – 1 CD		✔
World Family Tree – 5 CDs	£100	£270
Value of Data CDs when sold separately	3 months	6 months
Free Membership to Genealogy Library.com		

System requirements Windows 95/98 - Processor IBM or compatible 486 or faster (Pentium recommended), 16MB RAM (32MB recommended) 2x CD-ROM drive or faster, 70 MB free hard disk space, 640x480 display, 256 colours. Optional: Modem, Video capture board & soundboard, scanner.

Introducing Family Tree Maker® 7.0

Easier, More Accurate Searching© New FamilyFinder Centre is Family Tree Maker's "home base" for research. It integrates all of Family Tree Maker's powerful research features together for utmost convenience.

Improved FamilyFinder® Search combs through a database of over 200 CDs and the Internet for information on your family. With smart-match technology, Version 7.0 identifies more probable matches and weeds out more false leads.
Improved FamilyFinder Report© lists the best matches at the very top of the report and also prioritises other matches within their own sections, making the report much easier to read and work through.

Integrated, Versatile Printing Options© **New Maps** display key events in the lives of your family members on a selection of U.S. and world maps. Great for family reunions and Family Books, your family's history and where different groups settled. Version 7.0's fully integrated map feature plots individuals' birth, marriage, death – in fact, any event for which you've entered a location.

©Improved Fit-to-Page Ancestor Tree – Automatically formats your tree to fit 6 generations on a page, up from 4 generations in previous versions.

Family Tree Maker 7.0 20-CD Set £69.99
Includes: the Family Tree Maker 7.0 upgrade program CD
a new edition of the User's Manual
a CD entitling you to 4 months of free access to Genealogy Library.com the same CDs as the 12-CD set above, PLUS: Land Records: AL,AR, FL, MI, MN, OH,WI (CD No. 255)
Boston Passenger Lists (CD No. 256)
World Family Tree European Origins
World Family Tree Volumes 1 - 5

Family Tree Maker 7.0 Upgrade £30
Includes: the Family Tree Maker 7.0 upgrade program CD
a new edition of the User's Manual
an updated FamilyFinder Index on 3 CDs
a CD entitling you to 2 months of free access to Genealogy Library.com

Family Tree Maker 7.0 12-CD Set £49.99
Includes: the Family Tree Maker 7.0 upgrade program CD
a new edition of the User's Manual
an updated FamilyFinder Index on 3 CDs
a CD entitling you to 2 months of free access to Genealogy Library.com Social Security Death Index (CD No. 110)
U.S./International Marriage Records Index (CD No. 403)
Birth Records: U.S./Europe, 900-1880 (CD No. 17)
Military Records: U.S. Soldiers, 1784-1811 (CD No. 146)
Family Histories Mid-Atlantic Genealogies (CD No. 156)
Local & Family Histories: New England (CD No. 449)
Southern Biographies and Genealogies (CD No. 500)

System Requirements Family Tree Maker 7.0 requires a CD-ROM Drive; Microsoft® Windows 95 or higher; Pentium® 90 (Pentium 166 recommended); 16 MB RAM (32 MB RAM recommended);VGA display running in at least 256 colours; Mouse; and 95 MB free hard disk space (50 MB free HD space after install). Optional: Modem (for connecting to Family Tree Maker Online and Genealogy Library.com);Video capture board and sound board (for video or audio clips); Scanner (for digitising graphic images).As with all Windows programs, a faster processor, more RAM and more free disk space will enhance performance. 45 MB of program files will be copied to your hard drive; the rest of the data, including the FamilyFinder Index, will remain on the CD-ROMs to be accessed during program use. Family Tree Maker 7.0 will read files from all previous versions of Family Tree Maker through 3.0. However, earlier versions of Family Tree Maker will not be able to open files created or modified in Family Tree Maker 7.0 unless converted to GEDCOM. Please note that Family Tree Maker 7.0 is a 32-bit application and will not run under Windows 3.1 or earlier;Windows 95 or higher is required.

Family History Fairs

We specialise
in organising
Family History Fairs
around the country
The Fairs feature
Family History Societies,
Record Offices, and trade stalls
Our Fairs are for the beginner
& experienced Family Historian

Come ro a Family History Fair for help
& advice and to see the products before you buy

Visit our Web Site for the latest
venues and dates
http://www.3w.co.uk/familyhistoryfairs/

Tel: 01344 451479
Email
Fhfairs@aol.com

The Fairs featured on Radio 4's "Making History"

DATE BY CLOTHING SERVICE

Jayne Shrimpton
Trained dress expert offers assistance in dating clothing in old photographs plus a full analysis service detailing and discussing dress in historical context. See Page 161

100 Chester Terrace, Brighton, East Sussex, BN1 6GD
Tel No: 01273-386176
Email: JayneShrimpton@photographdating.freeserve.co.uk
Web Site: www.photographdating.freeserve.co.uk

FAMILY HISTORY FAIRS

Don Steel's Family History Affairs
A series of family and local history book fairs incorporating workshops and discussion sessions, held at numerous locations throughout the year. See Advert on Page 42

'Brooking', Jarvis Lane, East Brent, Highbridge,
Somerset, TA9 4HS   Tel No: 01278-760535

Family History Fairs
Family history fairs organised and arranged at many venues and held throughout the year. See Advert on Page 202

5 Cottesmore, Bracknall, Berkshire, RG12 7YL
Tel No: 01344-451479
Email: Fhfairs@aol.com
Web Site: www.3w.co.uk/familyhistoryfairs

North West Group of FHS Family History Fairs
Organisers of the premier FHS Family History Fair held in the North West in the Autumn each year. See Page 356
North West Group of Family History Societies

4 Lawrence Ave., Simonstone, Burnley, Lancs, BB12 7HX
Tel No: 01282-771999

Yorkshire Family History Fair
Organisers of the Yorkshire Family History Fair held at York Racecourse on the last Saturday in June each year. Contact for arrangements to have stands, etc. See Advert on Page 355

1 Oxgang Close, Redcar, Cleveland, TS10 4ND
Tel No: 01642-486615   Fax No: 01642-486615

HOUSE HISTORIES

Achievements (Established 1961)
To throw light on your ancestry, Coats of Arms, Family & House histories. See Advert on Page 60

Centre for Heraldic & Genealogical Research and Artwork,
79 - 82 Northgate, Canterbury, Kent, CT1 1BA (GSD)
Tel No: 01227-462618   Fax No: 01227-765617
Email: achievements@achievements.co.uk
Web Site: www.achievements.co.uk

Debrett Ancestry Research Limited
UK House Histories undertaken by reputable established professional researchers. Free information pack available.
See Advert on Page 46, 76, 90

Dept GSD, PO Box 7, New Alresford, Hants., SO24 9EN
Tel No: (0)1962-732676   Fax No: (0)1962-734040
Email: enquiry@debrettancestry.demon.co.uk
Web Site: www.debrettancestry.demon.co.uk

INSURANCE PROVISION

British Association for Local History
The BALH arranges insurance schemes specifically for family and local history societies. Adverts on Pages 235, 236
PO BOX 1576, 24 Lower St., Harnham, Salisbury SP2 8EY
Tel No: 01722-332158   Fax No: 017722-413242
Email: mail@balh.co.uk or info@balh.co.uk

INTERNET SERVICES AND MEDIA FACILITIES

BBC History 2000
History 2000 is a BBC Project to encourage viewers to find out more about history. See Article and Advert on Pages 242
BBC, History 2000 Dept., 201 Wood Lane, London W12 7TS
Web Site: www.bbc.co.uk/history

GENfair
Internet shop selling the publications and services of Family History Societies and other suppliers. Contact to arrange for your services to be listed. See Advert on Page 193

9 Fairstone Hill, Oadby, Leicester, LE2 5RL
Tel No: 0116-271-3494   Email: info@genfair.com
Web Site: www.genfair.com

Tree Tops
Internet and media publicity via Sky TV News features and teletext listings provided for genealogists and family history researchers. See Advert on Page 14, 54, 57

PO Box 116, , Swindon, Wiltshire, SN3 2SX
Tel No: 01793-538730   Fax No: 01793-538730
Email: tree.tops@virgin.net

For All Your Fiche Storage, Microfilm Supplies & Equipment Needs

Readers ☆ Storage Cabinets ☆ Fiche Panels ☆ Fiche Binders ☆ Microfiche ☆ Fiche Trays ☆ Reader/Printers ☆ Lamps ☆ etc. etc.

We always have a selection of second hand readers available

The Microfilm Shop

Hammond Close, Nuneaton, Warwickshire, CV11 6RY, U.K.
Tel: (024) 7638 3998/1196   Fax: (024) 7638 2319

www.microfilm.com

For the latest news, articles, our full product range & educational information on microfilm technology, visit our NEW web site.

MICROFICHE & MICROFILM

Family Tree Services
Suppliers of new and second-hand microfiche readers. For a free booklet detailing all services available from this well known business telephone or fax. See Advert on Page 20, 52

30 Eastfield Road, Peterborough, Cambridgeshire, PE1 4AN
Tel No: 01733-890458   Fax No: 01733-890458

Leicester Microdata Bureau Ltd
Service to convert paper, drawings and datafiles to CD-ROM, Microfilm and/or DVD. C.O.L.D. See Advert on Page 28

87 Avenue Road Extension, Leicester, LE2 3EQ
Tel No: 0116-270-9749   Fax: 0116-270-6298
Email: info@lmb-microdata.co.uk
Web Site: www.lmb-microdata.co.uk

MARATHON
MICROFILMING
LTD

NEW & REFURBISHED FICHE READERS AND PRINTERS FOR SALE AT REASONABLE PRICES.

LAMPS & SPARES FOR MOST MACHINES.

MASTER FICHE/FILMS & DIAZO COPIES PRODUCED.

CD ROM SERVICE.

MARATHON MICROFILMING LTD,
27/29 ST MARY'S PLACE,
KINGSWAY,
SOUTHAMPTON, SO14 3HY.

TEL: **023 80 220481** FAX: **023 80 230452**
E-mail: marathon_micro @ yahoo.com

Microfilm Shop
The Microfilm Shop has one of the largest available ranges of microfilm consumables, equipment and storage devices, with sales to over 60 countries worldwide. Advert on Page 204

15 Hammond Close, Attleborough Fields Industrial Est, Nuneaton, Warwickshire, CV11 6RY
Tel No: 024-7638-3998/1196   Fax No: 024-7638-2319
Email: sales@microfilm.com
Web Site: www.microfilm.com

MILITARY UNIFORM IDENTIFICATION

David J Barnes (Military & Aviation Research)
A British military uniform identification service @ £4 per photographic print to be identified. See Advert on Page 165

148 Parkinson Street, Burnley, Lancashire, BB11 3LL

MISSING PERSONS SEARCH

Brewster International
Missing People - Specialists in searching for missing friends, relatives and lost loves, etc, plus all adoption related searches. See Advert on Page Inside Front Cover

12 Avery Gardens, Ilford, Essex, IG2 6UJ
Tel No: 0208-550-0333   Fax No: 0208-550-7766
Email: 106422.164@compuserve.com
Web Site: www.missing-people-found.com

Gendocs
Genealogical, Missing Beneficiaries, Lost Family and Friends, House Histories researched at all London Archives. See Advert on Page 74

19 Mortar Pit Road, Northampton, NN3 5BL
Tel No: 01604-413025   Fax No: 01604-784281
Email: john@j-e-infotech.freeserve.co.uk
Web Site: www.gendocs.demon.co.uk

Link Investigations
Private and commercial investigations. Name tracing covering the UK. Missing friend and family. Plus many other investigative services. See Advert on Page 160

22 Swan Mill Gardens, Dorking, Surrey, RH4 1PN
Tel No: 01306-880707   Fax No: 01306-888077
Email: info@linkinvestigations.co.uk
Web Site: www.linkinvestigations.co.uk

People Search Tracing Services
Missing persons and living relatives traced in the UK. Current electoral registers searched by name, plus other specialist research. See Advert on Page 62

30A Bedford Place, Southampton, SO15 2DG
Tel No: 02380-562243   Fax No: 02380-562243
Email: info@people-search.co.uk
Web Site: www.people-search.co.uk

UK Tracing Services
Tracing Service Specialists in finding missing friends, family and beneficiaries, living in the UK. No find, no fee usually available. Enquiries welcome (SAE). See Advert on Page 74

11 Woodfield Ave, Bredbury, Stockport, Cheshire, SK6 1DB
Email: tracer@talk21.com.

Parchment (Oxford) Limited is a commercial printing company specialising in the production of short run booklets.

We have been printing for Family History and Genealogical Societies for over thirty years, and attend dozens of FHS and SOG exhibitions and fairs every year, all over the country.

Parchments are happy to provide estimates for newsletters or booklets by telephone, fax, post or email - and we won't bother you with sales people (*unless you ask*).

Some of the products we supply Societies at present, which you may find of interest include:

- DTP (*disks taken from PC or Mac's*)

- Magazines, Booklets and Newsletters

- Leaflets and Flyers

- Digital Printing from hard copy or disk
    (*full colour A4's from 27p per print*)

- Posters (*up to A0 and beyond*)

- Full Colour Printing

Estimates are free and we will be happy to provide references from satisfied customers. Send us a copy of your publication with quantities required and we'll send you an estimate by return.

Parchment (Oxford) Limited

Printworks, Crescent Road, Cowley, Oxford OX4 2PB
Tel: (01865) 747547 Fax: (01865) 747551
email: *parchmentoxford@compuserve.com*

Buy printing online with **www.PrintUK.com**

PHOTOGRAPHIC, REPRODUCTIVE & PRINTING

Ancestral Locations
Bring your family's story to life with professional location photography of your ancestors home town/village. See Advert on Page 60

9 Edgebury, Woolavington, Bridgwater, Somerset, TA7 8ES
Tel No: 01278-685255   Fax No: 01278-685255
Email: lesleyt@ancestorsuk.com
Web Site: www.amcestorsuk.com

Creative Digital Imaging
Photo restoration, digital imaging, photo repairs, photo enhancement, photo colourising and photo editing. See Advert on Page 28

3 Post Office Row, Station Road, Legbourne, Louth, Lincolnshire, LN11 8LL
Tel No: 01507-608700   Fax No: 01507-600059
Email: cdilouth@cs.com
Web Site: http://ourworld.cs.com/cdilouth/

CW & S Parkinson (GSD)
For the supply of purpose made certificate storage binders, photographic and memorabilia albums. Advert on Page 26

25 Stirling Cres., Totton, Southampton, Hants., SO40 3BN
Tel No: 01703-862611   Email: cws@sirdar.demon.co.uk
Web Site: www.sirdar.demon.co.uk/cws/

Photo Restoration

Photographs Copied And Restored

We can even put your photographs or slides onto a CD-Rom

David Walker Photography
PO Box 220
Barnsley
S75 3YG

Tel / Fax 01226 200788

www.davidwalkerphotography.freeserve.co.uk

Grandpa Staten's Family History Services
Photographic restoration service plus full printing services available eg. booklets, laminating, mounting, encapsulation to AO. See Advert on Page 46

37 Widgery Road, Exeter, Devon, EX4 8AX
Tel No: 01392-207259; 0771-902104
Email: staten@one-name.org.

Ian J Hilder, BA(Hons)
Photography service in Sussex by experienced ancestral researcher. See Advert on Page 76

23A Grantham Bank, Barcombe Cross, Lewes, BN8 5DJ
Tel No: 01273-400604   Email: HilderGen@aol.com

Leicester Microdata Bureau Ltd
Service to convert paper, drawings and datafiles to CD-ROM, Microfilm and/or DVD. C.O.L.D. See Advert on Page 28

87 Avenue Road Extension, Leicester, LE2 3EQ
Tel No: 0116-270-9749   Fax No: 0116-270-6298
Email: info@lmb-microdata.co.uk
Web Site: www.lmb-microdata.co.uk

Marathon Microfilming Ltd
Transfer of information to fiche or CD-Rom. Print-out service. See Advert on Page 205

27/29 St Mary's Place, Kingsway, Southampton, SO14 3HY
Tel No: 023-80-220481   Fax No: 023-80-230452
Email: marathon_micro@yahoo.com

Parchment Oxford Limited
See Advert on Page 206 opposite & Page 208

Printability Publishing Ltd
Printer, publisher and supplier of local interest items. Printing services incl single & full colour printing. Advert Page 102

10/11 Lower Church Street, Hartlepool, TS24 7DJ
Tel No: 01429-267849   Fax No: 01429-865416
Email: enquiries@atKinsonprint.freeserve.co.uk
Web Site: www.atKinsonprint.freeserve.co.uk

Vanessa Morgan
Location photography service at competitive rates by experienced Researcher who undertakes all from one name searches to complete family histories. See Advert on Page 88

33 Plymouth Road, Redditch, Worcestershire, B97 4PX
Tel No: 01527-62472   Fax No: 01527-457176
Email: Vanessa@snackbox.freeserve.co.uk

Victoria Walker
Family history research, adoption searches, access to parish registers, IGI, wills, monumental inscriptions, census returns, etc. Plus also location photographs. See Advert on Page 84

11 Belper Lane, Belper, Derbyshire, DE56 2UG
Tel No: 01773-826025   Email: vaw@belper.jireh.co.uk

War Research Society
Graves and memorials photographed as one of the services provided by the Society which organises WW1 & WW2 battlefield/pilgrimage tours. See Advert on Page 166

27 Courtway Avenue, Maypole, Birmingham B14 4PP
Tel No: 0121-430-5348   Fax No: 0121-436-7401
Email: battletour@aol.com
Web Site: www.battlefieldtours.co.uk

PRESENTATION SERVICES

Debrett Ancestry Research Limited
Respected and reliable research undertaking which also offers a service to produce A3 presentation pedigree charts based on clients own data. See Advert on Page 46, 76, 90

Dept GSD, PO Box 7, New Alresford, Hants. SO24 9EN
Tel No: (0)1962-732676   Fax No: (0)1962-734040
Email: enquiry@debrettancestry.demon.co.uk
Web Site: www.debrettancestry.demon.co.uk

Fine Detail Art
Family crests and mottoes produced. See Advert on Page 186

3 The Avenue, Churchdown, Gloucester, GL3 2HB
Tel No: 01452-713057   Fax No: 01452-715031

Grandpa Staten's Family History Services
Computer drawn family trees together with full printing services, booklets, laminating, mounting, encapsulation and photo restoration service. See Advert on Page 46

37 Widgery Road, Exeter, Devon, EX4 8AX
Tel No: 01392-207259; 0771-902104
Email: staten@one-name.org.

Heritage World Family History Services
For the supply of local history information; heritage items and products, etc. Member of the Irish Family History Foundation. Send for leaflet. See Advert on Page 145

The Heritage Centre, 26 Market Street, Dungannon, Co Tyrone, BT70 1AB, Northern Ireland
Tel No: 01868-724187   Fax No: 01868-752141
Email: irishwld@iol.ie   Web Site: www.iol.ie./irishworld

Marie Lynskey
Family trees, coats of arms, scrolls, certificates, maps, poems on vellum, parchment, etc. by the author of 'Family Trees - A Manual.' See Advert on Page 40

109 Nutcroft Grove, Fetcham, Surrey, KT22 9LD
Tel No: 01372-372334   Fax No: 01372-372334
Email: ml@clara.net   Web Site: www.ml.clara.net

Name Shop
Framed displays depicting Coats of Arms & detailing name histories beautifully produced for you and your ancestors to treasure. See Advert on Page 18

Unit 28, Parade Shops, St Marys Pl., Shrewsbury SY1 1DL
Tel: 01743-270220   Fax No: 01952-410689
Email: gary.huston@cableinet.co.uk
Web Site: www.family-name.co.uk/history

R-CRAFT Bookbinding and Restoration/Conservation
Family bibles, parchment deeds, paper documents, maps and plans, wax seals, whatever your requirements for restoration. See Advert on Page 29

7 Tammy Hall Street, Wakefield, West Yorkshire, WF1 2SX
Tel No: 01924-210052   Fax No: 01924-210052
Email: richard@r-craft.co.uk
Web Site: www.r-craft.co.uk

PRIVATE INVESTIGATORS

Brewster International
Full range of investigative services available including searching for missing friends, relatives and lost loves, etc, plus all adoption related searches. See Advert on Page Inside Front Cover

12 Avery Gardens, Ilford, Essex, IG2 6UJ
Tel No: 0208-550-0333   Fax No: 0208-550-7766
Email: 106422.164@compuserve.com
Web Site: www.missing-people-found.com

Link Investigations
Private and commercial investigations. Name tracing covering the UK. Missing friend and family. Plus many other investigative services. See Advert on Page 160

22 Swan Mill Gardens, Dorking, Surrey, RH4 1PN
Tel No: 01306-880707   Fax No: 01306-888077
Email: info@linkinvestigations.co.uk
Web Site: www.linkinvestigations.co.uk

SECRETARIAL & TYPING TRANSCRIPTION SERVICES

Christine Foley Secretarial & Transcription Services
Transcription of tape recordings to printed copy and computer disk, plus general secretarial and word processing support. See Advert on Page 211

Glyndedwydd, Login, Whitland, Carmarthenshire, SA34 0TN
Tel No: 01994-448414   Fax No: 01994-448414

Manufacturers and Stockist of Plain and Printed Polythene Mailing Envelopes, Polythene Bags and all Types of Flexible Packaging.

CLEAR LIGHTWEIGHT POLYTHENE MAILING ENVELOPES.

Plain - Unprinted
C4 (Code: CC9) 230mm x 305mm + Flap 38 micron
C5 (Code: CC65) 165mm x 230mm + Flap 38 micron

Printed with a White Franking Panel
(to accept lasting endorsements i.e. PPI, Return Address or a Logo.)

C4 (Code: PC9) 230mm x 305mm t Flap 38 micron
C5 (Code: PC65) 165mm x 230mm + Flap 38 micron

EXTRA STRONG OPAQUE POLYTHENE MAILING ENVELOPES.
Printed with a White Franking Panel

(Code: E524) 240mm x 320mm + Flap 75 micron
(Code: E540) 400mm x 320mm + Flap 75 micron

Unit 16, Deptford Trading Estate. Blackhorse Road, LONDON. SE8 5HY
Tel: 0208 692 4444   Fax: 0208 692 3851
e-mail: bayardplastics@mcmail.com

Visit our Web Site

www.bayardplastics.mcmail.com

STATIONERY & STORAGE

Back to Roots Family History Service
A well established company which sells a wide range of recording aids for Family Historians always at very competitive prices. See Advert on Page 198/199

16 Arrowsmith Drive, Stonehouse, Glos., GL10 2QR
Tel No: 01453-821300   Fax No: 01453-821300
Email: mike@backtoroots.co.uk
Web Site: www.backtoroots.co.uk

Bayard Plastics Ltd
Manufacturers and suppliers of plastic mailing envelopes, self sealing bags, etc. See Advert opposite for more information.

Church of Jesus Christ of Latter Day Saints
The Church which is well known for its International Genealogical Index (the IGI) also produces a very useful range of forms for recording family history details. The forms may be purchased by non-Church members at very reasonable charges from the Family History Centres usually located at the local Church premises (UK Centres listed later in the GSD)

LDS Church UK Distribution Centre
399 Garretts Green Lane, Birmingham. B33 0HU
Tel No: 0121-784-9555

LDS Church North America Distribution Center
Salt Lake Distribution Center, 1999 West 1700 South, Salt Lake City. Utah 84104 USA

CW & S Parkinson (GSD)
A well established concern which supplies purpose made certificate storage binders, photographic and memorabilia albums, etc. for family historians See Advert on Page 26

25 Stirling Crescent, Totton, Southampton SO40 3BN
Tel No: 01703-862611   Email: cws@sirdar.demon.co.uk
Web Site: www.sirdar.demon.co.uk/cws/

Don Steel: Family History Enterprises
Supplier of books, maps, charts, forms and stationery for use in genealogical and local history research. Extensive range of all material available. See Advert on Page 42

'Brooking', Jarvis Lane, East Brent, Highbridge,
Somerset TA9 4HS   Tel No: 01278-760535

P A & S Smith (Custodian)
Custodian - database software for the family historian with pre-defined forms for most U.K. sources, such as certificates, census returns, etc. See Advert on Page 197

PO Box 180, 2 Church Cottages, Bishopstone, Hereford, HR4 7YP
Tel No: 01981-590309; 07801-503144 (mobile)
Email: PandSSmith@aol.com
Web Site: www.members.aol.com/pandssmith/custodian.htm

TRANSCRIPTION & TRANSLATION

Canterbury Research Services
Research in London and Kent, plus other services including Palaeography and Latin translations. See Advert on Page 72

71 Island Wall, Whitstable, Kent, CT5 1EL
Tel No: 01227-275931

Ian J Hilder, BA(Hons)
Researcher who also undertakes abstracts and translations for various types of documents. See Advert on Page 76

23A Grantham Bank, Barcombe Cross, Lewes, BN8 5DJ
Tel No: 01273-400604   Email: HilderGen@aol.com.

Kin in Kent
Palaeographer, all hands read. Manorial documents, early parish registers and wills a speciality. Transcriptions, translations & abstracts supplied. See Advert on Page 93

Boundary Hse, Stodmarsh Rd, Canterbury, Kent, CT3 4AH
Tel No: 01227-455267   Fax No: 01227-455267

Simon Neal, MA, MScEcon
Transcription and translation of wills, inventories, deeds and other old documents, Latin and English, by qualified archivist and Latin graduate. See Advert on Page 98

1 Thrush Close, Booker, High Wycombe, Bucks, HP12 4RJ
Tel No: 01494-521380   Email: simon.neal@which.net
Web: http://homepages.which.net/~les.neal/SIMON.HTM

HILLINGDON
FAMILY HISTORY SOCIETY

Publications

Middlesex Sessions Records (Hillingdon extracts) on microfiche (2)	£2.00
Church School, Ickenham, Records of pupils & teachers1873-1929 on fiche (2)	£2.00
St Marys Church, Harefield, Middx. Monumental Inscriptions on fiche (3)	£3.00
St Laurence Church, Cowley, Middx. Monumental Inscriptions on fiche (2)	£2.00
Holy Trinity Church, Northwood, Middx. Monumental Inscriptions on fiche (2)	£2.00
St Martins Church, West Drayton, Middx. Monumental Inscriptions on fiche (1)	£1.00
Family History in Hillingdon, A Guide to Sources	£1.50
Directory of Members' interests 1997	£1.00

Any of the publications can be
obtained from the

**Publications Officer
Mrs G May
20 Moreland Drive
Gerrards Cross
Bucks. SL9 8BB**

Please add p&p to order
UK rates
25p - 1 booklet
35p - 2 booklets
45p - 3 booklets
50p - 4 booklets
Overseas – 50p surface
Or £1.25 airmail per booklet
**Cheques in Sterling to
Hillingdon FHS**

A series of 12 guides on Beginning Genealogy by Arthur Dark

1.	Why, What & Where?	£1.25
2.	Civil Registration	£1.00
3.	English & Welsh Census Returns 1841-1891	£1.00
4.	Wills & Administrations	£1.00
5.	Parish Registers	£1.00
6.	Parish Officers, Records & Surveys	£1.00
7.	Useful Civil Records	£1.00
8.	Military & Naval Records	£1.00
9.	Tudor & Stuart Sources	£1.00
10.	Writing & Presentation	£1.25
11.	Searching in London	£1.25
12.	Surnames & One-Name Studies	£1.00

HILLINGDON FAMILY HISTORY FAIR
10am to 4pm SUNDAY 6th AUGUST 2000
at THE GREAT BARN, RUISLIP, MIDDLESEX

SUSSEX FAMILY HISTORY GROUP

THE SOCIETY COVERS THE WHOLE OF SUSSEX
AND HAS SIX MEETING CENTRES AND A LIBRARY.

THERE ARE MANY INDICES AND PUBLICATIONS
AVAILABLE BY POST FOR YOUR RESEARCHES

Send a SAE to the Secretary for a full list of our publications, or
visit our Web site at http://www.sfhg.org.uk

The Honorary Secretary
Mrs J. R. Goddard
54 Shirley Drive
Hove
Sussex BN3 6UF

Tel: 01273 556382
E-mail: tonyh@sfhg.org.uk

Hillingdon Family History Society
Gill May

Hillingdon Family History Society is typical of a growing number of small local societies affiliated to the Federation of Family History Societies. It was founded in 1988 by a group of students who had attended Adult Education classes in genealogy mounted by the London Borough of Hillingdon (the Borough that contains Heathrow Airport). Once the course was completed they wanted to continue to meet together to explore their newly discovered interest (or addiction?). Other societies have originated in the same way. Although many of the founders joined larger county-wide societies representing the areas from which their ancestors hailed they did not want to travel long distances to monthly meetings. Like other peripheral London Boroughs Hillingdon is a collection of ancient Middlesex villages and modern suburbs with little in common with central London. To an extent that may surprise those who do not know London, loyalties and patterns of social life can be curiously local wherever one lives inside the M25. Also characteristic of the London area is the fact that only a minority of our members have ancestral connections within Hillingdon. Apart from differences of scale our activities are much the same as those of the larger societies, but the monthly meetings are the core activity. Here we have the advantage of congenial and comfortable surroundings, with lots of parking space, in a local golf centre. Our situation on the western edge of the metropolis adjacent to the M40 also means that we have little difficulty in attracting interesting and authoritative speakers. We have a very active President in the shape of Michael Gandy, who often contributes to our proceedings.

In 1998 we celebrated our tenth anniversary with a programmme of special events. We enter our twelfth year with membership approaching 300, a much expanded quarterly journal, seven publications relating to the local area, a newly inaugurated computer section, membership of GENFAIR and our own worldwide web page. In addition, our series "Beginning Genealogy" has been completed with the publication of Part 12, entitled "Surnames & One-Name Studies". We are confident that at £1.25p. per part this is the cheapest pocket sized introductory series on the market.Strenuous efforts are made to keep up to date by revising and amending every reprint.

Our two current projects, transcribing the parish registers of St. Giles (Ickenham) on behalf of the London Borough of Hillingdon and indexing the local 1910 Inland Revenue Valuation Books are proceeding apace. Between 80 and 90 members attend our monthly meetings at Ruislip Golf Centre. On August 22nd 1999 we mounted our most ambitious project yet; our own Family History Fair in the superb setting of Ruislip`s historic tithe barn.

We have always seen our relationships with the larger sister societies in the London area as being a complementary one.

To that end we have maintained a strict policy of confining our project activities to the nine ancient parishes that make up modern Hillingdon. At the same time we have not objected to other societies working within our Borough, as long as we do not duplicate each others efforts.

Two of our monthly meetings take the form of Open Evenings when members are encouraged to bring their old photographs, mementoes, family trees etc. , are given time to examine our microfiche collection, thoroughly browse through the library, obtain genealogical advice and listen to a half hour Brainstrust. No meetings take place in August and we finish the year with an Annual Dinner. These regular events are supplemented by occasional visits to places of interest to family historians.

For the future we would like to develop a collection of data bases on CD Rom which members can either borrow or interrogate at our open evenings on a Society provided computer. We would also like to make our first Family History Fair into an annual event. These are modest objectives but over the twelve years of our existence we have surprised ourselves by the extent to which such year on year building achieves results.

Family historians pursuing their ancestors within Hillingdon must be prepared to find their genealogical sources divided between the Borough`s own archive collections (Local Heritage Service, Uxbridge Central Library, 15/16 High Street, Uxbridge) and the London Metropolitan Archives (40, Northampton Road, London EC1R OHB). London Metropolitan Archives acts as a regional record office for the whole of the London area and there will be material at the L.M.A. relevant to Hillingdon which supplements that held in the Borough. The same is true of the Public Record Office at Kew and to a lesser extent at the Guildhall Library and Corporation of London Records Office. Such dispersal of source material is inevitable given the size and complexity of London and the connections that people develop between one part of the London area and another.

A booklet listing the sources held by the Borough entitled, "Family History in Hillingdon, A Guide to Sources" (price £1.50p.), can be obtained from the Local Heritage Service or the Society. Research into these holdings can be undertaken by the Society at modest rates.

The Society meets on the 3rd Tuesday of the month at Ruislip Golf Cente, doors open 7.30 p.m., except August when there is no meeting.

Further details available from the Secretary (sae) Gill May, 20 Moreland Drive, Gerrards Cross, Bucks SL9 8BB or e-mail: Gillmay@dial.pipex.com

The Societies web page address is:
http://dspace.dial.pipex.com/town/terrace/xmq42/

All Family History Societies have been circulated to confirm the information is correct & up to date. Some Societies have not responded (December 1999)

Society of Genealogists
14 Charterhouse Buildings, Goswell Road, London, EC1M 7BA, Tel: 020-7251-8799, Tel: 020-7250-0291, Fax: 020-7250-1800, Email: info@sog.org.uk - Sales at sales@sog.org.uk, WWW: http://www.sog.org.uk

Federation of Family History Societies
The Benson Room, Birmingham & Midland Institute, Margaret Street, Birmingham, B3 3BSTel: 070 41 492032 Fax: 01564 703100 Email: ukinfo@ffhs.org.uk

Institute of Heraldic & Genealogical Studies
79 - 82 Northgate, Canterbury, Kent CT1 1BA Tel: 01227-768664 Fax: 01227-765617 Email: ihgs@ihgs.ac.uk WWW: www.ihgs.ac.uk

Irish Ancestry Group
Clayton House, 59 Piccadilly, Manchester, M1 2AQ, Tel: 0161-236-9750 Fax: 0161-237-3512, Email: mlfhs.demon.co.uk

England

Avon
Bristol & Avon Family History Society
383 Southmead Road, Westbury on Trym, Bristol, BS10 5LT
Bristol
Bristol & Avon Family History Society
383 Southmead Road, Westbury on Trym, Bristol, BS10 5LT
Bedfordshire
Bedfordshire Family History Society
PO Box 214, Bedford, Bedfordshire, MK42 9RX Email: bfhs@bfhs.org.uk, WWW: http://www.bfhs.org.uk
Berkshire
Berkshire Family History Society
Purley Lodge Cottage, Purley Village, Purley on Thames, Reading, Berkshire, RG8 8AS, Tel: 0118-984-3995, Tel: 0118-950-3756, Fax: , Email: john.gurnett@btinternet.com, WWW: www.berksfhs.org.uk
Birmingham
Birmingham & Midland Soc for Genealogy & Heraldry
111 Kenilworth Court, Coventry, Warwickshire, CV3 6JD, Tel: 01203-505595 Email: , WWW: www.bmsgh.org
Buckinghamshire
Buckinghamshire Family History Society
12 Brackley Road, Hazlemere, High Wycombe, Buckinghamshire, HP15 7EW, Tel: 01494-712258 Email: society@bucksfhs.org.uk, WWW: http://www.bucksfhs.org.uk
Hillingdon Family History Society
20 Moreland Drive, Gerrards Cross, Buckinghamshire, SL9 8BB, Tel: 01753-885602 Email: gillmay@dial.pipex.com, WWW: http://dspace.dial.pipex.com/town/terrace/xmq42
Cambridgeshire
Cambridgeshire Family History Society
1 Ascham Lane, Whittlesford, Cambridgeshire, CB2 4NT, Tel: 01223 832680
Cambridge University H&GS
c/o Crossfield House, Dale Road, Stanton, Bury St Edmunds, Suffolk, IP31 2DY
Peterborough & District Family History Society
33 Farleigh Fields, Orton Wistow, Peterborough, Cambridgeshire, PE2 6YB, Tel: 01733 235956
East Anglian Group of Family History Societies
2 Burleigh Road, St Ives, Huntingdon, Cambridgeshire, PE17 6DF Email: 114040.3430@compuserve.com
(Covers: Suffolk, Norfolk, Essex, Huntingdon, Royston, Hertfordshire, Bedfordshire, Northampton, Peterborough)
Cheshire
South Cheshire Family History Society
PO Box 1990, , Crewe, Cheshire, CW2 6FF
Family History Society of Cheshire
Mayfield, 101 Irby Road, Heswall, Wirral, CH61 6UZ
North Cheshire Family History Society
2 Denham Drive, Bramhall, Stockport, Cheshire, SK7 2AT, Tel: 0161-439-9270
WWW: http://www.genuki.org.uk/big/eng/CHS/NorthChsFHS
North West Group of Family History Societies
4 Lawrence Avenue, Simonstone, Burnley, Lancashire, BB12 7HX, Tel: 01282-771999
Email: ed@gull66.freeserve.co.uk

Warrington Family History Group
9 Manor Road, Lymm, Cheshire, WA13 0AY
Cleveland
Cleveland Family History Society
1 Oxgang Close, Redcar, Cleveland, TS10 4ND
North East Group of Family History Societies
10 Hallam Grange Rd, Sheffield, South Yorkshire, S10 4BJ
Cornwall
Cornwall Family History Society
5 Victoria Square, Truro, Cornwall, TR1 2RS, Tel: 01872-264044 Email: secretary@cfhs.demon.co.uk
WWW: http://www.cfhs.demon.co.uk/Society/
Cornish Forefathers Society
Credville, Quakers Rd, Perranwell, Truro,Cornwall,TR3 7PJ
Fal Worldwide Family History
57 Huntersfield, South Tehidy, Camborne, Cornwall TR14 0HW, Tel: 01209-711557 Fax: 01209-711557, Email: cfdell@clara.net
WWW: www.stuartorgan.force9.co.uk/index.html
Coventry
Coventry Family History Society
61 Drayton Crescent, Eastern Green, Coventry, Warwickshire, CV5 7EL, Tel: 01203-464256
Cumbria
Cumbria Family History Society
"Ulpha", 32 Granada Road, Denton, Manchester, M34 2LJ WWW: http://SENTINEL.mcc.ac.uk/genuki/big/eng/WES/cumbFHS
Furness Family History Society
64 Cowlarns Road, Hawcoat, Barrow-in-Furness LA14 4HJ, Tel: 01229-830942 Email: julia.fairburn@virgin.net
Cumberland
Cumbria Family History Society (See Cumbria)
Derbyshire
Chesterfield & District Family History Society
Overholme Farm, Cutthorpe, Chesterfield, Derbyshire, S42 7AG, Tel: 01246-232230 Fax: 01246-558800
Email: cadfhs@mcmail.com
Derbyshire Ancestral Research Group
86 High Street, Loscoe, Heanor, Derbyshire, DE75 7LF, Tel: 01773-604916
Derbyshire Family History Society
Bridge Chapel House, St Mary's Bridge, Sowter Road, Derby, Derbyshire, DE1 3AT, Tel: 01332-608101
http://web.ukonline.co.uk/members/gjhadfield/dbyfhs.htm
Devon
Devon Family History Society
8 King Henry's Rd, Exeter EX2 6AL Tel: 01392-275917
Dorset
Dorset Family History Society
42 Evering Avenue, Parkstone, Poole, Dorset, BH12 4JQ, Tel: 01202-567419
Somerset & Dorset FHS (See Somerset)
County Durham
Cleveland Family History Society
1 Oxgang Close, Redcar, Cleveland, TS10 4ND

Elvet Local & Family History Groups
37 Hallgarth Street, Durham, Durham, DH1 3AT,
Tel: 0191-386-4098 Fax: 0191-386-4098, Email: Turnstone-Ventures@durham-city.freeserve.co.uk
Newton Aycliffe Family History Society
25 Anne Swyft Road, Newton Aycliffe, County Durham,
DL5 5HD, Tel: 01325-315538
North East Group of Family History Societies
10 Hallam Grange Rd, Sheffield, South Yorkshire, S10 4BJ
Northumberland & Durham FHS (see Northumberland)
East Sussex
Family Roots F H Society (Eastbourne & District)
6 Winchester Way, Willingdon, Eastbourne, East Sussex,
BN22 0JP, Tel: 01323 504412 Email: goward@mistral.co.uk
Hastings & Rother Family History Society
65 Vale Road, St Leonards on Sea, East Sussex, TN37 6PT,
Tel: 01424-425037 Email: 101526.547@compuserve.com
Essex
Essex Society for Family History
56 Armond Rd, Witham CM8 2HA, Tel: 01376 516315
Fax: 01376 516315, Email: gr.morris@btinternet.com
WWW: www.genuki.org.uk/big/eng/ESS/efhs
Waltham Forest Family History Society
1 Gelsthorpe Road, Romford, Essex, RM5 2NB
Gloucestershire
Gloucestershire Family History Society
14 Alexandra Road, Gloucester, Gloucestershire, GL1 3DR,
Tel: 01452-52344 Email: ejack@gloster.demon.co.uk,
WWW: http://www.cix.co.uk/~rd/genuki/gfhs.htm
Sodbury Vale Family History Group
36 Westcourt Drive, Oldland Common, Bristol, BS30 9RU,
Tel: 0117 932 4133 Email: sladekf@netlineuk.net (S. Glos)
Hampshire
Hampshire Genealogical Society
22 Portobello Grove, Portchester, Fareham, Hampshire,
PO16 8HU Email: projadm@hantsgensoc.demon.co.uk,
WWW: http://www.hantsgensoc.demon.co.uk
Herefordshire
Herefordshire Family History Society
6 Birch Meadow, Gosmore Road, Clehonger, Hereford,
Herefordshire, HR2 9RH, Tel: 01981-250974
Email: brian@BProsser.freeserve.co.uk
WWW: http://freespace.virgin.net/bruce.donaldson
Hertfordshire
Hertfordshire Family & Population History Society
2 Mayfair Close, St Albans, Hertfordshire, AL4 9TN
Email: hfphs@btinternet.com
WWW: http://www.btinternet.com/~hfphs/index.htm
Royston & District Family History Society
60 Heathfield, Royston, Hertfordshire, SG8 5BN
Welwyn & District Local History Society
9 York Way, Welwyn AL6 9LB, Tel: 01438 716415
Letchworth & District Family History Group
84 Kings Hedges, Hitchin, Hertfordshire, SG5 2QE
Codicote Local History Society
34 Harkness Way, Hitchin, Hertfordshire, SG4 0QL
Huntingdonshire
Huntingdonshire Family History Society
16 Kidmans Close, Hilton, Huntingdon PE18 9QB
Tel: 01480-830199 Email: ghb@brkr.freeserve.co.uk,
WWW: http://www.genuki.org.uk/big/eng/HUN/HFHS
Isle of Wight
Isle of Wight Family History Society
Westwards, Hulverstone, Newport, Isle of Wight, PO30
4EH, Tel: 01983-740421 Email: dina@clara.net
WWW: http://www.dina.clara.net
Roots Family & Parish History
San Fernando, Burnt House Lane, Alverstone, Sandown, Isle Of Wight, PO36 0HB,
Tel: 01983 403060 Email: peters.sanfernando@tesco.net

Kent
Folkestone & District Family History Society
41 Reachfields, Hythe, Kent, CT21 6LS, Tel: 01303-264561
Email: jennifer.killick@virgin.net
WWW: www.jmcrid.demon.co.uk/fdfhs
Kent Family History Society
29 The Mall, Faversham, Kent, ME13 8JL, Tel: 01795
537802 Fax: 01795 537802, Email: kfhs@centrenet.co.uk,
WWW: http://www.centrenet.co.uk/~cna49/kfhs.htm
Tunbridge Wells Family History Society
The Old Cottage, Langton Road, Langton Green, Tunbridge
Wells, Kent, TN3 0BA, Tel: 01982-521495 Email:
brian@kcckal.demon.co.uk, WWW:
http://www.kcckal.demon.co.uk
North West Kent Family History Society
6 Windermere Road, Barnehurst, Bexleyheath, Kent, DA7
6PW WWW: http://www.users.ox.ac.uk/~malcolm/nwkfhs
Woolwich & District Family History Society
132 Belverdere Road, Bexleyheath, Kent, DA7 4PF
Lancashire
North West Group of Family History Societies
4 Lawrence Avenue, Simonstone, Burnley, Lancashire,
BB12 7HX, Tel: 01282-771999
Email: ed@gull66.freeserve.co.uk
Bolton & District Family History Society
205 Crompton Way, Bolton, Lancashire, BL2 2RU
Lancashire Family History & Historical Society
17 Victoria Street, Haslingden, Rossendale, Lancashire,
BB4 5DL, Tel: 01706-2277561 Email: RitaHirst@ukgateway.net
WWW: http://www.lfhhs.mcmail.com
Lancaster Family History Group
94 Croston Road, Garstang, Preston, Lancashire, PR3 1HR
Email: , WWW: www.fhgroup.freeserve.co.uk
Liverpool & S W Lancashire Family History Society
8 Paltridge Way, Pensby, Wirral, CH61 5YG Email: ,
WWW: www.l&swlfhs.freeserve.co.uk
Manchester and Lancashire FHS (see Manchester)
North Meols Family History Society
108 High Park Road, Southport, Lancashire, PR9 7BY, Tel:
0171-228244
Oldham & District Branch(Man & Lancs FHS)
Clayton House, 59 Piccadilly, Manchester, M1 2QA,
Tel: 0161 236 9750 Fax: 0161 237 3512
Ormskirk & District Family History Society
85 Wigan Road, Westhead, Lathom, Lancashire, L40 6HY,
Tel: 01695-572669
Wigan Family History Society
464 Warrington Rd, Goose Green, Wigan WN3 6QF
North Lancashire
Cumbria Family History Society (See Cumbria)
Leicestershire
Leicester & Rutland Family History Society
11 Faldo Close, Leicester, Leicestershire, LE4 7TS
Lincolnshire
Lincolnshire Family History Society
135 Balderton Gate, Newark, Nottinghamshire NG24 1RY,
Tel: 01636-671192
South Holland Family & Local History Group
54 Wygate Road, Spalding , Lincolnshire, PE11 1NT
London
East of London Family History Society
18a Canewdon Gardens, Wickford, Essex, SS11 7BJ
London & North Middlesex Family History Society
7 Mount Pleasant Road, New Malden, Surrrey, KT3 3JZ,
Tel: 0181-949-6765
Westminster & Central Middlesex Family History Soc
2 West Avenue, Pinner, Middlesex, HA5 5BY
Tel: 020 8866 7017 Fax: 020 8866 7018
Email: rookledge@compuserve.com

Woolwich & District Family History Society
132 Belverdere Road, Bexleyheath, Kent, DA7 4PF
Yorkshire Consortium of F H Socs - London Group
20 Avon Close, Watford, Hertfordshire, WD2 6DN
Tel: 01923 672691
Manchester
Manchester and Lancashire Family History Society
Clayton House, 59 Piccadilly, Manchester, M1 2AQ, Tel: 0161-236-9750
Fax: 0161-237-3512 Email: office@mlfhs.demon.co.uk
WWW: www.mlfhs.demon.co.uk
Merseyside
Liverpool & S West Lancashire Family History Society
8 Paltridge Way, Pensby, Wirral, CH61 5YG
WWW: www.l&swlfhs.freeserve.co.uk
Middlesex
Hillingdon Family History Society
20 Moreland Drive, Gerrards Cross, Buckinghamshire, SL9
8BB, Tel: 01753-885602 Email: gillmay@dial.pipex.com,
WWW: http://dspace.dial.pipex.com/town/terrace/xmq42
West Middlesex Family History Society
10 West Way, Houslow, TW2 TW5 0JF
Westminster & Central Middlesex FHS (see London)
Norfolk
Norfolk Family History Society
Kirby Hall, 70 St Giles Street, Norwich, Norfolk, NR2 1LS,
Tel: 01603-763718 Email: nfhs@paston.co.uk
www.uea.ac.uk/~s300/genuki/NFK/organisations/nfhs/
Mid-Norfolk Family History Society
35 Colleen Close, Toftwood, Dereham, Norfolk, NR19 1NL
Northamptonshire
Northamptonshire Family History Society
5 Harrowick Lane, Earls Barton, Northampton, NN6 0HD,
Tel: 01604-811220 Email: northamptonshire_fhs@compuserve.com,
WWW: http://www.ourworld.compuserve.com/homepages/northamptonshire_fhs
Northumberland
Northumberland & Durham Family History Society
2nd Floor, Bolbec Hall, Westgate Road, Newcastle-on-Tyne NE1 1SE, Tel: 0191-
261-2159 WWW: http://www.geocities.com/athens/6549/
Nottinghamshire
Mansfield & District Family History Society
15 Cranmer Grove, Mansfield, Nottinghamshire, NG19 7JR
Email: flinthambe@aol.com
Nottinghamshire Family History Society
39 Brooklands Drive, Gedling, Nottingham,
Nottinghamshire, NG4 3GU
Email: secretary@nottsfhs.org.uk
WWW: http://www..nottsfhs.org.uk
Oxfordshire
Oxfordshire Family History Society
19 Mavor Close, Woodstock, Oxford OX20 1YL
Rutland
Leicester & Rutland Family History Society
11 Faldo Close, Leicester, Leicestershire, LE4 7TS
Shropshire
Shropshire Family History Society
Redhillside, Ludlow Road, Church Stretton, Shropshire, SY6
6AD, Tel: 01694-722949 Email: dothills@lineone.net
Cleobury Mortimer Historical Society
24 High Street, Cleobury Mortimer, Kidderminster, DY14
8BY, Tel: 01299 270110 Fax: 01299 270110
Email: history@mbaldwin.free-online.co.uk
Somerset
Burnham & Highbridge FHS - Disbanded April 1998
Somerset & Dorset Family History Society
Unit 10, Kent House, Wood St, Taunton TA1 1UW
Email: sdfhs@lds.co.uk
WWW: http://www.lds.co.uk/ajbrown/s&dfhs/
Weston-Super-Mare Family History Society
15 Stanhope Rd, Weston Super Mare, Somerset, BS23 4LP,
Tel: 01934-625622 Email: wsmfhs@pathase.demon.co.uk

South West Group of Family History Societies
41 Langford Rd,The Potteries, Weston Super Mare,
Somerset BS23 3PQ
Staffordshire
Ancestral Rescue Club
Briar Rose House, 109 Furness, Glascote, Tamworth,
Staffordshire, B77 2QH, Tel: 01827-65322
Email: ancestral@rescue.fsnet.co.uk
Audley & District Family History Society
20 Hillside Avenue, Endon, Stoke on Trent ST9 9HH
Burntwood Family History Group
10 Squirrels' Hollow, Burntwood, Staffordshire, WS7 8YS,
Tel: 01543-672946 Email: manlaw@freeuk.co.uk
Birmingham & Midland Soc for Genealogy & Heraldry
111 Kenilworth Court, Coventry, Warwickshire, CV3 6JD,
Tel: 01203-505595 WWW: www.bmsgh.org
Suffolk
Felixstowe Family History Society
Drenagh, 7 Victoria Road, Felixstowe, Suffolk, IP11 7PT,
Tel: 01394-275631 Fax: 01394-275631WWW:
http://midas.ac.uk/genuki/big/eng/SFK/ffhs
Suffolk Family History Society
123 Cedarcroft Road, Ipswich, Suffolk, IP1 6BP, Tel:
01473-748677 Fax: 01473-744854 WWW:
http://www.genuki.org.uk/big/eng/SFK/Sfhs/Sfhs.htm
Surrey
East Surrey Family History Society
27 Burley Close, London, SW16 4QQ
Email: stephenturner1@compuserve.com
WWW: http://scorpio.gold.ac.uk/genuki/sry/esfhs
West Surrey Family History Society
Deer Dell, Botany Hill, Sands, Farnham, Surrey, GU10 1LZ
WWW: http://www.surreyweb.org.uk/wsfhs/index.html
Sussex
Sussex Family History Group
54 Shirley Drive, Hove, Sussex, BN3 6UF
Tel: 01273-556382 Email: tonyh@sfhg.org.uk
WWW: http://www.sfhg.org.uk
Tyne & Wear
Northumberland & Durham FHS (see Northumberland)
Waltham Forest
Waltham Forest Family History Society
1 Gelsthorpe Road, Romford, Essex, RM5 2NB
Warwickshire
Birmingham & Midland Soc for Genealogy & Heraldry
111 Kenilworth Court, Coventry, Warwickshire, CV3 6JD,
Tel: 01203-505595 Email: , WWW: www.bmsgh.org
Coventry Family History Society
61 Drayton Crescent, Eastern Green, Coventry,
Warwickshire, CV5 7EL, Tel: 01203-464256
Nuneaton & North Warwickshire Family History Society
33 Buttermere Avenue, Nuneaton, Warwickshire, CV11
6ET Email: , WWW: members.aol.com/nnwfhs
Rugby Family History Group
17 St Mary's Close, Southam, Leamington Spa,
Warwickshire, CV33 0EW, Tel: 01926-817667 Email:
durnomitchell@Jamesdurno.swinternet.co.uk
Warwickshire Family History Society
7 Mersey Road, Bulkington, Warwickshire, CV12 9QB
Email: n.wetton.@virgin.net
Worcestershire
Birmingham & Midland Soc for Genealogy & Heraldry
111 Kenilworth Court, Coventry, Warwickshire, CV3 6JD,
Tel: 01203-505595 Email: , WWW: www.bmsgh.org
Malvern Family History Group
22 Jasmine Rd, Malvern Wells, Worcestershire, WR14 4XD
Westmorland
Cumbria Family History Society (See Cumbria)

Yorkshire
North East Group of Family History Societies
10 Hallam Grange Road, Sheffield, S Yorkshire, S10 4BJ
Yorkshire Archaeological Soc - Family History Section
Claremont, 23 Clarendon Road, Leeds, LS2 9NZ Email: ,
WWW: http://www.users.globalnet.co.uk/~gdl/yasfhs.htm
Yorkshire Consortium of F H Socs - London Group
20 Avon Close, Watford, Hertfordshire, WD2 6DN Tel: 01923 672691
East Yorkshire
City of York & District Family History Society
4 Orchard Close, Dringhouses, York, YO24 2NX
WWW: www.yorkfamilyhistory.org.uk
East Yorkshire Family History Society
12 Carlton Drive, Aldbrough, East Yorkshire, HU11 4SF
WWW: http://www.astrogfen.demon.co.uk/eyfhs.html
North Yorkshire
City of York & District Family History Society
4 Orchard Close, Dringhouses, York, YO24 2NX
WWW: www.yorkfamilyhistory.org.uk
Cleveland Family History Society
1 Oxgang Close, Redcar, Cleveland, TS10 4ND
Ripon Historical Society-Ripon, Harrogate & Dist FHG
18 Aspin Drive, Knaresborough, North Yorkshire, HG5
8HH, Tel: 01423-863728 Email: gdl@globalnet.co.uk,
WWW: www.users.globalnet.co.uk/~gdl/index.htm
Wharfedale Family History Group
47 Hill Park Avenue, Horsforth, Leeds, West Yorkshire,
LS18 5LR, Tel: 0113 258 5597 Email: gdl@globalnet.co.uk,
WWW: http://www.users.globalnet.co.uk/~gdl/index.htm
South Yorkshire
Isle of Axholme Family History Society
11 Barnet Green, Hatfield, Doncaster, South Yorkshire,
DN7 4HL, Tel: 01302 350849
Barnsley Family History Society
58A High Street, Royston, Barnsley, South Yorkshire, S71
4RN Email: kath@barnsleyfhs.freeserve.co.uk
WWW:
http://www.ourworld.compuserve.com/homepages/Ian_Tow
nend/bfhs01.htm
Boothferry Family & Local History Group
17 Airmyn Avenue, Goole, DN14 6PF
Doncaster & District Family History Society,
'Marton House', 125 The Grove, Wheatley Hills, Doncaster,
DN2 5SN, Tel: 01302-367257 Email: tonyjunes@aol.com
WWW: http://www.ourworld.compuserve.com/homepages/
doncasterfhs

Isle of Man
Isle of Man Family History Society
3 Minorca Hill, Laxey, Isle of Man, IM4 7DN
Tel: 01624-862088

Sheffield & District Family History Society
10 Hallam Grange Road, Sheffield, South Yorkshire, S10
4BJ Email: sdfhs@harbottle.demon.co.uk
WWW: http://mtx.net.au/~exy/family_history_research.html
West Yorkshire
Bradford Family History Society
2 Leaventhorpe Grove, Thornton, Bradford, West
Yorkshire, BD13 3BN, Tel: 01274 881309
Email: DFlax@aol.com
WWW: http://www.genuki.org.uk/big/eng/YKS/bfhs/
City of York & District Family History Society
4 Orchard Close, Dringhouses, York, YO24 2NX
WWW: www.yorkfamilyhistory.org.uk
Calderdale Family History Society inc Halifax & District
61 Gleanings Avenue, Norton Tower, Halifax, West
Yorkshire, HX2 0NU, Tel: 01422-360756
Huddersfield & District Family History Society
292 Thornhill Lane, Clifton, Brighouse, HD6 4JQ
Email: Alan_Starkey@compuserve.com
WWW: http://www.hdfhs.demon.co.uk
Keighley & District Family History Society
2 The Hallows, Shann Park, Keighley, West Yorkshire,
BD20 6HY, Tel: 01535-672144
Morley & District Family History Group
26 Wynyard Drive, Morley, Leeds, LS27 9NA
Pontefract and District Family History Society
1 Coltsfoot Close, Carleton Glen, Pontefract, West
Yorkshire, WF8 2RY WWW: www.genfair.com
Wharfedale Family History Group
47 Hill Park Avenue, Horsforth, Leeds, West Yorkshire,
LS18 5LR, Tel: 0113 258 5597 Email: gdl@globalnet.co.uk,
WWW: http://www.users.globalnet.co.uk/~gdl/index.htm
Wakefield Family History Society
46 Ledger Lane, Outwood, Wakefield, West Yorkshire,
WF2 WF1 2PH Email: wakefield.fhs@virgin.net
WWW: http://homepage.virgin.net/wakefield.fhs
Yorkshire Archaeological Soc - Family History Section
Claremont, 23 Clarendon Road, Leeds, LS2 9NZ Email: ,
WWW: http://www.users.globalnet.co.uk/~gdl/yasfhs.htm
Wiltshire
Wiltshire Family History Society
10 Castle Lane, Devizes, Wiltshire, SN10 1HU Email:
suekerrawn@aol.com
York
City of York & District Family History Society
4 Orchard Close, Dringhouses, York, YO24 2NX Email: ,
WWW: www.yorkfamilyhistory.org.uk

Channel Islands
Family History Section of La Société Guernesiaise
PO Box 314, Candie, St Peter Port, Guernsey GY1 3TG
Channel Islands Family History Society
PO Box 507, St Helier, Jersey JE4 5TN

Wales

London Branch of the Welsh Family History Societies
25 Broomfield Road, Sevenoaks, Kent, TN13 3EL, Tel:
01732-453964 Email: rd9@le.ac.uk
Brecknockshire
Powys Family History Society
Oaker's Lodge, The Vineyards, Winforton, Herefordshire,
HR3 6EA, Tel: 01544 327103 Fax: 01544 327103
Email: 114251,2276@compuserve.com, WWW:
http://ourworld.compuserve.com/homepages/michaelmacsor
ley/powys1.htm & also via Genuki
Cardiganshire
Cardiganshire Family History Society
PO Box 37, Aberystwyth, Cardiganshire, SY23 2WL
Tel: 01974-298 884 WWW:
http://www.celtic.co.uk/~heaton/cgnts
Dyfed Family History Society
13 Harold Street, Hereford, Herefordshire, HR1 2QU
WWW: http://www.westwales.co.uk/dfhs/dfhs.htm
Ceredigion
Dyfed Family History Society
13 Harold Street, Hereford, Herefordshire, HR1 2QU
WWW: http://www.westwales.co.uk/dfhs/dfhs.htm
Clwyd
Clwyd Family History Society
3 Heol Berwyn, Cefn Mawr, Wrexham, LL14 3NB
Tel: 01978-822218
Denbighshire
Clwyd Family History Society
3 Heol Berwyn, Cefn Mawr, Wrexham, LL14 3NB
Tel: 01978-822218
Dyfed
Dyfed Family History Society
13 Harold Street, Hereford, Herefordshire, HR1 2QU
WWW: http://www.westwales.co.uk/dfhs/dfhs.htm
Flintshire
Clwyd Family History Society
3 Heol Berwyn, Cefn Mawr, Wrexham, LL14 3NB
Tel: 01978-822218
Glamorgan
Glamorgan Family History Society
The Orchard, Penmark, Vale of Glamorgan, CF62 3BN,
Tel: 01446-710287 WWW:
http://www..hometown.aol.com/gfhsoc

Gwent
Gwent Family History Society
11 Rosser Street, Wainfelin, Pontypool, Gwent, NP4 6EA
Email: gwent.fhs@cableol.co.uk, WWW:
http://welcome.to/gwent.fhs
Gwynedd
Gwynedd Family History Society
36 Y Wern, Y Felinheli, Gwynedd, LL56 4TX, Tel: 01428-
670267 Email: Gwynedd.Roots@tesco.net, WWW:
http://www.nol.co.uk/~gwyfhs
Monmouthshire
Gwent Family History Society
11 Rosser Street, Wainfelin, Pontypool, Gwent, NP4 6EA
Email: gwent.fhs@cableol.co.uk, WWW:
http://welcome.to/gwent.fhs
Montgomeryshire
Montgomeryshire Genealogical Society
1 Moreton Road, South Croydon, Surrey, CR2 7DN Email:
montgensoc@freeuk.com, WWW:
http://home.freeuk.net/montgensoc
Powys Family History Society
Oaker's Lodge, The Vineyards, Winforton, Herefordshire,
HR3 6EA, Tel: 01544 327103, Tel: , Fax: 01544 327103,
Email: 114251,2276@compuserve.com, WWW:
http://ourworld.compuserve.com/homepages/michaelmacsor
ley/powys1.htm & also via Genuki
Pembrokeshire
Dyfed Family History Society
13 Harold Street, Hereford, Herefordshire, HR1 2QU
WWW: http://www.westwales.co.uk/dfhs/dfhs.htm
Powys
Powys Family History Society
Oaker's Lodge, The Vineyards, Winforton, Herefordshire,
HR3 6EA, Tel: 01544 327103, Tel: , Fax: 01544 327103,
Email: 114251,2276@compuserve.com, WWW:
http://ourworld.compuserve.com/homepages/michaelmacsor
ley/powys1.htm & also via Genuki
Radnorshire
Powys Family History Society
Oaker's Lodge, The Vineyards, Winforton, Herefordshire,
HR3 6EA, Tel: 01544 327103, Tel: , Fax: 01544 327103,
Email: 114251,2276@compuserve.com, WWW:
http://ourworld.compuserve.com/homepages/michaelmacsor
ley/powys1.htm & also via Genuki

Scotland

Scottish Genealogy Society
15 Victoria Terrace, Edinburgh, EH1 2JL, Tel: 0131-220-3677 Fax: 0131-220-3677, Email: scotgensoc@sol.co.uk, WWW: http://www.scotland.net/scotgensoc/

Aberdeen
Aberdeen & North East Scotland Family History Society
164 King Street, Aberdeen, AB24 5BD, Tel: 01224-646323 Fax: 01224-639096, Email: anesfhs@rsc.co.uk, WWW: http://www.rsc.co.uk/anesfhs

Alloway
Alloway & Southern Ayrshire Family History Society
Alloway Library, Doonholm Rd, Alloway, Ayr, KA7 4QQ

Ayrshire
Alloway & Southern Ayrshire Family History Society
c/o Alloway Public Library, Doonholm Road, Alloway, Ayr, Ayrshire, KA7 4QQ

East Ayrshire Family History Society
c/o Dick Institute, Elmbank Avenue, Kilmarnock, East Ayrshire, KA1 3BU Email: eastayrfhs@crosshoose.freeserve.co.uk, WWW: http://www.home.clara.net/tshaw/eastayrfhs.htm

Glasgow & West of Scotland FHS (see Glasgow)

Largs & North Ayrshire Family History Society
12 Kelvin Gardens, Largs, Ayrshire, KA30 8SX WWW: http://www.freeyellow.com/members7/lnafhs/index.html

Troon & District Family History Society
c/o M.E.R.C., Troon Public Library, South Beach, Troon, Ayrshire, KA10 6EF

Angus
Tay Valley Family History Society (see Fife)

Argyll
Glasgow & West of Scotland FHS (see Glasgow)

Berwickshire

Borders
Borders Family History Society
Pentennen, 15 Edinburgh Road, Greenlaw, Berwickshire, TD10 6XF

Bute
Glasgow & West of Scotland FHS (see Glasgow)

Central Scotland
Central Scotland Family History Society
4 Fir Lane, Larbert, Stirlingshire, FK5 3LW
WWW: http://www.dgnscrn.demon.co.uk/CSFHS

Dumfries
Dumfries & Galloway Family History Society
Family History Research Centre, 9 Glasgow Street, Dumfries, DG2 9AF, Tel: 01387-248093 Fax: WWW: http://www.users@labplnet.co.uk/mbrownfam/bgehs.html

Dunbartonshire
Glasgow & West of Scotland FHS (see Glasgow)

East Lothian
Lothians Family History Society (See Edinburgh)

Edinburgh
Lothians Family History Society
c/o Lasswade High School Centre, Eskdale Drive, Bonnyrigg, Midlothian, EH19 2LA, Tel: 0131-660-1933 Fax: 0131-663-6634, Email: anne_agnew@online.rednet.co.uk

Fife
Fife Family History Society
28 Craigearn Avenue, Kirkcaldy, Fife, KY2 6YS, Tel: 01592 642735 Email: Fife@ffhoc.freeserve.co.uk, WWW:

Scottish Association of Family History Societies
51/3 Mortonhall Road, Edinburgh   EH9 2HN
Tel: 0131-667-0437

Tay Valley Family History Society
Family History Research Centre, 179–181 Princes Street, Dundee, DD4 6DQ, Tel: 01382-461845 Email: tayvalleyfhs@sol.co.uk, WWW: http://www.sol.co.uk/t/tayvalleyfhs/

Glasgow
Glasgow & West of Scotland Family History Society
Unit 5, 22 Mansfield Street, Partick, Glasgow, G11 5QP, Tel: 0141-339-8303 Fax: 0141-339-4899 WWW: http://www.welcometo/gwsfhs

North East Scotland
Aberdeen & North East Scotland Family History Society
164 King Street, Aberdeen, AB24 5BD, Tel: 01224-646323 Fax: 01224-639096, Email: anesfhs@rsc.co.uk, WWW: http://www.rsc.co.uk/anesfhs

Highlands
Invernesshire
Highland Family History Society
c/o Reference Room, Inverness Public Library, Farraline Park, Inverness, IV1 1NH

Kinross-shire
Tay Valley Family History Society (see Fife)

Lanarkshire
Glasgow & West of Scotland FHS (see Glasgow)

Lanarkshire Family History Society
Ref Department, Hamilton Central Library, 98 Cadzow Street, Hamilton ML3 6HQ

Lothian
Borders Family History Society
Pentennen, 15 Edinburgh Road, Greenlaw, Berwickshire, TD10 6XF

Midlothian
Lothians Family History Society (See Edinburgh)

Orkney
Orkney Family History Society
Leckmelm, Annfield Cres, Kirkwall, Orkney, KW15 1NS

Perthshire
Tay Valley Family History Society (see Fife)

Renfrewshire
Glasgow & West of Scotland FHS (see Glasgow)

Renfrewshire Family History Society
Museum and Art Galleries, High Street, Paisley, PA1 2BA

Shetland
Shetland Family History Society
6 Hillhead, Lerwick, Shetland, ZE1 0EJ Email: shetland.fhs@zetnet.co.uk

Stirlingshire
Central Scotland Family History Society
4 Fir Lane, Larbert, Stirlingshire, FK5 3LW WWW: http://www.dgnscrn.demon.co.uk/CSFHS
Glasgow & West of Scotland FHS (See Glasgow)

West Lothian
Lothians Family History Society (See Edinburgh)

Ireland

English based Irish Genealogy

Irish Genealogical Research Society
c/o 82 Eaton Square, London, SW1W 9AJ

Irish Ancestry Group
Clayton House, 59 Piccadilly, Manchester, M1 2AQ, Tel: 0161-236-9750 Fax: 0161-237-3512, Email: mlfhs.demon.co.uk

Northern Ireland

Ulster Historical Foundation
Balmoral Buildings, 12 College Square East, Belfast, BT1 6DD, Tel: 01232-332288 Fax: 01232-239885, Email: enquiry@uhf.org.uk, WWW: http://www.uhf.org.uk
North of Ireland Family History Society

c/o Graduate School of Education, 69 University Street, Belfast, BT7 1HL Email: RCDavison@msn.com, WWW: http://www.mni.co.uk/nifhs/index
Irish Heritage Association
A.204 Portview, 310 Newtownards Road, Belfast, BT4 1HE, Tel: 01232-455325

Republic of Ireland

Council of Irish Genealogical Organisations
186 Ashcroft, Raheny, Dublin 5

Irish Family History Society
PO Box 36, Naas, Co Kildare, Tel: Email: heueston@iol.ie, WWW: http://www.mayo-ireland.ie/geneal/ifhissoc.htm

County Dublin
Ballinteer FHS
29 The View, Woodpark, Ballinteer, Dundrum, Dublin, 16, Tel: 01-298-8082 Email: ryanc@iol.ie
Dun Laoghaire Genealogical Society
14 Rochestown Park, Dun Laoghaire, Co Dublin
Raheny Heritage Society
68 Raheny Park, Raheny, Dublin 5, Dublin, Tel: 01-831-4729

County Cork
Cork Genealogical Society
c/o 4 Evergreen Villas, Evergreen Road, Cork City, Co Cork, Tel: Email: micaconl@tinet.ie, **County Wexford**
Wexford Family History Society
24 Parklands, Maudlintown, Co Wexford, Tel: 053-42273 Email: murphyh@tinet.ie
County Wicklow
Wicklow County Genealogical Society
1 Summerhill, Wicklow Town, Co Wicklow

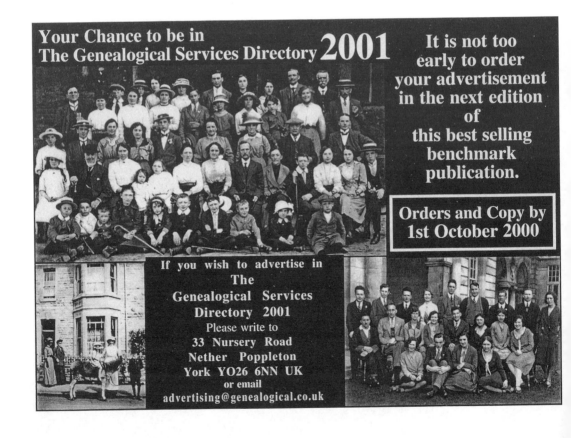

Specialist Family History Societies

Anglo-French Family History Society
31 Collingwood Walk, Andover, Hampshire, SP10 IPU
Anglo-German Family History Society
14 River Reach, Teddington, Middlesex, TW11 9QL,
Tel: 0181-977-2731 Fax: 0181-977-2731
Email: petertowey@compuserve.com
Anglo-Scottish Family History Society
Clayton House, 59 Piccadilly, Manchester, M1 2AQ
Tel: 0161-236-9750
Fax: 0161-237-3512, Email: mlfhs.demon.co.uk
British Assn for Cemeteries in S.Asia
76 1/2 Chartfield Avenue, London, SW15 6HQ
Tel: 0181-788-6953,
Catholic Family History Society
45 Gates Green Road, West Wickham, Kent, BR4 9DE
Cawdor Heritage Group
Wester Barevan, Cawdor, Nairn, Nairnshire, IV12 5XU
Email:106637,3442 (compuserve)
Genealogical Society of Utah (UK)
185 Penns Lane, Sutton Coldfield, West Midlands, B76 1JU,
Tel: 0121-384-2028 Fax: 0121-382-5948
Heraldry Society
PO Box 32, , Maidenhead, Berkshire, SL6 3FD
Tel: 0118-932-0210 Fax: 0118 932 0210
Email: heraldry-society@cwcom.net
The Historical Medical Equipment Society
14 The Avenue, Cliftonville, Northampton, NN1 5 BT
Hugenot & Walloon Research Association
Malmaison, Church St, Great Bedwyn, Wiltshire, SN8 3PE,
International Soc for British Genealogy & FH
P0 Box 3115, , Salt Lake City, Utah, 84110-3115, Tel: 801-
272-2178 WWW: http://www.homestart.com/isbgfh/
Jewish Genealogical Society of Great Britain
Finchley Synagogue, Kinloss Gardens, London, N3 3DU
Australia
Australian Society of the Lace Makers of Calais Inc
PO Box 946, , Batemans Bay, New South Wales, 2536,
Tel: 0244-718168 Tel: 0244-723421
Email: carolynb@acr.net.au
India
British Ancestors in India Society
2 South Farm Avenue, Harthill, Sheffield, South Yorkshire,
S31 8WY
Ireland
Clans of Ireland Ltd (Charity No 11585)
Grange Clare, Kilmeague, Naas, Co Kildare, Tel: 01365-
322353
Email: coolavin@indigo.ie, WWW:
http://www.irishclans.com

Police
Police History Society
37 Green Hill Road, Timperley, Altrincham, Cheshire,
WA15 7BG, Tel: 0161-980-2188 Fax: , Email:
alanhayhurst@compuserve.com Whilst the society is not
primarily interested in family history and has no personal
records to answer queries re individual officers, members
may contact each other
Railway
Railway Ancestors Family History Society
Lundy, 31 Tennyson Road, Eastleigh, Hampshire, SO50 9FS,
Tel: 01703 497465, Tel: 01703 900923, Fax: , Email:
alan@agldesign.freeserve.co.uk
WWW: www.railwayancestors.demon.co.uk

Lancashire Parish Register Society
16 Rothay Drive, Penketh, WarringtonWA5 2PG
Email: lprs@penketh.force9.co.uk,
WWW: http://www.genuki:org.uk/big/eng/LAN/lprs
Lighthouse Society of Great Britain
Gravesend Cottage, Gravesend, Torpoint, Cornwall
PL11 2LX Email: k.trethewey@btinternet.com,
WWW: http://www.lsgb.co.uk
Local Population Studies Society
78 Harlow Terrace, Harrogate, North Yorkshire, HG2 0PN,
Tel: 01423-560429 Fax: 01423-560429
Email: sir_david_cooke@compuserve.com
North East England Family History Club
5 Tree Court, Doxford Park, SunderlandSR3 2HR
Tel: 0191-522-8344,
Open University (DA3Ol)
Open University, Walton Hall, Milton Keynes, MK7 6AA
Quaker Family History Society
32 Ashburnham Road, Ampthill, Bedfordshire, MK45 2RH
Email: qfhs@mcmail.com, WWW: www.qfhs.mcmail.com
Rolls Royce Family History Society
25 Gisburn Road, Barnoldswick, Colne BB8 5HB
Romany & Traveller Family History Society
6 St James Walk, South Chailey, East Sussex, BN8 4BU
WWW: http://website.lineone.net/~mcgoa/rtfhs.html
Society of Brushmakers Descendants FHS
13 Asworth Place, Church Langley, Essex, CM17 9PU
Tel: 01279-629392 Email: socy-brush-desc@thenet.co.uk
WWW: http://www.thenet.co.uk/~socy-brush-desc
The Tennyson Society
Central Library, Free School Lane, Lincoln, Lincolnshire,
LN2 1EZ, Tel: 01522-552862 Fax: 01522-552858, Email:
lincs.lib@dial.pipex.com

Descendants of Convicts Group
PO Box 12224, A'Beckett Street, Melbourne 3000, Victoria,

Families in British India Society
81 Rosewood Avenue, Elm Park, Hornchurch, Essex, RM12
5LD

Irish Ancestry Group
Clayton House 59 Piccadilly, Manchester, M1 2AQ, Tel:
0161-236-9750
Fax: 0161-237-3512, Email: mlfhs.demon.co.uk
Irish Genealogical Research Society
c/o 82 Eaton Square, London, SW1W 9AJ

**International Police Association - British Section -
Genealogy Group**
Thornholm, Church Lane, South Muskham, Newark,
Nottinghamshire, NG23 6EQ, Tel: 01636-676997

London & North Western Railway Society
34 Falmouth Close, Nuneaton, Warwickshire, CV11 6GB

One Name Societies

Guild of One Name Studies
14 Charterhouse Buildings, Goswell Road, London, EC1M
7BA, Tel: 01293-411136 Email: guild@one-name.org,
WWW: www.one-name.org

Alabaster Society
No 1 Manor Farm Cottages, Bradenham, Thetford, Norfolk,
IP25 7QE, Tel: 01362-821243
Email: Laraine_Hake@compuserve.com, WWW:
http://ourworld.compuserve.com/homepages/Laraine_Hake
Alderson Family History Society
12 Masham Road, Harrogate, North Yorkshire, HG2 8QF,
Tel: 01423-884573
Allsop Family Group
86 High Street, Loscoe, Heanor, Derbyshire, DE75 7LF
Armstrong Clan Association, Gilnockie Tower, 7 Riverside
Park, Hollows, Canoubie, Dumfriesshire, DG14 0XB
Tel: 013873 71876 Email: ted.armclan@kencomp.net,
Beresford Family Society
5 Mill Close, Newton Solney, Burton-on-Trent,
Staffordshire, DE15 0SA
Blanchard Family History Society
Mill Farm, Church St, Bainton, East Yorkshire, YO25 9NJ
Bliss Family History Society
Spellowgrove Farm, Station Road, Clenchwarton, Kings
Lynn, Norfolk, PE34 4DH, Tel: 01553-772953
Email: bliss@one-name.org,WWW:
http://www.members.aol.com/keithbliss/fhs/main.htm
Braund Society
12 Ranelagh Road, Lake, Sandown, Isle of Wight, PO36
8NX, Tel: Email: braundsociety@fewiow.freeserve.co.uk,
Brooking Family History Society
37 Church Mead, Keymer, Hassocks, W Sussex, BN6 8BW
Bunting Society
'Firgrove', Horseshoe Lane, Ash Vale, Surrey, GU12 5LL,
Tel: 01252-325644 Fax: 01252-325644
Email: firgrove@compuserve.com WWW:
http://homepage.virgin.net/teebee.axeminster/BuntingSociety
.htm
Caraher Family History Society
142 Rexford Street, Sistersville, VA 26175
Cave Society
45 Wisbech Rd, Thorney, Peterborough PE6 0SA
Clan Davidson Association
Aisling, 67 Shore Road, Kircubbin, Newtownards
Co Down, BT22 2RP, Tel: 028 427-38402
Email: RCDavison@msn.com
WWW: http://www.phdavison.com/clandavison
Clan Gregor Society
2 Braehead, Alloa, Clackmannanshire, FK10 2EW
Tel: 01259-212076 Fax: 01259-720274
Email: clangregor@sol.co.uk
WWW: http://www.clangregor.com/macgregor
Cobbing Family History Society
89a Petherton Road, London, N5 2QT, Tel: 0171-226-2657
Cory Society
2 Pankhurst Close, Bexhill on Sea, East Sussex, TN39 5DL
Courtenay Society
Powderham Castle, Kenton, Exeter, Devon, EX6 8JQ
Tel: 01626-891554, Tel: 01626-891367, Fax: 01626-890729
Dalton Genealogical Society
30 Oxford Road, Cambridge, CB4 3PW, Tel: 01223-353987
Email: millicenty@aol.com
WWW: http://members.aol.com/daltongene/index.html
East Family History Society
64 Bearsdown Road, Eggbuckland, Plymouth, Devon, PL6
5TR, Tel: 01752-771157

Society for Name Studies in Britain & Ireland
22 Peel Park Avenue, Clitheroe, Lancashire, BB7 1ET, Tel:
01200-423771 Fax: 01200-423771

Family History Society of Martin
PO Box 9, , Rosanna, Victoria, 3084
Family History Society of Martin (UK)
202 Grangehill Road, Eltham, London, SE9 1ST
Gordon Clan
School Avenue, Huntley, Aberdeenshire,
Hamley, Hambly & Hamlyn FHS (International)
59 Eylewood Road, West Norwood, London, SE27 9LZ,
Tel: 0181-670-0683 Email: hamley@one-name.org
WWW: http://www.freespace.virgin.net/ham.famis/
Hards Family Society
Venusmead, 36 Venus Street, Congresbury, Bristol, BA49
5EZ, Tel: 01934 834780
Haskell Family History Society
73 Oakley Close, Holbury, Southampton SO45 2PJ
Holdich Family History Society
19 Park Crescent, Elstree, Hertfordshire, WD6 3PT
Tel: 0181 953 7105 Email: apogee@tesco.net
International Relf Society
Chatsworth House, Sutton Road, Haselbury Plucknett,
Somerton, Somerset, TA111 6QL, Tel: 01458-274015
Krans-Buckland Family Association
P0 Box 1025, North Highlands, California, 95660-1025
Tel: (916)-332-4359 Email: jkbfa@worldnet.att.net
Leather Family History Society
134 Holbeck, Great Hollands, Bracknell, Berkshire
RG12 8XG, Tel: 01344-425092 Email: s.leather@ic.ac.uk
Lin(d)field One Name Group
Southview, Maplehurst, Horsham, West Sussex, RH13 6QY,
Tel: 01403-864389 Email: lindfield@one-name.org WWW:
http://ourworld.compuserve.com/homepages/longweb
Mackman Family History Society
Chawton Cottage, 22a Long Ridge Lane, Nether Poppleton,
York, North Yorkshire, YO26 6LX
Tel: +44-(0)1904-781752 Email: mackman@one-name.org
Mayhew Ancestry Research
28 Windmill Road, West Croydon, Surrey, CR0 2XN
Morbey Family History Group
23 Cowper Crescent, Bengeo, Hertford SG14 3DZ
Morgan Society of England & Wales
11 Arden Drive, Dorridge, Solihull, W Midlands, B93 8LP
Moxon Family Research Trust
c/o 6 Halstone Avenue, Wilmslow, Cheshire, SK9 6NA
Moxon Society
59 Grantham Road, Sleaford., Lincolnshire, NG34 7NG,
Tel: 01529 304426
Offley, Offley Offler Offiler Family Society
2 The Green, Codicote, Hitchin, Hertfordshire, SG4 8UR,
Tel: 01438-820006
Orton Family History Society
25a Longwood Avenue, Bingley, West Yorkshire
BD16 2RX, Tel: Email: paul@orton.prestel.co.uk
WWW: http://www.prestel.co.uk/orton/fhs/
Palgrave Society
Crossfield House, Dale Road, Stanton, Bury St Edmunds,
Suffolk, IP31 2DY, Tel: 01359-251050 Fax: 01359-251050
Penty Family Name Society
Kymbelin, 30 Lych Way, Horsell Village, Surrey, GU21
4QG, Tel: 01483--764904 Email: pentytree@aol.com
Percy-Piercy Family History Society
'The Haven', 97 Manor Road South, Hinchley Wood, Esher,
Surrey, KT10 0QB, Tel: 0181-398-4991

Pomerology
The Keep, 3 Stokehouse Street, Poundbury, Dorchester, Dorset, DT1 3GP, Tel: 01305 257570, Tel: 01305 257912, Email: pomerology@compuserve.com

Rose Family Society
62 Olive Street, Grimsby, Ontario, L3M 2C4, Tel: 905-945-3352 Email: gordrose@vaxxine.com

Sermon, Surman Family History Society
Hill Rise House, Main Street, Hethe Village, Bicester, Oxfordshire, OX6 9HD, Tel: 01869-278105 Fax: 01869-278337, Email: design@johnsermon.demon.co.uk
WWW: www.johnsermon.demon.co.uk

Silverthorne Family Association
1 Cambridge Close, Lawn, Swindon, Wiltshire, SN3 1JQ

Society of Cornishes
216 Outland Road, Plymouth, Devon, PL2 3PE, Tel: 01752-773518 Fax: 01752 773518, Email: cornish@one-name.org

Sole Society
6 Hampden Close, Flitwick, Bedfordshire, MK45 1HR, Tel: 01525-716577 Email: timsoles@vossnet.co.uk
WWW: http://www.village.vossnet.co.uk/t/timsoles

Spencer Society
1303 Azalea Lane, Dekalb, Illinois, 60115

Stockdill Family History Society
6 First Avenue, Garston, Watford, Hertfordshire, WD2 6PZ, Tel: 01923-675292 Fax: 01923-675292, Email: roystock@compuserve.com WWW: http://ourworld.compuserve.com/homepages/roystock

Swinnerton Society
30 Coleridge Walk, London, NW11 6AT, Tel: 0181-458-3443 Email: roger.swynnerton@whichnet, WWW:

Talbot Research Organisation
42 Albemarle Avenue, Elson, Gosport., Hampshire PO12 4HY, Tel: 023 92589785
WWW: http://www.kiamara.demon.co.uk/index.html

The Goddard Association of Europe
2 Lowergate Road, Huncoat, Accrington, Lancashire BB5 6LN, Tel: 01254-235135
WWW: www.eese.qut.edu.au/~goddard/gae01.htm

The Metcalfe Society
31 Groves Lea, Mortimer, Berkshire, RG7 3SS, Tel: 0118-933-1244 Fax: 0118-933-1244, Email: diane.howarth@virgin.net, WWW: http://www.metcalfe.org.uk

The Stockton Society
101 Woodthorpe Dr, Bewdley, Worcestershire, DY12 2RL

Toseland Clan Society
40 Moresdale Lane, Seacroft, Leeds, West Yorkshire LS14 5SY Fax: 0113-225-9954

Watkins Family History Society
PO Box 1698, Douglas, Georgia, 31534-1698, Tel: 912-383-0839 Email: watkinsfhs@alltel.netbuzzwatk@aol.com
WWW: http://www.iinet.net.au/~davwat/wfhs/

Witheridge Family History Society
6 Nore Close, Gillingham., Kent, ME7 3DG

Australia

Society of Australian Genealogists
Richmond Villa, 120 Kent Street, Observatory Hill, Sydney 2000, New South Wales, Tel: 61-02-92473953 Fax: 61-02-92414872, Email: socgenes@ozemail.com.au

Australasian Federation of Family History Organisations (AFFHO)
6/48 May Street, Bayswater, Western Australia 6053

Genealogical Society of Victoria
Ancestor House, 179 Queen Street, Melbourne 3000, Victoria, Tel: +61-03-9670-7033 Fax: +61-03-9670-4490, Email: gsv@alphalink.com.au, WWW: http://www.alphalink.com.au/gsv/

Capital Territory

Historical & Genealogical Society of Canberra
GPO Box 585, Canberra, Capital Territory, ACT 2601

New South Wales

1788-1820 Pioneer Association
PO Box 57, Croydon, New South Wales, 2132, Tel: (02)-9797-8107

Australian Society of the Lace Makers of Calais Inc
PO Box 946, Batemans Bay, New South Wales, 2536, Tel: 0244-718168, Tel: 0244-723421, Email: carolynb@acr.net.au

Bega Valley Genealogical Society Inc
PO Box 19, Pambula, New South Wales, 2549

Berrima District Historical & Family History Society Inc
PO Box 851, Bowral, New South Wales, 2576

Blayney Shire Local & Family History Society Group Inc
c/o The Library, 48 Adelaide Street, Blayney, New South Wales, 2799 Email: blayney.library@cww.octec.org.au

Blue Mountains Family History Society
PO Box 97, Springwood, New South Wales, NSW 2777 Fax: 02-4751-2746

Botany Bay Family History Society Inc
PO Box 1006, Sutherland, New South Wales, 2232

Broken Hill Family History Group
PO Box 779, 75 Pell Street, Broken Hill, New South Wales, 2880, Tel: 08-80-881321

Burwood Drummoyne & District Family History Group
c/o Burwood Central Library, 4 Marmaduke Street, Burwood, New South Wales, 2134

Cape Banks Family History Society
PO Box 67, Maroubra, New South Wales, NSW 2035 Email: hazelb@compassnet.com.au, WWW: http://www.ozemail.com.au/mhazelb/capebank

Casino & District Family History Group Inc
PO Box 586, Casino, New South Wales, 2470 Email: hughsie@nor.com

Coffs Harbour District Family History Society Inc
PO Box 2057, Coffs Harbour, New South Wales, 2450

Cowra FHG Inc
PO Box 495, Cowra, New South Wales, 2794

Deniliquin Family History Group Inc
PO Box 144, Multi Arts Hall, Cressy Street, Denilquin, New South Wales, 2710, Tel: (03)-5881-3980 Fax: (03)-5881-1270

Dubbob & District FHS Inc
PO Box 868, Dubbo, New South Wales, 2830, Tel: 068-818635

Family History Society - Singleton Inc
PO Box 422, Singleton, New South Wales, 2330

Fellowship of First Fleeters
First Fleet House, 105 Cathedral Street, Woolloomooloo, New South Wales, 2000, Tel: (02)-9360-3988

Forbes Family History Group Inc
PO Box 574, Forbes, New South Wales, 2871, Tel: 0411-095311-(mobile)

Goulburn District Family History Society Inc
PO Box 611, Goulburn, New South Wales, 2580

Griffith Genealogical & Historical Society Inc
PO Box 270, Griffith, New South Wales, 2680

Gwydir Family History Society Inc
PO Box EM61, East Moree, New South Wales, 2400, Tel: (02)-67549235-(President)

Hastings Valley Family History Group Inc
PO Box 1359, Port Macquarie, New South Wales, 2444
Hawkesbury FHG, C/o Hawkesbury City Council Library,
Dight Street, Windsor, New South Wales, 2756
Hill End Family History Group
Sarnia, Hill End, New South Wales, 2850
Hornsbury Kuring-Gai FHS Inc
PO Box 680, Hornsby, New South Wales, 2077
Illawara Family History Group
PO Box 1652, South Coast Mail Centre, Wollongong, New
South Wales, 2521, Tel: (02)-42622212 WWW:
http://www.magna.com.au/~vivienne/ifhg.htm
Inverell District FHG Inc
PO Box 367, Inverell, New South Wales, 2360
Leeton Family History Society
PO Box 475, Centre Point, Pine Avenue, Leeton, New South
Wales, 2705, Tel: 02-6955-7199, Tel: 02-6953-2301, Fax:
Lithgow & District Family History Society
PO Box 516, Lithgow, New South Wales, 2790
Little Forest Family History Research Group
PO Box 87, 192 Little Forest Road, Milton, New South
Wales, 2538, Tel: 02-4455-4780, Tel: 02-4456-4223, Email:
cathyd@shoalhaven.net.au, WWW:
http://www.shoalhaven.net.au/~cathyd/groups.html
Liverpool & District Family History Society
PO Box 830, Liverpool, New South Wales, 2170
Manning Wallamba
c/o Greater Taree City Library, Pulteney Street, Taree,
New South Wales, 2430
Milton Ulladulla Genealogical Society Inc
PO Box 619, Ulladulla, New South Wales, 2539, Tel: 02-
4455-4206
Nepean Family History Society
PO Box 81, Emu Plains, New South Wales, 2750, Tel: (02)-

47-353-798 Email: istack@penrithcity.nsw.gov.au, WWW:
http://www.penrithcity.nsw.gov.au/nfhs/nfhshome.htm
New South Wales Association of Family History Societies
PO Box 48, Waratah, New South Wales, 2298
Newcastle Family History Society
PO Box 189, Adamstown, New South Wales, 2289
Orange Family History Society
PO Box 930, Orange, New South Wales, 2800
Port Stephens-Tilligerry & Districts FHS
PO Box 32, Tanilba Bay, New South Wales, 2319
Richmond River Historical Society Inc
PO Box 467, 165 Molesworth Street, Lismore, New South
Wales, 2480, Tel: 02-6621-9993
Richmond-Tweed Family History Society
PO Box 817, Ballina, New South Wales, 2478 Email:
warmer@nor.com.au
Ryde District Historical Society Inc
770 Victoria Road, Ryde, New South Wales, 2112, Tel:
(02)-9807-7137
Scone & Upper Hunter Historical Society Inc
PO Box 339, Kingdon Street, Upper Hunter, Scone, New
South Wales, 2337, Tel: 02-654-51218
Shoalhaven Family History Society Inc
PO Box 591, Nowra, New South Wales, 2541, Tel: 02-
44221253 Fax: 02-44212462, Email: jmoorley@shoal.net.au
Snowy Mountains Family History Group
PO Box 153, Cooma, New South Wales, 2630
Wagga Wagga & District Family History Society Inc
PO Box 307, Wagga Wagga, New South Wales, 2650
Wingham FHG, PO Box 72, Wingham, New South Wales,
2429
Young & District FHG Inc
PO Box 586, Young, New South Wales, 2594

Northern Territory

Genealogical Society of the Northern Territory
PO Box 37212, Winnellie, Northern Territory, 0821, Tel:
08-898-17363

Queensland

Queensland FHS
PO Box 171, Indooroonilly, Brisbane, Oueensland, 4O68
**Beaudesert Branch, Genealogical Society of Queensland
Inc**
PO Box 664, Beaudesert, Queensland, 4285
Bundaberg Genealocical Association Inc
PO Box 103, Bundaberg, Queensland, 4670
Burdekin Contact Group Family Hist Assn of N Qld Inc
PO Box 393, Home Hill, Queensland, 4806
Caboolture FH Research Group Inc
PO Box 837, Caboolture, Queensland, 4510
Cairns & District Family History Society Inc
PO Box 5069, Cairns, Queensland, 4870, Tel: 07-40537113
Central Queensland Family History Asociation
PO Box 6000, Rockhampton Mail Centre, Queensland, 4702
**Charters Towers & Dalrymple Family History
Association Inc**
PO Box 783, 54 Towers Street, Charters Towers,
Queensland, 4820, Tel: 07-4787-2124
**Cooroy Noosa Genealogical & Historical Research
Group Inc**
PO Box 792, Cooroy, Queensland, 4563 Email:
wefielder@bigpond.com.au
Dalby FHS Inc
PO Box 962, Dalby, Queensland, 4405
Darling Downs Family History Society
PO Box 2229, Toowoomba, Queensland, 4350
Genealogical Society of Queensland Inc
PO Box 8423, Woolloongabba, Queensland, 4102
Gladstone Branch G.S.Q.
PO Box 1778, Gladstone, Queensland, 4680

Gold Coast & Albert Gen Soc
PO Box 2763, Southport, Queensland, 4215
Gold Coast FH Research Group
PO Box 1126, Southport, Gold Coast, Queensland, 4215
Goondiwindi & District Family History Society
PO Box 190, Goondiwindi, Queensland, 4390, Tel:
0746712156 Fax: 0746713019, Email: pez@bigpond.com
Gympie Ancestral Research Society Inc
PO Box 767, Gympie, Queensland, 4570
Ipswich Genealogical Society Inc
PO Box 323, 1st Floor, Ipswich Campus Tafe, cnr.
Limestone & Ellenborough Streets, Ipswich, Queensland,
4305, Tel: (07)-3201-8770
Kingaroy Family History Centre
PO Box 629, James Street, Kingaroy, Queensland, 4610
Mackay Branch Genealogical Society of Queensland Inc
PO Box 882, Mackay, Queensland, 4740, Tel: (07)-
49426266
Maryborough District Family History Society
PO Box 408, Maryborough, Queensland, 4650
Mount Isa Family History Society Inc
PO Box 1832, Mount Isa, Queensland, 4825 Email:
krp8@+opend.com.au
**North Brisbane Branch - Genealogical Society of
Queensland Inc**
PO Box 353, Chermside South, Queensland, 4032
Queensland FHS Inc
PO Box 171, Indooroophilly, Queensland, 4068
Rockhampton Genealogical Society of Queensland Inc
PO Box 992, Rockhampton, Queensland, 4700

Roma & District Local & Family History Society
PO Box 877, Roma, Queensland, 4455
South Burnett Genealogical & Family History Society
PO Box 598, Kingaroy, Queensland, 4610
Southern Suburbs Branch - G.S.Q. Inc
PO Box 844, Mount Gravatt, Queensland, 4122
Sunshine Coast Historical & Genealogical Resource Centre Inc
PO Box 1051, Nambour, Queensland, 4560

South Australian Genealogical & Heraldic Society
GPO Box 592, Adelaide 5001, South Australia
Tel: (08)-8272-4222 Fax: (08)-8272-4910, Email:
saghs@dove.net.au, WWW: http://dove.net.au/~saghs
South East FHG Inc
PO Box 758, Millicent, South Australia 5280
Southern Eyre Peninsula FHG

Genealogical Society of Tasmania
PO Box 60, Prospect, Tasmania, 7250

Benalla & District Family History Group Inc
PO Box 268, St Andrews Church Hall, Church Street, Benalla, Victoria, 3672, Tel: (03)-57-644258
Bendigo Regional Genealogical Society Inc
PO Box 1049, Bendigo, Victoria, 3552
Cobram Genealogical Group
PO Box 75, Cobram, Victoria, 3643
East Gippsland Family History Group Inc
PO Box 1104, Bairnsdale, Victoria, 3875
Echuca/Moama Family History Group Inc
PO Box 707, Echuca, Victoria, 3564
Emerald Genealogy Group
62 Monbulk Road, Emerald, Victoria, 3782
Euroa Genealogical Group
43 Anderson Street, Euroa, Victoria, 3666
Geelong Family History Group Inc
PO Box 1187, Geelong, Victoria, 3220 Email:
flw@deakin.edu.au, WWW:
http://www.home.vicnet.net.au/wgfamhist/index.htm
Genealogical Society of Victoria
Ancestor House, 179 Queen Street, Melbourne 3000, Victoria, Tel: +61-03-9670-7033 Fax: +61-03-9670-4490, Email: gsv@alphalink.com.au, WWW:
http://www.alphalink.com.au/gsv/
Hamilton Family & Local History Group
PO Box 816, Hamilton, Victoria, 3300, Tel: 61-3-55-724933 Fax: 61-3-55-724933, Email: ham19.@mail.vicnet.net.au, WWW: http://www.freenet.com.au/hamilton
Kerang & District Family History Group
PO Box 325, Kerang, Victoria, 3579

Australasian Federation of Family History Organisations (AFFHO)
6/48 May Street, Bayswater, Western Australia 6053
Geraldton FHS
PO Box 2502, Geralton 6531, Western Australia WWW:
http://www.com.au/gol/genealogy/gfhs/gfhsmain.htm
Goldfields Branch, West Australian Genealogical Society Inc
PO Box 1462, Kalgoorlie, Western Australia 6430
Melville Family History Centre
PO Box 108 (Rear of Church of Jesus Christ Latter Day Saints, 308 Preston Point Road, Attadale, Melville, Western Australia 6156
Western Australia Genealogical Society
6/48 May Street, Bayswater, Western Australia 6053

Toowoomba Family History Centre
c/o South Town Post Office, South Street, Toowoomba, Queensland, 4350, Tel: 0746-355895
Townsville - Family History Association of North Queensland Inc
PO Box 6120, Townsville M.C., Queensland, 4810
Whitsunday Branch - Genealogical Soc Queensland Inc
PO Box 15, Prosperpine, Queensland, 4800

South Australia

26 Cranston Street, Port Lincoln, South Australia 5606
Whyalla FHG
PO Box 2190, Whyalla Norrie, South Australia 5608
Yorke Peninsula Family History Group
- 1st Branch SAGHS, PO Box 260, Kadina, South Australia 5554

Tasmania

Victoria

Mid Gippsland Family History Society Inc
PO Box 767, Morwell, Victoria, 3840
Mildura & District Genealogical Society Inc
PO Box 2895, Mildura, Victoria, 3502
Narre Warren & District Family History Group
PO Box 149, Narre Warren, Victoria, 3805 WWW:
http://www.ozemail.com.au/~narre/fam-hist.html
Nathalia Genealogical Group Inc
R.M.B. 1003, Picola, Victoria, 3639
Sale & District Family History Group Inc
PO Box 773, Sale, Victoria, 3850
Stawell Biarri Group for Genealogy Inc
PO Box 417, Stawell, Victoria, 3380
Swam Hill Genealogical & Historical Society Inc
PO Box 1232, Swan Hill, Victoria, 3585
Toora & District Family History Group Inc
PO Box 41, Toora, Victoria, 3962
Wangaratta Genealogical Soc Inc
PO Box 683, Wangaratta, Victoria, 3676
West Gippsland Genealogical Society Inc
PO Box 225, Old Shire Hall, Queen Street, Warragul, Victoria, 3820, Tel: 03-56252743 Email: watts@dcsi.net.au, WWW: http://www.vicnet.net.au/~wggs/
Wimmera Association for Genealogy
PO Box 880, Horsham, Victoria, 3402
Wodonga FHS Inc
PO Box 289, Wodonga, Victoria, 3689
Yarram Genealogical Group Inc
PO Box 42, 161 Commercial Road, Yarram, Victoria, 3971

Western Australia

Western Australia Genealogical Society Inc
6/48 May Street, Bayswater, Western Australia 6053, Tel: 08-9271-4311 Fax: 08-9271-4311, Email:
wags@cleo.murdoch.edu.au, WWW:
http://www.cleo.murdoch.edu.au/~wags

Canada

Canadian Federation of Genealogical & FH Societies
227 Parkville Bay, Winnipeg, Manitoba, R2M 2J6 WWW:
http://www.geocities.com/athens/troy/2274/index.html

Jewish Genealogical Society of Canada
PO Box 446, Station A, Willowdale, Ontario, M2N 5T1
Email: henry_wellisch@tvo.org

Alberta

Alberta Family Histories Society
PO Box 30270, Station B, Calgary, Alberta, T2M 4P1

Alberta Genealogical Society Drayton Valley Branch
PO Box 6358, Drayton Valley, Alberta, T7A 1R8, Tel: 403-542-2787 Fax: 403-542-2787, Email:
c_or_c@telusplanet.net

Alberta Genealogical Society (Edmonton Branch)
Room 116, Prince of Wales Armouries, 10440-108 Avenue,
Edmonton, Alberta, T5H 3Z9, Tel: (403)-424-4429 Fax:
(403)-423-8980, Email: agsedm@compusmart.ab.ca,
WWW:
http://www.compusmart.ab.ca/abgensoc/branches.html

Alberta Genealogical Society Fort McMurray Branch
PO Box 6253, Fort McMurray, Alberta, T9H 4W1

Alberta Genealogical Society Grande Prairie & District Branch
PO Box 1257, Grande Prairie, Alberta, T8V 4Z1

Alberta Genealogical Society Medicine Hat & District
PO Box 971, Medicine Hat, Alberta, T1A 7G8

Alberta Genealogical Society Red Deer & District
PO Box 922, Red Deer, Alberta, T4N 5H3 Email:
evwes@telusplanet.net

Brooks & District Branch, Alberta Genealogical Society
PO Box 1538, Brooks, Alberta, T1R 1C4

Ukrainian Genealogical & Historical Society of Canada
R.R.2, Cochrane, Alberta, T0L 0W0, Tel: (403) 932 6811
Fax: (403) 932 6811

British Columbia

British Columbia Gen Soc
PO Box 88054, Lansdowne Mall, Richmond, British
Columbia, V6X 3T6

Campbell River Genealogy Club
PO Box 884, Campbell River, British Columbia, V9W 6Y4
Email: rcase@connected.bc.ca, WWW:
http://www.connected.bc.ca/~genealogy/

Comox Valley Family History Research
c/o Courtenay & District Museum & Archives, 360 Cliffe
Street, Courtenay, British Columbia, V9N 2H9

Kamloops FHS
Box 1162, Kamloops, British Columbia, V2C 6H3

Kelowna & District Genealogical Society
PO Box 501, Station A, Kelowna, British Columbia, V1Y
7P1, Tel: 1-250-763-7159 Fax: 1-250-763-7159, Email:
doug.ablett@bc.sympatico.ca

Nanaimo FHS
PO Box 1027, Nanaimo, British Columbia, V9R 5Z2

Port Alberni Genealogy Club
Site 322, Comp. 6, R.R.3, Port Alberni, British Columbia,
V9Y 7L7

Powell River Genealogy Club
PO Box 446, Powell River, British Columbia, V8A 5C2

Prince George Genealogical Society
PO Box 1056, Prince George, British Columbia, V2L 4V2

Revelstoke Genealogy FHS
PO Box 2613, Revelstoke, British Columbia, V0E 2S0

Shuswap Lake Genealogical Society
R.R.1, Site 4, Com 4, Sorrento, British Columbia, V0E 2W0

South Okanagan Genealogical Society
c/o Museum, 785 Main Street, Penticton, British Columbia,
V2A 5E3

Vernon & District FHS
PO Box 1447, Vernon, British Columbia, V1T 6N7

Victoria Genealogical Society
PO Box 45031, Mayfair Place, Victoria, British Columbia,
V8Z 7G9

Manitoba

East European Genealogical Society
PO Box 2536, Winnipeg, Manitoba, R3C 4A7

La Societe Historique de Saint Boniface
220 Ave de la Cathedral, St Boniface, Manitoba, R2H 0H7

Manitoba Genealogical Society
Unit A, 1045 St James Street, Winnipeg, Manitoba, R3H 1B1

South West Branch of Manitoba Genealogical Society
53 Almond Crescent, Brandon, Manitoba, R7B 1A2, Tel:
204-728-2857 Fax: 204-725-1719
Email: mla@access.tkm.mb.ca

Winnipeg Branch of Manitoba Genealogical Society
PO Box 1244, Winnipeg, Manitoba, R3C 2Y4

New Brunswick

Centre de Etudes Acadiennes
Universite de Moncton, Moncton, New Brunswick, E1A
3E9

New Brunswick Genealogical Society
PO Box 3235, Station B, Fredericton, New Brunswick, E3A
5G9

Newfoundland

Newfoundland & Labrador Gen Soc
Colonial Building, Military Road, St John's, Newfoundland,
A1C 2C9

Nova Scotia

Archelaus Smith Historical Society
PO Box 291, Clarks Harbour, Nova Scotia, B0W 1P0 Email:
timkins@atcon.com

Cape Breton Genealogical Society
PO Box 53, Sydney, Nova Scotia, B1P 6G9

Genealogical Association of Nova Scotia
PO Box 641, Station Central, Halifax, Nova Scotia, B3J 2T3

Queens County Historical Society
PO Box 1078, Liverpool, Nova Scotia, B0T 1K0

Shelburne County Genealogical Society
PO Box 248 Town Hall, 168 Water Street, Shelburne, Nova
Scotia, B0T 1W0

Ontario

British Isles FHS of Greater Ottawa
Box 38026, Ottawa, Ontario, K2C 1N0

Bruce County Genealogical Society
PO Box 1083, Port Elgin, Ontario, N0H 2C0

Bruce & Grey Branch - Ontario Genealogical Society
PO Box 66, Owen Sound, Ontario, N4K 5P1

Elgin County Branch Ontario Genealogical Society
PO Box 20060, St Thomas, Ontario, N5P 4H4

Essex County Branch Ontario Genealogical Society
PO Box 2, Station A, Windsor, Ontario, N9A 6J5

Halton-Peel Branch Ontario Genealogical Society
PO Box 70030, 2441 Lakeshore Road West, Oakville, Ontario, L6L 6M9 Email: jwatt@ica.net, WWW: http://www.hhpl.on.c9/sigs/ogshp/ogshp.htm

Hamilton Branch Ontario Genealogical Society
PO Box 904, LCD 1, Hamilton, Ontario, L8N 3P6

Huron County Branch Ontario Genealogical Society
PO Box 469, Goderich, Ontario, N7A 4C7

Kawartha Branch Ontario Genealogical Society
PO Box 861, Peterborough, Ontario, K9J 7AZ

Kent County Branch Ontario Genealogical Society
PO Box 964, Chatham, Ontario, N7M 5L3

Kingston Branch, Ontario Genealogical Society
PO Box 1394, Kingston, Ontario, K7L 5C6

Lambton County Branch Ontario Genealogical Society
PO Box 2857, Sarnia, Ontario, N7T 7W1

Lanark County Genealogical Society
PO Box 512, Perth, Ontario, K7H 3K4 Email: gjbyron@magma.ca, WWW: http://www.globalgenealogy.com/LCGs

Marilyn Adams Genealogical Research Centre
PO Box 35, Ameliasburgh, Ontario, K0K 1A0, Tel: 613-967-6291

Niagara Peninsula Branch Ontario Genealogical Society
PO Box 2224, St Catharines, Ontario, L2R 7R8

Nipissing District Branch Ontario Genealogical Society
PO Box 93, North Bay, Ontario, P1B 8G8

Nor-West Genealogy & History Society
PO Box 35, Vermilion Bay, Ontario, P0V 2V0, Tel: 807-227-5293

Norfolk County Branch Ontario Genealogical Society
PO Box 145, Delhi, Ontario, N4B 2W9 Email: oxford.net/~mihaley/ogsnb/main.htm

Norwich & District Historical Society
c/o Archives, R.R. #3, Norwich, Ontario, N0J 1P0, Tel: (519)-863-3638

Ontario Genealogical Society
Suite 102, 40 Orchard View Boulevard, Toronto, Ontario, M4R 1B9 WWW: www.ogs.on.ca

Ontario Genealogical Society (Toronto Branch)
Box 513, Station Z, Toronto, Ontario, M4P 2GP

Ottawa Branch Ontario Genealogical Society
PO Box 8346, Ottawa, Ontario, K1G 3H8

Perth County Branch Ontario Genealogical Society
PO Box 9, Stratford, Ontario, N5A 6S8, Tel: 519-273-0399

Simcoe County Branch Ontario Genealogical Society
PO Box 892, Barrie, Ontario, L4M 4Y6

Sioux Lookout Genealogical Club
PO Box 1561, Sioux Lookout, Ontario, P8T 1C3

Societe Franco-Ontarienne D'Histoire et de Genealogie
C.P.720, succursale B, Ottawa, Ontario, K1P 5P8

Stormont, Dundas & Glengarry Genealogical Society
PO Box 1522, Cornwall, Ontario, K6H 5V5

Sudbury District Branch Ontario Genealogical Society
c/o Sudbury Public Library, 74 MacKenzie Street, Sudbury, Ontario, P3C 4X8, Tel: (705)-674-9991 Fax: (705)-670-6574, Email: fredie@isys.ca

Thunder Bay District Branch Ontario Gen Soc
PO Box 10373, Thunder Bay, Ontario, P7B 6T8

Upper Ottawa Genealogical
PO Box 972, Pembroke, Ontario, K8A 7M5

Waterdown East Flamborough Heritage Society
PO Box 1044, Waterdown, Ontario, L0R 2H0, Tel: 905-689-4074

Waterloo-Wellington Branch Ontario Genealogical Society
153 Frederick Street, Ste 102, Kitchener, Ontario, N2H 2M2 Email: lestrome@library.uwaterloo.ca, WWW: http://www.dos.iwaterloo.ca/~marj/genealogy/ww.html

West Elgin Genealogical & Historical Society
22552 Talbot Line, R.R.#3, Rodney, Ontario, N0L 2C0

Whitby - Oshawa Branch Ontario Genealogical Society
PO Box 174, Whitby, Ontario, L1N 5S1

Brome County Historical Society
PO Box 690, 130 Lakeside, Knowlton, Quebec, J0E 1V0, Tel: 450-243-6782

Quebec

Federation Quebecoise des Societies de Genealogie
C.P. 9454, Sainte Foy, Quebec, G1V 4B8

Les Patriotes Inc 105 Prince, Sorel, Quebec, J3P 4J9

Missisquoi Historical Society
PO Box 186, Stanbridge East, Quebec, J0J 2H0, Tel: (450)-248-3153 Fax: (450)-248-0420, Email: sochm@globetrotter.com

Quebec FHS
PO Box 1026, Postal Station, Pointe Claire, Quebec, H95 4H9, Tel: -1683

Societe de Genealogie de la Maurice et des Bois Francs
C.P. 901, Trois Rivieres, Quebec, G9A 5K2

Societe d'Histoire d'Amos
222 1ere Avenue Est, Amos, Quebec, J9T 1H3

Societe d'Histoire et d'Archeologie des Monts
C.P. 1192, 675 Chemin du Roy, Sainte Anne des Monts, Quebec, G0E 2G0

Societe d'Histoire et de Genealogie de Matane
145 Soucy, Matane, Quebec, G4W 2E1

Societe d'Histoire et de Genealogie de Riviere du Loup
800 rue St Pierre, Riviere du Loup, Quebec, G5R 3V3, Tel: (418)-867-4245 Email: shgrd@icrdl.net, WWW: http://www.icrdl.net/shgrdl/index.html

Societe d'Histoire et de Genealogie de Verdun
98 chemin de lÔAnce, Vaudreuil, Quebec, J7V 8P3

Societe d'histoire et de genealogie du Centre-du-Quebec
4-A, rue Laurier est, Victoriaville, Quebec, G6P 6P7, Tel: (819)-357-4029 Fax: (819)-357-9668, Email: geneatique@netscape.net WWW: http://www.geneatique.qc.ca

Societe d'Histoire et de Genealogie Maria Chapdeleine
1024 Place des Copains, C.P. 201, Dolbeau, Quebec, G8L 3N5

Societe d'Histoire et Genealogie de Salaberry de Valley Field
75 rue St Jean Baptiste, Valleyfield, Quebec, J6T 1Z6

Societe de Conservation du Patrimoine de St Fracois de la Riviere du Sud
C P 306, 534 Boul St Francois Ouest, St Francois, Quebec, G0R 3A0

Societe de Genealogie de Drummondville
545 des Ecoles, Drummondville, Quebec, J2B 8P3

Societe de Genealogie de Quebec
C.P. 9066, Sainte Foy, Quebec, G1V 4A8

Societe de Genealogie des Laurentides
C.P. 131, 185 Rue Du Palais, St Jerome, Quebec, J7Z 5T7, Tel: (450)-438-8158 WWW: http://www.societe-genealogie-laurentides.gc.ca

Societe de Genealogie et d'Histoire de Chetford Mines
671 boul. Smith Sud, Thetford Mines, Quebec, G6G 1N1

Societe Genealogie d'Argenteuil
378 Principale, Lachute, Quebec, J8H 1Y2

Societe Genealogique Canadienne-Francaise
Case Postale 335, Place de Armes, Montreal, Quebec, H2Y 2H1

Societie de Genealogie de L'Outaouaid Inc
C.P. 2025, Succ. ÒBÓ, Hull, Quebec, J8X 3Z2

Saskatchewan

Battleford's Branch Saskatchewan Genealogical Society
925 Gregory Drive, N Battleford, Saskatchewan, S9A W6

Central Butte Branch Saskatchewan Genealogical Society
P.O. Box 224, Central Butte, Saskatchewan, S0H 0T0

Grasslands Branch Saskatchewan Genealogical Society
P.O. Box 272, Mankota, Saskatchewan, S0H 2W0, Tel: 306-264-5149

Grenfell Branch Saskatchewan Genealogical Society
P.O. Box 61, Grenfell, Saskatchewan, S0G 2B0, Tel: (306)-697-3176
Moose Jaw Branch Saskatchewan Genealogical Society
1037 Henry Street, Moose Jaw, Saskatchewan, S6H 3H3
Pangman Branch Saskatchewan Genealogical Society
P.O. Box 23, Pangman, Saskatchewan, S0C 2C0
Radville Branch Saskatchewan Genealogical Society
P.O. Box 27, Radville, Saskatchewan, S0C 2G0

Regina Branch Saskatchewan Genealogical Society
95 Hammond Road, Regina, Saskatchewan, S4R 3C8
Saskatchewan Genealogical Society
1870 Lorne Street, Regina, Saskatchewan, S4P 3E1
South East Branch Saskatchewan Genealogical Society
P.O. Box 460, Carnduff, Saskatchewan, S0C 0S0
West Central Branch Saskatchewan Genealogical Society
P.O. Box 1147, Eston, Saskatchewan, S0L 1A0
Yorkton Branch Saskatchewan Genealogical Society
28 Dalewood Crescent, Yorkton, Saskatchewan, S3N 2P7

Yukon
Dawson City Museum & Historical Society
P.O. Box 303, Dawson City, Yukon, Y0B 1G0, Tel: 867-993-5291 Fax: 867-993-5839, Email: dcmuseum@yknet.yk.ca

United States of America

Alaska
Alaska Genealogical Society
7030 Dickerson Drive, Anchorage, Alaska, 99504
Anchorage Genealogical Society
PO Box 212265, Anchorage, Alaska, 99521-2265, Tel: 907-337-6377

Arizona
Apache Genealogy Society
PO Box 1084, Sierra Vista public Library, Sierra Vista, Arizona, 85636-1084, Tel: 602-458-7770
Arizona Society of Genealogists
6565 East Grant Road, Tucson, Arizona, 85715
Arizona State Genealogical Society
PO Box 42075, Tucson, Arizona, 85733-2075
Family History Society of Arizona
PO Box 310, Glendale, Arizona, 85311

Arkansas
Arkansas Genealogical Society
PO Box 908, Hot Springs, Arkansas, 71902-0908
North East Arkansas Genealogical Association
PO Box 936, 314 Vine Street, Newport, Arkansas, 72112

California
British Isles Family History Society
134, 2531 Sawtelle Boulevade, Los Angeles, California, 90064-3163
British Isles FHS - USA
2531 Sawtelle Boulevard, #134, Los Angeles, California, CA 90064-3163 Email: dotom2@aol.com, WWW: http://www.rootsweb.com/~bifhsusa
California Genealogical Society
Suite 200, Latham Office Building, 1611 Telegraph Avenue, Oakland, California, 94612-2152, Tel: 510-663-1358 Email: calgensoc@aol.com, WWW: www.calgensoc.com

Colorado
Association of Professional Genealogists
PO Box 40393, Denver, Colorado, 80204-393
Colorado Council of Genealogical Societies

Connecticut
Connecticut Society of Genealogists Inc
PO Box 435, Glastonbury, Connecticut, 06033-0435, Tel: 203-569-0002

District of Columbia
Association of Professional Genealogists
3421 M Street N W Suite 236, Washington, District of Columbia, 20007-3552
Florida
Florida Genealogical Society
PO Box 18624, Tampa, Florida, 33679-8624

Fairbanks Genealogical Society
PO Box 60534, Fairbanks, Alaska, 99706-0534, Tel: 907-479-2895
Genealogical Society of South East Alaska
PO Box 6313, Ketchikan, Alaska, 99901

Genealogical Society of Arizona
PO Box 27237, Tempe, Arizona, 85282
Mohave County Genealogy Society
400 West Beale Street, Kingman, Arizona, 864014, Tel: 602-458-7770
Northern Arizona Genealogical Society
PO Box 695, Prescott, Arizona, 86302

North West Arkansas Genealogical Association
PO Box 796, Rogers, Arkansas, 72757
Sevier County Genealogical Society
717 Maple Street, De Queen, Arkansas, 71832

California State Genealogical Alliance
4808 East Garland Street, Anaheim, California, 92807-1005, Tel: 714-777-0483
Professional Genealogists of California
5048 J Parkway, Sacramento, California, 95823
Santa Barbara County Genealogical Society
PO Box 1303, Goleta, Santa Barbara, California, CA 93116-1303, Tel: 1-805-884-9909, WWW: http://www.compuology.com/sbarbara

PO Box 24379, Denver, Colorado, 80224-0379 **Colorado Genealogical Society**
PO Box 9218, Denver, Colorado, 80209-0218

National Society Daughters of the American Revolution
1776 D Street NW, Washington, District of Columbia, 20006-5392

Florida, Florida Society for Genealogical Research
8461 54th Street North, Pinellas Park, Florida, 33565

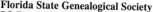

Florida State Genealogical Society
PO Box 10249, Tallahassee, Florida, 32302-2249 Email:
rootsweb.com/~flsgs/
Georgia
Georgia Genealogical Society
PO Box 54575, Atlanta, Georgia, 30308-0575, Tel: 404-475-
4404 Email: http://www.state.ga.us/SOS/Archives/
Idaho
Idaho Genealogical Society Inc
204, 4620 Overland Road, Boise, Idaho, 83705-2867, Tel:
208-384-0542

Indiana
Indiana Genealogical Society Inc
PO Box 10507, Fort Wayne, Indiana, 46852-0507, Tel: 219-
269-1782 Fax: 219-396-2136, Email: aiock@kconline.com,
WWW: http://www.indgensoc.org

Kansas
Jefferson County Gen Soc
Box 174, Oskalobsa, Kansas, 66066
Kansas Council of Genealogical Societies Inc
PO Box 3858, Topeka, Kansas, 66604-6858, Tel: 913-774-4411

Kentucky
Kentucky Genealogical Society Inc
PO Box 153, Frankfort, Kentucky, 40602, Tel: 502-875-
4452

Maine
Maine Genealogical Society
PO Box 221, Farmington, Maine, 04938-0221

Massachusetts
Massachusetts Genealogical Council
PO Box 5393, Cochituate, Massachusetts, 1778
Massachusetts Society of Genealogists Inc
PO Box 215, Ashland, Massachusetts, 01721-0215
Michigan
Michigan Genealogical Council
PO Box 80953, Lansing, Michigan, 48908-0953
Minnesota
Dakota County Genealogical Society
PO Box 74, 347 12th Avenue North, South St Paul, Minnesota, 55075, Tel: (651)-451-
6260, Tel: (651)-455-3626, Fax: (651)-455-2897, Email: valbu@worldnet.att.net

Mississippi
Historical & Genealogical Association of Mississippi
618 Avalon Road, Jackson, Mississippi, 39206, Tel: 601-
362-3079
Missouri
Missouri State Genealogical Association
PO Box 833, Columbia, Missouri, 65205-0803

Montana
Big Horn County Genealogical Society
PO Box 51, Hardin, Montana, 59034

Nebraska
Nebraska State Genealogical Society
PO Box 5608, Lincoln, Nebraska, 68505-0608

New Hampshire
New Hampshire Society of Genealogists
PO Box 633, Exeter, New Hampshire, 03833-0633, Tel:
603-432-8137

Hawaii
Sandwich Islands Genealogical Society
Hawii State Library, 478 South King Street, Honolulu,
Hawaii, 96813

Illinois
Illinois State Genealogical Society
PO Box 10195, Springfield, Illinois, 62791-0195, Tel: 217-
789-1968

Iowa
Iowa Genealogical Society
PO Box 7735, 6000 Douglas, Des Moines, Iowa, 50322-
7735, Tel: 515-276-0287 Email: igs@digiserve.com, WWW:
www.digiserve.com/igs/igs.htm

Kansas Genealogical Society Inc
PO Box 103, 2601 Central, Dodge City, Kansas, 67801-
0103, Tel: 316-225-1951

Louisiana
Louisiana Genealogical & Historical Society
PO Box 3454, Baton Rouge, Louisiana, 70821

Maryland
Maryland Genealogical Society
201 West Monument Street, Baltimore, Maryland, 21201,
Tel: 410-685-3750

New England Historic Genealogical Society
99 -101 Newbury Street, Boston, Massachusetts, 02116, Tel:
617-536-5740 Fax: 617-536-7307, Email:
membership@nehgs.org, WWW: http://www.nehgs.org

Irish Genealogical Society International
PO Box 16585, St Paul, Minnesota, 55116-0585, Tel: (612)-574-1436 Fax: (612)-574-
0316, Email: blmkerry@pclink.com, WWW: http://www.rootsweb.com/~irish
Minnesota Genealogical Society
5768 Olson Memorial Highway, Golden Valley, Minnesota,
55422, Tel: 612-595-9347

Mississippi Genealogical Society
PO Box 5301, Jackson, Mississippi, 39296-5301

Montana State Genealogical Society
PO Box 555, Chester, Montana, 59522

Carson City Genealogical Society
1509 Sharon Drive, Carson City, Nevada, 89701, Tel: 702-
687-4810
Nevada State Genealogical Society
PO Box 20666, Reno, Nevada, 89515

New Jersey
Genealogical Society of New Jersey
PO Box 1291, New Brunswick, New Jersey, 8903, Tel: 201-356-6920

New Mexico
New Mexico Genealogical Society
PO Box 8283, Alberquerque, New Mexico, 87198-8283,

New York
Irish Family History Forum
PO Box 67, Plainview, New York, 11803-0067

North Carolina
North Carolina Genealogical Society
PO Box 1492, Raleigh, North Carolina, 27602

Oklahoma
Federation of Oklahoma Genealogical Societies
PO Box 26151, Oklahoma City, Oklahoma, 73126

Oregon
Genealogical Forum of Oregon Inc
Room 812, 1410 S W Morrison Street, Portland, Oregon, 97205, Tel: 503-227-2398

Pennsylvania
Bucks County Genealogical Society
PO Box 1092, Doylestown, Pennsylvania, 18901, Tel: (215)-230-9410 Email: bucksgenpa.@erols.com
Genealogical Society of Pennsylvania
1300 Locust Street, Philadelphia, Pennsylvania, 19107-5699
South Carolina
South Carolina Genealogical Society
PO Box 16355, Greenville, South Carolina, 29606

Tennessee
Tennessee Genealogical Society
PO Box 111249, Memphis, Tennessee, 38111-1249, Tel: 901-327-3273

Texas
Amarillo Genealogical Society
PO Box 2171, 413 East Fourth Street, Amarillo, Texas, 79189-2171, Tel: 806-378-3054

Utah
Utah Genealogical Association
PO Box 1144, Salt Lake City, Utah, 84110-1144

Virginia
Genealogical Research Institute of Virginia
PO Box 29178, Richmond, Virginia, 23242-0178
National Genealogical Society
4527 17th Street North, Arlington, Virginia, 22207-2399, Tel: (703)-525-0050, Tel: (800)-473-0060, Fax: (703)-525-0052, Email: membership@ngsgenealogy.org, WWW: www.ngsgenealogy.org

Genealogy Club of the Library of the New Jersey Historical Society
230 Broadway, Newark, New Jersey, 7104, Tel: 201-483-3939
Tel: 505-256-3217

New York Genealogical & Biographical Society
122 East 58th Street, New York, New York, 10022-1939, Tel: 212-755-8532 Fax: 212-754-4218, Email: nygbs@sprynet.com, WWW: www.nygbs
Ohio
Ohio Genealogical Society
713 South Main Street, Mansfield, Ohio, 44907-1644, Tel: 419-756-7294 Fax: 419-756-8601, Email: ogs@ogs.org, WWW: http://www.ogs.org/

Genealogical Institute of Oklahoma
3813 Cashion Place, Oklahoma City, Oklahoma, 73112
Oklahoma Genealogical Society
PO Box 12986, Oklahoma City, Oklahoma, 73157-2986
WWW: http://www.rootsweb.com/~okgs/fftt.htm

Genealogical Heritage Council of Oregon Inc
PO Box 628, Ashland, Oregon, 97520-0021
Oregon Genealogical Society
PO Box 10306, Ashland, Oregon, 97440-2306, Tel: 503-746-7924

Rhode Island
Rhode Island Genealogical Society
13 Countryside Drive, Cumberland, Rhode Island, 02864-2601

South Dakota
South Dakota Genealogical Society
Rt 2 Box 10, Burke, South Dakota, 57523, Tel: 605-835-9364

Federation of Genealogical Societies
PO Box 830220, Richardson, Texas, 22207-2399, Tel: 972-907-9727
Texas State Genealogical Society
2507 Tannehill, Houston, Texas, 77008-3052, Tel: 713-864-6862

Vermont
Genealogical Society of Vermont
PO Box 422, Main Street, Pittsford, Vermont, 5763, Tel: 802-483-2900

Virginia Genealogical Society
Suite 115, 5001 West Broad Street, Richmond, Virginia, 23230-3023, Tel: 804-285-8954, WWW: http://www.vgs.org

Washington
Washington State Genealogical Society
PO Box 1422, Olympia, Washington, 98507
Tel: 206-352-0595

Wisconsin
Wisconsin Genealogical Council Inc
Rt 3 Box 253, Black River Falls, Wisconsin, 54615-9405,
Tel: 608-378-4388
Wisconsin State Genealogical Society
PO Box 5106, Madison, Wisconsin, 53705-0106,
Tel: 608-325-2609

West Virginia
West Virginia Genealogical Society Inc
PO Box 249, 5236 A Elk River Road North, Elk District, Elk
View, Kanawha County, West Virginia, 25071
Tel: 1-304-965-1179
Wyoming
Cheyenne Genealogical Society
Laramie County Library Service - Ge, 2800 Central
Avenue, Cheyenne, Wyoming, 82001, Tel: 307-634-3561

Europe

Austria
Heraldisch-Genealogische Gesellschaft 'Adler'
Universitatsstrasse 6, Wien, A-1096

Belgium
Cercle de Genealogie Juive de Belgique
74 Avenue Stalingrad, Bruxelles , B-1000, Tel: 32 0 2 512
19 63 Fax: 32 0 513 48 59, Email: mjb<d.dratwa@mjb-jmb.org>

Federation des Associations de Famille
Bruyeres Marion 10, Biez, B-1390
Federation Genealogique et Heraldique de Belgique
Avenue Parmentier 117, Bruxelles , B-1150
Office Genealogique et Heraldique de Belgique
Avenue C Thielemans 93, Brussels, B-1150

Finland
Genealogiska Samfundet i Finland
Fredsgatan 15 B , Helsingfors, SF-00170

Finland
Helsingfors Slaktforskare R.F.
Dragonvagen 10, Helsingfors, FIN-00330

France
Amicale des Familles d'alliance Canadiennne-Francaise
BP10, Les Ormes, 86220
Ancetres Italien
3 Rue de Turbigo, Paris, 75001, Tel: 01 4664 2722, WWW:
//members.aol.com/geneaita/
Assoc. Genealogique et Historique des Yvelines Nord
Hotel de Ville, Meulan, 78250
Association de la Bourgeoisie Ancienne Francaise
74 Avenue Kleber, Paris, 75116
Bibliotheque Genealogique
3 Rue de Turbigo, Paris, 75001, Tel: 01 4233 5821
Centre d'Entraide Genealogique de France
3 Rue de Turbigo, Paris, 75001, Tel: 33 4041 9909 Fax: 33
4041 9963, Email: cegf@usa.net, WWW:
www.mygale.org/04cabrigol/cegf/
Centre Genealogique Protestant
54 rue des Saints-Peres, Paris, 75007
Cercle d'Etudes Genealogiques et Heraldique d'Ile-de-France
46 Route de Croissy, Le Vesinet, 78110
Cercle de Genealogie et d'Heraldique de Seine et Marne
BP 113, Melun Cedex, 77002
Cercle de Genealogie Juive (Jewish)
14 rue St Lazare, Paris, 75009, Tel: 01 4023 0490 Fax: 01
4023 0490, Email: cgjgeniefr@aol.com
Cercle Genealogique Bull
rue Jean Jaures, BP 53, Les-Clayes-sous-Bois, 78340

Cercle Genealogique des P.T.T.
BP33, Paris Cedex 15, 75721
Cercle Genealogique du C.E. de la Caisse d'Epargne Ile de France-Paris
19 rue du Louvre, Paris, 75001
Cercle Genealogique Versailles et Yvelines
Archives Departementales, ⊦ avenue de Paris, Versailles,
78000, Tel: 01 3952 7239 Fax: 01 3952 7239
Club Genealogique Air France
CE Air France Roissy Exploitation , BP 10201, Roissy CDG
Cedex, 95703 Fax: 01 4864 3220
Club Genealogique Group IBM France
CE IBM St Jean de Braye-Ste Marie, 50-56 ave Pierre
Curie, St Jean de Braye Cedex, 45807
Confederation Internationale de Genealogie et d'Heraldique
Maison de la Genealogie, 3 rue Turbigo, Paris, F - 75001
Federation Francaise de Genealogie
3 Rue de Turbigo, Paris, 75001, Tel: 01 4013 0088 Fax: 01
4013 0089 WWW: www.karolus.org
Section Genealogique de l'Assoc. Artistique-Banque de France
2 rue Chabanais, Paris, 75002
Institut Francophone de Genealogie et d'Histoire
5 rue de l'Aimable Nanette , Le Gabut, La Rochelle, 17000,
Tel: 05 4641 9032 Fax: 05 4641 9032

Alsace
Centre Departemental d'Histoire des Familles
5 place Saint Leger, Guebwiller, Alsace, 68500 Email:
cdhf@telmat-net.fr, WWW: web.telemat-net-fr~cdhf

Cercle Genealogique d'Alsace
Archives du Bas-Rhin, 5 rue Fischart, Strasbourg, Alsace,
67000

Aquitaine
Amities Genealogiques Bordelaises
2 rue Paul Bert, Bordeaux, Aquitaine, 33000, Tel: 05 5644
8199 Fax: 05 5644 8199
Centre Genealogique des Landes
Societe de Borda, 27 rue de Cazarde, Dax, Aquitaine, 40100
Centre Genealogique des Pyrenees Atlantique
BP 1115, Pau Cedex, Aquitaine, 64011

Centre Genealogique du Sud Ouest
Hotel des Societes Savantes, 1 Place Bardineau, Bordeaux,
Aquitaine, 33000
Cercle d'Histoire et Genealogique du Perigord
2 rue Roletrou, Perigueux, Aquitaine, 24000
Cercle Genealogique et Historique du Lot et Garonne
13 rue Etienne Marcel, Villeneuve sur Lot, Aquitaine, 47340

Auvergne
Association Recherches Genealogiques Historique d'Auvergne
Maison des Consuls, Place Poly , Clermont Ferrand, Auvergne, 63100

Bourgogne
Cercle Genealogique Saone-et-Loire
115 rue des Cordiers, Macon, Bourgogne, 71000

Bretagne
Centre Genealogique des Cotes d'Armor
3bis rue Bel Orient, Saint Brieuc, Bretagne, 22000 Fax: 02 9662 8900
Cercle Genealogique d'Ille-et-Vilaine
6 rue Frederic Mistral, Rennes 35200, Tel: 02 9953 6363
Centre
Centre Genealogique de Touraine
BP 5951, Tours Cedex, Centre, 37059
Cercle Genealogique du Haut-Berry,
place Martin Luther King, Bourges, Centre, 18000 Fax: 02 4821 0483, Email: cgh-b@wanadoo.fr
Cercle Genealogique du Loir-et-Cher
11 rue du Bourg Neuf, Blois, Centre, 41000, Tel: 02 5456 0711

Champagne Ardennes
Centre Genealogique de la Marne
BP 20, Chalons-en-Champagne, Champagne Ardennes, 51005
Franche Comte
Centre Entraide Genealogique Franche Comte
35 rue du Polygone, Besancon, Franche Comte, 25000

France - Louisiana
France-Louisuane/Franco-Americanie
Commission Retrouvailles, Centre Commercial Gatie, 80 avenue du Maine, Paris 75014 Fax: 01 4047 8321 WWW: www.noconnet.com:80/forms/cajunews.htm
Languedoc Rousillon
Association Catalane de Genealogie
BP 1024, Perpignan Cedex, Languedoc Rousillon, 66101
Limousin
Brive-Genealogie
Maison des Associations, 11 place J M Dauaier, Brive, Limousin, 19100
Midi-Pyrenees
Cercle Genelogique du Rouergue
Archives Departementales, 25 av Victor Hugo, Rodez, Midi-Pyrenees, 12000
Nord-Pas de Calais
Association Genealogique du Pas de Calais
BP 471, Arras Cedex, Nord-Pas de Calais, 62028 Fax: 03 2107 8239
Association Genealogique Flandre-Hainaut
BP493, Valenciennes Cedex, Nord-Pas de Calais, 59321

Normandie
Association Genealogique du Pays de Bray
BP 62, Serqueux, Normandie, 76440 Fax: 02 3509 8756
Centre Genealogique du Perche
9 rue Ville Close, Bellame, Normandie, 61130, Tel: 02 3383 3789
Cercle de Genealogie du Calvados
Archives Departementales, 61 route de Lion-sur-Mer, Caen, Normandie, 14000
Cercle Genealogique d'Yvetot et du Pays de Caux
Pavillion des Fetes, Yvetot, Normandie, 76190

Salon Genealogique de Vichy et du Centre
48 Boulevard de Sichon, Vichy, Auvergne, 3200 WWW: www.genea.com

Genealogie Entraide Recherche en Cote d'Or
97 rue d'Estienne d'Orves, Clarmart, Bourgogne, 92140
Institut Genealogique de Bourgogne
237 rue Vendome, BP 7076, Lyon, Bourgogne, 69301

Cercle Genealogique du Finistere
Salle Municipale, rue du Commandant Tissot, Brest, Bretagne, 29000 Fax: 02 9843 0176, Email: cgf@eurobretagne.fr, WWW: www.karolus.org/membres/cgf.htm

Loiret Genealogique
BP 9, Orleans Cedex, Centre, 45016
Societe Genealogique du Bas-Berry
Maison des Associations, 30 Espace Mendez France, Chateauroux, Centre, 36000

Centre Genealogique et Heraldique des Ardennes
Hotel de Ville, Charleville Mezieres , Champagne Ardennes, 8000

Cercle Genealogique de la Region de Belfort
c/o F Werlen, 4 ave Charles de Gaulle, Valdoie, Franche Comte, 90300
France - Carribbean
Genealogie et Histoire de la Caraibe
Pavillion 23, 12 avenue Charles de Gaulle, Le Pecq, Overseas, 78230 Email: ghcaraibe@aol.com, WWW: //members.aol.com/ghcaraibe
Cercle Genealogique du Languedoc
18 rue de la Tannerie, Toulouse, Languedoc Rousillon, 31400, Tel: 05 6226 1530

Cercle Genealogique de la Meurthe et Moselle
4 rue Emile Gentil, Briey, Lorraine, 54150

Centre de Recherches Genealogiques Flandre-Artois
BP 76, Bailleul, Nord-Pas de Calais, 59270
Groupement Genealogique de la Region dy Nord
BP 62, Wambrechies, Nord-Pas de Calais, 59118

Cercle Genealogique de l'Eure
Archives Departementales, 2 rue de Verdun, Evreux Cedex Normandie, 27025
Cercle Genealogique de la Manche
BP 410, Cherbourg Cedex, Normandie, 50104
Cercle Genealogique Rouen Seine-Maritime
Archives Departementales, Cours Clemenceau, Normandie, 76101
Groupement Genealogique du Havre et de Seine Maritime
BP 80, Le Havre Cedex, Normandie, 76050, Tel: 02 3522 7633

Pays de la Loire
Association Genealogique de l'Anjou
75 rue Bressigny, Angers, Pays de la Loire, 49100
Association Genealogique de l'Oise
BP 626, Compiegne Cedex, Picardie, 60206

Poitou Charentes
Association Genealogique de la Charente
Archives Departementales, 24 avenue Gambetta,
Angouleme, Poitou Charentes, 16000
Cercle Genealogique d'Aunis et Saintonge
c/o Mr Provost, 10 ave de Metz, La Rochelle, Poitou
Charentes, 17000
Provence Alpes Cote d'Azur
Association Genealogique des Bouches-du-Rhone
BP 22, Marseilles Cedex, Provence Alpes Cote d'Azur, 1
Association Genealogique des Hautes Alpes
Archives Departementales, route de Rambaud, Gap,
Provence Alpes Cote d'Azur, 5000
Rhone Alpes
Centre Genealogique de Savoie
BP1727, Chambery Cedex, Rhone Alpes, 73017
Etudes Genealogique Drome-Ardeche
14 rue de la Manutention, Valence, Rhone Alpes, 26000

Cercle Genealogique Vendeen
Bat.H, 307bis, Cite de la Vigne aux Roses, La Roche-sur-
Yon, Pays de la Loire, 85000
Picardie

Cercle Genealogique de Saintonge
8 rue Mauny, Saintes, Poitou Charentes, 17100
Cercle Genealogique des Deux-Sevres
26 rue de la Blauderie, Niort, Poitou Charentes, 79000
Cercle Genealogique Poitevin
22bis rue Arsene Orillard, Poitiiers, Poitou Charentes, 86000

Association Genealogique du Var
BP 1022, Toulon Cedex, Provence Alpes Cote d'Azur, 83051
Cercle Genealogique de Vaucluse
Ecole Sixte Isnard , 31 ter Avenue de la Trillade, Avignon,
Provence Alpes Cote d'Azur, 84000

Societe Genealogique du Lyonnais
7 rue Major Martin, Lyon, Rhone Alpes, 69001

Germany

Deutsche Zentalstelle fur Genealogie,
Schongaver str. 1, Leipzig, D - 04329
**Herold - Verein fur Genealogie Heraldik und Reiwandte
Wissen-Scahaften**
Archiv Str. 12-14, Berlin, D -14195
Zentralstelle fur Personnen und Familiengeschichte
Birkenweg 13, Friedrichsdorf, D - 61381
Baden-Wuerttember
**Verein fur Familien-U. Wappenkunde in Wurttemberg
und Baden**
Postfach 105441, Stuttgart, Baden-Wuerttemberg, D - 70047
Bayern
Bayerischer Landesverein fur Familienkunde
Ludwigstrasse 14/1, Munchen, Bayern, D - 80539, Tel: 089
28638 398 Email: blf@rusch.m.shuttle.de, WWW:
www.genealogy.com/gene/reg/BAY/BLF-d.html

Greece
Heraldic-Genealogical Society of Greece
56 3rd Septemvriou Str. , Athens, GR - 10433

Iceland
The Genealogical Society
P O Box 829, Reykjavick, 121 Fax: 354 1 679840

Netherlands
Centraal Bureau voor Genealogie
P O Box 11755, The Hague, NL - 2502 AT, Tel: 070 315
0500 Fax: 070 347 8394 WWW: www.cbg.nl
Central Bureau voor Genealogie
PO Box 11755, 2502, The Hague,
**Koninklijk Nederlandsch Genootschap voor Geslacht-en
Wapen-Kunde**
P O Box 85630, Den Haag, 2508 CH

Niedersachsen
Niedersachsischer Gesellschaft fur Familienkunde e.V
Stadtarchiv, Am Bokemahle 14 - 16, Hannover,
Niedersachsen, D - 30171
Oldenburgische Gesellschaft fur Familienkunde
Lerigauweg 14, Oldenurg, Niedersachsen, D - 26131
Nordrhein Westfalen
Dusseldorfer Verein fur Familienkunde e.V
Krummenweger Strasse 26, Ratingen, Nordrhein Westfalen,
D - 40885
**Westdeutsche Gesellschaft fur Familienkunde e.V Sitz
Koln**
Unter Gottes Gnaden 34, Koln-Widdersdorf, Nordrhein
Westfalen, D - 50859, Tel: 49 221 50 48 88
Schleswig-Holstein
Arbeirkreis fur Familienforschung e.V
Muhlentorturm, Muhlentortplatz 2, Lubeck, Schleswig-
Holstein, D - 23552
Hungary
Historical Society of Hungary
University of Eoetveos Lorand, Pesti Barnabas utca 1,
Budapest, H - 1052, Tel: 267 0966
Norway
Norsk Slektshistorik Forening
Sentrum Postboks 59, Oslo, N - 0101, Tel: 2242 2204 Fax:
2242 2204
Nederlandse Genealogische Vereniging
Postbus 976, Amsterdam, NL - 1000 AZ Email: info@ngu.nl,
WWW: www.ngu.nl
Netherlands
Stichting 'Genealogisch Centrum Zeeland'
Wijnaardstraat, Goes, 4416DA, Tel: 0113 232 895
The Caledonian Society
Zuiderweg 50, Noordwolde, NL 8391 KH, Tel: 0561
431580

Spain

Asociacion de Diplomados en Genealogia y Nobilaria
Alcala 20, 2 Piso, Madrid, 28014, Tel: 34 522 3822 Fax: 34
532 6674

Asociacion de Hidalgos a Fuerto de Espana
Aniceto Marinas 114, Madrid, 28008

Cercle Genealogic del Valles
Roca 29, 5 2, Sabadell, Barcelona, 8208
Circulo de Estudios Genealogicos Familiares
Prado 21, Ateneo de Madrid, Madrid, 28014
Instituto Aragones de Investigaciones Historiograficas
Madre Sacremento 33, 1', Zaragoza, 50004
Instituto de Estudios Heraldicos y Genealogicos de

Extremadura
Lucio Cornelio Balbo 6, Caceres, 1004
Real Academia Matritense de Heraldica y Genealogia
Quintana 28, Madrid, 28008
Sociedad Toledana de Estudios Heraldicos y Genealogicos
Apartado de Correos No. 373, Toledo,
Sweden
Sveriges Slaktforskarforbund
Box 30222, Stockholm, 104 25, Tel: 08 695 0890 Fax: 08 695

Genealogical & Heraldry Association of Zurich
Dammbodenstrasse 1, Volketswil, CH-8604
Swiss Genealogical Society
Eggstr 46, Oberengstringen, CH 8102 WWW:
www.eye.ch/swissgen/SGFF.html

Societat Catalona de Genealogia, Heraldica, Sigillografia, Vexillologia
P O Box 2830, Barcelona, 8080
Societat Valenciana de Genealogia, Heraldica, Sigillografia, Vexillologia
Les Tendes 22, Oliva, 46780

0824, Email: genealog@genealogi.se

Switzerland

Swiss Society for Jewish Genealogy
P O Box 876, Zurich, CH-8021
Zentralstelle fur Genealogie
Vogelaustrasse 34, CH-8953 Fax: 44 1 742 20 84 , Email:
aicher@eyekon.ch

South Africa

Genealogical Institute of South Africa
115 Banheok Road, Stellenbosch, Western Cape, Tel: 021-887-5070, Email: gisa@renet.sun.ac.za
Genological Society of South Africa
Suite 143, Postnet X2600, Houghton, 2041

Human Sciences Research Council -Genealogy Information
HSRC Library & Information Service, Private Bag X41, Pretoria 0001, Tel: (012)-302-2636 Fax: (012)-302-2933, Email: ig@legii.hsrc.ac.za
West Rand Family History Society
The Secretary, PO Box 760, Florida 1710

Zimbabwe

Heraldry & Genealogy Society of Zimbabwe Harare Branch, 8 Renfrew Road, Eastlea, Harare

---

Did Forebears Lie ?

While watching for the umpteenth time Casablanca
and humming that wonderful song from the film I thought it might be fun
to write some new and appropriate lyrics to "As Time Goes By"

You must remember this...
Genealogy is bliss,
Yet oft we wonder why:
The fundamental rules apply,
Did Forebears lie?

And when with pen and book...
You go to sneak a look
Upon the IGI,
The facts sometimes belie
What your eyes spy.

Notebooks full of weddings, baptisms and fates,
Pages full of scribbles, family trees and dates:
The archivist takes a lunch break,
While the genealogist waits,
On that you can rely.

It's still the same old story...
We seek ancestors' glory,
And hold them up on high:
"The world will one days thank us,"
Is the genealogists' cry.

from *Rhyming Relations* Genealogy in Verse
by Roy Stockdill
Obtainable from the Author 6 First Avenue, Garston, Watford, Hertfordshire WD2 6PZ
Email: roystock@compuserve.com

BRITISH ASSOCIATION FOR LOCAL HISTORY

the national charity promoting local history

- books and pamphlets on local history
- regular conferences in London and the regions
- regular guided visits to major repositories, libraries and museums
- Local History Catalogue
- an annual conference for teachers of history
- prestigious annual lecture
- insurance scheme for local societies
- Web Site and mailbase for local history

Local history enriches our lives both as individuals and as whole communities and is an area where amateur and professional meet and work profitably together..

> The annual subscription is £19
> Members receive both *The Local Historian* and
> *Local History News*, four times a year

Write for **full details and a complimentary back number of** *The Local Historian* to
PO BOX 1576 SALISBURY SP2 8SY.
fax: 01722 413242

Registered Charity 285467

2000 Phillimore Lecture

Professor Margaret Spufford FBA
Roehampton Institute London (University of Surrey)

THE SCOPE OF LOCAL HISTORY
and the potential of the Hearth Tax Returns

The author of the much-acclaimed *Contrasting Communities* will describe how her personal interests expanded from purely economic history to issues such as literacy and religious belief. She will also address a problem faced by all local historians: how far were our localities 'typical', 'unusual' or even 'unique'? One solution is to use sources which enable us to make useful comparisons across parish boundaries. To this end Professor Spufford is currently directing a major project at Roehampton: the best surviving Hearth Tax returns from the reign of Charles II are being transcribed, analysed and mapped to show how counties varied in population, social composition and wealth.

at the Stationers' Hall, London
at 1.30pm on Saturday, 3 June, 2000

To obtain tickets please use this coupon, or a photocopy of it, or write to:

**BALH(L) PO Box 1576
SALISBURY SP2 8SY**

Please send me _____ tickets for the Annual Phillimore Lecture on 3 June 2000 at £12 each (or £8 for members); a cheque for £ _____ made out to BALH is enclosed

Please print your name and full postal address below to be used as a label to send your tickets and information:

Family History and Local History
– You can't have one without the other

Alan Crosby

I often give talks in this subject to organisations involved in both areas of research and I find that almost without exception people are excited by the challenge and the opportunities which linking these two themes can offer. It is in some ways obvious that the two subjects do go together, and are inextricably entwined. We cannot understand local communities - their origins, development and character - without giving the fullest possible attention to the people who made up those communities. After all, the farms and the fields, the streets and the houses, the industries and the churches, are all the product of untold human endeavour over the centuries. If we ignore the people we ignore the reason why, and that it absurd. Yet, at the same time, we cannot really understand the lives of individuals and the stories of families unless we consider their world, the environment they lived in and the lifestyles they enjoyed (or, maybe, didn't enjoy but rather suffered!).

How often, in researching your family history, have you wondered about what it was like for the people whose names, dates and brief historical record you have uncovered? What sort of housing did they live in, what clothes did they wear, what were their working conditions, what was the landscape which they knew from day to day and how did they fit into local society? Have you asked yourself why they moved from one place to another, what they felt about their fellow-citizens, how greater and lesser events impinged upon them, and what rituals and customs they encountered in birth,

Local History can answer many questions. It can set the lives of your forebear....

marriage and death. What sort of education was available to them - if any - and how did they tackle the burdens and oppressions of poverty, early and sudden death, natural disaster, illness and ill-health. What lightened their lives and what did they look forward to?

Local history can answer many such questions. It can set the lives of your forebears firmly in their proper context, helping to explain why they did what they did and what they met along life's path. All over the British Isles local history is a 'growth industry'. There are many hundreds of societies which are devoted to furthering the cause of local history - undertaking research, using original sources; holding lecture meetings and field visits; publishing the fruits of research and writing; campaigning for the extraordinarily rich heritage which is the legacy of the past and seeking to ensure its conservation and enhancement for future generations.

Local history is endlessly diverse, full of rewards and unexpected surprises, and something which is available and accessible to everybody. The British Association for Local History helps to further the cause of this fascinating and valuable subject. BALH promotes the study of, and interest in, our local heritage and history. All those who are interested in the history of the family will find that the study of local history can provide a much clearer and deeper understanding of where we came from and how it was in the past.

Brave New World
Alan Crosby

I grew up in a town which, despite fierce competition from many a dormitory clustered around a railway station, was alleged to be the most boring in Britain. Later, I wrote its history and proved that it (or at any rate its history) wasn't really boring, but during my childhood the town had a major image problem, exemplified by the sheer awfulness of its postcards. One which I vividly recall (though 'vivid' is hardly an appropriate term) depicted, in slightly smudged black and white, our famous roundabout, constructed in 1963. The picture was complete with a Ford Anglia, ungainly and evocative symbol of the early 60s. I would be untruthful if I suggested that tourists came to see the roundabout, but it did make a splendid sight with its towering concrete lamp standards and imposing direction signs. We in our town were very proud of it.

Another postcard showed the girls' grammar school (early 1950s), resplendent in concrete, while there also was a very fine view of the short (and, naturally, concrete) parade of shops in our local suburban village. There was, it is true, a postcard of the rather attractive early medieval church which survives, slightly bemused, in the midst of all the late twentieth century sprawl, and one of the then-derelict canal, but otherwise the emphasis was on progress with a capital C for concrete. We may speculate as to whether anybody ever sent these postcards, and if so, to whom, but in that town and hundreds of others what now seems ugly and mundane was then regarded with unalloyed enthusiasm.

Dreary views such as these featured in the national press during August because of the appearance of Martin Parr's entertaining book, Boring Postcards (Phaidon Press), devoted to the eccentric charms of these innocent pictures. As many commentators noted in their previews,

forty years ago to be progressive meant to tear down, rebuild and look forward. The past was dirty and depressing, the future shiny and clean.

In an age which is much more cynical, and when denigrating almost anything and everything has become a national pastime, it is hard to recapture the naive excitement which greeted the first roundabouts and multi-storey car parks, nuclear power stations and motorway service stations, holiday camps and rows of bungalows.

To the local historian, of course, such things are central features of twentieth century history, and as such postcards such as these have a special interest. There is also a new and to my mind somewhat contrived 'aesthetic' passion for the products of the 50s and early 60s. The everyday wares of those years have become collectors' items (I cannot lament the passing of all that hideous furniture and repellent crockery, thrown out with relief as soon as the cool lines of Swedish wood and Habitat appeared) and the postwar buildings are candidates for listing if they haven't been pulled down as unsafe and insanitary, or fallen down because of the vile diseases which afflict inferior concrete. And, in their turn, the cheap and dreary postcards, also thrown away in such quantities, have become collectable and desirable. They recapture the spirit of an age which seems much more than forty years ago and reflect the developments of a time crucial to the fabric of our environment and the history of our communities. When we write local histories in the future, pictures of the bus station and new town centre relief road, the holiday chalet and the 1960s civic centre, will be essential. The clothes look hilarious too - but even worse is the family photograph album. Did I really wear those flared trousers?

The past was dirty and depressing, the future shiny and clean

This item appeared in Local History News No 53 November 1999

Meeting the Ancestors
Alan Crosby

At home I hardly ever watch television (a familiar tale — too much to do and nothing worth watching) but sitting in a hotel room in January I was captivated by the first in the current BBC2 series *Meeting the Ancestors.* which discussed an archaeological excavation on the US airforce base at Lakenheath, Suffolk There. in an Anglo—Saxon cemetery, the grave of a 7th century warrior had been revealed. It was surrounded by the burials of children and babies(some, inexplicably, accompanied by weapons) and this perhaps implies that his role as protector of his people extended into the afterlife. There were two particularly powerful elements to the programme One was the reconstruction using computer technology of the appearance of the young man, in his early 30s. and of the horse (lame in one foot) which was slaughtered and laid in the crave beside him. The horse had been wearing full ornamental harness which survived *in situ.* including traces of its leather straps. For the first time it was possible to see how a complete set of Saxon horse-fittings was attached: the scenes where the individual components were replaced on a model of the horse's head were fascinating. Later, the warrior's face - having emerged from the screen - was painted as a portrait and a man 1300 years old came to life before us.

The other, and even more magical, process was the reconstruction, by a craftsman blacksmith, of the sword which the warrior had carried. X-rays of the long piece of rusted metal had shown it to be (if astonishingly complex and sophisticated construction. Bars of wrought iron were made by twisting thinner white-hot rods of metal together and then a set of bars was hammered and beaten into a single blade. incorporating separate pieces of carbon steel for the cutting edges. The blade was then polished which revealed, on the smooth surface of the metal an exquisite pattern of shimmering sinuous markings the fine lines formed by the arrangements of the original twisted rods. It was wonderful television emphasising not only the remarkable technological capacity of our ancestors 1300 years ago and extraordinary skills required too craft such an object) but also so the certainty that we still have very sore to learn about the past.

I have already covered the 'tingle factor' which comes from an sudden vivid insight into history perhaps through a phrase or document. Here I felt another 'tingle' from an different type oil' discovery History and archaeology on television can often be condemned. Many of us lament the trivialising gimmickry and the pretence that things are done and answers obtained in an instant, when we know that an long slog of preparation and background research has been necessary. We feel this, even though we know thee counter-argument that such programmes introduce so-called 'ordinary people' to a subject which they would otherwise not know at all. But television can also show us visions that the printed word simply cannot. The forging of a sword in the manner of a consummately skilful craftsman thirteen centuries ago was one such experience.

(This piece appeared originally in Local History News, No 50 Spring 1999)

Dead Language

Alan Crosby

Recent EU legislation requires medical products to be labelled in the language of Cicero so that everybody, from Turkü to Taranto, will understand what they contain. It's the irrepressible sense of quirky humour displayed by that lot in Brussels which is so endearing. English is now the *lingua franca* (I've always liked that joke, too) and another recent report (sociologist, Reading University, not 1 April) condemned, with awesome political incorrectness, the compulsory teaching of Welsh in the principality, arguing that it should be allowed to die because everybody west of Offa's Dyke speaks English anyway. Then, it was claimed, Welsh (once properly dead) could become the equivalent of Latin, a language used only for high-quality classical scholarship. Local historians, of course, don't see Latin as a classical language, and its deadness, like that of a monster in a horror film, is only partial. Instead, for most of us it is the last, and for many the insurmountable, vertical cliff-face on the uphill struggle towards the summit of total accomplishment.

Picture the hapless entrant into our world. He or she gets to grips with record office and library procedures, reads about county histories and pre-Conquest charters, Hooper's hedgerow dating and queenpost roofs, and then come the documents. Panic. Consternation. Funny writing, unintelligible script. Drunken spiders dipped in ink have crawled randomly across a page which starving mice have ravaged, chewing away corners and tattering the edges. What does document this say? How can I ever read this? Slowly, with much pain and humiliation, all becomes comparatively clear. The palaeography classes and the long evenings spent going over the same few words produce enlightenment. Seventeenth century wills hold fewer terrors, the delight of being able to read the original of something four centuries old replaces the longing for a nice clean bit of typescript circa 1930. But what's this at the top? I still can't read it.... or rather, I can read the letters but what do they say. Is it in 'Old English'. No, oh no, it's LATIN.

Why didn't I pay more attention at school. Why did I squander all those hours spent carving my name (in English) on the desk leg, or filling the ancient and dusty inkwell with even more bits of rubbish, or reading *Biggles* under the cover of an improving text. How on earth can I remember those endings, those agreements, those conjugations and declensions? Is being able to translate (badly) 'Having pitched camp near the enemy lines the troops were sent out to forage' going to help me in this exercise? The last is a fine example of a question which expects the answer 'no', for *amo amas amat* and *bellum bellum bellum* seem of questionable relevance when confronted by *Ad' Sess' pac' tent' apud Wigan in Com' lanc ' die lune vid'et vicesimo primo die Januar' Anno RR d'ni Caroli Ang '&c duod'mo*. Then come the subversive thoughts ... "I could just paraphrase", "Why not do only the date and leave the rest", "The endings don't really matter that much, it's the vocabulary which counts".

And those words, so familiar to so many and so much denounced by that happy band of local historians who have reached the summit and for whom 'doing the Latin bit at the top' no longer presents an obstacle: "Well, I can understand the gist of it". The only comfort in all this? Why did the clerk in 1637 abbreviate so many words. Could it really be true - did he not know the endings either!

Why didn't I pay more attention at school ?

(This piece first appeared in Local History News, No 52, Autumn 1999)

The Tingle Factor
Alan Crosby

In the *BBC Music Magazine* for November 1998 there was a fascinating and extremely well-written article by John Sloboda, Professor of Psychology at Keele University - (you don't often find the likes of me saying that the articles written by the likes of him have those qualities) - which describes, clearly and comprehensibly, why certain crucial elements in music -particular harmonies, changes of key, sequences of sounds or disruptions of progressions - produce very deep-seated reactions in most people. He concludes that the effects which create the 'tingle factor'- (he, too, puts it in inverted commas) - shivers down the spine, goose pimples, tears, lumps in the throat - are remarkably consistent among the population as a whole and involve the actions of a primitive part of the brain.

> No matter how familiar we may be with historical sources... local history can give us a... 'tingle factor'.

It set me thinking. No matter how familiar we may be with historical sources, no matter how routine it is to read, say, a 17th century will or 19th century account book, local history can give us a comparable 'tingle factor'. I vividly recall reading, ten years ago now, a Lancashire quarter sessions document. It concerned a not untypical case of petty thieving. A few items of clothing, which lay drying on some bushes one June day on the edge of the little market town of Poulton-le-Fylde, were allegedly stolen by two women - travelling stocking-sellers. Naturally, the accused were examined. One recounted her version of events, saying that she did not know the area at all because,'she was a stranger in that part of Lancashire' - she came from Standish near Wigan, twenty miles away - but she had gone to Poulton to sell stockings and had there been apprehended as a vagrant and set in the stocks. So far, interesting, full of detail. but not 'tingling'.

And then, amid the sonorous semi-legal language of the clerk who paraphrased her friend's tale, came the 'tingle factor'. They travelled, said Jane Clark, 'into Pulton parish and to the towne of great Pulton to get something for gods sake'. Just six words, but such powerful images came into my mind. An overbearing and bored magistrate. A hot day, that 12 June 1630; so tempers were fraying. A tired, harassed, frightened woman. Question after question after question. "And why were you going to Poulton town? Come on, tell me, you must have had a reason?"

"We went ... we went ... oh, to get something for god's sake". Damp strands of hair brushed back from her forehead, veins pulsing slightly. The magistrate, continuing the questioning,. not relaxing his interrogation. And the clerk, reticent and all-hearing, pen scratching, methodically translating from nigh-incomprehensible dialect to King's English, lets the formality of phrasing slip momentarily. Instead of filtering her speech through a courtly sieve, he gives the exact words of Jane's exasperated, impatient reply to that possibly stupid but, perhaps, so relevant question. We hear ourselves doing the same in such circumstances. We feel our muscles tighten slightly as, in our minds, we act her part, some 368 years later. Thus, people long dead live once more for us.

(This article appeared originally in Local History News (No 49 Winter 1998) – the magazine of The British Association for Local History)

BBC History 2000

BBC History 2000 is a BBC Millennium Project to encourage audiences in the UK, inspired by BBC programmes, to find out more about history.

To mark the millennium we are planning a rich and diverse choice of programmes. Highlights include a series about records and documents from the Domesday Book onwards, programmes about researching family history and Fred Dibnah's guide to magnificent monuments. In the autumn, Simon Schama presents a 16-part landmark television series on the history of Britain.

The BBC is working in partnership with our colleagues in the heritage community and there are a series of exciting History events planned across the UK for viewers who are inspired by programmes.

After each programme there is an invitation to visit the website or call the automated information line (08700 106060) for further details on places to go and things to do near you.

The *BBC History 2000* Website is an innovative and comprehensive source of additional information. Highlights include Timelines from 4000 BC to the present day, interactive games re-enacting the battles of Hastings and Waterloo, together with 3-D reconstructions of London Bridge during Medieval times and a World War One trench.

The Website also holds details of partners and planned activities up and down the country and will act as a portal to other history sites.

http://www.bbc.co.uk/history/

Archaeological Societies and Organisations

British Archaeological Association,
Burlington House, Piccadilly, London, W1V 0HS
Council for British Archaeology,
Bowes Morrell House, 111 Walmgate, York, YO1 9WA
Tel: 01904 671417, Fax: 01904 671384,
WWW: http:www.britarch.ac.uk/cba

England

Bedfordshire
Ampthill & District Archaeological & Local History Soc
63 Ampthill Road, Maulden, Bedford, MK45 2DH
Bedfordshire Archaeological and Local History Society
7 Lely Close, Bedford, MK41 7LS, Tel: 01234 365095
Berkshire
Middle Thames Archaeological & Historical Society
Merry Lea, Wexham Park Lane, Slough, SL3 6LX
Berkshire Archaeological Society
30 Salcombe Drive, Earley, RG6 5HU
Buckinghamshire
Buckinghamshire Archaeological Society,
Museum, Church St, Aylesbury, HP20 2QP Tel: 01296-331441
Bristol
Bristol & Avon Archaeological Society
14 Goldney Road, Clifton, Bristol, BS8 4RB
Cambridgeshire
Cambridgeshire Archaeology Society
Castle Court, Shire Hall, Cambridge, CB3 0AP
Cheshire
Chester Archaeology Society
The Museum, 27 Grosvenor St, Chester CH1 20D, Tel: 01244 402009
Chester Archaeological Society
Ochor House, Porch Lane, Hope Mountain, L12 9LS
Cumbria
**Cumberland & Westmorland Antiquarian &
Archaeological Society,**
2 High Tenterfell, Kendal, LA9 4PG, Tel: 01539 773542
Fax: 01539 773439, Email: info@cwaas.org.uk
WWW: www.cwaas.org.uk
Derbyshire
Council for British Archeology - East Midlands
Southfield House, Portway, Coxbench DE21 5BE, Tel: 01332 880600
Derbyshire Archaeological Society
25 Bridgeness Road, Heatherton, Derby, DE23 7UJ
Tel: 01332 510566 Email: christine@suggy.softnet.co.uk
WWW: http://www.ccc.nottingham.ac.uk/~aczsjm/das/das.html
Devon
Council for British Archeaology - South West
Old Orchard, Village Road, Christow, Exeter, EX6 7LX
Dorset
Dorset Natural History & Archaeological Society
Dorset County Museum, High West St, Dorchester DT1 1XA
County Durham
Architectural & Archaeological Soc of Durham & Northumberland
5 Girton Close, Peterlee, SR8 2NF, Tel: 0191-586-6259
East Sussex
Eastbourne Natural History and Archaeological Society
1 Brown Jack Avenue, Polegate, BN26 5HN, Tel: 01323 486014
East Sussex Archaeology Project
Anne of Cleves House, 52 Southover High Street, Lewes,
BN7 1JA, Tel: 01273 486959
Lewes Archaeological Group
Rosemary Cottage, High St, Barcombe, Lewes, BN8 5DM
Tel: 01273 400878
Sussex Archaeological Society
Barbican House, 169 High Street, Lewes, BN7 1YE Tel: 01273 405738
Essex
Essex Archaeological & Historical Congress
Birds Hill House, 59 Wroths Park, Loughton, IG10 1SH, Tel:

The Prehistoric Society
UCL Institute of Archaeology, 31 -34 Gordon Square,
London, WC1H 0PY
Royal Archaeological Institute
c/o English Heritage, 23 Savile Row, London, W1X 1AB

0181 508 5582 Email: 1001104.1041@compuserve.com
Ingatestone & Fryerning Historical & Archaeological Soc
20 Marks Close, Ingatestone, CM4 9AR, Tel: 01277 353550
Billericay Archaeological and Historical Society
24 Belgrave Rd, Billericay, CM12 1TX, Tel: 01277 658989
Colchester Archaeological Group
172 Lexden Road, Colchester, CO3 4BZ, Tel: 01206 575081
Burnham & District Local History & Archealogical Soc
The Museum, The Quay, Burnham On Crouch, CM0 8AS
Gloucestershire
Bristol and Gloucestershire Archaeological Society
22 Beaumont Rd, Gloucester, GL2 0EJ, Tel: 01452 302610
Campden and District Hiostorical & Archaeological Soc
14 Pear Tree Close, Chipping Campden, GL55 6DB
Cirencester Archaeological and Historical Society
Corinium Museum, Park Street, Cirencester, GL7 2BX
Hampshire
Aldershot Historical and Archaeological Society
10 Brockenhurst Road, Aldershot, GU11 3HH, Tel: 01252 26589
Andover History and Archaeology Society
140 Weyhill Road, Andover, SP10 3BG, Tel: 01264 324926
Basingstoke Archaeological and Historical Society
16 Scotney Road, Basingstoke, RG21 2SR
Tel: 01256 322090 Email: JTHerring@aol.com
Guildford Archaeology Group
6 St Omer Road, Guildford, GU1 2DB, Tel: 01483 532201
Hampshire Field Club and Archaeological Society
28 Harvest Close, Badger Farm, Winchester, S022 4DW
NE Hampshire Historical and Archaeological Society
36 High View Road, Farnborough, GU14 7PT Tel: 01252-543023
Email: nehhas@netscape.net WWW: www.hants.org.uk/nehhas
Hertfordshire
Council for British Archeology - Mid Anglia
34 Kingfisher Close, Wheathampstead, AL4 8JJ, Tel: 01582
629433 Fax: 01582 629433, Email: derek.hills@virgin.net
Welwyn Archaeological Society
The Old Rectory, 23 Mill Lane, Welyn, AL6 9EU
Tel: 01438 715300 Fax: 01438 715300
East Herts Archaeological Society
1 Marsh Lane, Stanstead Abbots, Ware, SG12 8HH Tel: 01920 870664
Hertfordshire Archaeological Trust
Seed Warehouse, Maidenhead Yard, The Wash, Hertford,
SG14 1PX, Tel: 01992 558 170, Fax: 01992 553359
Isle of Wight
Isle of Wight Natural History & Archaeological Society
Island Countryside Centre, Rylstone Gardens, Shanklin,
PO37 6RG, Tel: 01983 867016
Kent
Ashford Archaeological and Historical Society
9 Wainwright Place, Newtown, Ashford, TN24 0PF Tel: 01233 631017
Canterbury Archaeology Society
Dane Court, Adisham, Canterbury, CT3 3LA
Council for Kentish Archaeology
32 Birling Road, Tunbridge Wells, TN2 5LY
Crayford Manor House Historical & Archaeological Soc
17 Swanton Road, Erith, DA8 1LP
The Kent Archaeological Society
Three Elms, Woodlands Lane, Shorne, Gravesend, DA12 3HH,
Tel: 01474 822280 Email: ai_moffat@csi.com, WWW:
http://ourworld.compuserve.com/homepages/ai_moffat
Kent Archaeological Society
Three Elms, Woodland Lane, Shorne, Gravesend

DA12 3HH, Tel: 01474 822280
Maidstone Area Archaeological Group
14 The Quarter, Cranbrook Road, Staplehurst, TN12 0EP
Sedgeford Historical & Archaeological Research Project
Church Villa, Church St, Tilehurst, Wadhurst, TN5 7AB,
Tel: 01580 201290
Lancashire
Council for British Archeaology - North West
The Museum,Le Mans Crescent, Bolton, BL1 1SE, Tel: 01204 522311
Littleborough Historical and Archaeological Society
8 Springfield Avenue, Littleborough, LA15 9JR Tel: 01706 377685
Leicestershire
Glenfield & Western Archaeological & Historical Group
50 Chadwell Road, Leicester, LE3 6LF, Tel: 1162873220
Leicestershire Archaeological & Historical Society
The Guildhall,Leicester, LE1 5PQ, Tel: 0116 2703031
WWW: http://www.le.ac.uk/archaeology/lahs/lahs.html
Vaughan Archaeological and Historical Society
Vaughan College, St Nicholas Circle, Leicester, LEl 4LB
Lincolnshire
Society for Lincolnshire History & Archaeology
Jews' Court, Steep Hill, Lincoln, LN2 ILS Tel: 01522-521337
London
Hendon and District Archaeological Society
13 Reynolds Close, London, NW11 7EA Tel: 0181 458 1352
London & Middlesex Archaeological Society
University of N London, 62-66 Highbury Grove, London, N5 2AD
Walthamstow Historical Society
173 Brettenham Road, Walthamstow, London, E17 5AX,
Tel: 0181 523 2399 Fax: 0181 523 2399
Merseyside
Merseyside Archaeological Society
20 Osborne Road, Formby, Liverpool, L37 6AR Tel: 01704 871802
Norfolk
Federation of Norfolk Historical & Archaeological Orgs
14 Beck Lane, Horsham St Faith, Norwich, NR10 3LD
Feltwell Historical and Archaeological Society
16 High Street, Feltwell, Thetford, IP26, Tel: 01842 828448
Lowestoft Archaeological and Local History Society
1 Cranfield Close, Pakefield, Lowestoft, NR33 7EL Tel: 01502 586143
Norfolk Archaeological and Historical Research Group
50 Cotman Road, Norwich, NR1 4AH, Tel: 01603 435470
Norfolk and Norwich Archaeological Society
30 Brettingham Ave, Cringleford, Norwich, NR4 6XG, Tel: 01603 455913
North Yorkshire
Scarborough Archaeological and Historical Society
10 Westbourne Park, Scarborough, YO12 4AT
 Tel: 01723 354237 Email: archaelogy@scarborough.co.uk
Northamptonshire
Bozeat Historical and Archaeological Society
44 Mile Street, Bozeat, NN9 7NB, Tel: 01933 663647
Nottinghamshire
Nottingham Historical and Archaeological Society
48 Banks Road, Toton, Beaston, NG9 6HA Tel: 0115 9734284
Redford and District Historical & Archaeological Soc
Cambridge House, 36 Alma Road, Redford, DN22 6LW
Tel: 01777 701902, Fax: 01777 707784
Email: joan@j.a+esewell.demon.co.uk
Oxfordshire
Abingdon Area Archaeological and Historical Society
4 Cherwell Close Abingdon, OX14 3TD Tel: 01235 528835
Chinnor Historical & Archealogical Society
7 Cherry Tree Road, Chinnor, OX9 4QY
Faringdon Archaeological & Historical Society
1 Orchard Hill, Faringdon, SN7 7EH

Council for British Archaeology - Wales
7A Church Street, Welshpool, SY21 7DL, Tel: 01938 552035
Fax: 01938 552719, Email: BobSilvester@cpat.demon.co.uk

Wallingford Historical and Archaeological Society
Flint House, 52a High Street, Wallingford, OX1O 0DB, Tel: 01491 837720
Shropshire
Council for British Archeaology - West Midlands
c/o Rowley's House Museum, Barker Street, Shrewsbury,
SY1 1QH, Tel: 01743 361196, Tel: 01743 358411
Kidderminster & District Archaeology & History Soc
178 Birmingham Road, Kidderminster, DY1O 2SJ
Shropshire Archaeological & Historical Society
Lower Wallop Farm, Westbury, Shrewsbury, SY5 9RT
Whitchurch History and Archaeology Group
The Field House, Wirswall, Whitchurch, SY13 4LA Tel: 01948 662623
Somerset
Somerset Archaeological & Natural History Society
Taunton Castle Taunton, TA1 4AD, Tel: 01823 272429
Axbridge Archaeological and Local History Society
King John's Hunting Lodge, The Square, Axbridge
BS26 2AR, Tel: 01934 732012
South East Somerset Archaeological & Historical Society
Abbascombe Barn, Templecombe, BA8 OHN, Tel: 01963 371163
Yeovil Archaeological and Local History Society
Plantagenet Chase, Yeovil, Tel: 01935 78258
South Yorkshire
Doncaster Group of the Yorkshire Archaeological Soc
Merrylees, 1b Ellers Road, Doncaster, DN4 7BE, Tel: 01302 531581
Staffordshire
Staffordshire Archaeological and Historical Society
38 Knighton Dr, Four Oaks, Sutton Coldfield, B74 4QP, Tel: 0121 3081072
Suffolk
Suffolk Institute of Archaeology and History Roots
Church Lane, Playford, Ipswich, IP6 9DS Tel: 01473-624556
Surrey
Nonsuch Antiquarian Society
17 Seymour Avenue, Ewell, Epsom, KT17 2RP Tel: 0181 3930531
Surrey Archaeological Society
Castle Arch, Guildford, GU1 3SX, Tel: 01483 532454, Fax: 01483 532454,
Email: surreyarch@compuserve.com
WWW: ourworld.compuserve.com/homepages/surreyarch
Croydon Natural History & Scientific Society Ltd
96a Brighton Rd, South Croydon CR2 6AD Tel: 0181 688 4539
Sussex,
Council for British Archeaology - South East
47 Durrington Gardens, The Causeway, Goring, Worthing,
BN12 6BX, Tel: 01903 504510
West Yorkshire
Yorkshire Archaeological Society
Claremont, 23 Clarendon Rd, Leeds, LS2 9NZ, Tel: 0113-245-6342, Tel:
0113 245 7910, Fax: 0113-244-1979 Email: j.heron@shej.ac.uk
Wiltshire
Wiltshire Archaeological and Natural History Society
WANHS Library, 41 Long Street, Devizes, SN1O 1NS
Tel: 01380 727369, Fax: 01380 722150
Worcestershire
Droitwich History and Archaeology Society
45 Moreland Road, Droitwich Spa, WR9 8RN Tel: 01905-773420
Worcestershire Archaeological Society
Mount Pleasant, Pound Ln Clifton-on-Jeme, WR6 6EE Tel: 01886 812326
Worcestershire Archaeological Service
Woodbury Hall, University College of Worcester, Henwick
Grove, Worcester, WR2 6AJ Tel: 01905 855494
Fax: 01905 29054 Email: arcgaeology@worcestershire.gov.uk
Yorkshire
East Riding Archaeological Society
455 Chanterland Ave, Hull, HU5 4AY, Tel: 01482 445232
South Yorkshire Archaeology Unit and Museum
Ellin Street, Sheffield, Tel: 0114 2734230

Wales

Clwyd Powys Archaeological Trust
7A Church Street, Welshpool, SY21 7DL
Tel: 01938 552035, Fax: 01938 552179

History Societies

British Association for Local History
PO Box 1576, 24 Lower Street, Harnham, Salisbury, SP2
8EY Tel: 01722-332158 Fax: 01722-413242
Current Archaeology
9 Nassington Road, London, NW3 2TX Tel: 0171-435-7517
Fax: 0171-916-2405, Email: editor@archaeology.co.uk,
WWW: http://www.archaeology.co.uk
Black and Asian Studies Association
28 Russell Square, London, WC1B 5DS Tel: 0171 862 8844
Email: marikas@sas.ac.uk
Brewery History Society
Manor Side East, Mill Lane, Byfleet, West Byfleet, Surrey,
KT14 7RS Email: jsechiari@rmcbp.co.uk
British Archaeological Association
Burlington House, Piccadilly, London, W1V 0HS
British Brick Society
9 Bailey Close, High Wycombe, Buckinghamshire, HP13
6QA Tel: 01494-520299 Fax: 01344-890129
Email: brick@brick.org.uk
British Library National Sound Archive
96 Euston Road, London, NW1 2DB Tel: 0171-412-7405
Tel: 0171-412-7440, Fax: 0171-412-7441
Email: rob.perks@bl.uk
WWW: http://www.essex.ac.uk/sociology/oralhis.htm
British Deaf History Society
288 Bedfont Lane, Feltham, Middlesex, TW14 9NU
Friends of War Memorials
4 Lower Belgrave Street, London, SW1W 0LA Tel: 0171-
259-0403 Fax: 0171-259-0296, Email: enquirics@war-
memorials.com, WWW: http://www.war-memorials.com
Garden History Society
77 Cowcross Street, London, EC1M 6BP Tel: 0171-608-
2409 Fax: 0171-490-2974
Email: gardenhistorysociety@compuserve.com
The Historical Association (Local History)
59A Kennington Park Road, London, SE11 4JH
Tel: 0171-735-3901 Fax: 0171 582 4989,
Email: enquiry@history.org.uk
WWW: http://www..history.org.uk
Historical Medical Equipment Society
14 The Avenue, Cliftonville, Northampton NN1 5 BT
Social History of Learning Disability Research Group
School of Health & Social Welfare, Open University, Milton
Keynes, Bedfordshire, MK7 6AA
Labour Heritage
13 Grovewood, Sandycombe Road, Kew, Surrey, TW9 3NF
Lighthouse Society of Great Britain
Gravesend Cottage, Gravesend, Torpoint PL11 2LX Email:
k.trethewey@btinternet.com, WWW: http://www.lsgb.co.uk
Local Population Studies Society
78 Harlow Terrace, Harrogate HG2 0PN Tel: 01423-560429
Fax: 01423-560429 Email: sir_david_cooke@compuserve.com
Open University History Society
111 Coleshill Drive, Chapel End, Nuneaton CV10 0PG
Tel: 01203 397668
The Anglo-Zulu War Historical Society
Woodbury House, Woodchurch Road, Tenterden, Kent,
TN30 7AE Tel: 01580-764189 Fax: 01580-766648
WWW: www.web-marketing.co.uk/anglozuluwar
The Yorkshire Heraldry Society
35 Holmes Carr Road, West Bessacarr, Doncaster, South
Yorkshire, DN4 7HJ Tel: 01302-539993
British Association of Paper Historians
2 Manor Way, Kidlington, Oxfordshire, OX5 2BD
WWW: www.baph.freeserve.co.uk

Police History Society
37 Green Hill Road, Timperley, Altrincham, Cheshire,
WA15 7BG Tel: 0161-980-2188
Email: alanhayhurst@compuserve.com
Postal History Society
60 Tachbrook Street, London, SW1V 2NA
Tel: 0171-821-6399
The Railway & Canal Historical Society
The National Waterways Museum, Llanthony Warehouse,
Gloucester Docks, Gloucester, Gloucestershire, GL1 2EH
Tel: 01452 318053
British Records Association
40 Northampton Road, London, EC1R 0HB Tel: 0171 833
0428 Fax: 0171 833 0416
Richard III Society
20 Rowington Road, Norwich, NR1 3RR
Museum of the Royal Pharmaceutical Society
1 Lambeth High Street, London, SE1 7JN Tel: 0171-735-
9141-ext-354 Email: museum@rpsgh.org.uk, WWW:
http://www.rpsgb.org.uk
Royal Society of Chemistry Library & Info Centre
Burlington House, Piccadilly, London, W1V 0BN Tel: 0207
437 8656 Tel: 0207 287 9798 Email: library@rsc.org,
www.rsc.org
Society of Antiquaries
Burlington House, Piccadilly, London, W1V 0HS
Society For Genealogy and History of The Family
136 Lennard Road, Beckenham, BR3 1QT
Society for Name Studies in Britain & Ireland
22 Peel Park Avenue, Clitheroe, Lancashire, BB7 1ET Tel:
01200-423771 Fax: 01200-423771
British Society for Sports History
Dept of Sports & Science, John Moore's University, Byrom
Street, Liverpool L3 3AF
Tennyson Society
Central Library, Free School Lane, Lincoln LN2 1EZ
Tel: 01522-552862 Fax: 01522-552858
Email: lincs.lib@dial.pipex.com
United Reformed Church History Society
Westminster College, Madingley Road, Cambridge, CB3
0AA Tel: 01223-741084
The Victorian Society
1 Priory Gardens, Bedford Park, London, W4 1TT Tel: 0181
994 1019 Fax: 0181 995 4895, Email: admin@victorian-
society.org.uk, WWW: http://www.btinternet.com/~vss
Voluntary Action History Society
National Centre for Volunteering, Regent's Wharf, 8 All
Saints Street, London, N1 9RL Tel: 0171 520 8900 Fax:
0171 520 8910, Email: instvolres.aol.com
The West of England Costume Society
4 Church Lane, Long Aston, Nr. Bristol, BS41 9LU
Tel: 01275-543564 Fax: 01275-543564
Society of Brushmakers Descendants Fam Hist Soc
13 Asworth Place, Church Langley, Essex, CM17 9PU Tel:
01279-629392 Email: socy-brush-desc@thenet.co.uk,
WWW: http://www.thenet.co.uk/~socy-brush-desc
War Research Society
27 Courtway Avenue, Birmingham, West Midlands, B14 4PP
Tel: 0121-430-5348 Fax: 0121 436 7401, Email:
battletour@aol.com, WWW: www.battlefieldtours.co.uk
Wesley Historical Society
34 Spiceland Road, Northfield, Birmingham, West Midlands,
B31 1NJ Email: 106364.3456@compuserve.com
Association of Friends of Waterloo Committee
2 Coburn Drive, Four Oaks, Sutton Coldfield, West
Midlands, B75 5N

Avon
Avon Local History Association
5 Parry's Grove, Bristol, Bristol, BS9 1TT Tel: 01179 684974
Bristol & Avon Archaeological Society
14 Goldney Road, Clifton, Bristol, BS8 4RB
Congresbury History Group
36 Venus Street, Congresbury, Bristol, BS49 5EZ
Tel: 01934 834780
Bath & NE Somerset
Avon Local History Association (see Avon)
Bedfordshire
Bedfordshire Archaeological and Local History Society
7 Lely Close, Bedford, MK41 7LS Tel: 01234 365095
Luton & District Historical Society
22 Homerton Rd, Luton, LU3 2UL
Bedfordshire Local History Association
7 Castle Close, Totternhoe, Dunstable LU6 1QJ
Bedfordshire Historical Record Society
50 Shefford Road, Meppershall SG17 5LL Tel: 01462 813363
Ampthill & District Archaeological & Local Hist Soc
63 Ampthill Road, Maulden, Bedford MK45 2DH
Ampthill & District Preservation Society
Seventh House, 43 Park Hill, Ampthill MK45 2LP
Caddington Local History Group
98 Mancroft Road, Caddington, Nr. Luton LUL 4EN
Dunstable Historic and Heritage Society
184 West Street, Dunstable, Bedfordshire, LU6 1 NX
Harlington Heritage Trust
Happy Haven, Sundon Road, Harlington LU5 6L5
Biggleswade History Society
6 Pine Close, Biggleswade, Bedfordshire, 5G18 QEF
Dunstable & District Local History Society
12 Friars Walk, Dunstable LU6 3JA Tel: 01525 659955
Bedfordshire Local History
14 Glebe Avenue, Flitwick, Bedfordshire, MK45 1HS
Ampthill & District Local History
14 Glebe Avenue, Flitwick, Bedfordshire, MK45 1HS
Carlton & Chellington Historical Society
3 High Street, Carlton, Bedfordshire, MK43 7JX
Toddington Historical Society
25 Gorham Way, Dunstable, Bedfordshire, LU5 4NJ
Berkshire
Heraldry Society
PO Box 32, Maidenhead, Berkshire, SL6 3FD Tel: 0118-932-0210 Fax: 0118 932 0210
Email: heraldry-society@cwcom.net
Berkshire Record Society
Berkshire Record Office, Shinfield Park, Reading, Berkshire, RG2 9XD Tel: 0118-901-5130 Fax: 0118-901-5131
Cox Green Local History Group
29 Bissley Drive, Maidenhead SL6 3UX Tel: 01628 823890
Middle Thames Archaeological & Historical Society
Merry Lea, Wexham Park Lane, Slough, Berkshire, SL3 6LX
Berkshire Local History Association
181 Church Road, Earley, Reading, Berkshire, RG6 1HN
Wargrave Local History Society
6 East View Close, Wargrave, Berkshire, RG10 8BJ
Hungerford Historical Association
11 Regent Close, Hungerford, Berkshire, RG17 0LF
Berkshire Industrial Archaeological Group
6 Harefield Close, Winnersh, Wokingham RG11 5NP
Association of Local History Tutors
47 Ramsbury drive, Earley, Reading, Berkshire, RG6 7RT
Goring & Streatley Local History Society
45 Springhill Road, Goring On Thames, Reading, RG8 OBY
Tel: 01491 872625
Oxfordshire
Newbury District Field Club
Glenwood, 30 Monkswood Close, Newbury RG14 6N5

Bracknell & District Historical Society
7 Hambledon Court, Woodmere, BracknellRG12 9QG
Oxfordshire (South)
Berkshire Local History Association
181 Church Road, Earley, Reading, Berkshire, RG6 1HN
Goring & Streatley History Society (see Berkshire)
Chiltern Heraldry Group
Magpie Cottage, Pondwood Lane Shottesbrooke SL6 3SS
Birmingham
Birmingham & District Local History Association
112 Brandwood Road, Kings Heath, Birmingham, B14 6BX
Tel: 0121-444-7470
Barr & Aston Local Historical Society
17 Booths Farm Road, Great Barr, Birmingham, B42 2NJ
Alvechurch Historical Society
Bearhill House, Alvechurch, Birmingham, B48 7JX
Small Heath Local History Society
381 St Benedicts Road, Small Heath, Birmingham, B10 9ND
Quinton Local History Society
15 Worlds End Ave, Quinton, Birmingham, B32 1JF
Tel: 0121-422-1792
Bristol
Downend Local History Society
141 Overndale Road, Downend, Bristol, B516 2RN
Keynsham & Saltford Local History Society
33 Martock Road, Keynsham, Bristol, B531 IXA
Whitchurch Local History Society
62 Nailsea Park, Nailsea, Bristol, B519 1BB
Yatton Local History Society
21 Westaway Park, Yatton, Bristol, BS20 4JU
Bristol & Avon Archaeological Society
14 Goldney Road, Clifton, Bristol, BS8 4RB
Alveston Local History Society
1 Greenhill Down, Alveston, Bristol, BS35 3PA
Buckinghamshire
Buckinghamshire Archaeological Society
County Museum, Church Street, Aylesbury, HP20 2QP
Tel: 01296-331441-(Wed-only) Extension 217
Buckinghamshire Record Society
County Record Office, County Hall, Aylesbury, HP20 1UU
Tel: 01296-303013 Fax: 01296-382274
Buckinghamshire Archaeological Society
c/o Buckinghamshire County Museum, Church Street,
Aylesbury, Buckinghamshire, HP2O 2QP Tel: 01296 331441
Pitstone Local History Society
Vicarage Road, Pitstone, Nr Ivinghoe Tel: 01582 605464
Chesham Society
54 Church Street, Chesham, Buckinghamshire, HP5 IHY
Chess Valley Archealogical & Historical Society
16 Chapmans Crescent, Chesham, Buckinghamshire, NP5 2QU
Princes Risborough Area Heritage Society
Martin's Close, 11 Wycombe Rd, Princes Risborough
HP27 0EE Tel: 01844 343004 Email:
sandymac@risboro35.freeserve.co.uk
Cambridgeshire
Cambridgeshire Local History Society
1A Archers Cl, Swaffham Bulbeck, Cambridge, CB5 0NG
Cambridgeshire Archaeology Society
Castle Court, Shire Hall, Cambridge, CB3 0AP
Sawston Village History Society
21 Westmoor Avenue, Sawston, Cambridge, CB2 4BU
Upwood & Raveley History Group
The Old Post Office, 71-73 High Street, Upwood, Huntingdon PE17 1QE
Cambridgeshire Records Society
Fitzwilliam College, Cambridge, Cambridgeshire, CB3 0DG
Cambridge Antiquarian Society
Madingley Hall, Madingley, Cambridge CB3 8AQ
Huntingdonshire Local History Society
2 Croftfield Road, Godmanchester PE18 8ED

Oundle Historical Society
13 Lime Avenue, Oundle, Peterborough PE8 4PT
Huntingdonshire Local History
2 Croftfield Road, Godmanchester PEL8 8ED
Cheshire
Chester Archaeology Society
Grosvenor Museum, 27 Grosvenor Street, Chester, CH1 20D
Tel: 01244 402009
Chester Archaeological Society
Ochor House, Porch Lane, Hope Mountain, Caegwrle, L12 9LS
County Palatine of Chester Local History Committee
Department of History, University College Chester,
Cheveney Road, Chester CH1 4BJ
Lancashire & Cheshire Antiquarian Society
59 Malmesbury Road, Cheadle Hulme, Cheshire, SK8 7QL
Lawton Heritage Society
9 Woodgate Avenue, Church Lawton, Stoke on Trent,
Staffordshire, ST7 3EF Tel: 01270-878386
Email: dmcall12280@aol.com
Cheshire Local History Association
Cheshire Record Office, Duke Street, Chester, Cheshire, CH1
1RL Tel: 01224 602559 Tel: 01244 603812, Fax:
recordoffice@cheshire.gov.uk
Lancashire/Cheshire Antiquarian Society
59 Malmesbury Road, Cheadle Hulme, Cheshire, SK8 7QL
Altrincham History Society
10 Willoughby Close, Sale, Cheshire, M33 6PJ
Ashton & Sale History Society
Tralawney House, 78 School Road, Sale M33 7XB
Congleton History Society
10 Coronation Road, Congleton, Cheshire, CWI2 3HA
Lymm Local History Society
2 Statham Drive, Lymm, Cheshire, WA13 9NW
Stockport Historical Society
45 Dovedale Road, Offerton, Stockport, Cheshire, 5K2 5DZ
Wilmslow Historical Society
2 Tranmere Drive, Handforth, Wilmslow 5K9 3BW
Tel: 01625 522290 Email: morton@first-net.co.uk
Poynton Local History Society
33 Beech Crescent, Poynton, Cheshire, SK12 1AW
Macclesfield Historical Society
Little Hough, 5 Pinehurst, Prestbury, Cheshire, SK10 4BA
Cheshire Heraldry Society
24 Malvern Close, Congleton, Cheshire, CW12 4PD
Christleton Local History Group
25 Croft Close, Rowton CH3 7QX Tel: 01244 332410
Weaverham History Society
Ashdown, Sandy Lane, Weaverham, Northwich CW8 3PX
Tel: 01606 852252
Cleveland
Cleveland, Cleveland & Teeside Local History Society
150 Oxford Road, Linthorpe, Middlesbrough TS5 6AY
Cornwall
The Devon & Cornwall Record Society
7 The Close, Exeter, Devon, EX1 1EZ Tel: , Fax: WWW:
www.gendex.com/users/branscombe/genuki/devon.htm
Cornwall Family History Society
5 Victoria Square, Truro, Cornwall, TR1 2RS Tel: 01872-
264044 Email: secretary@cfhs.demon.co.uk
WWW: http://www.cfhs.demon.co.uk/Society/
Cornwall Association of Local Historians
St Margaret's Cottage, St Margaret's Lane, Polgooth, St
Austell, Cornwall, PL26 7AX
Email: backhouse.dodds@btinternet.com
Royal Institution of Cornwall
Royal Cornwall Museum, River Street, Truro TR1 2SJ Tel: 01872 72205
Fal Family History Group
4 Downside Close, Treloggan, Newquay, Cornwall, TR7 2TD

County Durham
Mercia Cinema Society
5 Arcadia Avenue, Chester le Street DH3 3UH
Durham County Local History Society
3 Briardene, Margery Lane, Durham DH1 4QU
Tel: 0191 386 1500
Durham Victoria County History Trust
Redesdale, The Oval, North Crescent, Durham DH1 4NE
Architectural & Archaeological Soc of Durham & Northumberland
6 Girton Close, Peterlee SR8 2NF Tel: 0191-586-6259
Tow Law History Society
27 Attleee Estate, Tow Law, County Durham, DL13 4LG
Tel: 01388-730056 Email:
RonaldStorey@storey42.freeserve.co.uk
Teesdale Heritage Group
26 Wesley Terrace, Middleton in Teesdale DL12 0SW
Tel: 01833 641104
Lanchester Local History Society
11 St Margaret's Drive, Tanfield Village, Stanley DH9 9QW
Tel: 01207-236634
Wheatley Hill History Club
57 Birkdale Gardens, Belmont, Durham DH1 2UL Tel: 0191-
384-8885 Email:
WHEATHISTORY@ORANGENET.CO.UK
North-East England History Institute (NEEHI)
Department of History University of Durham, 43 North
Bailey, Durham DH1 3EX Tel: 0191-374-2004
Fax: 0191-374-4754, Email: S.F.Ketelaar@durham.ac.uk,
WWW: http://chic.tees.ac.uk/neehi/ (Covers Northumberland,
Teesside, Tyne & Wear, Cleveland)
Croydon
Croydon Natural History & Scientific Society
20 Queenhill Road, Selsdon, South Croydon, CR2 8DN
Croydon Local Studies Forum
Flat 2, 30 Howard Road, South Norwood, London
SE25 5BY Tel: 0181-654-6454
Cumbria
Staveley and District History Society
1 Oakland, Windermere, WA23 1AR
Cumbria Industrial History Society
Coomara, Carleton, Carlisle CA4 0BU Tel: 01228-357379
Fax: 01228-596986, Email: gbrooksvet@compuserve.com
Cumbria Local History Federation
Sidegarth, Staveley, Kendal LA8 9NN
Email: joescott@clara.net
Sedbergh & District History Society
c/o 27a Main Street, Sedbergh, Cumbria, LA10 5AD Tel:
015396 20504 Email: history@sedberghcomoff.force9.co.uk
**Cumberland and Westmorland Antiquarian and
Archaeological Society**
2 High Tenterfell, Kendal LA9 4PG Tel: 01539 773542
Fax: 01539 773439, Email: info@cwaas.org.uk, WWW:
www.cwaas.org.uk
Appleby-In-Westmorland Society
67 Glebe Road, Appleby-In-Westmorland CA16 6EU
Cartmel Peninsula Local History Society
Fairfield, Cartmel, Grange Over Sands, Cumbria, LA11 6PY
Friends of Cumbria Archives
Redbourne House, 52 Main Street, St Bees CA27 0AD
Cartmel & District Local History Society
1 Barton Hse, Kents Bank Rd, Grange-Over-Sands LA11 7HD
Cumberland & Westmoreland Local Hisatory Society
10 Stewart Close, Arnside, Cumbria, LAS QES
Derbys, Ilkeston & District Local History Society
c/o 28 Kensington, Ilkeston, Derbys, DE7 5NZ
Derbyshire
Derbyshire Record Society
9 Caernarvon Close, Chesterfield, Derbyshire, S40 3DY
Derby & District Local History Forum
230 Woodbridge Close, Chellaston, Derby DE73 1QW

Derbyshire Local History Societies Network
Derbyshire Record Office, Libraries & Heritage Dept, County Hall,
MatlockDE4 3AG Tel: 01629-580000-ext-3520-1 Fax: 01629-57611
Derbyshire Archaeological Society
25 Bridgeness Road, Heatherton, Derby DE23 7UJ Tel:
01332 510566 Email: christine@suggy.softnet.co.uk, WWW:
http://www.ccc.nottingham.ac.uk/~aczsjm/das/das.html
Holymoorside and District History Society
12 Brook Close, Holymoorside, Chesterfield S42 7HB
Tel: 01246 566799
Arkwright Society
Cromford Mill, Mill Lane, Cromford, Derbyshire, DE4 3RQ
Tel: 01629 823256 Fax: 01629 823256
Chesterfield & District Local History Society
Melbourne House, 130 Station Road, Bimington,
Chesterfield, Derbyshire, S43 1LU Tel: 01246 229085
Old Dronfield Society
2 Gosforth Close, Dronfield, Derbyshire, S18 INT
New Mills Local History Society
High Point, Cote Lane, Hayfield, High Peak SK23 Tel: 01663-742814
Allestree Local Studies Group
30 Kingsley Road, Allestree, Derby, Derbyshire, DE22 2JH
Devon
Ogwell History Society
East Ogwell, Newton Abbott Devon, TQI2 6AR
Old Plymouth Society
625 Budshead Road, Whiteleigh, Plymouth, PL5 4DW
Tavistock & District Local History Society
10 Parkwood Rd, Tavistock, PL19 0HH Tel: 01822 615554
Thorverton & District History Society
Lime Tree Cottage, Thorverton, Devon, EX5 5LS
The Devon & Cornwall Record Society
7 The Close, Exeter, Devon, EX1 1EZ WWW:
www.gendex.com/users/branscombe/genuki/devon.htm
The Devon History Society
82 Hawkins Avenue, Torquay TQ2 6ES Tel: 01803 613336
Modbury Local History Society
Cawte Cottage, Brounston Street, Modbury PL21 ORH
Moretonhampstead History Society
School House, Moreton, Hampstead, Devon, TQ13 8NX
Wembury Amenity Society
5 Cross Park Road, Wembury, Plymouth, Devon, PL9 OEU
Yelverton & District Local History Society
4 The Coach House, Grenofen, Tavistock, Devon, PL19 9ES
Holbeton Yealmpton Brixton Local History Society
32 Cherry Tree Drive, Brixton, Plymouth, Devon, PL8 2DD
Newton Tracey & District Local History Society
Home Park, Lovacott , Newton Tracey, Barnstaple EX31 3PY
Dorset
Dorset Natural History & Archaeological Society
Dorset County Museum, High West Street, Dorchester DT1 1XA
Dorset Record Society
Dorset County Museum, High West Street, Dorchester,
Dorset, DT1 1XA Tel: 01305-262735
Bournemouth Local Studies Group
6 Sunningdale, Fairway Drive, Christchurch, Dorset, BH23
1JY Tel: 01202 485903 Email: mbhall@tinyonline.co.uk
Dorset
Dorchester Association For Research into Local History
68 Maiden Castle Road, Dorchester, Dorset, DT1 2ES
William Barnes Society
Pippins, Winterborne Zelston, Blandford Forum DT1 1 9EU
Friends of East Sussex Record Office
The Maltings, Castle Precincts, Lewes, BN7 LYT Tel: 01273-482349 Fax:
01273-482341 WWW: www.essole.freeserve.co.uk
Sussex History Forum
Barbican House, 169 High Street, Lewes, East Sussex, BN7
1YE Tel: 01273-405736 Fax: 01273-486990
Email: research@sussexpast.co.uk, WWW:
www.sussexpast.co.uk

Family & Community Historical Research Society
56 South Way, Lewes, East Sussex, BN7 1LY
Eastbourne Natural History and Archaeological Society
11 Brown Jack Avenue, Polegate BN26 5HN Tel: 01323 486014
East Sussex
The Sussex History Forum
Anne of Cleves House, 52 Southover High St, Lewes BN7 1JA
Sussex Archaeological Society
Barbican House, 169 High St Lewes BN7 1YE
Tel: 01273 405738
Blackboys & District Historical Society
6 Palehouse Common, Framfield, Nr Uckfield TN22 5QY
Brighton & Hove Archealogical Society
115 Braeside Avenue, Patcham, Brighton BN1 8SQ
Forest Row Local History Group
32 Freshfield Bank, Forest Row, East Sussex, RH18 HG
Peacehaven & Telscombe Historical Society
2 The Compts, Peacehaven BN1O 75Q Tel: 01273 588874
Fax: 01273 589881 Email: sbernard@mcafeemail.com
Warbleton History Group
Hillside Cottage, Bodle Street Green, Hailsham, East Sussex,
BN27 4RG Tel: 01323 832339
Maresfield Parish Historical Society
Hockridge House, London Road, Maresfield TN22 2EH
East Yorkshire
East Riding Archaeological Society
455 Chanterland Avenue, Hull, HU5 4AY Tel: 01482 445232
East Yorkshire Local History Society
13 Oaktree Drive, Molescroft, Beverley HU17 7BB
Essex
Essex Archealogical and Historical Congress
Lowe Hill House, Stratford St Mary, Suffolk, C07 6JX
Barking & District Historical Society
9 Armstrong Close, Dagenham, RM8 1TF Tel: 0208 590
9694 Email: pgibbs9@tesco.net
Friends of Historic Essex
11 Milligans Chase, Galleywood, Chelmsford, CM2 8QD
Tel: 01245 430076 Fax: 01245 430085
Barking Historical Society
9 Armstrong Close, Dagenham, RM8 LTF
The Colne Smack Preservation Society
76 New Street, Brightlingsea CO7 0DD Tel: 012065 304768
Essex Archaeological & Historical Congress
Birds Hill House, 59 Wroths Park, Loughton, Essex, IG10
1SH Tel: 0181 508 5582 Email:
1001104.1041@compuserve.com
Waltham Abbey History Society
29 Hanover Court, Waltham Abbey EN9 1HE
Tel: 01992 716830
Wanstead Historical Society
28 Howard Road, Ilford, Essex, IG1 2EX
Walthamstow Historical Society
173 Brettenham Road, Walthamstow, London, E17 5AX
Tel: 0181 523 2399 Fax: 0181 523 2399
**Ingatestone and Fryerning Historical and Archaeological
Soc**
20 Marks Close, Ingatestone, Essex, CM4 9AR Tel: 01277
353550
Billericay Archaeological and Historical Society
24 Belgrave Road, Billericay CM12 1TX Tel: 01277 658989
Colchester Archaeological Group
172 Lexden Road, Colchester CO3 4BZ Tel: 01206 575081
Burnham & District Local History & Archealogical Soc
The Museum, The Quay, Burnham On Crouch CM0 8AS
Dunmow & District Historical and Literary Society
18 The Poplars, Great Dunmow, Essex, CM6 2JA
Essex Architectural Research Society
4 Nelmes Way, Hornchurch RM11 2QZ Tel: 01708 473646
Essex Society for Archeaology & History
2 Landview Gardens, Ongar, Essex, CM5 9EQ

Friends of The Hospital Chapel
174 Aldborough Road, Seven Kings, Ilford, Essex, IG3 8HF
Friends of Thomas Plume Library
West Bowers Hall, Woodham, Maldon, Essex, CM9 6RZ
Halstead & District Local History Society
Y Magnolia, 3 Monklands Court, Halstead, Essex, C09 LAB
Loughton & District Historical Society
97 Staples Road, Loughton IG10 1HR Tel: 0181 508 0776
Nazeing History Workshop
16 Shooters Drive, Nazeing EN9 2QD Tel: 01992 893264
Witham History Group
35 The Avenue, Witham CM8 2DN Tel: 01376 512566
Brentwood & District Historical Society
51 Hartswood Rd, Brentwood CM14 5AG Tel:01277 221637
Thurrock Local History Society
13 Rosedale Road, Thurrock Grays, Essex, RM17 6AD
Romford & District Historical
5 Rosemary Avenue, Romford, Essex, RM1 4HB
Tel: 01708 730150 Fax: 01708 730150
Maldon Society
15 Regency Court, Heybridge, Maldon, Essex, CM9 4EJ
East London History Society
13 Three Crowns Road, Colchester, Essex, CO4 5AD,
Gloucestershire
Leckhampton Local History Society
15 Arden Road, Leckhampton, Cheltenham, GL53 OHG
Moreton-In-Marsh & District Local History Society
5 The Row, Donnington, Moreton-In-Marsh, GL56 OYA
Swindon Village Society
3 Swindon Hall, Swindon Village, Cheltenham, GL51 9QR
Tel: 01242 521723
Gloucestershire County Local History Committee
Gloucestershire RCC, Community House, 15 College Green,
Gloucester, Gloucestershire, GL1 2LZ Tel: 01452-309783
Fax: 01452-528493, Email: grcc@grcc.ndirect.co.uk
Bristol and Gloucestershire Archaeological Society
22 Beaumont Road, Gloucester GL2 0EJ Tel: 01452 302610
Cheltenham Local History Society
39 Tivoli Road, Cheltenham, Gloucestershire, GL50 2TD
Campden and District Historical & Archaeological Soc
14 Pear Tree Close, Chipping Campden GL55 6DB
Cirencester Archaeological and Historical Society
Corinium Museum, Park Street, Cirencester GL7 2BX
Charlton Kings Local History Society
19 Lyefield Road West, Charlton Kings, Cheltenham,
Gloucestershire, GL53 8EZ Tel: 01242 524258
Forest of Dean Local History Society
51 Lancaster Drive, Lydney, Gloucestershire, GL15 5SJ Tel:
01594 843310 Email: keith.walker3@which.net
Painswick Local History Society
Valley Lodge Lower, Washwell, Painswick GL6 6XW
Stroud Civic Society
Blakeford House,Broad St,Kings Stanley,Stonehouse GL10 3PN
Stroud Local History Society
Coombe House, 213 Slad Road, Stroud GL5 1RJ
Friends of Gloucestershire Archives
72 Swindon Lane, Prestbury, Cheltenham GL50 4PA
Tel: 01242 528790
Tewkesbury Historical Society
7 Moulder Rd, Tewkesbury GL20 8ED Tel: 01684 292633
Newent Local History Society
Arron, Ross Road, Newent, Gloucestershire, GL18 1BE
Frenchay Tuckett Society and Local History Museum
247 Frenchay Park Road, FrenchayBS16 ILG Tel: 0117 956 9324
Email: raybulmer@compuserve.com WWW:
http://ourworld.compuserve.com/homepages/raybutler
South Gloucestershire
Avon Local History Association (see Avon)

Hampshire
Botley & Curdridge Local History Society
38 Bryony Gardens, Horton Heath, Eastleigh, SO50 7PT
Milford on Sea Historical Records Society
New House, New Road, Keyhaven, Lymington, S041 0TN
Newchurch Parish History Society
1 Mount Pleasant, Newport Road, Sandown, P036 OLS
History of Thursley Society
50 Wyke Lane, Ash, Aldershot GU12 6EA
Email: old.norm@clara.net
WWW: http://home.clara.net/old.norm/Thursley
Bitterne Local History Society
Heritage Centre, 225 Peartree Avenue, Bitterne, Southampton,
Tel: 01703-444837 Fax: 01703-444837
Email: richardsheaf@compuserve.com
WWW: http://www.bitterne2.freeserve.co.uk
Hampshire FC & A Society (Local History Section)
Hampshire C R O , Sussex Street, Winchester, SO23 8TH
**North East Hampshire Historical and Archaeological
Society**
36 High View Road, Farnborough, Hampshire, GU14 7PT
Tel: 01252-543023 Email: nehhas@netscape.net
WWW: www.hants.org.uk/nehhas
Hampshire Field Club and Archaeological Society
28 Harvest Close, Badger Farm, Winchester S022 4DW
Aldershot Historical and Archaeological Society
10 Brockenhurst Road, Aldershot GU11 3HH Tel: 01252
26589
Andover History and Archaeology Society
140 Weyhill Road, Andover SPIO 3BG Tel: 01264 324926
Basingstoke Archaeological and Historical Society
16 Scotney Road, Basingstoke RG21 2SR,
Tel: 01256 322090 Email: JTHerring@aol.com
Fleet & Crookham Local History Group
5 Rosedene Gardens, Fleet, Hampshire, GU13 8NQ
Fordingbridge Historical Society
26 Lyster Road,, Manor Park, Fordingbridge SP6 IQY
Tel: 01425 655417
Havant Museum
Havant Museum, 56 East Street, Havant P09 1BS Tel: 023
9245 1155 Fax: 023 9249 8707
Lymington & District Historical Society
47 Rowans Park, Lymington, Hampshire, S041 9GE
Somborne & District Society
Forge House, Winchester Road, Kings Somborne,
Stockbridge, Hampshire, S020 6NY Tel: 01794 388742
West End Local History Society
20 Orchards Way, West End, Southampton S030 3FB
Lymington & District Hist Soc
47 Rowans Park, Lymington, Hampshire, S041 9GE
Costume Society South of England Branch
173 Abbotstone, Alresford, Hampshire, S024 9TE
Fleet & Crookham Local History
29 Woodcote Green, Fleet, Hampshire, GUI3 8EY
Botley & Curdridge Local History
38 Bryony Gardens, Horton Heath, Eastleigh SO50 7PT
Stubbington & Hillhead History Society
34 Anker Lane, Stubbington, Fareham PO14 3HE,
Tel: 01329 664554
Bishops Waltham Museum Trust
8 Folly Field, Bishop's Waltham, Southampton S032 1GF
Tel: 01489 894970
Milford-on-Sea Historical Record Society
New House, New Road, Keyhaven, Lymington S041 OTN
Herefordshire
Eardisland Oral History Group
Eardisland, Leominster, Herefordshire, HR
Ewyas Harold & District WEA
c/o Hillside, Ewyas Harold, Hereford HR2 0HA

Kington History Society
Kington Library, Kington, Herefordshire, HR5 3BD
Leominster Historical Society
Fircroft, Hereford Rd, Leominster HR6 8JU Tel: 01568 612874
Weobley & District Local History Society and Museum
Back Lane, Weobley HR4 8SG Tel: 01544 340292
Hertfordshire
Hertford & Ware Local History Society
10 Hawthorn Close, Hertford, SG14 2DT
1st or Grenadier Foot Guards 1803 -1823
39 Chatterton, Letchworth, Hertfordshire, SG6 2JY
Tel: 01462-670918 Email: BJCham2809@aol.com
Welwyn & District Local History Society
9 York Way, Welwyn AL6 9LB Tel: 01438 716415
Baptist Historical Society
60 Strathmore Avenue, Hitchin SG5 1ST
Tel: 01462-431816 Tel: 01462-442548
Email: slcopson@dial.pipex.com
Hertfordshire Association for Local History
Ashwell Education Services, Merchant Taylors' Centre,
Ashwell, Baldock SG7 5LY Tel: 01462-742385 Fax: 01462-
743024, Email: aes@ashwell-education-services.co.uk
Hertfordshire Record Society
119 Winton Drive, Croxley Green, Rickmansworth,
Hertfordshire, WD3 3QS Tel: 01923-248581
Machine Breakers, Rioters & Protesters
4 Quills, Letchworth, Hertfordshire, SG6 2RJ Tel: 01462-
483706 Email: J_M_Chambers@compuserve.com
Welwyn Archaeological Society
The Old Rectory, 23 Mill Lane, Welyn AL6 9EU
Tel: 01438 715300 Fax: 01438 715300
Potters Bar and District History Society
23 Osborne Road, Potters Bar, Hertfordshire, EN6 IR2
Hertfordshire Local History Council
Lamb Cottage, Whitwell, Hitchin, Hertfordshire, SG4 3HQ
East Herts Archaeological Society
1 Marsh Lane, Stanstead Abbots, Ware SG12 8HH
Tel: 01920 870664
Hertfordshire Archaeological Trust
The Seed Warehouse, Maidenhead Yard, The Wash, Hertford
SG14 1PX Tel: 01992 558 170 Fax: 01992 553359
Abbots Langley Local History Society
80 Abbots Road, Abbots Langley, Hertfordshire, WD5 0BH
Harpenden & District Local History Society
The History Centre, 19 Arden Grove, Harpenden AL5 45J
Hitchin Historical Society
c/o Hitchin Museum, Paynes Park, Hitchin SG5 2EQ
Kings Langley Local History & Museum Society
The Library, The Nap, Kings Langley, WD4 8ET
Tel: 01923 263205 Email: alan@Penwardens.freeserve.co.uk
London Colney Local History Society
51A St Annes Rd, London Colney, Nr. St. Albans AL2 1PD
Middlesex Heraldry Society
4 Croftwell, Harpenden, Hertfordshire, AL5 1JG
Rickmansworth Historical Society
20 West Way, Rickmansworth, Hertfordshire, WD3 2EN
Tel: 01923 774998 Email: geoff@gmsaul.freeserve.co.uk
Codicote Local History Society
34 Harkness Way, Hitchin, Hertfordshire, SG4 0QL
Royston & District Local History Society
8 Chilcourt, Royston SG8 9DD Tel: 01763 242677
St. Albans & Herts Architectural & Local History Society
28 Faircross Way, St Albans, Hertfordshire, AL1 4SD
London Colney Local History Society
51a St Annes Road, London Colney, Nr. St Albans AL2 ILQ
Royal Photographic Society Historical Group
PO Box 28, Borehamwood, Hertfordshire, WD6 4SY

Isle of Wight
Isle of Wight Natural History & Archaeological Society
Island Countryside Centre, Rylstone Gardens, Shanklin, Isle
of Wight, PO37 6RG Tel: 01983 867016
Isle Of Wight, Roots Family & Parish History
San Fernando, Burnt House Lane, Alverstone, Sandown PO36 0HB Tel:
01983 403060 Email: peters.sanfernando@tesco.net
Isle Of Wight
St. Helens Hist Soc
The Castle, Duver Rd, St Helens, Ryde, Isle Of Wight, PO33 1XY
Kent
Ashford Archaeological and Historical Society
9 Wainwright Place, Newtown, Ashford, TN24 0PF Tel: 01233 631017
Canterbury Archaeology Society
Dane Court, Adisham, Canterbury, CT3 3LA
Maidstone Historical Society
37 Bower Mount Road, Maidstone ME16 8AX Tel: 01622 676472
Tonbridge Historical Society
8 Woodview Cresent, Hildenborough, Tonbridge, TN11 9HD
Tel: 01732 838698 Fax: 01732 838522
Email: s.broomfield@dial.pipex.com
Legion of Frontiersmen of Commonwealth
4 Edwards Road, Belvedere, Kent, DA17 5AL
The Kent Archaeological Society
Three Elms, Woodlands Lane, Shorne, Gravesend, Kent,
DA12 3HH Tel: 01474 822280 Email: ai_moffat@csi.com,
WWW: http://ourworld.compuserve.com/homepages/ai_moffat
Kent History Federation
48 Beverley Avenue, Sidcup, Kent, DA15 8HE
Kent Archaeological Society
Three Elms, Woodland Lane, Shorne, Gravesend DA12 3HH
Tel: 01474 822280
Crayford Manor House Historical & Archaeological Soc
17 Swanton Road, Erith, Kent, DA8 1LP
Maidstone Area Archaeological Group
14 The Quarter, Cranbrook Road, Staplehurst TN12 0EP
Council for Kentish Archaeology
32 Birling Road, Tunbridge Wells, Kent, TN2 5LY
Fawkham & District Historical Society
6 Nuthatch, New Barn, Longfield, Kent, DA3 7NS
Fleur De Lis Heritage Centre
13 Preston Street, Faversham, Kent, ME13 8NS
Gravesend Historical Society
58 Vicarage Lane, Chalk, Gravesend DA12 4TE Tel: 01474 3693998
Maidenhead Archealogical & Historical Society
43 Bannard Road, Maidenhead, Kent, 5L6 4NP
Romney Marsh Research Trust
Langley Farm, Bethersden, Ashford, Kent, TN26 3HF
Sandwich Local History Society
Clover Rise, 14 Stone Cross Lees, Sandwich CT13 OBZ
Tel: 01304 613476 Email: frankandrews@FreeNet.co.uk
Tonbridge History Soc
33 Bramble Close, Hildenborough, Tonbridge TN1 1 9HQ
Wealden Buildings Study Group
64 Pilgrims Way, East Otford, Sevenoaks, Kent, TN14 5QW
Society of Genealogy & History of Beckenham
136 Lennard Road, Beckenham, Kent, BR3 IQT
Kingston upon Hull
Hull Central Library Family and Local History Club
Hull Central Library, Albion Street, Kingston upon Hull,
HU1 3TF Tel: 01482-616828 Fax: 01482-883080
Email: gwatkins@kuhcc.demon.co.uk
WWW: http://www.hullcc.gov.uk/genealogy/fhclub.htm
Lancashire
Ewecross History Society
Farr House, Lowgill, Lancaster, LA2 8RA Tel: 01524 261382
Lancashire Parish Register Society
16 Rothay Drive, Penketh, Warrington WA5 2PG
Email: lprs@penketh.force9.co.uk
WWW: http://www.genuki.org.uk/big/eng/LAN/lprs

North West Sound Archive
Old Steward's Office, Clitheroe Castle, Clitheroe BB7 1AZ
Tel: 01200-427897 Fax: 01200-427897
WWW: www.nw-soundarchive.co.uk
Lancashire Local History Federation
101 Todmorden Road, Littleborough, Lancashire, OL15 9EB
Tel: 01706 379949 Email: mai..llhf@virgin.net
Saddleworth Historical Society
7 Slackcote, Delph, Oldham OL3 5TW Tel: 01457 874530
Lancashire History
4 Cork Road, Lancaster, Lancashire, LA1 4AJ
Littleborough Historical and Archaeological Society
8 Springfield Ave, Littleborough LA15 9JR Tel: 01706 377685
Aspull and Haigh Historical Society
3 Pennington Close, Aspull, Wigan, Lancashire, WN2 2SP
Blackburn Civic Society
20 Tower Road, Blackburn, Lancashire, BB2 5LE
Burnley Historical Society
Central Library, Grimshaw Street, Burnley BB11 2BD
Chadderton Historical Society
18 Moreton St, Chadderton 0L9 0LP Tel: 0161 652 3930
Garstang Historical & Archealogical Society
2 Lakeland Close, Forton, Preston, Lancashire, PR3 QAY
Lancashire Family History/Heraldry Society
66 Glenluce Drive, Farringdon Park, Preston PRI 5TD
Fleetwood & District Historical Society
54 The Esplanade, Fleetwood, Lancashire, FY7 6QE
Leyland Historical Society
172 Stanifield Lane, Farington; Leyland, Preston PR5 2QT
Nelson Local History Society
5 Trent Road, Nelson, Lancashire, BB9 ONY
Leicestershire
Glenfield & Western Archaeological & Historical Group
50 Chadwell Road, Leicester LE3 6LF Tel: 1162873220
Leicestershire Archaeological and Historical Society
The Guildhall, Leicester LE1 5PQ Tel: 0116 2703031
WWW: http://www.le.ac.uk/archaeology/lahs/lahs.html
Vaughan Archaeological and Historical Society
Vaughan College, St Nicholas Circle, Leicester LEl 4LB
Desford & District Local History Group
Lindridge House, Lindridge Lane, Desford LE9 9FD
East Leake & District Local History
35 Sycamore Road, East Leake, Loughborough LE12 6PP
Lincolnshire
South Holland Family & Local History Group
54 Wygate Road, Spalding , Lincolnshire, PE11 1NT
Society for Lincolnshire History & Archaeology
Jews' Court, Steep Hill, Lincoln LN2 1LS Tel: 01522-521337
Stamford Historical Society
14 Castle Rise, Belmesthorpe, Stamford PE9 4JL Tel: 01780 64213
Mourholme Local History Society
173a Main Street, Warton, Carnforth, Lincolnshire, LAS 9QF
Liverpool
Merseyside Archaeological Society
20 Osborne Rd, Formby, Liverpool, L37 6AR Tel: 01704 871802
London
London & Middlesex Archaeological Society
University of N London, 62-66 Highbury Grove, London, N5 2AD
London Record Society
c/o Institute of Historical Research, Senate House, Malet Street, London,
WC1E 7HU Tel: 0171-862-8798 Email: creaton@sas.ac.uk
WWW: http://www.ihr.sas.ac.uk/ihr/associnstits/lrsmnu.html
Centre for Metropolitan History
Institute of Historical Research, Senate House, Malet Street, London, WC1E
7HU Tel: 0171 862 8790 Fax: 0171 862 8793, Email: o-myhill@sas.ac.uk,
WWW: www.ihrinfo.ac.uk/cmh/cmh.main.html
Haringey/Hornsey
Hornsey Historical Society
The Old Schoolhouse, 136 Tottenham Lane, London, N8 7EL
Tel: 0181 348 8429

Wandsworth Historical Society
7 Coalecroft Road, London, SW15 6LW Tel: 0181 7880015
Acton History Group
48 Perryn Road, London, W3 7NA Tel: 0181 743 3476
Brentford & Chiswick Local History Society
25 Hartington Road, London, W4 3TL
Mill Hill Historical Society
41 Victoria Rd, Mill Hill, London, NW7 4SA Tel: 0181 959 7126
Pwmvs Local History Group
19a Randolph Road, Maida Vale, London, W9 1AN
Fulham And Hammersmith Historical Soceity
6 Ariel Court, Ashchurch Park Villas, London, W12 95R
Walthamstow Historical Society
173 Brettenham Road, Walthamstow, London, E17 5AX
Tel: 0181 523 2399 Fax: 0181 523 2399
Brixton Society
82 Mayall Road, London, SE24 0PJ
Newham History Society
52 Eastbourne Road, East Ham, London, E6 6AT
Croydon Local Studies Forum
208 Turnpike Lane, London, London, CR0 5NZ
Birkbeck College Department of History
Malet Street, London, London, WC1E 7HU Tel: 0171 6316299
Fulham & Hammersmith History Society
85 Rannoch Road, Hammersmith, London, W6 9SX
London Borough of Barnet, Hendon & Dist Arch So
13 Reynolds Close, London, NW11 7EA Tel: 0181 458 1352
Manchester
Stretford Local History Society
26 Sandy Lane, Stretford, Manchester, M32 9DA
Denton Local History Society
94 Edward Street, Denton, Manchester, M34 3BR
Merseyside
Maghull And Lydiate Local History Society
15 Brendale Avenue, Maghull, Liverpool, L31 7AX
Historic Society of Lancashire & Cheshire
Liverpool Hope University College, Hope Park, Liverpool,
Merseyside, L16 9JD Tel: 0151-291-3062
Friends of Williamson's Tunnels
15-17 Chatham Place, Edge Hill, Liverpool, Merseyside, L7
3HD Tel: , Email: tunnels@mail.cybase.co.uk, WWW:
http://ourworld.compuserve.com/homepages/bill_douglas
Birkdale & Alnsdale Historical Research Society
14 The Lawns, Southport, Merseyside, PR9 PNS
Merseyside Archaeological Society
20 Osborne Road, Formby, Liverpool, L37 6AR Tel: 01704 871802
Middlesex
London and Middlesex Archaeological Society
University of London, 62-66 Highbury Grove, N5 2AD
Hounslow & District History Society
142 Guildford Avenue, Feltham, Middlesex, TW13 4EL
Ruislip Northwood & Eastcote Local History Society
7 The Greenway, Ickenham, Uxbridge UB10 8L5
Borough of Twickenham Local History Society
258 Hanworth Road, Hounslow, Middlesex, TW3 3TY
Edmonton Hundred Historical Society
7 Park Crescent, Enfield EN2 6HT Tel: 0181 367 2211
Pinner Local History Society
8 The Dell, Pinner, Middlesex, HAS 3EW
Tel: 0208 866 1918 Email: mwg@pinnerlhs.freeserve.co.uk,
WWW: www.pinnerlhs.freeserve.co.uk/index.html
Sunbury and Shepperton Local History
95 Gaston Way, Shepperton, Middlesex, TW17 8ET
Northwood & Eastcote Local History Society
7 The Greenway, Ickenham, Uxbridge, Ruislip UB10 8LS
Norfolk
Norfolk Archaeological and Historical Research Group
50 Cotman Road, Norwich, NR1 4AH Tel: 01603 435470
Norfolk Heraldry Society
22 Cintra Road, Norwich, NR1 4AE

Federation of Norfolk Historical and Archaeological Organisations
14 Beck Lane, Horsham St Faith, Norwich NR10 3LD
Feltwell Historical and Archaeological Society
16 High'Street, Feltwell, Thetford IP26 Tel: 01842 828448
Lowestoft Archaeological and Local History Society
1 Cranfield Close, Pakefield, Lowestoft, Norfolk, NR33 7EL
Tel: 01502 586143
Norfolk and Norwich Archaeological Society
30 Brettingham Ave, Cringleford, Norwich NR4 6XG
Tel: 01603 455913
Narborough Local History Society
101 Westfields, Narborough, Kings Lynn PE32 ISY
Blakeney Area Historical Society
Hillside, Morston Road, Blakeney NR25 7BG Tel: 01263-740589
North Somerset, Nailsea & District Local History Society
13 Fosse Lane, Nailsea, North Somerset, BS48 2AR
North Yorkshire
Local Population Studies Society
78 Harlow Terrace, Harrogate HG2 0PN Tel: 01423-560429
Fax: 01423-560429 Email: sir_david_cooke@compuserve.com
Upper Wharfedale Field Society (Local History Section)
Old School House, Conistone, Skipton BD23 5HS Tel: 01756-752953
Poppleton History Society
44 Millfield Gardens, Nether Poppleton, York YO26 6NZ
Tel: 01904-785945 Email: susan.major@virgin.net, WWW:
http://freespace.virgin.net/susan.major/PHS
Stokesley & District Local History Study Group
21 Cleveland Avenue, Stokesley, North Yorkshire, TS9 5EZ
Scarborough Archaeological and Historical Society
10 Westbourne Park, Scarborough YO12 4AT
 Tel: 01723 354237 Email: archaelogy@scarborough.co.uk
Northallerton and District Local History Society
17 Thistle Close, Romanby Park, Northallerton DL7 8FF
Snape Local History Group
Garthland, Snape, Bedale, North Yorkshire, DL8 2DF
Tel: 01677 470769 Email: debbie.fiona@ukgateway.net
Northamptonshire
Weedon Bec History Society
35 Oak Street, Weedon, Northampton, NN7 4RR
Northamptonshire Association for Local History
12 Frog Lane, Upper Boddington, Daventry NN11 6DJ
Northamptonshire Record Society
Wooton Park Hall, Northampton NN4 8BQ
Bozeat Historical and Archaeological Society
44 Mile Street, Bozeat NN9 7NB Tel: 01933 663647
Brackley & District Historical Society
32 Church Lane, Evenley, Brackley NNL3 5SG
Northants Record Society
Wootton Hall Park, Northampton NN4 9BQ Tel: 01604 762297
Houghtons & Brafield Local History Society
c/o 5 Lodge Road, Little Houghton NN7 1AE
Rushden & District History Society
25 Byron Crescent, Rushden NN10 6BL Email: rdhs.rushden@virgin.net,
WWW: http://freespace.virgin.net/bob.safford/rdhs/home.htm
Brackley & District History Society
32 Church Lane, Evenley, Brackley NN13 5SG Tel: 01280 703508
Houghtons & Brafield History
The, 5 Lodge Road, Little Houghton NN7 IAE
West Haddon Local History Group
Bramley House, 12 Guilsborough Rd, West Haddon, NN6 7AD
Higham Chichele Society
1 Hachenburg Place, Higham, Ferrers NN10 8HJ
Northumberland
Felton & Swarland Local History Society
23 Benlaw Grove, Felton, Morpeth NE65 9NG Tel: 01670 787476
Morpeth Antiquarian Society
14 Southgate Wood, Morpeth, Northumberland, NE61 2EN
Morpeth Nothumbrian Gathering
Westgate House, Dogger Bank, Morpeth NE61 1RF

Stannington Local History Society
Glencar House, 1 Moor Lane, Stannnington, Morpeth, NE61 6BB
War Memorials Survey N E Bilsdale
Ulgham, Morpeth, Northumberland, NE61 3AR Tel: 01670 790465
(Tyne & Wear, North & South Tyneside, Gateshead)
Hexham Local History Society
Dilstone, Burswell Villas, Hexham NE46 3LD Tel: 01434 603216
Nottinghamshire
Ruddington Local History Society
36 Brook View Drive, Keyworth, Nottingham, NG12 5JN
Keyworth & District Local History Society
Innisfree, Thelda Avenue, Keyworth, Nottingham, NG12 5HU
Tel: 0115 937908 Fax: 0115 9372908
Nottinghamshire Local History Association
128 Sandhill Street, Worksop S80 1SY Tel: 01909 488878
Thoroton Society of Nottinghamshire
59 Briar Gate, Long Eaton, Nottingham NG10 4BQ
Tel: 0115-972-6590 Email: keithgoodman@compuserve.com
WWW: www.cthulu.demon.co.uk
Nottingham Historical and Archaeological Society
48 Banks Road, Toton, Beaston NG9 6HA Tel: 0115 9734284
Redford & District Historical & Archaeological Society
Cambridge House, 36 Alma Road, Redford, Nottinghamshire,
DN22 6LW Tel: 01777 701902 Fax: 01777 707784
Email: joan@j.a+esewell.demon.co.uk
Beeston & District Local History Society
16 Cumberland Ave, Beeston, Nottinghamshire, NG9 4DH
Numismatic Society of Nottinghamshire
43 Park Street, Beeston, Nottinghamshire, NG9 1DF
Oxfordshire
Wallingford Historical and Archaeological Society
Flint House, 52a High Street, Wallingford, OX1O 0DB Tel: 01491 837720
Banbury History Society
c/o Banbury Museum, 8 Horsefair, Banbury, OX16 OAA
Wychwood's Local History Society
The Old Till House, Shipton-Under-Wychwoood 0X7 6DQ
Volunteer Corps of Frontiersmen
Archangels' Rest, 26 Dark Lane, Witney OX8 5LE
Oxfordshire Local History Association
12 Meadow View, Witney OX8 6TY Tel: 01993 778345
Oxfordshire Record Society
Bodelian Library, Oxford, Oxfordshire, OX1 3BG
Faringdon Archaeological & Historical Society
1 Orchard Hill, Faringdon, Oxfordshire, SN7 7EH
Oxford Local History Association
Windrush Cottage, Ducklington, Oxfordshire, OX8 7UD
Abingdon Area Archaeological and Historical Society
4 Cherwell Close, Abingdon OX14 3TD Tel: 01235 528835
Oxfordshire Architectural and Historical Society
c/o Centre for Oxfordshire Studies, Westgate, Oxford,
OX1 1DJ WWW: http://ww.demon.co.uk/adodd/oahs
Blewbury Local History Group
Spring Cottage, Church Road, Blewbury OX11 9PY
Chinnor Historical & Archealogical Society
7 Cherry Tree Road, Chinnor, Oxfordshire, 0X9 4QY
Cumnor History Society
4 Kenilworth Road, Cumnor, Nr Oxford OX2 9QP
Oxfordshire Local History Society
3 The Square, Aynho, Nr Banbury 0X17 3BL
Longworth Local History Society
10 Bellamy Close, Southmoor, Oxfordshire, OX13 5AB
Rutland
Rutland Local History & Record Society
c/o Rutland County Museum, Catmos Street, Oakham,
Rutland, LE15 6HW Tel: 01572-723654 Fax: 01572 757576
Isle Of Wight
St Helens Historical Society
Gloddaeth, Westfield Rd, St. Helens,Ryde Isle Of Wight P033 LUZ

Shropshire
Cleobury Mortimer Historical Society
24 High Street, Cleobury Mortimer, Kidderminster, DY14
8BY Tel: 01299 270110 Fax: 01299 270110
Email: history@mbaldwin.free-online.co.uk
Council for British Archeaology - West Midlands
c/o Rowley's House Museum, Barker Street, Shrewsbury,
SY1 1QH Tel: 01743 361196 Tel: 01743 358411
(Herefordshire, Shropshire, Staffordshire, Warwickshire, Worcestershire,
West Midlands, Herefordshire, Shropshire, Staffordshire)
Shropshire Archaeological and Historical Society
Lower Wallop Farm, Westbury, Shrewsbury SY5 9RT
Whitchurch History and Archaeology Group
The Field House, Wirswall, Whitchurch SY13 4LA
Tel: 01948 662623
Field Studies Council
Central Services, Preston Montford, Montford Bridge,
Shrewsbury, Shropshire, SY4 1HW Tel: 01743 850674
Somerset
Somerset Archaeological & Natural History Society
Taunton Castle, Taunton TA1 4AD Tel: 01823 272429
Somerset Record Society
Somerset Studies Library, Paul Street, Taunton, Somerset
TA1 3XZ Tel: 01823-340300 Fax: 01823-340301
Axbridge Archaeological and Local History Society
King John's Hunting Lodge, The Square, Axbridge, Somerset
BS26 2AR Tel: 01934 732012
South East Somerset Archaeological & Historical Society
Abbascombe Barn, Lilly Lane, Templecombe, Somerset
BA8 OHN Tel: 01963 371163
Yeovil Archaeological and Local History Society
Plantagenet Chase, Yeovil, Somerset Tel: 01935 78258
Bathford Society
36 Bathford Hill, Bathford, Somerset, BA1 7SL
Castle Cary & District Museum & Monymusk
March Lane, Galhampton, Yeovil, Somerset, BA22 7AN
Oakhill & Ashwick Local History Society
Bramley Farm, Bath Road, Oakhill, Somerset, BA3 5AF
South Petherton Local History Group
Cobbetts Droveway, South Petherton, Somerset, TAI3 5DA
Ogwell History Society
East Ogwell, Newton Abbott, South Devon, TQI2 6AR
North Somerset
Alveston Local History Society (see Bristol)
Avon Local History Association (see Avon)
South Yorkshire
Doncaster Group of the Yorkshire Archaeological Society
Merrylees, 1b Ellers Road, Doncaster, DN4 7BE Tel: 01302 531581
South Yorkshire Archaeology Unit and Museum
Ellin Street, Sheffield Tel: 0114 2734230
Bentley with Arksey Heritage Society
45 Finkle Street, Bentley, Doncaster DN5 0RP
Staffordshire
Staffordshire Archaeological and Historical Society
38 Knighton Drive, Four Oaks, Sutton Coldfield, B74 4QP
Tel: 0121 3081072
Staffordshire
Birmingham Canal Navigation's Society
37 Chestnut Close, Handsacre, Rugeley WS15 4TH
Lawton Heritage Society
9 Woodgate Avenue, Church Lawton, Stoke on Trent, ST7
3EF Tel: 01270-878386 Email: dmcall12280@aol.com
Staffordshire Local Studies
PO Box 23, Stafford, Staffordshire, ST17 4AY
Staffordshire, British Records Society
Stone Barn Farm, Sutherland Road, Longsdon ST9 9QD
Tel: 01782 385446/01538 385024
Email: carolyn@cs.keele.ac.uk
Staffordshire Local Studies Forum
POBox 23, Stafford ST17 4AY Tel: 01785 278353

Berkswich Local History Group
1 Greenfield Road, Stafford, Staffordshire, ST17 OPU
Landor Society
38 Fortescue Lane, Rugeley, Staffordshire, WS15 2AE
Ridware History Society
Priory Farm, Blithbury, Nr. Rugeley WSI5 3JA Tel: 01889 504269
Stafford Historical & Civic Society
86 Bodmin Avenue, Weeping Cross, Stafford ST17 OEQ
Tel: 01785 662565
Suffolk
Framlingham & Dist Local History & Preservation Soc
28 Pembroke Road, Framlingham IP13 9HA Tel: 01728 723214
Suffolk Local History Council
2nd Floor, Orchard House, St Helens Street, Ipswich IP4 2JL
Suffolk Institute of Archaeology and History
Roots,Church Lane, Playford, Ipswich IP6 9DS Tel: 01473-624556
Brett Valley History Society
17 Manor Road, Bildeston, Ipswich, Suffolk, IP7 7BG
Elmswell Parish Council Village Recorder
Hill Court, Church Road, Elmswell, Suffolk, P30 9DY
Surrey
Guildford Archaeology Group
6 St Omer Road, Guildford, GU1 2DB Tel: 01483 532201
Surrey
Shere Gomshall & Peaslake Local History Society
Twiga Lodge, Wonham Way, Gomshall, Guildford, GUS 9NZ
Richmond Local History Society
9 Bridge Road, St Margarets, Twickenham, TWI IRE
Centre for Local History Studies
Faculty of Human Sciences, Kingston University, Penrhyn
Road, Kingston, Surrey, KT1 2EE Tel: 0181 547 2000
Surrey Local History Council
University of Surrey, Ward Street, Guildford GU1 4LH
Surrey Record Society
History Centre, 130 Goldsworth Rd, Woking GU21 1ND
Send and Ripley History Society
St Georges Farm House, Ripley, Surrey, GU23 6AF
Nonsuch Antiquarian Society
17 Seymour Avenue, Ewell, Epsom KT17 2RP Tel: 0181 3930531
Surrey Archaeological Society
Castle Arch, Guildford GU1 3SX Tel: 01483 532454
Fax: 01483 532454, Email: surreyarch@compuserve.com
WWW: ourworld.compuserve.com/homepages/surreyarch
Addlestone History Society
53 Liberty Lane, Addlestone, Weybridge, Surrey, KT15 1NQ
Beddington Carshalton & Wallington History Society
57 Brambledown Road, Wallington, Surrey, SM6 0TF
Carshalton Society
43 Denmark Road, Carshalton, Surrey, SM5 2JE
Croydon Natural History & Scientific Society Ltd
96a Brighton Road, South Croydon CR2 6AD Tel: 0181 688 4539
Domestic Buildings Research Group (Surrey)
Meadow Cottage, Brook Hill, Albury, Guildford GUS 9DJ
Farnham and District Museum Society
Tanyard House, 13a Bridge Square, Farnham GU9 7QR
Leatherhead District Local History Society
Leatherhead Museum, 64 Church Street, Leatherhead, Surrey,
KT22 8DP Tel: 01372 386348
Walton On The Hill District Local History Society
5 Russell Close, Walton On The Hill, Tadworth, Surrey
KT2O 7QH Tel: 01737 812013
Sedgeford Historical & Archaeological Research Project
Church Villa, Church Street, Tilehurst, Wadhurst, TN5 7AB
Tel: 01580 201290
Bourne Society
46 Beverley Road, Whyteleafe, Surrey, CR3 0DX
Carshalton & Beddington History Society
75 Beddington Gardens, Carshalton Beeches SM5 3HL
Danehill Parish Historical Society
1 Danehurst Cottages, Church Lane, Danehill RH17 7EY

Walton & Weybridge Local History Society
9 Weybridge House, Queen's Road, Weybridge KTI3 0AP
Sussex
East Sussex Archaeology Project
Anne of Cleves House, 52 Southover High Street, Lewes,
BN7 1JA Tel: 01273 486959
Lewes Archaeological Group
Rosemary Cottage, High St Barcombe, nr Lewes, BN8 5DM,
Tel: 01273 400878
Sussex History Study Group
Colstock, 43 High Street, Ditchling, Sussex, BN5 8SY
Forest Row History Group
32 Freshfield Bank, Forest Row, Sussex, RH18 5HG
Tyne and Wear
Association of Northumberland Local History Societies
Centre for Lifelong Learning, King George VI Building,
University of Newcastle upon Tyne, Newcastle upon Tyne,
NE1 7RU Tel: 0191-222-7458 Tel: 0191-222-5680,
North Eastern Police History Society
Brinkburn Cottage, 28 Brinkburn Street, High Barnes,
Sunderland, Tyne and Wear, SR4 7RG Tel: 0191-565-7215
Email: harry.wynnne@virgin.net
WWW: http://freespace.virgin.net/carol.almond/index.htm
North East Labour History Society
Department of Historical & Critical Studies, University of
Northumbria, Newcastle upon Tyne, Tyne and Wear, NE1
8ST Tel: 0191-227-3193 Fax: 0191-227-4630
Email: joan.hugman@unn.ac.uk
Cullercoats Local History Society
33 St Georges Rd, Cullercoats, North Shields NE30 3JZ,
Tel: 0191 252 7042
Society of Antiquaries of Newcastle upon Tyne
Black Gate, Castle Garth, Newcastle upon Tyne, NE1 1RQ
Tel: 1912615390 Tel: 0771 216 0431
Northumberland Local History
University Of Newcastle, Newcastle Upon Tyne NE1 7RL
Northumbria Historic Churches Trust
The Vicarage, South Hylton, Sunderland, Tyne and Wear
Warwickshire
Warwickshire Local History Society
9 Willes Terrace, Leamington Spa CV31 1DL
Kineton and District Local History Group
The Glebe House, Lighthorne Road, Kineton, Warwickshire,
CV35 0JL Tel: 01926 690298 Fax: 01926 690298
Alcester & District Local History Society
43 Seymour Road, Alcester, Warwickshire, B49 6JY
Shakespeare Birthplace Trust Records Office
Henley Street, Stratford Upon Avon, Warwickshire, CV37
6QW Tel: 01789 201816 Tel: 01789 204016, Fax: 01789
296083, Email: records@sharespeare.org.uk
WWW: www.shakespeare.org.uk
Kineton & District Local History
The Glebe House, Lighthouse Road, Kineton CV35 OJL
Watford
Watford and District Industrial History Society
79 Kingswood Road, Garston, Watford, WD2 6EF
West Dorset
Bridport History Society
c/o 22 Fox Close, Bradpole, Bridport, West Dorset, DT6 3JF
Smethwick Local History Society
94 Victoria Court, Messenger Road, Smethwick, B66 3DY
West Midlands
Local History Consortium
The Black Country Living Museum, Tipton Road, Dudley,
West Midlands, DY1 4SQ Tel: 0121 557 9643
Birmingham War Research Society
43 Norfolk Place, Kings Norton, Birmingham, West
Midlands, B30 3LB Tel: 0121-459-9008
Aldridge Local History Society
45 Erdington Road, Walsall, West Midlands, WS9 8UU

Smethwick Local History Society
47 Talbot Road, Smethwick, Warley B66 4DX
Barr & Ashton Local History
17 Booths Farm Road, Great Barr, Birmingham 642 2NJ
Romsley & Hunnington History Society
Port Erin, Green Lane, Chapmans Hill, Romsley, Halesowen
West Midlands, B62 0HB Tel: 01562 710295
West Sussex
The Angmering Society
Holly Lodge, Rectory Lane, Angmering, West Sussex
BNI6 4JU Tel: 01903-775811 Fax: 01903-775811
Beeding & Bramber Local History Society
23 Primrose Court, Goring Rd, Steyning, BN44 3FY
Tel: 01903 816480
Billingshurst Local History
27 Carpenters, Billingshurst, West Sussex, RH14 9RA
Bolney Local History Society
Challoners, Jeremy's Lane, Bolney, Haywards RH17 5QE
Chichester Local History Society
20 Cavendish Street, Chichester, West Sussex, P019 3BS
Horsham Museum Society
Horsham Museum, 9 The Causeway, Horsham RH12 1HE
Tel: 01403 254959
Midland Railway Society
4 Canal Road, Yapton, West Sussex, BN18 0HA
Tel: 01243-553401 Email: BeeFitch@aol.com
Mid Sussex Local History Group
15 Welbeck Drive, Burgess Hill, West Sussex, RH15 0BB
Steyning Society
30 St Cuthmans Road, Steyning, West Sussex, BN44 3RN
Sussex Record Society
West Sussex Archive Society
c/o West Sussex County County Hall, Chichester, P019 IRN
Tel: 01243 533911 Fax: 01243 533959
Email: records.office@westsussex.gov.uk
Wivelsfield Historical Society
Middlefield Cottage, Fox Hill, Haywards Heath RH16 4QY
West Yorkshire
Lowertown Old Burial Ground Trust
16 South Close, Guisley, Leeds, West Yorkshire, LS20 8TD
Halifax Antiquarian Society
7 Hyde Park Gardens, Haugh Shaw Road, Savile Park,
Halifax, West Yorkshire, HX1 3AH Tel: 01422-250780
Olicana Historical Society
54 Kings Road, Ilkley LS29 9AT Tel: 01943-609206
Ossett & District Historical Society
29 Prospect Road, Ossett Tel: Ossett 279449
Thoresby Society
23 Clarendon Road, Leeds, LS2 9NZ
Wetherby & District Historical Society
27 Marston Way, Wetherby, West Yorkshire, LS22 6XZ
Yorkshire Archaeological Society
Claremont, 23 Clarendon Rd, Leeds, West Yorkshire, LS2
9NZ Tel: 0113-245-6342 Tel: 0113 245 7910, Fax: 0113-
244-1979, Email: j.heron@shej.ac.uk
Yorkshire Archaeological Soc - Local History Study
(See above) Email: blong@historyas.force9.co.uk
Westmoreland
Cumberland & Westmoreland Antiquarian & Archeological Society
10 Stewart Close, Arnside, LA5 OES
Wiltshire
Redlynch & District Local History Society
Hawkstone, Church Hill, Redlynch, Salisbury, SP5 2PL Tel: ,
Email: pat.mill@btinternet.com
Wiltshire
Mid Thorngate Society
Yewcroft, Stoney Batter, West Tytherley, Salisbury, SP5 ILD
Swindon Society
4 Lakeside, Swindon SN3 1QE Tel: 01793-521910

Local History Forum
Tanglewood, Laverstock Park, Salisbury SP1 1QJ
Tel: 01722-328922
Wiltshire Record Society
County Hall, Trowbridge BA14 8JG Tel: 01225-713136
Asbury Local History Society
Claremont House, Asbury, Swindon, Wiltshire, SN6 8LN
Archaeological and Natural History Society
WANHS Library, 41 Long Street, Devizes, Wiltshire, SN10
1NS Tel: 01380 727369 Fax: 01380 722150
Marshfield & District Local History Society
150 High Street, Marshfield, Chippenham 5N14 8LU
Salisbury Civic Society
4 Chestnut Close, Laverstock, Salisbury, Wiltshire, SP1 1SL
Trowbridge Civic Society
43 Victoria Road, Trowbridge, Wiltshire, BA14 7LD
Archaeology & Natural History Society
41 Long Street, Devizes, Wiltshire, SN1O INS
Marshfield & District Local History Society
150 High Street, Marshfield, Chippenham SN14 8LU
Worcestershire
Alvechurch Historical Society
Bearhill House, Alvechurch, Birmingham, B48 7JX
Kidderminster and District Archaeology & History Soc
178 Birmingham Road, Kidderminster, DYlO 2SJ
Droitwich History and Archaeology Society
45 Moreland Road, Droitwich Spa WR9 8RN Tel: 01905-773420

Wales
Carmarthenshire
Carmarthenshire Antiquarian Society
16 Heol Morfa, Brenin, Carmarthen, SA31 3PA
Gwendraeth Val History Society
19 Grugos Avenue, Pontyberem, Llanelli SA15 5AF
Caegwrle
Chester Archaeological Society
Ochor House, Porch Lane, Hope Mountain, Caegwrle, L12 9LS
Cardiff
Pentyrch & District Local History Society
34 Castell Coch View, Tongwynlais, Cardiff, CF15 7LA
South Wales Record Society
12 The Green, Radyr, Cardiff, CF4 8BR
Ceredigion
Ceredigion Antiquarian Society
Henllys, Lôn Tyllwyd, Llanfarian, AberystwythSY23 4UH
Ceredigion Archives
Swyddfa'r Sir , Glan-Y-Mor, Aberystwyth, Ceredigion,
SY23 2DE Tel: 01970 633697 Fax: 01970 633663 Email:
archives@ceredigion.gov.uk
Clwyd
Friends of The Clwyd Archives
16 Bryntirion Avenue, Rhyl, LL18 3NP Tel: 01745 342168
Denbighshire
Flintshire History Society
69 Pen y Maes Avenue, Rhyl LL18 4ED Tel: 01745 332220
Ruthin Local History Group
61 Clwyd Street, Ruthin, Denbighsire, LL15 1HH
Denbighshire Historical Society
1 Green Park, Erdigg, Wrexham, Wrexham, LL13 7YE
Conwy County Boro
Denbighshire Historical Society
1 Green Park, Erdigg, Wrexham, Wrexham, LL13 7YE
Abergele Field Club Historical
3 Lon Kinmel, Pensarn, Abergele, North Wales, LL22 7SG

Worcestershire Archaeological Society
Mount Pleasant, Pound Lane, Clifton-on-Jeme
WR6 6EE Tel: 01886 812326
Worcestershire Local History Forum
45 Moreland Road, Droitwich WR9 8RN Tel: 01905-773420
Pershore Heritage & History Society
6 Abbey Croft, Pershore, Worcestershire, WR10 1JQ
Worcestershire Archaeological Service
Woodbury Hall, University College of Worcester, Henwick
Grove, Worcester WR2 6AJ Tel: 01905 855494
Fax: 01905 29054 Email: arcgaeology@worcestershire.gov.uk
Worstershire Local History Forum
45 Moreland Road, Droitwich, Worcestershire, WR9 8RN
Bewdley Historical Research
8 Ironside Close, Bewdley, Worcestershire, DY12 2HX
Email: purcell@graftonf.freeserve.co.uk
Feckenham Forest History Society
Lower Grinsty Farmhouse, Callow Hill, Redditch, B97 5PJ
Tel: 01527-542063 Fax: 01527-542063
Kidderminster Field Club
7 Holmwood Avenue, Kidderminster DYL 1 6DA
Wolverley & Cockley History Society
18120 Caunsall Road, Cookley, Nr Kidderminster,
Worcestershire Archealogical & Local History Society
19 Grayling Close, Broomhall, Worcestershire, WR5 3HY
Wolverley & Cockley Historical
18/20 Caunsall Road, Cookley, Kidderminster DYL 1 5YB
Kidderminster & District Local History Society
110 Woodland Avenue, Kidderminster DYL 1 5AN

Glamorgan
Kenfig Society
4 Glan-Y-Llyn, North Cornelly, Nr Bridgend, CF33 4EF
Llantrisant & District Local History Society
Y Bwthyn School Road, Miskin, Pontyclun CF72 8JH
Glamorgan History Society
5 Plasdraw Place, Aberdare, Mid Glamorgan, CF44 0NS
Merthyr Tydfil Historical Society
Ronamar, Ashlea Drive, Twynyrodyn, Merthyr Tydfil, Mid
Glamorgan, CF47 0NY Tel: 01685 385871
Gwent
Gwent Local History Council
8 Pentonville, Newport, Gwent, NP9 5XH
Abertillery & District Museum Society
5 Harcourt Terrace, Glandwr Street, Abertillery NP3 1TS
Pontypool Local History Society
24 Longhouse Grove, Henllys, Cwmbran NP44 6HQ Tel: 01633 865662
Gwynedd
Meirioneth Historicial and Record Society
Archifdy Meirion Cae Penarlag, Dolgellau LL40 2YB
Cymdeithas Hanes Beddgeler
Creua,Llanfrothen, Penrhyndevdraeth, Gwynedd, LL4B 6SH
Newport
Newport Local History Society
72 Risca Road, Newport, South Wales, NP9 4JA
Pembrokeshire
Pembrokeshire History Society
The Castle, Haverford West, SA61 2EF
Powys
Radnorshire Society
Pool House, Discoed, Presteigne, Powys, LD8 2NW
Email: sadie@cole.kc3ltd.co.uk
Wrexham
Wrexham Maelor Hisory Society
37 Park Avenue, Wrexham, LL12 7AL

Scotland

Airdrie
Monklands Historical Society
141 Cromarty Road, Cairnhill, Airdrie, ML6 9RZ
Ayrshire
Ayrshire Federation of Historical Societies
11 Chalmers Road, Ayr, Ayrshire, KA7 2RQ
Dundee
Abertay Historical Society
27 Pitcairn Road, Downfield, Dundee DD3 9EE Tel: 01382
858701 (Angus, Fife, Perthshire)
Friends of Dundee City Archives
21 City Square, Dundee, DD1 3BY Tel: 01382 434494
Fax: 01382 434666 Email: richard.cullen@dundeecity.gov.uk
WWW: http://www.dundeecity.gov.uk/dcchtml/sservices/archives-html
Perthshire
Dunning Parish Historical Society
May Cottage, Newtown-Of-Pitcairns, Dunning, Perth PH2 0SL
Renfrewshire
Bridge of Weir History Society
41 Houston Road, Bridge Of Weir, Renfrewshire, PA11 3QR

Renfrewshire Local History Forum
388 Glasgow Road, Paisley PAL 3BG Tel: 0141 883 8685
Fax:
Paisley Philosophical Institution
388 Glasgow Road, Paisley, Renfrewshire, PAL 3BG
Society of Antiquaries of Scotland
Royal Museum of Scotland, Chambers Street, Edinburgh,
EH1 1JF Tel: 0131 247 4115 Tel: 0131 247 4133, Fax: 0131
247 4163
Scottish Records Association
H M General Register House, Edinburgh, EH1 3YY
West Lothian
Scottish Local History Forum
45 High Street, Linlithgow, West Lothian, EH54 6EW Tel:
01506 844649 Fax: 0131 260 6610, Email:
chantal.hamill@dial.pipex.com
Linlithgow Union Canal Society
Manse Road Basin, Linlithgow, West Lothian, EH49 6AJ
Tel: 01506-671215 Email: lucs@linnet.co.uk, WWW:
www.linet.co.uk/luc

Isle of Man

Isle of Man Natural History & Antiquarian Society
Ballacrye Stream Cottage, Ballaugh, Isle of Man, IM7 5EB
Tel: 01624-897306
Isle of Man Natural History & Local History Society
Argan Peveril Avenue, Peel, Isle Of Man, MS

Channel Islands

Jersey
Societe Jersiase
7 Pier Road, St Helier, Jersey, JE2 4XW
Email: societe@siciete-jersiaise.org,
WWW: http://www.societe-jersiaise.org

Ireland

Federation of Local History Societies
Rothe House, Kilkenny,
County Mayo
Mayo North Family Heritage Centre
Enniscoe, Castlehill, Ballina, County Mayo Tel: 353 96
31809 Fax: 353 96 31885 Email: normayo@iol.ie
South Mayo Family Research Centre
Main Street, Ballinrobe, County Mayo Tel: 353 92 41214
Email: soumayo@iol.ie WWW: http:/mayo.irish-roots.net/

Northern Ireland

Presbyterian Historical Society of Ireland
Church House, Fisherwick Place, Belfast, BT1 6DW Tel:
01232-322284
Federation of Ulster Local Studies
18 May Street, Belfast, BT1 4NL Tel: 01232 235254 Fax:
Co Tyrone
Ulster American Folk
Mellon Road, Castletown, Omagh, Co Tyrone, BT78 8QY

South Africa

The Anglo-Zulu War Historical Society
Woodbury House, Woodchurch Road, Tenterden, Kent,
TN30 7AE Tel: 01580-764189 Fax: 01580-766648 WWW:
www.web-marketing.co.uk/anglozuluwar

United States of America

Alabama,
Alabama Genealogical Society Inc
800 Lakeshore Drive, Birmingham, Alabama, 35229 Tel:
205-870-2749 Fax:
Southern Society of Genealogists Inc
PO Box 295, Stewart University, Centre, Alabama, 35960
Tel: 205-447-2939 Fax:
Arizona
Arizona Historical Society
949 East Second Street, Tucson, Arizona, 85719 Tel: 602-
628-5774 Fax:
Arizona Historical Society
Box 704, Rt 4, North Fort Valley Road, Flagstaff, Arizona,
86001 Tel: 602-774-6272 Fax:

California
Augustan Society Inc
PO Box P, Torrance, California, 320-7766 Tel: 310-320-7766
Massachusetts
New England Historic Genealogical Society
99 -101 Newbury Street, Boston, Massachusetts, 02116 Tel:
617-536-5740 Fax: 617-536-7307
Email: membership@nehgs.org,
WWW: http://www.nehgs.org
Missouri
American Family Records Association
Po Box 15505, Kansas City Missouri 64106-0505
Tel: 816-252-0950
Pennsylvania
The Daguerreian Society
Suite 9, 3045 West Libert Avenue, Pittsburgh, Pennsylvania,
15216-2460 Tel: 412-343-5525 Email: DagSocPgh@aol.com
WWW: http://www.dagurre.org

Following is a list of Superintendent Registrars of Births, Marriages and Deaths in alphabetical order by County. Where there are other local authority administrative areas such as Metropolitan Districts within a County area they are listed in that geographical county. For the first time we have included details of Registration Sub Districts.
Note: Many of the Registration Officers listed here share Office accommodation with other parties. When using the addresses given they must be prefixed "Superintendent Registrar, Register Office ...."

a heartfelt plea from a Registrar for our readers
The volume and page number references which are found on the microfiche and film indexes of the General Register Office must only be used when applying for certificates from the GRO. These reference numbers bear no resemblance to the filing system used at local register offices and do not assist Superintendent Registrars in any way to find the entry. The General Register Office hold the records for the whole of England and Wales and therefore have their own filing system, whereas the majority of register offices are still manually searching handwritten index books which is extremely time consuming. Most offices only became computerised in the early 1990s and do not hold records before this date on computer and will never have the staff for time to backlog 150 years of records. Finally, many offices are only part time, some just open 6 hours per week. Unlike the larger offices they do not have receptionists or staff employed specifically to assist people researching their family history, and have to devote the majority of their time to providing certificates urgently required for passport applications, marriage bookings and pension applications.

Once the applicant has carried out their research fully using all the records and data widely available to them at no cost, they can apply to their local office with sufficient information for the Registrar to trace the entry within minutes instead of hours. The Registrars have asked that these guidelines be included in the Directory as a means of providing a more efficient service to their customers

England
Bath & North East Somerset
12 Charlotte St, Bath, BA1 2NF
Tel: 01225-312032 Fax: 01225-334812
Bath & North East Somerset (Norton Radstock SD)
The Library, 119 High St, Midsomer Norton, Bath, BA3 2DA Tel: 01761-418768 Fax:
Bedfordshire
Ampthill Court House, Woburn St, Ampthill, MK45 2HX Tel: 01525-403430 Fax: 01525-841984
Email: denmanm@csd.bedfordshire.gov.uk
Bedford Pilgrim House, 20 Brickhill Drive, MK41 7PZ Tel: 01234-354554 Fax: 01234 270215
Biggleswade 142 London Rd, Biggleswade, SG18 8EL Tel: 01767-312511 Fax: 01767-315033
Dunstable Grove House, 76 High Street North, Dunstable, LU6 1NF Tel: 01582-660191 Fax: 01582-471004
Leighton Buzzard Bossard House, West St, Leighton Buzzard, LU7 7DA Tel: 01525-851486 Fax: 01525-381483
Luton
Luton 6 George Street West, Luton, LU1 2BJ Tel: 01582-722603 Fax: 01582-429522
Berkshire
Windsor & Maidenhead Town Hall, St Ives Rd, Maidenhead, SL6 1RF Tel: 01628-796101 Fax: 01628-796625
(Ascot SD) Bridge House, 18 Brockenhurst Rd, Ascot, SL5 9DL Tel: 01344-628135 Fax: 01344-628135
(Maidenhead SD) Town Hall, St Ives Rd, Maidenhead, SL6 1RF Tel: 01628-796181
(Windsor SD) York House, Sheet St, Windsor, SL4 1DD Tel: 01628-683652 Fax: 01682-683629
Wokingham
Wokingham (Wokingham SD) Council Offices, Shute End, Wokingham, RG40 1BN Tel: 0118-978-2514 Fax: 0118-978-2813
Bracknell Forest, Easthampstead House, Town Square, Bracknell, RG12 1AQ Tel: 01344-352027 Fax: 01344-352010
Kingsclere & Whitchurch Council Offices, Swan St, Kingsclere, Nr Newbury, RG15 8PM Tel: 01635-298714
Newbury, Peake House, 112 Newtown Rd, Newbury, RG14 7EB Tel: 01635-48133 Fax: 01635-524694
Slough, 'Revelstoke House', 1-5 Chalvey Park, Slough, SL1 2HX Tel: 01753-520485 Fax: 01753-787605
Bournemouth
Bournemouth The Register Office,159 Old Christchurch Rd, Bournemouth, BH1 1JS Tel: 01202-551668 Fax: 01202-789456
City of Bristol \
Quakers Friars, Bristol, BS1 3AR Tel: 0117-929-2461 Fax: 0117-925-8861

Buckinghamshire
Aylesbury Vale County Ofices, Walton St, Aylesbury, HP20 1XF Tel: 01296-382581 Tel: 01296-395000 Fax: 01296-382675
Chiltern & South Bucks Transferred to Chiltern Hills RD wef November 1998
Chiltern Hills Wycombe Area Offices, Easton St, High Wycombe, HP11 1NII Tel: 01494-475209 Fax: 01494-475040
Cambridgeshire
Cambridge Castle Lodge, Shire Hall, Castle Hill, Cambridge, CB3 0AP Tel: 01223-717021 Fax: 01223-717888
Ely Old School House, 74 Market St, Ely, CB7 4LS Tel: 01353-663824
Fenland The Old Vicarage, Church Terrace, Wisbech, PE13 1BW Tel: 01945-463128
Huntingdon Wykeham House, Market Hill, Huntingdon, PE18 6NR Tel: 01480-425822 Fax: 01480-375725
Peterborough, The Lawns, 33 Thorpe Rd, Peterborough, PE3 6AB Tel: 01733-566323 Fax: 01733-566049
Cheshire
Cheshire East Park Green, Macclesfield, SK11 6TW Tel: 01625-423463 Fax: 01625-619225
Cheshire Vale Royal Transferred to Cheshire Central wef April 1998
Chester West Goldsmith House, Goss St, Chester, CH1 2BG Tel: 01244-602668 Fax: 01244-602934
Halton Heath Rd, Runcorn, WA7 5TN Tel: 01928-576797 Fax: 01928-573616
Cheshire Central Delamere House, Chester Street Crewe CW1 2LL Tel: 01270-505106 Fax: 01270 505107
Warrington Museum St, Warrington, WA1 1JX Tel: 01925-442762 Fax: 01925-442739
Stockport MD
Greenhale House, Piccadilly, Stockport, SK1 3DY Tel: 0161-474-3399 Fax: 0161-474-3390
Tameside MD
Town Hall, King St, Dukinfield, SK16 4LA Tel: 0161-330-1177 Fax: 0161 342 2625
Trafford MD
Trafford Town Hall, tatton Rd, Sale, M33 1ZF Tel: 0161-912-3025 Fax: 0161 912 3031
Cleveland
Middlesbrough Corporation Rd, Middlesbrough, TS1 2DA Tel: 01642-262078 Fax: 01642 262091
Redcar & Cleveland Westgate, Guisborough, TS14 6AP Tel: 01287-632564 Fax: 01287 630768
Stockton-on-Tees Nightingale House, Balaclava St, Stockton-on-Tees, TS18 2AL Tel: 01642-393156 Fax: 01642-393159
Cornwall
Bodmin Lyndhurst, 66 Nicholas St, Bodmin, PL31 1AG Tel: 01208-73677 Fax: 01208-73677

Camborne-Redruth Roskear, Camborne, TR14 8DN Tel: 01209-612924 Fax: 01209-612924

Falmouth Berkeley House, 12-14 Berkeley Vale, Falmouth, TR11 3PH Tel: 01326-312606 Fax: 01326-312606

Kerrier The Willows, Church St, Helston, TR13 8NJ Tel: 01326-562848 Fax: 01326-562848

Launceston 'Hendra', Dunheved Rd, Launceston, PL15 9JG Tel: 01566-777464 Fax: 01566-777464

Liskeard, 'Graylands', Dean St, Liskeard, PL14 4AH Tel: 01579-343442 Fax: 01579-343442

Penzance St. John's Hall, Penzance, TR18 2QR Tel: 01736-330093 Fax: 01736-330067

St. Austell 12 Carlyon Rd, St. Austell, PL25 4LD Tel: 01726-68974 Fax: 01726-67048

St. Germans Plougastel Drive, St Germans, Saltash, PL12 6DL Tel: 01752-842624 Fax: 01752-848556

Stratton The Parkhouse Centre, Ergue Gaberic Way, Bude, EX23 8LD Tel: 01288-353209 Fax: 01288-353209

Truro The Leats, Truro, TR1 3AH Tel: 01872-72842 Fax: 01872-261625

Darlington
Central House, Gladstone St, DL3 6JX Tel: 01325-346600 Fax: 01325-346605

County Durham
Durham Central 40 Old Elvet, Durham, DH1 3HN Tel: 0191-3864077

Durham Eastern Acre Rigg, York Rd, Peterlee, SR8 2DP Tel: 0191-5866147 Fax: 0191-51846007

Durham Northern 7 Thorneyholme Terrace, Stanley, DH9 0BJ Tel: 01207-235849 Fax: 01207-235334

(Chester le Street SD) Civic Centre, Chester le St, DH3 3UT Tel: 0191-388-3240

(Consett SD) 39 Medomsley Rd, Consett, DH8 5HE Tel: 01207-502797

(Stanley SD) 7 Thorneyholme Terrace, Stanley, DH9 0BJ Tel: 01207-235849

Durham South Western 30 Galgate, Barnard Castle, DL12 8BH Tel: 01833-637997

Durham Western, Cockton House, Waddington St, Bishop Auckland, DL14 6HG Tel: 01388-607277 Fax: 01388-603404

(Bishop Auckland SD) Cockton House, Waddington St, Bishop Auckland, DL14 6HG Tel: 01388-603404

(Crook SD) The Community Health Clinic, Hope St, Crook, DL15 9HU Tel: 01388-767630

(Weardale SD) The Health Centre, Dales St, Stanhope, Bishop Auckland, DL13 2XD Tel: 01388-527074

Hartlepool
Raby Rd, Hartlepool, TS24 8AF Tel: 01429-236369 Fax: 01429-236373, Email: registrar@hartlepool.gov.uk

Coventry MD
Cheylesmore Manor House, Manor House Drive, CV1 2ND Tel: 01203-833137 Fax: 01203-833110

Cumbria
Cockermouth 67 Wood St, Maryport, CA15 6LD Tel: 01900-325960

(Maryport SD) 67 Wood St, Maryport, CA15 6LD Tel: 01900-812637

(Workington SD) Hill Park, Ramsay Brow, Workington, CA14 4AR Tel: 01900-325160

Kendal County Offices, Kendal, LA9 4RQ Tel: 01539-773567

(Kirkby Lonsdale SD) 15 Market Square, Kirkby Lonsdale, Carnforth, LA6 2AN Tel: 01542-71222

(Lakes SD) Windermere Library, Ellerthwaite, Windermere, LA23 2AJ Tel: 015394-62420

Penrith Friargate, Penrith, CA11 7XR Tel: 01768-242120 Fax: 01768-242122

(Alston SD) Alston Register Office Townhead, Alston, CA9 3SL Tel: 01434-381784 Fax: 01434-381784

(Appleby SD) Shire Hall, The Sands, Appleby in Westmorland, CA16 6XN Tel: 017683-52976

Barrow-in-Furness 74 Abbey Rd, Barrow-in-Furness, LA14 5UB Tel: 01229-894511 Fax: 01229-894513

Carlisle 23 Portland Square, Carlisle, CA1 1PE Tel: 01228-607432 Fax: 01228-607434

Millom The Millom Council Centre, St Georges Rd, Millom, LA14 4DD Tel: 01229-772357 Fax: 01229-773412

Ulverston Town Hall, Queen St, Ulverston, LA12 7AR Tel: 01229-894170 Fax: 01229-894172

Whitehaven 75 Lowther St, Whitehaven, CA28 7RB Tel: 01946-693554

Wigton Council Offices, South End, Wigton, CA7 9QD Tel: 016973-42155 Fax: 016973-49967

Derbyshire
Amber Valley Market Place, Ripley, DE5 3BT Tel: 01773-841380 Fax: 01773-841382

Ashbourne Town Hall, Market Place, Ashbourne, DE6 1ES Tel: 01335-300575 Fax: 01335-345252

Bakewell Town Hall, Bakewell, DE45 1BW Tel: 0162-981-2261

(Matlock SD) Firs Parade, Matlock, DE4 3AS Tel: 01629-582870

Chesterfield New Beetwell St, Chesterfield, S40 1QJ Tel: 01246-234754 Fax: 01246-274493

Derby 9 Traffic St, Derby, DE1 2NL Tel: 01332-363609 Fax: 01332-368310

Erewash 87 Lord Haddon Rd, Ilkeston, DE7 8AX Tel: 0115-932-1014 Fax: 0115-932-6450

High Peak, Council Offices, Hayfield Rd, Chapel-en-le-Frith, High Peak, SK23 0QJ Tel: 01663-750473

(Buxton SD) The Registrar's Office, Hardwick Square West, Buxton, SK17 6PX Tel: 01298-25075

(Chapel en le Frith SD) The Town Hall, Chapel en le Frith, SK23 0HB Tel: 01298-813559

Glossop SD) 46-50 High Street West, Glossop, SK13 8BH Tel: 01457-852425

South Derbyshire Traffic St, Derby, DE1 2NL Tel: 01332-363618 Fax: 01332-368310

(Sub-district) The Registrars Office, Civic Way, Swadlincote, DE11 0AB Tel: 01283-213976 Fax: 01283-213976

Devon
East Devon Dowell St, Honiton, EX14 8LZ Tel: 01404-42531 Fax: 01404-41475

Exeter, 1 Lower Summerlands, Heavitree Rd, Exeter, EX1 2LL Tel: 01392-270941 Fax: 01392-499540

Holsworthy 8 Fore St, Holsworthy, EX22 6ED Tel: 01409-253262

Mid Devon The Great House, 1 St Peter St, Tiverton, EX16 6NY Tel: 01884-255255 Fax: 01884-255255

North Devon Civic Centre, Barnstaple, EX31 1ED Tel: 01271-388456

Okehampton, Transferred to West Devon wef July 1997

Plymouth
Lockyer St, Plymouth, PL1 2QD Tel: 01752-268331 Fax: 01752-256046

South Hams, Follaton House, Plymouth Rd, Totnes, TQ9 5NE Tel: 01803-861234 Fax: 01803-868965

Teignbridge 15 Devon Square, Newton Abbot, TQ12 2HR Tel: 01626-353642 Fax: 01626-353636

Torbay Oldway Mansion, Paignton, TQ3 2TU Tel: 01803-207130 Fax: 01803-525388

Torridge Council Offices, Windmill Lane, Northam, Bideford, EX39 1BY Tel: 01237-474978 Fax: 01237-473385

West Devon Town Council Offices, Drake Rd, Tavistock, PL19 8AJ Tel: 01822-612137 Fax: 01822-618935

Dorset
East Dorset, King George V Pavillion, Peter Grant Way, Ferndown, BH22 9EN Tel: 01202-892325 Fax:

North Dorset Salisbury Rd, Blandford Forum, DT11 7LN Tel: 01258-484096 Fax: 01258-484095

Poole Civic Centre Annexe, Park Rd, Poole, BH15 2RN Tel: 01202-633744 Fax: 01202 633725

South Dorset, The Guildhall, St Edmund St, Weymouth, DT4 8AS Tel: 01305-760899 Fax: 01305-772611

West Dorset 32 South St, Bridport, DT6 3NQ Tel: 01308-456047

East Yorkshire

Beverley 34 Lairgate, Beverley, HU17 8ES Tel: 01482-864205 Fax: 01482-679155

(Withernsea SD) The Court House, Railway Crescent, Withernsea, HU19 2HF Tel: 01964-612344 Fax: 01964-612344

(Beverley B SD) The Council Offices, Market Green, Cottingham, HU16 5QG Tel: 01482-883510 Fax: 01482-883510

Beverley (Hornsea SD) The Court House, off Railway St, Hornsea, HU18 1PS Tel: 01964-534111 Fax: 01964-534111

Bridlington, Town Hall, Quay Rd, Bridlington, YO16 4LP Tel: 01262-422662 Fax: 01262-422664

(Driffield SD) 51 Manorfield Rd, Driffield, YO25 5JE Tel: 01377-254051 Fax: 01377-254051

Pocklington Burnby Hall, Pocklington, YO4 2QQ Tel: 01759-303614 Fax: 01759-306722

Goole Council Offices, Church St, Goole, DN14 5BG Tel: 01405-722371 Fax: 01405- 722379

East Sussex

Eastbourne, Town Hall, Grove Rd, Eastbourne, BN21 4UG Tel: 01323-410000 Fax: 01323-431386

Hastings & Rother

Bohemia Rd, Hastings, TN34 1EX Tel: 01424-721722 Fax: 01424-465296

Brighton & Hove

Royal York Buildings, Old Steine, Brighton, BN1 1NH Tel: 01273-292016 Fax: 01273-292019

Hove Transferred to Brighton & Hove RD wef November 1998

Lewes, Southover Grange, Southover Rd, Lewes, BN7 1TP Tel: 01273-475916 Fax: 01273-488073

Uckfield Beaconwood, Beacon Rd, Crowborough, TN6 1AR Tel: 01892-653803 Fax: 01892-669884

Essex

Brentwood 1 Seven Arches Rd, Brentwood, CM14 4JG Tel: 01277-233565 Fax: 01277-262712

(Basildon SD) Burghstead Lodge, 143 High St, Billericay, CM12 9AB Tel: 01277-623939 Fax: 01277-636162

Castle Point & Rochford, Civic Centre, Victoria Avenue, Southend-on-Sea, SS2 6ER Tel: 01702-343728

(Sub-district) District Council Offices, Hockley Rd, Rayleigh, SS6 8EB Tel: 01268-776362 Fax: 01268-776362

Barking & Dagenham

Barking & Dagenham Arden House, 198 Longbridge Rd, Barking, IG11 8SY Tel: 0181-270-4742 Fax: 0181-270-4745

Braintree, John Ray House, Bocking End, Braintree, CM7 9RW Tel: 01376-323463 Fax: 01376-342423

Chelmsford 17 Market Rd, Chelmsford, CM1 1GF Tel: 01245-430701 Fax: 01245-430707

Colchester Stanwell House, Stanwell St, Colchester, CO2 7DL Tel: 01206-572926 Fax: 01206-540626

Epping Forest St Johns Rd, Epping, CM16 5DN Tel: 01992-572789 Fax: 01992-571236

Harlow Watergarden Ofices, College Square, The High, Harlow, CM20 1AG Tel: 01279-427674 Fax: 01279-444594

Havering LB

'Langtons', Billet Lane, Hornchurch, RM11 1XL Tel: 01708-773403 Fax: 01708-444180

Redbridge LB

Queen Victoria House, 794 Cranbrook Rd, Barkingside, Ilford, IG6 1JS Tel: 0181-478-9497 Fax: 0181 478 9483

Southend-on-Sea Civic Centre, Victoria Avenue, Southend-on-Sea, SS2 6ER Tel: 01702-343728 Fax: 01702-612610

Thurrock 2 Quarry Hill, Grays, RM17 5BT Tel: 01375-375245 Fax: 01375-392649

Uttlesford, Council Offices, London Rd, Saffron Walden, CB11 4ER Tel: 01799-510319 Fax: 01799-510332

Gloucestershire

Cheltenham St. Georges Rd, Cheltenham, GL50 3EW Tel: 01242-532455 Fax: 01242-254600

Cirencester Old Memorial Hospital, Sheep St, Cirencester, GL7 1QW Tel: 01285-650455 Fax: 01285-640253

Forest of Dean Belle Vue Centre, 6 Belle Vue Rd, Cinderford, GL14 2AB Tel: 01594-822113 Fax: 01594-826352

Gloucester, Maitland House, Spa Rd, Gloucester, GL1 1UY Tel: 01452-425275 Fax: 01452-385385

North Cotswold, North Cotswold Register Office, High St, Moreton-in-Marsh, GL56 0AZ Tel: 01608-651230 Fax: 01608-651226

Stroud Parliament St, Stroud, GL5 1DY Tel: 01453-766049 Fax: 01453-752961

Hampshire

Winchester (Eastleigh SD) 101 Leigh Rd, Eastleigh, SO50 9Dr Tel: 01703-612058 Fax: 01703-612058

Alton 4 Queens Rd, Alton, GU34 1HU Tel: 01420-85410

Andover, Wessex Chambers, South St, Andover, SP10 2BN Tel: 01264-352513 Fax: 01264-366849

Basingstoke 60 New Rd, Basingstoke, RG21 7PW Tel: 01256-350745 Fax: 01256-350745

New Forest, Hillcroft, New St, Lymington, SO41 9BQ Tel: 01590-673425 Fax: 01590-688509

(Lymington SD) Public Offices, 65 Christchurch Rd, Ringwood, BH24 1DH

(New Forest SD) Totton Health Centre, Testwood Lane, Totton, Southampton, SO4 3AP Tel: 01703-863168 Fax: 01703-863168

North-East Hampshire 30 Grosvenor Rd, Aldershot, GU11 3EB Tel: 01252-322066 Fax: 01252-338004

Petersfield, The Old College, College St, Petersfield, GU31 4AG Tel: 01730-265372 Fax: 01730-265396

Ringwood & Fordingbridge Public Office, Ringwood, BH24 1DJ Tel: 01425-470150 Fax: 01425-471732

Romsey, Hayter House, Hayter Gardens, Romsey, SO51 7QU Tel: 01794-513846 Fax: 01794-830491

South-East Hampshire 4-8 Osborn Road South, Fareham, PO16 7DG Tel: 01329-280493 Fax: 01329-823184

(Fareham SD) 4 - 8 Osborn Road South, Fareham, PO16 7DG Tel: 01329-280493

(Gosport SD) 3 Thorngate Way, Gosport, PO12 1DX Tel: 01705-580629 Fax: 01705-580629

(Havant SD) Fernglen, Town Hall Rd, Havant, PO9 1AN Tel: 01705-482533 Fax: 01705-482533

Winchester Station Hill, Winchester, SO23 8TJ Tel: 01962-869608 Tel: 01962-869594 Fax: 01962-851912

Southampton

Southampton 6A Bugle St, Southampton, SO14 2LX Tel: 01703-631422 Fax: 01703-633431

Herefordshire

Bromyard, Council Offices, 1 Rowberry St, Bromyard, Hereford, HR7 4DU Tel: 01885-482730

Hereford, County Offices, Bath St, Hereford, HR1 2HQ Tel: 01432-350461 Fax: 01432-363264

Kington Market Hall St, Kington, HR5 3DP Tel: 01544-230156 Fax: 01544-231385

Ledbury Town Council Offices, Church St, Ledbury, HR8 1DH Tel: 01531-632306

Leominster The Old Priory, Leominster, HR6 8EQ Tel: 01568-610131

Ross, The Old Chapel, Cantilupe Rd, Ross on Wye, HR9 7AN Tel: 01989-562795 Fax: 01989 564869

Hertfordshire

Barnet

29 Wood St, Barnet, EN5 4BD Tel: 0181-731-1100 Fax: 0181-731-1111

Hertfordshire

Bishops Stortford 2 Hockerill St, Bishops Stortford, CM23 2DL Tel: 01279-652273 Fax: 01279-461492, Email: gill.wenzer@hertscc.gov.uk

Broxbourne, Borough Offices, Churchgate, Cheshunt, EN8 9XQ Tel: 01992-623107

Dacorum, The Bury, Queensway, Hemel Hemstead, HP1 1HR Tel: 01442-228600 Fax: 01442-243974

Hatfield 19b St Albans Road East, Hatfield, AL10 0NG Tel: 01707-283920

Hertford & Ware, County Hall, Pegs Lane, Hertford, SG13 8DE Tel: 0192-555590

Hitchen & Stevenage Danesgate, Stevenage, SG1 1WW Tel: 01438-316579 Fax: 01438-357197

St Albans, Hertfordshire House, Civic Close, St. Albans, AL1 3JZ Tel: 01727-816806 Fax: 01727-816804

Watford 36 Clarendon Rd, Watford, WD1 1JP Tel: 01923-231302 Fax: 01923 246852

Hull

Kingston-upon-Hull
Municipal Offices, 181-191 George St, Hull, HU1 3BY Tel: 01482-615400 Fax: 01482 615411

Isle of Wight
County Hall, High St, PO30 1UD Tel: 01983-823230 Tel: 01983-823233 Fax: 01983-823227

Kent

Ashford with Shepway, Elwick House, Elwick Rd, Ashford, TN23 1NR Tel: 01233-62466 Fax: 01233-642962

Bexley LB
Bexley, Manor House, The Green, Sidcup, DA14 6BW Tel: 0181-303-7777 Ext 32 Fax: 0181-308-4967

Canterbury with Swale Wellington House, 4 StStephen's Rd, Canterbury, CT2 7RD Tel: 01227-470480 Fax: 01227-780176

Chatham Ingleside, 114 Maidstone Rd, Chatham, ME4 6DJ Tel: 01634-844073 Fax: 01634-840165

Gravesend 132 Windmill St, Gravesend, DA12 1BE Tel: 01474-333451 Fax: 01474-564428

Maidstone The Archbishop's Palace, Palace Gardens, Mill St, Maidstone, ME15 6YE Tel: 01622-752891 Fax: 01622 663690

Thanet with Dover, Aberdeen House, 68 Ellington Rd, Ramsgate, CT11 9ST Tel: 01843-591417

Tunbridge Wells, Divisional County Offices, 39 Grove Hill Rd, Tunbridge Wells, TN1 1SL Tel: 01892-527332 Fax: 01892 528518

Lancashire

Blackburn with Darwen
(Darwen & Turton SD) Town Hall, Croft St, Darwen, BB3 2RN Tel: 01254-702443

Garstang,
Fleetwood & Fylde South King St, Blackpool, FY1 4AX Tel: 01253-477177 Fax: 01253-477170

(Fleetwood SD) Fleetwood Central Library, North Albert St, Fleetwood, FY7 6AJ Tel: 01253-874580

(Fylde SD) The Library, Clifton St, Lytham, FY8 5ED Tel: 01253-737530

Hyndburn & Rossendale The Mechanics Institute, Willow St, Accrington, BB5 1LP Tel: 01254-871360 Fax: 01254 239391

(Rossendale SD) 1 Grange St, Rawtenstall, Rossendale, BB4 7RT Tel: 01706-215496

Blackburn Jubilee St, Blackburn, BB1 1EP Tel: 01254-57602 Fax: 01254 587524 Fax: 01254 587538

Blackpool & Fylde South King St, Blackpool, FY1 4AX Tel: 01253-477177 Fax: 01253-477176

Bolton MD
Bolton Mere Hall, Merehall St, Bolton, BL1 2QT Tel: 01204-525165 Fax: 01204-525125

Burnley & Pendle 12 Nicholas St, Burnley, BB11 2AQ Tel: 01282-36116 Fax: 01282 412221

Bury MD
Bury, Town Hall, Manchester Rd, Bury, BL9 0SW Tel: 0161-253-6027 Fax: 0161-253-6028

Chorley 16 St. George's St, Chorley, PR7 2AA Tel: 012572-63143 Fax: 01257-263808

Lancaster 4 Queen St, Lancaster, LA1 1RS Tel: 01524-65673 Fax: 01524-842285

(Garstang SD) Croston Villas, High St, Garstang, PR3 1EA Tel: 01995-603330

(Preesall SD) The Over Wyre Medical Centre, Pilling Lane, Preesall, FY6 0FA Tel: 01253-810722

Oldham MD
Oldham, Metropolitan House, Hobson St, Oldham, OL1 1PY Tel: 0161-678-0137 Fax: 0161 911 3729

Preston & South Ribble Guildhall Offices, Guildhall St, Preston, PR1 3PR Tel: 01772-823739 Fax: 01772 263809

Ribble Valley Off Pimlico Rd, Clitheroe, BB7 2BW Tel: 01200-425786 Fax: 01200-425786

Rochdale MD
Rochdale, Town Hall, The Esplanade, Rochdale, OL16 1AB Tel: 01706-864779 Fax: 01706-864786

Calderdale MD
Todmorden, Municipal Offices, Rise Lane, Todmorden, OL14 7AB Tel: 01706-814811

West Lancashire, Greetby Buildings, Derby St, Ormskirk, L39 2BS Tel: 01695-576009 Fax: 01695 585819

Wigan MD
Wigan & Leigh, New Town Hall, Library St, Wigan, WN1 1NN Tel: 01942-705000 Fax: 01942-705013

Leicestershire
Coalville 41 Ravenstone Rd, Coalville, LE67 3NB Tel: 01530-832007 Fax: 01530-815802

Hinckley, The Chestnuts, 25 Mount Rd, Hinckley, LE10 1AD Tel: 01455-637259 Fax: 01455-612817

Leicester 5 Pocklington's Walk, Leicester, LE1 6BQ Tel: 0116-253-6326 Fax: 0116 253 3008

Loughborough 202 Ashby Rd, Loughborough, LE11 3AG Tel: 01509-611954

Market Harborough 42 Coventry Rd, Market Harborough, LE16 9BZ Tel: 01858-431124 Fax: 01858-432955

Melton Mowbray, County Council Area Offices, Leicester Rd, Melton Mowbray, LE13 0DG Tel: 01664-482267 Fax: 01664-481910

Rutland
Rutland Catmore, Oakham, Rutland, E15 6JU Tel: 01572-756547

Lincolnshire
East Elloe 25 West St, Long Sutton, PE12 9BN Tel: 01406-363874 Fax: 01406 365325

(Holbeach SD) 33 Boston Rd, Holbeach, Spalding, PE12 7LR Tel: 01406-423166 Fax: 01406-422812

(Long Sutton SD) 25 West St, Long Sutton, PE12 9BN Tel: 01406-363874

Boston County Hall, Boston, PE21 6LX Tel: 01205-310010 Fax: 01205-356690

Bourne, Saxonhurst, 35 West St, Bourne, PE10 9NE Tel: 01778-422269 Fax: 01778-421081

Caistor Council Offices, Caistor, LN7 6LX Tel: 01472-851153 Fax: 01472-852678

Gainsborough 156 Trinity St, Gainsborough, DN21 1JP Tel: 01427-612312 Fax: 01427-678185

Grantham, The Priory, Market Place, Grantham, NG31 6LJ Tel: 01476-561061 Fax: 01476 562235

Horncastle, Holmeleigh, Foundry St, Horncastle, LN9 6AQ Tel: 01507-522576 Fax: 01507 524849

Lincoln 4 Lindum Rd, Lincoln, LN2 1NN Tel: 01522-552501/2 Fax: 01522-589524

Louth, Louth Town Hall, Eastgate, Louth, LN11 9NH Tel: 01507-603529 Fax: 01507-608346

Sleaford, PO Box 2, Council Offices, Eastgate, Sleaford, NG34 7EB Tel: 01529-414144-Ext.-2520 Fax: 01529 413728

Spalding, Sessions House, Sheep Market, Spalding, PE11 1BB Tel: 01775-769064 Fax: 01775-714392

Spilsby, Offord House, Church St, Spilsby, PE23 5EF Tel: 01790-752550 Fax: 01790-752162

(Skegness SD) 30 Roman Bank, Skegness, PE25 2SG

Stamford 2 St Mary's Hill, Stamford, PE9 2DR Tel: 01780-756004 Fax: 01780 752659

London
Bromley LB
Room S101, Bromley Civic Centre, Stockwell Close, Bromley, BR1 3UH Tel: 0181-313-4666 Fax: 0181-313-4699
Camden LB
Camden Register Office, Camden Town Hall, Judd St, WC1H 9JE Tel: 0171-314-1900 Fax: 0171-860-5792
City of London
Finsbury Town Hall, Roseberry Avenue, EC1R 4QT Tel: 0171-833-3210 Fax: 0171-477-3744
City of Westminster LB
Westminster Council House, Marylebone Rd, NW1 5PT Tel: 0171-641-1161/2/3 Fax: 0171-641-1246
Croydon LB
Mint Walk, Croydon, CR0 1EA Tel: 0181-760-5617 Fax: 0181-760-5633
Ealing LB
Ealing Town Hall, New Broadway, Ealing, W5 2BY Tel: 0181-758-8946 Fax: 0181-758-8722
Greenwich LB
Town Hall, Wellington St, SE18 6PW Tel: 0181-854-8888 Fax: 0181-317-5747
Hackney LB
Town Hall, Mare St, E8 1EA Tel: 0181-356-3376 Fax: 0181-356-3552
Hammersmith & Fulham LB
Fulham Register Office, Old Town Hall, 553/561 Fulham Rd, London, SW6 1ET Tel: 0181-576-5217 Fax: 0181-576-5072
Hammersmith & Fulham LB
Nigel Playfair Avenue, London, W6 9JY Tel: 0181-748-3020 Tel: 0181-576-5032 Fax: 0181-748-6619
Haringey LB
Civic Centre, High Rd, Haringey, N22 4LE Tel: 0181-528-0186 Fax: 0181-862-2912
Islington LB
Finsbury Town Hall, Roseberry Avenue, EC1R 4QT Tel: 0171-837-4941 Tel: 0171 527 6350 Fax: 0171 527 6355
Kensington & Chelsea LB
The Kensington & Chelsea Register Office, Chelsea Old Town Hall, Kings Rd, London, SW3 5EE Tel: 0171-361-4100 Fax: 0171-361-4054
Lambeth MB
357-361 Brixton Rd, London, SW9 7DA Tel: 0171-926-9420 Fax: 0171 926 9426
Lewisham LB
368 Lewisham High St, London, SE13 6LQ Tel: 0181-690-2128 Fax: 0181 314 1078
Newham LB
Passmore Edwards Building, 207 Plashet Grove, East Ham, London, E6 1BT Tel: 0181-471 5128 Fax: 0181 557 8973
Southwark LB
34 Peckham Rd, London, SE5 8QA Tel: 0171-525-7669 Fax: 0171 525 7652
Tower Hamlets LB
Bromley Public Hall, Bow Rd, E3 3AA Tel: 0181-980-8025 Fax: 0181 981 9931
Waltham Forest LB
106 Grove Rd, Walthamstow, E17 9BY Tel: 0181-520-8617 Fax: 0181 509 1388
Wandsworth LB
The Town Hall, Wandsworth High St, SW18 2PU Tel: 0181-871-6120 Fax: 0181 871 8100
Manchester
Manchester MD
Cumberland House, Spinningfield, Off Deansgate, M60 3RG Tel: 0161-234-7878 Fax: 0161-234-7888, Email: register-office@manchester.gov.uk
Salford MD
'Kingslea', Barton Rd, Swinton, M27 5WH Tel: 0161-793-0077 Fax: 0161-794-4797

Merseyside
Knowsley MD
District Council Offices, High St, Prescot, L34 3LH Tel: 0151-443-5210 Fax: 0151-443-5216
Liverpool MD
7 Brougham Terrace, West Derby Rd, Liverpool, L6 1AF Tel: 0151-225-4977 Fax: 0151-225-4944
Sefton MD
Sefton North, Town Hall, Corporation St, Southport, PR8 1DA Tel: 01704-533133 Fax: 0151-934-2014
Sefton South, Crosby Town Hall, Great Georges Rd, Waterloo, Liverpool, L22 1RB Tel: 0151-934 3045 Fax: 0151 934 3044
St Helens MD
St. Helens Central St, St Helens, WA10 1UJ Tel: 01744-23524 Tel: 01744-732012 Fax: 01744 23524
Wirral MD
Wallasey Town Hall, Wallasey, L44 8ED Tel: 0151-691-8505
Wirral, Town Hall, Mortimer St, Birkenhead, L41 5EU Tel: 0151-666-3953 Fax: 0151-666-3955
Middlesex
Brent LB
Brent Town Hall, Forty Lane, Wembley, HA9 9EZ Tel: 0181-937-1010 Fax: 0181-937-1021, Email: "name"@brent.gov.uk
Enfield LB
Public Offices, Gentlemen's Row, Enfield, EN2 6PS Tcl: 0181-367-5757 Fax: 0181-379-8562
Harrow LB
The Civic Centre, Station Rd, Harrow, HA1 2UX Tel: 0181-424-1618 Fax: 0181-424-1414
Hendon
182 Burnt Oak, Broadway, Edgware, HA8 0AU Tel: 0181-952-0876 Tel: 0181-952-0024 Fax: 0181-381-2346, Transferred to Barnet wef April 1999
Hillingdon LB
Hillingdon Civic Centre, Uxbridge, UB8 1UW Tel: 01895-250418 Fax: 01895-250678
Hounslow LB
88 Lampton Rd, Hounslow, TW3 4DW Tel: 0181-862-5022 Fax: 0181-577-8798
Milton Keynes
Milton Keynes
Bracknell House, Aylesbury St, Bletchley, MK2 2BE Tel: 01908-372101 Fax: 01908 645103
Norfolk
North Walsham 18 Kings Arms St, North Walsham, NR28 9JX Tel: 01692-403075 Tel: Fax: 01692-406220
(Erpingham SD) Council Offices, North Lodge Park, Overstrand Rd, Cromer, NR27 0AH Tel: 01263-513078
(Smallburgh SD) 18 Kings Arms St, North Walsham, NR28 9JX Tel: 01692-403075
Depwade, Council Offices, 11-12 Market Hill, Diss, IP22 3JX Tel: 01379-643915 Fax: 01379 643915
Downham 15 Paradise Rd, Downham Market, PE38 9HS Tel: 01366-388080 Fax: 01366 387105
East Dereham, 59 High St, Dereham, NR19 1DZ Tel: 01362-698021 Fax: 01362 698021
Fakenham 37 Market Place, Fakenham, NR21 9DN Tel: 01328-855910 Fax: 01328-855910
Great Yarmouth 'Ferryside', High Rd, Southtown, Great Yarmouth, NR31 0PH Tel: 01493-662313 Tel: Fax: 01493-602107
King's Lynn St Margaret's House, St Margaret's Place, King's Lynn, PE30 5DW Tel: 01553-669251 Tel: Fax: 01553 669251
Norwich, Churchaman House, 71 Bethel St, Norwich, NR2 1NR Tel: 01603-767600 Fax: 01603 632677
Wayland, Kings House, Kings St, Thetford, IP24 2AP Tel: 01847-754115 Tel: Fax: 01847-765996

North East Lincolnshire
Town Hall Square, Grimsby, DN31 1HX Tel: 01472-324860
Tel: Fax: 01472-324867
North Lincolnshire
92 Oswald Rd, Scunthorpe, DN15 7PA Tel: 01724-843915
Tel: Fax: 01724 872668
North Somerset
North Somerset 41 The Boulevard, Weston-super-Mare,
BS23 1PG Tel: 01934-627552 Fax: 01934-412014
(Clevedon SD) 37a Old Church Rd, Clevedon, BS21 6NN
(Weston Super Mare SD) 41 The Boulevard, Weston Super
Mare, BS23 1PG
North Yorkshire
North Yorkshire Registration Service Bilton House, 31 Park
Parade, Harrogate, HG1 5AG Tel: 01423-506949 Fax: 01423-502105
(Malton Out Station) Ryedale House, Malton, YO17 0HH
Tel: 01653-692285
(Northallerton Out Station) County Hall, Northallerton,
DL7 8XE Tel: 01609-780780
(Pickering Out Station) 38 The Mount, Potter Hill,
Pickering, YO18 8AE Tel: 01751 476708
(Richmond Out Station) 12 Queens Rd, Richmond, DL10
4AJ Tel: 01748-823008
(Scarborough Out Station) 14 Dean Rd, Scarborough,
YO12 7SN Tel: 01723-360309
(Selby Out Station) The Annexe, Brook Lodge, Union Lane,
Selby, YO8 0AL Tel: 01757-706590
(Settle Out Station) Council Offices, Castle Hill, Settle,
BD24 9EU Tel: 01729-823624
(Skipton Out Station) Area Offices, Water St, Skipton,
BD23 1PB Tel: 01756 793005
(Whitby Out Station) 'Eskholme', Upgang Lane, Whitby,
YO21 3DR Tel: 01947-602731 Fax: 01947-602731
Northamptonshire
Brackley, Brackley Lodge, High St, Brackley, NN13 5BD
Tel: 01280-702949
Corby Civic Centre, Corby, NN17 1QB Tel: 01536-203141
Daventry, Council Offices, Lodge Rd, Daventry, NN11 5AF
Tel: 01327-302209 Fax: 01327-300011
Kettering 75 London Rd, Kettering, NN15 7PQ Tel: 01536-
514792 Fax: 01536 411359
Northampton, The Guildhall, St Giles Square, Northampton,
NN1 1DE Tel: 01604-233500 Fax: 01604 238507
Towcester, Old Town Hall, Watling Street East, Towcester
Tel: 01327-350774
Wellinborough, Council Offices, Swanspool,
Wellingborough, NN8 1BP Tel: 01933-442553
Northumberland
Northumberland Central 94 Newgate St, Morpeth, NE61
1BU Tel: 01670-513232
(Blyth Valley SD) 107a Waterloo Rd, Blyth, NE24 1AD Tel:
01670-352450
(Morpeth SD) 94 Newgate St, Morpeth, NE61 1BU
Tel: 01670 513232
(Wansbeck SD) Post Office Chambers, Station Rd,
Ashington, NE63 8RJ Tel: 01670-812243
Northumberland North First 49-51 Bridge St, Berwick
upon Tweed, TD15 1ES Tel: 01289-306479
(Belford SD) Linhope, 29 King St, Seahouses, NE68 7XW
Tel: 01665-721676
(Berwick SD) 49-51 Bridge St, Berwick on Tweed, TD15
1ES Tel: 01289-307373
(Wooler SD) 33 Glendale Rd, Wooler, NE71 6DN
Tel: 01668-281656
Northumberland North Second 6 Market Place, Alnwick,
NE66 1HP Tel: 01665-602363 Fax: 01665 510079
(Alnwick SD) 6 Market Place, Alnwick, NE66 1HP Tel:
(Rothbury SD) Court House, Front St, Rothbury, NE65 2TZ
(Warkworth SD) 73 Queen St, Amble, Morpeth, NE65 0DA
Tel: 01665-710744/5

Northumberland West, Abbey Gate House, Market St,
Hexham, NE46 3LX Tel: 01434-602355 Tel: 01434 602605
Fax: 01434 604957
(Bellingham SD) Sutherland House, 3 St Cuthbert's Terrace,
Bellingham, Hexham, NE48 2JR Tel: 01434-220321
(Haltwhistle SD) Haltwhistle Library, Westgate,
Haltwhistle, NE49 0AX Tel: 01434-602355 Tel: 01434-602605
(Hexham SD) Abbey Gate House, Market St, Hexham,
NE46 3LX Tel: 01434-602355 Tel: 01434-602605
(Prudhoe SD) Prudhoe Fire Station, Front St, Prudhoe,
NE42 5DQ Tel: 01661-832248
Nottinghamshire
Basford Highbury Rd, Bulwell, NG6 9DA Tel: 0115-927-
1294 Fax: 0115 977 1845
(Beeston & Stapleford SD) Register Office, Marvin Rd, off
Station Rd, Beeston, NG9 2AP Tel: 0115-925-5530
Carlton Sub-district) County Council Offices, Carlton
Square, Carlton, NG4 3BP Tel: 0115-961-9663
(Eastwood SD) Eastwood Health Clinic, Nottingham Rd,
Eastwood, NG16 3GL Tel: 01773-712449
Newark, County Offices, Balderton Gate, Newark, NG24
1UW Tel: 01636-705455 Fax: 01636 705455
Southwell SD) North Muskham Prebend, Church St,
Southwell, NG25 0HG Tel: 01636-814200
East Retford, Notts County Council Offices, Chancery
Lane, Retford, DN22 6DG Tel: 01777-708631 Fax: 01777
860667
Mansfield, Notts CC Offices, St John St, Mansfield, NG18
1QH Tel: 01623-476564 Fax: 01623 636284
Nottingham 50 Shakespeare St, Nottingham, NG1 4FP Tel:
0115-947-5665 Fax: 0115-941-5773
Rushcliffe, The Hall, Bridgford Rd, West Bridgford, NG2
6AQ Tel: 0115-981-5307 Fax: 0115-969-6189
Worksop, Queens Buildings, Potter St, Worksop, S80 2AH
Tel: 01909-535534 Fax: 01909 501067
Oxfordshire
Abingdon, Roysse Court, Bridge St, Abingdon, OX14 3HU
Tel: 01235-520156
Banbury, Bodicote House, Bodicote, Near Banbury, OX15
4AA Tel: 01295-263268 Fax: 01295-263268
Bullingdon Littleworth Rd, Wheatley, OX33 1NR Tel:
01865-874702
Henley, Easby House, Northfield End, Henley-on-Thames,
RG9 2JW Tel: 01491-573047 Fax: 01491 573047
Oxford Tidmarsh Lane, Oxford, OX1 1NS Tel: 01865-
815167 Fax: 01865 815632
Ploughley, Waverley House, Queen's Avenue, Bicester, OX6
8PY Tel: 01869-252917
Wallingford 197 The Broadway, Didcot, OX11 8RU Tel:
01235-818706
Wantage, The Civic Centre, Portway, Wantage, OX12 9BX
Tel: 012357-65796
West Oxfordshire Welch Way, Witney, OX8 7HH Tel:
01993-703062
Peterborough
Cundle & Thrapston 17 Mill Rd, Cundle, PE8 4BW Tel:
01832-273413
Portsmouth
Milldam House, Burnaby Rd, PO1 3AF Tel: 01705-829041
Fax: 01705 831996
Reading
Reading & Wokingham Yeomanry House, 131 Castle Hill,
RG1 7TA Tel: 0118-957-1213 Fax: 0118-951-0212
Shropshire
Ludlow Stone House, Corve St, Ludlow, SY8 1DG Tel:
01584-874941 Fax: 01584-872971
(Craven Arms SD) The Library, School Rd, Craven Arms,
SY7 9PE Tel: 01588-673455
(Ludlow SD) The Red Cross Centre, The Smithfield, Lower
Galdeford, Ludlow, SY8 1SB Tel: 01584-874422

North Shropshire, Edinburgh House, New St, Wem, Shrewsbury, SY4 5DB Tel: 01939-238418

(Market Drayton SD) Health Centre, Cheshire St, Market Drayton, TF9 3AA Tel:

North Shropshire (Whitchurch SD) 29 St Mary's St, Whitchurch, SY13 1RA Tel: 01948-663402

(Wem SD) Edinburgh House, New St, Wem, Shrewsbury, SY4 5DB Tel: 01939-238418 Fax:

Bridgnorth 12 West Castle St, Bridgnorth, WV16 4AB Tel: 01746-762589 Fax: 01746 764270

Clun, The Pines, Colebatch Rd, Bishop's Castle, SY9 5JZ Tel: 01588-638588

Oswestry Holbache Rd, Oswestry Tel: 01691-652086

Shrewsbury The Shirehall, Abbey Foregate, Shrewsbury, SY2 6LY Tel: 01743-259921 Fax: 01743 252922

Wrekin, The Beeches, 29 Vineyard Rd, Wellinton, Telford, TF1 1HB Tel: 01952-248292

Somerset

Mendip 19b Commercial Rd, Shepton Mallet, BA4 5BU Tel: 01749-343928 Fax: 01749 343928

(Frome SD) West Hill House, West End, Frome, BA11 3AD Tel: 01373-462887

(Shepton Mallet SD) 19 Commercial Rd, Shepton Mallet, BA4 5BU Tel: 01749-342268

(Wells SD) Town Hall, Market Place, Wells, BA5 2RB Tel: 01749-675355

Yeovil, Maltravers House, Petters Way, Yeovil, BA20 1SP Tel: 01935-422230 Fax: 01935-413993

(Chard SD) Holyrood Lace Mill, Holyrood St, Chard, TA20 2YA Tel: 01460-63139 Fax: 01460-260402

(Wincanton SD) Council Offices, Churchfield, Wincanton, BA9 9AG Tel: 01963-435008 Fax: 01963-34182

Sedgemoor, Morgan House, Mount St, Bridgewater, TA6 3ER Tel: 01278-422527

Taunton, Flook House, Belvedere Rd, Taunton, TA1 1BT Tel: 01823-282251 Fax: 01823 351173

West Somerset, 2 Long St, Williton, Taunton, TA4 4QN Tel: 01984-633116

South Gloucestershire

Poole Court, Poole Court Drive, Yate, BS37 5PY Tel: 01454-863140 Fax: 01454-863145

South Yorkshire

Doncaster MD

Elmfield Park, South Parade, Doncaster, DN1 2EB Tel: 01302-364922 Fax: 01302-364922

Mexborough SD) Council Offices, Main St, Mexborough, S64 9LU Tel: 01302-735705

Barnsley, Barnsley, Town Hall, Church St, Barnsley, S70 2TA Tel: 01226-773085 Tel: 01226 773080

Rotherham MD

Rotherham, Bailey House, Rawmarsh Rd, Rotherham, S60 1TX Tel: 01709-382121

Sheffield MD

Sheffield Surrey Place, Sheffield, S1 1YA Tel: 0114-203-9423 Fax: 0114-203-9424

Southampton

Hampshire, Droxford, Bank House, Bank St, Bishop's Waltham, SO32 1GP Tel: 01489-894044 Fax: 01489-892219

Staffordshire

South Staffordshire, Civic Centre, Gravel Hill, Wombourne, Wolverhampton, WV5 9HA Tel: 01902-895829 Fax: 01902-326779

(Seisdon SD) Civic Centre, Gravel Hill, Wombourne, Wolverhampton, WV5 9HA Tel: 01902-895829 Fax: 01902-326779

(Penkridge SD) Haling Dene Centre, Cannock Rd, Penkridge, ST19 5DT Tel: 01785-715260 Fax: 01785-715260

Cannock Chase 5 Victoria St, Cannock, WS11 1AG Tel: 01543-503255 Fax: 01543-468306

(Rugeley SD) Council Offices, Anson St, Rugeley, WS15 2BH Tel: 01889-585322

East Staffordshire, Rangemore House, 22 Rangemore St, Burton-upon-Trent, DE14 2ED Tel: 01283-538701 Fax: 01283 547338

(Burton on Trent SD) Rangemore House, 22 Rangemore St, Burton on Trent, DE14 2ED Tel: 01283-538701 Fax: 01283-547338

(Uttoxeter SD) 63 High St, Uttoxeter, ST14 7JD Tel: 01889-562168 Fax: 01889-569935

Lichfield (Tamworth SD) 26 Albert Rd, Tamworth, B79 7JS Tel: 01827-62295 Fax: 01827-62295

Newcastle-under-Lyme 20 Sidmouth Avenue, The Brampton, Newcastle-under-Lyme, ST5 0QN Tel: 01782-297581 Fax: 01782-297582

(Kidsgrove SD) The Town Hall, Liverpool Rd, Kidsgrove, ST7 4EH

Stafford, Eastgate House, 79 Eastgate St, Stafford, ST16 2NG Tel: 01785-277880 Fax: 01785 277884

(Stone SD) 15 Station Rd, Stone, ST15 8JR Tel: 01785-812087 Fax: 01785-286123

Staffordshire Moorlands High St, Leek, ST13 5EA Tel: 01538-373166 Fax: 01538-386985

(Biddulph SD) Biddulph Library Annexe, Tunstall Rd, Biddulph, ST8 6HH Tel: 01782-512619

(Cheadle & Alton SD) Council Offices, Leek Rd, Cheadle, ST10 1JF Tel: 01538-752435 Fax: 01538-752435

Leek & Cheddleton SD) High St, Leek, ST13 5EA Tel: 01538-373191

Lichfield, The Old Library Buildings, Bird St, Lichfield, WS13 6PN Tel: 01543-510771 Fax: 01543-510773

Stoke-on-Trent Town Hall, Albion St, Hanley, Stoke on Trent, ST1 1QQ Tel: 01782-295640 Fax: 01782-295648

Suffolk

Bury St. Edmunds St. Margarets, Shire Hall, Bury StEdmunds, IP33 1RX Tel: 01284-352373 Fax: 01284 352376

Deben Council Offices, Melton Hill, Woodbridge, IP12 1AU Tel: 01394-444331 Tel: 01394-444682 Fax: 01394-383171

Gipping & Hartismere, Milton House, Milton Road South, Stowmarket, IP14 1EZ Tel: 01449-612060 Fax: 01449-775103

Ipswich, St Peters House, 16 Grimwade St, Ipswich, IP4 1LP Tel: 01473-583050 Fax: 01473-584331

Sudbury 14 Cornard Rd, Sudbury, CO10 6XA Tel: 01787-372904

Waveney, St Margarets House, Gordon Rd, Lowestoft, NR32 1JQ Tel: 01502-405325 Fax: 01502-508170

Surrey

Kingston-upon-Thames LB

Kingston upon Thames 35 Coombe Rd, Kingston upon Thames, KT2 7BA Tel: 0181-546-7993 Fax: 0181 287 2888

Merton LB

Merton, Morden Cottage, Morden Hall Rd, Morden, SM4 5JA Tel: 0181-540-5011 Fax: 0181-543-2906

Mid Surrey, Ashley House, Ashley Rd, Epsom, KT18 5AB Tel: 01372-721747 Fax: 01372-747308

North Surrey, 'Rylston', 81 Oatlands Drive, Weybridge, KT13 9LN Tel: 01932-254360 Fax: 01932 227139

Richmond Upon Thames LB

Richmond upon Thames 1 Spring Terrace, Richmond, TW9 1LW Tel: 0181-940-2853 Fax: 0181-940-8226

South-East Surrey 44 Reigate Hill, Reigate, RH2 9NG Tel: 01737-243359 Fax: 01737 223163

Sutton LB

Sutton, Russettings, 25 Worcester Rd, Sutton, SM2 6PR Tel: 0181-770-6790 Fax: 0181-770-6772

West Surrey, Artington House, Portsmouth Rd, Guildford, GU2 5DZ Tel: 01483-562841 Fax: 01483-573232

Wokingham Yeomanry House, 131 Castle Hill, Reading, RG1 7TA Tel: 0118-957-1213 Fax: 0118-951-0212

Tyne & Wear
Gateshead MD
Gateshead Civic Centre, Regent St, Gateshead, NE8 1HH
Tel: 0191-477-1011 Fax: 0191-477-9978
South Tyneside, Jarrow Suffolk St, Jarrow, NE32 5BJ Tel:
0191-489 7595 Fax: 0191 428 0931
Newcastle-upon-Tyne MD
Newcastle-upon-Tyne Civic Centre, Barras Bridge, Newcastle-upon-
Tyne, NE1 8PS Tel: 0191-232-8520 Fax: 0191 211 4970
North Tyneside MD
North Tyneside, Maritime Chambers, Howard St. North
Shields, NE30 1LZ Tel: 0191-2006164
South Tyneside MD
South Shields 18 Barrington St, South Shields, NE33 1AH
Tel: 0191-455-3915 Fax: 0191-427-7564
Sunderland MD
Sunderland Town Hall & Civic Centre, PO Box 108, Sunderland, SR2
7DN Tel: 0191-553-1760 Fax: 0191 553 1769
Warwickshire
Mid Warwickshire, Pageant House, 2 Jury St, Warwick,
CV34 4EW Tel: 01926-494269 Fax: 01926 496287
(Leamington Spa SD) 1 Euston Square, Leamington Spa,
CV32 4NE Tel: 01962-428807 Fax: 01962-339923
(Southam SD) The Grange, Coventry Rd, Southam, CV33
0ED Tel: 01926-812636
South Warwickshire 7 Rother St, Stratford-on-Avon, CV37
6LU Tel: 01789-293711 Fax: 01789 261423
(Alcester SD) The Court House, Priory Rd, Alcester, B49
5DZ Tel: 01789-765441
(Shipston on Stour SD) Clark House, West St, Shipston on
Stour, CV36 4HD Tel: 01608-662839
Stratford on Avon SD) Register Office, 7 Rother St,
Stratford on Avon, CV37 6LU Tel: 01789-293397 Fax:
01789-261423
North Warwickshire, Warwick House, Ratcliffe St,
Atherstone, CV9 1JP Tel: 01827-713241 Fax: 01827 720467
Nuneaton & Bedworth Riversley Park, Coton Rd, Nuneaton, CV11
5HA Tel: 01203-348948 Fax: 01203-350988
Rugby 5 Bloxam Place, Rugby, CV21 3DS Tel: 01788-
571233 Fax: 01788-542024
West Midlands
Birmingham MD
Birmingham 300 Broad St, Birmingham, B1 2DE Tel: 0121-
235-3421 Fax: 0121-303-1396
Dudley MD
Dudley, Priory Hall, Priory Park, Dudley, DY1 4EU Tel:
01384-815373 Fax: 01384-815339
Sandwell MD
Sandwell, Highfields, High St, Sandwell, B70 8RJ Tel:
0121-569-2480 Fax: 0121-569-2473
Solihull MD
Solihull North The Library, Stephenson Drive, Chelmsley Wood,
Birmingham, B37 5TA Tel: 0121-788-4376 Fax: 0121 788 4379
Solihull South Homer Rd, Solihull, B9 3QZ Tel: 0121-704-
6100 Fax: 0121 704 6123
Dudley MD
Stourbridge, Crown Centre, Crown Lane, Stourbridge, DY8
1YA Tel: 01384-815384 Fax: 01384-815397
Walsall MD
Walsall Hatherton Rd, Walsall, WS1 1TN Tel: 01922-
652260
Wolverhampton Civic Centre, St Peters Square, Wolverhampton,
WV1 1RU Tel: 01902-554989 Fax: 01902-554987
West Sussex
Crawley, Town Hall, The Boulevard, Crawley, RH10 1UZ
Tel: 01293-438341 Fax: 01293-526454
(Sub-district) County Buildings, Northgate Avenue,
Crawley, RH10 1XB Tel: 01293-514545 Fax: 01293-553832
Chichester, Greyfriars, 61 North St, Chichester, PO19 1NB
Tel: 01243-782307 Fax: 01243-773671

(Bognor SD) Health Centre, West St, Bognor Regis, PO21
1UT Tel: 01243-823453 Fax: 01243-823453
(Midhurst SD) Capron House, North St, Midhurst, GU29
9XX Tel: 01730-813245 Fax: 01730-813245
Worthing, County Buildings, 15 Mill Rd, Worthing, BN11
4JY Tel: 01903-708250 Fax: 01903-708263
(Chanctonbury SD) 26 West St, Storrington, RH20 4EE
Tel: 01903-744275
(Shoreham by the Sea SD) Shoreham Health Centre, Pond
Rd, Shoreham by the Sea, BN4 5US Tel: 01273-440550
(Littlehampton SD) County Buildings, East St, Littlehampton, BN17
6AP Tel: 01903-715460 Fax: 01903-715460
Haywards Heath, West Sussex County Council Offices,
Oaklands Rd, Haywards Heath, RH16 1SU Tel: 01444-
452157 Fax: 01444-410128
Horsham, Town Hall, Market Square, Horsham, RH12 1EU
Tel: 01403-265368 Fax: 01403-2170778
West Yorkshire
Bradford MD
Bradford 22 Manor Row, Bradford, BD1 4QR Tel: 01274-
752151 Fax: 01274-305139
Keighley, Town Hall, Bow St, Keighley, BD21 3PA Tel:
01535-618060 Fax:
Kirklees MD
Dewsbury Wellington St, Dewsbury, WF13 1LY Tel:
01924-324880 Fax: 01924 324882
Huddersfield, Civic Centre, 11 High St, Huddersfield, HD1
2PL Tel: 01484-221030
Leeds MD
Leeds, Belgrave House, Belgrave St, Leeds, LS2 8DQ Tel:
0113-247-6711 Fax: 0113-247-4192
Calderdale MD
Halifax 4 Carlton St, Halifax, HX1 2AH Tel: 01422-353993
Fax: 01422-252370
Wakefield MD
Pontefract Town Hall, Pontefract, WF8 1PG Tel: 01977-
722670 Fax: 01977-722676
Wakefield 71 Northgate, Wakefield, WF1 3BS Tel: 01924-
361635 Fax: 01924-371859
Wiltshire
Chippenham 10-11 Market Place, Chippenham, SN15 3HF
Tel: 01249-654361 Fax: 01249-658850
Devizes & Marlborough, The Beeches, Bath Rd, Devizes,
SN10 2AL Tel: 01380-722162 Fax: 01380-728933
Marlborough 1 The Green, Marlborough, SN8 1AL Tel:
01672-512483
Salisbury, The Laburnums, 50 Bedwin St, Salisbury, SP1
3UW Tel: 01722-335340 Fax: 01722 326806
Trowbridge, East wing Block, County Hall, Trowbridge,
BA14 8JQ Tel: 01225-713000 Fax: 01225 713097
Warminster 3 The Avenue, Warminster, BA12 9AB Tel:
01985-213435 Fax: 01985 217688
Thamesdown, Swindon, 1st Floor Aspen House, Temple St,
Swindon, SN1 1SQ Tel: 01793-521734 Fax: 01793 433887
Worcestershire
Bromsgrove School Drive, Bromsgrove, B60 1AY Tel:
01527-578759 Fax: 01527-578750
Droitwich, Council Offices, Ombersley St, Droitwich, WR9
8QX Tel: 01905-772280 Fax: 01905-776841
Evesham, County Offices, Swan Lane, Evesham, WR11 4TZ
Tel: 01386-443945 Fax: 01386-448745
Kidderminster Council Offices, Bewdley Rd, Kidderminster, DY11
6RL Tel: 01562-829100 Fax: 01562-60192
Malvern, Hatherton Lodge, Avenue Rd, Malvern, WR14
3AG Tel: 01684-573000 Fax: 01684-892378
Pershore, Civic Centre, Queen Elizabeth Drive, Pershore,
WR10 1PT Tel: 01386-565610 Fax: 01386-553656
Redditch 29 Easmore Rd, Redditch, B98 8ER Tel: 01527-60647
Tenbury, Council Buildings, Teme St, Tenbury Wells Tel:
01584-810588

Worcester 29-30 Foregate St, Worcester, WR1 1DS Tel: 01905-765350 Fax: 01905-765355

Isles of Scilly
Isles of Scilly Town Hall, St Marys, TR21 0LW Tel: 01720

Wales
Rhondda Cynon Taff
Pontypridd Court House St, Pontypridd, CF37 1JS Tel: 01443-486869 Fax: 01443 406587
Cynon Valley SD) The Annexe, Rock Grounds, Aberdare, CF44 7AE Tel: 01685-871008
(Rhondda No1 SD) De Winton Field, Tonypandy, CF40 2NJ
(Rhondda No 2 SD) Crown Buildings, 69 High St, Ferndale, Rhondda, CF43 4RR Tel: 01443-730369
(Taff Ely SD) Courthouse St, Pontypridd, CF37 1LJ Tel: 01443-486870 Fax: 01443-406587
Bridgend
Bridgend, County Borough Offices, Sunnyside, Bridgend, CF31 4AR Tel: 01656-642391 Fax: 01656-642391
Caerphilly
Caerphilly, The Council Offices, Ystrad Fawr, Ystrad Mynach, CF82 7SF Tel: 01443-863478 Fax: 01443-863385
Cardiff
Cardiff 48 Park Place, Cardiff, CF1 3LU Tel: 01222-871690 Fax: 01222-871689
Neath Port Talbot
119 London Rd, Neath, Neath Port Talbot, SA11 1HL Tel: 01639-643696 Fax: 01639 760023
Swansea
Swansea The Swansea Register Office, County Hall, Swansea, SA1 3SN Tel: 01792-636188 Fax: 01792-636909
Wrexham
Wrexham 2 Grosvenor Rd, Wrexham, LL11 1DL Tel: 01978-265786 Fax: 01978-262061
Anglesey Ynys Môn, Shire Hall, Glanhwfa Rd, Llangefni, LL77 7TW Tel: 01248-725264
Caerphilly
Bargoed SD) Register Office, Hanbury Square, Bargoed, CF8 8QQ Tel: 01443-875560 Fax: 01443-822535
(Islwyn SD) Council Offices, Pontllanfraith, Blackwood, NP2 2YW Tel: 01495-226622 Ext 5188
Ceredigion
Cardiganshire Central 21 High St, Lampeter, SA48 7BG Tel: 01570-422558 Fax: 01570-422558
Cardiganshire North, Swyddfar Sir, Marine Terrace, Aberystwyth, SY33 2DE Tel: 01970-633580
Comwy
Conwy CB Public Protection Department Civic Offices, Colwyn Bay, LL29 8AR Tel: 01492 575183 Fax: 01492 575204
Colwyn
New Clinic & Offices, 67 Market St, Abergele, LL22 7BP Tel: 01745-823976 Fax: 01745-823976
(Sub-district) Bod Alaw, Rivieres Avenue, Colwyn Bay, LL29 7DP Tel: 01492-530430
Aberconwy, Muriau Buildings, Rose Hill St, Aberconwy, LL32 8LD Tel: 01492-592407 Fax: 01492-2315
DenbighshireDenbighshire North, Morfa Hall, Church St, Rhyl, LL18 3AA Tel: 01745-353428 Fax: 01745-361424
Denbighshire South Station Rd, Ruthin, LL15 1BS Tel: 01824-703782 Fax: 01824-704399
Dyfed
Ceredigion
Cardiganshire South, Glyncoed Chambers, Priory St, Cardigan, SA43 1BX Tel: 01239-612684 Fax: 01239-612684
Carmarthenshire
St Peters St, Carmarthen, SA31 1LN Tel: 01267-230875 Fax: 01267-221974

York
56 Bootham, York, YO30 7DA Tel: 01904-654477 Fax: 01904-638090 422537 Fax: 01720-422202

Llanelli
County Council Offices, Swansea Rd, Llanelli, SA15 3DJ Tel: 01554-774088 Fax: 01554-749424
Pembrokeshire
South Pembroke East Back, Pembroke, SA71 4HL Tel: 01646-682432 Fax: 01646 621433
Flintshire
Flintshire East, The Old Rectory, Rectory Lane, Hawarden, CH5 3NN Tel: 01244-531512 Fax: 01244-534628
Flintshire West Park Lane, Holywell, CH8 7UR Tel: 01352-711813 Fax: 01352-713292
Glamorgan
Vale of Glamorgan, Vale of Glamorgan 2-6 Holton Rd, Barry, CF63 4HD Tel: 01446-700809 Fax: 01446 746861
Gwent
Blaenau Gwent
Blaenau Gwent, The Grove, Church St, Tredegar, NP2 3DS Tel: 01495-722305
(Abertilley SD) Council Offices, Mitre St, Abertilley, NP3 1AE Tel: 01495-216082
(Ebbw Vale & Tredegar SD) The Grove, Church St, Tredegar, NP2 3DS Tel: 01495-72269
Newport
8 Gold Tops, Newport, NP9 4PH Tel: 01633-265547 Fax: 01633 220913
Torfaen
Hanbury Rd, Pontypool, NP4 6YG Tel: 01495-762937 Fax: 01495 769049
Gwynedd
Ardudwy, Bryn Marian, Church St, Blaenau Ffestiniog, LL41 3HD Tel: 01766-830217
Bangor
Town Hall, Bangor, LL57 2RE Tel: 01248-362418
Caernarfon
Swyddfa Arfon, Pennrallt, Caernarfon, LL55 1BN Tel: 01286-682661
De Meirionndd
Bridge St, Dolgellau, LL40 1AU Tel: 01341-424341
Dwyfor
35 High St, Pwllheli, LL53 5RT Tel: 01758-612546 Fax: 01758-701373
Penllyn
5 Plasey St, Bala, LL23 7SW Tel: 01678-520428 Fax: 01678-520474
Merthyr Tydfil
Oldway House, Castle St, CF47 8BJ Tel: 01685-723318 Fax: 01685 721849
Mid Glamorgan
see **Rhondda Cynon Taff**
Monmouthshire
Monmouth, Coed Glas, Firs Rd, Abergavenny, NP7 5LE Tel: 01873 735435 Fax: 01837 735841
(Abergavenny SD) 26a Monk St, Abergavenny, NP7 5NP Tel: 01873-735435
(Chepstow SD) High Trees, Steep St, Chepstow, NP6 6RL
Pembrokeshire
Haverfordwest Tower Hill, Haverfordwest, SA61 1SS Tel: 01437-762579 Fax: 01437 763543
(Fishguard & Cemaes SD) Town Hall, Fishguard, SA65 9HE Tel: 01348-872875 Fax: 01348-872875
(Haverfordwest & Milford Haven SD) Tower Hill, Haverfordwest, SA61 1SS Tel: 01437-762579
Powys
Mid Powys, Powys County Hall, Llandrindod Wells, LD1 5LG Tel: 01597-826386 Fax: 01597-826220

(Builth SD) The Strand hall, Strand St, Builth Wells, LD2 3AA Tel: 01982-552134
(Radnorshire West SD) Register Office, Powys County Hall, Llandrindod Wells, LD1 5LG Tel: 01597-826382
Newtown Room 4 Council Offices, The Park, Newtown, SY16 2NZ Tel: 01686-627862
(Llanidloes SD) Town Hall, Llanidloes, SY18 6BN Tel: 01686-412353
Welshpool & Llanfyllllin
Neuadd Maldwyn, Severn Rd, Welshpool, SY21 7AS Tel: 01938-552828-ext-228 Fax: 01938 551233
(Llanfyllin SD) Old County School, Llanfyllin, SY22 5AA Tel: 01691-648794

Northern Ireland
General Register Office of Northern Ireland Oxford House, 49 - 55 Chichester St, Belfast, BT1 4HL Tel: 028 90 252033 Fax: 028 90 252044, Email: stanley.campbell@dfpni.gov.uk

Brecknock, Neuadd Brycheiniog, Cambrian Way, Brecon, LD3 7HR Tel: 01874-624334 Fax: 01874 625781
Hay, The Borough Council Offices, Broad St, Hay-on-Wye, HR3 5BX Tel: 01479-821371 Fax: 01479 821540
Machynlleth 11 Penrallt St, Machynlleth, SY20 8AG Tel: 01654-702335 Fax: 01654-703742
Radnorshire East 2 Station Rd, Knighton, LD7 1DU Tel: 01547-528332
Swansea
Ystradgynlais
County Council Offices, Trawsffordd, Ystradgynlais, SA9 1BS Tel: 01639-843104

Superintendent Registars Scotland

ABERCHIRDER 91 Main Street, Aberchirder, AB54 5TB Tel: 01466-780735
ABERDEEN St Nicholas House Upperkirkgate, Aberdeen, AB10 1EY Tel: 01224-522616, Fax: 01224-522616
ABERFELDY, DULL & WEEM Municipal Buildings Crieff Road, Aberfeldy, PH15 2BJ Tel: 01887-820773
ABERFOYLE + MENTHEITH 4 Montrose Road, Aberfoyle, FK8 3UL Tel: 01877-382311
ABERLOUR 46 High Street, Aberlour, AB38 9QD Tel: 01340-871635
ABOYNE District Council Offices Bellwood Road, Aboyne, AB34 5HQ Tel: 01339-886109, Fax: 01339-86798
AIRDRIE Area Registration Office 37 Alexander Street, Airdrie, ML6 0BA Tel: 01236-763322
AIRTH 100 South Green Drive Airth Falkirk, FK8 8JR Tel: 01324-831538
ALFORD Council Office School Road, Alford, AB33 8PY Tel: 01975-652421, Fax: 01975-563286
ALLOA Marshill House, Marshill Alloa, FK10 1 AD Tel: 01259-123850
ANNAN Moat House Bruce Street, Annan, DG12 5DE Tel: 01461-204914
APPLECROSS Coire-ringeal Applecross, Kyle Ross-shire IV54 8LU Tel: 01520-744248
ARBROATH Academy Lane, Arbroath, DD11 1EJ Tel: 01241-873752
ARDGOUR 9 Clovullin Ardgour by Fort William, PH33 7AB Tel: 01855-841261
ARROCHAR 1 Cobbler View, Arrochar, G83 1 AD Tel: 01301-702289
ASSYNT Post Office House, Lochinvar by Lairg, IV27 4JY Tel: 01571-844201
AUCHINLECK 154 Main Street Auchlinleck Cummock, KA18 2AS Tel: 01290-420582
AUCHTERARDER 187 High Street, Auchterarder, PH3 1AF Tel: 01764-663581
AUCHTERDERRAN 145 Station Road, Cardenden, KY5 0BN Tel: 01592-414800
AUCHTERMUCHTY Town House High Street, Auchtermuchty, KY14 7AP Tel: 01337-828329, Fax: 01337-821166
AVIEMORE Tremayne Dalfaber Road, Aviemore, PH22 1PU Tel: 01479-810694
AYR Sandgate House 43 Sandgate, Ayr, KY7 1JW Tel: 01292-284988, Fax: 01292-885643
BAILLIESTON Council Office 89 Main Street, Baillieston, G69 6AB Tel: 0141-771-1901
BALLACHULISH 5 Wades Rood Kinlochleven, Argyll, PA4O 4QX Tel: 01855-831350
BALLATER An Creagan S Queens Road., Ballater, AB35 5RJ Tel: 01339-755535
BANCHORY Aberdeenshire Council The Square High Street Banchory, AB3 1 Tel: 01330-822878
BANFF Seafield House 37 Castle Street, Banff, AB4S DQ Tel: 01261-812001
BARRA Council Offices, Castlebay Dana, HS9 5XD Tel: 01871-810431

BARRHEAD Council Office 13 Lowndes Street, Barrhead, 078 2QX Tel: 0141-8813551/2, Fax: 0141-5773553
BATHGATE 76 Mid Street, Bathgate, EH48 1QD Tel: 01506-653162
BEAULY 7 Viewfield Avenue, Beauly, 1V4 7BW Tel: 01463-782264
BELLSHILL 20/22 Motherwelt Road, Bellshill, ML4 1RB Tel: 01698-747145
BENBECULA Council Offices Balivanich Benbecula South Uist, HS7 5LA Tel: 01870-602425
BIGGAR 4 Ross Square, Biggar, MLI2 EAT Tel: 01899-220997
BIRSAY Sandveien Dounby, Orkney, KW15 2118 Tel: 01856-771226
BISHOPDRIOGS Council Office 1 Balmuildy Road, Bishopbriggs, G64 2RR Tel: 0141-772-1154/5
BLACK ISLE (NORTH) Operating from Dingwall, , Tel: 01349-863113, Fax: 01349-866164
BLACK ISLE (SOUTH) Black Isles Centre, Service Point Office Deans Road, Fortrose, IV10 8TJ Tel: 01381-620797/8, Fax: 01381-621085
BLAIR ATHOLL Lauchope The Terrace, Blair Atholl, PH15 5SZ Tel: 01796-481242
BLAIRGOWRIE Council Buildings 46 Leslie Street, Blairgowrie, PH10 6AW Tel: 01250-872051, Fax: 01250-876029
BO'NESS + CARRIDEN 12 Corbiehail, Bo'ness, EH51 0AP Tel: 01506-778990
BOISDALE Post Office Hse Daliburgh, South Uist, PA81 5SS Tel: 01878-700300
BONAR + KINCARDINE Post Office Bonar Bridge, Ardgay, IV24 3EA Tel: 01863-766219
BONNYBRIDGE Operating from Denny., , Tel: 01324-504280
BRAEMAR Piedmont 9 Auchendryne Square, Eraemar, AB35 5YS Tel: 01339-741501
BRECHIN 32 Panmure Street, Brechin, DD9 6AP Tel: 01356-622107
BRESSAY No 2 Roadside Bressay, Lerwick Shetland ZE2 9BL Tel: 01595-820356
BROADEORD Fairwinds, Broadford Skye 1V49 9AB Tel: 01471-822270
BUCKIE 1 West Church Street, Buckie, AB56 1UN Tel: 01542-832691
BUCKNAVEN Council Office 96 Wellesley Road, Buckhaven, KY8 1HT Tel: 01592-414444, Fax: 01592-414490
BUCKSBURN Nea Office 23 Inverurie Rd., Bucksburn, AB2 9LJ Tel: 01224-712866
BURRA ISLES Roadside Hannavoe, Lerwick Shetland ZEZ 9LA Tel: 01595-859201
CALLANDER 1 South Church Street, Callander, FKI7 B2N Tel: 01877-330166
CAMBUSLANG Council Office 6 Glasgow Rd, Cambuslang, G72 7BW Tel: 0141-641-8178
CAMPBELTOWN Council Office Witchburn Road, Campbeltown, PA28 6313 Tel: 01586-555253
CARLO WAY The Registry, Carloway Lewis PA86 9AU Tel: 01851-643264
CARLUKE 25 High Street., Carluke, MLB 4A3 Tel: 01555-772273

CARNOCH Bridgend, Strathconon Muir Of Ord 1V6 7QQ Tel: 01997-477254

CARNOUSTIE Council Chambers, Carnoustie, DDV 6AP Tel: 01241-853335/6

CASTLE DOUGLAS District Council 5 Street Andrew Street, Castle Douglas, D07 1DE Tel: 01557-330291

CASTLETON Dalkeith House 13 Douglas Square, Newcastleton, TD9 OQD Tel: 01387-375835

CATRINE 9 Co-operative Aye, Catrine, KA5 6SG Tel: 01290-551638

CHIRNSIDE White House, Chirnside Duns, TD11 3XL Tel: 01890-818339

CHRYSTON Lindsaybeg Road Muirhead Glasgow, G69 9HW Tel: 0141-779-1714

CLYNE Gower Lane, Brora, KW9 6NT Tel: 01408-621233

COALBURN 'Pretoria 200 Coalburn Road, Coolburi, ML11 0LT Tel: 01555-820664

COATBRIDGE 183 Main Street, Coatbridge, ML5 3HH Tel: 01236-422133

COIGACH The Stores, Achilibuie Ullapool, IV26 2Y0 Tel: 01854-622256

COLDSTREAM Operating from Duns, , Tel: 01361-882600

COLL 9 Carnan Road, Isle Of Coll PA78 6TA Tel: 01879-230329

COLONSAY & ORONSAY Scalasaig Farm, Colonsay, PA6 1 7YW Tel: 01951-200357

COUPAR-ANGUS Union Bank Buildings, Coupar- Angus, PH13 9AJ Tel: 01828-628395

COWDENBEATH 320 High Street, Cowdenbeath, KY4 9QX Tel: 01383-313131

CRAWFORD 76 Carlisle Road Crawford Biggar, ML12 6TW Tel: 01864-502633

CRIEFF 14 Comrie Street, Crieff, PH7 4AZ Tel: 01764-655151

CUMBERNAULD Fleming House Tryst Road, Cumbernauld, G67 1JW Tel: 01236-616390, Fax: 01236-616386

CUMBRAE 49 Stuart Street, Millport, KMS GAG Tel: 01475-53074112, Fax: 01475-530891

CUPAR County Buildings St Catherine Street, Cupar, KYl5 4TA Tel: 01334-412200, Fax: 01334-412110

CURRIE 133 Lanark Road West, Currie, EH14 5NY Tel: 0131-449-5318

DALBEATTIE Town Hall Buildings Water Street, Dalbeattie, DG5 '41X Tel: 01557-330291-Ext323

DALKEITH 2-4 Buccieuch Street, Dalkeith, EH22 IHA Tel: 0131-660-7570/1

DALMELLINGTON Area Office 1 New Street, Dalmellington, KA6 7QX Tel: 01292-550229, Fax: 01292-550229

DALRY 42 Main Street Daly, Castle Douglas, DG7 3UW Tel: 01644-430310

DARVEL Operating from Galston., , Tel: 01563-820218

DELTING Soibakkan, Mossbank Shetland ZE2 9R13 Tel: 01806-242209

DENNY Carronbank House Carronbank Crescent, Denny, PK4 2DE Tel: 01324-504280

DING WALL Council Offices Ferry Road, Dingwall, IV15 Tel: 01349-863113, Fax: 01349-866164

DORNOCH Cathedral Square, Dornoch, 1V25 3SW Tel: 01862-810202, Fax: 01862-810166

DOUGLAS Post Office Ayr Road, Douglas, ML1 I OPU Tel: 01555-851227

DUFFTOWN Brentwood Villa Albert Place, Dufftown, AB55 4AY Tel: 01340-820663

DUMBARTON 18 College Way, Dumbarton, G82 1LJ Tel: 01389-767515

DUMFRIES Municipal Chambers Buccleuch Street, Dumfries, DO 1 2AD Tel: 01387-260000, Fax: 01387-269605

DUNBAR Town House 79/85 High Street, Dunbar, EH42 IER Tel: 01368-863434, Fax: 01368-865728

DUNBLANE Municipal Buildings, Dunblane, FK15 OAG Tel: 01786-822214, Fax: 01786-822214

DUNDEE 89 Commercial Street, Dundee, DD1 2AO Tel: 01382-435222/3, Fax: 01382-435224

DUNFERMLINE 34 Viewfield Terrace, Dunfermline, KY12 7HZ Tel: 01383-3-12121

DUNKELD Buchanans Bridge Street, Dunkeld, P118 OAR Tel: 01350-727268

DUNOON Council Offices Hill Street, Dunoon, PA23 7AP Tel: 01369-704374, Fax: 01369-705948

DUNROSSNESS Wiltrow, Dunrossness Shetland 2E2 930 Tel: 01950-460792

DUNS 8 Newtown Street, Duns, TD11 3AS Tel: 01361-882600

DUNVEGAN Tigh-na- Bruaich, Dunvegan Isle Of Skye IV55 8WA Tel: 01470-521296

DURNESS Mid Villa Durine, Durness by Lairg, 1W4 7PN Tel: 01971-511340

EALKIRK Old Burgh Buildings Newmarket Street, Falkirk, FK1 lIE Tel: 01324-506580, Fax: 01324-506581

EAST CALDER East Calder Library 200 Main Street, East Calder, EH53 0EJ Tel: 01506-884680, Fax: 01506-883944

EAST KILBRIDE Civic Centre Cornwall Street East Kilbride Glasgow, G74 1AF Tel: 01355-220841

EAST NEUK Municipal Office Ladywalk, Anstruther, KYID 3EY Tel: 01333-31227R

EASTWOOD + MEARNS Council Offices Easiwood Park Roukenglen Rd Giffnock, G46 7JS Tel: 0141-638-7588

EDAY + PHARAY Redbanks, Eday Orkney, KW1 2AA Tel: 01857-622239

EDINBURGH 2 India Buildings Victoria Street, Edinburgh, EH1 2EX Tel: 0131-220-0349, Fax: 0131-220-0351

EDINBURGH (L) 30 Ferry Road, Edinburgh, EH6 4AE Tel: 0131-554-8452

ELGIN 240 High Street, Elgin, IV30 1BA Tel: 01343-541202, Fax: 01343-541202

ELLON Area Office Schoolhill Road, Ellon, AB41 9AN Tel: 01358-720295

ERASERBURGH 14 Saltoun Square, Fraserburgh, AB43 5DB Tel: 01346-513281

EYEMOUTH Community Centre Albert Road, Eyemoulh, TD14 5DE Tel: 01890-750690

FAIR ISLE Field, Fair Isle Shetland ZE2 9JU Tel: 01595-760224

FETLAR Lower Toft Funzie, Fetlar Shetland 7E2 9DJ Tel: 01957-733273

FIRTH & STENNESS Langbigging, Stenness Orkney KWI6 3LB Tel: 01856-850320

FLOTTA Post Office, Flotta Kirkwall Orkney KWI6 3NP Tel: 01856-701252

FORFAR The Cross, Forfar, DD8 1BX Tel: 01307-464973

FORRES Forres House High Street, Fortes, 1V36 0BU Tel: 01309-672792

FORT AUGUSTUS Cich Collage, Fort Augustus, PH32 4DH Tel: 01320-366245

FORT WILLIAM Tweeddale Buildings High Street, Fort William, PH33 EEU Tel: 01397-704583, Fax: 01397-702757

FORTH 4 Cloglands, Forth, ML11 8ED Tel: 01535-811631

FOULA Magdala Foula, Shetland 7E2 9PN Tel: 01595-753236

GAIRLOCH (NORTH) 12 Bualnaluib, Aultbea, IV22 2JH Tel: 01445-731320

GAIRLOCH (SOUTH) District Office Poolewe, Achnasheen Ross-shire IV22 2JU Tel: 01445-781243, Fax: 01445-781315

GALASHIELS Library Buildings Lawyers Brac, Galashiels, TU1 3JQ Tel: 01896-752822

GALSTON 11 Cross Streel, Galston, KA4 8AA Tel: 02563-820218

GIGHA The Post Office, Gigha, PA4 17AA Tel: 01583-505251

GIRTHON & ANWOTH Bleachfield Birtwhistle Street, Gatehouse Of Fleet, DG7 2JJ Tel: 01557-814046

GIRVAN 22 Dalrymple Street, Girvan, KA26 9AE Tel: 01465-712894, Fax: 01465-715576

GLASGOW 1 Martha Street, Glasgow, G1 1JJ Tel: 0141-287-7677, Fax: 0141-225-7666

GLASGOW (PC) 22 Park Circus, Glasgow, G3 6BE Tel: 0141-287-8350, Fax: 0141-225-8357

GLENELG Taobl Na Mara, Gleneig Kyle Ross-shire IV40 8JT Tel: , Fax: 01599-522310

GLENROTHES Albany House Albany Gate Kingdom Centre, Glenrothes, KY7 5NX Tel: 01592-414141-Ext-4900

GOLSPIE Murrayfield Main Street, Golspie, KW10 6TG Tel: 01408-633150

GORDON Operating from Kelso, , Tel: 01573-225659

GRANGEMOUTH Municipal Chambers Bo'ness Road, Grangemouth, FK3 3AY Tel: 01324-504499

GRANTOWN-ON-SPEY Council Offices The Square, Grangetown On Spey, PH26 3HP Tel: 01479-872539

GREENOCK 40 West Stewart St., Greenock, PA15 1YA Tel: 01475-720084, Fax: 01415-781647

GRETNA Central Avenue, Orcina, DG16 5AQ Tel: 01461-337648, Fax: 01461-338459

HADDINGTON 25 Court Street, Haddington, EH41 3HA Tel: 01620-827308/368

HAMILTON 21 Beckford Street, Hamilton, ML3 0BT Tel: 01698-454211

HARRAY New Breckan, Harray Orkney KW17 2JR Tel: 01856-771233

HARRIS Council Offices, Tarbert Harris HS3 3DJ Tel: 01859-502367, Fax: 01859-502283

HAWICK Council Offices 12 High Street, Hawick, TD9 9EF Tel: 01450-364710, Fax: 01450-364720

HELENSBURGH Council Offices 25 West King Street, Helensburgh, G84 8UW Tel: 01436-673909

HELMSDALE 12 Dunrobin Street, Helmsdale, KW8 6LA Tel: 01431-821751

HOLM & PAPLAY The Register Office, Netherbreck Holm Orkney KWI7 2RX Tel: 01856-382130

HOY Laundry House Melsetter, Longhope Orkney KWI6 3NZ Tel: 01856-791337

HUNTLY 25 Gordon Street, Huntly, AB54 5AN Tel: 01466-794488

INSCH Marbert George Street, Insch, AB52 6JL Tel: 01464-820964

INVERARAY Municipal Office, Inveraray, PA32 8UZ Tel: 01499-302124

INVERBERVIB Area Office Church Street, Inverbervie, DD10 0RU Tel: 01561-361255, Fax: 01561-362802

INVERESK Brunton Hall Ladywell Way, Musselburgh, EH21 6AF Tel: 0131-665-3711

INVERKEITHING 6 Fleriot Street, Inverkeithing, KY11 1ND Tel: 01383-411742

INVERNESS Farraline Park, Inverness, IV1 1NH Tel: 01463-239798

INVERURIE Gordon House Blackhall Road, Inverurie, AB51 3WA Tel: 01467-620981, Fax: 01467-628012

IRVINE 106-108 Bridgegate Hse, Irvine, KA12 8BD Tel: 01294-279333, Fax: 01294-312879

ISLAY Council Office Jamieson Street Bowmore Islay, PA43 7HL Tel: 01496-810332

ISLE OF BUTE Council Office Mount Pleasant Road, Rothesay, PA20 9HH Tel: 01700-5033l/551

JEDBURGH Library Building Castlegate, Jedburgh, TD8 6AS Tel: 01835-863670

JOHNSTONE 16-18 Mc Dowall Street, Johnstone, PA5 8QL Tel: 01505-320012, Fax: 01505-382130

JURA Forestry Cottage Craighouse, Jura, PA60 7AY Tel: 01496-820326

KEITH Area Office Mid Street, Keith, AE55 5DY Tel: 01542-882166-Ext-39, Fax: 01542-882014

KELSO Rose Lane, Kelso, TD5 7AP Tel: 01573-225659

KELTY Kelly Local Services Sanjana Court 51 Main Street Kelty, KY4 0AA Tel: 01383-839999

KENMORE The Old Schoolhouse, Acharn by Aberfeldy, PH15 2HS Tel: 01887-830307, Fax: Same-as-tel-no

KENNOWAY Sandybrae Community Centre, Kennoway Fife, KY8 5JW Tel: 01333-351721

KILBIRNIE, BEITH & DALRY 19 School Wynd, Kilbirnie, KA25 7AY Tel: 01505-682416, Fax: 01505-684334

KILBRANDON + KILCHATTAN Cnoc Groin, Isle Of Seil by Oban PA34 4RF Tel: 01852-300380

KILFINICHEN & KILVICKEON The Anchorage, Fionnphori Isle Of Mull PA66 6BL Tel: 01681-700241

KILLIN Ardlun 17 Monemore, Killin, FK21 8XD Tel: 01567-820618

KILMARNOCK Civic Centre John Dickie Street, Kilnianiock, KA1 1HW Tel: 01563-576695/6

KILSYTH Health Centre Burngreen Park, Kilsyth, G65 0HU Tel: 01236-822151

KILWINNING 32 Howgale, Kilwinning Ayrshire KAI3 6EJ Tel: 01294-55226112

KINGUSSIE Town Hall Spey Street, Kingussie, PH21 1EH Tel: 01540-661867

KINLOCHBERVIE 114 Inshegra, Rhiconich Lairg, IV27 4RH Tel: 01971-521388

KINLOCHLUICHART The Old Manse, Garve Ross-shire IV23 2PX Tel: 01997-414201

KINROSS 40 High Street, Kinross, KY13 7AN Tel: 01577-862405

KIRKCALDY 7 East Fergus Place, Kirkcaldy, KY1 1XT Tel: 0I592-412121, Fax: 01592-412123

KIRKCONNEL Nith Buildings Greystone Avenue Kelloholm Kirkconnel, DG4 6RX Tel: 01659-67206, Fax: 01659-66052

KIRKCUDBRIGHT District Council Offices, Kirkcudbrigbt, DG6 4JG Tel: 01557-330291-Ext-234

KIRKINTILLOCH Council Office 21 Southbank Road, Kirkintilloch, G66 1NH Tel: 0141-776-2109

KIRKLISTON 19 Station Road, Kirkliston, EH29 9BB Tel: 0131-333-3210

KIRKMABRECK The Bogxie Creetowm, Newton Stewart, DG8 73W Tel: 01671-820266

KIRKTON (FARR) 47 Crask, Bettyhill by Thurso, KW14 7SZ Tel: 01641-521335

KIRKWALL Council Offices School Place, Kirkwall Orkney KW15 1NY Tel: 01856-873535-Ext-2109

KIRRIEMUIR CouncilChambers, Kirriemuir, DD8 8BJ Tel: 01575-572845

KNOYDART Knoydari Estate Office, Inverie Knoydart by Mallaig, PH41 4PL Tel: 01681-462331, Fax: 01687-462243

LAIRG 4 Lochside, Lairg Sutherland IV27 4EG Tel: 01549-402424

LAMLASH District Council Office, LamLash Isle Of Arran KA27 8LB Tel: 01770-600338, Fax: 01770-600028

LANARK 25 Hope Streel, Lanark, ML7 7NN Tel: 01555-664679

LANGHOLM Town Hall, Langholm, DG13 0JQ Tel: 01387-380255

LARBERT 318 Main Street, Lathed, FK5 3BE Tel: 01324-503580

LARGS Macturn 24 Greenock Road, Largs, KA30 8NE Tel: 01475-674521, Fax: 01475-689227

LARKHALL Council Office 55 Victoria Street, Larkhall, ML9 2BN Tel: 01698-882454/5

LATHERON Post Office, Latheron, KW5 6DG Tel: 01593-741201

LAUDER Session House Old Causeway East High St Lauder, TD2 6FX Tel: 01578-722795

LAURENCEKIRK Royal Bank Buildings, Laurencekirk, AB30 1AF Tel: 01561-377245, Fax: 01561-378020

LEADHILLS Violet Bank 30 Station Road, Leadhills, ML12 6XS Tel: 01659-74260

LENNOXTOWN Council Office 132 Main Street, Lennoxtown, 065 7DA Tel: 01360-311362

LERWICK County Buildings, Lerwick Shetland ZE1 OHD Tel: 01595-693535-Ext-368

LESMAHAGOW 40/42 Abbeygreen, Lesmahagow, ML11 0DE Tel: 01555-893314

LEVEN 12 Station Road, Leven, KYS 4NH Tel: 01333-592538

LINLITHGOW 29 The Vennel, Linlithgow, EH49 7EX Tel: 01506-775373, Fax: 01506-775374

LISMORE Bachuil, Lismore Oban PA34 5UL Tel: 01631-760256

LIVINGSTON Lammermuir House Owen Sq, Almondvale S. Livingston, EH54 6PW Tel: 01506-414218, Fax: 01506-462575

LOCH DUICH Aird View Dornie, Kyle Of Lochalsh, IV40 8EZ Tel: 01599-555201

LOCHALSH Hamilton House Plock Road, Kyle, IV40 8BL Tel: 01599-534270

LOCHCARRON Curaig Lochcarron, Strathcarron, IV54 8YD Tel: 01520-722390

LOCHGELLY Lochgelly Local Office Town House Hall Street Lochgelly, KY5 911 Tel: 01592-782614

LOCHGILPHEAD Dairiada House Lochnell Street, Lochgilphead, PA31 8ST Tel: 01546-604511

LOCHGOILHEAD The Register Office, Creiganiver Lochgoilhead, PA14 8AJ Tel: 01301-703222

LOCHHROOM Locality Office 29 Market Street, Ullapool, 1V26 2XE Tel: 01854-612426, Fax: 01854-612717

LOCHORE The Register Office, Rosewell Lochore by Lochgelly, KY5 SDA Tel: 01592-860237

LOCHRANZA Operating from Larnlash, , 01770-600338 Tel: 01770-600028

LOCKERBIE Town Hall High Street, Lockerbie, DG11 2ES Tel: 01576-204267/8

LOGIERAIT Operating from Pitlochry, , Tel: 01796-472409

LONGFORGAN 8 Norval Place Longforgan Dundee, DD2 5ER Tel: 01382-360283

LUNNASTING Vidlin Farm, Vidlin Shetland, 7E2 9QB Tel: 01806-577204

MALLAIG Golden Sands Morar, Mallaig Inverness-shire PH40 4PA Tel: 01687-462383

MAUCHLINE 2 The Cross, Mauchline Ayrshire KA5 5DA Tel: 01290-550231, Fax: 01290-551991

MAUD County Offices, Maud Aberdeenshire AB4 SND Tel: 01771-613667

MAYBOLE Council Office 64 High Street, Maybole, KAI 713Z Tel: 01655-882124

MELROSE Public Library \Iarket Square, Meirose, T06 9PN Tel: 01896-823114

MEY Operating from Thurso, , Tel: 01847-892786, Fax: 01847-894611

MID + SOUTH YELL Schoolhouse, Ulsia Yell, ZE2 98D Tel: 01957-722260

MILNATHORT Rowallan' 21 Church Street, Milnathort, KY13 7XE Tel: 01577-862536

MOCHRUM Granite House 85 Main Street, Fort William, DG8 9HR Tel: 01988-700265

MOFFAT Town Hall High Street., Moffat, DG10 9HF Tel: 01683-220536

MONTROSE . 51 John Street, Montrose Angus DD10 8LZ Tel: 01674-672351

MORVERN Dungrianach, Morvern by Oban PA34 5XW Tel: 01961-421662

MOTHER WELL & WISHAW Civic Centre Windmillhill Street, Motherwell, ML1 1TW Tel: 01698-302222

MUCKHART + GLENDEVON Operating from Alloa, , Tel: 01259-723850

MUIRKIRK 33 Main Street, Muirkirk, KA18 39R Tel: 01290-661227

NAIRN The Court House, Nairn, IV12 4AU Tel: 01667-458510

NESTING Laxfirth Brettabister, Lerwick Shetland ZE2 9PR Tel: 01595-694737

NETHYBRIDGE Operating from Grantown-on-Spey, , Tel: 01479-872539

NEW ABBEY 1 Ingleston View New Abbey Dumfries, DG2 8BZ Tel: 01387-850343

NEW CUMNOCK Town Hall The Castle, New Cumnock, KA18 4AN Tel: / Fax: 01290-338214

NEW KILPATRICK Council Office 38 Roman Road, Bearsden, G61 2SH Tel: 0141-942-2352/3

NEW MI LN S Operating from Galston, , Tel: 01563-820218/9

NEWBURGH Tayside Institute High Street, Newburgh, KY4 6DA Tel: 01337-840917

NEWPORT-ON-TAY Blyth Hall Blyth Street, Newport On Tay, DD6 8BJ Tel: 01382-542839

NEWTON STEWART AREA The Old Town Hall 79 Victoria Street, Newton Stewart, DG8 6NL Tel: 01671-404187

NORTH BER WICK 2 Quality Street, North Berwick, EH39 4HW Tel: 01620-893957

NORTH RONALDSAY Waterhouse, North Ronaldsay Orkney KW17 2BE Tel: 01857-633263

NORTH UIST Fairview' Lochmaddy, North Uist, HS6 5AW Tel: 01876-500239

NORTH YELL Breckon, Cullivoe Yell, ZE2 9DD Tel: 01957-744244

NORTHMAVEN Uradell, Eshaness Shetland ZEZ 9RS Tel: 01806-503362

OBAN Council Office Albany Street, Oban, PA34 4AR Tel: 01631-562137

OLD CUMNOCK Council Office Millbank 14 Lugar Street., Cummock, KA18 1AB Tel: 01290-420666, Fax: 01290-426164

OLD KILPATRICK 57 Kilbowie Road, Clydebank, G81 1BL Tel: 0141-952-1330

OLD MELORUM Gordon Cottage Urquhart Road, Oldmeldrum, AB51 0EX Tel: 01651-873028, Fax: 01651-872060

ORPHIR The Bu, Orphir Kirkwall, KW17 2RD Tel: 01856-811319

PAISLEY Registration Ornce Cotton Street, Paisley, PA1 1BU Tel: 0141-889-1030

PAPA STOUR North House Papa Stout, Lerwick Shetland ZE2 9PW Tel: 01595-873238

PAPA WESTRAY Backaskaill, Papa Westray Kirkwall, KW17 2BU Tel: 01857-644221

PEEBLES Chambers Institute High Street., Peebles, EH45 8AF Tel: 01721-720123

PENICUIK & GLENCORSE 33 High Street, Penicuik, EH26 8HS Tel: 01963-672281

PERTH Rose Terrace, Perth, PH1 5HA Tel: 01738-632486, Fax: 01738-444133

PERTH Rose Terrace, Perth, PH1 5HA Tel: 01738-632486, Fax: 01738-444133

PETERCULTER Lilydale 102 North Deeside Road, Peterculter, AB1 0QB Tel: 01224-732648/9

PETERHEAD County Offices 88 King Street, Peterhead, AB42 6UH Tel: 01779-472761/2, Fax: 01779-476435

PITLOCHRY District Area Office 21 Atholl Road, Pitlochry, PH16 5BX Tel: 01796-472409

POLMONT + MUIRAVONSIDE Council Offices Redding Road Brightons Falkirk, FK2 0HG Tel: 01324-712745

PORT GLASGOW Scarlow Street., Port Glasgow, PA14 5EY Tel: 01475-742140

PORTREE Registrars Office King's House The Green Portree, IV51 9BS Tel: 01478-613277, Fax: 01478-613277

PORTSOY 2 Main Street, Portsoy Banffshire AB45 2RT Tel: 01261-843843

PRESTONPANS Aldhammer House High Street, Prestonpans, EH32 9SE Tel: 01875-810232

PRESTWICK 2 The Cross, Prestwick, KA9 1AJ Tel: 01292-671666

QUEENSFERRY Council Office 53 High Street, South Queensferry, EH30 9HN Tel: 0131-331-1590

RAASAY Operating from Portee, , Tel: 01478-613217, Fax: 01478-613277

RANNOCH + FOSS Bridgend Cottages, Kinloch-rannoch Pitlochry, PH16 5PX Tel: 01882-632359

RATHO Operating from India Buildings, Ratho, Tel: 0131-220-0349, Fax: 0131-2200351

RENFREW Town Hall, Renfrew, PA4 8PF Tel: 0141-886-3589

ROSNEATH Willowbury Clynder by Helensburgh, G84 0QQ Tel: 01436-831212, Fax: 01436-831212

ROSSKEEN Invergordon Service Point 62 High St, Invergordon, IV18 0DH Tel: 01349-853139

ROUSAY + EGILSAY Braehead Rousay, Kirkwall, KW17 2PT Tel: 01856-821222

RUTHERGLEN Town Hall Buildings King Street, Rutherglen, G73 1BD Tel: 0141-647-1072

SALTCOATS 45 ARoadrossan Road, Saltcoats, KA21 5BS Tel: 01294-463312/604868

SANDAY 2 Lettan, Sanday Kirkwall KWI7 2BP Tel: 01857-600280

SANDNESS 13 Melby, Sandness Shetland ZE2 9PL Tel: 01595-870257

SANDSTING + AITHSTING Modesty, West Burrafirth Aithsting ZE2 9NT Tel: 01595-809428

SANDWICK Yeldabreck, Sandwick Stromness KWI6 3LP Tel: 01856-841596

SANDWICK+CUNNINGSBUR Pytaslee Leebitton, Sandwick Shetland ZE2 9HP Tel: 01950-431367

SANQUHAR Council Offices 100 High Street, Sanquhar, DG4 6DZ Tel: 01659-50347

SAUCHEN Fresta Cottage 6 Main Street, Sauchen, AB51 7JP Tel: 01330-833254

SCOURIE 12 Park Terrace, Scourie by Lairg IV27 4TD Tel: 01971-502425

SELKIRK Municipal Buildings High Street, Selkirk, TD7 4JX Tel: 01750-23104

SHAPINSAY Girnigoe, Shapinsay Orkney KWI7 2EB Tel: 01856-711256

SHIELDAIG The Register Office, Baramore Shieldaig Strathcarron IV54 8XN Tel: 01520-755296

SHOTTS Council Ornee 106 Station Road, Shells, ML7 8BH Tel: 01501-823349

SKENE & ECHT 25 Glebe Land Kirkion Of Skene, Westhill Aberdeenshire AB32 6XX Tel: 01224-743371

SLAMANNAN Operating from Falkirk, , Tel: 01324-506580

SMALL ISLES Kildonan House, Isle Of Eigg PH42 4RL Tel: 01687-482446

SOUTH COWAL Copeswood Auchenlochan High Rd, Tighnabruaich, PA21 2BE Tel: 01700-811601

SOUTH LOCHS 7 Kershader, South Lochs Isle Of Lewis PA86 9QA Tel: 01851-880339

SOUTH RONALDSAY West Cara Grimness South Ronaldsay, KWI7 2TH Tel: 01856-831509

ST ANDREWS Area Office St Man's Place, St Andrews, KY16 9UY Tel: 01334-412525

STIRLING Municipal Buildings Corn Exchange Road, Stirling, FK8 2HU Tel: 01786-432343

STONEHAVEN Viewrnount Arduthie Road, Stonehaven, AB39 2DQ Tel: 01569-762001-EXT:-8360

STORNOWAY Town Hall 2 Cromwell Street, Stornoway, HS1 2BW Tel: 01851-709438

STRACHUR Memorial Hall, Strachur Argyll PA27 8DG Tel: 01369-860316

STRANRAER AREA 23 Lewis Street, Stranraer, DG9 7AB Tel: 01776-702151-Ext-254

STRATHAVEN R Bank Of Scot Blds 36 Common Green, Strathaven, ML10 6AF Tel: 01357-520316

STRATHDON Old Engine House Candacraie Nursery Garden, Strathdon, AB36 8XT Tel: 01975-651226

STRATHENDRICK District Office 32 Buchanan St., Balfron, G63 0TR Tel: 01360-440315

STRATHY Hillside Portskerra Melvich Thurso, KWI4 7YL Tel: 01641-531231

STROMNESS 5 Whitehouse Lane, Stromness Orkney KW16 3EY Tel: 01856-850854

STRONSAY Strynie Stronsay Kirkwall, KWI7 2AR Tel: 01857-616239

STRQNTIAN Easgadail Longrigg Road, Strontian Acharacle Argyll PH36 4HY Tel: 01967-402037

TAIN Operating from Rosskeen, , Tel: 01862-853139

TARBAT The Bungalow Chaplehill Portmahomack Portmathom Tain, IV20 1XJ Tel: 01862-871328

TARBERT Argyll House School Road, Tarbert, PA29 6UJ Tel: 01880-820374

TARRADALE Service Point Office Seaforth Road, Muir Of Ord, IV6 7TA Tel: 01463-870201

TARVES Post Office Udny, Ellon Aberdeenshire AB4 I 0PQ Tel: 01651-842253

TAYINLOAN Bridge House, Tayinloan Tarbert, PA29 6XG Tel: 01583-441239

TAYPORT Burgh Chambers, Tayport, DD6 9JY Tel: 01382-552544

THORNHILL 15 Dalgarnock Road, Thornhill Dumfriesshire DG3 4JW Tel: 01848-330108

THURSO District Office Davidson's Lane, Thurso, KW14 7AF Tel: 01847-892786, Fax: 01847-894611

TINGWALL 20 Meadowfleld Road Scalloway Lerwick Shetland ZEI 0UT Tel: 01595-880732

TOBERMORY Council Offices Breadalbane Street, Tobennory, PA75 6PX Tel: 01688-302051

TOMINTOUL Jubilee Cottage 51 Main Street, Tomintoul, AB37 9HA Tel: 01807-580207

TONGUE The Kyle Centre, Tongue Lairg, IV27 4XB Tel: 01847-601330

TORPHINS Willowbank, Kincardine O' NeilI, AB34 5AX Tel: 01339-884308

TRANENT 8 Civic Square, Tranent, EH33 1LH Tel: 01875-610278

TROON Municipal Buildings 8 South Beach, Troon, KA10 6EF Tel: 01292-313555, Fax: 01292-318009

TURRIFF Towie House Manse Road, Turiff, AB53 7AY Tel: 01888-562427, Fax: 01888-568559

TYREE The Register Office, Crossapol Isle Of Tyree PA77 6UP Tel: 01879-220349

UIG(LEWIS) 10 Valtos Uig Lewis, PA86 9HR Tel: 01851-672213

UIG(SKYE)(INVERNESS) 3 Ellishadder Staffin Portree, IV51 9JE Tel: 01410-562303

UNST New Noose, Ballsound Unst, ZE2 9DX Tel: 01957-711348

UPHALL 99 East Main Street, Broxburn, EH52 5JA Tel: 01506-775500, Fax: 01506-775505

VALE OF LEVEN 77 Bank Street, Alexandria, G83 0LE, Fax: 01389-752413

WALLS Victoria Cottage, Walls Lerwick Shetland ZE2 9PD Tel: 01595-809384

WANLOCKHEAD Operating from Sanquhar, , Tel: 01659-74287

WEST CALDER 1 East End, West Calder, EH55 8AB Tel: 01506-871763

WEST FIFE The Health Centre Chapel St High Valleyfield, Dunferrnline, KY12 8SJ Tel: 01383-880682

WEST KILBRIDE Kirktonhall 1 Glen Road, West Kilbride, KA23 9BL Tel: / Fax: 01294-823569

WEST LINTON Council Office, West Linton, EH46 7ED Tel: 01968-660267

WESTERN ARDNAMURCHAN Post Office, Kilchoan Acharacle, PH36 4LL Tel: 01972-510209

WESTRAY Myrtle Cottage, Pierowall Westray Orkney KW1 2DH Tel: 01857-677278

WHALSAY Conamore Brough, Whalsay Shetland ZE2 9AL Tel: 01806-566544

WHALSAY-SKERRIES Fairview, East Isle Skerries Lerwick ZE2 9AS Tel: 01806-515224

WHITBURN 5 East Main Street, Whitburn, EH47 0RA Tel: 01501-678000, Fax: 01506-678026

WHITENESS & WEISDALE Vista, Whiteness Shetland ZE2 9LJ Tel: 01595-830332

WHITHORN AREA 75 George Street, Whithom, DG8 8NU Tel: 01988-500458

WICK Town Hall Bridge Street, Wick, KW1 4AN Tel: 01955-605713

WIGTOWN AREA Council Sub-office County Buildings, Wigtown, DG8 9HR Tel: 01988-402624

Clothing the bones - future access to minor records
Rita Freedman - York City Archivist

York Art Gallery & Archives by kind permission of Rita Freedman

I would like to write about the possibilities of making minor series or even one-off records more generally available to the public. The present time is an exciting period of progress for genealogy, made possible by the increasing availability of technology and the ultimate international access via the Internet. There are numerous sources of unlisted name which can make a very valuable contribution both to family research and also to local and national history. Whilst there are many published guides to record office and library collections which include specific types of records, it is simply not worth while searching these records on the off-chance that there might be something relevant. Therefore the next stage is to actually list and index their contents and to make those lists generally available. The result will be that for the first time, there is a serious possibility of using them without wasting an inordinate amount of time.

Records which can be described as "difficult" rather than "minor" are Poor Law (Board of Guardians) records. If they exist (and many have been lost), they provide a rich source of names and family circumstances. In York, there is a massive series of records. The actual workhouse registers (which do have indexes), do not start until near the end of the 19th century. However the "application and report books" in which people make claims for relief, start in 1837 and continue until 1880 and the weekly outdoor relief lists cover the period and continue (with a few gaps) until 1930. The latter however, do not give nearly as much information as the application series.
None of these records have their own indexes and the volumes are set out under parishes. People appear under the parish responsible for them, which is often not the same parish as their given address, because the claimant has been put in lodgings (or in the workhouse). This means that researchers looking through a parish in which they think their ancestors lived may well not pick them up. There are two or even three books for each year and searching is interminable. The records are severely under-used and not generally found rewarding.

Much progress has been made by one of our volunteers in the last three years. She started inputting for 1837, did the entries for 1845 and then commenced filling in. There are now over 5,500 entries on a database (1837-41, 1845). Clustering around the 1841 Census period, this work is invaluable. The application and report books mainly give name; age or date of birth; address; parish (responsible for claimant); occupation (about half the entries filled in - includes "bastard", "deceased" etc. under this heading); reason (only one quarter inputted); marital status; children's names and ages. Not all remarks about the circumstances of the claimants have been entered, but a substantial part of each entry is entered. I hope that another volunteer will take on the task of carrying on the database. I originally thought that only names and ages of each claimant should be entered in order to speed up the work. But not only is this not really interesting enough to keep a volunteer committed, the results of a virtually full listing are startling. The realisation that there are many studies to be made and many conclusions to be drawn is immediately apparent from scrolling up and down each column in turn, rearranged into alphabetical or numeric order. I did not expect to find a substantial body of workhouse residents in these records. I assumed that the volumes only contained people who had not yet entered the system and have not yet ascertained whether workhouse inmates are listed (in their scattered parishes) all the way through the series. None of this was apparent until the information was entered on a database which revealed, (when the address column was put into alphabetical order) that there were about 100 people citing the institution as their current or former address.

Occupations include a plethora of washerwomen and charwomen, pages of labourers and the 55 comb makers claiming relief reflect the downturn in their business as does the 50 or so glove makers. Surprisingly there are even a handful of gravediggers, strange in view of the inevitability of the trade. To be a tailor was on the borderline of poverty at that time and even 18 schoolmasters and schoolmistresses could not keep the wolf from the door in spite of their intellect.
Under the "Reason" heading, the sad litany of desertion, funeral costs (many claimants are listed as "deceased"), infirmity, illness, lameness, lunacy, "low earnings" and unemployed - is the odd sharp comment "has 2 pigs/does she need relief?" (a note in 1840 on the claim of Mary Robinson, aged 34 charwoman). Another claimant,

Elizabeth Bell whose occupation in 1839 is given as keeping a cow, is subject to no such censure. Unfortunate "John Steels bastard" from Goole and aged 14 is dismissed with "blind in one eye/end relief". John and Julian *BPickerdike of Clancy's Buildings, Walmgate are summarily dismissed as "Bad characters/to workhouse or no relief" and on another occasion as "both rogues". (Incidentally the database picked up the entries as "Pickerdike" and "Bickerdike" and so made correction possible).

What is interesting is the number of people whose address is given as another town or village. There are many from York or nearby, but more distant towns and cities feature; Bradford, Barnsley, Cleckheaton, Darlington, Doncaster, Hull (over 100 with street names often given), Leeds (similar to Hull), Liverpool (c 70 names), London and Sheffield. Some seemed to fare better than York citizens as in the case of James Fallon a weaver of Idle near Bradford, aged 34, who along with his wife and three children obtained a "Loan to buy loom/Doctor's bill" in 1841. Other incomers included Ann Watson, aged 50, a former well attendant from Harrogate, who was widowed with a son and a daughter aged 14 and 15 and sought relief in 1845; an oyster seller from Leeds; two stocking weavers from Mansfield; weavers from Knaresborough; and surprisingly, William Henry Kilby "ex Leeds/Father Governor City Gaol" and his young family in 1838. A pawnbroker's pledge book covering seventeen months of 1777-78, can certainly be classed as a minor record. However the book contains nearly 11,000 entries, giving name, address (street), items pawned, amounts and redemption date, (if redeemed). The shop was in the centre of the city. Another volunteer has transcribed and indexed nearly 3,500 entries and written a fascinating article called "The Wormeaten Waistcoat", (as the entry appears!). She has analysed the entries, described the background to pawnbroking and followed the history of the business and its owners. *(York Historian no 14:1997 - Alison Backhouse "The Wormeaten Waistcoat - the Pledge Book and Owners of a Pawnbroker's Business". Yorkshire Architectural and York Archaeological Society).*

Some idea of the central role the pawnbroker played in society is conveyed in the typical case of Mary Prince of Thursday Market who went to the shop some thirty five times during the five months which the index covers. A variety of his, hers and a boy's garments were pawned, including "1 pr of old leather breeches" pawned on 22nd December 1777 for 6_d and redeemed on the 24th, Christmas Eve. Her husband therefore, was able to look decent, if not smart for any Christmas activities which he might be expected to participate in. Mary also brought in household items, a coarse sheet, a checked apron and the pawnbroker included a pewter dish and a Bible within the household category. Under jewellery, the pawnbroker counted in and out on several occasions, a pair of plaited buckles which Mary proffered. These surprisingly fetched only 8d, the same amount as a shirt.

The article notes that the annual race meetings in York brought new visitors to the shop from a much wider area, but on the whole the clientele was not only local, but essentially regular. A few poor souls such as Mary Birch, pocketing 1/- for a muslin apron, (never collected) would nip in with one or two small goods and return (or not) to redeem them and were never seen again. But most were impelled, reluctantly, to be regular customers to a greater or lesser degree.

Another volunteer has agreed to continue with indexing the book and it will be interesting to see how many new names there are. As far as I know, the above source is unique for the eighteenth century, although I find it hard to believe that the pawnbroking business, so widespread nationally, has left so meagre a record.

A small cache of debtor prisoner's account books (52 for named debtors) came to light in York Guildhall a few years ago and details of about half of the cases have been linked up with the local newspapers. Covering the period 1795-1854, there survive the daily account books of men and women in York and Yorkshire who struggled and finally sunk under the weight of adverse financial circumstances, (although some appear to have been rogues). They represent many of the trades and indeed, the professional services. There is a sprinkling of publicans, including the landlord of the well known Starr Inn, Stonegate (John James Anderson). He was already bankrupt, owing £2,500, when he took over the Starr and borrowed money on pretence of ownership of the property. He received six months when brought before the courts for fraud in 1841.

There is even an account book of a veterinary surgeon, John Stephenson, apparently working in the North Riding; the business records of an apothecary; and also a schoolmaster, John Rippon, of Blake Street in York. He writes "This book contains entry of Scholars etc. to 1826 I have not seen since I was sold up, they were lost or taken away". The account book containing scholars names (mainly surnames only), commences in 1795 and must contain over 1,000 names (but many will be repeated as they are entered when paying their fees). No work yet has been done on indexing this record. Rippon was discharged by the Court of Insolvent Debtors in 1830. The problem of imprisonment for debt, where the poor, but honest debtors could languish in gaol for long periods had come to a head by 1813, when there was " a crowd of insolvent debtors multiplying so fast that the prisons are hardly capacious enough to hold them". A permanent court " for the relief of insolvent debtors" was set up with provincial branches to eradicate corrupt administration and so that those eligible might be discharged more speedily. In York, the court met in the Guildhall and at the Castle at irregular intervals. The account books would have been shown to the court when the debtor made a full disclosure of his estate.

Criminal records are not indexed in any way as yet. However on the fringes of less salubrious activities there exists a wonderful list of 141 prostitutes for 1843, with their residence in York, age and place where they belong. A number have come in from other towns and villages. The presence of the army base in York would no doubt have influenced their choice of town. A second list records the houses of ill fame, proprietress and number of prostitutes residing there. (It is known that the Chief Constable of around that time owned a brothel, but as the list was prepared by the police, it would no doubt have seemed prudent to omit this fact). Mrs Morgantroy of St Andrew's

Churchyard is noted on this list as having no girls. However Maria Midgley, aged 20 from Acomb is on the other list as residing in St Andrew's Churchyard and no other house of ill fame appears to exist in that hallowed precinct. Yet a third list of 1842 simply states bluntly "A Return of the Persons in York who have no visible means of Gaining an Honest Livelihood" and notes 58 persons, residence, trade and remarks, (either " Associate of Thieves" or "Poacher" - the latter description sounds an odd note in the City York). All these lists will go on a database fairly soon.

At York City Archives the key to unlocking these records has been the use of volunteers. The staff cannot give time to such detailed work however enthusiastic they might be. Although there is an element of monotony in the data entering, manipulating the results can point to several lines of interesting research. Hopefully, as in the case of the pawnbrokers book, the volunteer will go on to write about the results. Our databases (in "ACCESS") have developed in a rather ad hoc fashion over the years. But linking by name and reference is possible to form the basis of an overall names list. A local historian, Professor Philip Stell has a database of some 600,000 entries (nearly all pre 1550) from a variety of sources in the three York record offices *(telephone York Minster Archives for details - 01904/611118),*

and Brian Jones, from Bradford is working on our 1741 City of York poll book having already published indexes to the 1774 poll book, 1723 oath of allegience, and the extant parts of the 1801, 1811 and 1821 censuses for York (three parishes only).*(For details telephone 01274/638792).*

Not all subjects lend themselves to a database. Several of our volunteers are expanding letters, diaries, miscellaneous solicitors' collections etc. on a word processor, (or typescript which can be scanned in). Word processing packages allow word searches, very helpful as some expanded lists have now grown to one hundred or more pages. The process of putting lists directly onto the Internet is in its early stages and hopefully linked databases will become available. Progress should come in leaps and bounds (millennium bug permitting!). The delight of discovering an ancestor last heard of in London, living in York; or bringing in a silver watch carefully listed by the pawnbroker with its manufacturer and serial number; or the pathos of family circumstances leading to a claim to the Board of Guardians for relief, should become more frequent as an increasing body of information is brought into the light of day by the means of long and hard graft and the indispensible computer.

YORK CITY ARCHIVES
ART GALLERY BUILDING, EXHIBITION SQUARE, YORK YOI 7EW
TEL 01904/551878 FAX 01904/551877 www.york.gov.uk/learning/libraries/archives/index.html

---

LANCASHIRE RECORD OFFICE
Now including the Lancashire Local Studies Collection

TIMES OF OPENING
Mon: 0900-1700; Tue: 0900-2030; Wed: 0900-1700; Thu: 0900-1700; Fri: 0900-1600

Please note that the Public Search Room is closed for the first full week of each calendar month.

The Office will be closed during the following weeks in 2000:

3 - 7 JANUARY
7 - 11 FEBRUARY
6 - 10 MARCH
3 - 7 APRIL
1 - 5 MAY
5 - 9 JUNE
3 - 7 JULY
7 - 11 AUGUST
4 - 8 SEPTEMBER
2 - 6 OCTOBER
6 - 10 NOVEMBER

The Office is also closed on Bank Holidays, the Tuesday after the Easter and Spring Bank Holidays and for an extra day at Christmas

If you have any queries, please phone the Record Office on 01772 263039.

The Central Index of Decrees Absolute

The Central Index is a record of all decrees absolute granted by Courts in England and Wales since 1858. It is kept and controlled by the Principal Registry of the Family Division and anyone is entitled to apply for a search to be carried out, and to receive a certificate of the result and any decree absolute traced. People may wish to apply for a search of the Central Index for a number of reasons, the most common of which are:-

• To obtain a copy of their decree absolute, if they have lost the original

• To find out whether they have been divorced, following a long separation from their spouse

• To find out whether a friend or relative has been divorced to help trace a family tree or other historical reasons

To apply for a search complete a Form D440 and send it to the address below. Form D440 can be obtained from the above address or you can attend in person at the office. Staff can only search a three year period whilst you wait, if the years to be searched are prior to 1981. In such cases, the result of the remainder of the period requested to be searched, will be sent to you within 10 working days.

There is a fee of £20.00 to pay for each ten year period or part thereof searched. For example, if you wish a thirteen year period to be searched (ie 1958 to 1970 inclusive), the fee would be £40.00. The fee can be paid by cash, cheque or postal order. Cheques and postal orders should be made payable to "HM Paymaster General" or "HMPG". Cash should not be sent through the post. You may be exempt from paying a fee if you are receiving Income Support or Family Credit. You will need to fill in a form entitled "Application for Fees Exemption" and supply the Court with a copy of your benefit book, if you wish to apply for exemption. The Form "Application for Fees Exemption" is available from the above address. The questions on Form D440 are straightforward and you should try to answer as many as you can. The court requires the full names of both parties to the marriage, ensure that the names are spelt correctly. Incorrect spelling may result in an unsuccessful search! Once completed the form should be sent to the Principal Registry together with the fee or the Form "Application for Fees Exemption" and a copy of any benefit book, if appropriate.

If all is in order, a certificate of the result of the search will be sent within 10 working days. If there is anything wrong with the application, it will be returned with a letter giving reasons for its return. In the case of a successful search where the divorce proceedings are found to have taken place in the Principal Registry of the Family Division, you will also receive with your certificate a "sealed" or sealed and certified copy" of the decree absolute. If the divorce took place other than at this Court, you will be notified of the name of the court and the case number, and we will write to that court, on your behalf, to instruct them to send you a copy of the decree absolute. A sealed and certified copy will only be supplied if you state in your application that the decree absolute is required in connection with matters outside of England and Wales. If there is no trace of a decree having been granted, you will be issued with a "no trace" certificate.

The Principal Registry does not keep any documents in relation to cases issued in other Courts, it simply holds a record of any decrees absolute granted by them. If, therefore, you require a copy of a decree absolute and already know the case number and name of the court which granted the decree, you should write direct to that court for a copy thereof and for any other information you may require.

General Information

If you are submitting your documents by post please address them to:
Principal Registry of the Family Division
First Avenue House, 42 - 49 High Holborn
London, WC1V 6NP
Tel: 0171 936 6000 (Switchboard)
Opening Hours: 1 0.00.a.m. to 4.30pm Monday to Friday
The offices are closed on public and certain other holidays.
The main entrance to the building is on High Holborn

Public Record Office
Ruskin Avenue, Kew, Richmond, Surrey, TW9 4DU
Tel: 0181 876 3444 Fax:, WWW: http://www.pro.gov.uk
Family Records Centre
1 Myddleton Street, London, EC1R 1UW Tel: 0181 392 5300 Fax: 0181 392 5307
WWW: http://www.open.gov.uk/pro/prohome.htm
BT Archives
3rd Floor, Holborn Telephone Exchange, 268 270 High
Holborn, London, WC1V 7EE Tel: 0171 492 8792
Fax: 0171 242 1967, Email: archives@bt.com
WWW: http://www.bt.com/archives
British Coal Corporation Records & Archive
Provincial House, Solly Street, Sheffield, South Yorkshire,
S11 7BS Tel: 0114 279 9643 Fax: 0114 279 9641
**Department of Special Collections & Western
Manuscripts**
Bodleian Library Oxford, Oxfordshire, OX1 3BG
Tel: 01865 277152 Fax: 01865 277187
National Monuments Record Centre
Great Western Village, Kemble Drive, Swindon, Wiltshire,
SN2 2GZ Tel: 01793 414600 Fax: 01793 414606, Email:
info@rchme.gov.uk, WWW: www.english heritage.org.uk
Barnardo's Film & Photographic Archive
Barnardo's, Tanner Lane, Barkingside, Ilford, Essex, IG6
1QG Tel: 0181 550 8822 Fax: 0181 550 0429
Lloyds Register of Shipping
100 Leadenhall St, London, EC3A 3BP Tel: 0171 423 2475
Personal callers only. Reserarch cannot be undertaken
Registry of Shipping & Seamen
PO Box 165, St Agnes Road, Cardiff, Glamorgan, CF4 5FU
Tel: 029 2076 8227
Institution of Electrical Engineer
Savoy Place, London, WC2R 0BL Tel: 0171 240 1871
Fax: 0171 240 7735, WWW: http://www.iee.org.uk
Institution of Mechanical Engineers
1 Birdcage Walk, London, SW1H 9JJ Tel: 0171 222 7899
Institution of Mining & Metallurgy
Hallam Court, 77 Hallam Street, London, W1N 5LR, **The
Institution of Civil Engineers**
Great George St,London, SW1P 3AA Tel: 0171 222 7722
Deed Poll Records
Rm E16 Royal Courts of Justice,Strand, London, WC2A 2LL
Commonwealth War Graves Commission
2 Marlow Road, Maidenhead, Berkshire, SL6 7DX
Tel: 01628 634221 Fax: 01628 771208,
Email: cwgc@dial.pipex.com, WWW: www.cwgc.org
Documents Register
Quality House, Quality Court, Chancery Lane, London,
WC2A 1HP Tel: 0171 242 1198 Fax: 0171 831 3550,
Email: nra@hmc.gov.uk
Probate Service
Probate Sub Registry, Duncombe Place, York, YO1 7EA
Tel: 01904 624210
Institute of Heraldic & Genealogical Studies
79 82 Northgate, Canterbury, Kent, CT1 1BA Tel: 01227
768664 Fax: 01227 765617, Email: ihgs@ihgs.ac.uk
WWW: www.ihgs.ac.uk

Specialist Records & Indexes

British Library Newspaper Library
Colindale Avenue, London, NW9 5HE Tel: 020 7412 7353
Fax: 020 7412 7379, Email: newspaper@bl.uk
WWW: http://www.bl.uk/collections/newspaper/
British Waterways Archives & The Waterways Trust
Llanthony Warehouse, Gloucester Docks, Gloucester, GL1
2EJ Tel: 01452 318041 Fax: 01452 318076
Email: archivist@dial.pipex.com
WWW: http://www.britishwaterways.org.uk
British Deaf History Society
288 Bedfont Lane, Feltham, Middlesex, TW14 9NU

The Documentary Photography Archive
7 Towncroft Lane, Bolton BL1 5EW Tel: 01204 840439
Traceline
Smedley Hydro, Trafalgar Road, Birkdale, Southport,
Lancashire, PR8 2HH Tel: 01704 569824
Fax: 01704 563354, Email: traceline@ons.gov.uk
Bank of England Archive
Archive Section HO SV, The Bank of England,
Threadneedle Street, London, EC2R 8AH
Tel: 0171 601 5096 Fax: 0171 601 4356
Email: archive@bankofengland.co.uk
British Library Western Manuscripts Collections
96 Euston Road, London, NW1 2DB Tel: 0171 412 7513
Fax: 0171 412 7511, Email: mss@bl.uk
WWW: http://www.bl.uk/
British Red Cross Museum & Archives
9 Grosvenor Crescent, London, SW1X 7EJ Tel: 0171 201
5153 Fax: 0171 235 0876, Email: enquiry@redcross.org.uk,
WWW: www.redcross.org.uk
British Empire & Commonwealth Museum
Clock Tower Yard, Temple Meads, Bristol, BS1 6QH Tel:
0117 925 4980 Fax: 0117 925 4983
Email: staff@empiremuseum.demon.co.uk
Manorial Documents Register
Quality House, Quality Court, Chancery Lane, London,
WC2A 1HP Tel: 0171 242 1198 Fax: 0171 831 3550
Email: nra@hmc.gov.uk
Archives of Royal College of Surgeons of England
35 43 Lincoln's Inn Fields, London, WC2A 3PN
Tel: 0171 405 3474 ext 3011 Fax: 0171 405 4438
Email: archives@rseng.ac.uk
Museum of the Royal Pharmaceutical Society
1 Lambeth High Street, London, SE1 7JN Tel: 0171 735 9141 ext 354
Email: museum@rpsgb.org.uk, WWW: http://www.rpsgb.org.uk
Research fee charged to non members of the Society (Genealogical Enquiries)
**National Army Museum Department of Archives
(Photographs, Film & Sound)**
Royal Hospital Road, London, SW3 4HT Tel: 0171 730 0717
Ext 2222 Fax: 0171 823 6573, Email: nam@enterprise.net,
WWW: http://www.failte.co./nam/
National Register of Archives
Quality House, Quality Court, Chancery Lane, London,
WC2A 1HP Tel: 0171 242 1198 Fax: 0171 831 3550, Email:
nra@hmc.gov.uk, WWW: http://www.hmc.gov.uk
Post Office Archives
Freeling Hse Mount Pleasant Complex, Farringdon Road
(Phoenix Place Entrance), London, EC1A 1BB Tel: 0171
239 2570 Fax: 0171 239 2576, Email:
Catherine.Orton@postoffice.co.uk
Principal Registry of the Family Division
First Avenue House, 42 49 High Holborn, London, WC1V
6NP Tel: 0171 936 7000
Society of Genealogists - Library
14 Charterhouse Buildings, Goswell Road, London, EC1M
7BA Tel: 020 7251 8799 Tel: 020 7250 0291, Fax: 020 7250
1800, Email: info@sog.org.uk sales@sog.org.uk
WWW: http://www.sog.org.uk

Department of Manuscripts & Special Collections
Hallward Library, Nottingham University, University Park, Nottingham,
NG7 2RD Tel: 0115 951 4565 Fax: 0115 951848
Lambeth Palace Library
Lambeth Palace Road, London, SE1 7JU Tel: 0171 898 1400
Fax: 0171 928 7932
Library of the Religious Society of Friends (Quakers)
Friends House, 173-177 Euston Rd, London, NW1 2BJ
Tel: 0207 663 1135 Tel: 0207 663 1001
Email: library@quaker.org.uk WWW: http://www.quaker.org.uk

Coal Miners Records
Cannock Record Centre, Old Mid Cannock (Closed) Colliery Site, Rumer Hill Road, Cannock WS11 3EX Tel: 01543 570666 Fax: 01543 578168

College of Arms
Queen Victoria St, London, EC4V 4BT Tel: 0171 248 2762 Fax: 0171 248 6448
WWW: http://www.kwtelecom.com/heraldry/collarms

House of Lords Record Office
House of Lords, London, SW1A 0PW Tel: 0171 219 3074 Fax: 0171 219 2570
Email: hlro@parliament.uk WWW: www.parliament.uk

Huguenot Library
University College, Gower Street, London, WC1E 6BT
Tel: 0171 380 7094 Fax:, Email: a.massilk@ucl.ac.uk,
WWW: http://www.ucl.ac.uk/library/hugenot.htm

Images of England Project
National Monuments Records Centre Kemble Drive,
Swindon SN2 2GZ Tel: 01793 414779
WWW: www.imagesof england.org.uk

Imperial War Museum Department of Documents
Department of Documents, Lambeth Road, London, SE1
6HZ Tel: 0171 416 5221/2/3/6 Fax: 0171 416 5374
Email: docs@iwm.org.uk, WWW: http://www.iwm.org.uk

John Rylands University Library Special Collections
150 Deansgate, Manchester, M3 3EH Tel: 0161 834 5343
Fax: 0161 834 5343, Email: j.r.hodgson@man.ac.uk
WWW: http://rylibweb.man.ac.uk

Liverpool University Special Collections & Archives
University of Liverpool Library, PO Box 123, Liverpool,
L69 3DA Tel: 0151 794 2696 Fax: 0151 794 2081
Email: archives@liv.ac.uk WWW: http://www.lsca.lib.liv.ac.uk

National Inventory of War Memorials
Imperial War Museum, Lambeth Road, London, SE1 6HZ
Tel: 0171 416 5353 Tel: 0171 416 5281, Fax: 0171 416 5379,
Email: memorials@iwm.org.uk, WWW: www.iwm.org.uk

National Museum of Labour History
103 Princess Street, Manchester, M1 6DD Tel: 0161 228
7212 Fax: 0161 237 5965, Email: info
nmlh@pop3.poptel.org.uk

England
Bedfordshire
Bedfordshire & Luton Archives & Record Service
County Hall, Cauldwell Street, Bedford MK42 9AP
Tel: 01234 228833 Tel: 01234 228777, Fax: 01234 228854,
Email: archive@csd.bedfordshire.gov.uk
WWW: http://www.bedfordshire.gov.uk

Berkshire
Berkshire Record Office
Shinfield Park, Reading, RG2 9XD Tel: 0118 901 5132 Fax: 0118 901 5131, Email: arch@reading.gov.uk 1st April 2000 Moves to: Yeomanry House, Castle Hill, Reading, Berkshire

Rural History Centre
University of Reading, Whiteknights PO Box 229, Reading,
RG6 6AG Tel: 0118 931 8664 Fax: 0118 975 1264
Email: jis.creasey@reading.ac.uk
WWW: http://www.reading.ac.uk/fnstits/im/

The Museum of Berkshire Aviation Trust
6 Richmond Rd, Caversham Heights, Reading RG7 7PP Tel: 0118 947 3924

Buckinghamshire
Buckinghamshire Record Office
County Offices, Walton Street, Aylesbury HP20 1UU
Tel: 01296 382587 Fax: 01296 382274
Email: archives@buckscc.gov.uk, WWW: www.buckscc.gov.uk/leisure/archives

Cambridgeshire
Cambridgeshire Archive Service (Huntingdon)
Grammar School Walk, Huntingdon PE18 6LF Tel: 01480
375842 Fax: 01480 459563 Email: county.records.hunts@camcnty.gov
WWW: www.camcnty.gov.uk

Cambridgeshire Archives Service County Record Office
Shire Hall, Castle Hill, Cambridge CB3 0AP Tel: 01223 717281 Fax: 01223 717201,
Email: County.Records.Cambridge@camcnty.gov.uk

National Railway Museum
Leeman Road, York, YO26 4XJ Tel: 01904 621261 Fax:
01904 6111112, Email: nrm@nmsi.ac.uk, WWW:
www.nmsi.ac.uk/nrm/

National Sound Archive
British Library Building, 96 Euston Road, London, NW1
2DB Tel: 0171 412 7440 Fax: 0171 412 7441
Email:Reader/admissions@bl.uk WWW:http://www.portico.bl.uk

Northern Region Film & Television Archive
Blandford House, Blandford Square, Newcastle upon Tyne,
Tyne & Wear, NE1 4JA Tel: 0191 232 6789 ext 456
Fax: 0191 230 2614, Email: chris.galloway@dial.pipex.com

Royal Commission on Historical Manuscripts
Quality House, Quality Court, Chancery Lane, London,
WC2A 1HP Tel: 0171 242 1198 Fax: 0171 831 3550
Email: nra@hmc.gov.uk, WWW: http://www.hmc.gov.uk

Royal Marines Museum Archive
Eastney, Southsea, Hampshire, PO4 9PX Tel: 01705 819385
Exts 244/239 Fax: 01705 838420
Email: matthewlittle@royalmarinesmuseum.co.uk

Tennyson Research Centre
Central Library, Free School Lane, Lincoln, Lincolnshire,
LN2 1EZ Tel: 01522 552862 Fax: 01522 552858
Email: sue.gates@lincolnshire.gov.uk

The Royal College of Physicians
11 St Andrews Place, London, NW1 4LE

United Reformed Church History Society
Westminster College, Madingley Road, Cambridge, CB3
0AA Tel: 01223 741084

Wellcome Institute for the History of Medicine
183 Euston Road, London, NW1 2BE Tel: 0171 611 8582
Fax: 0171 611 8369, Email: library@wellcome.ac.uk,
WWW: www.wellcome.ac.uk/library
Library catalogue is available through the internet:telnet://wihm.ucl.ac.uk

Centre for Regional Studies
Anglia Polytechnic University, East Road, Cambridge,
Cambridgeshire, CB1 1PT Tel: 01223 363271 ext 2030 Fax:
01223 352973, Email: t.kirby@anglia.ac.uk

Cheshire
Cheshire & Chester Archives & Local Studies
Duke Street, Chester CH1 1RL Tel: 01244 602574
Fax: 01244 603812 Email: recordoffice@cheshire.gov.uk,
WWW: http://www.u net.com/cheshire/recoff/home.htm
From 2000 management of all original archives will be transferred to Cheshire & Chester Archives & Local Studies, Duke Street, Chester. All archives must be consulted there. However, secondary sources such as Census, Cemetery Registers, Parish Records etc & Local History Library will be available at the Town Hall

Chester Archives
Town Hall Chester CH1 2HJ Tel: 01244 402110 Fax: 01244
312243, Email: j.halewood@chestercc.gov.uk
http://www.chestercc.gov.uk/htmls/heritage.htm
From 2000 management of all original archives will be transferred to Cheshire & Chester Archives & Local Studies, Duke Street, Chester. All archives must be consulted there. However, secondary sources such as Census, Cemetery Registers, Parish Records etc & Local History Library will be available at the Town Hall

Port Sunlight Heritage Centre
5 Greendale R d, Port Sunlight, L62 4XE Tel: 0151 6446466

Stockport Archive Service
Central Library, Wellington Road South, Stockport,
Cheshire, SK1 3RS Tel: 0161 474 4530 Fax: 0161 474 7750,
Email: stockport.cenlibrary@dial.pipex.com

Tameside Local Studies Library
Stalybridge Library, Trinity Street, Stalybridge, Cheshire,
SK15 2BN Tel: 0161 338 2708 Tel: 0161 338 3831, Fax:
0161 303 8289, Email: tamelocal@dial.pipex.com
WWW: http://www.tameside.gov.uk

The Boat Museum
South Pier Rd, Ellesmere Port CH65 4FW Tel: 0151 355 5017
Fax: 0151 355 4079 Info on some boatmen & boatwomen
Cheshire
Trafford Local Studies Centre
Public Library, Tatton Road, Sale, M33 1YH Tel: 0161 912
3013 Fax: 0161 912 3019
City & County Bristol
Bristol Record Office
"B" Bond Warehouse, Smeaton Road, Bristol, BS1 6XN Tel:
0117 922 5692 Fax: 0117 922 4236
Cleveland
Teesside Archives
Exchange House, 6 Marton Road, Middlesbrough,
Cleveland, TS1 1DB Tel: 01642 248321 Fax: 01642 248391
Cornwall
Cornish Studies Library
2 4 Clinton Road, Redruth, Cornwall, TR15 2QE
Tel: 01209 216760 Fax: 01209 210283
Cornwall Record Office
County Hall Truro, Cornwall, TRI 3AY Tel: 01872 323127
Fax: 01872 270340, Email: cro@ceo.cornwall.gov.uk
WWW: http://www.cornwall.gov.uk
County Durham
Centre For Local Studies
The Library, Crown Street, Darlington, County Durham,
DL1 1ND Tel: 01325 349630 Fax: 01325 381556
Email: library@dbc lib.demon.co.uk
County Record Office
County Hall Durham, County Durham, DH1 5UL Tel: 0191
383 3474 Tel: 0191 383 3253, Fax: 0191 383 4500, Email:
record.office@durham.gov.uk, WWW:
http:www.durham.gov.uk/CL/LIBS/REC.HTM
Durham University Library Archives & Special Collections
Palace Green Section, Palace Green, Durham, DH1 3RN
Tel: 0191 374 3032
Durham University Library Archives & Special Collections
5 The College, Durham, County Durham, DH1 3EQ Tel:
0191 374 3610
Cumbria
Cumbria Archive Service
County Offices, Kendal, Cumbria, LA9 4RQ Tel: 01539 814430
Cumbria Archive Service
Cumbria Record Office The Castle, Carlisle CA3 8UR
Tel: 01228 607285 Tel: 01228 607284 Fax: 01228 607274
Cumbria Record Office
County Offices, Stricklandgate, Kendal, Cumbria, LA9 4RQ
Tel: 01539 773540 Fax: 01539 773439
Cumbria Record Office
140 Duke St, Barrow in Furness, Cumbria, LA14 1XW Tel:
01229 894363 Fax: 01229 894371
Cumbria Record Office & Local Studies Library (Whitehaven)
Scotch Street, Whitehaven, Cumbria, CA28 7BJ Tel: 01946
852920 Fax: 01946 852919
Email: whitehaven.record.office@cumbriacc.gov.uk
Derbyshire
Chesterfield Local Studies Dept
Chesterfield Library, New Beetwell Street, Chesterfield,
Derbyshire, S40 1QN Tel: 01246 209292 Fax: 01246 209304
Derby Local Studies Library inc Derby City
25b Irongate, Derby DE1 3GL Tel: 01332 255393
Derby Museum & Art Gallery
The Strand, Derby, Derbyshire, DE1 1BS
Tel: 01332 716659 Fax: 01332 716670
Derbyshire Record Office
County Hall Matlock, Derbyshire, DE4 3AG
Tel: 01629 580000 ext 35207 Fax: 01629 57611
Erewash Museum
The Museum, High Street, Ilkeston, Derbyshire, DE7 5JA
Tel: 0115 907 1141 Fax:, WWW: www.erewash.gov.uk

Devon
Beaford Photograph Archive
Barnstaple, Devon, EX32 7EJ Tel: 01271 288611
Devon Record Office
Castle Street, Exeter, Devon, EX4 3PU Tel: 01392 384253
Fax: 01392 384256, Email: devrec@devon cc.gov.uk,
WWW: http://www.devon cc.gov.uk/dro/homepage.html
North Devon Record Office
Tuly Street, Barnstaple, Devon, EX31 1EL Tel: 01271
388607 Tel: 01271 388608
WWW: www.devon cc.gov.uk/dro/homepage
Plymouth & West Devon Record Office
3 Clare Place, Coxside, Plymouth, Devon, PL4 0JW Tel:
01752 305940 Fax: 01752 223939
Email: pwdro@plymouth.gov.uk
Dorset
Dorset Archives Service
9 Bridport Road, Dorchester DT1 1RP Tel: 01305 250550
Fax: 01305 257184 Email: dcc_archives@dorset cc.gov.uk,
WWW: http://www.dorset cc.gov.uk
Poole Local Studies Collection
Dolphin Centre Poole BH15 1QE Tel: 01202 671496 Fax: 01202 670253 Email:
poolereflib@hotmail.com, WWW: www.poole.gov.uk
East Yorkshire
East Yorkshire Archives & Record Service
County Hall, Champney Road, Beverley, East Yorkshire,
HU17 9BA Tel: 01482 885007 Fax: 01482 885463
 Email: archives.service@east riding of yorkshire.gov.uk
Essex
Chelmsford Library
PO Box 882, Market Road, Chelmsford, Essex, CM1 1LH
Tel: 01245 492758 Fax: 01245 492536
Email: answers.direct@essexcc.gov.uk, WWW: www.essexcc.gov.uk
Essex Record Office
Wharf Road, Chelmsford, CM2 6YT Tel: 01245 244644
Fax: 01245 244655 Email: ero.search@essexcc.gov.uk,
WWW: http://www.essexcc.gov.uk
Essex Record Office, Colchester & NE Essex Branch
Stanwell House, Stanwell Street, Colchester, Essex, CO2
7DL Tel: 01206 572099 Fax: 01206 574541
 WWW: www.essexcc.gov.uk
Essex Record Office, Southend Branch
Central Library, Victoria Avenue, Southend on Sea, Essex,
SS2 6EX Tel: 01702 464278 Fax: 01702 464253
L B of Barking & Dagenham Local History Studies
Valence Library & Museum, Becontree Avenue, Dagenham RM8 3HT
Tel: 020 8592 6537 Tel: 020 822 75294, Fax: 020 822 75297
Email: fm019@viscount.org.uk
WWW: http://www.earl.org.uk/partners/barking/index.html
L B of Barking & Dagenham Local History Studies
Central Library, Barking, Dagenham, Essex, IG11 7NB Tel:
0181 517 8666
L B of Havering Reference Library
Reference Library, St Edward's Way, Romford, Essex, RM1
3AR Tel: 01708 772393 Tel: 01708 772394
Fax: 01708 772391 Email: romfordlib2@rmplc.co.uk
Redbridge Library
Central Library, Clements Road, Ilford, Essex, IG1 1EA
Tel: 0187 478 9421 Fax: 0181 553 3299
 Email: Local.Studies@redbridge.gov.uk
Gloucestershire
Gloucester Library, Brunswick Rd, Gloucester GL1 1HT
Tel: 01452 426979 Fax: 01452 521468, Email:
clams@gloscc.gov.uk WWW: http://www.gloscc.gov.uk
Gloucestershire Record Office
Clarence Row, Alvin St, Gloucester, GL1 3DW Tel: 01452
425295 Fax: 01452 426378, Email: records@gloscc.gov.uk,
WWW: www.gloscc.gov.uk/pubserv/gcc/corpserv/archives

Greater Manchester
Bury Archive Service
1st Floor, Derby Hall Annexe, Edwin Street off Crompton Street, Bury BL9 0AS Tel: 0161 797 6697
Email: info@bury.gov.uk, WWW: www.bury.gov.uk
Greater Manchester County Record Office
56 Marshall St, New Cross, Manchester M4 5FU
Tel: 0161 832 5284 Fax: 0161 839 3808
Email: archives@gmcro.u net.com, WWW: http://www.gmcro.u net.com
Hampshire
Hampshire Record Office
Sussex St, Winchester, Hampshire, SO23 8TH Tel: 01962 846154 Fax: 01962 878681, Email: sadeax@hants.gov.uk, WWW: http://www.hants.gov.uk/record office
Portsmouth City Libraries
Central Library, Guildhall Square, Portsmouth, Hampshire, PO1 2DX Tel: 01705 819311 X232 (Bookings) Tel: 01705 819311 X234 (Enquiries), Fax: 01705 839855
Email: reference.library@portsmouthcc.gov.uk
Portsmouth City Museum & Record Office
Museum Road, Portsmouth, Hampshire, PO1 2LJ Tel: 01705 827261 Fax: 01705 875276
Email: portmus@compuserve.com
Portsmouth Roman Catholic Diocesan Archives
St Edmund House, Edinburgh Road, Portsmouth PO1 3QA
Royal Marines Museum Archive
Eastney, Southsea, Hampshire, PO4 9PX Tel: 01705 819385 Exts 244/239 Fax: 01705 838420, Email: matthewlittle@royalmarinesmuseum.co.uk
Southampton City Archives
Civic Centre, Southampton, Hampshire, SO14 7LW Tel: 023 8083 2205 Fax: 023 8033 6305, Email: localstudies@southampton.gov.uk
WWW: www.southampton.gov.uk
Southampton City Record Office
Civic Centre, Southampton SO14 7LY Tel: 01703 832251
Fax: 01703 832156 Email: city.archives@southampton.gov.uk
Winchester Local Studies Library
Winchester Library, Jewry Street, WinchesterSO23 8RX
Tel: 01962 841408 Email: clceloc@hants.gov.uk
Herefordshire
Hereford Cathedral Archives & Library
5 College Cloisters, Cathedral Close, Hereford, HR1 2NG Tel: 01432 359880 Fax: 01432 355929 Email: archives@herefordcathedral.co.uk
Herefordshire Record Office
The Old Barracks, Harold Street, Hereford HR1 2QX
Tel: 01432 265441 Fax: 01432 370248 WWW: http://www.open.gov.uk/hereford/pages/hfd rec2.htm
Ashwell Education Services
Merchant Taylor's Centre, Ashwell, Baldock, SG7 5LY
Tel: 01462 742385 Fax: 01462 743024 Email: aes@ashwell education services.co.uk
WWW: www.ashwell education services.co.uk
Hertfordshire
Hertfordshire Archives & Local Studies
County Hall, Pegs Lane, Hertford SG13 8EJ Tel: 01992 555105 Fax: 01992 555113, Email: hals@hertscc.gov.uk, WWW: http://hertslib.hertscc.gov.uk, Hertfordshire Archives & Local Studies is comprised of the former Herts County Record Office & Herts Local Studies Library
Hull
Hull City Archives
79 Lowgate, Kingston upon Hull, HU1 1HN Tel: 01482 615102 Tel: 01482 615110, Fax: 01482 613051
WWW: www.hullcc.gov.uk
Local History Unit
Hull College, Park Street Centre, Hull, HU2 8RR Tel: 01482 598952
Huntingdonshire
Cambridgeshire Archive Service (Huntingdon)
County Record Office, Grammar School Walk, Huntingdon PE18 6LF Tel: 01480 375842 Fax: 01480 459563
Email: county.records.hunts@camcnty.gov WWW: www.camcnty.gov.uk

Isle of Wight
Isle of Wight Record Office
26 Hillside, NewportPO30 2EB Tel: 01983 823820/1 Fax: 01983 823820
Kent
Bethlem Royal Hospital
Archives & Museum, Monks Orchard Road, Beckenham, Kent, BR3 3BX Tel: 0181 776 4307 Fax: 0181 776 4045
Bexley Local Studies Centre
Hall Place, Bourne Rd, Bexley DA5 1PQ Tel: 01322 526574
Fax: 01322 522921, Email: bexlibs@dial.pipex.com
Canterbury City & Cathedral Archives
The Precincts, Canterbury, Kent, CT1 2EH Tel: 01227 865330 Fax: 01227865222
Canterbury Library & local Studies Collection
18 High Street, Canterbury, Kent, CT1 2JF Tel: 01227 463608 Fax: 01227 768338
Centre for Kentish Studies
Sessions House, County Hall, Maidstone, Kent, ME141XQ
Tel: 01622 694363 Fax: 01622 694379
Email: archives@kent.gov.uk
East Kent Archives Centre
Enterprise Business Park, Honeywood Road, Whitfield, Dover, Kent, CT16 3EH Tel: 01304 829306 Fax: 01304 829306 (Thanet, Dover, Shepway, Kent Councils)
Hythe Archives
Council Offices, Oaklands, Stade Street, Hythe, Kent Tel: 01303 266152 Fax: 01303 262912, Email: admin@hythe kent.demon.co.uk, WWW: www.hythe kent.demon.co.uk
Institute of Heraldic & Genealogical Studies
79 82 Northgate, Canterbury, Kent, CT1 1BA Tel: 01227 768664 Fax: 01227 765617, Email: ihgs@ihgs.ac.uk, WWW: www.ihgs.ac.uk
L B of Bromley Local Studies Library
Central Library, High Street, Bromley, Kent, BR1 1EX Tel: 020 8460 9955 Fax: 020 8313 9975
Margate Library Local History Collection
Cecil Square, Margate, Kent, CT9 1RE Tel: 01843 223626 Fax: 01843 293015
Medway Archives & Local Studies Centre
Civic Centre, Strood, Rochester, Kent, ME2 4AU Tel: 01634 332714 Fax: 01634 297060, Email: archives@medway.gov.uklocal.studies@medway.gov.uk
Pembroke Lodge Family History Centre & Museum
4 Station Approach, Birchington on Sea CT7 9RD Tel: 01843 841649
Ramsgate Library Local Strudies Collection & Thanet Branch Archives
Ramsgate Library, Guildford Lawn, Ramsgate, Kent, CT11 9AY Tel: 01843 593532 (Archives at this library moved to the New East Kent Archives Centre a Local Studies Collection remains)
Sevenoaks Archives Office
Central Library, Buckhurst Lane, Sevenoaks, TN13 1LQ
Tel: 01732 453118 Tel: 01732 452384, Fax: 01732 742682
Sevenoaks Branch Archive Office
Central Library, Buckhurst Lane, Sevenoaks TN13 1LQ
Tel: 01732 452384 Tel: 01732 453118, Fax: 01732 742682
Lancashire
Blackburn Central Library
Town Hall Street, Blackburn BB2 1AG Tel: 01254 587930
Fax: 01254 690539
Bolton Archive & Local Studies Service
Civic Centre, Le Mans Cres, Bolton BL1 1SE Tel: 01204 332185
Lancashire Record Office & Local Studies Library
Bow Lane, Preston PR1 2RE Tel: 01772 264021 Tel: 01772 264020, Fax: 01772 264149 Email: lancsrecord@treas.lancscc.gov.uk locstuds@lb.lancs.cc.gov.uk WWW:
http://www.lancashire.com/lcc/edu/ro/index.htm
http://www.earl.org.uk/earl/members/lancashire
(The Lancashire Local Studies Collection is now housed here)

North West Sound Archive
Old Steward's Office, Clitheroe Castle, Clitheroe, BB7 1AZ
Tel: 01200 427897 Fax: 01200 427897 WWW: www.nw soundarchive.co.uk
Oldham Local Studies & Archives
Local Studies Library, 84 Union Street, Oldham, OL1 1DN
Tel: 0161 911 4654 Fax: 0161 911 4654
Email: archives@oldham.gov.uklocalstudies@oldham.gov.uk, WWW:
http://www.oldham.gov.uk/archiveshttp://www.oldham.gov.uk/local studies
The Documentary Photography Archive
c/o 7 Towncroft Lane, Bolton BL1 5EW Tel: 01204 840439
Rochdale Local Studies Library
The Esplanade, Rochdale, OL16 4TY Tel: 1706 864915
Salford City Archives
Salford Archives Centre, 658/662 Liverpool Rd, Irlam,
Manchester, M44 5AD Tel: 0161775 5643
Salford Local History Library
Peel House, Salford, M5 4WU Tel: 0161 736 2649
Tameside Local Studies Library
Stalybridge Library, Trinity Street, Stalybridge, Cheshire,
SK15 2BN Tel: 0161 338 2708 Tel: 0161 338 3831, Fax:
0161 303 8289, Email: tamelocal@dial.pipex.com, WWW:
http://www.tameside.gov.uk
Wigan Heritage Service
Town Hall, Leigh, Wigan, Greater Manchester, WN7 2DY
Tel: 01942 404431 Fax: 01942 404425, Email:
heritage@wiganmbc.gov.uk, WWW:
http://www.wiganmbc.gov.uk

London

Bethlem Royal Hospital
Archives & Museum, Monks Orchard Road, Beckenham,
Kent, BR3 3BX Tel: 0181 776 4307 Fax: 0181 776 4045,
British Library Oriental & India Collections
197 Blackfriars Rd, London, SE1 8NG Tel: 0171 412 7873 Fax: 0171 412 7641,
Email: oioc enquiries@bl.uk WWW: http://www.bl.uk/collections/oriental
Centre for Metropolitan History
Institute of Historical Research, Senate House, Malet St
London, WC1E 7HU Tel: 0171 862 8790
Fax: 0171 862 8793 Email: myhill@sas.ac.uk,
WWW: www.ihrinfo.ac.uk/cmh/cmh.main.html
Chelsea Public Library
Old Town Hall, King's Road, London, SW3 5EZ Tel: 0171
352 6056 Tel: 0171 361 4158, Fax: 0171 351 1294 (Local Studies
Collection on Royal Borough of Kensington & Chelsea south of Fulham Road)
City of Westminster Archives Centre
10 St Ann's Street, London, SW1P 2DE Tel: 0171 641 5180
Fax: 0171 641 5179, WWW: www.westminster.gov.uk
Corporation of London Records Office
PO Box 270, Guildhall, London, EC2P 2EJ Tel: 0171 332 1251 Fax: 0171 710 8682,
Email: clro@ms.corpoflondon.gov.uk
Dr Williams's Library
14 Gordon Square, London, WC1H 0AG Tel: 0171387 3727
Fax: 0171 388 1142 Email: 101340.2541@compuserve.com
Ealing Local History Library
Central Library, 103 Broadway Centre, Ealing, London, W5 5JY Tel: 0181 567 3656
ext 37 Fax: 0181 840 2351 Email: localhistory@hotmail.com
Galton Institute
19 Northfields Prospect, London, SW18 1PE
Guildhall Library, Manuscripts Section
Aldermanbury, London, EC2P 2EJ Tel: 0171 332 1863 Fax: 0171 600 3384 Email:
manuscripts.guildhall@ms.corpoflondon.gov.uk,
WWW: http://www.ihr.sas.ac.uk/ihr/ghmnu.html
Hackney Archives Department
43 De Beauvoir Road, Hackney, London, N1 5SQ Tel: 0171 241
2886 Fax: 0171 241 6688 Email: archives@hackney.gov.uk WWW:
http://www.hackney.gov.uk/archives/first1.htm
Hillingdon Heritage Service
Central Library, High Street, Uxbridge, London, UB8 1HD
Tel: 01895 250702 Fax: 01895 811164
Email: ccotton@lbhill.gov.uk WWW: http://www.hillingdon.gov.uk

Leicestershire,
Melton Mowbray Library
Wilton Road, Melton Mowbray, Leicestershire, LE13 0UJ
Tel: 01664 560161 Fax: 01664 410199
Record Office for Leicestershire, Leicester & Rutland
Long Street, Wigston Magna, Leicestershire, LE18 2AH
Tel: 0116 257 1080 Fax: 0116 257 1120
Lincolnshire
Lincolnshire Archives
St Rumbold Street, Lincoln LN2 5AB Tel: 01522 526204
Fax: 01522 530047, Email: archives@lincolnshire.gov.uk,
WWW: http://www.lincs archives.com
Lincolnshire County Library, Local Studies Section
Lincoln Central Library, Free School Lane, Lincoln,
Lincolnshire, LN1 1EZ Tel: 01522 510800 Fax: 01522
575011, Email: lincoln.library@dial.pipex.com, WWW:
www.lincolnshire.gov.uk/library/services/family.htm
N E Lincolnshire
North East Lincolnshire Archives
Town Hall, Town Hall Square, Grimsby DN31 1HX
Tel: 01472 323585 Fax: 01472 323582
Liverpool
Liverpool Record Office & Local History Department
Central Library, William Brown Street, Liverpool, L3 8EW
Tel: 0151 233 5817 Fax: 0151 207 1342
Email: recoffice.central,library@liverpool.gov.uk
WWW: http://www.liverpool.gov.uk

Hounslow Library & Local Studies
24 Treaty Centre, High Street, Hounslow, London, TW3 1ES Tel: 0181 570 0622
Islington History Collection
Central Library, 2 Fieldway Cres, Islington, London, N5 1PF
Tel: 0171 619 6931 Fax: 0171 619 6939
Email: is.loc.hist.@dial.pipex.com WWW: http://www.islington.gov.uk
L B of Hammersmith & Fulham Archives & Local History Centre
The Lilla Huset, 191 Talgarth Road, London, W6 8BJ
Tel: 0208 741 5159 Fax: 0208 741 4882
WWW: http://www.lbhf.gov.uk
Local Studies Collection for Chiswick & Brentford
Chiswick Public Library, Dukes Avenue, Chiswick, London,
W4 2AB Tel: 0181 994 5295 Fax: 0181 995 0016 (Restricted
opening hours for local history room: please telephone before visiting)
L B of Barking & Dagenham Local History Studies
Valence Library & Museum, Becontree Ave, Dagenham, RM8 3HT Tel: 020
8592 6537 Tel: 020 822 75294 Fax: 020 822 75297 Email: fm019@viscount.org.uk
WWW: http://www.earl.org.uk/partners/barking/index.html
L B of Barking & Dagenham Local History Studies
Valence Library & Museum, Becontree Ave Dagenham,
Essex, RM8 3HT Tel: 020 8592 6537 Tel: 020 822 75294
Fax: 020 822 7529 Email: fm019@viscount.org.uk
WWW: http://www.earl.org.uk/partners/barking/index.html
L B of Barking & Dagenham Local History Studies
Central Library, Barking, Dagenham, Essex, IG11 7NB
Tel: 0181 517 8666
L B of Bromley Local Studies Library
Central Library, High Street, Bromley, Kent, BR1 1EX
Tel: 020 8460 9955 Fax: 020 8313 9975
L B of Barnet, Archives & Local Studies Department
Hendon Library, The Burroughs, Hendon, London NW4 3BQ
Tel: 0181 359 2876 Fax: 0181 359 2885
Email: hendon.library@barnet.gov.uk
L B of Camden Local Studies & Archive Centre
Holborn Library, 32-38 Theobalds Road, London, WC1X
8PA Tel: 020 7974 6342 Fax: 020 7974 6284
L B of Croydon Library & Archives Service Central Library,
Katharine Street, Croydon, CR9 1ET Tel: 0181 760 5400
Fax: 0181 253 1004
Email: localstudies@library.croydon.gov.uk
WWW: http://www.croydon.gov.uk/cr libls.htm

L B of Enfield Archives & Local History Unit
Southgate Town Hall, Green Lanes, Palmers Green, London, N13 4XD Tel: 0181 379 2724

L B of Greenwich Local History Library
Woodlands, 90 Mycenae Road, Blackheath, London, SE3 7SE Tel: 0181 858 4631 Fax: 0181 293 4721

L B of Haringey Archives Department
Bruce Castle Museum, Lordship Lane, Tottenham, London, N17 8NU Tel: 0181 808 8772 Fax: 0181 808 4118

L B of Havering Reference Library
Reference Library, St Edward's Way, Romford, Essex, RM1 3AR Tel: 01708 772393 Tel: 01708 772394, Fax: 01708 772391, Email: romfordlib2@rmplc.co.uk

L B of Lambeth Archives Department
Minet Library, 52 Knatchbull Road, Lambeth, London, SE5 9QY Tel: 0171 926 6076 Fax: 0171 936 6080

L B of Lewisham Local Studies Centre
Lewisham Library, 199 201 High Sreet, Lewisham, London, Kent, SE13 6LG Tel: 0181 297 0682 Fax: 0181 297 1169, Email: local.studies@lewisham.gov.uk, WWW: http://www.lewisham.gov.uk

L B of Newham Archives & Local Studies Library
Stratford Library, Water Lane, London, E15 4NJ Tel: 0181 557 8856 Fax: 0181 503 1525

L B of Newham Local Studies Library
Stratford Library, Water Lane, London, E15 4NJ Tel: 0181 557 8856 Fax: 0181 503 1525

L B of Wandsworth Local History Collection
Battersea Library, 265 Lavender Hill, London, SW11 1JB Tel: 020 8871 7753 Fax: 0171 978 4376

London Metropolitan Archives
40 Northampton Road, London, EC1R 0HB Tel: 020 7332 3820 Tel: Mini com 020 7278 8703, Fax: 020 7833 9136, Email: ask.lma@ms.corpoflondon.gov.uk, WWW: www.cityoflondon.gov.uk

Metropolitan Police Archives
Wellington House, 67-73 Buckingham Gate London SW1E 6BE

Museum in Docklands Project Library & Archive
Unit C14, Poplar Business Park, 10 Prestons Road, London, E14 9RL Tel: 0171 515 1162 Fax: 0171 538 0209, Email: docklands@museum london.org.uk

Royal Borough of Kensington & Chelsea
Central Library, Phillimore Walk, Kensington, London, W8 7RX Tel: 0171 361 3036 Tel: 0171 361 3007 WWW: www.rbkc.gov.uk

Royal London Hospital Archives & Museum
Royal London Hospital, Newark Whitechapel, London, E1 1BB Tel: 0171 377 7608 Fax: 0171 377 7413 Email: r.j.evans@mds.qmw.ac.uk

Southwark Local Studies Library
211 Borough High Street, Southwark, London, SE1 1JA Tel: 0207 403 3507 Fax: 0207 403 8633

St Bartholomew's Hospital Archives & Museum
Archives & Museum, West Smithfield, London, EC1A 7BE Tel: 0171 601 8152

The Archives of Worshipful Company of Brewers
Brewers' Hall, Aldermanbury Square, London, EC2V 7HR Tel: 0171 606 1301

Tower Hamlets Local History Library & Archives
Bancroft Library, 277 Bancroft Road, London, E1 4DQ Tel: 0181 980 4366 ext 129 Fax: 0181 983 4510

Twickenham Local Studies Library
Garfield Rd, Twickenham, TW1 3JS Tel: 0181 891 7271

Waltham Forest Archives
Vestry House Museum, Vestry Road, Walthamstow, London, E17 9NH Tel: 020 8509 1917 Email: Vestry.House@al.lbwf.gov.uk
WWW: http://.www.lbwf.gov.uk/vestry/vestry.htm

Westminster Abbey Library & Muniment Room
Westminster Abbey London, SW1P 3PA Tel: 0171 222 5152 Ext 228 Fax: 0171 226 6391, Email: library@westminster abbey.org, WWW: www.westminster abbey.org

Westminster Diocesan Archives
16a Abingdon Road, Kensington, London, W8 6AF Tel: 0171 938 3580

Manchester
Local Studies Unit Manchester Central Library
St Peter's Square, Manchester, M2 5PD Tel: 0161 234 1980

Merseyside
Crosby Library (South Sefton Local History Unit)
Crosby Road North, Waterloo, Liverpool, Merseyside, L22 0LQ Tel: 0151 928 6401 Fax: 0151 934 5770 (The Local History Units serve Sefton Borough Council area. The South Sefton Unit covers Bootle, Crosby, Maghull & other communities south of the River Alt. The North Sefton Unit covers Southport, Formby)

Huyton Central Library
Huyton Library, Civic Way, Huyton, Knowsley, L36 9GD Tel: 0151 443 3738 Fax: 0151 443 3739 Email: http://www.history.knowsley.gov.uk
WWW:http://www.knowsley.gov.uk/leisure/libraries/huyton/index.html

Merseyside Maritime Museum Archives & Library
Albert Dock, Liverpool, Merseyside, L3 4AQ Tel: 0151 478 4613 Fax: 0151 478 777

Southport Library (North Sefton Local History Unit)
Lord Street, Southport, Merseyside, PR8 1DJ Tel: 0151 934 2119 Fax: 0151 934 2115 (The Local History Units serve Sefton Borough Council area. The North Sefton Unit covers Southport, Formby. The South Sefton Unit covers Bootle, Crosby, Maghull & other communities south of the River)

St Helen's Local History & Archives Library
Central Library, Gamble Institute, Victoria Square, St Helens, Merseyside, WA10 1DY Tel: 01744 456952

Wirral Archives Service
Central Library, Borough Road, Birkenhead, Merseyside, CH41 2XB Tel: 0151 652 6106/7/8 Fax: 0151 653 7320

Middlesex
L B of Harrow Local History Collection
PO Box 4, Civic Centre Library, Station Rd,Harrow HA1 2UU Tel: 02084241055 Tel: 0208 421056 Fax: 01814241971

Norfolk
Kings Lynn Borough Archives
The Old Gaol House, Saturday Market Place, Kings Lynn, Norfolk, PE30 5DQ Tel: 01553 774297

Norfolk Record Office
Gildengate House, Anglia Square, Upper Green Lane, Norwich, Norfolk, NR3 1AX Tel: 01603 761349 Fax: 01603 761885, Email: norfrec.nro@norfolk.gov.uk, WWW: http://archives.norfolk.gov.uk

North Yorkshire
North Yorkshire County Record Office
County Hall, Northallerton DL7 8AF Tel: 01609 777585

Whitby Pictorial Archives Trust
Whitby Archives & Heritage Centre, 17/18 Grape Lane, Whitby, North Yorkshire, YO22 4BA Tel: 01947 600170 Email: whitby.archiv@zetnet.co.uk
WWW: http://www.users.zetnet.co.uk/whitby archives/

Yorkshire Film Archive
The University College of Ripon & York st John, College Rd, Ripon HG4 2QX Tel: 01765 602691 Fax: 01765 600516

Northamptonshire
Northampton Central Library
Abington Street, Northampton NN1 2BA Tel: 01604 462040 Fax: 01604 462055, WWW: http://www.northamptonshire.gov.uk

Northamptonshire Record Office
Wootton Hall Park, Northampton NN4 8BQ Tel: 01604 76129 Fax: 01604 767562 Email: archivist@nro.northamtonshire.gov.uk, WWW: http://www.nro.northamptonshire.gov.uk

Northumberland
Berwick upon Tweed Record Office
Council Offices, Wallace Green, Berwick Upon Tweed, Northumberland, TD15 1ED Tel: 01289 330044 Ext 230 Fax: 01289 330540, Email: lb@berwickc.demon.co.uk, WWW: www.swinhope.demon.co.uk/genuki/NBL/Northumberland RO/Berwick.html

Northumberland Archive Service
Morpeth Records Centre, The Kylins, Loansdean, Morpeth, Northumberland, NE61 2EQ Tel: 01670 504084 Fax: 01670 514815, WWW: http://www.swinhope.demon.co.uk/genuki/nbl/northumberlandro/

Nottinghamshire

Nottingham Central Library : Local Studies Centre
Angel Row, Nottingham, Nottinghamshire, NG1 6HP Tel: 0115 915 2873 Fax: 0115 915 2850, Email: localstudies@notlib.demon.co.uk, WWW: www.notlib.demon.co.uk

Nottingham R.C. Diocese Nottingham Diocesan Archives
Willson House, Derby St, Nottingham, Nottinghamshire, NG1 5AW Tel: 0115 953 9803

Nottinghamshire Archives
Castle Meadow Rd, Nottingham NG2 1AG Tel: 0115 950 4524 Admin Tel: 0115 958 1634 Enquiries Fax: 0115 941 3997

Southwell Minster Library
Trebeck Hall, Bishop's Dr, Southwell NG25 0JP Tel: 01636 812649

Oxfordshire

Centre for Oxfordshire Studies
Central Library, Westgate, Oxford, Oxfordshire, OX1 1DJ Tel: 01865 815749 Fax: 01865 810187 Email: enquiries@oxst.demon.co.uk, WWW: www.oxfordshire.gov.uk

Oxfordshire Archives
County Record Office County Hall, New Road, Oxford, Oxfordshire, OX1 1ND Tel: 01865 815203 Tel: 01865 810801, Fax: 01865 815429, Email: archives.occla@dial.pipex.com, WWW: http://www.oxfordshire.gov.uk

Rutland

Record Office for Leicestershire, Leicester & Rutland
Long Street, Wigston Magna, Leicestershire, LE18 2AH Tel: 0116 257 1080 Fax: 0116 257 1120

Shropshire

Ironbridge Gorge Museum, Library & Archives
The Wharfage, Ironbridge, Telford, TF8 7AW Tel: 01952 432141 Fax: 01952 432237

Shropshire Records & Research Centre
Castle Gates, Shrewsbury, Shropshire, SY1 2AQ Tel: 01743 255350 Fax: 01743 255355, Email: research@shropshire cc.gov.uk

Wrekin Local Studies Forum
Madeley Library, Russell Square, Telford, Shropshire, TF7 5BB Tel: 01952 586575 Fax:, Email: library@madeley.uk, WWW: www.madeley.org.uk

Somerset

Bath & North East Somerset Record Office
Guildhall, High St, Bath, Somerset, BA1 5AW Tel: 01225 477421 Fax: 01225 477439**Somerset Archive & Record Service Somerset RO**
Obridge Road, Taunton, Somerset, TA2 7PU Tel: 01823 337600 Appointments Tel: 01823 278805 Enquiries, Fax: 01823 325402, Email: Somerset_Archives@csi.com, WWW: http://www.somerset.gov.uk

The Jane Austen Centre
40 Gay Street, Bath, Somerset, BA1 2NT Tel: 01225 443000 Fax:, Email: info@janeausten.co.uk

South Yorkshire

Rotherham Archives & Local Studies
Central Library, Walker Place, Rotherham, South Yorkshire, S65 1JH Tel: 01709 823616 Fax: 01709 823650, Email: archives@rotherham.gov.uk, WWW: www.rotherha.gov.uk/pages/living/learning/islib/callib.htm

Barnsley Archives & Local Studies Department
Central Library, Shambles Street, Barnsley, South Yorkshire, S70 2JF Tel: 01226 773950 Tel: 01226 773938, Fax: 01226 773955, Email: Archives@Barnsley.ac.uklibrarian@barnsley.ac.uk, WWW: http://www.barnsley.ac.uk/sites/library

Sheffield Central Library
Surrey Street, Sheffield, South Yorkshire, S1 1XZ Tel: 0114 273 4711 Fax: 0114 273 5009, Email: sheffield.libraries@dial.pipex.com

Doncaster Archives Department
King Edward Road, Balby, Doncaster, DN4 0NA Tel: 01302 859811

Sheffield Archives
52 Shoreham Street, Sheffield, South Yorkshire, S1 4SP Tel: 0114 203 9395 Fax: 0114 203 9398, Email: sheffield.archives@dial.pipex.com, WWW: http://www.earl.org.uk/earl/members/sheffield/arch.htm

Staffordshire

Burton Archives
Burton Library, Riverside, High Street, Burton on Trent, Staffordshire, DE14 1AH Tel: 01283 239556 Fax: 01283 239571, Email: burton.library@staffordshire.gov.uk

Lichfield Record Office
Lichfield Library, The Friary, Lichfield, Staffordshire, WS13 6QG Tel: 01543 510720 Fax: 01543 510715, Email: lichfield.record.office@staffordshire.gov.uk, WWW: www.staffordshire.gov.uk/archives/

Staffordshire Record Office
Eastgate Street, Stafford, Staffordshire, ST16 2LZ Tel: 01785 278373 Fax: 01785 278384, Email: staffordshire.record.office@staffordshire.co.uk, WWW: www.staffordshire.gov.uk/archives

Staffordshire & Stoke on Trent Archive Service

Stoke on Trent City Archives
Hanley Library, Bethesda Street, Hanley, Stoke on Trent, Staffordshire, ST1 3RS Tel: 01782 238420 Fax: 01782 238499, Email: stoke.archives@stoke.gov.uk

Tamworth Library
Corporation Street, Tamworth, Staffordshire, B79 7DN Tel: 01827 475645 Fax: 01827 475658, Email: tamworth.library@staffordshire.gov.uk

William Salt Library
Eastgate Street, Stafford, Staffordshire, ST16 2LZ Tel: 01785 278372 Fax: 01785 278414, Email: william.salt.library@staffordshire.gov.uk, WWW: www.staffordshire.gov.uk/archives/saly.htm

Suffolk

Suffolk Record Office   Bury St Edmunds Branch
77 Raingate Street, Bury St Edmunds, Suffolk, IP33 2AR Tel: 01284 352352 Fax: 01284 352355, Email: bury.ro@libher.suffolkcc.gov.uk, WWW: http://www.suffolkcc.gov.uk/libraries_and_heritage/

Suffolk Record Office Ipswich Branch
Gatacre Road, Ipswich, Suffolk, IP1 2LQ Tel: 01473 584541 Fax: 01473 584533, Email: ipswich.ro@libher.suffolkcc.gov.uk, WWW: http://www.suffolkcc.gov.uk/libraries_and_heritage/

Suffolk Record Office Lowestoft Branch
Central Library, Clapham Road, Lowestoft, Suffolk, NR32 1DR Tel: 01502 405357 Fax: 01502 405350, Email: lowestoft.ro@libher.suffolkcc.gov.uk., WWW: http://www.suffolkcc.gov.uk/Libraries_and_heritage/

Suffolk Regiment Archives
Suffolk Record Office 77 Raingate Street, Bury St Edmunds, Suffolk, IP33 2AR Tel: 01284 352352 Fax: 01284 352355, Email: bury.ro@libher.suffolkcc.gov.uk, WWW: http://www.suffolkcc.gov.uk/libraries_and_heritage/

Surrey

Kingston Museum & Heritage Service
North Kingston Centre, Richmond Road, Kingston upon Thames, Surrey, KT2 5PE Tel: 0181 547 6738 Fax: 0181 547 6747, Email: king.mus@rbk.kingston.gov.uk

L B of Merton Local Studies Centre
Merton Civic Centre, London Road, Morden, Surrey, SM4 5DX Tel: 0181 545 3239 Fax: 0181 545 4037, Email: mertonlibs@compuserve.com

L B of Sutton Archives
Central Library, St Nicholas Way, Sutton, Surrey, SM1 1EA Tel: 0181 770 4747 Fax: 0181 770 4777, Email: archives@sutton.gov.uk, WWW: www.sutton.gov.uk

Surrey History Service
Surrey History Centre, 130 Goldsworth Road, Woking, Surrey, GU21 1ND Tel: 01483 594594 Fax: 01483 594595, Email: shc@surreycc.gov.uk, WWW: http://www.shs.surreycc.gov.uk

Sussex

East Sussex Record Office
The Maltings, Castle Precincts, Lewes, Sussex, BN7 1YT Tel: 01273 482349 Fax: 01273 482341

Tameside

Tameside Local Studies Library
Stalybridge Library, Trinity Street, Stalybridge, Cheshire, SK15 2BN Tel: 0161 338 2708 Tel: 0161 338 3831, Fax: 0161 303 8289 Email: tamelocal@dial.pipex.com WWW: http://www.tameside.gov.uk

Tyne & Wear
Local Studies Centre, Central Library, Northumberland Square, North Shields, NE3O 1QU Tel: 0191 200 5424

South Tyneside Library
Prince Georg Square, South Shields, Tyne & Wear, NE33 2PE Tel: 0191 427 1818 Ext 2135 Fax: 0191 455 8085 Email: reference.library@s tyneside mbc.gov.uk, WWW: www.s tyneside mbc.gov.uk

Central Library & Local Studies Department
Prince Consort Road, Gateshead, Tyne & Wear, NE8 4LN Tel: 0191 477 3478 Fax: 0191 477 7454, Email: Local@gateslib.demon.co.uk, WWW: http://ris.niaa.org.uk

Northumberland County Record Office
Melton Park, North Gosforth, Newcastle upon Tyne, NE3 5QX Tel: 0191 236 2680 Fax: 0191 217 0905, WWW: http://www.swinnhopc.demon.co.uk/genuki/NBL/

Newcastle City Library Local Studies Section
Princess Square, Newcastle upon Tyne, NE99 1DX Tel: 0191 261 0691

Tyne & Wear Archives Service
Blandford House, Blandford Square, Newcastle upon Tyne, Tyne & Wear, NE1 4JA Tel: 0191 232 6789 Fax: 0191 230 2614, Email: twas@dial.pipex.com, WWW: www.thenortheast.com/archives/

Warwickshire

Coventry City Archives
Mandela House, Bayley Lane, Coventry, West Midlands, CV1 5RG Tel: 01203 832418 Fax: 01203 832421, Email: coventryarchives@discover.co.uk

Modem Records Centre
University of Warwick Library Coventry, Warwickshire, CV4 7AL Tel: 01203 524219 from 1/4/2000 024 7652 4219 Fax: 01203 524211 from 1/4/2000 024 7657 2988, Email: archives@warwick.ac.uk, WWW: http://warwick.ac.uk/services/library/mrc/mrc.html

Shakespeare Birthplace Trust Records Office
Henley Street, Stratford upon Avon, Warwickshire, CV37 6QW Tel: 01789 201816 Tel: 01789 204016, Fax: 01789 296083, Email: records@shakespeare.org.uk, WWW: http://www.shakespeare.org.uk

Sutton Coldfield Library & Local Studies Centre
43 Lower Parade, Sutton Coldfield B72 1XX
Tel: 0121 354 2274 Tel: 0121 464 0164 Fax: 0121 464 0173

Warwick County Record Office
Priory Park, Cape Road, Warwick CV34 4JS
Tel: 01926 412735 Fax: 01926 412509
Email: recordoffiuce@warwickshire.gov.uk
WWW: http://www.warwickshire.gov.uk

West Midlands

Birmingham City Archives
Floor 7, Central Library, Chamberlain Square, Birmingham, West Midlands, B3 3HQ Tel: 0121 303 4217 Fax: 0121 212 9397 WWW: http://www.birmingham.gov.uk/libraries/archives/home.htm

Birmingham Roman Catholic Archdiocesan Archives
Cathedral House, St Chad's Queensway, Birmingham, West Midlands, B4 6EU Tel: 0121 236 2251 Fax: 0121 233 9299, Email: archives@rc birmingham.org

Connexional Archives for the Methodist Church
34 Spiceland Road, Northfield, Birmingham B31 1NJ Email: 106364.3456@compuserve.com (Genealogical Research is not undertaken but advice on sources given. Methodist queries only)

Dudley Archives & Local History Service
Mount Pleasant Street, Coseley, Dudley, West Midlands, WV14 9JR Tel: 01384 812770 Fax: 01384 812770 Email: archives.pls@mbc.dudley.gov.uk WWW: http://dudleygov.uk/council/library/archives/archive1.htm

Sandwell Community History & Archives Service
Smethwick Library, High Street, Smethwick, West Midlands, B66 1AB Tel: 0121 558 2561 Fax: 0121 555 6064

Solihull Library
Homer Road, Solihull, West Midlands, B91 3RG Tel: 0121 704 6977 Fax: 0121 704 6212 (NOT an archive repository, secondary sources only for Solihull MBC area only)

Solihull MBC Walsall Local History Centre
Essex Street, Walsall WS2 7AS Tel: 01922 721305
Fax: 01922 634594, Email: ruthvyse@walsplsm.demon.uk, WWW:http://www.walsall.gov.uk/culturalservices/library/welcome.htm

Wolverhampton Archives & Local Studies
42 50 Snow Hill, Wolverhampton, West Midlands, WV2 4AG Tel: 01902 552480 Fax: 01902 552481
Email: wolvarch.and.ls@dial.pipex.com
WWW: http://www.wolverhampton.gov.uk/library/archives

West Sussex

West Sussex Record Office
County Hall Chichester PO19 1RN Tel: 01243 533911 Fax: 01243 533959, Email: records.office@westsussex.gov.uk, WWW: www.westsussex.gov.uk/cs/ro/rohome.htm

Worthing Reference Library
Worthing Library, Richmond Road, Worthing, BN11 1HD Tel: 01903 212060 Fax: 01903 821902
Email: mhayes@westsussex.gov.uk

West Yorkshire

Bradford District Archives
West Yorkshire Archive Service, 15 Canal Street, Bradford, BD1 4AT Tel: 01724 731931 Fax: 01274 734013

John Goodchild Collection Local History Study Centre
Below Central Library, Drury Lane, Wakefield, West Yorkshire, WF1 2DT Tel: 01924 298929

Local Studies Library, Leeds Central Library
Calverley Street, Leeds LS1 3AB Tel: 0113 247 8290 Fax: 0113 247 8290, Email: local.studies@leeds.gov.uk, WWW: www.leeds.gov.uk/library/services/loc_reso.html, (Located in Leeds Town Hall Spring 2000 whilst essential repair work is carried out to the Central Library. Phone 0113 247 8290 for details)

Wakefield Library Headquarters Local Studies Dept
Balne Lane, Wakefield WF2 0DQ Tel: 01924 302224 Fax: 01924 302245, Email: localstudies@talk21.com WWW: www.wakefield.gov.uk

West Yorks Archive Service Kirklees
Central Library, Princess Alexandra Walk, Huddersfield, HD1 2SU Tel: 01484 221966 Fax: 01484 518361
Email: kirklees@wyashq.demon.co.uk
WWW: http://www.archives.wyjs.org.uk

West Yorkshire Archive Service Registry of Deeds
Newstead Road, Wakefield, WF1 2DE Tel: 01924 305982 Fax: 01924 305983, Email: hq@wyashq.demon.co.uk, WWW: http://www.archives.wyjs.org.uk

West Yorkshire Archive Service Bradford
15 Canal Road, Bradford BDI 4AT Tel: 01274 731931 Fax: 01274 734013, Email: enquiries@bradfordarchives.freeserve.co.uk WWW: http://www.archives.wyjs.org.uk

West Yorkshire Archive Service, Calderdale
Central Library, Northgate House, Northgate, Halifax, HX1 1UN Tel: 01422 392636 Fax: 01422 341083
Email: calderdale@wyashq.demon.co.uk, WWW: http://www.archives.wyjs.org.uk

West Yorkshire Archive Service Leeds
Chapeltown Road, Sheepscar, Leeds LS7 3AP Tel: 0113 214
5814 Fax: 0113 2145815 Email:leeds@wyashq.demon.co.uk
WWW: http://www.archives.wyjs.org.uk
West Yorkshire Archive Service, Wakefield HQ
Registry of Deeds, Newstead Road, Wakefield WF1 2DE Tel: 01924 305980 Fax:
01924 305983, Email: enquiries@wakefieldarchives.freeserve.co.uk
hq@wyashq.demon.co.uk, WWW: http://www.archives.wyjs.org.uk
Yorkshire Archaeological Society
Claremont, 23 Clarendon Rd, Leeds LS2 9NZ Tel: 0113 245 6342
Tel: 0113 245 7910, Fax: 0113 244 1979, Email: j.heron@shej.ac.uk
Wiltshire
Salisbury Local Studies Library
Market Place, Salisbury SP1 1BL Tel: 01722 410073
Wiltshire & Swindon Record Office
County Hall East, Bythesea Road, Trowbridge BA14 8BS
Tel: 01225 713709 Fax: 01225 71371501225 713993
Wiltshire Studies Library
Bythesea Rd, Trowbridge BA14 8BS Tel: 01225 713732 Tel: 01225 71372, Fax:
01225 713715, Email: trowref@compuserve.uk
Worcestershire
St Helens Record Office Worcestershire
Fish Street, Worcester WR1 2HN Tel: 01905 765922 Fax:
01905 765925, Email: corr@worcestershire.gov.uk

Wales
National Library of Wales
Penglais, Aberystwyth, Ceredigion, SY23 3BU Tel: 01970
632800 Tel: 01970 623811, Fax: 01970 623852 & 01970
615709, Email: holi@llgc.org.uk, WWW:
http://www.llgc.org.uk
National Monuments Record of Wales
Crown Building, Plas Crug, Aberystwyth, Ceredigion, Wales
Tel: 01970 621200 Fax: 01970 627701, Email:
nmr.wales@rcahmw.org.uk, WWW: www.rcahmw.org.uk
Department of Manuscripts
Main Library, University of Wales, College Road, Bangor,
Gwynedd, LL57 2DG Tel: 01248 382966 Fax: 01248
382979, Email: iss177@bangor.ac.uk
Anglesey
Anglesey County Archives Service
Shirehall, Glanhwfa Road, Llangefni, Anglesey, LL77 7TW
Tel: 01248 752080 Fax:, WWW: www.anglesey.gov.uk
Carmarthenshire
Carmarthenshire Archive Service
County Hall Carmarthen, Carmarthenshire, SA31 1JP Tel:
01267 224184 Fax: 01267 224104, Email:
archives@carmarthenshire.gov.uk
Ceredigion
Archifdy Ceredigion, Ceredigion Archives
Swyddfa'r Sir, County Offices, Glan y Mor, Marine
Terrace, Aberystwyth SY23 2DE Tel: 01970 633697
Fax: 01970 633663, Email: archives@ceredigion.gov.uk
Denbighshire
Denbighshire Record Office
46 Clwyd Street, Ruthin LL15 1HP Tel: 01824 708250
Fax: 01824 708258, Email: archives@denbighshire.go.uk,
WWW: http://www.denbighshire.gov.uk
Flintshire
Flintshire Record Office
The Old Rectory, Rectory Lane, Hawarden CH5 3NR
Tel: 01244 532364 Fax: 01244 538344 Email: archives@flintshire.gov.uk
WWW: http://www.llgc.org.uk/cac/
Glamorgan
Glamorgan Record Office
Glamorgan Building, King Edward VII Avenue, Cathays Park, Cardiff CF1 3NE
Tel: 01222 780282 Fax: 01222 780284, WWW: http://www.llgc.org.uk/cac/
Glamorgan West
Neath Central Library (Local Studies Department)
29 Victoria Gardens, Neath, Glamorgan Tel: 01639 620139

Worcesterhire Record Office
Record Office, County Hall, Spetchley Road, Worcester, WR5 2NP Tel: 01905
766351 Fax: 01905 766363, Email: record.office@worcestershire.gov.uk
Worcestershire Regimental Archives
RHQ The Worcestershire & Sherwood Foresters Regiment, Norton Barracks,
Worcester WR5 2PA Tel: 01905 354359 Fax: 01905 353871
York
**City of York Libraries Local History & Reference
Collection**
York Central Library, Library Square, Museum Street,
York, YO1 7DS Tel: 01904 655631 Fax: 01904 611025,
Email: reference.library@york.gov.uk
WWW: http://www.york.gov.uk
York City Archives
Exhibition Square, Bootham, York, YO1 2EW
Tel: 01904 551879 Fax: 01904 551877
York Minster Archives
Library & Archives Dean's Park, York, YO1 2JQ Tel:
01904 611118 Fax: 01904 611119
Borthwick Institute of Historical Research
St Anthony's Hall, Peasholme Green, York, YO1 7PW Tel:
01904 642315 Fax:, WWW: www.york.ac.uk/inst/bihr,
Appointment necessary to use Archives

West Glamorgan Archive Service Port Talbot Access Point
Port Talbot Library, Aberafan Centre, Port Talbot, West
Glamorgan, SA13 1PJ Tel: 01639 763430 Fax:, WWW:
http://www.swansea.gov.uk/culture/laarindex.html
West Glamorgan Archive Service
County Hall, Oystermouth Road, Swansea, West Glamorgan, SA1 3SN Tel: 01792
636589 Fax: 01792 637130, Email: archives@swansea.gov.uk, WWW:
http://www.swansea.gov.uk
Swansea Reference Library
Alexandra Road, Swansea, SA1 5DX Tel: 01792 516753
Fax: 01792 516759 (Extensive holdings of trade directories,
local census returns, newspapers (partially indexed)
Gwent
Gwent Record Office
County Hall, Croesyceiliog, Cwmbran, Gwent, NP44 2XH
Tel: 01633 644886 Fax: 01633 648382, Email:
113057.2173@compuserve.com
Gwynedd
Archifdy Meirion Archives
Swyddfeydd y Cyngor, Cae Penarlag, Dolgellau, Gwynedd,
LL40 2YB Tel: 01341 424444 Fax: 01341 424505, Email:
EinionWynThomas@gwynedd.gov.uk, WWW:
http://www.llgc.org.uk
Gwynedd Archives Caernarfon Area Record Office
Victoria Dock, Caernarfon, Gwynedd, LL55 1SH Tel:
01286 679095 Fax: 01286 679637, Email:
AnnRhydderch@gwynedd.gov.uk, WWW:
http://www.llgc.org.uk/cac/cac0053.html
Newport
Newport Library & Information Service
Newport Central Library, John Frost Square, Newport, South
Wales, NP20 1PA Tel: 01633 211376 Fax: 01633 222615,
Email: central.library@newport.gov.uk, WWW:
http://www.earl.org.uk/partners/newport/index.html
Pembrokeshire
Pembrokeshire Libraries
The County Library, Dew Street, Haverfordwest,
Pembrokeshire, SA61 1SU Tel: 01437 762070 Fax: 01437
769218, Email: anita.thomas@pembrokeshire.gov.uk (The
Local Studies Library covers people, places & events realting to The County of
Pembrokeshire past & present. The Library also houses The Francis Green
Genealogical Collection consisting of over 800 pedigree sheets & 35 volumes of
information relating to the prominent families of Pembraokeshier, Cardiganshire &
Carmarthenshire)

Pembrokeshire Record Office
The Castle Haverfordwest, Pembrokeshire, SA61 2EF Tel: 01437 763707
Tenby Museum
Tenby Museum & Art Gallery, Castle Hill, Tenby, SA70 7BP Tel: 01834 842809 Fax: 01834 842809

Scotland

General Register Office for Scotland
New Register House Edinburgh, EH1 3YT Tel: 0131 334 0380 Fax: 0131 314 4400, Email: nrh.gros@gtnet.gov.uk, WWW: http://www.open.gov.uk/gros/[groshome.htm]
National Archives of Scotland
HM General Register House, 2 Princes Street, Edinburgh, EH1 3YY Tel: 0131 535 1334 Fax: 0131 535 1328, Email: research@nas.gov.uk
National Archives of Scotland   West Search Room
West Register House, Charlotte Square, Edinburgh, EH2 4DF Tel: 0131 535 1413 Fax: 0131 535 1411, Email: wsv@nas.gov.uk All correspondence to: National Archives of scotland, HM general Register House, Edinburgh EH1 3YY
Department of Manuscripts National Library of Scotland
George IV Bridge, Edinburgh, EH1 1EW Tel: 0131 226 4531 Fax: 0131 622 4803, Email: mss@nls.uk, WWW: http://www.nls.uk (Will answer general enquiries but cannot undertake detailed genealogical research)
National Register of Archives(Scotland)
H M General Register House, 2 Princes Street, Edinburgh, EH1 3YY Tel: 0131 535 1405 Tel: 0131 535 1430 Fax: nra@nas.gov.uk
Scottish Genealogy Society Library
15 Victoria Terrace, Edinburgh, EH1 2JL Tel: 0131 220 3677 Fax: 0131 220 3677, Email: scotgensoc@sol.co.uk, WWW: http://www.scotland.net/scotgensoc/
Scottish Jewish Archive
The Synagogue, 125 Niddrie Road, Garnet Hill, Glasgow, G42 8QA Tel: 0141 332 4911
Scottish Catholic Archives
Columba House, 16 Drummond Place, Edinburgh, EH3 6PL Tel: 0131 5563661
Aberdeen
Aberdeen City Archives
Town House, Broad St, Aberdeen, AB10 1AQ Tel: 01224 522513 Fax: 01224 522491, Email: archives@legal.aberdeen.net.uk
Aberdeen City Archives
Old Aberdeen House, Dunbar Street, Aberdeen, AB24 1UE Tel: 01224 481775 Fax: 01224 495830
Reference & Local Studies Library
Central Library, Rosemount Viaduct, Aberdeen, AB25 1GW Tel: 01224 652511 Fax: 01224 624118 Email: refloc@arts rec.aberdeen.net.uk
Angus
Angus Archives
Montrose Library, 214 High Street, Montrose, Angus, DD10 8PH Tel: 01674 671415 Fax: 01674 671810 Email: anguscularch@sol.co.uk, WWW: www.angus.gov.uk/history/history.htm
Dundee City Council - Genealogy Unit
89 Commercial Street, Dundee, DD1 2AF Tel: 01382 435222 Fax: 01382 435224 Email: grant.law@dundeecity.gov.uk
Argyll
Argyll & Bute District Archives
Kilmory, Lochgilphead, Argyll, PA31 8RT Tel: 1546604120
Ayrshire
Ayrshire Archives
Ayrshire Archives Centre, Craigie Estate, Ayr KA8 0SS Tel: 01292 287584 Fax: 01292 284918, Email: archives@south ayrshire.gov.uk, WWW: http://www.south ayrshire.gov.uk/archives/index.htm

Powys
Powys County Archives Office
County Hall, Llandrindod Wells, Powys, LD1 5LG Tel: 01597 826087/8 Fax: 01597 827162 Email: archives@powys.gov.uk, WWW: http://archives.powys.gov.uk
Wrexham
Wrexham Archives Service
County Buildings, Regent Street, Wrexham, LL11 1RB Tel: 01978 358916 Fax: 01978 353882

East Ayrshire Council District History Centre & Museum
Baird Institute, 3 Lugar Street, Cumnock KA18 1AD Tel: 01290 421701 Fax: 01290 421701
North Ayrshire Libraries
Library Headquarters, 39 41 Princes Street, Ardrossan, Ayrshire, KA22 8BT Tel: 01294 469137 Fax: 01924 604236, Email: reference@naclibhq.prestel.co.uk
Clackmannanshire
Alloa Registration Office
Marshill House, Marshill, Alloa, Clackmannanshire, FK10 1AB Tel: 01259 723850 Fax: 01259 723850, Email: clack.lib@mail.easynet.co.uk
Clackmannanshire Archives
Alloa Library, 26/28 Drysdale Street, Alloa, Clackmannanshire, FK10 1JL Tel: 01259 722262 Fax: 01259 219469, Email: clack.lib@mail.easynet.co.uk
Dumfries & Galloway
Dumfries & Galloway Library & Archives
Archive Centre, 33 Burns Street, Dumfries, DG1 1PS Tel: 01387 269254 Fax: 01387 264126, Email: libsxi@dumgal.gov.uk, WWW: www.dumgal.gov.uk (Dumfrieshire, Kirkcudbrightshire, Wigtownshire)
Ewart Library
Catherine Street, Dumfries, DG1 1JB Tel: 01387 260285 Tel: 01387 252070, Fax: 01387 260294, Email: ruth_airley@dumgal.gov.uklibsxi@dumgal.gov.uk, WWW: www.dumgal.gov.ukf
Dundee
Dundee City Archives
21 City Square, (callers use 1 Shore Terrace), Dundee, DD1 3BY Tel: 01382 434494 Fax: 01382 434666 Email: iain.flett@dundeecity.gov.uk WWW: http://www.dundeecity.gov.uk/dcchtml/sservices/archives.html
Dundee Central Library & Local History Suite
The Wellgate, Dundee, DD1 1DB Tel: 01382 23141
Dundee City Council - Genealogy Unit
89 Commercial Street, Dundee, DD1 2AF Tel: 01382 435222 Fax: 01382 435224 Email: grant.law@dundeecity.gov.uk
East Dunbartonshire
East Dunbartonshire Record Offices & Ref Libraries
William Patrick Library, 2 West High Street, Kirkintilloch, East Dunbartonshire, G66 1AD Tel: 0141 776 8090 Fax: 0141 776 0408, Email: ref@edlib.freeserve.co.uk
East Renfrewshire
Record Offices East Renfrewshire District Council
Rouken Glen Road Road, Glasgow, East Renfrewshire, G46 6JF Tel: 0141 577 4976
Edinburgh
Edinburgh City Archives
City Chambers, High St, Edinburgh, EH1 1YJ Tel: 0131 529 4616 Fax: 0131 529 4957
Falkirk
Falkirk Library
Hope Street, Falkirk, FK1 5AU (Holds Local Studies Collection)

Falkirk Museum History Research Centre
Callendar House, Callendar Park, Falkirk, FK1 1YR Tel: 01324 503779 Fax: 01324 503771, Email: callandarhouse@falkirkmuseums.demon.co.uk, WWW: www.falkirkmuseums.demon.co.uk
(Records held: Local Authority, business, personal & estate records, local organisations, trade unions, over 28,000 photographs Falkirk District)
Glasgow
Glasgow City Archives
Mitchell Library, North Street, Glasgow, G3 7DN Tel: 0141 287 2913 Fax: 0141 226 8452, Email: archives@gel.glasgow.gov.uk WWW: http://users.colloquium.co.uk/~glw_archives/src001.htm
Invernesshire
Highland Region Archives
Farraline Park, Inverness, IV11NH Tel: 01463 220330
Isle of Lewis
Stornoway Record Office
Town Hall, South Beach Street, Stornoway, Isle of Lewis, HS1 2QG Tel: 01851 703773
Kinross shire
Perth & Kinross Council Archives
A K Bell Library, 2 8 York Place, Perth PH2 8EP Tel: 01738 477012 Tel: 01738 477022, Fax: 01738 477010, Email: archives@pkc.gov.uk WWW: http://www.pkc.gov.uk
Midlothian
Midlothian Archives
2 Clerk Street, Loanhead, Midlothian, EH20 9DR Tel: 0131 440 2210 Fax: 0131 440 4635 Email: mc_libhq_blossoming@compuscrve.com
Midlothian Council Libraries Local History Centre
2 Clerk Street, Loanhead, Midlothian, EH20 9DR
Moray
Local Heritage Centre
Grant Lodge, Cooper Park, Elgin, Moray, IV30 1HS Tel: 01343 544475 Tel: 01343 563413, Fax: 01343 549050, Email: graeme.wilson@techleis.moray.gov.uk
North Lanarkshire
Lenziemill Archives
10 Kelvin Road, Cumbernauld, G67 2BA Tel: 01236 737114

Isle of Man
Civil Registry, Registries Building
Bucks Road, Douglas IM1 3AR Tel: 01624 687039 Fax: 01624 687004

Isles of Scilly
Islands of Scilly Museum
Church Street, St Mary's, Isles of Scilly, TR21 0JT Tel: 01720 422337 Fax: 01720 422337

Channel Islands
Guernsey
Guernsey Island Archives Service
29 Victoria Rd, St Peter Port, Guernsey, GYI 1HU Tel: 01481 724512

Northern Ireland
Public Record Office of Northern Ireland
66 Balmoral Avenue, Belfast, BT9 6NY Tel: 01232 255905 Fax: 01232 255999, Email: proni@nics.gov.uk WWW: http://www.nics.gov.uk/index.htm
General Register Office of Northern Ireland
Oxford House, 49-55 Chichester Street, Belfast, BT1 4HL Tel: 028 90 252033 Fax: 028 90 252044 Email: stanley.campbell@dfpni.gov.uk WWW: www.nics.gov.uk/nisra/grohome.htm

Orkney
Orkney Archives
The Orkney Library, Laing Street, Kirkwall, Orkney, KWI5 1NW Tel: 01856 873166 Fax: 01856 875260
Email: alison.fraser@orkney.gov.uk
Perthshire
Perth & Kinross Council Archives
A K Bell Library, 2-8 York Place, Perth, PH2 8EP Tel: 01738 477012 Tel: 01738 477022, Fax: 01738 477010, Email: archives@pkc.gov.uk WWW: http://www.pkc.gov.uk
Renfrewshire
Renfrewshire Archives
Central Library & Museum Complex, High Street, Paisley, PA1 2BB Tel: 0141 889 2350 Fax: 0141 887 6468
Scottish Borders
Scottish Borders Archive & Local History Centre
Library Headquarters, St Mary's Mill, Selkirk, Scottish Borders, TD7 5EW Tel: 01750 20842 Fax: 01750 22875, Email: Library1@netcomuk.co.uk
Shetland
Shetland Archives
44 King Harald St, Lerwick, Shetland, ZE1 0EQ Tel: 01595 696247 Fax: 01595 696533 Email: shetland.archives@zetnet.co.uk
Stirlingshire
Stirling Council Archives
Unit 6, Burghmuir Industrial Estate, Stirling, FK7 7PY Tel: 01786 450745 Fax: 01786 473713, Email: archives@stirling.council.demon.co.uk
Tayside
Dundee University Archives
Tower Building, University of Dundee, Dundee, DD1 4HN Tel: 01382 344095 Fax: 01382 345523, Email: p.e.whatley@dundee.ac.uk, WWW: http://www.dundee.ac.uk/archives/
West Lothian
Archives & Records Management
7 Rutherford Square, Brucefield Industrial Estate, Livingston EH54 9BU Tel: 01506 460 020 Fax: 01506 416 167
General Registry
The Registries, Registries Building, Deemster's Walk, Bucks Road, Douglas IM1 3AR Tel: 01624 687039 Fax: 01624 687004
Manx National Heritage Library
Douglas IM1 3LY Tel: 01624 648000 Fax: 01624 648001

Jersey
Jersey Archives Service
Jersey Museum, The Weybridge, St Helier, Jersey, JE2 3NF Tel: 01534 633303 Fax: 01534 633301
Judicial Greffe
Morier House, Halkett Place, St Helier, Jersey, JE1 1DD Tel: 01534 502300 Fax: 01534 502399/502390, Email: jgreffe@super.net.uk, WWW: www.jersey.gov.uk
Presbyterian Historical Society of Ireland
Church House, Fisherwick Place, Belfast, BT1 6DW Tel: 01232 322284
Belfast Central Library Irish & Local Studies Dept
Royal Ave, Belfast, BT1 1EA Tel: 01232 243233 Fax: 01232 332819
Belfast Family History & Cultural Heritage Centre
64 Wellington Place, Belfast, BT1 6GE Tel: 01232 235392 Fax: 01232 239885
Co Londonderry
Derry City Council Heritage & Museum Service
Harbour Museum, Harbour Square, Derry, Co Londonderry, BT48 6AF Tel: 01504 377331 Fax: 01504 377633

Ireland

National Archives
Bishop Street, Dublin 8 Tel: 01 407 2300 Fax: 01 407 2333,
Email: mail@nationalarchives.ie WWW: http://www.nationalarchives.ie
Registrar General for Ireland
Joyce House, 8-11 Lombard Street East, Dublin 2 Tel: Dublin 711000
Dublin City Archives
City Assembly House, 58 South William Street, Dublin, 2
Tel: (01) 677 5877 Fax: (01) 677 5954
Genealogical Office
Kildare Street, Dublin 2, Co Dublin Tel: Dublin 6030300 Fax: Dublin 6621062
Church of Ireland Archives
Representative Church Body Library, Braemor Park,
Churchtown, Dublin 14 Tel: 01 492 3979 Fax: 01 492 4770
Email: library@ireland.anglican.org, WWW: http://www.ireland.anglican.org/
Co Mayo
Local Record Offices
The Registration Office, New Antrim Street, Castlebar, Co
Mayo Tel: 094 23249 Fax: 094 23249
County Clare
Clare County Archives
Clare County Council, New Road, Ennis, Co Clare Tel: 065
28525 Tel: 065 21616 WWW: www.clare.ie
County Donegal
Donegal County Council Archive Centre
The Courthouse, The Diamond, Lifford Tel: 00353 7421968

Donegal Ancestry
Old Meeting House, Back Lane, Ramleton, Letterkenny,
County Donegal Tel: 00353 74 51266 Fax: 00353 74 51702,
Email: donances@indigo.ie
WWW: http://www.indigo.ie/~donances
Donegal Local Studies Centre
Central Library & Arts Centre, Oliver Plunkett Road,
Letterkenny, County Donegal Tel: 00353 74 24950 Fax:
00353 74 24950, Email: dgcolib@iol.ie, WWW: donegal.ie
County Dublin
Dublin Heritage Group
Ballyfermot Library, Ballyfermot Road, Ballyfermot, Dublin,
10 Tel: 6269324 Fax:, Email: dhgeneal@iol.ie
County Limerick
Limerick City Library Local History Collection
The Granary, Michael Street, Limerick Tel: 061 314668
Fax: 061 415266, Email: noneill@citylib.limerickcorp.ie,
WWW: http://www.limerickcorp.ie
Limerick Regional Archives
The Granary, Michael Street, Limerick Tel: 061 410777
Fax: 061 415125
Co Waterford
Waterford Archives & Local Records
St Joseph's Hospital Dungarvan, Co Waterford Tel: 058
42199

Australia

Capital Territory
National Archives of Australia, PO Box 7425, Canberra Mail Centre, Canberra,
ACT, 2610 Tel: 02 6212 3600 Fax: 02 6212 3699, Email: archives@naa.gov.au,
WWW: http://www.naa.gov.au
New South Wales
National Archives of Australia Sydney Office
120 Miller Road, Chester Hill, Sydney, New South Wales, 2162 Tel: 02 96450 100
Fax: 02 96450 108, Email: refnsw@naa.gov.au, WWW: http://www.naa.gov.uk
State Archives Office
2 Globe Street, Sydney, New South Wales, 2000 Tel: 02 9237 0254 Fax: 02 9237
0142
State Library of New South Wales
Macquarie Street, Sydney, New South Wales, 2000 Tel: 02 9230 1414 Fax: 02 9223
3369, Email: slinfo@slsw.gov.au
Northern Territories
Australian Archives Northern Territories
Kelsey Crescent, Nightcliffe, N T 810 Tel: 08 8948 4577 Fax: 08 8948 0276
Queensland
National Archives of Australia Queensland
996 Wynnum Road, Cannon Hill, Queensland, 4170 Tel: 07 3249 4226 Fax: 07 3399
6589, WWW: http://www.naa.gov.au
Queensland State Archives
PO Box 1397, Sunnybanks Hills, Brisbane, Queensland, 4109 Tel: 61 7 3875 8755
Fax: 61 7 3875 8764, Email: qsa@ipd.pwh.qld.gov.au, WWW:
http://www.archives.qld.gov.au
South Australia
Australian Archives South Australia
11 Derlanger Ave, Collingwood, South Australia, 5081
Tel: 08 269 0100 Fax: 08 269 3234
South Australia State Archives
PO Box 1056, Blair Athol West, South Australia, 5084 Tel: 08 8226 8000
Fax: 08 8226 8002

New Zealand
National Archives of New Zealand
PO Box 10 050, 10 Mulgrave Street, Thorndon, Wellington Tel: 04 499 5595 Fax: 04
495 6210, Email: national.archives@dia.govt.nz, WWW:
http://www.archives.dia.govt.nz

Tasmania
National Archives of Australia Hobart Office
4 Rosny Hill Road, Rosny Park, Tasmania, 7018 Tel: 03 62 440101
Fax: 03 62 446834, Email: reftas@naa.gov.au, WWW: http://www.naa.gov.au
State Archives Archives Office of Tasmania
77 Murray Street, Hobart, Tasmania, 7000 Tel: (03) 6233 7488
Fax: (03) 6233 7471 Email: archives.tasmania@central.tased.edu.au
WWW: http://www.tased.edu.au/archives
Victoria
Bendigo Regional Genealogical Society Inc
PO Box 1049 Bendigo, Victoria, 3552
National Archives of Australia Victoria
PO Box 8005 Burwood Heights, Victoria, 3151 Tel: 03 9285 7900
Fax: 03 9285 7979
Victoria State Archives
57 Cherry Lane, Laverton North, Victoria, 3028 Tel: 03 9360 9665 Fax: 03 9360 9685
Victoria State Archives
Level 2 Casselden Place, 2 Lonsdale Street, Melbourne, Victoria, 3000
Tel: 03 9285 7999 Fax: 03 9285 7953
Victoria State Archives
State Offices, Corner of Mair & Doveton Streets, Ballarat, Victoria, 3350 Tel: 03 5333
6611 Fax: 03 5333 6609
Western Australia
Australian Archives Western Australia
384 Berwick Street East, Victoria Park, Western Australia, 6101 Tel: 09 470 7500 Fax:
09 470 2787
State Archives & Public Record Office
Alexander Library, Perth Cultural Centre, Perth, Western Australia, 6000 Tel: 09 427
3360 Fax: 09 427 3256

Canada

Alberta

Glenbow Library & Archives
130 9th Avenue SE, Calgary, Alberta, T2G 0P3 Tel: 403 268 4197
Fax: 403 232 6569

Manitoba

Hudson's Bay Company Archives
200 Vaughan Street, Winnipeg, Manitoba, R3C 1T5 Tel: 204 945 4949
Fax: 204 948 3236, Email: hbca@chc.gov.mb.ca, WWW:
http://www.gov.mb.ca/chc/archives/hbca/index.html

Manitoba Provincial Archives
200 Vaughan Street Winnepeg, Manitoba, R3C 1T5 Tel: 204 945 4949
Fax: 204 948 3236

New Brunswick

Archives & Special Collections
PO Box 7500, Fredericton, New Brunswick, E3B 5H5 Tel: 506 453 4748
Fax: 506 453 4595

Loyalist Collection & Reference Department
PO Box 7500, Fredericton, New Brunswick, E3B 5H5 Tel: 506 453 4749
Fax: 506 453 4596

New Brunswick Provincial Archives
PO Box 6000, Fredericton, New Brunswick, E3B 5H1 Tel: 506 453 2122
Fax: 506 453 3288, Email: provarch@gov.nb.ca, WWW:
http://www.gov.nb.ca/supply/archives

Newfoundland & Labrador Archives
Colonial Building, Military Road, St Johns, Newfoundland, A1C 2C9
Tel: 709 729 0475 Fax: 709 729 0578

Nova Scotia State Archives
6016 University Avenue, Halifax, Nova Scotia, B3H 1W4 Tel: 902 424 6060

United States of America

Alaska

National Archives & Records Administration Pacific Alaska Region
654 West 3rd Avenue, Anchorage, Alaska, 99501 2145 Tel: 011 1 907 271 2443
Fax: 011 1 907 271 2442, Email: archives@alaska.nara.gov
WWW: http://www.nara.gov?regional/anchorage.html

State Archives
141 Willoughby Avenue, Juneau, Alaska, 99801 1720 Tel: 907 465 2270
Fax: 907 465 2465, Email: sou@bham.lib.al.usarchives@educ.state.ak.us

Arizona

Arizona Department of Library, Archives & Public Records
State Capitol,1700 W Washington, Phoenix, Arizona, 85007 Tel: 602 542 3942

Arizona Historical Foundation Library
Hayden Library, Arizona State Univeristy, Tempe, Arizona, 85287
Tel: 602 966 8331

Arkansas

Arkansas History Commission
1 Capitol Mall,Little Rock,Arkansas 72201 Tel: 501682 6900

California

California State Archives
1020 O Street, Sacramento, California, 95814 Tel: (916) 653 7715
Fax: (916) 653 7363, Email: archivesweb@ss.ca.gov
WWW: http://www.ss.ca.gov/archives/archives.htm

National Archives & Records Administration (Pacific Region)
1st Floor East, 24000 Avila Road, Orange County, Laguna Niguel, California, 92677
Tel: (949) 360 2641 Fax: (949) 360 2624, Email: archives@laguna.nara.gov
WWW: www.nara.gov/regional/laguna.html

National Archives
100 Commodore Drive, San Bruno, California, 94066 2350

Colorado

National Archives
PO Box 25307 Denver, Colorado, 80225 0307 Tel: 303 866 2390

State Archives
Room 1b 20, 1313 Sherman Street, Denver, Colorado, 80203 2236 Tel: 303 866 2390

Connecticut

Connecticut State Archives
231 Capitol Avenue, Hartford, Connecticut, 6106 Tel: 203 566 5650

National Archives
Pennsylvania Avenue, Washington, District of Colombia, 20408

Yarmouth County Museums & Archives
22 Collins Street, Yarmouth, Nova Scotia, B5A 3C8 Tel: (902) 742 5539
Fax: (902) 749 1120, Email: ycn0056@ycn.library.ns.ca
WWW: http://www.ycn.library.ns.ca/museum/yarcomus.htm

Ontario

National Archives of Canada
395 Wellington Street, Ottawa, Ontario, K1A 0N3 Tel: 613 996 7458
Fax: 613 995 6274, Email: http://www.archives.ca

Ontario Archives
Unit 300, 77 Grenville Street, Toronto, Ontario, M5S 1B3 Tel: 416 327 1582
Fax: 416 327 1999, Email: reference@archives.gov.on.ca,
WWW: http://www.gov.on.ca/MCZCR/archives

Prince Edward Island

Public Archives & Record Office
PO Box 1000 Charlottetown, Prince Edward Island, C1A 7M4 Tel: 902 368 4290
Fax: 902 368 6327, Email: archives@gov.pe.ca
WWW: http://www.gov.pe.ca/educ/

Quebec

Archives Nationales
PO Box 10450 Sainte Foy, Quebec, G1V 4N1 Tel: 418 643 8904 Fax: 418 646 0868

Saskatchewan

Saskatchewan Archives Board
3303 Hillsdale Street, Regina, Saskatchewan, S4S 0A2 Tel: 306 787 4068
Fax: 306 787 1197, Email: sabreg@sk.sympatico.ca,
WWW: http://www.gov.sk.ca/govt/archives

Saskatchewan Archives Board
Room 91, Murray Building, University of Saskatchewan, 3 Campus Drive,
Saskatoon, Saskatchewan, S7N 5A4 Tel: 306 933 5832 Fax: 306 933 7305, Email:
sabsktn@sk.sympatico.ca, WWW: http://www.gov.sk.ca/govt/archives

Daughters of the American Revolution Library
1776 D Street N W, Washington, District of Columbia, 20006 5392 Tel: 202 879 3229

District of Columbia Archives
1300 Naylor Court North West, Washington, District of Columbia, 20001 4225 Tel:
Tel: 203 566 3690

Georgia

Georgia State Archives
330 Capital Avenue SE, Atlanta, Georgia, 30334 9002 Tel: 404 656 2350
Fax:, Email: http://www.state.ga.us/SOS/Archives/

National Archives Georgia
1557 St Joseph Avenue, East Point, Georgia, 30344 Tel: 404 763 7477
Fax: 404 763 7059

Hawaii

Hawaii State Library
478 South King Street, Honolulu, Hawaii, 96813

Illinois

National Archives Illinois
7358 South Pulaski Road, Chicago, Illinois, 60629

Indiana

Indiana Archives,
The, Room117, 140 N Senate Avenue, Indianapolis, Indiana, 46204 2296
Tel: 317 232 3660 Fax: 317 233 1085

Kansas

Kansas State Historical Society Archives
6425 SW Sixth Street, Topeka, Kansas, 66615 1099 Tel: 913 272 8681
Fax: 913 272 8682, Email: reference@hspo.wpo.state.ks.us
WWW: http://www.kshs.org

Maryland

Maryland State Archives
Hall of Records Building, 350 Rowe Boulevard, Annapolis, Maryland, 21401
Tel: 410 974 3914

Massachusetts

National Archives Massachusetts
380 Trapelo Road, Waltham, Massachusetts, 2154

National Archives Massachusetts
100 Dan Fox Drive, Pittsfield, Massachusetts, 01201 8230

Missouri
Missouri State Archives
PO Box 778 Jefferson City, Missouri, 65102 Tel: 314 751 3280
National Archives
2306 East Bannister Road, Kansas City, Missouri, 64131
Nevada
Nevada State Archives
100 Stewart Street, Carson City, Nevada, 89710 Tel: 702 687 5210
New Jersey
New Jersey State Archives
PO Box 307, 185 West State Street, Trenton, New Jersey, 08625 0307
Tel: 609 292 6260
New Mexico
New Mexico State Archives
1205 Camino carlos Rey, Sante Fe, New Mexico, 87501 Tel: (505) 827 7332
Fax: (505) 476 7909, Email: cmartine@rain.state.nm.us,
WWW: http://www.state.nmus/cpr
New York
National Archives
201 Varick Street, New York, New York, 10014   4811
Ohio
Ohio State Archives
1982 Velma Avenue, Columbus, Ohio, 43211 2497 Tel: 614 297 2510
Oregon
Gallipoli Campaign 1915 16 Biographical Index
3966 Robin Avenue, Eugene, Oregon, 97402 Tel: Email: patrickg@efn.org
Pennsylvania
National Archives
Room 1350, 900 Market Street, Philadelphia, Pennsylvania, 19144
Pennsylvania State Archives
PO Box 1026, 3rd & Forster Streets, Harrisburg, Pennsylvania, 17108 1026
Tel: 717 783 3281
South Carolina
South Carolina Department Archives & History
8301 Parklane Road, Columbia, South Carolina, 292223 Tel: 803 896 6100
South Carolina State Archives
PO Box 11669, 1430 Senate Street, Columbia, South Carolina, 29211 1669 Tel: 803
734 8577
South Dakota
South Dakota Archives
Cultural Heritage Center, 900 Governors Drive, Pierre South Dakota, 57501 2217
Tel: 605 773 3804

South Africa
Albany Museum
Somerset Street, Grahamstown, 6139 Tel: 046 622 2312 Fax: 046 622 2398,
Email: w.jervois@ru.ac.za
Cape Town Archives Repository
Private Bag X9025, Cape Town, 8000 Tel: 021 462 4050 Fax: 021 465960
Dutch Reformed Church Archive
PO Box 398 Bloemfontein, 9301 Tel: 051 448 9546
Dutch Reformed Church Records Office
PO Box 649 Pietermaritzburg, 3200 Tel: 0331 452279 Fax: 0331 452279
Dutch Reformed Church Archive of Orange Free State
P O Box 398, Bloemfontein, 9301 Tel: 051 448 9546
Dutch Reformed Church Synod Records Office of Kwa Zulu Natal
P O Box 649, Pietermaritzburg, 3200 Tel: 0331 452279 Fax: 0331 452279, Email:
ngntlargrief@alpha.futurenet.co.za

Namibia
National Archives of Namibia
Private Bag, Windhoek, 13250 Tel: 061 293 4386 Fax: 061 239042, Email:
Renate@natarch.mec.gov.na, WWW: www.witbooi.natarch.mec.gov.na
Belgium
Archives de l'Etat a Liege
79 rue du Chera, Liege, B 4000 Tel: 04 252 0393 Fax: 04 229 3350
Email: archives.liege@skynet.be
De Kerk van Jezus Christus van den Heiligen
Der Laaste Dagen, Kortrijkse Steenweg 1060, Sint Deniss Westrem, B 9051
Tel: 09 220 4316

Tennessee
Tennessee State Library & Archives
403 7th Avenue North, Nashville, Tennessee, 37243 0312 Tel: 615 741 2764
Fax:, Email: reference@mail.state.tn.us
WWW: http://www.state.tn.us/sos/statelib
Texas
National Archives
Box 6216, 4900 Hemphill Road, Fort Worth, Texas, 76115
Texas State Archives
PO Box 12927, Austin, Texas, 78711 2927 Tel: 512 463 5463
Vermont
Vermont Public Records Division
PO Drawer 33, U S Route 2, Middlesex, Montpelier, Vermont, 05633 7601
Tel: 802 828 3700 Tel: 802 828 3286, Fax: 802 828 3710
Vermont State Archives
Redstone Building, 26 Terrace Street, Montpelier, Vermont, 05609 1103
Tel: 802 828 2308
Virginia
Virginia State Archives
11th Street at Capitol Square, Richmond, Virginia, 23219 3491 Tel: 804 786 8929
Washington
National Archives Northwest Pacific Region
6125 Sand Point Way NE, Seattle, Washington, 98115 Tel: 206 524 6501
Fax:, Email: archives@seattle.nara.gov
West Virginia
West Virginia State Archives
The Cultural Center, 1900 Kanawha Boulevard East, Charleston, West Virginia,
25305 0300 Tel: 304 558 0230
Wisconsin
Wisconsin State Archives
816 State Street, Madison, Wisconsin, 53706 Tel: 608 264 6460 Fax: 608 264 6742,
Email: archives.reference@ccmail.adp.wisc.edu
WWW: http://www.wisc.edu/shs archives
Wyoming
Wyoming State Archives
Barrett State Office Building, 2301 Central Avenue, Cheyenne, Wyoming, 82002
Tel: 307 777 7826

Free State Archives Repository
Private Bag X20504, Bloemfontein, 9300 Tel: 051 522 6762 Fax: 051 522 6765
Huguenot Museum
P O Box 37, Franschhoek, Western Cape, 7690 Tel: 021 876 2532
Kaffrarian Museum
P O Box 1434, King Williamstown, 5600 Tel: 0433 24506
National Archives Pretoria
Private Bag X236, Pretoria, 1 Tel: 323 5300 Fax: 323 5287
Free State Archives
Private Bag X20504 Bloemfontein, Free State, 9300 Tel: 051 522 6762
Fax: 051 522 6765

Zimbabwe
National Archives of Zimbabwe
Hiller Road, off Borrowdale Road, Gunhill, Harare Tel: 792741/3 Fax: 792398
Private Bag 7729, Causeway, Harare Tel: 792741 Fax: 792398
Provinciebestuur Limburg
Universititslaan 1, Afdeling 623 Archief, Hasselt, B 3500
Rijks Archief te Brugge
Academiestraat 14, Brugge, 8000 Tel: 050 33 7288 Fax: 050 33 7288, Email:
rijksarchief.brugge@skynet.be
Rijksarchief in Beveren
Kruibekesteenweg 39/1, Beveren, B 9210 Tel: 03 775 3839

Service de Centralisation des Etudes Genealogique et Demographiques Belgique
Chaussee de Haecht 147, Brussels, B 1030 Tel: 02 374 1492
Staatsarchiv in Eupen

Kaperberg 2 4, Eupen, B 4700 Tel: 087 55 4377
Stadsarchief te Veurne
Grote Markt 29, Veurne, B 8630 Tel: 058 31 4115 Fax: 058 31 4554

Cyprus

Cyprus Center of Medievalism & Heraldry
P O Box 80711, Piraeus Greece 185 10 Tel: 42 26 356

Denmark

Association of Local History Archives
P O Box 235, Enghavevej 2, Vejle, DK 7100 Tel:, Fax: 45 7583 1801, WWW:
www.lokalarkiver.dk
Cadastral Archives
Rentemestervej 8, Copenhagen NV, DK 2400 Tel:, Fax: 45 3587 5064, WWW:
www.kms.min.dk
Danish Data Archive
Islandsgade 10, Odense C, DK 5000 Tel:, Fax: 45 6611 3060, WWW: www.dda.dk
Danish Emigration Archives
P O Box 1731, Arkivstraede 1, Aalborg, DK 9100 Tel: 045 9931 4221 Fax: 45 9810
2248, Email: bfl kultur@aalbkom.dk, WWW: www.cybercity.dk/users/ccc13656
Danish Genealogical Research Guide
Kildevaenget 37, Copenhagen O, DK 2100 Tel:, Fax: 45 3927 2433, WWW:
www.hvemforskerhvad.dk/index_us.htm
Danish National Archives
Rigsdagsgaarden 9, Copenhagen, DK 1218 Tel: 45 3392 3310 Fax: 45 3315 3239,
WWW: www.sa.dk/ra/uk/uk.htm
Danish Soc. for Local History
Colbjornsensvej 8, Naerum, DK 2850

Kobenshavns Stadsarkiv
Kobenhavns Radhus Kobenhavn, DK01599 Tel: 3366 2374 Fax: 3366 7039
National Business Archives
Vester Alle 12, Aarhus C, DK 8000 Tel: 45 8612 8533 Fax: 45 8612 8560, Email:
mailbox@ea.sa.dk, WWW: www.sa.dk/ea/engelsk.htm
Provincial Archives Funen
Jernbanegade 36, Odense C, DK 5000 Tel: 6612 5885 Fax: 45 6614 7071, WWW:
www.sa.dk/lao/default.htm
Provincial Archives North Jutland
Lille Sct. Hansgade 5, Viborg, DK 8800 Tel: 45 8662 1788 Fax: 45 8660 1006,
WWW: www.sa.dk/lav/default.htm
Provincial Archives Southern Jutland
Haderslevvej 45, Aabenraa, DK 6200 Tel: 45 7462 5858 Fax: 45 7462 3288,
WWW: www.sa.dk/laa/default.htm
Provincial Archives Zealand
Jagtvej 10, Copenhagen, DK 2200 Tel:, Fax: 45 3539 0535, WWW:
www.sa.dk/lak.htm
Society for Danish Genealogy & Biography
Grysgardsvej 2, Copenhagen NV, DK 2400 Tel: WWW: www.genealogi.dk

Finland

Institute of Migration
Piispankatu 3, Turku, 20500 Tel: 2 231 7536 Fax: 2 233 3460, Email:
jouni.kurkiasaaz@utu.fi, WWW: www.utu.fi/erill/instmigr/

France

Centre d'Accueil et de Recherche des Archives Nationales
60 rue des Francs Bourgeois, Paris Cedex, 75141 Tel: 1 40 27 6000 Fax: 1 40 27 6628,
Email:
Centre des Archives d'Outre Mer
29 Chemin du Moulin de Testas, Aix en Provence, 13090

Service Historique de l'Armee de l'Air
Chateau de Vincennes Vincennes Cedex, 94304
Service Historique de l'Armee de Terre
BP 107, Armees, 481
Service Historique de la Marine
Chateau de Vincennes Vincennes Cedex, 94304

Germany

Historic Emigration Office
Steinstr. 7, Hamburg, (D) 20095 Tel: 4940 300 51 282 Fax: 4940 300 51 220, Email:
ESROKAHEA@aol.com, WWW:
users.cybercity.dk/gccc13652/addr/ger_heo.htm
Research Centre Lower Saxons in the USA
Postfach 2503, Oldenburg, D 2900 Tel: 0441 798 2614 Fax: 0441 970 6180, Email:
holtmann@hrzl.uni oldenburg.de, WWW: www.uni oldenburg.de/nausa

The German Emigration Museum
Inselstrasse 6, Bremerhaven, D 2850 Tel: 0471 49096
Zentralstelle fur Personen und Familiengeschichte
Birkenweg 13, Friedrichsdorf, D 61381 Tel: 06172 78263 Fax:, WWW:
www.genealogy.com/gene/genealogy.html

Greece

Cyprus Center of Medievalism & Heraldry
P O Box 80711, Piraeus, 185 10 Tel: 42 26 356

Netherlands

Amsterdam Municipal Archives
P O 51140, Amsterdam, 1007 EC
Brabant Collectie
Tilburg University Library, P O Box 90153, Warandelaan, Tilburg, NL 5000 LE Tel:
0031 134 662127
Gemeentelijke Archiefdienst Amersfoort
P O Box 4000, Amersfoort, 3800 EA Tel: 033 4695017 Fax: 033 4695451
Het Utrechts Archief
Alexander Numankade 199/201, Utrecht, 3572 KW Tel: 030 286 6611 Fax: 030
286 6600, Email: Utrecht@acl.archivel.nl**Rijksarchief in Drenthe**
P O Box 595, Assen, 9400 AN Tel: 0031 592 313523 Fax: 0031 592 314697, Email:
RADR@noord.bart.nl, WWW: obd server.obd.nl/instel/enderarch/radz.htm

Rijksarchief in Overijssel
Eikenstraat 20, Zwolle, 8021 WX Tel: 038 454 0722 Fax: 038 454 4506, Email:
RAO@euronet.nl, WWW: www.obd.nl/instel/arch/rkarch.htm
Zealand Documentation
P O Box 8004, Middelburg, 4330 EA**Spain**
Archivo Historico National
Serrano 115, Madrid, 28006 Tel: 261 8003 Tel: 2618004, Fax:
Instituucion Fernando el Catolico
Plaza de Espagna 2, Zaragoza, 50071 Tel: 09 7628 8878 Fax: 09 7628 8869, Email:
ifc@isendanet.es.mail

Norway

Norwegian Emigration Centre
Strandkaien 31, Stavanger, 4005 Tel: 47 51 53 88 63 Fax:, Email: detnu@telepost.no,
WWW: www.emigrationcenter.com

Sweden

City & Provincial Archives
Box 22063, Stockholm, S 104 22 Tel: 8 508 283 00 Fax: 8 508 283 01
House of Emigrants
Box 201, Vaxjo, S 351 04 Tel: 470 201 20 Fax:, Email:
info@svenskaemigrantinstitulet.g.se
Kinship Centre
Box 331, Karlstad, S 651 08 Tel: 54 107720
Military Archives
Banergatan 64, Stockholm, S 115 88 Tel: 8 782 4! 00
National Archives
Box 12541, Stockholm, S 102 29 Tel: 8 737 63 50
Orebro Stadsarkiv
Box 300, Orebro, S 701 35 Tel: 19 21 10 75 Fax: 19 21 10 50
Provincial Archive
Arkivvagen 1, Ostersund, S 831 31 Tel: 63 10 84 85 Fax:, Email:
landsarkivet@landsarkivet ostersund.ra.se, WWW: www.ra.se/ola/
Provincial Archive
Visborgsgatan 1, Visby, 621 57 Tel: 498 2129 55
Provincial Archive
Box 126, Vadstena, S 592 23 Tel: 143 130 30
Provincial Archive
Box 135, Uppsala, SE 751 04 Tel: 18 65 21 00
Provincial Archive
Box 2016, Lund, S 220 02 Tel: 046 197000 Fax: 046 197070, Email:
landsarkivet@landsarkivet lund.ra.se

Poland

State Archives
Ul Dluga6 Skr, Poczt, Warsaw, 1005 00 950 Tel:, Fax: 0 22 831 9222

Provincial Archive
Box 161, Harnosand, S 871 24 Tel: 611 835 00 Fax:, Email: landsarkivet@landsarkivet
harnosand.ra.se, WWW: www.ra.se/hla
Provincial Archive
Box 19035, Goteborg, S 400 12 Tel: 31 778 6800

Switzerland

Achives de la Ville de Geneve
Palais Eynard, 4 rue de la Croix Rouge, Geneve 3, 1211 Tel: 22 418 2990 Fax: 22 418
2901, Email: didier.grange@seg.ville ge.ch
Archives d'Etat de Geneve
Casa Postale 3964, Geneve 3, 1211 Tel: 022 319 3395 Fax: 319 3365
Archives de l'Ancien Eveche de Bale
10 rue des Annonciades, Porrentruy, CH 2900
Archives Canonales Vaudoises
rue de la Mouline 32, Chavannes pres Renens, CH 1022 Tel: 021 316 37 11 Fax: 021
316 37 55
Staatsarchiv Appenzell Ausserhoden
Obstmarkt, Regierungsgebaede, Herisau, CH 9100 Tel: 071 353 6111 Fax: 071 352
1277, Email: Peter.Witschi@kk.ar.ch
Staatsarchiv des Kantons Basel Landschaft
Wiedenhubstrasse 35, Liestal, 4410 Tel: 061 921 44 40 Fax: 061 921 32, Email:
baselland@lka.bl.ch
WWW: www.baselland.ch
Staatsarchiv des Kantons Solothurn
Bielstrasse 41, Solothurn, CH 4509 Tel: 032 627 08 21 Fax: 032 622 34 87
Staatsarchiv Luzern
Postfach 7853, Luzern, 6000 Tel: 41 41 2285365 Fax: 41 41 2286663, Email:
archiv@staluzern.ch, WWW: www.staluzern.ch

But Not For Me

You know the feeling we all get when you spend hours searching records and find everybody's
ancestors but your own? This expresses that kind of feeling, to the tune of But Not for Me.

I'm finding forebears fine,
But not for me,
A strong ancestral line,
But not for me;
How could I miss
A golden chance like this
To trace my family tree.

I was a fool to think
I really should
Find a family link
To Robin Hood;
What can I say?
Perhaps one day,
I'll meet someone who could.

I'm growing tired now
And feeling rather blue,
I'm left wondering how
To start anew;
But I won't give in,
I know I'll find my kin,
It's my ancestral due.

from *Rhyming Relations* Genealogy in Verse
by Roy Stockdill
Obtainable from the Author 6 First Avenue, Garston, Watford, Hertfordshire WD2 6PZ
Email: roystock@compuserve.com

THE OPEN REGISTER – A GUIDE TO INFORMATION HELD BY THE LAND REGISTRY AND HOW TO OBTAIN IT

Ken Young Head of Information

Since 3 December 1990 the register of title in England and Wales has been open for inspection by the Public. The object of registering title to land is to create and maintain a register of land owners whose title is guaranteed by the State and thus simplifying the sale (transfer) and mortgage of such land. Anybody can now obtain information which is held on the register of a registered title. Prior to December 1990 only registered owners and persons with the owner's consent could inspect the register.

A registered title is the legal evidence of title to land which has been registered at HM Land Registry. When a title is registered the register provides an up-to-date official record of the legal ownership and certain other matters relating to the property or piece of land in question.

How do I find out if land is registered? The Registry holds a series of large scale Ordnance Survey maps covering the whole of England and Wales on which is shown the extent of land in every registered title. These maps are called Index Maps and each single map is called a 'Section'. Index Maps will indicate whether or not a particular piece of land is registered and, if it is, the registered title number and whether the registration is of freehold or leasehold land.

An application for an official search (inspection) of the Index Map should preferably be made by post and must be on Land Registry Form 96. In some instances, for example when information is required in respect of land sited on a rural area, it may be necessary for you to supply a plan to enable its precise whereabouts on the Index Map to be established. Further details of this service may be obtained from HM Land Registry Practice Leaflet No. 15. Alternatively, a copy of an Index Map Section may be obtained on application in Land Registry Form 96B. The title numbers of all registered properties falling within the area covered by the Section would be shown on the copy Index Map supplied. Further information concerning this service is provided in HM Land Registry Explanatory Leaflet No. 16.

The Property Register identifies the geographical location and extent of the registered property by means of a short verbal description (usually the address) and a reference to an official plan which is prepared for each title. it may also give particulars of any rights that benefit the land, for example, a right of way over adjoining land. In the case of a leasehold title, it gives brief details of the lease. The official title plan is based on the large scale maps of the Ordnance Survey. Further information regarding boundaries in land registration is provided in HM Land Registry Explanatory Leaflet No. 18.

The Proprietorship Register specifies the quality of the title. It also gives the name and address of the legal owner and shows whether there are any restrictions on their power to sell, mortgage or otherwise deal with the land. Where the Land Registry is entirely satisfied about the ownership of the property "absolute title" will have been given. In some cases, however, a more limited class of title will have been given.

The charges register contains identifying particulars of registered mortgages and notice of other financial burdens secured on the property (but does not disclose details of the amounts of money involved). It also gives notice of other rights and interests to which the property is subject such as leases, rights of way or covenants restricting the use of the property.

How can I inspect the register? The best and most convenient method of obtaining information from the register is to apply by post on Land Registry Form 109 for a copy of the register entries and/or a copy of the title plan, as required. One form is required for each registered title inspected. If you think the property is probably registered but do not know the title number you may, should you wish, dispense with applying for an official search of the Index Map in Form 96 (in the manner described in paragraph 5 above) and instead complete Form 109 applying for a copy of the register and/or title plan but leaving the title number box blank. A fee to cover the cost of the additional work for the Registry in checking the Index Map on your behalf may be payable. The fee will be refunded if the title proves to be unregistered. If application is made in this manner please write in capitals at the head of the Form 109 "PLEASE SUPPLY THE TITLE NUMBER".

Can I inspect copies of documents referred to on the register?
Yes; once you have received a copy of the register you may, if you wish, apply by post on Land Registry Form 110 specifying which documents you require. Copies of such documents will be forwarded to you. See below regarding the fee payable. Please note that copies of documents not actually referred to on the register are not generally open to inspection. Also copies of Leases or Charges (mortgages) referred to on the register of title are not generally open to inspection.

Can I make a personal inspection of the register, title plan or copies of documents referred to on the register? Yes; a personal inspection can be made by completing a Land Registry Form 111 when you visit a Land Registry office. One form is required for each registered title inspected It is requested that at least four days notice of intention to make a personal inspection be given to the registry office concerned. Without such notice – which may be provided by telephone – there is a risk that the register, title plan or documents might not be available when you arrive. If you do not know the title number you may, if you wish, dispense with applying for an official search of the Index Map in Land Registry Form 96 (in the manner described above) and instead complete Land Registry Form 111 leaving the title number box blank. A fee to cover the cost of the additional work for the Registry in checking the Index Map on your behalf may be payable. Visits to registry offices may be made between the hours of 9am and 4.30pm, Mondays to Fridays only. Alternatively, a postal application is strongly recommended.

Where do I apply? You should send your application to the district land registry serving the area in which the property the subject of your enquiry is situated. If in doubt you should telephone your nearest Land Registry office and ask them to advise you. A personal inspection can be made at any district land registry or at the Registry's headquarters office. The four days notice of intention to make such a search as mentioned above should be given at the office where you intend to made the search.

Is there a simpler way that I can obtain the name and address of the owner of a property? If a property is registered and can be identified by a single postal address, (for example, 23, Coniston Drive, Kerwick) and you only want to know the name and address of the registered owner, you may apply by post on Land Registry form 313.

This service although covering all registered properties in England and Wales, **is currently only available from The Customer Information Centre, Room 105, The Harrow District Land Registry, Lyon House, Lyon Road, Harrow, Middx, HA1 2EU**, to which office Land Registry forms 313 should be addressed.

If the land does not have a single postal address, (for example, land lying to the west of Augustine Way, Kerwick) or information other than details of the registered owner is wanted, then application should be made for an office copy or a personal inspection of the register as set out above.

What fees are payable?
The fees payable under the current Land Registration Fees Order to cover the cost of the services are:
(a) Postal search of the Index Map
> (1) Where any part of the land to which the search relates is registered, and until further notice, the Chief Land Registrar has exercised his discretion and has waived this fee where a result of search discloses up to and including 10 registered titles.Where more than 10 registered titles are disclosed, the application for search will be charged only for the excess over 10 titles. E.g.15 registered titles disclosed will attract a fee of 5 x £4 = £20.
> (2) Where no part of the land to which the search relates is registered until further notice, the Chief Land Registrar has exercised his discretion and has waived this fee.

(b)Copy of the register or any part thereof – per copy £4
(c) Copy of the title plan – per copy £4
(d) Copy of any or all of the documents referred to in the register - per copy or set £4
(e) Personal inspection of the register or any part thereof – per title £4
(f)Personal inspection of the title plan – per title £4
(g) Personal inspection of any or all of the documents referred to in the register –per title £4
(h) The supply of a copy of an Index Map Section – per copy £40
(h) Where the applicant does not know the title number and endorses the application form "Please supply title number" a £4 fee will be payable if more than 10
> registered titles are disclosed.

(j) The supply of the name and address of the registered
> proprietor of land identified by its postal address
> – per application £4

These fees may change from time to time
The appropriate fee payable must accompany the relevant application form. Fees should be paid by cheque or postal order drawn in favour of HM LAND REGISTRY. Bank notes or coins should not be sent through the post. Credit cards cannot be used.

What documents are not held by the registry and cannot therefore be inspected?
Amongst documents that are **not** held by the Land Registry Re:-
(a) Title deeds dated prior to the date of first registration of the property other than those referred to on the register as filed. [When a property is first registered with the Land Registry the title deeds existing at that time are lodged at the Registry. After registration has been completed such deeds are returned to the person applying for registration or their solicitors.]
(b) Copies of deeds not referred to on the register
(c) Court Orders
(d) Birth, Marriage or Death Certificates
(e) Grants of Probate or Letters of Administration
N.B. Items (c), (d) and (e) are documents of public record and copies can be obtained from the appropriate court officials, the Registrar of Births, Deaths and Marriages or the Probate Registry.

What information relating to land cannot be obtained from the registry?
There are many matters which relate to land and property for which the Land Registry is not responsible and does not hold records. Amongst such matters are:
(a) Individual land or property values
(b) Matters relating to planning permission, compulsory purchase, land redevelopment, road charges, public health charges, building lines or tree conservations. (Such matters should be recorded as local land charges by the local authority.)
(c) Unregistered titles
(d) Tenancy agreements
(e) Land held under a Lease for a term of 21 years or less
(f) Land or property outside England and Wales
(g) Matters relating to the Community Charge/Council Tax/Rating assessment

Copies of all Land Registry forms and other leaflets may be obtained by writing to any
District Land Registry
or from
HM Land Registry, Lincoln's Inn Fields, London WC2A 3PH
(Tel: 0171 917 8888)

Areas Served by The District Land Registries for England & Wales

HM Land Registry, HM Land Registry, Lincoln's Inn Fields, London, WC2A 3PH

England

Birkenhead District Land Registry
Rosebrae Court, Woodside Ferry Approach, Birkenhead, Merseyside, L41 6DU, Tel: 0151 473 1110
Tel: 0151 473 1106 Enquiries Fax: 0151 473 0366
Cheshire; London Boroughs of Kensington, Chelsea, Hammersmith, Fulham

Birkenhead District Land Registry
Old Market House, Hamilton Street, Birkenhead, Merseyside, L41 5FL, Tel: 0151 473 1110
Tel: 0151 473 1106 Enquiries, Fax: 0151 473 0251
Merseyside; Staffordshire; Stoke on Trent

Coventry District Land Registry
Leigh Court, Torrington Ave, Tile Hill, Coventry, CV4 9XZ, Tel: 01203 860860, Tel: 01203 860864 Enquiries
Fax: 01203 860021
West Midlands

Croydon District Land Registry
Sunley House, Bedford Park, Croydon, CR9 3LE, Tel: 0181 781 9100, Tel: 0181 781 9103 Enquiries, Fax: 0181 781 9110
London Boroughs of Croydon, Sutton, Bromley, Bexley,

Durham (Boldon House) District Land Registry
Boldon House, Wheatlands Way, Pity Me, Durham, County Durham, DH1 5GJ, Tel: 0191 301 2345 Fax: 0191 301 2300
Cumbria; Surrey

Durham (Southfield House) District Land Registry
Southfield House, Southfield Way, Durham, County Durham, England Tel: 0191 301 3500, Tel: 0191 301 0020
Darlington; Durham; Hartlepool; Middlesbrough; Northumberland; Redcar & Cleveland; Stockton on Tees
Tyne & Wear

Gloucester District Land Registry
Twyver House, Bruton Way, Gloucester, Gloucestershire, GL1 1DQ, Tel: 01452 511111 Fax: 01452 510050
Berkshire; Bristol; Gloucestershire; Oxfordshire; South Gloucestershire; Warwickshire

Harrow District Land Registry
Lyon House, Lyon Road, Harrow, Middlesex, HA1 2EU, Tel: 0181 235 1181 Fax: 0181 862 0176
London Boroughs of Barnet, Brent, Camden, Islington City of London; City of Westminster; Harrow
Inner & Middle Temples

Kingston Upon Hull District Land Registry
Earle House, Portland Street, Hull, HU2 8JN, Tel: 01482 223244 Fax: 01482 224278
East Riding of York; Kingston Upon Hull; Lincolnshire
Norfolk; N E Lincolnshire; North Lincolnshire; Suffolk

Leicester District Land Registry
Westbridge Place, Leicester, Leicestershire, LE3 5DR
Tel: 0116 265 4000, Tel: 0116 265 4001 Enquiries
Fax: 0116 265 4008
Buckinghamshire; Leicester; Leicestershire; Milton Keynes
Rutland

Lytham District Land Registry
Birkenhead House, East Beach, Lytham St Annes FY8 5AB, Tel: 01253 849 849, Tel: 01253 840012 Enquiries
Fax: 01253 840001 (Manchester, Salford, Stockport, Tameside & Trafford)
Fax: 01253 840002 (Bolton, Bury, Oldham, Rochdale & Wigan)
Fax: 01253 840013 (Lancashire)
Greater Manchester; Lancashire

Wales

District Land Registry for Wales
Ty Cwm Tawe, Phoenix Way, Llansamlet, Swansea
SA7 9FQ, Tel: 01792 355000, Tel: 01792 355095 Enquiries
Fax: 01792 355055

Nottingham District Land Registry
Chalfont Drive, Nottingham, Nottinghamshire, NG8 3RN, Tel: 0115 935 1166 Fax: 0115 936 0036 for Nottinghamshire
Derby; Derbyshire; Nottinghamshire; South Yorkshire
West Yorkshire

Peterborough District Land Registry
Touhill Close, City Road, Peterborough, PE1 1XN
Tel: 01733 288288 Fax: 01733 280022
Bedfordshire; Cambridgeshire; Essex; Luton; Northamptonshire

Plymouth District Land Registry
Plumer House, Tailyour Road, Crownhill, Plymouth, Devon, PL6 5HY, Tel: 01752 636000, Tel: 01752 636123 Enquiries, Fax: 01752 636161
Bath; North Somerset; Cornwall; Isles of Scilly; North Somerset; Somerset

Portsmouth District Land Registry
St Andrews Court, St Michael's Road, Portsmouth, Hampshire, PO1 2JH, Tel: 01705 768888
Tel: 01705 768880 Enquiries, Fax: 01705 768768
Brighton & Hove; East Sussex; Isle of Wight; West Sussex

Stevenage District Land Registry
Brickdale House, Swingate, Stevenage, Hertfordshire, SG1 1XG, Tel: 01438 788888, Tel: 01438 788889 Enquiries
Fax: 01438 780107
Hertfordshire
London Boroughs of Barking & Dagenham, Enfield, Hackney, Haringey, Havering, Newham, Redbridge, Tower Hamlets, Waltham Forest

Swansea District Land Registry
Ty Bryn Glas, High Street, Swansea, SA1 1PW
Tel: 01792 458877 Fax: 01792 473236
London Boroughs of Ealing, Hillingdon, Hounslow

Telford District Land Registry
Parkside Court, Hall Park Way, Telford TF3 4LR
Tel: 01952 290355 Fax: 01952 290356
Hereford; Worcester; Shropshire, Greenwich
Kingston upon Thames
London Boroughs of Lambeth, Lewsiham, Merton, Richmond upon Thames, Southwark, Wandsworth

Tunbridge Wells District Land Registry
Curtis House, Forest Road, Tunbridge Wells TN2 5AQ
Tel: 01892 510015 Fax: 01892 510032
Kent

Weymouth District Land Registry
Melcombe Court, 1 Cumberland Drive, Weymouth, Dorset, DT4 9TT, Tel: 01305 363636 Fax: 01305 363646
Hampshire Poole; Portsmouth; Southampton; Swindon
Wiltshire; Dorset

York District Land Registry
James House, James Street, York, YO1 3YZ
Tel: 01904 450000 Fax: 01904 450086
North Yorkshire; York

THE NORTH OF ENGLAND OPEN AIR MUSEUM

The Development of an Open Air Museum

Beamish is a museum which tells the story of the people of the North East of England at two distinct points in their history:- 1825 and 1913.

The early 1800s was a period of agricultural improvement and pioneering in livestock breeding and 1825 saw the opening of the Stockton and Darlington Railway. 1913 was peak year of coal production in the Great Northern Coalfield, the area which was geographically Northumberland and Durham, and of course the year before the outbreak of the First World War which was to affect many regional patterns of culture and tradition.

Beamish was largely the brainchild of Frank Atkinson, a Yorkshireman who had come to the North East of England in 1958, to be the Director of the Bowes Museum at Barnard Castle, a museum largely representing Continental Fine and Applied Art. Realising at that time that little social history was being recorded about the people of the North East, Frank persuaded his Committee that he build up a "collection of objects for a future museum of the life and work of ordinary people". Frank, as an "outsider" saw more clearly the magnitude and speed of social change than most people within the North East. Urgency was the watchword. Frank adopted a policy of "unselective collecting".......""you offer it to us and we'll collect it". The imagination of the people of the region was immediately captured; they donated objects of all sizes, from steam engines and complete shop interiors to old photographs of people, and tape recordings and information about them.

At Brancepeth, a disused army camp was taken over and about 22 huts and hangars were rapidly filled. The public wanted to know more and demanded more information. An interior of a miner's cottage, a chemist's shop and bar were set up and shown to visitors on open days. Frank gave hundreds of lectures to societies, W.I.s and other groups and the media backed him up with enthusiastic support for the project. Meanwhile an army of volunteers were at work gathering further material for the museum. The collecting of objects from the community, on such a large scale, was to create a future bond between museum and community which has never been lost.

In 1968 a Working Party drew up a list of possible sites for the development of an open air museum. These were for the most part situated in the Counties of Northumberland and Durham, and took into account the main centres of population in the North East, good road communications, the geographical nature of the land and any geographical features or buildings already on the site. The site chosen of about 200 acres was based on Beamish Hall, situated on the northern boundary of County Durham in a well contained "bowl" of land. The topography ranged from steep slopes of woodland to gentler more undulating land in the valley bottom. The land was largely agricultural but also contained an area of 19th century parkland around Beamish Hall, once the home of the Eden and Shafto families. The importance of the Beamish Valley cannot be underestimated. The site chosen for the museum has proved to be even more ideal than ever could have been envisaged in those early days. Later acquisitions of a 19th century

estate farmstead, an important medieval strong house and manor house, a series of mills, mill sites and forges dotted around the Beamish Burn as well as two sites of Special Scientific Interest and some mature woodland have since been added to the original landholding, the total now being some 300 acres.

In 1970 Beamish as an open air museum came into being, with the first few staff being appointed and Frank Atkinson as the first Director. The purpose of the museum was set out and now includes "the studying, collecting, preserving, interpreting and exhibiting to the public, buildings machinery, objects and information illustrating the development of industry and agriculture and way of life in the North East of England."

Now nearly 30 years on, Beamish is recognised as a museum not just of the region, but of international importance. It is a Registered museum and one of the first 26 museums throughout the Country to be "Designated" as a museum with an outstanding collection. It has won numerous awards including "Museum of Europe", and now attracts some 300-400,000 visitors each year from all over the world.

Beamish is not a traditional museum. Some of the buildings in the Beamish valley such as Home Farm, Pockerley Manor and the Drift Mine were on site already. Most of the other buildings, however, which can now be seen have been rescued from elsewhere in the North East. They have been carefully dismantled and rebuilt along with typical furnishings and fittings, Beamish has now recreated a typical North Eastern Railway station with associated buildings, a Colliery Village with Board School, Chapel and Pit cottages and a Vertical 1855 steam winding engine. There are also two working farms with Durham Shorthorn cattle, pigs, poultry and heavy horses. One of the largest areas at Beamish is its Town with park; bandstand, town houses, pub, co-op store, garage and working sweet shop producing hand made boiled sweets. All these areas are linked by 1 1/2 miles of working electric tramway. Beamish is a museum of living history where visitors of all ages can come along and talk to the costumed demonstrators and find out what life was like in the region. Newest developments include an 1825 area where visitors can go to Pockerley Manor a lovely Georgian House with parterre garden and 1820s plants, Pockerley also incorporates a medieval stronghouse dating back to the 1400s. Pockerley was mentioned in the Great Survey undertaken by the Bishop of Durham, Hugh de Pudsey in 1183, known as Boldon Book.

Across the Beamish Valley runs the working replica of George Stephenson's Engine, Locomotion, which carries passengers as did the original on the opening of the Stockton and Darlington railway in 1825. The Great Shed at Beamish houses displays on early railways up to the 1820 period.

Beamish, therefore plays a major part in the preservation of the heritage of the North East of England. Its collections are remarkable; the early years of development resulted in some wonderful material relating to the region's history being collected. Whilst the period areas can be seen by all the visitors, few people realise that a wealth of information exists behind the scenes without which, the staff at Beamish would not be able to create the period areas.

The Resource collection includes a reference library, which has been built up of recently published books, together with a wide ranging collection of 19th and early 20th century books. Often, though out of date as textbooks, they are invaluable for providing information on the collections and their use. A substantial proportion of the 20,000 volumes comprises rare antiquarian books and other collections of agricultural, industrial and social history interest. The collection does not duplicate the work of local libraries but rather complements it. The library also houses a large and nationally important collection of trade catalogues of suppliers and manufacturers of products supplied into the region. These are now a comprehensive reference source, which is proving of great value to students, researchers, publishers and other investigators. The library also includes a collection of printed posters, leaflets and ephemera.

An oral history collection of several hundred tape recordings have been made of the memories of North Eastern people from all walks of life. Since much of our heritage is preserved only in people's memories, it is essential that we record as much of this information before it is lost. The value of oral history cannot be underestimated, whether it is for recording historical fact, family information, stories, dialects, songs or music. It is invaluable for project work for schools or for reminiscence and recall with the elderly, forging a powerful link between the generations.

One of Beamish's most exciting "behind the scenes" development is the Photographic Archive, which is a visual record of life as it was in the counties of Cleveland, Durham, Northumberland and Tyne & Wear. The collections consist of a very wide range of old photographs illustrating towns, street scenes, shops and advertising material, villages, rural life and farming scenes as well as studies of old livestock in photo and engraving. There is also a fine collection of industrial scenes illustrating coal mining above and below ground, lead mining, iron and steel and other northern industries.

The photographs largely illustrate people at work and play and some 200,000 images cover a period from the 1860s up until the present day. Unlike many public collections, which are built around the work of a single photographer of acknowledged skill, the Beamish collection is a popular contribution to historical record. The Archive also includes many modern record photographs showing buildings of interest in the North East region. The photos include black and white prints, magic lantern slides, negatives and transparencies. Some 100 films relating to the events and activities in the North East, 8mm to 16mm have now been copied onto video format and these are held within the archive.

The development of Beamish's photo archive has been one of the most important features of the museum's activity since its foundation in 1970. The archive follows the museum's underlying philosophy in contributing knowledge, information and resources to the community served by the museum. Several years ago, the museum decided that information technology could be employed to make the archive more accessible, facilitate its growth and improve efficiency without significantly increasing the staff required to service and manage the collection. The result was an innovative highly flexible system which was based on Sony Analogue write once optical laser disc, under computer control, linked to a large computer data base. The system gave total control over editing of copy discs. All data was microfilmed from the existing manual card index and transferred during 1991-92.

Since then the archive has been made available to everyone with an interest in the material or a need to acquire images for use in school projects, reference study material, publications and for display. Current users include schools and colleges, social historians, publishers and television companies.

Technology is changing rapidly and Beamish was leading the field in 1991/92 with its original Analogue laser disc system. Digitisation has improved dramatically over the last few years and Beamish is now in the process of converting the Photo Archive to a new Digital system where images can be stored and compressed but at the same time where excellent quality can be retained. Large volumes of images can be stored in a system which is now faster and less expensive.

The museum has come full circle. We have been successful in going back in time to the early 1800s and yet we have also come right up to date in being able to harness present day technology to access even more of the past.

Beamish is delighted to welcome researchers who may have access to the Resource Centre, including Reference Library, Oral History Collection and Photographic Archive, by appointment during weekdays. At present these collections are housed within Beamish Hall but are due to be moved to new accommodation over the next two years.

Any enquiries may be addressed to
The Senior Keeper
Rosemary E Allan
BEAMISH
The North of England Open Air Museum
Beamish, Co. Durham. DH9 0RG
Tel: 01207 231811 Fax: 01207 290933

British Empire & Commonwealth Museum
Clock Tower Yard, Temple Meads, Bristoil, BS1 6QH Tel:
0117 925 4980 Fax: 0117 925 4983, Email:
staff@empiremuseum.demon.co.uk
National Museum of Labour History
103 Princess Street, Manchester, M1 6DD Tel: 0161-228-
7212 Fax: 0161-237-5965, Email: info-
nmlh@pop3.poptel.org.uk

England
Bedfordshire
Bedford Museum
Castle Lane, Bedford, MK40 3XD Tel: 01234 353323
Cecil Higgins Art Gallery & Museum
Castle Close, Castle Lane, Bedford, MK40 3RP
Tel: 01234 211222
Elstow Moot Hall,
Elstow, Bedford, MK42 9 Tel: 01234 266889
John Dony Field Centre
Hancock Drive, Bushmead, Luton, LU2 7SF Tel: 01582 486983
Luton Museum & Art Gallery
Wardown Park, Old Bedford Rd, Luton, LU2 7HA Tel:
01582 546722
Shuttleworth Collection
Old Warden Aerodrome, Old Warden, Biggleswade,
SG18 9ER Tel: 01767 627288
Shuttleworth Veteran Aeroplane Society
Old Warden Aerodrome, Old Warden, Biggleswade,
SG18 9ER Tel: 01767 627398
Berkshire
Blake's Lock Museum
Gasworks Rd, Reading, RG1 3DS Tel: 0118 939 0918
Slough Museum
278-286 High St, Slough, SL1 1NB Tel: 01753 526422
The Museum of Berkshire Aviation Trust
6 Richmond Road, Caversham Heights, Reading, RG7 7PP
Tel: 0118 947 3924
West Berkshire Museum
The Wharf, Newbury, RG14 5AS Tel: 01635 30511
Bristol
Ashton Court Visitor Centre
Ashton Court, Long Ashton, Bristol, BS41 8JN
Tel: 117 963 9174
Blaise Castle House Museum
Henbury, Bristol, BS10 7QS Tel: 0117 950 6789
Bristol Industrial Museum
Princes Wharf, Wapping Road, Bristol, BS1 4RN Tel: 0117
925 1470
British Empire & Commonwealth Museum
Clock Tower Yard, Temple Meads, Bristoil, BS1 6QH
Tel: 117 925 4980 Fax: 0117 925 4983, Email:
staff@empiremuseum.demon.co.uk
City Museum & Art Gallery
Queens Road, Bristol, BS8 1RL Tel: 0117 921 3571
Fax: 117 922 2047 Email: general_museum@bristol-
city.gov.uk WWW: www.bristol-city.gov.uk/museums
Clevedon Story Heritage Centre
Waterloo House, 4 The Beach, Clevedon, BS21 7QU Tel:
01275 341196
Clifton Suspension Bridge Visitor Centre
Bridge House, Sion Place, Bristol, BS8 4AP
Tel: 117 974 4664
Exploratory Hands on Science Centre
Bristol Old Station, Temple Meads, Bristol, BS1 6QU
Tel: 117 907 9000
Harveys Wine Museum
12 Denmark St, Bristol, BS1 5DQ Tel: 0117 927 5036
Maritime Heritage Centre
Wapping Wharf, Gasferry Road, Bristol, BS1 6TY
Tel: 117 926 0680

National Railway Museum
Leeman Road, York, YO26 4XJ Tel: 01904 621261 Fax:
01904 6111112, Email: nrm@nmsi.ac.uk, WWW:
www.nmsi.ac.uk/nrm/

Red Lodge
Park Row, Bristol, BS1 5LJ Tel: 0117 921 1360
The Georgian House
7 Great George Street, Bristol, BS1 5RR Tel: 0117 921 1362
Buckinghamshire
Amersham Local History Museum
49 High Street, Amersham Tel: 01494 725754
Bletchley Park Trust
The Mansion, Bletchley Park, Bletchley, Milton Keynes,
MK3 6EB Tel: 01908 640404
Blue Max
Wycombe Air Park, Booker, Marlow, SL7 3DP
Tel: 1494 449810
Buckinghamshire County Museum
Church Street, Aylesbury, HP20 2QP Tel: 01296 331441
Fax: 01296 334884, Email: museum@buckscc.gov.uk
Chesham Town Museum Project
Chesham Library, Elgiva Lane, Chesham, HP8 2JD
Tel: 1494 783183
Chiltern Open Air Museum Ltd
Newland Park, Gorelands Lane, Chalfont St. Giles, HP8 4AD
Tel: 01494 871117
Milton Keynes Museum
Stacey Hill Farm, Southern Way, Wolverton, Milton Keynes,
MK12 5EJ Tel: 01908 316222
Wycombe Local History & Chair Museum
Priory Avenue, High Wycombe, HP13 6PX Tel: 01494
421895 Fax: 01494 421897 Email:
enquiries@wycombemuseum.demon.co.uk WWW:
www.wycombe.gov.uk/museum
Cambridgeshire
Cambridge Brass Rubbing
The Round Church, Bridge St, Cambridge, CB2 1UB Tel:
01223 871621
Cambridge Museum of Technology
Old Pumping Station, Cheddars Lane, Cambridge, CB5 8LD
Tel: 01223 368650
Duxford Aviation Society
Duxford Airfield, Duxford, CB2 4QR Tel: 01223 835594
Duxford Displays Ltd
Duxford Airfield, Duxford CB2 4QR Tel: 01223 836593
Ely Museum
The Old Gaol, Market St, Ely, CB7 4LS Tel: 01353-666655
Farmland Museum
Denny Abbey, Ely Rd, Waterbeach, Cambridge, CB5 9PQ
Tel: 01223 860988
Fenland & West Norfolk Aviation Museum
Lynn Rd, West Walton, Wisbech, PE14 7 Tel: 01945 584440
Fighter Collection
Imperial War Museum, The Airfield, Duxford, Cambridge,
CB2 4QR Tel: 01223 834973
Folk Museum
2 Castle St, Cambridge, CB3 0AQ Tel: 01223 355159
Imperial War Museum Duxford
The Airfield , Duxford, Cambridge, CB2 4QR Tel: 01223-
835000, WWW: www.iwm.org.uk
March & District Museum Society,
Museum, High St, March, PE15 9JJ Tel: 01354 655300
National Dragonfly Museum
Ashton Mill, Ashton, Peterborough, PE8 5LB
Tel: 1832 272427

Norris Library and Museum
The Broadway, St Ives, Huntingdon, PE17 4BX Tel: 01480-465101 Fax: 01480 497314
Octavia Hill Birthplace Museum Trust
1 South Brink Place, Wisbech, PE13 1JE Tel: 01945 476358
Peterborough Museum & Art Gallery
Priestgate, Peterborough, PE1 1LF Tel: 01733 343329
Prickwillow Drainage Engine Museum
Main St, Prickwillow, Ely, CB7 4UN Tel: 01353 688360
Ramsey Rural Museum
The Woodyard, Wood Lane, Ramsey, Huntingdon, PE17 1XD Tel: 01487 815715
Sedgwick Museum
Downing St, Cambridge, CB2 3EQ Tel: 01223 333456
Wisbech and Fenland Museum
Museum Square, Wisbech, PE13 1ES Tel: 01945-583817 Fax: 1945-589050,
Wisbech & Fenland Museum
Museum Square, Wisbech, PE13 1ES Tel: 01945 583817
Cheshire
Catalyst
Gossage Building, Mersey Rd, Widnes, WA8 0DF Tel: 0151 420 1121
Cheshire Military Museum
The Castle, Chester, CH1 2DN Tel: 01244 327617
Chester Heritage Centre
St. Michaels Church, Bridge St, Chester, CH1 1NQ Tel: 01244 317948
Grosvenor Museum
27 Grosvenor St, Chester, CH1 2DD Tel: 01244 321616
Lion Salt Works Trust
Ollershaw Lane, Marston, Northwich, CW9 6ES Tel: 01606 41823
Macclesfield Heritage Centre Museum
Roe St, Macclesfield, SK11 6UT Tel: 01625 613210
Nantwich Museum
Pillory St, Nantwich, CW5 5BQ Tel: 01270 627104
Norton Priory Museum Trust Ltd
Tudor Rd, Manor Park, Runcorn WA7 1SX Tel: 1928 569895
On The Air, 42 Bridge St Row, Chester, CH1 1NN Tel: 1244 348468
Paradise Mill, Park Lane, Macclesfield, SK11 6TJ Tel: 1625 618228
Port Sunlight Heritage Centre
95 Greendale Road, Port Sunlight, L62 4XE Tel: 151-6446466
Warrington Museum & Art Gallery
Bold St, Warrington, WA1 1JG Tel: 01925 442392
West Park Museum
Prestbury Rd, Macclesfield, SK10 3BJ Tel: 01625 619831
Cleveland
Captain Cook Birthplace Museum
Stewart Park, Marton, Middlesbrough, TS7 8AT Tel: 1642 311211
Captain Cook & Staithes Heritage Centre
High St, Staithes, Saltburn-By-The-Sea, TS13 5BQ Tel: 1947 841454
Dorman Musuem,
Linthorpe Rd, Middlesbrough, TS5 6LA Tel: 01642 813781
Green Dragon Museum
Theatre Yard, High St, Stockton-On-Tees, TS18 1AT Tel: 1642 393938
Margrove Heritage Centre
Margrove Park, Boosbeck, Saltburn-By-The-Sea, TS12 3BZ Tel: 01287 610368
Museums and Gallery Service
Gloucester House, Church Road, Stockton on Tees, TS18 1YB Tel: 01642-393983 Fax: 01642-393983,

Preston Hall Museum
Yarm Rd, Stockton-On-Tees, TS18 3RH Tel: 01642 781184
Cornwall
Automobilia
The Old Mill, Terras Rd, St. Austell, PL26 7RX Tel: 01726 823092
Bodmin Museum
Mount Folly, Bodmin, PL31 2DB Tel: 01208 77067
Cable & Wireless Telecomunication Museum plc
Eastern House, Porthcurno, St. Levan, Penzance, TR19 6 Tel: 01736 810477
Charlestown Shipwreck & Heritage Centre
Quay Rd, Charlestown, St. Austell, PL25 3NX Tel: 01726 69897
Duke of Cornwall's Light Infantry Museum
The Keep, Bodmin, Cornwall, PL31 1EG Tel: 01206-72610
Helston Folk Museum
Market Place, Helston, TR13 8TH Tel: 01326 564027
John Betjeman Centre
Southern Way, Wadebridge, PL27 7BX Tel: 01208 812392
Lanreath Farm & Folk Museum
Lanreath, Looe, PL13 2NX Tel: 01503 220321
Lawrence House Museum
9 Castle St, Launceston, PL15 8BA Tel: 01566 773277
Maritime Museum
19 Chapel St, Penzance, TR18 4AW Tel: 01736 368890
Mevagissey Museum Society
Frazier Ho, The Quay, Mevagissey, Cornwall PL26 6QU Tel: 01726 843568
Merlin's Cave Crystal Mineral & Fossil Museum & Shop
Molesworth St, Tintagel, PL34 0BZ Tel: 01840 770023
Military Museum
The Keep, Bodmin, PL31 1EG Tel: 01208 72810
National Maritime Museum (Falmouth, Cornwall)
48 Arwenack St, Falmouth, TR11 3SA Tel: 01326 313388
National Maritime Museum (Saltash, Cornwall), Cotehele Quay, Cotehele, Saltash, PL12 6TA Tel: 01579 350830
Penryn Museum
Town Hall, Higher Market St, Penryn, TR10 8LT Tel: 01326 372158
Potter's Museum
Jamaica Inn, Bolventor, Launceston, PL15 7TS Tel: 01566 86838
Royal Cornwall Museum
River St, Truro, TR1 2SJ Tel: 01872 272205
County Durham
Beamish Museum
Beamish Tel; 01207 231811 Fax: 01207 290933
Bowes Museum
Newgate, Barnard Castle, DL12 8NP Tel: 01833 690606
Darlington Museum & Art Gallery
Tubwell Row, Darlington, DL1 1PD Tel: 01325 463795
Darlington Railway Centre & Museum
North Road Station , Station Rd, Darlington, DL3 6ST Tel: 01325 460532
Darlington Railway Preservation Society
Station Rd, Hopetown, Darlington, DL3 6ST Tel: 01325 483606
Discovery Centre
Grosvenor House, 29 Market Place, Bishop Auckland, DL14 7NP Tel: 01388-662666 Fax: 01388-661941
Email: west.durham@groundwork.org.uk
Durham Arts
Library and Museums Department, County Hall, Durham DH1 5TY Tel: 0191-383-3595
Durham Heritage Centre
St Mary le Bow, North Bailey, Durham, DH1 5ET Tel: 191-384-5589
Durham University Library Archives and Special Collections
Palace Green, Durham, DH1 3RN Tel: 0191-374-3032

Fulling Mill Museum of Archaeology
The Banks, Durham Tel: 0191 374 3623
Killhope Lead Mining Centre
Cowshill, Weardale, DL13 1AR Tel: 01388-537505 Fax:
01388-537617 Email: killhope@durham.gov.uk
WWW: http://www.durham.gov.uk/killhope/index.htm
Timothy Hackworth Victorian & Railway Museum
Shildon, DL4 1PQ Tel: 01388-777999 Fax: 01388-777999,
Weardale Museum
Ireshopeburn, DL13 1EY Tel: 1388-537417
Cumbria
Aspects of Motoring Western Lakes Motor Museum
The Maltings, The Maltings, Brewery Lane, Cockermouth
CA13 9ND Tel: 01900 824448
Dove Cottage & The Wordsworth Museum
Town End, Grasmere, Ambleside, LA22 9SH
Tel: 015394 35544
Guildhall Museum
Green Market, Carlisle, CA3 8JE Tel: 01228 819925
Haig Colliery Mining Museum
Solway Rd, Kells,Whitehaven,CA28 9BG Tel: 01946 599949
Keswick Museum & Art Gallery
Station Rd, Keswick, CA12 4NF Tel: 017687 73263
Lakeland Motor Museum
Holker Hall, Cark In Cartmel, Grange-Over-Sands,
LA11 7PL Tel: 015395 58509
Laurel & Hardy Museum
4c Upper Brook St, Ulverston,LA12 7BH Tel: 01229 582292
Maryport Steamship Museum
Elizabeth Dock South Quay, Maryport, CA15 8AB
Tel: 1900 815954
Penrith Museum
Middlegate, Penrith, CA11 7PT,
Roman Army Museum
Carvoran House, Greenhead, Carlisle,CA6 7JB
Tel: 16977 47485
Ruskin Museum
Coniston Institute, Yewdale Rd, Coniston, LA21 8DU
Tel: 15394 41164
Senhouse Roman Museum
The Battery, Sea Brows, Maryport, CA15 6JD
Tel: 01900 816168
Solway Aviation Museum
Carlisle Airport, Carlisle, CA6 4NW Tel: 01228 573823
The Dock Museum
North Rd, Barrow-In-Furness,LA14 2PWTel: 01229 894444
Tullie House Museum and Art Gallery
Castle Street, Carlisle, CA3 8TP Tel: 01228-534781
Fax: 1228-810249,
Ulverston Heritage Centre
Lower Brook St, Ulverston, LA12 7EE Tel: 01229 580820
William Creighton Mineral Museum & Gallery
2 Crown St, Cockermouth, CA13 0EJ Tel: 01900 828301
Windermere Steamboat Museum
Rayrigg Rd, Windermere, LA23 1BN Tel: 015394 45565
Derbyshire
Chesterfield Museum & Art Gallery
St Mary's Gate, Chesterfield, S41 7TY Tel: 01246 345727
Fax: 01246 345720, No archive or library material held. The
Museum tells the story of the developement of Chesterfield
from Roman times to the present day.
Derby Industrial Museum
Silk Mill Lane, Derby, DE1 3AR Tel: 01332 255308
Derby Museum & Art Gallery
The Strand, Derby, DE1 1BS Tel: 01332-716659
Fax: 01332-716670,
Derwent Valley Visitor Centre
Belper North Mill, Bridge Foot, Belper, DE56 1YD
Tel: 1773 880474

Donington Grandprix Collection
Donington Park, Castle Donington, Derby, DE74 2RP
Tel: 01332 811027
Donington Park Racing Ltd
Donington Park, Castle Donnington, Derby, DE74 2RP Tel:
01332 814697
Elvaston Castle Estate Museum
Elvaston Castle Country Park, Borrowash Rd, Elvaston,
Derby, DE72 3EP Tel: 01332 573799
Erewash Museum
The Museum High Street, Ilkeston, DE7 5JA
Tel: 0115 907 1141 WWW: www.erewash.gov.uk
Glossop Heritage Centre
Bank House, Henry St, Glossop, SK13 8BW
Tel: 1457 869176
High Peak Junction Workshop
High Peak Junction, Cronford, Matlock, DE4 5HN
Tel: 1629 822831
High Peak Trail
Middleton Top, Rise End, Middleton, Matlock, DE4 4LS
Tel: 01629 823204
Midland Railway Centre
Butterley Station, Ripley, DE5 3QZ Tel: 01773 570140
National Stone Centre
Porter Lane, Wirksworth, Matlock, DE4 4LS
Tel: 1629 824833
Peak District Mining Museum
Pavilion, South Parade, Matlock, DE4 3NR
Tel: 1629 583834
Pickford's House Museum
41 Friar Gate, Derby, DE1 1DA Tel: 01332 255363
Devon
Allhallows Museum of Lace & Antiquities
High St, Honiton, EX14 8PE Tel: 01404 44966
Century of Playtime
30 Winner St, Paignton, TQ3 3BJ Tel: 1803 553850
Devon & Cornwall Constabulary Museum
Middlemoor, Exeter, EX2 7HQ Tel: 01392 203025
Dunkeswell Memorial Museum
Dunkeswell Airfield, Dunkeswell Ind Est, Dunkeswell,
Honiton, EX14 0RA Tel: 01404 891943
Fairlynch Art Centre & Museum
27 Fore St, Budleigh Salterton, EX9 6NP Tel: 01395 442666
Finch Foundary Museum of Rural Industry
Sticklepath, Okehampton, EX20 2NW Tel: 01837 840046
Ilfracombe Museum
Wilder Rd, Ilfracombe, EX34 8AF Tel: 01271 863541
Museum of North Devon
The Square, Barnstaple, EX32 8LN Tel: 01271 346 747
Newhall Equestrian Centre
Newhall, Budlake, Exeter, EX5 3LW Tel: 01392 466030
Newton Abbot Town & Great Western Railway Museum
2A St. Pauls Rd, Newton Abbot, TQ12 2HP
Tel: 1626 201121
North Devon Maritime Museum
Odun House, Odun Rd, Appledore, Bideford, EX39 1PT
Tel: 1237 422064
North Devon Museum Service
St.Anne's Chapel, Paternoster Row, Barnstaple, EX32 8LN
Tel: 01271 378709
North Devon Museum Service, The Square, Barnstaple,
EX32 8LN Tel: 01271 346747
Otterton Mill Centre
Otterton, Budleigh Salterton, EX9 7HG Tel: 01395 568521
Park Pharmacy Trust
Thorn Park Lodge, Thorn Park , Mannamead, Plymouth,
PL3 4TF Tel: 01752 263501
Plymouth City Museum
Drake Circus, Plymouth, PL4 8AJ Tel: 01752 304774

Royal Albert Memorial Museum
Queen St, Exeter, EX4 3RX Tel: 01392 265858
Sidmouth Museum
Hope Cottage, Church St, Sidmouth, EX10 8LY
Tel: 1395 516139
Teignmouth Museum
29 French St, Teignmouth, TQ14 8ST Tel: 01626 777041
The Dartmouth Museum
The Butterwalk, Dartmouth, TQ6 9 Tel: 01803 832923
Dorset
Bournemouth Aviation Museum
Hanger 600 South East Sector, Bournemouth International
Airport Hurn, Christchurch, BH23 6SE Tel: 01202 580858
Cavalcade of Costume
Lime Tree House, The Plocks, Blandford Forum, DT11 7AA
Tel: 01258 453006
Christchurch Motor Museum
Matchams Lane, Hurn, Christchurch, BH23 6AW
Tel: 1202 488100
Dinosaur Land
Coombe St, Lyme Regis, DT7 3PY
Tel: 1297 443541
Dinosaur Museum
Icen Way, Dorchester, DT1 1EW Tel: 01305 269880
Dorset County Museum
66 High West St, Dorchester, DT1 1XA Tel: 01305 262735
Harbour Museum
West Bay, Bridport, DT6 4SA Tel: 01308 420997
Lyme Regis Philpot Museum
Bridge St, Lyme Regis, DT7 3QA Tel: 01297 443370
Merley House Model Museum
Merley Park, Wimborne, BH21 3AA Tel: 01202 886533
Nothe Fort
Barrack Rd, Weymouth, DT4 8UF Tel: 01305 787243
Portland Museum
Wakeham, Portland, DT5 1HS Tel: 01305 821804
Priest's House Museum
23-27 High St, Wimborne, BH21 1HR Tel: 01202 882533
Red House Museum & Gardens
Quay Rd, Christchurch, BH23 1BU Tel: 01202 482860
Russell-Cotes Art Gallery & Museum
East Cliff, Bournemouth, BH1 3AA Tel: 01202 451800
Shaftesbury Abbey Museum & Garden
Park Walk, Shaftesbury, SP7 8JR Tel: 01747 852910
Shaftesbury Town Museum
Gold Hill, Shaftesbury, SP7 8JW Tel: 01747 852157
Shelley Rooms
Shelley Park, Beechwood Avenue, Bournemouth, BH5 1NE
Tel: 01202 303571
Sherborne Museum Association
Abbey Gate House, Church Avenue, Sherborne, DT9 3BP
Tel: 01935 812252
Wareham Town Museum
5 East St, Wareham, BH20 4NN Tel: 01929 553448
Waterfront Musuem
4 High St, Poole, BH15 1BW Tel: 01202 683138
Weymouth & Portland Museum Service
The Esplanade, Weymouth, DT4 8ED Tel: 01305 765206
East Sussex
Anne of Cleves House Museum
52 Southover, High St, Lewes, BN7 1JA Tel: 01273 474610
Battle Museum
Langton Memorial Hall, High St, Battle, TN33 0AQ
Tel: 1424 775955
Bexhill Museum
Egerton Rd, Bexhill-On-Sea, TN39 3HL Tel: 01424 787950
Bexhill Museum of Costume & Social History Association
Manor Gardens, Upper Sea Rd, Bexhill-On-Sea, TN40 1RL
Tel: 01424 210045

Visual Arts Project
Brighton Media Centre
9-12 Middle St, Brighton, BN1 1AL Tel: 01273 384242
Booth Musuem
194 Dyke Rd, Brighton, BN1 5AA Tel: 01273 292777
Dave Clarke Prop Shop
Long Barn, Cross In Hand, Heathfield, TN21 0TP
Tel: 1435 863800
Eastbourne Heritage Centre
2 Carlisle Rd, Eastbourne, BN21 4BT Tel: 01323 411189
Filching Manor Motor Museum
Filching Manor, Jevington Rd, Polegate, BN26 5QA Tel:
01323 487838
Fishermans Museum
Rock A Nore Rd, Hastings, TN34 3DW Tel: 01424 461446
Hastings Museum & Art Gallery
Johns Place, Bohemia Rd, Hastings, TN34 1ET
Tel: 1424 781155
Hove Musuem & Art Gallery
19 New Church Rd, Hove, BN3 4AB Tel: 01273 290200
How We Lived Then Museum of Shops
20 Cornfield Terrace, Eastbourne, BN21 4NS
Tel: 1323 737143
Newhaven Local & Maritime Museum
Garden Paradise, Avis Way, Newhaven, BN9 0DH
Tel: 1273 612530
Preston Manor Musuem
Preston Drove, Brighton, BN1 1 Tel: 01273 292770
Rye Castle Museum
East St, Rye, TN31 7JY Tel: 01797 226728
Seaford Museum of Local History
Martello Tower, The Esplanade, Seaford, BN25 1JH
Tel: 1323 898222
The Engineerium
The Droveway, Nevill Rd, Hove, BN3 7QA
Tel: 1273 554070
Wish Tower Puppet Museum
Tower 73, King Edwards Parade, Eastbourne, BN21 4BY
Tel: 01323 411620
East Yorkshire
East Riding Heritage Library & Museum
Sewerby Hall, Church Lane, Sewerby, Bridlington, YO15
1EA Tel: 01262-677874 Tel: 01262-674265
Email: museum@pop3.poptel.org.uk
WWW: www.bridlington.net/sew
The Hornsea Museum
Burns Farm, 11 Newbegin, Hornsea, HU18 1AB
Tel: 1964 533443
Withernsea Lighthouse Museum
Hull Rd, Withernsea, HU19 2DY Tel: 01964 614834
Essex
Barleylands Farm Museum & Visitors Centre
Barleylands Farm, Billericay, CM11 2UD Tel: 01268 282090
Battlesbridge Motorcycle Museum
Muggeridge Farm, Maltings Road, Battlesbridge, Wickford,
SS11 7RF Tel: 01268 560866
Castle Point Transport Museum Society
105 Point Rd, Canvey Island, SS8 7TJ Tel: 01268 684272
Chelmsford & Essex Museum
Oaklands Park, Moulsham St, Chelmsford, CM2 9AQ
Tel: 1245 353066
East England Tank Museum
Oak Business Park, Wix Rd, Beaumont, Clacton-On-Sea,
CO16 0AT Tel: 01255 871119
Epping Forest District Museum
39-41 Sun St, Waltham Abbey, EN9 1EL Tel: 01992 716882
Essex Police Museum
Police Headquarters, PO Box 2, Springfield, Chelmsford,
CM2 6DA Tel: 01245-491491-ext-50771

Harlow Museum
Passmores House, Third Avenue, Harlow, CM18 6YL Tel:
01279 454959
Hollytrees Museum
High St, Colchester, CO1 1DN Tel: 01206 282940
Leigh Heritage Centre & Museum
13a High St, Leigh-On-Sea, SS9 2EN Tel: 01702 470834
Valence Library & Museum
London Borough of Barking & Dagenham Local History
Studies, Becontree Avenue, Dagenham, RM8 3HT Tel: 20-
8592-6537 Tel: 20-822-75294 Fax: 20-822-75297, Email:
fm019@viscount.org.uk, WWW:
http://www.earl.org.uk/partners/barking/index.html
Maldon District Museum
47 Mill Rd, Maldon, CM9 5HX Tel: 01621 842688
Mark Hall Cycle Museum
Muskham Rd, Harlow, CM20 2LF Tel: 01279 439680
National Motorboat Museum
Wattyler Country Park, Pitsea Hall Lane, Pitsea, Basildon,
SS16 4UH Tel: 01268 550077
Prittlewell Priory Museum
Priory Park, Victoria Avenue, Southend-On-Sea, SS2 6NB
Tel: 01702 342878
Saffron Walden Museum
Museum St, Saffron Walden, CB10 1JL Tel: 01799 510333
The Cater Museum
74 High St, Billericay, CM12 9BS Tel: 01277 622023
Valence House Museum
Becontree Avenue, Dagenham, RM8 3HS Tel: 0181
595 8404
Gloucestershire
Corinium Museum
Park Street, Cirencester, GL7 2BX,
Dean Heritage Centre
Soudley, Cinderford, Forest of dean, GL14 2UB
Tel: 01594 822170
Frenchay Tuckett Society and Local History Museum
247 Frenchay Park Road, Frenchay, BS16 ILG Tel: 0117 956
9324, Email: raybulmer@compuserve.com, WWW:
http://ourworld.compuserve.com/homepages/raybutler
Gloucester City Museum & Art Gallery
Brunswick Rd, Gloucester, GL1 1HP Tel: 01452 524131
Gloucester Folk Museum
93-103 Westgate St, Gloucester, GL1 2PG
Tel: 01452 526467
Guild of Handicraft Trust
Silk Mill, Sheep St, Chipping Campden, GL55 6DS
Tel: 1386 841417
Holst Birthplace Museum
4 Clarence Rd, Cheltenham, GL52 2AY Tel: 01242 524846
Jenner Museum
Church Lane, Berkeley, GL13 9BN Tel: 01453 810631
John Moore Countryside Museum
42 Church St, Tewkesbury, GL20 5SN Tel: 01684 297174
Nature In Art
Wallsworth Hall, Tewkesbury Rd, Twigworth, Gloucester,
GL2 9PG Tel: 01452 731422
Robert Opie Collection
Albert Warehouse, The Docks, Gloucester, GL1 2EH
Tel: 01452 302309
Shambles Museum
20 Church St, Newent, GL18 1PP Tel: 01531 822144
The Great Western Railway Museum (Coleford)
The Old Railway Station, Railway Drive, Coleford,
GL16 8RH Tel: 01594 833569
The National Waterways Museum
Llanthony Warehouse, Gloucester Docks, Gloucester
GL1 2EH Tel: 01452 318053

Greater Manchester
The History Shop
Wigan Council Heritage Service Centre, Library Street ,
Wigan, WN1 1NU Tel: 01942-828128 Fax: 01942-827645
Manchester Jewish Museum
190 Cheetham Hill Road, Manchester, M8 8LW,
Hampshire
Andover Museum & Iron Age Museum
6 Church Close, Andover, SP10 1DP Tel: 01264 366283
Bishops Waltham Museum Trust
8 Folly Field, Bishop's Waltham, Southampton, S032 1GF
Tel: 01489 894970
Eastleigh Museum
25 High St, Eastleigh, SO50 5LF Tel: 01703 643026
Eling Tide Mill Trust Ltd
The Tollbridge, Eling Hill, Totton, Southampton, SO40 9HF
Tel: 01703 869575
Gosport Museum
Walpole Rd, Gosport, PO12 1NS Tel: 01705 588035
Hampshire County Museums Service
Chilcomb House, Chilcomb Lane, Winchester, SO23 8RD
Tel: 01962 846304
Havant Museum
56 East Street, Havant, P09 1BS Tel: 23 9245 1155
Fax: 23 9249 8707
HMS Warrior (1860)
Victory Gate, HM Naval Base, Portsmouth, PO1 3
Tel: 1705 291379
Hollycombe Steam Collection
Iron Hill, Midhurst Rd, Liphook, GU30 7LP
Tel: 1428 724900
Maritime Museum
Bugle St, Southampton , SO14 2AJ Tel: 01703 223941
Mary Rose Trust
1-10 College Rd, HM Naval Base, Portsmouth, PO1 3LX
Tel: 01705 750521
New Forest Museum & Visitor Centre
High St, Lyndhurst, SO43 7NY Tel: 01703 283914
Portsmouth City Museum
Museum Rd, Old Portsmouth, Portsmouth, PO1 2LJ
Tel: 01705 827261
Priddy's Hard Armament Museum
Priory Rd, Gosport, PO12 4LE Tel: 01705 502490
Rockbourne Roman Villa, Rockbourne, Fordingbridge,
SP6 3PG Tel: 01725 518541
Royal Armouries
Fort Nelson Down End Rd, Fareham PO17 6AN
Tel: 1329 233734
Sammy Miller Motor Cycle Museum
Bashley Manor Farm, Bashley Cross Rd, New Milton,
BH25 5SZ Tel: 01425 620777
Search
50 Clarence Rd, Gosport, PO12 1BU Tel: 01705 501957
The Bear Museum
38 Dragon St, Petersfield, GU31 4JJ Tel: 01730 265108
Westbury Manor Museum
West St, Fareham, PO16 0JJ Tel: 01329 824895
Whitchurch Silk Mill
28 Winchester St, Whitchurch, RG28 7AL
Tel: 01256 892065
Willis Museum Of Basingstoke Town & Country Life
Old Town Hall, Market Place, Basingstoke, RG21 7QD
Tel: 01256 465902
Winchester Museums Service, 75 Hyde St, Winchester,
SO23 7DW Tel: 01962 848269
Herefordshire
Churchill House Museum
Venns Lane, Aylestone Hill, Hereford, HR1 1DE
Tel: 01432 267409

Cider Museum & King Offa Distillery
21 Ryelands St, Hereford, HR4 0LW Tel: 01432 354207
Leominster Museum
Etnam St, Leominster, HR6 8 Tel: 01568 615186
Teddy Bears of Bromyard
12 The Square, Bromyard, HR7 4BP Tel: 01885 488329
Waterworks Museum,
Broomy Hill, Hereford Tel: 01432-361147
Weobley & District Local History Society and Museum
Weobley Museum
Back Lane, Weobley, HR4 8SG Tel: 01544 340292
Hertfordshire
First Garden City Heritage Museum
296 Norton Way South, Letchworth Garden City, SG6 1SU
Tel: 01462 482710 Fax: 01462 486056, Email:
fgchm@letchworth.com
Hertford Museum
18 Bull Plain, Hertford, SG14 1DT Tel: 01992 582686
Hertford Museum
18 Bull Plain, Hertford, SG14 1DT ,
Hitchin British Schools
41-42 Queen St, Hitchin, SG4 9TS Tel: 01462 452697
Hitchin Museum
Paynes Park, Hitchin, SG5 1EQ Tel: 01462-434476 Fax:
01462-431318,
Kingsbury Water Mill Museum
St. Michaels St, St. Albans, AL3 4SJ Tel: 01727 853502
Letchworth Museum & Art Gallery
Broadway, Letchworth, SG6 3PF Tel: 01462 685647
Mill Green Museum & Mill
Mill Green, Hatfield, AL9 5PD Tel: 01707 271362
Rhodes Memorial Museum & Commonwealth Centre
South Rd, Bishop's Stortford, CM23 3JG Tel: 01279 651746
Royston & District Museum
5 Lower King St, Royston, SG8 5AL Tel: 01763 242587
The De Havilland Aircraft Museum Trust
P.O Box 107, Salisbury Hall, London Colney, St. Albans,
AL2 1EX Tel: 01727 822051
The Environmental Awareness Trust
23 High St, Wheathampstead, St. Albans, AL4 8BB
Tel: 01582 834580
The Forge Museum
High St, Much Hadham, SG10 6BS Tel: 01279 843301
Verulamium Museum
St. Michaels St, St. Albans, AL3 4SW Tel: 01727 751810
Walter Rothschild Zoological Museum
Akeman St, Tring, HP23 6AP Tel: 01442 824181
Ware Museum
Priory Lodge, 89 High St, Ware, SG12 9AD
Tel: 1920 487848
Watford Museum
194 High St, Watford, WD1 2DT Tel: 01923 232297
Welwyn Hatfield Museum Service
Welwyn Roman Baths, By-Pass-Road, Welwyn, AL6 0
Tel: 01438 716096
Isle Of Wight
Bembridge Maritime Museum & Shipwreck Centre
Providence House, Sherborne St, Bembridge, PO35 5SB
Tel: 01983 872223
Calbourne Water Mill
Calbourne Mill, Newport, PO30 4JN Tel: 01983 531227
Carisbrooke Castle Museum
Carisbrooke Castle, Newport, PO30 1XY Tel: 01983 523112
East Cowes Heritage Centre
8 Clarence Rd, East Cowes, PO32 6EP Tel: 01983 280310
Front Line Britain at War Experience
Sandown Airport, Scotchells Brook Lane, Sandown,
PO36 0JP Tel: 01983 404448
Guildhall Museum
High St, Newport, PO30 1TY Tel: 01983 823366

Lilliput Museum of Antique Dolls & Toys
High St Brading, Sandown, PO36 0DJ Tel: 01983 407231
Natural History Centre
High St, Godshill, Ventnor, PO38 3HZ Tel: 01983 840333
The Classic Boat Museum
Seaclose Wharf, Town Quay, Newport, PO30 2EF
Tel: 1983 533493
Ventnor Heritage Museum
11 Spring Hill, Ventnor, PO38 1PE Tel: 01983 855407
Kent
Bethlem Royal Hospital
Archives and Museum
Monks Orchard Road, Beckenham, BR3 3BX Tel: 0181-776-
4307 Fax: 0181-776-4045,
Canterbury Roman Museum
Butchery Lane, Canterbury, CT1 2JR Tel: 01227 785575
Chatham Dockyard Historical Society Museum
Cottage Row, Barrack Rd, Chatham Dockyard, Chatham,
ME4 4TZ Tel: 01634 844897
Dickens House Museum
2 Victoria Parade, Broadstairs, CT10 1QS Tel: 01843 861232
Dolphin Sailing Barge Museum
Crown Quay Lane, Sittingbourne, ME10 3SN
Tel: 1795 423215
Dover Museum
Market Square, Dover, CT16 1PB Tel: 01304 201066
Dover Transport Museum
Old Park Barracks, Whitfield, Dover, CT16 2HQ
Tel: 1304 822409
Drapers Museum of Bygones
4 High St, Rochester, ME1 1PT Tel: 01634 830647
Faversham Society
13 Preston St, Faversham, ME13 8NS Tel: 01795 534542
Guildhall Museum
High St, Rochester, ME1 1PY Tel: 01634 848717
Herne Bay Museum Centre
12 William St, Herne Bay, CT6 5EJ Tel: 01227 367368
Kent Battle of Britain Museum
Aerodrome Rd, Hawkinge, Folkestone, CT18 7AG Tel:
01303 893140
Maidstone Museum & Art Gallery
St. Faith St, Maidstone, ME14 1LH Tel: 01622 75449
Mander & Mitchenson Theatre Collection
The Mansion Beckenham, Place Park, Beckenham, BR3 5BP
Tel: 0181 658 7725
Margate Old Town Hall Museum
Old Town Hall, Market Place, Margate, CT9 1ER
Tel: 01843 231213
Maritime Museum
Clock House, Pier Yard, Royal Harbour, Ramsgate,
CT11 8LS Tel: 01843 587765
Masonic Library & Museum
St. Peters Place, Canterbury, CT1 2DA Tel: 01227 785625
Minster Abbey Gatehouse Museum
Union Rd, Minster On Sea, Sheerness, ME12 2HW
Tel: 1795 872303
Minster Museum Craft & Animal Centre
Bedlam Court Lane, Minster, Ramsgate, CT12 4HQ
Tel: 1843 822312
Pembroke Lodge Family History Centre and Museum
4 Station Approach, Birchington on Sea, CT7 9RD
Tel: 1843-841649
Phanet Movie Centre Ltd
United Reform Church Buildings, Meeting St, Ramsgate,
CT11 9RT Tel: 01843 850103
Powell-Cotton Museum
Quex Park, Birchington, CT7 0 Tel: 01843 842168
Royal Museum & Art Gallery
18 High St, Canterbury, CT1 2RA Tel: 01227 452747

SECTION 9
Museums

Sheerness Heritage Centre
10 Rose St, Sheerness, ME12 1AJ Tel: 01795 663317
Tenterden Museum
Station Rd, Tenterden, TN30 6HE Tel: 01580 764310
The Royal Museum & Art Gallery
18 High Street, Canterbury, CT1 2RA Tel: 01227-452747
Fax: 1227-455047,
The C.M Booth Collection Of Historic Vehicles
63-67 High St, Rolvenden, Cranbrook, TN17 4LP
Tel: 1580 241234
The Charles Dickens Centre
Eastgate House, High St, Rochester, ME1 1EW
Tel: 1634 844176
Victoriana Museum
Deal Town Hall, High St, Deal, CT14 6BB
Tel: 01304 380546
Watts Charity
Poor Travellers House, 97 High St, Rochester, ME1 1LX
Tel: 01634 845609
Whitstable Museum & Gallery
5a Oxford St, Whitstable, CT5 1DB Tel: 01227 276998
Lancashire
Blackburn Museum and Art Gallery
Museum Street, Blackburn, BB1 7AJ Tel: 01254-661730
Bolton Museum & Art Gallery
Le Mans Crescent, Bolton, BL1 1SE Tel: 01204 522311
Ellenroad Engine House
Elizabethan Way, Milnrow, Rochdale, OL16 4LG Tel:
01706 881952
Fleetwood Museum
Queens Terrace, Fleetwood, FY7 6BT Tel: 01253 876621
Gawthorpe Hall, Habergham Drive, Padiham, Burnley,
BB12 8UA Tel: 01282 771004
Hall I'Th' Wood Museum
Tonge Moor, Bolton, BL1 8UA Tel: 01204 301159
Heaton Park Tramway (Transport Museum)
Tram Depot, Heaton Park, Prestwich, Manchester, M25 2SW
Tel: 0161 740 1919
Helmshore Textile Museums, Holcombe Road, Helmshore,
Rossendale, BB4 4NP These museums deal with the history
of cotton manufacture in the area, people and the machinery.,
Heritage Trust for the North West
Pendle Heritage Centre Colne Rd, Barrowford, Nelson,
BB9 6JQ Tel: 01282 661704
Judge's Lodgings Museum
Church St, Lancaster, LA1 1LP Tel: 01524 32808
Keighley Bus Museum Trust
47 Brantfell Drive, Burnley, BB12 8AW Tel: 01282 413179
Kippers Cats, 51 Bridge St, Ramsbottom, Bury, BL0 9AD
Tel: 01706 822133
Lancashire Mining Museum
Buile Hill Park, Eccles Old Rd, Salford, M6 8GL
Tel: 161 736 1832
Lancaster City Museum
Market Square, Lancaster, LA1 1HT Tel: 01524 64637
Lytham Heritage Group
2 Henry St, Lytham St. Annes, FY8 5LE Tel: 01253 730767
Manchester Jewish Museum
190 Cheetham Hill Rd, Cheetham Hill, Manchester, M8 8LW
Tel: 0161 834 9879
Manchester Museum
Oxford Rd, Manchester, M13 9PL Tel: 0161 275 2634
Museum of Lancashire
Stanley Street, Preston PR1 4YP Tel: 01772-264075
Museum of the Manchesters
Ashton Town Hall, Market Place, Ashton-u-Lyne, OL6 6DL,
Tel:0161 342 3078/3710 or 343 1978

North West Sound Archive
Old Steward's Office, Clitheroe Castle, Clitheroe, BB7 1AZ
Tel: 01200-427897 Fax: 01200-427897
WWW: www.nw-soundarchive.co.uk
Oldham Museum
Greaves St, Oldham, OL1 1 Tel: 0161 911 4657
Ordsall Hall Museum
Taylorson St, Salford, M5 3HT Tel: 0161 872 0251
Pendle Heritage Centre
Park Hill, Colne Rd, Barrowford, Nelson, BB9 6JQ Tel:
01282 661702
Portland Basin Museum
Portland Place, Ashton-Under-Lyne, OL7 0QA
Tel: 161 343 2878
Pump House Peoples History Museum
Bridge St, Manchester, M3 3ER Tel: 0161 839 6061
Queen St Mill
Harle Syke, Queen St, Briercliffe, Burnley, BB10 2HX Tel:
01282 459996
Ribchester Roman Bath-House
Riverside, Preston, PR3 3XS Tel: 01772 264080
Ribchester Roman Museum
Riverside, Ribchester, Preston, PR3 3XS Tel: 01254 878261
Rochdale Museum Service
The Arts & Heritage Centre
The Esplanade, Rochdale, OL16 1AQ Tel: 01706 641085
Rochdale Pioneers Museum
Toad Lane, Rochdale, OL12 0NU Tel: 01706 524920
Rochdale Pioneers' Museum
31 Toad Lane, Rochdale Tel: 01706-524920
Saddleworth Museum & Art Gallery
High St, Uppermill, Oldham, OL3 6HS Tel: 01457 874093
Salford Museum & Art Gallery
Peel Park, Salford, M5 4WU Tel: 0161 736 2649
Salford Quays Heritage Centre
3 The Quays, Salford, M5 2SQ Tel: 0161 876 5359
Slaidburn Heritage Centre
25 Church St, Slaidburn, Clitheroe, BB7 3ER
Tel: 1200 446161
Smithills Hall Museum
Smithills, Dean Rd, Bolton, BL1 7NP Tel: 01204 841265
The Greater Manchester Police Museum
57 Newton St, Manchester, M1 1ET Tel: 0161 856 3287
The Museum of Science & Industry In Manchester
Liverpool Rd, Castlefield, Manchester, M3 4JP
Tel: 161 832 2244
Weavers Cottage Heritage Centre
Weavers Cottage, Bacup Rd, Rawtenstall, Rossendale,
BB4 7NW Tel: 01706 229828
Leicestershire
Abbey Pumping Station
Corporation Rd, Abbey Lane, Leicester, LE4 5PX
Tel: 116 299 5111
Ashby De La Zouch Museum
North St, Ashby-De-La-Zouch, LE65 1HU Tel:
01530 560090
Belgrave Hall & Gardens
Church Rd, Belgrave, Leicester, LE4 5PE Tel:
0116 266 6590
Bellfoundry Museum
Freehold St, Loughborough, LE11 1AR Tel: 01509 233414
Charnwood Museum
Granby St, Loughborough, LE11 3DU Tel: 01509 233754
Foxton Canal Museum
Middle Lock, Gumley Rd, Foxton, Market Harborough,
LE16 7RA Tel: 0116 279 2657
Hinckley & District Museum Ltd
Framework Knitters Cottage, Lower Bond St, Hinckley,
LE10 1QU Tel: 01455 251218

Jewry Wall Museum
St. Nicholas Circle, Leicester, LE1 4LB Tel: 0116 247 3021
Leicester City Museum & Art Gallery
53 New Walk, Leicester, LE1 7EA Tel: 0116 255 4100
Leicester Gas Museum
Aylestone Rd, Leicester, LE2 7LF Tel: 0116 250 3190
Leicestershire Ecology Centre
216 Birstall Rd, Birstall, Leicester, LE4 4DG Tel:
0116 267 1950
Melton Carnegie Museum
Thorpe End, Melton Mowbray, LE13 1RB Tel:
01664 569946
Rutland Railway Museum
Iron Ore Mine Sidings, Ashwell Rd, Cottesmore, Oakham,
LE15 7BX Tel: 01572 813203
Snibston Discovery Park, Ashby Rd, Coalville, LE67 3LN
Tel: 01530 510851
The Guildhall
Guildhall Lane, Leicester, LE1 5FQ Tel: 0116 253 2569
The Manor House
Manor Rd, Donington Le Heath, Coalville, LE67 2FW
Tel: 1530 831259
Lincolnshire
Manor House Museum
West St, Alford Tel: 01507 463073
Ayscoughfee Hall Museum
Churchgate, Spalding, PE11 2RA Tel: 01775 725468
Boston Guildhall Museum
South St, Boston, PE21 6HT Tel: 01205 365954
Church Farm Museum
Church Rd South, Skegness, PE25 2HF Tel: 01754 766658
Gainsborough Old Hall
Parnell St, Gainsborough, DN21 2NB Tel: 01427 612669
Gordon Boswell Romany Museum
Hawthorns Clay Lake, Spalding, PE12 6BL
Tel: 1775 710599
Grantham Museum
St. Peters Hill, Grantham, NG31 6PY Tel: 01476 568783
Lincolnshire Aviation Heritage Centre
East Kirkby Airfield, East Kirkby, Spilsby, PE23 4DE
Tel: 1790 763207
Lincs Vintage Vehicle Society
Whisby Rd, North Hykeham, Lincoln, LN6 3QT
Tel: 1522 500566
Louth Naturalists Antiquarian & Literary Society
4 Broadbank, Louth, LN11 0EQ Tel: 01507 601211
Museum of Lincolnshire Life
Old Barracks, Burton Road, Lincoln, LN1 3LY
Tel: 01522-528448 Fax: 01522-521264
Email: finchj@lincolnshire.gov.uk
National Fishing Heritage Centre
Alexander Dock, Great Grimsby, DN31 1UZ
Tel: 1472-323345
The Incredibly Fantastic Old Toy Show
26 Westgate, Lincoln, LN1 3BD Tel: 01522 520534
Liverpool
Maritime Museum
William Brown Street, Liverpool, L3 8EN
Tel: 0151-2070001
London
Alexander Fleming Laboratory Museum
St Mary's Hospital, Praed Street, Paddington, London, W2
1NY Tel: 0171-886-6528 Fax: 0171-886-6739,
Bank of England Archive
Archive Section HO-SV, The Bank of England,
Threadneedle Street, London, EC2R 8AH Tel: 0171-601-
5096 Fax: 0171-601-4356, Email:
archive@bankofengland.co.uk
Bethnal Green Museum of Childhood
Cambridge Heath Rd, London, E2 9PA Tel: 0181 980 2415

Black Cultural Archives
378 Coldharbour Lane, London, SW9 8LF Tel: 0171
738 4591
British Dental Association Museum (CLOSED UNTIL FURTHER NOTICE)
64 Wimpole Street, London, W1M 8AL Tel: 0171-935-0875-
British Museum
Great Russell St, London, WC1B 3DG Tel: 0171 580 9215
British Red Cross Museum and Archives
9 Grosvenor Crescent, London, SW1X 7EJ Tel: 0171-201-
5153 Fax: 0171-235-0876, Email: enquiry@redcross.org.uk,
WWW: www.redcross.org.uk
Cabaret Mechanical Theatre
Unit 33 , The Market, Covent Garden, WC2E 8RE
Tel: 171 379 7961
Cabinet War Rooms
Clive Steps, King Charles St, SW1A 2AQ Tel: 0171
930 6961
Church Farmhouse Museum
Greyhound Hill, Hendon, NW4 4JR Tel: 208203 0130
Cutty Sark
King William Walk, London, SE10 9HT Tel: 0181 858 2698
Design Museum
Butlers Wharf 28, Shad Thames, London, SE1 2YD Tel:
0171 403 6933
Dickens House Museum
48 Doughty St, London, WC1N 2LF Tel: 0171 405 2127
Doctor Johnson's House
17 Gough Square, London, EC4A 3DE Tel: 0171 353 3745
Eastside Community Heritage
The Old Town Hall, 29 Broadway, E15 4BQ
Tel: 181 519 7364
Florence Nightingale Museum
2 Lambeth Palace Road, London, SE1 7EW Tel: 0171-620-
0374 Fax: 0171-928-1760, Email: curator@florence-
nightingale.co.uk
WWW: http://www.florence-nightingale.co.uk
Freud Museum
20 Maresfield Gardens, Hampstead, London, NW3 5SX
Tel: 171 435 2002
Geffrye Museum
Kingsland Rd, London, E2 8EA Tel: 0171 739 9893
Geological Museum
Cromwell Rd, London, SW7 5BD Tel: 0171 938 8765
Golden Hinde
St. Mary Overie Dock, Cathedral St, SE1 9DE Tel:
8700 118700
Grange Museum of Community History
The Grange, Neasden Lane, Neasden, London, NW10 1QB
Tel: 20 8452 8311
Gunnersbury Park Museum
Gunnersbury Park, Popes Lane, W3 8LQ Tel: 0181 992 1612
Hackney Museum Service
Parkside Library, Victoria Park Rd, London, E9 7JL
Tel: 181 986 6914
Handel House Trust Ltd
10 Stratford Place, London, W1N 9AE Tel: 0171 495 1685
Hogarth's House
Hogarth Lane, Chiswick, London, W4 2QN
Tel: 0181 994 6757
Horniman Museum
100 London Rd, Forest Hill, London, SE23 3PQ
Tel: 0181 699 1872
House Mill
Three Mills Island, Three Mill Lane, Bromley by Bow,
London, E3 3DU Tel: 0181-980-4626
Imperial War Museum
Lambeth Road, London, SE1 6HZ Tel: 0171-416-5000
Island History Trust
St. Matthias Old Church, Woodstock Terrace, Poplar High
St, London, E14 0AE Tel: 0171 987 6041

Islington Museum
Foyer Gallery, Town Hall, Upper St, N1 2UD
Tel: 171 354 9442
Iveagh Bequest
Kenwood House, Hampstead Lane, London, NW3 7JR
Tel: 0181 348 1286
Jewish Museum
The Sternberg Centre for Judaism, 80 East End Road,
Finchley, London, N3 2SY Tel: 20 8349 1143
WWW: www.jewmusm.ort.org
Jewish Museum
129 Albert St, London, NW1 7NB Tel: 0171 284 1997
Keats House Museum
Wentworth Place, Keats Grove, NW3 2RR Tel: 0171
435 2062
Kensington Palace State Apartments
Kensington Palace, London, W8 4PX Tel: 0171 937 9561
Leighton House Museum & Art Gallery
12 Holland Park Rd, London, W14 8LZ Tel: 207602 3316
Livesey Museum
682 Old Kent Rd, London, SE15 1JF Tel: 0171 639 5604
London Canal Museum
12-13 New Wharf Rd, London, N1 9RT Tel: 0171 713 0836
London Fire Brigade Museum
94 Southwark Bridge Rd, London, SE1 0EG
Tel: 171 587 2894
London Gas Museum
Twelvetrees Crescent, London, E3 3JH Tel: 0171 538 4982
London Toy & Model Museum
21-23 Craven Hill, London, W2 3EN Tel: 0171 706 8000
London Transport Museum
Covent Garden Piazza, London, WC2E 7BB
Tel: 171 379 6344
Markfield Beam Engine & Museum
Markfield Rd, London, N15 4RB Tel: 0181 800 7061
Metropolitan Police Museum
Room 1317, New Scotland Yard, Broadway, London, SW1H
Tel: BG Tel: 0181-305-2824 Tel: 0181-305-1676
Fax: 181-293-6692,
Museum of the Royal College of Surgeons of England
35-43 Lincoln's Inn Fields, London, WC2A 3PN Tel: 0171-
405-3474-ext-3011 Fax: 0171 405 4438
Email: archives@rseng.ac.uk
Museum in Docklands Project Library & Archives
Unit C14, Poplar Business Park, 10 Prestons Road, London,
E14 9RL Tel: 0171-515-1162 Fax: 0171-538-0209, Email:
docklands@museum-london.org.uk
Museum of London
London Wall, London, EC2Y 5HN, Fax: 0171-600-1058,
Email: kstarling@museumoflondon.org.uk
Museum of the Order of St John
St John's Gate, St John's Lane, London, EC1M 4DA
Tel: 171-253-6644
Museum of the Royal Pharmaceutical Society
1 Lambeth High Street, London, SE1 7JN Tel: 0171-735-
9141-ext-354, Email: museum@rpsgb.org.uk
WWW: http://www.rpsgb.org.uk Research fee charged to
non members of the Society (Genealogical Enquiries)
Museums Association
42 Clerkenwell Close, London, EC1R Tel: PA Tel: 0171 250
1789 Fax: 0171 250 1929
National Gallery
St. Vincent House, 30 Orange St, London, WC2H 7HH
Tel: 171 747 5950
National Maritime Museum & Memorial Index
Romney Road, Greenwich, London, SE10 9NF
Tel: 0181-858-4422 Fax: 0181-312-6632
WWW: http://www.nmm.ac.uk
National Portrait Gallery
2 St. Martins Place, London, WC2H 0HE Tel: 0171 306 0055

National Postal Museum
King Edward Building, King Edward St, London, EC1A 1LP
Tel: 0171 776 3636
Newham Museum Service
The Old Town Hall, 29 The Broadway, Stratford, E15 4BQ
Tel: 0181 534 2274
North Woolwich Old Station Musuem
Pier Rd, North Woolwich, London, E16 2JJ Tel: 0171
474 7244
Old Operating Theatre Museum & Herb Garret
9a St. Thomas's St, London, SE1 9RY Tel: 0171 955 4791
Percival David Foundation of Chinese Art
53 Gordon Square, London, WC1H 0PD Tel: 0171 387 3909
Petrie Museum of Egyptian Archaeology
University College London, Gower St, WC1E 6BT
Tel: 171 504 2884
Pitshanger Manor & Gallery
Mattock Lane, London, W5 5EQ Tel: 208567 1227
Polish Institute & Sikorski Museum
20 Princes Gate, London, SW7 1PT Tel: 0171 589 9249
Pollock's Toy Museum
1 Scala St, London, W1P 1LT Tel: 0171 636 3452
Pump House Educational Museum
Lavender Pond & Nature Park, Lavender Rd, Rotherhithe,
SE16 1DZ Tel: 0171 231 2976
Ragged School Museum Trust, 46-50 Copperfield Rd,
London, E3 4RR Tel: 0181 980 6405
Royal Armouries
H.M Tower Of London, Tower Hill, London, EC3N 4AB
Tel: 0171 480 6358
Royal London Hospital Archives and Museum
Royal London Hospital, Newark Whitechapel, London, E1
1BB Tel: 0171-377-7608 Fax: 0171 377 7413
Email: r.j.evans@mds.qmw.ac.uk
Sam Uriah Morris Society
136a Lower Clapton Rd, London, E5 0QJ Tel: 0181
985 6449
Science For Life, 183 Euston Rd, London, NW1 2BN
Tel: 171 611 8727
Science Museum
Exhibition Rd, London, SW7 2DD Tel: 0171 938 8000
Sherlock Holmes Museum
221b Baker St, London, NW1 6XE Tel: 0171 935 8866
Sir John Soane's Museum
13 Lincolns Inn Fields, London, WC2A 3BP
Tel: 171 430 0175
St Bartholomew's Hospital Archives & Museum
West Smithfield, London, EC1A 7BE Tel: 0171-601-8152
The British Museum
Great Russell St, London, WC1B 3DG Tel: 0171 636 1555
The Clink Prison Museum
1 Clink St, London, SE1 9DG Tel: 0171 403 6515
The Fan Museum
12 Crooms Hill, London, SE10 8ER Tel: 208858 7879
The Museum of Women's Art
11 Northburgh St, London, EC1V 0AN Tel: 0171 251 4881
Vestry House Museum
Vestry Road, Walthamstow, London, E17 9NH Tel: 0181-
509-1917 Fax: 0181-509-9539
Email: vestry.house@ql.lbwf.gov.uk
WWW: www.lbwf.gov.uk/vestry/vestry.htm
Veterinary Museum
Royal Vetinary College, Royal College Street, London,
NW1 Tel: TU Tel: 0171-468-5165/6 Fax: 0171 468 5162,
Email: fhouston@rvc.ac.uk
Victoria & Albert Museum
Cromwell Rd, South Kensington, London, SW7 2RL
Tel: 171 938 8500
Wallace Collection, Hertford House, Manchester Square,
London, W1M 6BN Tel: 0171 935 0687

Wellington Museum
Apsley House, 149 Piccadilly Hyde Park Corner, London, W1V 9FA Tel: 0171 499 5676
Westminster Abbey Museum
Westminster Abbey, Deans Yard, SW1P 3PA
Tel: 171 233 0019
Wimbledon Lawn Tennis Museum
Church Rd, Wimbledon, London, SW19 5AE
Tel: 181 946 6131
Wimbledon Museum
26 Lingfield Rd, London, SW19 4QD Tel: 0181 296 9914
Merseyside
Beatle Story Ltd
Britannia Vaults, Albert Dock, Liverpool, L3 4AA
Tel: 151 709 1963
Botanic Gardens Museum
Churchtown, Southport, PR9 7NB Tel: 01704 227547
Merseyside Maritime Museum
Maritime Archives and Library, Albert Dock, Liverpool
L3 4AQ Tel: 0151-478-4613 Fax: 0151-478-777,
Merseyside Maritime Museum
Mann Island Pier, Liverpool, L3 1DG Tel: 0151 236 5567
Merseyside Maritime Museum
Albert Dock, Liverpool , L3 4AQ Tel: 0151 478 4499
National Museums & Galleries on Merseyside
127 Dale St, Liverpool, L2 2JH Tel: 0151 207 0001
Prescot Museum
34 Church St, Prescot, L34 3LA Tel: 0151 430 7787
Shore Road Pumping Station
Shore Rd, Birkenhead, CH41 1AG Tel: 0151 650 1182
Western Approaches
1 Rumford St, Liverpool, L2 8SZ Tel: 0151 227 2008
Middlesex
Forty Hall Museum
Forty Hill, Enfield, EN2 9HA Tel: 0181 363 8196
Harrow Museum & Heritage Centre
Headstone Manor, Pinner View, Harrow, HA2 6PX
Tel: 20 8861 2626
Kew Bridge Steam Museum
Green Dragon Lane, Brentford, TW8 0EN
Tel: 0181 568 4757
The Musical Museum
368 High St, Brentford, TW8 0BD Tel: 0181 560 8108
Scots D.G Museum Shop
The Castle, Edinburgh, EH1 2YT Tel: 0131 220 4387
Norfolk
Castle Museum
Castle Hill, Norwich, NR1 3JU Tel: 01603 493624
City of Norwich Aviation Museum Ltd
Old Norwich Rd, Horsham St. Faith, Norwich, NR10 3JF
Tel: 01603 893080
Diss Museum
The Market Place, Diss, IP22 3JT Tel: 01379 650618
Elizabethan House Museum
4 South Quay, Great Yarmouth, NR30 2QH
Tel: 1493 855746
Feltwell Historical and Archaeological Society
16 High Street, Feltwell, Thetford, IP26 Tel: 01842 828448
Glandford Shell Museum
Church House, Glandford, Holt, NR25 7JR
Tel: 01263 740081
Iceni Village & Museums
Cockley Cley, Swaffham, PE37 8AG Tel: 01760 721339
Inspire Hands On Science Centre
Coslany St, Norwich, NR3 3DJ Tel: 01603 612612
Lynn Museum
Old Market St, King's Lynn, PE30 1NL Tel: 01553 775001
Maritime Museum for East Anglia
25 Marine Parade, Great Yarmouth, NR30 2EN
Tel: 1493 842267

Norfolk Motorcycle Museum
Station Yard, Norwich Rd, North Walsham, NR28 0DS Tel: 01692 406266
Norfolk Rural Life Museum & Union Farm
Beach House, Gressenhall, Dereham, NR20 4DR
Tel: 1362 860563
Sheringham Museum
Station Rd, Sheringham, NR26 8RE Tel: 01263 821871
Shirehall Museum
Common Place, Walsingham, NR22 6BP Tel: 01328 820510
North Lincolnshire
Baysgarth House Museum
Caistor Rd, Barton-Upon-Humber, DN18 6AH
Tel: 1652 632318
Immingham Museum
Immingham Resorce Centre
Margaret St, Immingham, DN40 1LE Tel: 01469 577066
North Lincolnshire Museum
Oswald Rd, Scunthorpe, DN15 7BD Tel: 01724 843533
North Yorkshire
Archaeological Resource Centre
St.Saviour Church, St.Saviourgate, York, YO1 8NN
Tel: 1904 654324
Aysgarth Falls Carriage Museum
Yore Mill , Asgarth Falls, Leyburn, DL8 3SR
Tel: 1969 663399
Beck Isle Museum of Rural Life, Bridge St, Pickering, YO18 8DT Tel: 01751 473653
Captain Cook Memorial Museum
Grape Lane, Whitby, YO22 4BA Tel: 01947 601900
Captain Cook Schoolroom Museum
Great Ayton Tel: 01642-722030
Dales Countryside Museum
Station Yard, Burtersett Rd, Hawes, DL8 3NT
Tel: 01969 667494
Embsay Steam Railway
Embsay Railway Station, Embsay, Skipton, BD23 6QX
Tel: 1756 794727
Life In Miniature
8 Sandgate, Whitby, YO22 4DB Tel: 01947 601478
Malton Museum
The Old Town Hall, Market Place, Malton, YO17 7LP
Tel: 1653 695136
Micklegate Bar Museum
Micklegate, York, YO1 6JX Tel: 01904 634436
Nidderdale Museum
Council Offices, King Street, Pateley Bridge, HG3 5LE
Tel: 1423-711225
Old Courthouse Museum
Castle Yard, Knaresborough Tel: 01423-556188
Fax: 1423-556130,
Richard III Museum
Monk Bar, York, YO1 7LH Tel: 01904 634191
Richmondshire Museum
Ryder's Wynd, Richmond, DL10 4JA Tel: 01748 825611
Ripon Prison & Police Museum
St Marygate, Ripon, HG4 1LX Tel: 01765-690799
Email: ralph.lindley@which.net
Rotunda Museum
Vernon Rd, Scarborough, YO11 2 Tel: 01723 374839
Royal Pump Room Museum
Crown Place, Harrogate Tel: 01423-556188 Fax: 01423 556130
Ryedale Folk Museum
Hutton le Hole, YO62 6UA Tel: 01751 417367, Email: library@dbc-lib.demon.co.uk
The World of James Herriott
23 Kirkgate, Thirsk, YO7 1PL Tel: 01845 524234 Fax: 01845 525333, WWW: www.hambleton.gov.uk

Whitby Lifeboat Museum
30 Ruswarp Lane, Whitby, YO21 1ND Tel: 01947 606094
Whitby Lifeboat Museum
Pier Rd, Whitby, YO21 3PU Tel: 01947 602001
Whitby Museum
Pannet Park, Whitby, YO21 1RE Tel: 01947 602908
Yorkshire Museum of Farming
Murton Park, Murton Lane, York, YO19 5UF Tel: 01904
489966 Fax: 01904 489159,
Northamptonshire
Abington Museum
Abington Park, Northampton, NN1 5LW Tel: 01604 631454
Canal Museum
Stoke Bruerne, Towcester, NN12 7SE Tel: 01604 862229
Museum of The Northamptonshire Regiment
Park Museum Abington, NN1 5LW Tel: 01604 635412
Northampton Iron Stone Railway Trust
Hunsbury Hill Country Park, Hunsbury Hill Rd, West
Hunsbury, Northampton, NN4 9UW Tel: 01604 702031
Rushden Historical Transport Society
The Station, Station Approach, Rushden, NN10 0AW
Tel: 1933 318988
Wellingborough Heritage Centre
Croyland Hall, Burystead Place, Wellingborough, NN8 1AH
Tel: 01933 276838
Northumberland
Berwick Borough Museum
The Barracks, The Parade, Berwick-Upon-Tweed,
TD15 1DG Tel: 01289 330933
Bewick Studios
Mickley Square, Mickley, Stocksfield, NE43 7BL
Tel: 1661 844055
Border History Museum
The Old Gaol, Hallgate, Hexham, NE46 3NH Tel: 01434-
652349 Fax: 01434-652425, Email: lted@tynedale.gov.uk
Border History Museum and Library
Moothall, Hallgate, Hexham, NE46 3NH Tel: 01434-652349
Fax: 01434-652425, Email: lted@tynedale.gov.uk
Marine Life Centre & Fishing Museum
8 Main St, Seahouses, NE68 7RG Tel: 01665 721257
North East Mills Group
Blackfriars, Monk Street, Newcastle upon Tyne, NE1 4XN
Tel:191 2329279
WWW: //welcome.to/North.East.Mill.Group
The Heritage Centre
Front St, Bellingham, Hexham, NE48 2AU Tel:
01434 220050
Vindolanda Trust
Chesterholm Museum Bardon Mill, Hexham, NE47 7JN
Tel: 1434 344277
Nottinghamshire
Department of Manuscripts and Special Collections
Hallward Library, Nottingham University , University Park,
Nottingham, NG7 2RD Tel: 0115 951 4565 Fax: 0115
951848,
D.H Lawrence Heritage
Durban House Heritage Centre
Mansfield Rd, Eastwood, Nottingham, NG16 3DZ
Tel: 1773 717353
Galleries of Justice
Shire Hall, High Pavement, Nottingham, NG1 1HN Tel:
0115 952 0555
Great Central Railway
Nottingham Heritage Centre
Mere Way, Ruddington, Nottingham, NG11 6JS
Tel: 115 940 5705
Greens Mill & Science Musuem
Windmill Lane, Sneinton, Nottingham, NG2 4QB
Tel: 115 915 6878

Harley Gallery
Welbeck, Worksop, S80 3LW Tel: 01909 501700
Industrial Musuem
Wollaton Hall, Wollaton Park, Nottingham, NG8 2AE
Tel: 115 915 3910
Mansfield Museum & Art Gallery
Leeming Street, Mansfield, NG18 1NG Tel: 01623-463088
Fax: 01623-412922,
Millgate Museum of Folk Life
48 Millgate, Newark, NG24 4TS Tel: 01636 679403
Natural History Museum
Wollaton Hall, Wollaton Park, Nottingham, NG8 2AE
Tel: 115 915 3900
Newark Museum
Appleton Gate, Newark, NG24 1JY Tel: 01636 702358
Newark (Notts & Lincs) Air Museum
The Airfield, Lincoln Rd, Winthorpe, Newark, NG24 2NY
Tel: 01636 707170
Newstead Abbey Museum
Newstead Abbey Park, Nottingham, NG15 8GE
Tel: 1623 455900
Nottingham Castle Museum & Art Gallery
Castle Rd, Nottingham, NG1 6AA Tel: 0115 915 3700
Nottingham Museum Shops
Canal St, Nottingham, NG1 7HG Tel: 0115 915 6871
Ruddington Frame Work Knitter's Museum
Chapel St, Ruddington, Nottingham, NG11 6HE
Tel: 115 984 6914
Ruddington Village Museum
St. Peters Rooms, Church St, Ruddington, Nottingham,
NG11 6HD Tel: 0115 914 6645
The Museum of Nottingham Lace
3-5 High Pavement, Nottingham, NG1 1HF
Tel: 115 989 7365
Whaley Thorn Heritage & Environment Centre
Portland Terrace, Langwith, Mansfield, NG20 9HA
Tel: 1623 742525
Oxfordshire
Abingdon Museum
Market Place, Abingdon, OX14 3HG Tel: 01235 523703
Ashmolean Museum
Beaumont St, Oxford, OX1 2PH Tel: 01865 278000
Great Western Society Ltd
Didcot Railway Station Rd, Didcot, OX11 7NJ Tel:
01235 817200
Oxfordshire County Museum
Fletchers House, Park St, Woodstock, OX20 1SN
Tel: 1993 811456
Pitt Rivers/University Museums Information Line
South Parks Rd, Oxford, OX1 3PP Tel: 01865 270949
River & Rowing Museum
Mill Meadows, Henley on Thames, RG9 1BF Tel: 01491
415610 Fax: 01491 415601, Email: museum@rrm.co.uk,
WWW: www..rrm.co.uk
Vale & Downland Museum Centre
19 Church St, Wantage, OX12 8BL Tel: 01235 771447
Wallingford Museum
Flint House, High St, Wallingford, OX10 0DB
Tel: 1491 835065
Witney & District Museum
Gloucester Court Mews, High St, Witney, OX8 6LX
Tel: 1993 775915
Rutland
Rutland County Museum
Catmose Street, Oakham, LE15 6HW Tel: 01572-723654
Fax: 1572-757576,
Shropshire
Acton Scott Historic Working Farm
Wenlock Lodge, Acton Scott, Church Stretton, SY6 6QN
Tel: 01694 781306

Blists Hill Open Air Museum
Ironbridge Gorge Museum Trust Ltd, Legges Way, Madeley, Telford, TF7 5DU Tel: 01952 586063
Coalport China Museum
Ironbridge Gorge Museum Trust Ltd, High St, Coalport, Telford, TF8 7AW Tel: 01952 580650
Ironbridge Gorge Museum, Library & Archives
The Wharfage, Ironbridge, Telford, TF8 7AW
Tel: 1952-432141 Fax: 01952-432237,
Jackfield Tile Museum
Ironbridge Gorge Museum Trust Ltd, Jackfield, Telford, TF8 7AW Tel: 01952 882030
Ludlow Museum
Castle St, Ludlow, SY8 1AS Tel: 01584 875384
Ludlow Museum Store
47 Old St, Ludlow, SY8 1NW Tel: 01584 873857
Midland Motor Museum
Stanmore Hall, Stourbridge Rd, Stanmore, Bridgnorth, WV15 6DT Tel: 01746 762992
Museum Of Iron
Ironbridge Gorge Museum Trust Ltd, Coach Rd, Coalbrookdale, Telford, TF8 7EZ Tel: 01952 433418
Museum Of The River Visitor Centre
Ironbridge Gorge Museum Trust Ltd, The Wharfage, Ironbridge, TF8 7AW Tel: 01952 432405
Oswestry Transport Museum
Oswald Rd, Oswestry, SY11 1RE Tel: 01691 671749
Rosehill House
Ironbridge Gorge Museum Trust Ltd, Darby Rd, Coalbrookdale, Telford, TF8 7AW Tel: 01952 432551
Rowley's House Museum
Barker Street, Shrewsbury, SY1 1QH Tel: 01743 361196 Fax: 1743 358411,
Royal Air Force Museum
Cosford, Shifnal, TF11 8UP Tel: 01902 376200
Somerset
Abbey Barn - Somerset Rural Life Museum
Abbey Barn, Chilkwell St, Glastonbury, BA6 8DB
Tel: 1458 831197
Admiral Blake Museum
Blake St, Bridgwater, TA6 3NB Tel: 01278 456127
American Museum
Claverton Manor, Bath, BA2 7BD Tel: 01225 460503
Tel: 1225 463538 Fax: 01225 480726,
Area Museum Council For The South West
Hestercombe House, Cheddon Fitzpaine, Taunton, TA2 8LQ
Tel: 01823 259696
Bakelite Museum
Orchard Mill, Bridge St Williton, Taunton, TA4 4NS
Tel: 1984 632133
Bath Industrial Heritage Centre
Camden Works, Julian Road, Bath, BA1 2RH
Tel: 1225 318348 Fax: 01225 318348, Email:
BathIndHeritage@Camdenworks.swinternet.com.uk
Bath Postal Museum
8 Broad St, Bath, BA1 5LJ Tel: 01225 460333
Bath Royal Literary & Scientific Institution
16-18 Queen Square, Bath, BA1 2HN Tel: 01225 312084
Blazes Fire Museum
Sandhill Park, Bishops Lydeard, Taunton, TA4 3DE
Tel: 1823 433964
Chard & District Museum
Godworthy House, High St, Chard, TA20 1QB
Tel: 1460 65091
Glastonbury Lake Village Museum
9 High St, Glastonbury, BA6 9DP Tel: 1458 832949
Haynes Motor Museum
Castle Cary Rd, Sparkford, Yeovil, BA22 7LH
Tel: 1963 440804

Holburne Museum & Crafts Study Centre
Great Pulteney St, Bath, BA2 4DB Tel: 01225 466669
John Judkyn Memorial
Garden Thorpe, Freshford, Bath, BA3 6BX Tel:
01225 723312
Lambretta Scooter Museum
77 Alfred St, Weston-Super-Mare, BS23 1PP
Tel: 1934 822075
No.1 Royal Crescent
1 Royal Crescent, Bath, BA1 2LR Tel: 01225 428126
North Somerset Museum Service
Burlington St, Weston-Super-Mare, BS23 1PR Tel:
01934 621028
Radstock, Midsomer Norton & District Museum
Barton Meade House, Haydon, Radstock, Bath
Tel: 1761 437722
Roman Baths Museum
Abbey Churchyard, Bath, BA1 1LZ Tel: 01225 477785
Somerset County Museum Service, Taunton Castle,
Taunton, TA1 4AA Tel: 01823 320200
Somerset & Dorset Railway Trust, Washford Station,
Washford, Watchet, TA23 0PP Tel: 01984 640869
The Building of Bath Museum
The Countess of Huntingdon's Chapel, The Vineyards, Bath,
BA1 5NA Tel: 01225 333 895 Fax: 01225 445 473
WWW: www.bath-preservation-trust.org.uk
The Helicopter Museum
Locking Moor Rd, Weston-Super-Mare, BS22 8PL
Tel: 1934 635227
The Jane Austen Centre
40 Gay Street, Bath, BA1 2NT Tel: 01225 443000
Email: info@janeausten.co.uk
The Museum Of East Asian Art
12 Bennett St, Bath, BA1 2QJ Tel: 01225 464640
Wells Museum
8 Cathedral Green, Wells, BA5 2UE Tel: 01749 673477
West Somerset Museum
The Old School, Allerford, Minehead, TA24 8HN
Tel: 1643 862529
William Herschel Museum
19 New King St, Bath, BA1 2BL Tel: 01225 311342
South Yorkshire
Abbeydale Industrial Hamlet, Abbeydale Road South,
Sheffield, S7 2 Tel: 0114 236 7731
Bishops House Museum
Meersbrook Park, Nortin Lees Lane, Sheffield, S8 9BE
Tel: 114 255 7701
Cannon Hall Museum
Cannon Hall, Cawthorne, Barnsley, S75 4AT
Tel: 1226 790270
Clifton Park Museum
Clifton Lane, Rotherham, S65 2AA Tel: 01709 823635
Fire Museum (Sheffield)
Peter House, 101-109 West Bar, Sheffield, S3 8PT Tel:
0114 249 1999
Kelham Island Museum
Alma St, Kelham Island, Sheffield, S3 8RY
Tel: 114 272 2106
Sandtoft Transport Centre Ltd
Belton Rd, Sandtoft, Doncaster, DN8 5SX Tel:
01724 711391
Sheffield City Museum
Weston Park, Sheffield, S10 2TP Tel: 0114 276 8588
South Yorkshire Archaeology Unit and Museum
Ellin Street, Sheffield Tel: 0114 2734230
Staffordshire
Borough Museum & Art Gallery
Brampton Park, Newcastle, ST5 0QP Tel: 01782 619705

Clay Mills Pumping Engines Trust Ltd
Sewage Treatment Works, Meadow Lane, Stretton, Burton-On-Trent, DE13 0DB Tel: 01283 509929
Etruria Industrial Museum
Lower Bedford St, Etruria, Stoke-On-Trent, ST4 7AF
Tel: 1782 233144
Gladstone Pottery Museum
Uttoxeter Rd, Longton, Stoke-On-Trent, ST3 1PQ
Tel: 1782 319232 Fax: Fax: 01782 598640,
Hanley Museum & Art Gallery
Bethesda St, Hanley, Stoke-On-Trent, ST1 3DW
Tel: 1782 232323
Hanley Museum & Art Gallery
Broad St, Hanley, Stoke-On-Trent, ST1 4HS
Tel: 1782 202173
Samuel Johnson Birthplace Museum
Breadmarket St, Lichfield, WS13 6LG Tel: 01543 264972
Uttoxeter Heritage Centre
34-36 Carter St, Uttoxeter, ST14 8EU Tel: 01889 567176
Suffolk
Christchurch Mansion & Wolsey Art Gallery
Christchurch Park, Soane St, Ipswich, IP4 2BE
Tel: 1473 253246
Dunwich Museum
St. James's St, Dunwich, Saxmundham, IP17 3DT
Tel: 1728 648796
East Anglia Transport Museum
Chapel Rd, Carlton Colville, Lowestoft, NR33 8BL
Tel: 1502 518459
Felixstowe Museum
Landguards Fort, Felixstowe, IP11 8TW Tel: 01394 674355
Gainsborough House Society
Gainsborough St, Sudbury, CO10 2EU Tel: 01787 372958
International Sailing Craft Assoc Maritime Museum
Caldecott Rd, Oulton Broad, Lowestoft, NR32 3PH
Tel: 1502 585606
Ipswich Museum & Exhibition Gallery
High St, Ipswich, IP1 3QH Tel: 01473 213761
Ipswich Transport Museum Ltd
Old Trolley Bus Depot, Cobham Rd, Ipswich, IP3 9JD Tel: 01473 715666
Long Shop Steam Museum
Main St, Leiston, IP16 4ES Tel: 01728 832189
Lowestoft Museum
Broad House, Nicholas Everitt Park, Oulton Broad,
Lowestoft, NR33 9JR Tel: 01502 511457
Maritime Museum Sparrows Nest
Whapload Rd, Lowestoft, NR32 1XG Tel: 01502 561963
Mid Suffolk Light Railway
Brockford Station, Wetheringsett, Stowmarket, IP14 5PW
Tel: 01449 766899
Mildenhall & District Museum
6 King St, Mildenhall, Bury St. Edmunds, IP28 7EX
Tel: 1638 716970
National Horseracing Museum & Tours
99 High St, Newmarket, CB8 8JH Tel: 01638 667333
Norfolk & Suffolk Aviation Museum
The Street, Flixton, Bungay, NR35 1NZ Tel: 01986 896644
Rougham Tower Association
Rougham Estate Office, Ipswich Rd Rougham, Bury St.
Edmunds, IP30 9LZ Tel: 01359 271471
Surrey
Bourne Hall Museum
Bourne Hall, Spring St, Ewell, Epsom, KT17 1UF
Tel: 181 394 1734
Chertsey Museum
The Cedars, 33 Windsor St, Chertsey, KT16 8AT
Tel: 1932 565764

Dorking & District Museum
The Old Foundry, 62a West St, Dorking, RH4 1BS
Tel: 01306 876591
East Surrey Museum
1 Stafford Rd, Caterham, CR3 6JG Tel: 01883 340275
Elmbridge Museum
Church St, Weybridge, KT13 8DE Tel: 01932 843573
Godalming Museum
109a High St, Godalming, GU7 1AQ Tel: 01483 426510
Guildford Museum
Castle Arch, Quarry St, Guildford, GU1 3S Tel:
01483 444750
Haslemere Educational Museum
78 High St, Haslemere, GU27 2LA Tel: 01428 642112
Kingston Museum & Heritage Service
North Kingston Centre
Richmond Road, Kingston upon Thames, KT2 5PE
Tel: 181-547-6738 Fax: 0181-547-6747
Email: king.mus@rbk.kingston.gov.uk
Merton Heritage Centre
The Cannons, Madeira Rd, Mitcham, CR4 4HD
Tel: 181 640 9387
Reigate Priory Museum
Reigate Priory, Bell St, Reigate, RH2 7RL Tel:
01737 222550
Rural Life Centre
Old Kiln Museum The Reeds, Tilford, Farnham, GU10 2DL
Tel: 01252 792300
Wandle Industrial Museum
Vestry Hall Annex, London Rd, Mitcham, CR4 3UD Tel:
0181 648 0127
Woking Museum & Arts & Craft Centre
The Galleries, Chobham Rd, Woking , GU21 1JF Tel:
01483 725517
Sussex
Brighton Fishing Museum
201 Kings Road, Arches, Brighton, BN1 1NB Tel: 01273-723064 Fax: 01273-723064,
Tyne and Wear
Arbeia Roman Fort
Baring St, South Shields, NE33 2BB Tel: 0191 4561369
Bede's World Museum
Church Bank, Jarrow, NE32 3DY Tel: 0191 4892106
Castle Keep
St. Nicholas St, Newcastle Upon Tyne, NE1 1RE
Tel: 191 2327938
Hancock Museum
Barras Bridge, Newcastle Upon Tyne, NE2 4PT
Tel: 191 2227418
Joicey Museum
City Rd, Newcastle Upon Tyne, NE1 2AS
Tel: 0191 2324562
Newburn Motor Museum
Townfield Gardens, Newburn, Newcastle Upon Tyne,
NE15 8PY Tel: 0191 2642977
Newcastle Discovery
Blandford House, Blandford Square, Newcastle Upon Tyne,
NE1 4JA Tel: 0191 2326789
North East Aircraft Museum
Old Washington Rd, Sunderland, SR5 3HZ Tel:
0191 5190662
North East Museums
House of Recovery, Bath Lane, Newcastle Upon Tyne,
NE4 5SQ Tel: 0191 2221661
Ryhope Engines Trust
Pumping Station, Stockton Rd, Ryhope, Sunderland,
SR2 0ND Tel: 0191 5210235
South Shields Museum & Art Gallery
Ocean Road, South Shields, NE33 2JA Tel: 0191-456-8740
Fax: 0191 456 7850,

Sunderland Museum & Art Gallery
Borough Road, Sunderland, SR1 1PP,
The Bowes Railway Co.Ltd
Springwell Rd, Springwell Village, Gateshead, NE9 7QJ
Tel: 191 4161847
Washington F Pit
Albany Way, Washington, NE37 1BJ Tel: 0191 4167640
Warwickshire
Leamington Spa Art Gallery & Musuem
Avenue Rd, Leamington Spa, CV31 3PP Tel: 01926 426559
Nuneaton Museum & Art Gallery
Riversley Park, Nuneaton, CV11 5TU Tel: 01203 376473
Rugby School Museum
10 Little Church St, Rugby, CV21 3AW Tel: 01788 574117
Shakespeare Birthplace Trust
Henley Street, Stratford upon Avon, CV37 6QW
Tel: 1789-204016
St. Johns House
St. Johns, Warwick, CV34 4NF Tel: 01926 412021
Warwick Doll Museum
Okens House, Castle St, Warwick, CV34 4BP
Tel: 1926 495546
Warwickshire Market Hall Museum
Market Place, Warwick, CV34 4SA Tel: 01926 412500
West Midlands
Aston Manor-Road Transport Museum Ltd
208-216 Witton Lane, Birmingham, B6 6QE
Tel: 121 322 2298
Bantock House & Park
Bantock Park, Finchfield Rd, Wolverhampton, WV3 9LQ
Tel: 01902 552195
Birmingham & Midland Museum Of Transport
Chapel Lane, Wythall, Birmingham, B47 6JX
Tel: 1564 826471
Birmingham Museum & Art Gallery
Chamberlain Square, Birmingham, B3 3DH
Tel: 121 235 2834
Birmingham Railway Museum Ltd
670 Warwick Rd, Tyseley, Birmingham, B11 2HL
Tel: 121 707 4696
Black Country Living Museum
Tipton Rd, Dudley, DY1 4SQ Tel: 0121 557 9643
Black Country Museum Development Trust
Canal St, Tipton Rd, Dudley, DY1 4SQ Tel: 0121 522 2277
Blakesley Hall
Blakesley Rd, Yardley, Birmingham, B25 8RN
Tel: 121 783 2193
Dudley Museum & Art Gallerey
St JamesÕs Road, Dudley, DY1,
Haden Hall, Haden Hill Park, Barrs Rd, Cradley Heath,
B64 7JX Tel: 01384 635846
Haden Hill House, Haden Hill Park, Barrs Rd, Cradley
Heath, B64 7JX Tel: 01384 569444
Herbert Art Gallery & Museum
Jordan Well, Coventry, CV1 5QP Tel: 24 76832381
Jewellery Quarter Discovery Centre
75-79 Vyse St, Hockley, Birmingham, B18 6HA
Tel: 121 554 3598
Midland Air Museum
Coventry Airport, Coventry Rd, Baginton, Coventry,
CV8 3AZ Tel: 01203 301033
Oak House Museum
Oak Rd, West Bromwich, B70 8HJ Tel: 0121 553 0759
Selly Manor Museum
Maple Rd, Birmingham, B30 2AE Tel: 0121 472 0199
The Lock Museum
55 New Rd, Willenhall, WV13 2DA Tel: 01902 634542
Walsall Leather Museum
Littleton St West, Walsall, WS2 8EN Tel: 01922 721153

West Midlands Police Museum
Sparkhill Police Station, Stratford Rd, Sparkhill,
Birmingham, B11 4EA Tel: 0121 626 7181
Whitefriars Gallery
London Rd, Coventry, CV3 4AR Tel: 01203 832432
Whitlocks End Farm, Bills Lane, Shirley, Solihull,
B90 2PL Tel: 0121 745 4891
West Sussex
Amberley Museum
Station Rd, Amberley, Arundel, BN18 9LT Tel:
01798 831370
Chichester District Museum
29 Little London, Chichester, PO19 1PB Tel: 01243 784683
Ditchling Museum
Church Lane, Ditchling, Hassocks, BN6 8TB
Tel: 01273 844744
Fishbourne Roman Palace
Roman Way, Salthill Rd, Fishbourne, Chichester, PO19 3QR
Tel: 01243 785859
Horsham Museum
9 The Causeway, Horsham, RH12 1HE Tel: 01403-254959
Marlipins Museum
High St, Shoreham-By-Sea, BN43 5DA Tel: 01273 462994
Petworth Cottage Museum
346 High St, Petworth, GU28 0AU Tel: 01798 342100
The Doll House Museum
Station Rd, Petworth, GU28 0BF Tel: 01798 344044
The Mechanical Music & Doll Collection
Church Rd, Portfield, Chichester, PO19 4HN
Tel: 01243 372646
West Yorkshire
Armley Mills
Canal Rd, Leeds, LS12 2QF Tel: 0113 263 7861
Bankfield Museum
Boothtown Rd, Halifax, HX3 6HG Tel: 01422 354823
Bolling Hall Museum
Bowling Hall Rd, Bradford, BD4 7 Tel: 01274 723057
Brackenhall Countryside Centre
Glen Rd, Baildon, Shipley, BD17 5ED Tel: 01274 584140
Bradford Industrial Museum & Horses at Work
Moorside Rd, Eccleshill, Bradford, BD2 3HP Tel:
01274 631756
Calderdale Museums & Arts, Piece Hall, Halifax,
HX1 1RE Tel: 01422 358087
Castleford Museum Room, Carlton St, Castleford,
WF10 1BB Tel: 01977 559552
Cliffe Castle Museum
Spring Gardens Lane, Keighley, BD20 6LH Tel:
01535 618230
Eureka The Museum For Children
Discovery Rd, Halifax, HX1 2NE Tel: 01422 330069
Manor House Art Gallery & Museum
Castle Yard, Castle Hill, Ilkley, LS29 9D Tel: 01943 600066
National Museum of Photography, Film and Television
Bradford, BD1 1NQ Tel: 01274-202030 Fax: 01274 -723155,
WWW: http://www.nmpft.org.uk
Royal Armouries
Armouries Drive, Leeds, LS10 1LT Tel: 990 106666
Shibden Hall
Lister Rd, Shibden, Halifax, HX3 6AG Tel: 01422 352246
Skopos Motor Museum
Alexandra Mills, Alexandra Rd, Batley, WF17 6JA Tel:
01924 444423
Thackray Medical Museum
Beckett Street, Leeds, LS9 7LN Tel: 0113-244-4343 Fax:
0113-247-0219, Email: medical_museum@msn.com
The Colour Museum
1 Providence St, Bradford, BD1 2PW Tel: 01274 390955

Vintage Carriages Trust
Station Yard, South St, Ingrow, Keighley, BD21 1DB
Tel: 01535 680425
Wakefield Museum
Wood St, Wakefield, WF1 2EW Tel: 01924 305351
Yorkshire & Humberside Museums Council
Farnley Hall Hall Lane, Leeds, LS12 5HA Tel:
0113 263 8909
Yorkshire Mining Museum
Caphouse Colliery, New Rd, Overton, Wakefield, WF4 4RH
Tel: 01924 848806
Wiltshire
Alexander Keiller Museum
High St, Avebury, Marlborough, SN8 1RF Tel:
01672 539250
Atwell-Wilson Motor Museum Trust
Stockley Lane, Calne, SN11 0 Tel: 01249 813119
Great Western Railway Museum
Faringdon Rd, Swindon, SN1 5BJ Tel: 01793 466555
Lydiard House, Lydiard Park, Lydiard Tregoze, Swindon,
SN5 9PA Tel: 01793 770401
Salisbury & South Wiltshire Museum
The King's House, 65 The Close, Salisbury, SP1 2EN Tel:
01722 332151
Sevington Victorian School, Sevington, Grittleton,
Chippenham, SN14 7LD Tel: 01249 783070
Yelde Hall Museum
Market Place, Chippenham , SN15 3HL Tel: 01249 651488
Worcestershire
Almonry Museum
Abbey Gate, WR11 4BG Tel: 01386 446944
Avoncroft Museum of Historic Buildings
Redditch Rd, Bromsgrove By-Pass, Stoke Heath,
Bromsgrove, B60 4JR Tel: 01527 831363

Bewdley Museum
Load Street, Bewdley, DY12 2AE Tel: 01229-403573
Kidderminster Railway Museum
Station Drive, Kidderminster, DY10 1QX Tel: 01562 825316
Malvern Museum
Abbey Gateway, Abbey Rd, Malvern, WR14 3ES Tel:
01684 567811
The Commandery Civil War Museum
Sidbury, Worcester, WR1 2HU Tel: 01905 361821
The Elgar's Birthplace Museum
Crown East Lane, Lower Broadheath, Worcester, WR2 6RH
Tel: 01905 333224
West Midlands Regional Museums Council
Hanbury Rd, Stoke Prior, Bromsgrove, B60 4 Tel:
01527 872258
Worcester City Museum & Art Gallery
Foregate St, Worcester, WR1 1DT Tel: 01905 25371
Worcestershire City Museum
Queen Elizabeth House, Trinity Street, Worcester, WR1
2PW,
Worcestershire County Museum
Hartlebury Castle, Hartlebury, DY11 7XZ Tel: 01229-
250416 Fax: 01299-251890, Email:
museum@worcestershire.gov.uk, WWW:
http://www.worcestershire.gov.uk/museum
York
Bar Convent
17 Blossom Street, York, YO24 1AQ Tel: 01904 643238
Fax: 01904 631792,
York Castle Museum
The Eye of York, York, YO1 9RY Tel: 01904 653611 Fax:
01904 671078, WWW: www.york.gov.uk
Yorkshire Museum
Museum Gardens, York, YO1 7FR Tel: 01904 629745 Fax:
01904 651221, WWW: www.york.gov.uk

Isles of Scilly
Isles of Scilly Museum
Church Street, St Mary's, TR21 Tel: JT Tel: 01720-422337

Wales
Caernarfon
Welsh Slate Museum
Padarn Country Park, Llanberis, Gwynedd LL55 4TY
Tel: 01286 870630
Ceredigion
Ceredigion Museum
Coliseum, Terrace Rd, Aberystwyth, SY23 2AQ
Tel: 01970 633088
Mid-Wales Mining Museum Ltd
15 Market St, Aberaeron, SA46 0AU Tel: 01545 570823
Llywernog Silver Mine
Ponterwyd, Aberystwyth, SY23 3AB Tel: 01970 890620
Clwyd
Cae Dai Trust
Cae Dai Lawnt, Denbigh, LL16 4SU Tel: 01745 812107
Llangollen Motor Museum
Pentrefelin, Llangollen, LL20 8EE Tel: 01978 860324
Dyfed
Cardigan Heritage Centre
Bridge Warehouse, Castle St, Cardigan, SA43 3AA
Tel: 01239 614404
Haverfordwest Town Museum
Castle St, Haverfordwest, SA61 2EF Tel: 01437 763087
Kidwelly Industrial Museum
Broadford, Kidwelly, SA17 4 Tel: 01554 891078
Parc Howard Museum & Art Gallery
Mansion House, Parc Howard, Llanelli, SA15 3LJ Tel:
01554 772029

Pembrokeshire Motor Museum
Keeston Hill, Haverfordwest, SA62 6EH Tel: 01437 710950
Pembrokeshire Museum Service
Castle Gallery, Castle St, Haverfordwest, SA61 2EF Tel:
01437 760460
Wilson Museum of Narberth
Market Square, Narberth, SA67 7AX Tel: 01834 861719
Gwent
Abergavenny Museum
The Castle, Castle St, Abergavenny, NP7 5EE Tel:
01873 854282
Big Pit Mining Museum
Blaenavon, Torfaen, NP4 9XP Tel: 01495-790311
Castle & Regimental Museum
Monmouth Castle, Monmouth, NP25 3BS Tel:
01600 772175
Chepstow Musuem
Bridge St, Chepstow, NP16 5EZ Tel: 01291 625981
Drenewydd Museum
26-27 Lower Row, Bute Town, Tredegar, NP22 5QH Tel:
01685 843039
Newport Museum & Art Gallery
John Frost Square, Newport, NP9 1PA Tel: 01633-840064
Pillgwenlly Heritage Community Project,
within Baptist Chapel, Alexandra Rd, Newport, NP20 2JE
Tel: 01633 244893
Roman Legionary Museum
High St, Caerleon, Newport, NP18 1AE Tel: 01633 423134

Valley Inheritance
Park Buildings, Pontypool, Torfaen, NP4 6JH Tel: 01495-752036 Fax: 01495-752036,
Gwynedd
Beaumaris Gaol Museum
Bunkers Hill, Beaumaris, LL58 8EP Tel: 01248 810921
Betws-y-Coed Motor Museum
Museum Cottage, Betws-Y-Coed, LL24 0AH Tel: 01690 710760
Gwynedd Museums Service
Victoria Dock, Caernarvon, LL55 1SH Tel: 01286-679098 Fax: 01286-679637, Email: amgueddflydd-museums@gwynedd.gov.uk
Porthmadog Maritime Museum
Oakley Wharf 1, The Harbour, Porthmadog, LL49 9LU Tel: 01766 513736
Regimental Museum
Royal Welch Fusiliers, Caernarfon Castle, Caernarfon, LL55 2AY Tel: 01286 673362
Segontium Roman Museum
Beddgelert Rd, Caernarfon, LL55 2 Tel: 01286 675625
Teapot Museum
25 Castle St, Conwy, LL32 8AY Tel: 01492 596533
The Maritime Museum
Beach Rd, Newry Beach, Holyhead, LL65 1YD Tel: 01407 769745
Mid Glamorgan, Joseph Parrys Cottage
4 Chapel Row, Merthyr Tydfil, CF48 1BN Tel: 01685 383704
Pontypridd Historical & Cultural Centre
Bridge St, Pontypridd, CF37 4PE Tel: 01443 409512
Ynysfach Iron Heritage Centre
Merthyr Tydfil Heritage Trust, Ynysfach Rd, Merthyr Tydfil, CF48 1AG Tel: 01685 721858
Monmouthshire
Nelson Museum & Local History Centre
Priory St, Newport, NP5 3XA 1600 713519
Gwent Rural Life Museum
The Malt Barn, New Market Street, Usk, Monmouth, NP5 1AU Tel: 01291-673777
National Collection, Museum of Welsh Life, St Fagans, Cardiff, CF5 6XB Tel: 01222-573500-Ext-437 Fax: 01222-573490,

Pembrokeshire
Milford Haven Museum
Old Customs House, The Docks, Milford Haven, SA73 3AF Tel: 01646 694496
Tenby Museum
Tenby Museum & Art Gallery, Castle Hill, Tenby, SA70 7BP Tel: 01834-842809 Fax: 01834-842809,
Powys
Amgueddfa'R Hen Gapel
Tre-r-Ddol, Machynlleth, SY20 8PN Tel: 01970 832407
Llandrindod Wells Museum
Temple St, Llandrindod Wells, LD1 5DL Tel: 01597 824513
Llanidloes Museum
Great Oak St, Llanidloes, SY18 6BN Tel: 01686 412375
Powysland Museum & Montgomery Canal Centre
Canal Yard, Welshpool, SY21 7AQ Tel: 01938 554656
The Judge's Lodging
Broad St, Presteigne, LD8 2AD Tel: 01544 260651
Water Folk
Old Store House, Llanfrynach, Brecon, LD3 7LJ Tel: 01874 665382
South Glamorgan
National Museum & Galleries of Wales
Cathays Park, Cardiff, CF10 3NP Tel: 01222 397951
Techniquest
Stuart St, Cardiff, CF10 5BW Tel: 01222 475475
West Glamorgan
Cefn Coed Colliery Museum
Blaenant Colliery, Crynant, Neath, SA10 8SE Tel: 01639 750556
Glynn Vivian Art Gallery
Alexandra Rd, Swansea, SA1 5DZ Tel: 01792 655006
Maritime & Industrial Museum
Museum Square, Maritime Quarter, Victoria Rd, Swansea, SA1 1SN Tel: 01792 650351
Neath Museum
4 Church Place, Neath, SA11 3LL Tel: 01639 645741
Wrexham
Wrexham Museum
Regent Street, Wrexham, LL11 1RB Tel: 01978-358916 Fax: 01978-353882

Scotland

Museum of Scotland
Chambers Street, Edinburgh, EH1 1JF Tel: 0131-225-7534 Tel: 0131-247-4027 (Text), WWW: www.nms.ac.uk
Royal Museum of Scotland
Chambers Street, Edinburgh, EH1 1JF Tel: 0131 247 4115, WWW: www.nms.ac.uk
Huntly House Museum
142 Canongate, Edinburgh, EH8 8DD,
Scottish Museum Council
County House, 20-22 Torphichen Street, Edinburgh, EH3 8JB Tel: 0131 229 7465
Scottish United Services Museum
The Castle, Museum Square, Edinburgh, EH1 2NG Tel: 0131-225-7534 Fax: 0131-225-7534, Email:
Stranraer Museum
55 George Street, Stranraer, DG9 7JP Tel: 01776-705088 Fax: 01776-705835, Email: John.Pic@dumgal.gov.uk
Aberdeenshire
Aberdeen Maritime Museum
52-56 Shiprow, Aberdeen, AB11 5BY Tel: 01224 337700
Alford & Donside Heritage Association
Mart Rd, Alford, AB33 8AA Tel: 019755 62906
Arbuthnot Museum
St. Peter St, Peterhead, AB42 1DA Tel: 01779 477778

Fraserburgh Heritage Society
Heritage Centre Quarry Rd, Fraserburgh, AB43 9DT Tel: 01346 512888
Grampian Transport Museum
Alford, AB33 8AE Tel: 019755-62292
Hamilton T.B
Northfield Farm, New Pitsligo, Fraserburgh, AB43 6PX Tel: 01771 653504
Provost Skene's House
Guestrow, Aberdeen, AB10 1AS Tel: 01224 641086
Satrosphere, 19 Justice Mill Lane, Aberdeen, AB11 6EQ Tel: 01224 213232
The Museum of Scottish Lighthouses, Kinnaird Head, Fraserburgh, AB43 9DU Tel: 01346-511022 Fax: 01346-511033,
Angus, Arbroath Museum
Signal Tower, Ladyloan, Arbroath, DD11 1PU Tel: 01241 875598
Barrack Street Museum
Barrack St, Dundee, DD1 1PG Tel: 01382 432067
Glenesk Folk Museum
The Retreat, Glenesk, Brechin, DD9 7YT Tel: 01356 670254
Meffan Institute
20 High St., West, Forfar, DD8 1BB Tel: 01307 464123

Argyll
Campbeltown Heritage Centre
Big Kiln, Witchburn Rd, Campbeltown, PA28 6JU Tel:
01586 551400
Campbeltown Museum
Hall St, Campbeltown, PA28 6BU Tel: 01586 552366
Castle House Museum
Castle Gardens, Argyll St, Dunoon, PA23 7HH Tel:
01369 701422
Kilmartin House Trust
Kilmartin House, Kilmartin, Lochgilphead, PA31 8RQ Tel:
01546 510278
Ayrshire
Dalgarven Mill
Dalry Rd, Dalgarven, Kilwinning, KA13 6PL Tel:
01294 552448
East Ayrshire Council District History Centre & Museum
Baird Institute, 3 Lugar Street, Cumnock, KA18 1AD Tel:
01290-421701 Fax: 01290-421701,
Glasgow Vennel Museum
10 Glasgow, Vennel, Irvine, KA12 0BD Tel: 01294 275059
Irvine Burns Club & Burgh Museum
28 Eglinton St, Irvine, KA12 8AS Tel: 01294 274511
Largs Museum
Kirkgate House, Manse Court, Largs, KA30 8AW Tel:
01475 687081
McKechnie Institute
Dalrymple St, Girvan, KA26 9AE Tel: 01465 713643
North Ayrshire Museum
Manse St, Saltcoats, KA21 5AA Tel: 01294 464174
Rozelle House
Rozelle Park, Ayr, KA7 4NQ Tel: 01292 445447
Banffshire
The Buckie Drifter Maritime Heritage Centre
Freuchny Rd, Buckie, AB56 1TT Tel: 01542 834646
Berwickshire
Jim Clark Room
44 Newtown St, Duns, TD11 3DT Tel: 01361 883960
Caithness
Clangunn Heritage Centre & Museum
Old Parish Kirk, Latheron, KW5 6DL Tel: 01593 741700
Dunbeath Preservation Trust
Old School, Dunbeath, KW6 6EG Tel: 01593 731233
The Last House
John O'Groats, Wick, KW1 4YR Tel: 01955 611250
Dumfriesshire
Dumfries Museum
The Observatory, Dumfries, DG2 7SW Tel: 01387 253374
Ellisland Trust
Ellisland Farm, Dumfries, DG2 0RP Tel: 01387 740426
Gretna Museum
Headless Cross, Gretna, DG16 5EA Tel: 01461 338441
John Paul Jones Birthplace Museum
Arbigland, Kirkbean, Dumfries DG2 8B Tel: 01387 880613
Old Bridge House Museum
Mill Rd, Dumfries, DG2 7BE Tel: 01387 256904
Robert Burns Centre
Mill Rd, Dumfries, DG2 7BE Tel: 01387 264808
Sanquhar Tolbooth Museum
High St, Sanquhar, DG4 6BL Tel: 01659 50186
Savings Banks Museum
Ruthwell, Dumfries, DG1 4NN Tel: 01387 870640
Shambellie House Museum of Costume, New Abbey,
Dumfries, DG2 8HQ Tel: 01387 850375
Dunbartonshire, Scottish Maritime Museum
Castle St, Dumbarton, G82 1QS Tel: 01389 763444

Dundee
Verdant Works - A Working Jute Mill
West Henderson's Wynd, Dundee, DD1 5BT
Tel: 01382-225282 Fax: 01382-221612
Email: dundeeheritage@sol.co.uk
WWW: www.verdant-works.co.uk
East Lothian
Dunbar Museum
High St, Dunbar, EH42 1ER Tel: 01368 863734
John Muir House Museum
126-128 High St, Dunbar, EH42 1JJ Tel: 01368 862585
Museum of Flight
The Airfield, East Fortune , EH39 5LF Tel: 01620-880308
Fax: 01620-880355, WWW: www.nms.ac/flight
North Berwick Museum
School Rd, North Berwick, EH39 4JU Tel: 01620 895457
Edinburgh
Heritage Projects (Edinburgh) Ltd
Castlehill, Royal Mile, Edinburgh, Midlothian EH1 2NE
Tel: 0131 225 7575
Falkirk
Falkirk Museum History Research Centre
Callendar House, Callendar Park, Falkirk, FK1 1YR Tel:
01324 503779 Fax: 01324 503771, Email:
callandarhouse@falkirkmuseums.demon.co.uk, WWW:
www.falkirkmuseums.demon.co.uk
Fife
Andrew Carnegie Birthplace Museum
Moodie St, Dunfermline, KY12 7PL Tel: 01383 724302
Inverkeithing Museum
The Friary, Queen St, Inverkeithing, KY11 1 Tel:
01383 313595
John McDouall Stuart Museum
Rectory Lane, Dysart, Kirkcaldy, KY1 2TP Tel:
01592 653118
Kirkcaldy Museum and Art Gallery
War Memorial Gardens, Kirkcaldy, KY1 1YG Tel: 01592-
412860 Fax: 01592-412870,
Kirkcaldy Museum & Art Gallery
War Memorial Gardens, Abbotshall Rd, Kirkcaldy,
KY1 1YG Tel: 01592 412860
Methil Heritage Centre
272 High St, Methil, Leven, KY8 3EQ Tel: 01333 422100
Pittencrieff House Museum
Pittencrieff Park, Dunfermline, KY12 8QH
Tel: 01383 722935
Scotland's Secret Bunker
Underground Nuclear Command Centre
Crown Buildings (Near St Andrews), KY16 8QH
Tel: 01333-310301
Scottish Fisheries Museum
St. Ayles, Harbourhead, Anstruther, KY10 3AB
Tel: 01333 310628
The Fife Folk Museum
High St, Ceres, Cupar, KY15 5NF Tel: 01334 828180
Glasgow
Museum of Piping, The Piping Centre
30-34 McPhater Street, Cowcaddens, Glasgow
Tel: 0141-353-0220
Inverness-Shire
Highland Folk Museum
Duke St, Kingussie, PH21 1JG Tel: 01540 661307
Highland Folk Park
Aultlarie Croft, Kingussie Rd, Newtonmore, PH20 1AY
Tel: 01540 673551
Highland Railway Museum
5 Druimlon, Drumnadrochit, Inverness, IV63 6TY
Tel: 01456 450527

Inverness Museum & Art Gallery
Castle Wynd, Inverness, IV2 3ED Tel: 01463 237114
Mallaig Heritage Centre
Station Rd, Mallaig, PH41 4PY Tel: 01687 462085
The Clansman Centre
Canalside, Fort Augustus, PH32 4AU Tel: 01320 366444
West Highland Museum
Cameron Square, Fort William, PH33 6AJ Tel: 01397 702169
Lanarkshire
Low Parks Museum
129 Muir St, Hamilton, ML3 6BJ Tel: 01698 283981
Weavers' Cottages Museum
23-25 Wellwynd, Airdrie, ML6 0BN Tel: 01236 747712
West Lothian
Linlithgow's Story, Annet House, 143 High St, Linlithgow,
EH49 7EJ Tel: 01506 670677
Isle Of Arran
Arran Heritage Museum
Rosaburn House, Brodick, KA27 8DP Tel: 01770 302636
Isle Of Islay
Finlaggan Trust The, The Cottage, Ballygrant, PA45 7QL
Tel: 01496 840644
Isle Of Mull
The Columba Centre
Fionnphort, Isle Of Mull, PA66 6BN Tel: 01681 700660
Isle Of North Uist
Taigh Chearsabhagh Trust, Taigh Chearsabhagh,
Lochmaddy, HS6 5AE Tel: 01876 500293
Isle Of South Uist
Kildonan Museum
Kildonan, Lochboisdale, HS8 5RZ Tel: 01878 710343
Lanarkshire
Auld Kirk Musuem, The Cross, Kirkintilloch, Glasgow,
G66 1 Tel: 0141 578 0144
Barrhead Museum
Main St, Barrhead, Glasgow, G78 1SW Tel: 0141 876 1994
Biggar Museum Trust, Moat Park Kirkstyle, Biggar,
ML12 6DT Tel: 01899 221050
Discover Carmichael Visitors Centre
Warrenhill Farm, Warrenhill Rd, Thankerton, Biggar,
ML12 6PF Tel: 01899 308169
Fossil Grove Museum
Victoria Park, Glasgow, G65 9AH Tel: 0141 950 1448
Gladstone Court Museum
Kirksyle, Biggar, ML12 6DT Tel: 01899 221573
Greenhill Covenanters House Museum
Kirkstyle, Biggar, ML12 6DT Tel: 01899 221572
Heatherbank Museum
Within Caledonian University, 1 Park Drive, Glasgow,
G3 6LP Tel: 0141 337 4402
Heritage Engineering, 22 Carmyle Avenue, Glasgow,
G32 8HJ Tel: 0141 763 0007
Hunter House
Maxwellton Rd, East Kilbride, Glasgow, G74 3LW
Tel: 01355 261261
John Hastie Museum
Threestanes Rd, Strathaven, ML10 6EB Tel: 01357 521257
Lanarkshire, Lanark Museum
8 Westport, Lanark, ML11 9HD Tel: 01555 666680
New Lanark Conservation Trust
Visitors Centre Mill No 3, New Lanark Mills, Lanark,
ML11 9DB Tel: 01555 661345
People's Palace
Glasgow Green, Glasgow, G40 1AT Tel: 0141 554 0223
Scotland Street School Museum
225 Scotland St, Glasgow, G5 8QB Tel: 0141 287 0500
Scotland Street School Museum of Education
225 Scotland St, Glasgow, G5 8QB Tel: 0141 429 1202
Low Parks Museum
129 Muir Street, Hamilton, ML3 6BJ Tel: 01698 455714

The Lighthouse, 11 Mitchell Lane, Glasgow, G1 3NU
Tel: 0141 221 6362
Midlothian
History of Education Centre
East London St, Edinburgh, EH7 4BW Tel: 0131 556 4224
Lauriston Castle
2a Cramond Rd South, Edinburgh, EH4 5QD
Tel: 0131 336 2060
Nelson Monument
Calton Hill, Edinburgh, EH7 5AA Tel: 0131 556 2716
Newhaven Heritage Museum
Pier Place, Edinburgh, EH6 4LP Tel: 0131 551 4165
Portobello Tower Project
47 Figgate Lane, Edinburgh, EH15 1HJ Tel: 0131 657 3001
Royal Museum of Scotland
Commercial Street, Edinburgh, EH6 6EJ Tel: 0131 553 7679
Scottish Agricultural Museum
Ingliston, Newbridge, EH28 8NB Tel: 0131-333-2674
Scottish Mining Museum Trust
Lady Victoria Colliery, Newtongrange, Dalkeith, EH22 4QN
Tel: 0131 663 7519
Scottish Mining Museum Trust
Lady Victoria Colliery, Newtongrange, EH22 4QN Tel:
0131-663-7519 Fax: 0131-654-1618, WWW:
www.scottishminingmuseum.com
Morayshire
Elgin Museum
1 High St, Elgin, IV30 1EQ Tel: 01343 543675
Falconer Museum
Tolbooth St, Forres, IV36 1PH Tel: 01309 673701
Grantown Museum & Heritage Trust
Burnfield House, Burnfield Avenue, Grantown-On-Spey,
PH26 3HH Tel: 01479 872478
Lossiemouth Fisheries Museum
Pitgaveny St, Lossiemouth, IV31 6TW Tel: 01343 813772
Nairn Museum
Viewfield House, King St, Nairn, IV12 4EE
Tel: 01667 456791
Orkney
Orkney Farm & Folk Museum
Corrigall Farm Museum Harray, KW17 2LQ
Tel: 01856 771411
Orkney Farm & Folk Museum
Kirbister Farm, Birsay, KW17 2LR Tel: 01856 771268
Orkney Fossil & Vintage Centre
Viewforth Burray, KW17 2SY Tel: 01856 731255
Orkney Museum
Tankerness House, Broad Street, Kirkwall, KW15 1DH
Tel: 01856-873191 Fax: 01856 871560,
Orkney Wireless Museum
Kiln Corner, Kirkwall, KW15 1LB Tel: 01856-871400
Scapa Flow Visitor Centre
Lyness, Stromness, KW16 3NT Tel: 01856 791300
Scapa Flow Visitor Centre
Lyness, Hoy,
Stromness Museum
52 Alfred Street, Stromness Tel: 01856-850025
Perthshire
Atholl Country Collection, The Old School, Blair Atholl,
PH18 5SP Tel: 01796-481232
Clan Donnachaidh (Robertson) Museum
Clan Donnachaidh Centre
Bruar, Pitlochry, PH18 5TW Tel: 01796-483338
Email: clandonnachaidh@compuserve.com
Clan Menzies Museum
Castle Menzies, Weem, by Aberfeldy, PH15 2JD Tel: 01887-
820982
Meigle Museum
Dundee Rd, Meigle, Blairgowrie, PH12 8SB
Tel: 01828 640612

Dunkeld Cathedral Chapter House Museum
Dunkeld, PH8 Tel: AW Tel: 01350-727601/727249
The Hamilton Toy Collection
11 Main St, Callander, FK17 8BQ Tel: 01877 330004
Renfrewshire
Mclean Museum & Art Gallery
15 Kelly St, Greenock, PA16 8JX Tel: 01475 715624
Old Paisley Society
George Place, Paisley, PA1 2HZ Tel: 0141 889 1708
Paisley Museum
Paisley Museum & Art Galleries, High Street, Paisley, PA1
2BA Tel: 0141-889-3151
Ross-Shire
Dingwall Museum Trust
Town Hall, High St, Dingwall, IV15 9RY Tel: 01349 865366
Highland Museum of Childhood
The Old Station, Strathpeffer, IV14 9DH Tel: 01997 421031
Tain & District Museum
Castle Brae, Tain, IV19 1AJ Tel: 01862 893054
Tain Through Time, Tower St, Tain, IV19 1DY Tel:
01862 894089
The Groam House Museum
High St, Rosemarkie, Fortrose, IV10 8UF Tel: 01381 620961
Ullapool Museum & Visitor Centre
7 & 8 West Argyle St, Ullapool, IV26 2TY
Tel: 01854 612987
Roxburghshire, Hawick Museum & Scott Gallery, Wilton
Lodge Park, Hawick, TD9 7JL Tel: 01450 373457
Jedburgh Castle Jail Museum
Castlegate, Jedburgh, TD8 6BD Tel: 01835 863254
Mary Queen of Scots House
Queens St, Jedburgh, TD8 6EN Tel: 01835 863331
Selkirkshire
Halliwells House Museum
Halliwells Close, Market Place, Selkirk, TD7 4BL
Tel: 01750 20096
Shetland Islands
Fetlar Interpretive Centre
Beach Of Houbie, Fetlar, Shetland ZE2 9DJ Tel:
01957 733206
Old Haa Museum
Burravoe Yell, Shetland, ZE2 9AY Tel: 01957 722339

Pod of Gremista Museum
Gremista, Lerwick, ZE1 0PX Tel: 01595 694386
Shetland Textile Working Museum
Weisdale Mill, Weisdale ZE2 9LW Tel: 01595 830419
Tangwick HAA Museum
Tangwick, Hillswick, Shetland, ZE2 9RW Tel:
01806 503389
Unst Heritage Centre
Haroldswick, Unst, Shetland, ZE2 9EF Tel: 01957 711528
Stirlingshire
Regimental Museum Argyll and Sutherland Highlanders
Stirling Castle, Stirling, FK8 1EH Tel: 01786 475165 Fax:
01786 446038,
Sutherland, Strathnaver Museum
Bettyhill, KW11, , The museum tells the story of the
Highland Clearances in 18th Century dealing mainly with the
Strathnaver area
Tayside
Perth Museum & Art Gallery
George Street, Perth, PH1 5LB Tel: 01738-632488 Fax:
01738 443505, Email: museum@pkc.gov.uk
Kinross-shire
Perth Museum & Art Gallery
West Lothian
Almond Valley Heritage Trust, Livingston Mill Farm,
Millfield, Livingston, EH54 7AR Tel: 01506 414957
Bennie Museum
Mansefield St, Bathgate, EH48 4HU Tel: 01506 634944
Kinneil Museum
Kinneil Estate, Bo'Ness, EH51 0AY Tel: 01506 778530
Queensferry Museum
53 High St, South Queensferry, EH30 9HP Tel: 0131
331 5545
Wigtownshire
Taylor's Tradition
Barraer, Newton Stewart, DG8 6QQ Tel: 01671 404890
Caithness
Wick Hertiage Centre
18 Bank Row, Wick, KW1 5EY Tel: 01955 605393

Northern Ireland
Ulster Museum
Botanic Gardens, Belfast, BT9 5AB Tel: 01232-381251
County Antrim
Ballymoney Museum & Heritage Centre
33 Charlotte St, Ballymoney, BT53 6AY Tel: 012656 62280
Friends of the Ulster Museum Botanic Gardens
Botanic Gardens, Stranmillas Rd, Belfast, BT9 5AB
Tel: 01232 681606
Odyssey Science Centre Project Office
Project Office NMGNI, Botanic Gardens, Belfast, BT9 5AB
NI Museums Council
66 Donegall Pass, Belfast, BT7 1BU Tel: 01232 550215
Ulster American Folk Park Project Team Belfast
4 The Mount Albert Bridge Rd, Belfast, BT5 4NA
Tel: 01232 452250
Ulster Aviation Society
Langford Lodge Airfield 97, Largy Rd, Crumlin, BT29 4RT
Tel: 01849 454444
Ulster Museum
Botanic Gardens, Stranmelis Rd, Belfast, BT9 5AB Tel:
01232 383000
County Armagh
Armagh County Museum
The Mall East, Armagh, BT61 9BE Tel: 01861 523070

County Down
Down County Museum
The Mall, Downpatrick, BT30 6AH Tel: 01396 615218
Downpatrick Railway Museum
Railway Station, Market St, Downpatrick, BT30 6LZ Tel:
01396 615779
Route 66 American Car Museum
94 Dundrum Rd, Newcastle, BT33 0LN Tel: 013967 25223
Somme Heritage Centre
233 Bangor Rd, Newtownards, BT23 7PH Tel:
01247 823202
Ulster Folk and Transport Museum
Cultra, Holywood, BT18 Tel: EU Tel: 01232-428728
County Fermanagh
Fermanagh County Museum
Enniskillen Castle Castle Barracks, Enniskillen, BT74 7HL
Tel: 28 66325000
Roslea Heritage Centre
Church St, Roslea, Enniskillen, BT74 7DW Tel:
28 67751750
County Londonderry
Garvagh Museum
142 Main St, Garvagh, Coleraine, BT51 5AE Tel:
28 29557924

County Tyrone
Ulster American Folk Park, Mellon Rd, Castletown, Omagh, BT78 5QU Tel: 01662 243292
Ulster History Park
150 Glenpark Rd, Cullion, Omagh, BT79 7SU Tel: 016626 48188
Londonderry
Foyle Valley Railway Museum
Foyle Rd, Londonderry, BT48 6SQ Tel: 01504 265234
Harbour Museum
Harbour Square, Londonderry, BT48 6AF Tel: 01504 377331

Belgium
In Flanders Fields Museum
Lakenhallen, Grote Markt 34, Ieper, B-8900
Tel: 0-32-(0)-57-22-85-84 Fax: 0-32-(0)-57-22-85-89
WWW: www.inflandersfields.be

South Africa
Albany Museum
Somerset Street, Grahamstown, 6140 Tel: 461-22312 Fax: 461-22398,
Kafframan Museum
PO Box 1434, King William's Town, 5600 Tel: 430-24506 Fax: 433-21569 Email: stephani@hubertd.ry.ac.2a

United States of America
Arizona
Arizona Historical Society Pioneer Museum, The, PO Box 1968, 2340 North Fort Valley Road, Flagstaff, 86002
Tel: 602-774-6272
Phoenix Museum of History, PO Box 926, 1002 West Van Buren Street, Phoenix, 85001
Tel: 602-253-2734

Republic of Ireland
Dublin Civic Museum
58 South William Street, Dublin, 2 Tel: 679-4260
Irish Jewish Museum
3 - 4 Walworth Road, South Circular Road, Dublin, 8
Tel: 453-1797

Western Cape
Huguenot Memorial Museum
PO Box 37, Franschoek, 7690 Tel: 21-876-2532

Nevada
Nevada State Museum
Division of Museums & History, 600 North Carson Street, Carson City, 89710 Tel: 702-687-4810
Nevada, Nevada State Museum
Division of Museums & History, 700 Twin Lakes Drive, Las Vegas, 89107 702-486-520

Military Museums

England
Bedfordshire
Bedford Museum Bedfordshire Yeomanry
Castle Lane, Bedford, MK40 3XD Tel: 01234 353323
Fax: 01234 273401
Bedfordshire and Hertfordshire Regimental Museum
Luton Museum, Wardown Park, Luton, LU2 7HA
Tel: 01582 546719
Berkshire
R.E.M.E. Museum of Technology
Isaac Newton Road, Arborfield, Reading, RG2 9NJ
Tel: 0118-976-3567 Fax: 0118-976-3672
Email: reme-museum@gtnet.gov.uk
WWW: http://www.eldred.demon.co.uk/reme-museum/index.htm
Royal Berkshire Yeomanry Cavalry Museum
T A Centre, Bolton Road, Windsor, SL4 3JG
Tel: 01753-860600
The Household Cavalry Museum
Combermere Barracks, Windsor Tel: 01753 868222
Buckinghamshire
Royal Army Education Corps Museum
HQ Beaconsfield Station, Wilton Park, Beaconsfield HP9 2RP Tel: 01494 683232
Cambridgeshire
Cambridgeshire Regimental Collection
Ely Museum, The Old Goal, Market Street, Ely, CB7 4LS
Tel: 01353-666655
Cheshire
Cheshire Military Museum (Cheshire Regiment)
The Castle, Chester, CH1 2DN Tel: 01244 327617
Cornwall
Duke of Cornwall's Light Infantry Museum
The Keep, Bodmin, Cornwall, PL31 1EG Tel: 01206-72610

County Durham
Durham Light Infantry Museum
Aykley Heads, Durham, DH1 5TU Tel: 0191-384-2214
Fax: 0191-386-1770, Email: dli@durham.gov.uk
Cumbria
Border Regiment & Kings Own Royal Border Regt Museum
Queen Mary's Tower, The Castle, Carlisle, CA3 8UR Tel: 01228-532774 Fax: 01228-521275, Email: rhq@kingsownborder.demon.co.uk
Derbyshire
Regimental Museum of the 9th/12th Royal Lancers
Derby City Museum and Art Gallery, The Strand, Derby, DE1 1BS Tel: 01332 716657 Fax: 01332 716670
Devon
Devonshire Regimental Museum, Wyvern Barracks, Barrack Road, Exeter, EX2 6AE Tel: 01392 218178
Dorset
Military Museum of Devon and Dorset, The Keep Museum, Bridport Road, Dorchester, DT1 1RN Tel: 01305-264066 Fax: 01305-250373
Royal Armoured Corps and Royal Tank Museum,
Bovington, BH20 6JG Tel: 01929 405096 Fax: 01929 405360 Email: admin@tankmuseum.co.uk
WWW: www.tankmuseum.co.uk
Royal Signals Museum
Blandford Camp, Nr Blandford Forum, DT11 8RH Tel: 01258-482248 Tel: 01258-482267 Fax: 01258-482084,
WWW: www.royalsignalsarmy.org.uk/museum/
The Devon and Dorset Regimental Museum
The Keep, Bridport Road, Dorchester, DT1 1RN Tel: 01305 264066, Fax:1305 250373

East Yorkshire
Museum of Army Transport
Flemingate, Beverley, HU17 0NG Tel: 01482-860445
Essex
Essex Regiment Museum
Oaklands Park, Moulsham Street, Chelmsford, CM2 9AQ
Tel: 01245-353066 Tel: 01245-260614 Fax: 01245-280642,
Email: pompadour@chelsfordbc.gov.uk
WWW: http://www.chelmsfordbc.gov.uk
Gloucestershire
Soldiers of Gloucestershire Museum
Gloucester Docks, Commercial Road, Gloucester, GL1 2EH
Tel: 01452 522682 Fax: 01452 311116
Hampshire
Airborne Forces Museum
Browning Barracks, Aldershot, GU11 2BU
Tel: 01252 349619
Aldershot Military Museum
Queens Avenue, Aldershot, GU11 2LG Tel: 01252-314598
Fax: 01252-34294, Email: musim@hants.gov.uk
Aldershot Military Historical Trust
Evelyn Woods Rd, Aldershot, GU11 2LG Tel: 01252 314598
Army Medical Services Museum
Keogh Barracks, Mychett Place Road, Ash Vale, Aldershot,
GU12 5RQ Tel: 01252 340212 Fax: 01252 340224
Army Physical Training Corps Museum
ASPT, Fox Line, Queen's Avenue, Aldershot, GU11 2LB
Tel: 01252 347168 Fax: 01252 340785
Museum of Army Flying
Middle Wallop, Stockbridge, SO20 8DY Tel: 01980 674421
Fax: 01264 781694, Email: daa@flying-museum.org.uk,
WWW: www.flying-museum.org.uk
Queen Alexandra's Royal Army Nursing Corps Museum
Keogh Barracks, Ash Vale, Aldershot, GU12 5RQ,
Royal Marines Museum
Eastney, Southsea, PO4 9PX Tel: 01705-819385-Exts-
244/239 Fax: 01705-838420
Royal Marines Museum
Southsea, Portsmouth, PO4 9PX Tel: 01705 819385
Fax: 01705 838420
Royal Naval Museum
H M Naval Base (PP66), Portsmouth, PO1 3NH Tel: 01705-
723795 Fax: 01705-727575
Royal Navy Submarine Museum
Haslar Jetty Road, Gosport, PO12 2AS Tel: 01705-510354
The Gurkha Museum
Peninsula Barracks, Romsey Road, Winchester, SO23 8TS
Tel: 01962 842832 Fax: 01962 877597
**The King's Royal Hussars Museum (10th Royal Hussars
PWO 11th Hussars PAO and Royal Hussars PWO)**
Tel: 01962 828540 Fax: 01962 828538
The Light Infantry Museum
Tel: 01962 868550
**The Royal Green Jackets Museum (Oxford & Bucks
Light Infantry King's Royal Rifle Corps & Rifle Brigade)**
Peninsula Barracks, Romsey Road, Winchester, SO23 8TS
Tel: 01962 863658
Royal Hampshire Regimental Museum
Serle's House, Southgate Street, Winchester, SO23 9EG Tel:
01962 863658
Hertfordshire
Hertford Museum (Hertford Regiment)
18 Bull Plain, Hertford, SG14 1DT ,
Kent, Buffs Regimental Museum
The Royal Museum & Art Gallery, 18 High Street,
Canterbury, CT1 2RA Tel: 01227-452747 Fax: 01227-
455047
Princess of Wales and Queen's Regiment Museum
Inner Bailey, Dover Castle, Dover, CT16 1HU Tel: 01304-
240121

Princess of Wales's Royal Regt & Queen's Regt Museum
Howe Barracks, Canterbury, CT1 1JY Tel: 01227-818056
Fax: 01227-818057
Royal Engineers Library
Brompton Barracks, Chatham, ME4 4UG Tel: 01634-822416
Fax: 01634-822419
Royal Engineers Museum
Prince Arthur Road, Gillingham, ME4 4UG
Tel: 01634 406397
The Buffs Regimental Museum
18 High Street, Canterbury Tel: 01227 452747
The Queen's Own Royal West Kent Regiment Museum
Maidstone Museum and Art Gallery, St. Faith's Street,
Maidstone, ME14 1LH Tel: 01622 754497
Fax: 01622 602193
Lancashire
King's Own Royal Regimental Museum
The City Museum, Market Square, Lancaster, LA1 1HT Tel:
01524 64637 Fax: 01524 841692
**Museum of Lancashire (Queen's Lancashire Regiment
Duke of Lancaster's Own Yeomanry Lancashire Hussars
14th/20th King's Hussars)**
Stanley Street, Preston, PR1 4YP Tel: 01772 264075
Museum of the Manchesters
Ashton Town Hall, Market Place, Ashton-u-Lyne, OL6 6DL,
Tel:0161 342 3078/3710 or 343 1978
**Museum of the Queen's Lancashire Regiment (East South
and Loyal North LancashireRegiments)**
Fulwood Barracks, Preston, PR2 8AA Tel: 01772 260362
Fax: 01772 260583
**South Lancashire Regiment Prince of Wales Volunteers
Museum**
Peninsula Barracks, Warrington,
The Fusiliers Museum Lancashire
Bury, BL8 2PL Tel: 0161 764 2208
Leicestershire
Battle of Britain Memorial Flight Visits
R.A.F Coningsby Lincoln, LN4 4SY Tel: 01526 344041
Royal Leicestershire Regiment Museum
New Walk Museum, 53 New Walk, Leicester, LE1 7AE,
Lincolnshire
Museum of Lincolnshire Life
Royal Lincolnshire Regiment Lincolnshire Yeomanry
Old Barracks, Burton Road, Lincoln, LN1 3LY Tel: 01522
528448 Fax: 01522 521264
**The Queen's Royal Lancers Regimental Museum
(16th/5th and 17th/21st Lancers)**
Belvoir Castle, nr Grantham , NG32 1PD Tel: 0115 957 3295
Liverpool
King's Regiment Collection
Museum of Liverpool Life, Pier Head, Liverpool, L3 1PZ
Tel: 0151-478-4062 Fax: 0151-478-4090
London
Imperial War Museum
Lambeth Road, London, SE1 6HZ Tel: 0171-416-5000
Middlesex Regiment Museum (inc National Army Museum)
Royal Hospital Road, Chelsea, London, SW3 4HT,
National Army Museum
Royal Hospital Road, London, SW3 4HT Tel: 0171-730-
0717 Fax: 0171-823-6573, Email: nam@enterprise.net,
WWW: http://www.failte.co./nam/
National Maritime Museum
Romney Road, Greenwich, London, SE10 9NF Tel: 0181-
858-4422 Fax: 0181-312-6632 WWW:
http://www.nmm.ac.uk
Royal Air Force Museum
Grahame Park Way, Hendon, London, NW9 5LL Tel: 0181-
205-2266 Fax: 0181 200 1751 WWW:
http://www.rafmuseum.org.uk

Norfolk
Royal Norfolk Regimental Museum
Shirehall, Market Avenue, Norwich, NR1 3JQ Tel: 01603 493649 Fax: 01603 765651
100 Bomb Group
Memorial Museum Common Rd, Dickleburgh, Diss, IP21 4PH Tel: 01379 740708
Air Defence Battle Command & Control Museum
Neatishead, Norwich, NR12 8YB Tel: 01692 633309
North Yorkshire
Eden Camp Museum
Malton, YO17 6RT Tel: 01653-697777 Fax: 01653-698243, Email: admin@edencamp.co.uk, WWW: http://www.edencamp.co.uk
Green Howards Regimental Museum
Trinity Church Square, Richmond, DL10 4QN Tel: 01748-822133 Fax: 01748-826561
Prince of Wales' Own Regiment of Yorkshire Military Museum (West & East Yorkshire Regiments)
Royal Dragoon Guards Military Museum (4th/7th Dragoons & 5th Inniskilling Dragoons)
3A Tower Street, York, YO1 1SB Tel: 01904-662790 Tel: Tel: 01904 642036 Tel: 01904 658051
Yorkshire Air Museum
Elvington, York, YO41 5AU Tel: 01904-608595
Northamptonshire
Museum of The Northamptonshire Regiment
Abington Park Museum, Abington, NN1 5LW
Tel: 01604 635412
Northumberland
Fusiliers Museum of Northumberland, The Abbot's Tower, Alnwick Castle, Alnwick, NE66 1NG Tel: 01665-602151 Fax: 01665-603320, Email: fusmusnorthld@btinternet.com
King's Own Scottish Borderers Museum
The Barracks, Berwick-upon-Tweed, TD15 1DG, Tel:01289 307426
Nottinghamshire
Sherwood Foresters Museum and Archives
RHQ WFR, Foresters House, Chetwynd Barracks, Chilwell, Nottingham, NG9 5HA Tel: 0115-946-5415
Fax: 0115-946-5712
Sherwood Foresters (Notts and Derbys. Regt. Museum)
The Castle, Nottingham, NG1 6EL Tel: 0115 946 5415
Fax: 0115 946 5712
Oxfordshire
Oxfordshire and Buckinghamshire Light Infantry Regimental Museum
Slade Park, Headington, Oxford, OX3 7JL Tel: 01865 780128
Shropshire
Shropshire Regimental Museum (King's Shropshire Light Infantry, Shropshire Yeomanry)
The Castle, Shrewsbury, SY1 2AT Tel: 01743-358516 Tel: 01743-262292
Somerset
Fleet Air Arm Museum Records Research Centre
Box D61, RNAS Yeovilton, Nr Ilchester, BA22 8HT Tel: 01935-840565 Fax: 01935-840181
Somerset Military Museum (Somerset Light Infantry Yeomanry
The Castle, Taunton, TA1 4AA Tel: 01823 333434
South Yorkshire
King's Own Yorkshire Light Infantry Regimental Museum
Doncaster Museum & Art Gallery, Chequer Road, Doncaster, DN1 2AE Tel: 01302 734292 Fax: 01302 735409
Regimental Museum 13th/18th Royal Hussars and The Light Dragoons
Cannon Hall, Cawthorne, Barnsley, S75 4AT Tel: 01226 790270

York and Lancaster Regimental Museum
Library and Arts Centre, Walker Place, Rotherham, S65 1JH Tel: 01709 382121 ext 3625/3632
Staffordshire
Museum of The Staffordshire Regiment
Whittington Barracks, Lichfield, WS14 9PY
Tel: 0121 311 3240
Museum of the Staffordshire Yeomanry
The Ancient High House, Greengate Street, Stafford, ST16 2HS Tel: 01785 40204 (Tourist Info. Office)
Suffolk
Suffolk Regiment Museum
Suffolk Record Office, 77 Raingate Street, Bury St Edmunds, IP33 2AR Tel: 01284-352352 Fax: 01284-352355
Email: bury.ro@libhev.suffolkcc.gov.uk
Surrey
Queen's Royal Surrey Regiment Museum (Queen's Royal Surrey East Surrey & Queen's Royal Surrey Regiments)
Clandon Park, West Clandon, Guildford, GU4 7RQ Tel: 01483 223419 Fax: 01483 224636
Regimental Museum Royal Logistical Corps
Deepcut, Camberley, Surrey, GU16 6RW
Tel: 01252-340871-&-01252-340984
Sussex
Royal Military Police Museum
Roussillon Barracks, Chichester, PO19 4BN Tel: 01243 534225 Fax: 01243 534288
Sussex Combined Services Museum (Royal Sussex Regiment and Queen's Royal Irish Hussars)
Redoubt Fortress, Royal Parade, Eastbourne, BN22 7AQ Tel: 01323 410300
Tyne & Wear
A Soldier's Life 15th/19th King's Royal Hussars Northumberland Hussars and Light Dragoons
Newcastle Discovery, Blandford Square, Newcastle-upon-Tyne, NE1 4JA Tel: 0191 232 6789 Fax: 0191 230 2614
Military Vehicles Museum
Exhibition Park Pavilion, Newcastle Upon Tyne, NE2 4PZ Tel: 0191 2817222
Warwickshire
Regimental Museum of The Queen's Own Hussars (3rd King's Own and 7th Queen's Own Hussars)
The Lord Leycester Hospital, High Street, Warwick, CV34 4EW, Tel:01926 492035
Royal Warwickshire Regimental Museum
St. John's House, Warwick , CV34 4NF, Tel:01926 491653
Warwickshire Yeomanry Museum
The Court House, Jury Street, Warwick, CV34 4EW
Tel: 01926 492212 Fax: 01926 494837
West Yorkshire, Duke of Wellington's Regimental Museum Bankfield Museum, Akroyd Park, Boothtown Road, Halifax, HX3 6HG Tel: 01422 354823 Fax: 01422 249020
Wiltshire
Duke of Edinburgh's Royal Regiment (Berks & Wilts) Museum
The Wardrobe, 58 The Close, Salisbury, SP1 2EX Tel: 01722-414536
Royal Army Chaplains Department Museum
Netheravon House, Salisbury Road, Netheravon, SP4 9SY Tel: 01980-604911 Fax: 01980-604908
Worcestershire
The Worcestershire Regiment Museum
Worcester City Museum & Art Gallery, Foregate Street, Worcester, WR1 1DT Tel: 01905-25371 Museum Tel: 01905 354359 Office Fax: 01905-616979 Museum 01905 353871 Office, Postal Address: The Curator, The Worcestershire Regimental Museum Trust, RHQ WFR, Norton Barracks, Worcester WR5 2PA

Worcestershire Regiment Archives (Worcester and Sherwood Forester's Regiment)
RHQ WFR Norton Barracks, Worcester, WRS 2PA Tel: 01905-354359

Northern Ireland

Royal Inniskilling Fusiliers Regimental Museum, The Castle, Enniskillen, Co Fermanagh, BT74 7BB Tel: 01365-323142 Fax: 01365-320359
Royal Irish Fusiliers Museum
Sovereign's House, Mall East, Armagh, BT61 9DL Tel: 01861 522911 Fax: 01861 522911

Royal Ulster Rifles Regimental Museum
RHQ Royal Irish Rifles, 5 Waring Street, Belfast, BT1 2EW Tel: 01232-232086
The Museum Of The Royal Irish Regiment
St. Patricks Barracks, Demesne Avenue, Ballymena, BT43 7BH Tel: 01266 661355

Scotland

Queen's Own Highlanders (Seaforths & Camerons) Regimental Museum Archives
Fort George, Ardersier, Inverness, IV1 2TD Tel: 01463-224380
Royal Scots Regimental Museum
The Castle, Edinburgh, EH1 2YT Tel: 0131-310-5014 Fax: 0131-310-5019
Scottish United Services Museum
The Castle, Museum Square, Edinburgh, EH1 2NG Tel: 0131-225-7534 Fax: 0131-225-7534
Aberdeenshire
Gordon Highlanders Museum
St Lukes, Viewfield Road, Aberdeen, AB15 7XH Tel: 01224 311200 Fax: 01224 319323
Ayrshire
Ayrshire Yeomanry Museum
Rozelle House, Monument Road, Alloway by Ayr, KA7 4NQ Tel: 01292 264091
Berwickshire
Museum of Coldstream Guards, Coldstream
Glasgow
Museum of The Royal Highland Fusiliers (Royal Scots Fusiliers and Highland Light Infantry)
518 Sauchiehall Street, Glasgow, G2 3LW Tel: 0141 332 961
Inverness-Shire

Queen's Own Highlanders (Seaforths & Camerons) Regimental Museum Archives
Fort George, Ardersier, Inverness, IV1 2TD Tel: 01463-224380
Lanarkshire
The Cameronians (Scottish Rifles) Museum, c/o Low Parks Museum, 129 Muir Street, Hamilton, ML3 6BJ Tel: 01698 455714
Midlothian
Royal Scots Dragoon Guards (Carabiniers and Greys)
Edinburgh, EH1 2YT Tel: 0131 220 4387 Fax: 0131 310 5101
Perthshire
Regimental Archives of Black Watch
Balhousie Castle, Hay Street, Perth, PH1 5HS Tel: 0131-3108530 Fax: 01738-643245
Scottish Horse Regimental Museum
The Cross, Dunkeld, PH8 0AN,
The Black Watch Museum
Perth (on the North Inch), PH1 5HS Tel: 01738 621281 ext 8530 Fax: 01738 623245
Stirlingshire
Regimental Museum Argyll and Sutherland Highlanders
Stirling Castle, Stirling, FK8 1EH Tel: 01786 475165 Fax: 01786 446038

Wales

Caernarfon
The Royal Welch Fusiliers Regimental Museum
The Queen's Tower, The Castle, Caernarfon, LL55 2AY Tel: 01286-673362 Fax: 01286-677042
Welch Regiment Museum (41st/69th Foot)
The Castle, Cardiff, CF1 2RB Tel: 01222-229367
Cardiff
1st The Queen's Dragoon Guards Regimental Museum
Cardiff Castle, Cardiff, CF1 2RB Tel: 01222 222253 Tel: 01222 781232 Fax: 01222 781384
The Welch Regiment Museum of the Royal Regiment of Wales
The Black and Barbican Tower, Cardiff Castle, Cardiff, CF1 2RB Tel: 01222 229367

Monmouth
Monmouthshire Royal Engineers (Militia)
Castle and Regimental Museum, The Castle, Monmouth, NP5 3BS Tel: 01600-712935
Nelson Museum & Local History Centre, Priory St, Newport, NP5 3XA Tel: 1600 713519
Powys
Powys, South Wales Borderers & Monmouthshire Regimental Museum of the Royal Regiment of Wales (24th/41st Foot), The Barracks, Brecon, LD3 7EB Tel: 01874-613310 Fax: 01874-613275, Email: rrw@ukonline.co.uk, WWW: http://www.ukonline.co.uk/rrw/index.htm

Belgium

In Flanders Fields Museum, Lakenhallen, Grote Markt 34, Ieper, B-8900 Tel: 00-32-(0)-57-22-85-84 Fax: 00-32-(0)-57-22-85-89 WWW: www.inflandersfields.be

Libraries and Genealogical Research
Stuart A. Raymond

Where would we be without libraries? They are storehouses of information - not just books and journals, but also microfiche, microfilm, and, increasingly these days, CD-roms. Public libraries are there for everyone, and although the perception in some quarters may be that they merely offer light reading, in fact they provide information on every subject under the sun -- and beyond! Whether your interests are astronomy or cake making, the law or motoring, the public library is there to provide whatever information you need.

Libraries are one of the first places that genealogists should visit in their research. A vast amount of genealogical information has been published, and is available in print. Genealogists should check whether the information they require is in printed form before they consult the archives. Archives are unique and irreplaceable; any use may damage them, and they should be consulted as little as possible. If the information contained in them has been published, then you should go to the printed book first - although you may need to check its accuracy later against the original manuscript.

Virtually all of the information contained in published sources may be accessed via the public library network. Very few published books fail to find their way onto public library shelves. And the network of libraries is worldwide: I was able to write a book on Cornish genealogy by using the resources of the State Library of Victoria in Melbourne. In addition to public libraries, the genealogist will also find the libraries of family history societies - and especially of the Society of Genealogists - to be invaluable for research purposes. The libraries of county institutions such as the Yorkshire Archaeological Society or the Somerset Archaeological and Natural History Society hold many useful works, not just for the counties in which they are situated. Relevant material may also be found in University libraries - especially runs of the major county record society publications and local history society transactions. Institutions such as the British Library, the Library of Congress, and the National Library of Australia may also be worth visiting to locate elusive titles; these national libraries should have copies of every book published in their respective countries. The best guide to libraries for genealogists in England is probably Susannah Guy's *English Local Studies Handbook* (University of Exeter Press, 1992 - new edition in preparation).

Libraries can appear to be intimidating places to enter. They should not be. You, the taxpayer, fund them in order to meet your informational needs, and you should make sure that they do so. If you have a question you need answered, ask it! The librarian sitting at the information desk is there to provide an answer, and if you do not ask, you are preventing the librarian from doing his job. Be sure, however, that you ask the right person; it is no good asking the junior assistant about indexes to probate records; she may be able to direct you to the 929s, but is unlikely to be able to help you further. Horses for courses! Make sure that you ask the professional librarian, who should have a good knowledge of the collection, and ought to be able to point you to the reference work you need, to find addresses for you, to identify books on specific subjects, to direct you to other more appropriate libraries, or to explain the use of the catalogue. Do not, however, expect the reference librarian to do your research for you. He/she is expert in finding published information, but is not necessarily an experienced genealogist.

The catalogue provides you (usually) with a full list of the books in a library. Nowadays it is likely to be computerised, although it is always worth checking whether parts of the collection are still listed on cards. As I write this, the Society of Genealogists' old card catalogue is in the process of being replaced by a computerised system, but you must still check the card catalogue for some items. You can usually search catalogues by author, title, or subject. Many computerised catalogues also permit you to search by a combination of author and title, or by keywords found in either.

> **Libraries are one of the first places that genealogists should visit ...**

The catalogue record will tell you where the book is shelved, and may also indicate whether it is on loan. Most libraries shelve their books in accordance with the Dewey decimal classification (genealogy is at 929), although a number of other classification schemes are also in use. In larger library systems, the catalogue may include details of books in many library; if you do not understand what it is telling you, ask a librarian! An increasing number of library catalogues are available via the internet. At present, these are mainly university library catalogues, which should not be neglected; however, the most useful catalogue on the internet for genealogists is probably the British Library. Amongst much, much else, the library holds thousands of family histories -- so type in your surname, and see what comes up! If you cannot actually get to London, take a copy of the citation - you need author, title, and date as a minimum - and check it against the catalogues of libraries you are able to visit. Or ask your local librarian if you can obtain the book you need via Inter library loan.

Identifying the particular item you need generally involves more than just using the library catalogue - especially if it is an article in a journal, which is unlikely to be separately listed in most catalogues. How do you identify useful guides to sources? Which parish registers have been published? What monumental inscriptions are available on microfiche? Too often, genealogists rely on serendipity for answers to questions like these. If you are attempting a systematic search, however, and wish to check all available sources, then you need to consult bibliographies. Don't let the word put you off. Bibliographies simply list the books and journal articles etc that are available, and enable you to make a systematic study of the works listed.

A number of current genealogical bibliographies are available; these list works currently available for purchase (of course they may also be found in libraries). My own *British Genealogical Books in Print* (F.F.H.S., 1999) and *British Genealogical Microfiche* (F.F.H.S., 1999) list the publications of hundreds of commercial publishers, libraries, record offices, historical societies, and private publishers. The publications of family history societies are listed in John Perkins' *Current Publications on Microfiche by Member Societies* (4th ed., F.F.H.S., 1997), and in the forthcoming 10th edition of *Current Publications by Member Societies* (F.F.H.S.) All of these titles should be checked for information on the many thousand works currently available. Of course, each month sees many more titles published; to keep up to date, the book reviews in *Family History Monthly, Family Tree Magazine, Family History News & Digest,* and the *Genealogists magazine* should all be checked.

These titles cover the whole country; however, most genealogists are likely to be researching in specific areas, and need information on all the publications relating to that area. The county volumes of my *British Genealogical Library guides* series (formerly *British Genealogical Bibliographies*) provide the information needed to conduct systematic searches of the genealogical lterature for specific counties. Counties covered to date include Buckinghamshire, Cheshire, Cornwall*, Cumberland & Westmorland*, Devon*, Dorset, Essex, Gloucestershire*, Hampshire, Kent, Lancashire, Lincolnshire, London & Middlesex, Norfolk, Oxfordshire, Somerset*, Suffolk* and Wiltshire* (* indicates out of print). These volumes complement my *English Genealogy: a Bibliography* (3rd ed. F.F.H.S., 1996), which lists publications of national importance. *English Genealogy* identifies innumerable handbooks on the whole range of genealogical topics, as well as numerous biographical dictionaries, pedigree collections, surname dictionaries, archival guides, handwriting manuals, *etc., etc* ., also many indexes to sources which are national in scope, e.g. Prerogative Court of Canterbury records,

The range of genealogical material revealed by these bibliographies is enormous; to try to dip into it without consulting them may be likened to searching for a needle in a haystack. And to try to describe that literature in an article of this length taxes the brain somewhat! The authoritative guide to our hobby is now Mark Heber's *Ancestral Trails* (Sutton, 1997). This is relatively expensive, and runs to 674 pages. There are many briefer, less expensive guides for beginners, for example, George Pelling's *Beginning your Family History* (7th ed., F.F.H.S. 1998), or Colin Chapman's *Tracing your British ancestors* (2nd ed. Lochin, 1996). Encyclopaedias are also useful; Terrick Fitzhugh's *Dictionary of Genealogy*, and Pauline Saul's *Family Historians Enquire Within* (5th ed., F.F.H.S., 1995) may both be recommended.

Much invaluable information is to be found in genealogical journals. Reference has already been made to the major current journals; these are complemented by the journals or newsletters of family history societies. These generally provide lists of their members interests, together with details of society activities, and brief articles on topics of interest - including many notes on the histories of particular families. Articles in these journals are regularly indexed in the digest section *of Family History News and Digest*. A number of genealogical journals published in the late 19th and early 20th centuries are also worth consulting. The most important of these were *The Genealogist* (1877-1921) and *Miscellanea genealogica et heraldica* (1868-1938). These include numerous extracts from original sources such as parish registers and monumental inscriptions, as well as many pedigrees and articles on particular families. I have indexed them, together with a number of other titles, in my *British Genealogical Periodicals: a bibliography of their contents* (3 vols. in 5; F.F.H.S., 1991-3), and also in my county bibliographies.

Historical journals also have much to offer the genealogist. In particular, the transactions of county historical and archaeological societies frequently contain many works of relevance. For example, between 1882 and 1908, the *Yorkshire Archaeological Journal* published many abstracts from the marriage allegations of York diocese. County record society series are also of considerable importance. These societies publish edited transcripts of important records, such as deed collections, probate records, diaries, ecclesiastical records, etc., etc. A full list of their publications may be found in E. L. C. Mullins' *Texts and Calendars: an analytical guide to serial publications* (Royal Historical Society, 1958). A supplement to Mullins was published in 1982, and an online update is available on the internet. Relevant items are also listed in my county bibliographies.

The majority of genealogical publications relate to specific sources, and the remainder of this essay will be devoted to discussing these. Parish registers are of major importance to the genealogist, and especially to those researching prior to the 19th century. Many record offices have produced listings of their own holdings; however, the most comprehensive guides are the county volumes of the *National Index of Parish Registers*, published by the Society of Genealogists. *Phillimore's Atlas and Index of Parish Registers* is also valuable, especially for its parish maps. Many registers have been published; these are listed in detail in my county bibliographies. In the early years of this century, many registers were printed by the Parish Register Society, and in *Phillimore's Parish Register series*. There are or have been a number of county parish register societies; those for Lancashire and Yorkshire have each produced over 100 volumes. Registers have also been published by bodies such as the Devon and Cornwall Record Society and, for London & Middlesex, the Harleian Society (see Mullins for details), by record offices (Bedfordshire is the best example), and by private individuals such as F. Crisp for East Anglia, E. Dwelly for Somerset and S.H.A. Hervey for Suffolk. Today, family history societies are increasingly publishing registers on microfiche, as a glance at Perkins work mentioned above will reveal.

Family history societies are also leading the way in transcribing and microfiching monumental inscriptions (see Perkins again) - although it is regrettable that most transcripts of inscriptions remain unpublished. Prior to the 1980s, although a small number of collections of inscriptions were published privately, most published inscriptions appeared either as appendices to parish registers, as chapters of local histories, or as individual inscriptions in journals such as *Miscellanea genealogica et heraldica*. Full lists of published inscriptions are provided in my county bibliographies

Probate records are much better documented. The standard guide to them is Jeremy Gibson's *Probate Jurisdictions: where to look for wills* (4th ed. F.F.H.S. 1997). Numerous published indexes to wills and probate inventories are available: the British Record Society's *Index library*, which now runs to over 100 volumes, is almost entirely devoted to probate indexes; these are listed in Mullins, as are a number of similar works published by county record societies. The latter have also published many edited transcripts of wills and probate inventories, as have a few university history departments and commercial publishers. Many individual wills etc., appear in journals such as *Miscellanea genealogica et heraldica*. Detailed listings of what is available are given in my county bibliographies. Probate records provide one of the best examples of genealogical sources that are also of great

interest to historians in general; many studies of particular communities have been based upon them, and numerous aspiring Ph.Ds have mined them for information.

Official lists of names, such as tax lists, protestation returns, muster rolls, census returns, etc., have also been the subjects of much publishing effort. Jeremy Gibson has been responsible for a number of guides in this area, for example, *The Hearth Tax, other late Stuart tax lists, and the association oath rolls* (2nd ed. F.F.H.S., 1996); *The Protestation Returns 1641--2, and other contemporary listings* (with Alan Dell; F.F.H.S., 1995). Record societies have issued numerous editions of subsidy rolls, hearth tax returns, muster rolls, etc., these are listed by Mullins.

The major guide to census records is Susan Lumas's *Making Use of the Census* (PRO Publications 1997). In the last decade, the indexing of census records has been a major growth industry amongst genealogists. The 1881 census indexing project was one of the biggest projects of its kind, but it was not alone; numerous census indexes are now available from family history societies and other publishers; these are listed in the current bibliographies mentioned above, and in my county bibliographies.

Trade directories of the 19th and early 20th centuries provide unofficial lists of names which can be very useful. These are rarely found outside of the libraries for the areas they cover; however, a number of commercial publishers now have extensive lists of directories reprinted on microfiche; my *British genealogical microfiche* provides the relevant details. There are probably over 1,000 directories currently available; it is worth noting that one of the major publishers in this field, Nick Vine Hall, is based in Australia.

This article inevitably skims the surface of the material available; no mention has been made, for example, of ecclesiastical records other than parish registers, of school registers, of estate archives, or of guides to particular record offices. Many other bibliographies could have been mentioned; e.g., my *Occupational Sources for Genealogists*, or Michael Gandy's *Catholic Family History: a Bibliography of General Sources* (Michael Gandy, 1996).

Using bibliographies, libraries, and the published literature of genealogy effectively could considerably reduce the time you spend searching for information in the archives; that time, however, is likely to be more than used up checking the sources you identify. At least you should be able to do much of the work at home, and in local libraries. If you need more information, just check as many bibliographies as you can find!

Stuart Raymond may be contacted at P.O.Box 35, Exeter, EX4 5EF.
Email: stuart@samjraymond.softnet.co.uk. Phone (01392) 252193.

Let's get FAMILIA!

Many public library authorities are now targeting family history researchers as one of the most important user groups that we serve. More sources, often beyond the local, are being made available, specialist publications produced, staff training undertaken and facilities improved.

But how does the public find out what libraries throughout the UK and Ireland hold? For those genealogists with a PC and an internet connection, the answer is now, quite literally at your fingertips! In 1997 the FAMILIA website (Family History Resources in Public Libraries in Britain and Ireland) was launched under the auspices of EARL, a partnership of library authorities established to develop the role of public libraries in providing electronic internet services for the public.

The FAMILIA site can be found at : http://earl.org.uk/familia

The site is very easy to use. There is a list of all the library authorities – those which have supplied data for the project are in bold; those which have not yet contributed are in italics. So far over 160 library authorities have joined the FAMILIA project and clicking on the name of the authority leads to details of the family history resource material held by each individual authority. Additional detail of contact names, addresses and email addresses is given. All information is updated at regular intervals.

Sections within the listings include:
- Principal libraries with family history resources
- Details of the Registrar General's index to births, deaths and marriages; census returns; trade directories; electoral registers and poll books; IGI; unpublished in-house indexes; parish registers; periodicals; published transcripts of archival material; published guides to collections
- Details of local record offices
- Details of any research service provided

A series of pages headed 'Guides' have practical tips on using libraries, a basic book list and so on. The FAMILIA Working Group is adding to this section with the co-operation of the Public Record Office.

Clicking on 'Maps' allows access to a series of maps, most of which are hotlinked from the GENUKI (UK and Ireland Genealogy) website with their permission. The maps show both pre-1974 English counties and also those counties as at 1998 (Perry-Castaneda Library map Collection, University of Texas). There are also separate maps for Ireland, Scotland and Wales, the last two supplied by the Scottish Office and Data Wales respectively. The Working Group is also developing an alphabetical index linking towns with their current authority in order to assist access for genealogists who will not be aware of the present geography of the country.

Many public libraries are continually improving and increasing the range of family history sources easily available to the public. Library staff are pleased to welcome researchers, especially those who contact them in advance to check on opening hours, conditions of access and the types of material that they can provide. The FAMILIA website is designed to help genealogists identify the authorities and enable them to prepare for a visit in a planned manner. Most libraries now have email addresses. Log on to the site – http://www.earl.org.uk/familia – surf, and see!

This information has been kindly provided by Elizabeth Anne Melrose, Information Services Adviser for North Yorkshire County Libraries who is a member of The FAMILIA Working Group.

British Library
British Library Building, 96 Euston Road, London, NW1
2DB Tel: 0171 412 7677 Email:
http://www.portico.bl.ukReader/admissions@bl.uk
British Library
Boston Spa, Wetherby, West Yorkshire, LS23 7BY Tel:
01937 546212
British Library   Early Printed Collections
96 Euston Road, London, NW1 2DB Tel: 0171 412 7673
Fax: 0171 412 7577 Email: rare books@bl.uk WWW:
http://www.bl.uk
The Bodelian Library
Broad Street, Oxford, Oxfordshire, OX1 3BG Tel: 01865
277000 Fax: 01865 277182 WWW: www.bodley.ox.ac.uk

Specialist Records
Department of Manuscripts and Special Collections,
Hallward Library Nottingham University , University Park,
Nottingham, NG7 2RD Tel: 0115 951 4565
Fax: 0115 951848
Lambeth Palace Library
Lambeth Palace Road, London, SE1 7JU
Tel: 0171 898 1400 Fax: 0171 928 7932
Library of the Religious Society of Friends (Quakers)
Friends House, 173   177 Euston Rd, London, NW1 2BJ Tel:
0207 663 1135 Tel: 0207 663 1001 Email:
library@quaker.org.uk WWW: http://www.quaker.org.uk
British Library Newspaper Library
Colindale Avenue, London, NW9 5HE Tel: 020 7412 7353
Fax: 020 7412 7379 Email: newspaper@bl.uk WWW:
http://www.bl.uk/collections/newspaper/
British Library Oriental and India Office Collections
96 Euston Road, London, NW1 2DB Tel: 0171 412 7873
Fax: 0171 412 7641 Email: oioc enquiries@bl.uk WWW:
http://www.bl.uk/collections/oriental
Catholic Central Library
Lancing Street, London, NW1 1ND Tel: 0171 383 4333 Fax:
0171 388 6675 Email: librarian@catholic
library.demon.co.uk WWW: www.catholic
library.demon.co.uk
Huguenot Library
University College, Gower Street, London, WC1E 6BT Tel:
0171 380 7094 Email: a.massilk@ucl.ac.uk WWW:
http://www.ucl.ac.uk/library/hugenot.htm

England
Bedfordshire
Bedford Central Library
Harpur Street, Bedford, MK40 1PG Tel: 01234 350931
Fax: 01234 342163 Email: stephenson@bedfordshire.co.uk
Luton Central & Local Studies Library
St George's Square, Luton, Bedfordshire, LU1 2NG
Tel: 01582 547420 Tel: 01582 547421 Fax: 01582 547450
Berkshire
County Local Studies Library
3rd Floor, Central Library, Abbey Square, Reading,
Berkshire RG1 3BQ Tel: 0118 950 9243
Birkenhead
Wirral Central Library
Borough Road, Birkenhead L41 2XB Tel: 0151 652 6106/7/8
Birmingham
Birminham Central Library Local Studies & History
Floor 6, Central Library, Chamberlain Square, Birmingham,
B3 3HQ Tel: 0121 303 4549 Fax: 0121 233 4458
Bolton
Central Library
Civic Centre, Le Mans Crescent, Bolton, BL1 1SE
Tel: 01204 522311 Ext 2179

House of Commons Library
House of Commons, 1 Derby Gate, London, SW1A 2DG
Tel: 0171 219 5545 Fax: 0171 219 3921
Society of Genealogists   Library
14 Charterhouse Buildings, Goswell Road, London, EC1M
7BA Tel: 020 7251 8799 Tel: 020 7250 0291 Fax: 020 7250
1800 Email: info@sog.org.uk   Sales at sales@sog.org.uk
WWW: http://www.sog.org.uk
Institute of Heraldic and Genealogical Studies
79   82 Northgate, Canterbury, Kent, CT1 1BA Tel: 01227
768664 Fax: 01227 765617 Email: ihgs@ihgs.ac.uk WWW:
www.ihgs.ac.uk

Jewish Museum, The Sternberg Centre for Judaism
80 East End Road, Finchley, London, N3 2SY Tel: 020 8349
1143 Fax: WWW: www.jewmusm.ort.org
John Rylands University Library
Special Collections Division, 150 Deansgate, Manchester,
M3 3EH Tel: 0161 834 5343 Fax: 0161 834 5343 Email:
j.r.hodgson@man.ac.uk WWW: http://rylibweb.man.ac.uk
Liverpool University Special Collections & Archives
University of Liverpool Library
PO Box 123, Liverpool, L69 3DA Tel: 0151 794 2696 Fax:
0151 794 2081 Email: archives@liv.ac.uk WWW:
http://www.lsca.lib.liv.ac.uk
**Royal Society of Chemistry Library & Information
Centre**
Burlington House, Piccadilly, London, W1V 0BN Tel: 0207
437 8656 Tel: 0207 287 9798 Fax: library@rsc.org Email:
www.rsc.org
**Trades Union Congress Library Collections   University
of North London**
236   250 Holloway Road, London, N7 6PP Tel: Fax: 0171
753 3191 Email: tuclib@unl.ac.uk
United Reformed Church History Society
Westminster College, Madingley Road, Cambridge, CB3
0AA Tel: 01223 741084
Wellcome Institute for the History of Medicine
183 Euston Road, London, NW1 2BE Tel: 0171 611 8582
Fax: 0171 611 8369 Email: library@wellcome.ac.uk WWW:
www.wellcome.ac.uk/library, Library catalogue is available
through the internet:telnet://wihm.ucl.ac.uk

Bristol
Bristol Central Library
Reference Section, College Green, Bristol, BS1 5TL
Tel: 0117 929 9147
Buckinghamshire
County Reference Library
Walton Street, Aylesbury HP20 1UU Tel: 01296 382250
Fax: 01296 382405
High Wycombe Reference Library
Queen Victoria Road, High Wycombe HP11 1BD Tel: 01494
510241 Fax: 01494 533086
Milton Keynes Reference Library
555 Silbury Boulevard, Milton Keynes MK9 3HL
Cambridgeshire
Norris Library and Museum
The Broadway, St Ives, Huntingdon, Cambridgeshire, PE17
4BX Tel: 01480 465101 Fax: 01480 497314
Peterborough Local Studies Collection
Broadway, Peterborough, PE1 1RX Tel: 01733 348343
Fax: 01733 555277

Cheshire

John Rylands University Library
Special Collections Division, 150 Deansgate, Manchester,
M3 3EH Tel: 0161 834 5343 Fax: 0161 834 5343 Email:
j.r.hodgson@man.ac.uk WWW: http://rylibweb.man.ac.uk

Chester Library
Northgate Street, Chester CH1 2EF Tel: 01244 312935 Fax:
01244 315534

Crewe Library
Prince Albert Street, Crewe, Cheshire, CW1 2DH Tel: 01270
211123 Fax: 01270 256952

Ellesmere Port Library
Civic Way, Ellesmere Port, South Wirral, Cheshire, L65 0BG
Tel: 0151 355 8101 Fax: 0151 355 6849

Stockport Local Heritage Library
Central Library, Wellington Road South, Stockport,
Cheshire, SK1 3RS Tel: 0161 474 4530 Fax: 0161 474 7750
Email: stockport.cenlibrary@dial.pipex.com

Macclesfield Library
Jordongate, Macclesfield, Cheshire, SK10 1EE
Tel: 01625 422512 Fax: 01625 612818

Runcorn Library
Runcorn Shopping City, Runcorn, Cheshire, WA7 2PF Tel:
01928 715351 Fax: 01928 790221

Tameside Local Studies Library - Stalybridge Library
Trinity Street, Stalybridge SK15 2BN Tel: 0161 338 2708
Tel: 0161 338 3831 Fax: 0161 303 8289
Email: tamelocal@dial.pipex.com,
WWW: http://www.tameside.gov.uk

Trafford Public Library
Tatton Road, Sale, Cheshire, M33 1YH Tel: 0161 9123013

Warrington Library
Museum Street, Warrington WA1 1JB Tel: 01925 442889
Fax: 01925 411395 Email: library@warrington.gov.uk

Cleveland

Middlesbrough Libraries & Local Studies Centre
Central Library, Victoria Square, Middlesbrough, Cleveland,
TS1 2AY Tel: 01642 263358 Fax: 01642 648077

Stockton Reference Library
Church Road, Stockton on Tees, Cleveland, TS18 1TU Tel:
01642 393994 Fax: 01642 393929

Cornwall

Cornish Studies Library
2 4 Clinton Road, Redruth, Cornwall, TR15 2QE Tel:
01209 216760 Fax: 01209 210283

County Durham

Centre For Local Studies
The Library, Crown Street, Darlington DL1 1ND
Tel: 01325 349630 Fax: 01325 381556 Email: library@dbc
lib.demon.co.uk

Durham Arts, Library and Museums Department
County Hall, Durham DH1 STY Tel: 0191 383 3595

Durham City Library
Reference & Local Studies South Street, Durham DH1 4QS
Tel: 0191 386 4003 Fax: 0191 386 0379

Durham University Library Archives & Special
Collections Palace Green Section, Palace Green, Durham,
DH1 3RN Tel: 0191 374 3032

Cumbria

Carlisle Library
Globe Lane, Carlisle, Cumbria, CA3 8NX Tel: 01228 607310
Fax: 01228 607333 Email: carlib.staff@dial.pipex.com
WWW: http://dspace.dial.pipex.com/cumherit/index.htm

Cumbria RO & Local Studies Library (Whitehaven)
Scotch Street, Whitehaven, Cumbria, CA28 7BJ Tel: 01946
852920 Fax: 01946 852919
Email: whitehaven.record.office@cumbriacc.gov.uk

Kendal Library
Stricklandgate, Kendal LA9 4PY Tel: 01539 773520
Fax: 01539 773530 Email: Kendal.library@dial.pipex.com

Penrith Library
St Andrews Walk, Penrith CA11 7YA Tel: 01768 242100
Fax: 01768 242101 Email: penrith.library@dial.pipexcom

Workington Library
Vulcans Lane, Workington CA14 4ND Tel: 01900 325170
Fax: 01900 325181 Email:
workington.library@dial.pipex.com

Derbyshire

Chesterfield Local Studies Department, Chesterfield
Library
New Beetwell Street, Chesterfield, Derbyshire, S40 1QN Tel:
01246 209292 Fax: 01246 209304

Derby Local Studies Library
25b Irongate, Derby DE1 3GL Tel: 01332 255393

Family History Research
5 Old Houses, Piccadilly Road, Chesterfield, Derbyshire, S41
0EH Tel: 01246 557033 Email: 1maskell@compuserve.com

Local Studies Library   Matlock
County Hall, Smedley Street, Matlock DE4 3AG
Tel: 01629 585579 Fax: 01629 585049

Devon

Westcountry Studies Library
Exeter Central Library, Castle Street, Exeter, Devon, EX4
3PQ Tel: 01392 384216 Fax: 01392 384228 WWW:
http://www.devon cc.gov.uk/library/locstudy

Devon & Exeter Institution Library
7 The Close, Exeter, Devon EX1 1EZ Tel: 01392 251017
Fax: 01392 263871 Email: m.midgley@exeter.ac.uk WWW:
http://www.ex.ac.uk/~ijtilsed/lib/devonex.html

Dorset

Dorchester Reference Library
Colliton Park, Dorchester, Dorset, DT1 1XJ Tel: 01305
224448 Fax: 01305 266120

Poole Local Studies Collection
Dolphin Centre, Poole, Dorset, BH15 1QE Tel: 01202
671496 Fax: 01202 670253 Email: poolereflib@hotmail.com
WWW: www.poole.gov.uk

East Sussex

Brighton Local Studies Library
Church Street, Brighton BN1 1 UD Tel: 01273 296971 Fax:
01273 296962 Email: brightonlibrary@pavilion.co.uk

Hove Reference Library
182   186 Church Road, Hove, East Sussex, BN3 2EG
Tel: 01273 296942 Fax: 01273 296947

East Yorkshire

Beverley Local Studies Library
Beverley Library Champney Road, Beverley HU17 9BG Tel:
01482 885358 Fax: 01482 881861
Email: user@bevlib.karoo.co.uk

Bridlington Local Studies Library
Bridlington Library King Street, Bridlington, East Yorkshire,
YO15 2DF Tel: 01262 672917 Fax: 01262 670208

East Riding Heritage Library & Museum
Sewerby Hall, Bridlington YO15 1EA Tel: 01262 677874
Tel: 01262 674265 Email: museum@pop3.poptel.org.uk
WWW: www.bridlington.net/sew

Goole Local Studie Library
Goole Library Carlisle Street, Goole DN14 5AA
Tel: 01405 762187 Fax: 01405 768329

Essex

Chelmsford Library
PO Box 882, Market Road, Chelmsford, Essex, CM1 1LH
Tel: 01245 492758 Fax: 01245 492536 Email:
answers.direct@essexcc.gov.uk WWW:
www.essexcc.gov.uk

Colchester Central Library
Trinity Square, Colchester, Essex, CO1 1JB Tel: 01206
245917 Fax: 01206 245901

L B of Barking & Dagenham Local History Studies
Valence Library & Museum
Becontree Avenue, Dagenham, Essex, RM8 3HT Tel: 020 8592 6537 Tel: 020 822 75294 Fax: 020 822 75297 Email: fm019@viscount.org.uk WWW: http://www.earl.org.uk/partners/barking/index.html
Central Library, Barking
Dagenham, Essex, IG11 7NB Tel: 0181 517 8666
L B of Havering Reference Library
St Edward's Way, Romford RM1 3AR Tel: 01708 772393 Fax: 01708 772391 Email: romfordlib2@rmplc.co.uk
Redbridge Library
Central Library, Clements Road, Ilford IG1 1EA Tel: 0187 478 9421 Fax: 0181 553 3299 Email: Local.Studies@redbridge.gov.uk
Southend Library
Central Library, Victoria Avenue, Southend on Sea, Essex, SS2 6EX Tel: 01702 612621 Fax: 01792 612652 and 01702 469241 Email: library@southend.gov.uk WWW: www.southend.gov.uk/libraries/, Minicom 01702 600579
Thomas Plume Library
Market Hill, Malden, Essex, CO9 2AR Tel: , Fax:
Gloucestershire
Cheltenham Local Studies Centre
Cheltenham Library Clarence Street, Cheltenham, Gloucestershire, GL50 3JT Tel: 01242 532678
Gloucester County Library
Brunswick Road, Gloucester, GL1 1HT Tel: 01452 426979 Fax: 01452 521468 Email: clams@gloscc.gov.uk WWW: http://www.gloscc.gov.uk
Gloucester Library, Arts & Museums, County Library
Quayside, Shire Hall, Gloucester, Gloucestershire, GL1 1HY Tel: 01452 425037 Fax: 01452 425042 Email: clams@gloscc.gov.uk
Gloucestershire Family History Society
14 Alexandra Road, Gloucester, Gloucestershire, GL1 3DR Tel: 01452 52344 Email: ejack@gloster.demon.co.uk WWW: http://www.cix.co.uk/~rd/genuki/gfhs.htm
Yate Library
44 West Walk, Yate, Gloucestershire, BS17 4AX Tel: 01454 865661 Fax: 01454 319178
Hampshire
Basingstoke Library
19 20 Westminster House, Potters Walk, Basingstoke, RG21 7LS Tel: 01256 473901 Fax: 01256 470666
Fareham Library
Osborn Road, Fareham, Hampshire, PO16 7EN Tel: 01329 282715 Fax: 01329 221551 Email: clsoref@hants.gov.uk
Hampshire County Library
The Old School, Cannon Street, Lymington, Hampshire, SO41 9BR Tel: 01590 675767 Fax: 01590 672561 Email: clwedhq@hants.gov.uk WWW: http://www.hants.gov.uk
Portsmouth City Libraries, Central Library
Guildhall Square, Portsmouth PO1 2DX Tel: 01705 819311 X232 (Bookings) Tel: 01705 819311   X234 (Enquiries) Fax: 01705 839855
Email: reference.library@portsmouthcc.gov.uk
Royal Marines Musem Library
Eastney, Southsea, Hampshire, PO4 9PX Tel: 01705 819385 Exts 244/239 Fax: 01705 838420
Southampton City Archives, Civic Centre
Southampton SO14 7LW Tel: 023 8083 2205 Fax: 023 8033 6305 Email: localstudies@southampton.gov.uk WWW: www.southampton.gov.uk
Winchester Local Studies Library
Winchester Library, Jewry Street, Winchester SO23 8RX Tel: 01962 841408 Email: clceloc@hants.gov.uk
Winchester Reference Library
81 North Walls, Winchester SO23 8BY Tel: 01962 846059 Fax: 01962 856615 Email: clceref@hants.gov.uk

Herefordshire
Belmont Library
Eastholme Community Centre, Belmont, Hereford, Herefordshire, HR21 7UQ Tel: 01432 342648
Bromyard Library
34 Church Street, Bromyard, Herefordshire, HR7 4DP Tel: 01885 482657 (No Genealogical information held)
Colwall Library
Humphrey Walwyn Library, Colwall, Malvern, Herefordshire, WR13 6QT Tel: 01684 540642
Broad Street Library Hereford
Hereford HR4 9AU Tel: 01432 272456 Fax: 01432 359668
Hereford Cathedral Archives & Library
5 College Cloisters, Cathedral Close, Hereford, Herefordshire, HR1 2NG Tel: 01432 359880 Fax: 01432 355929 Email: archives@herefordcathedral.co.uk
Ledbury Library
The Homend, Ledbury HR8 1BT Tel: 01531 632133
Leominster Library
8 Buttercross, Leominster, Herefordshire, HR6 8BN Tel: 01568 612384 Fax: 01568 616025
Ross Library
Cantilupe Road, Ross on Wye HR9 7AN Tel: 01989 567937
Hertfordshire
Hertfordshire Archives and Local Studies
County Hall, Pegs Lane, Hertford, Hertfordshire, SG13 8EJ Tel: 01992 555105 Fax: 01992 555113 Email: hals@hertscc.gov.uk WWW: http://hertslib.hertscc.gov.uk, (Hertfordshire Archives and Local Studies is comprised of the former Herts County Record Office and Herts Local Studies)
Welwyn Garden City Central Library
Local Studies Section, Campus West, Welwyn Garden City, Hertfordshire, AL8 6AJ
Hull
Hull Family History Unit, Central Library
Albion Street, Kingston upon Hull, HU1 3TF Tel: 01482 616828 Tel: 01482 616827
Email: gareth.watkins@hullcc.gov.uk
WWW: http://www.hullcc.gov.uk/genealogy
Isle of Wight
Isle of Wight County Library
Lord Louis Library
Orchard Street, NewportPO30 1LL Tel: 01983 823800 Fax: 01983 825972 Email: reflib@llouis.demon.co.uk
Kent
Broadstairs Library
The Broadway, Broadstairs, Kent, CT10 2BS Tel: 01843 862994 Fax: 01843 861938
Canterbury Cathedral Library
The Precincts, Canterbury, Kent, CT1 2EH Tel: 01227 865287 Fax: 01227 865222 Email: catlib@ukc.ac.uk WWW: www.canterbury cathedral.org
Canterbury Library & Local Studies Collection
18 High Street, Canterbury, Kent, CT1 2JF Tel: 01227 463608 Fax: 01227 768338
Dartford Central Library   Reference Department
Market Street, Dartford, Kent, DA1 1EU Tel: 01322 221133 Fax: 01322 278271
Dover Library
Maison Dieu House, Biggin Street, Dover, Kent, CT16 1DW Tel: 01304 204241 Fax: 01304 225914
Faversham Library
Newton Road, Faversham, Kent, ME13 8DY Tel: 01759 532448 Fax: 01795 591229
Folkestone Library & Local Heritage Studies
Heritage Room, 2 Grace Hill, Folkestone, Kent, CT20 1HD Tel: 01303 850123 Fax: 01303 242907 Email: janet.adamson@kent.gov.uk

Gillingham Library
High Street, Gillingham, Kent, ME7 1BG Tel: 01634 281066
Fax: 01634 855814
Email: Gillingham.Library@medway.gov.uk
Medway
Gravesend Library
Windmill Street, Gravesend DA12 1BE Tel: 01474 352758
Fax: 01474 320284
Greenhill Library
Greenhill Road, Herne Bay CT6 7PN Tel: 01227 374288
Herne Bay Library
124 High Street, Herne Bay CT6 5JY Tel: 01227 374896
Fax: 01227 741582
L B of Bromley Local Studies Library
Central Library, High Street, Bromley BR1 1EX
Tel: 020 8460 9955 Fax: 020 8313 9975
Margate Library Local History Collection
Cecil Square, Margate, Kent, CT9 1RE Tel: 01843 223626
Fax: 01843 293015
Medway Archives and Local Studies Centre
Civic Centre Strood, Rochester, Kent, ME2 4AU
Tel: 01634 332714 Fax: 01634 297060 Email:
archives@medway.gov.uklocal.studies@medway.gov.uk
Ramsgate Library and Museum
Guildford Lawn, Ramsgate, Kent, CT11 9QY Tel: 01843
593532 Fax: 01843 852692 Archives at this library will move
to the New East Kent Archives Centre in winter 1999. A
Local Studies Collection will remain
Royal Engineers Library
Brompton Barracks, Chatham, Kent, ME4 4UG
Tel: 01634 822416 Fax: 01634 822419
Sevenoaks Library
Buckhurst Lane, Sevenoaks, Kent, TN13 1LQ
Tel: 01732 453118 Fax: 01732 742682
Sheerness Library
Russell Street, Sheerness, Kent, ME12 1PL
 Tel: 01795 662618 Fax: 01795 583035
Sittingbourne Library
Central Avenue, Sittingbourne, Kent, ME10 4AH
Tel: 01795 476545 Fax: 01795 428376
Sturry Library
Chafy Crescent, Sturry, Canterbury, Kent, CT2 0BA
Tel: 01227 711479 Fax: 01227 710768
Tunbridge Wells Library
Mount Pleasant, Tunbridge Wells, Kent, TN1 1NS
Tel: 01892 522352 Fax: 01892 514657
Whitstable Library
31 33 Oxford Street, Whitstable, Kent, CT5 1DB
Tel: 01227 273309 Fax: 01227 771812
Lancashire
Barnoldswick Library
Fernlea Avenue, Barnoldswick, Lancashire, BB18 5DW
Tel: 01282 812147 Fax: 01282 850791
Blackburn Central Library
Town Hall Street, Blackburn, Lancashire, BB2 1AG
Tel: 01254 587930 Fax: 01254 690539
Lancashire, Burnley Central & Local Studies Library
Grimshaw Street, Burnley, Lancashire, BB11 2BD
Tel: 01282 437115 Fax: 01282 831682
Colne Library
Market Street, Colne, Lancashire, BB8 0AP
Tel: 01282 871155 Fax: 01282 865227
Heywood Local Studies Library
Church Street, Heywood, Lancashire, OL10 1LL
Tel: 01706 360947 Fax: 01706 368683
Lancashire,
Hyndburn Central Library
St James Street, Accrington, Lancs, BB5 1NQ
Tel: 01254 872385 Fax: 01254 301066

Lancashire Record Office and Local Studies Library
Bow Lane, Preston, Lancashire, PR1 2RE Tel: 01772 264021
Tel: 01772 264020 Fax: 01772 264149
Email: lancsrecord@treas.lancscc.gov.uk
Email: locstuds@lb.lancs.cc.gov.uk
WWW: http://www.lancashire.com./lcc/edu/ro/index.htm
WWW: http://www.earl.org.uk/earl/members/lancashire
The Lancashire Local Studies Collection is now housed here
Leigh Library
Turnpike Centre, Civic Centre, Leigh WN7 1EB
Tel: 01942 404559 Fax: 01942 404567
Email: heritage@wiganmbc.gov.uk
Middleton Local Studies Library
Long Street, Middleton, Lancashire, M24 6DU
Tel: 0161 643 5228 Fax: 0161 654 0745
Oldham Local Studies and Archives Library
84 Union Street, Oldham, Lancashire, OL1 1DN Tel: 0161
911 4654 Fax: 0161 911 4654
Email: archives@oldham.gov.uk   localstudies@oldham.gov.uk WWW:
http://www.oldham.gov.uk/archiveshttp://www.oldham.gov.u
k/local studies
Bury Central Library
Manchester Road, Bury, Lancashire, BL9 0DG
Tel: 0161 253 5871 Fax: 0161 253 5857
Email: information@bury.gov.uk
WWW: www.bury.gov.uk/culture.htm
Rochdale Local Studies Library
Arts & Heritage Centre, The Esplanade, Rochdale,
Lancashire, OL16 4TY Tel: 1706 864915
Salford Local History Library
Peel Park, Salford, Lancashire, M5 4WU Tel: 0161 736 2649
Warrington Library & Local Studies Centre
Museum Street, Warrington, Cheshire, WA1 1JB Tel: 01925
571232 Fax: 01925 411395
Wigan Heritage Service Library
Turnpike Centre Civic Square Leigh WN7 1EB
Tel: 01942 404559
Working Class Movement Library
51 The Crescent, Salford, Lancashire, M5 4WX
Tel: 0161 736 2649 Fax: 0161 745 9490
Leicestershire
Hinckley Library Local Studies Collection
Lancaster Road, Hinckley, Leicestershire, LE10 0AT
Tel: 01455 635106 Fax: 01455 251385
Leicestershire Libraries & Information Service
929 931 Loughborough Road, Rothley, Leicestershire
LE7 7NH Tel: 0116 267 8023 Fax: 0116 267 8039
Loughborough Library Local Studies Collection
Granby Street, Loughborough, Leicestershire, LE11 3DZ
Tel: 01509 238466 Fax: 01509 212985
Email: slaterjohn@hotmail.com
Market Harborough Library & Local Studies Collection
Pen Lloyd Library, Adam and Eve St, Market Harborough
LE16 7LT Tel: 01858 821272 Fax: 01858 821265
Melton Mowbray Library
Wilton Road, Melton Mowbray, Leicestershire, LE13 0UJ
Tel: 01664 560161 Fax: 01664 410199
Boston Library
County Hall, Boston, Lincolnshire, PE21 6LX Tel: 01205
310010 ext 2874 Fax: 01205 357760
Gainsborough Library
Cobden Street, Gainsborough, Lincolnshire, DN21 2NG
Grantham Library
Issac Newton Centre, Grantham, Lincolnshire, NG1 9LD
Tel: 01476 591411 Fax: 01476 592458
Lincoln Cathedral Library
The Cathedral, Lincoln, Lincolnshire, LN2 1PZ England
Tel: 01522 544544 Fax: 01522 511307

Lincolnshire County Library
Local Studies Section, Lincoln Central Library
Free School Lane, Lincoln LN1 1EZ Tel: 01522 510800
Fax: 01522 575011 Email: lincoln.library@dial.pipex.com
WWW: www.lincolnshire.gov.uk/library/services/family.htm
Stamford Library
High Street, Stamford PE9 2BB Tel: 01780 763442
Fax: 01780 482518
Liverpool
Liverpool Record Office & Local History Department
Central Library, William Brown Street, Liverpool, L3 8EW
Tel: 0151 233 5817 Fax: 0151 207 1342
Email: recoffice.central,library@liverpool.gov.uk
WWW: http://www.liverpool.gov.uk
London
Bishopsgate Institute
230 Bishopsgate, London, ECM 4QH Tel: 0171 247 6844
Fax: 0171 247 6318
Chelsea Public Library
Old Town Hall, King's Road, London, SW3 5EZ Tel: 0171
352 6056 Tel: 0171 361 4158 Fax: 0171 351 1294 (Local
Studies Collection on Royal Borough of Kensington & Chelsea south of
Fulham Road)
Ealing Local History Centre
Central Library, 103 Broadway Centre, Ealing, London, W5
5JY Tel: 0181 567 3656 ext 37 Fax: 0181 840 2351
Email: localhistory@hotmail.com
L B of Bromley Local Studies Library
Central Library, High Street, Bromley, Kent, BR1 1EX
Tel: 020 8460 9955 Fax: 020 8313 9975
Fawcett Library
London Guildhall University, Old Castle Street London, E1
7NT Tel: 0171 320 1189 Fax: 0171 320 1188
Email: fawcett@lgu.ac.uk
WWW: http://www.lgu.ac.uk/phil/fawcett.htm
Guildhall Library, Manuscripts Section
Aldermanbury, London, EC2P 2EJ Tel: 0171 332 1863
Fax: 0171 600 3384
Email: manuscripts.guildhall@ms.corpoflondon.gov.uk
WWW: http://www.ihr.sas.ac.uk/ihr/ghmnu.html
Hounslow Library & Local Studies
24 Treaty Centre, High Street, Hounslow, London TW3 1ES
Tel: 0181 570 0622
Lewisham Local Studies & Archives Lewisham Library
199 201 Lewisham High Street, Lewisham, London, SE13
6LG Tel: 0181 297 0682 Fax: 0181 297 1169
Email: local.studies@lewisham.gov.uk
WWW: http://www.lewisham.gov.uk
Local Studies Collection for Chiswick & Brentford
Chiswick Public Library Dukes Avenue, Chiswick, London,
W4 2AB Tel: 0181 994 5295 Fax: 0181 995 0016 Restricted
opening hours for local history room: please telephone before visiting
L B of Barnet, Archives & Local Studies Hendon Library
The Burroughs, Hendon, London, NW4 3BQ Tel: 0181 359
2876 Fax: 0181 359 2885Email: hendon.library@barnet.gov.uk
Dr Williams's Library
14 Gordon Square, London, WC1H 0AG Tel: 0171 387 3727
Fax: 0171 388 1142 Email: 101340.2541@compuserve.com
L B of Newham Archives & Local Studies Stratford
Water Lane, London, E15 4NJ Tel: 0181 557 8856
Fax: 0181 503 1525
Museum in Docklands Project Library & Archives
Unit C14, Poplar Business Park, 10 Prestons Road, London,
E14 9RL Tel: 0171 515 1162 Fax: 0171 538 0209
Email: docklands@museum london.org.uk
L B of Barking & Dagenham Local History Studies
Valence Library & Museum, Becontree Avenue, Dagenham RM8 3HT
Tel: 020 8592 6537 Tel: 020 822 75294 Fax: 020 822 75297 Email:
fm019@viscount.org.uk
WWW: http://www.earl.org.uk/partners/barking/index.html

L B of Barking & Dagenham Local History Studies
Central Library, Barking, Dagenham IG11 7NB
Tel: 0181 517 8666
L B of Havering Reference & Information Library
St Edward's Way, Romford, Essèx, RM1 3AR Tel: 01708
772393 Tel: 01708 772394 Fax: 01708 772391 Email:
romfordlib2@rmplc.co.uk
L B of Brent, Cricklewood Library
152 Olive Road, London, NW2 6UY Tel: 0181 908 7430 or
0181 450 5211
L B of Camden Local Studies & Archive Centre
Holborn Library 32 38 Theobalds Road, London, WC1X
8PA Tel: 020 7974 6342 Fax: 020 7974 6284
L B of Croydon Library and Archives Service
Central Library Katharine Street, Croydon, CR9 1ET Tel:
0181 760 5400 ext 1112 Fax: 0181 253 1004 Email:
localstudies@library.croydon.gov.uk WWW:
http://www.croydon.gov.uk/cr libls..htm
L B of Enfield Libraries
Southgate Town Hall, Green Lanes, Palmers Green, London,
N13 4XD Tel: 0181 379 2724
L B of Greenwich Local History Library
Woodlands, 90 Mycenae Road, Blackheath, London, SE3
7SE Tel: 0181 858 4631 Fax: 0181 293 4721
L B of Islington Central Reference Library
Central Reference Library 2 Fieldway Crescent, London, N5
1PF Tel: 0171 619 6931 Fax: 0171 619 6939 Email:
is.loc.his@dial.pipex.com WWW:
http://www.w3.co.uk/isling/localinfo/libraries/
L B of Islington Finsbury Library
245 St John Street, London, EC1V 4NB Tel: 0171 689 7994
Fax: 0171 278 8821 WWW: www.islington.gov.uk/htm
L B of Lambeth Archives Department, Minet Library
52 Knatchbull Road, Lambeth, London, SE5 9QY Tel: 0171
926 6076 Fax: 0171 936 6080
L B of Waltham Forest Local Studies Library
Vestry House Museum, Vestry Road, Walthamstow, London,
E17 9NH Tel: 020 8509 1917 Email:
Vestry.House@al.lbwf.gov.uk WWW:
http://www.lbwf.gov.uk/vestry/vestry.htm
L B of Wandsworth, Local History Collection, Battersea Library
265 Lavender Hill, London, SW11 1JB Tel: 020 8871 7753
Fax: 0171 978 4376
London Hillingdon Borough Libraries, Central Library
High Street, Uxbridge, UB8 1HD Tel: 01895 250702
Southwark Local Studies Library
211 Borough High Street, Southwark, London, SE1 1JA Tel:
0207 403 3507 Fax: 0207 403 8633
Tower Hamlets L History Library & Archives Bancroft
277 Bancroft Road, London, El 4DQ Tel: 0181 980 4366 ext
129 Fax: 0181 983 4510
Westminster Abbey Library & Muniment Room
Westminster Abbey, London, SW1P 3PA
Tel: 0171 222 5152 Ext 228 Fax: 0171 226 6391
Email: library@westminster abbey.org
WWW: www.westminster abbey.org
Manchester
Manchester Central Library
St Peter's Square, Manchester, M2 5PD Tel: 0161 234 1979
Fax: 0161 234 1927 Email:
mclib@libraries.manchester.gov.uk WWW:
http://www..manchester.gov.uk/mccdlt/index.htm
John Rylands University Library
Special Collections Division, 150 Deansgate, Manchester,
M3 3EH Tel: 0161 834 5343 Fax: 0161 834 5343 Email:
j.r.hodgson@man.ac.uk WWW: http://rylibweb.man.ac.uk

Merseyside
Crosby Library (South Sefton Local History Unit)
Crosby Road North, Waterloo, Liverpool, Merseyside, L22
0LQ Tel: 0151 928 6401 Fax: 0151 934 5770(The Local History
Units serve Sefton Borough Council area. The South Sefton Unit covers
Bootle, Crosby, Maghull and other communities south of the River Alt. The
North Sefton Unit covers Southport, Formby.)
Huyton Central Library
Huyton Library, Civic Way, Huyton, Knowsley, Merseyside,
L36 9GD Tel: 0151 443 3738 Fax: 0151 443 3739 WWW:
http://www.knowsley.gov.uk/leisure/libraries/huyton/index.ht
ml
Southport Library (North Sefton Local History Unit)
Lord Street, Southport, Merseyside, PR8 1DJ Tel: 0151 934
2119 Fax: 0151 934 2115 The Local History Units serve
Sefton Borough Council area.(The North Sefton Unit covers
Southport, Formby. The South Sefton Unit covers Bootle, Crosby, Maghull
and other communities south of the River Alt)
St Helen's Local History & Archives Library
Central Library, Gamble Institute, Victoria Square, St
Helens, Merseyside, WA10 1DY Tel: 01744 456952
Middlesex
L B of Harrow Local History Collection
PO Box 4, Civic Centre Library Station Road, Harrow,
Middlesex, HA1 2UU Tel: 0208 424 1055 Tel: 0208 424
1056 Fax: 0181 424 1971
L B of Richmond upon Thames Twickenham Local
Studies Library Twickenham Library Garfield Road,
Twickenham, Middlesex, TW1 3JS Tel: 0181 891 7271 Fax:
0181 891 5934 Email: twicklib@richmond.gov.uk
WWW: http://www.richmond.gov.uk
British Library
British Library Building, 96 Euston Road, London, NW1
2DB Tel: 0171 412 7677 Email:
http://www.portico.bl.ukReader/admissions@bl.uk
British Library Early Printed Collections
96 Euston Road, London, NW1 2DB Tel: 0171 412 7673
Fax: 0171 412 7577 Email: rare books@bl.uk WWW:
http://www.bl.uk
House of Commons Library
House of Commons, 1 Derby Gate, London, SW1A 2DG
Tel: 0171 219 5545 Fax: 0171 219 3921
Society of Genealogists   Library
14 Charterhouse Buildings, Goswell Road, London, EC1M
7BA Tel: 020 7251 8799 Tel: 020 7250 0291 Fax: 020 7250
1800 Email: info@sog.org.uk   Sales at sales@sog.org.uk
WWW: http://www.sog.org.uk
Norfolk
Family History Shop & Library
The Family History Shop, 24d Magdalen Street, Norwich,
Norfolk, NR3 1HU Tel: 01603 621152 Email:
jenlibrary@aol.com WWW: http://www.jenlibrary.u net.com
Great Yarmouth Central Library
Tolhouse Street, Great Yarmouth, Norfolk, NR30 2SH Tel:
01493 844551 Tel: 01493 842279 Fax: 01493 857628
Kings Lynn Library
London Road, King's Lynn, Norfolk, PE30 5EZ Tel: 01553
772568 Tel: 01553 761393 Fax: 01553 769832 Email:
kings.lynn.lib@norfolk.gov.uk
Norfolk Library & Information Service
Gildengate House, Anglia Square, Norwich, Norfolk
NR3 1AX Tel: 01603 215254 Fax: 01603 215258
Thetford Library
Raymond Street, Thetford, Norfolk, IP24 2EA Tel: 01842
752048 Fax: 01842 750125
North East Lincolnshire
Reference Department Central Library
Central Library, Town Hall Square, Great Grimsby, North
East Lincolnshire, DN31 1HG Tel: 01472 323635
Fax: 01472 323634

North Lincolnshire
Scunthorpe Central Library
Carlton Street, Scunthorpe, North Lincolnshire, DN15 6TX
Tel: 01724 860161 Fax: 01724 859737 Email:
scunthorpe.ref@central library.demon.co.uk WWW:
www.nothlincs.gov.uk/library
North Yorkshire
Harrogate Reference Library
Victoria Avenue, Harrogate, North Yorkshire, HG1 1EG Tel:
01423 502744 Fax: 01423 523158
North Yorkshire County Libraries
21 Grammar School Lane, Northallerton, North Yorkshire,
DL6 1DF Tel: 01609 776271 Fax: 01609 780793
WWW: http://www.northyorks.gov.uk
Northallerton Reference Library
1 Thirsk Road, Northallerton, North Yorkshire, DL6 1PT
Tel: 01609 776202 Fax: 01609 780793 Email:
northallerton.libraryhq@northyorks.gov.uk
Pickering Reference Library
The Ropery, Pickering YO18 8DY Tel: 01751 472185
Scarborough Reference Library
Vernon Road, Scarborough, North Yorkshire, YO11 2NN
Tel: 01723 364285 Fax: 01723 353893 Email:
scarborough.library@northyorks.gov.uk
Selby Reference Library
52 Micklegate, Selby YO8 4EQ Tel: 01757 702020
 Fax: 01757 705396
Skipton Reference Library
High Street, Skipton BD23 1JX Tel: 01756 794726
Fax: 01756 798056
Whitby Library
Windsor Terrace, Whitby, North Yorkshire, YO21 1ET Tel:
01947 602554 Fax: 01947 820288
Northumberland
Alnwick Library
Green Batt, Alnwick, Northumberland, NE66 1TU
Tel: 01665 602689 Fax: 01665 604740
Berwick upon Tweed Library
Church Street, Berwick upon Tweed, Northumberland
TD15 1EE Tel: 01289 307320 Fax: 01289 308299
Blyth Library
Bridge Street, Blyth NE24 2DJ Tel: 01670 361352
Border History Museum and Library
Moothall, Hallgate, Hexham, Northumberland, NE46 3NH
Tel: 01434 652349 Fax: 01434 652425 Email:
lted@tynedale.gov.uk
Northumberland, Hexham Library
Queens Hall, Beaumont Street, Hexham, Northumberland,
NE46 3LS Tel: 01434 603156 Fax: 01434 606043
Nottinghamshire
Arnold Library
Front Street, Arnold NG5 7EE Tel: 0115 920 2247 Fax: 0115
967 3378
Beeston Library
Foster Avenue, Beeston NG9 1AE Tel: 0115 925 5168 Fax:
0115 922 0841
Eastwood Library
Wellington Place, Eastwood, Nottinghamshire, NG16 3GB
Tel: 01773 712209
Mansfield Library, Four Seasons Centre
Westgate, Mansfield, Nottinghamshire, NG18 1NH Tel:
01623 627591 Fax: 01623 629276 Email:
mansfield@ncclibria.demon.co.uk
Newark Library
Beaumont Gardens, Newark, Nottinghamshire, NG24 1UW
Tel: 01636 703966 Fax: 01636 610045
Nottingham Central Library : Local Studies Centre
Angel Row, Nottingham NG1 6HP Tel: 0115 915 2873 Fax:
0115 915 2850 Email: localstudies@notlib.demon.co.uk
WWW: www.notlib.demon.co.uk

Retford Library
Denman Library, Churchgate, Retford, Nottinghamshire,
DN22 6PE Tel: 01777 708724 Fax: 01777 710020
Southwell Minster Library
Trebeck Hall, Bishop's Drive, Southwell, Nottinghamshire,
NG25 0JP Tel: 01636 812649
Sutton in Ashfield Library
Devonshire Mall, Sutton in Ashfield, Nottinghamshire, NG17
1BP Tel: 01623 556296 Fax: 01623 551962
University of Nottingham, Hallward Library
University Park, Nottingham, NG7 2RD Tel: 0115 951 4514
Fax: 0115 951 4558 WWW:
http://www.nottingham.ac.uk/library/
West Bridgford Library
Bridgford Road, West Bridgford, Nottinghamshire, NG2
6AT Tel: 0115 981 6506 Fax: 0115 981 3199
Oxfordshire
Abingdon Library
The Charter, Abingdon OX14 3LY Tel: 01235 520374
Banbury Library
Marlborough Road, Banbury, Oxfordshire, OX16 8DF Tel:
01295 262282 Fax: 01295 264331
Centre for Oxfordshire Studies, Central Library
Westgate, Oxford, Oxfordshire, OX1 1DJ Tel: 01865 815749
Fax: 01865 810187 Email: enquiries@oxst.demon.co.uk
WWW: www.oxfordshire.gov.uk
Henley Library
Ravenscroft Road, Henley on Thames, Oxfordshire, RG9
2DH Tel: 01491 575278 Fax: 01491 576187
River & Rowing Museum, Rowing & River Museum
Mill Meadows, Henley on Thames, Oxfordshire, RG9 1BF
Tel: 01491 415610 Fax: 01491 415601 Email:
museum@rrm.co.uk WWW: www..rrm.co.uk
The Bodelian Library
Broad Street, Oxford, Oxfordshire, OX1 3BG Tel: 01865
277000 Fax: 01865 277182 WWW: www.bodley.ox.ac.uk
Wantage Library
Stirlings Road, Wantage OX12 7BB Tel: 01235 762291
Witney Library
Welch Way, Witney, Oxfordshire, OX8 7HH Tel: 01993
703659 Fax: 01993 775993
Shropshire
Wrekin Local Studies Forum, Madeley Library
Russell Square, Telford TF7 5BB Tel: 01952 586575
Email: library@madeley.uk WWW: www.madeley.org.uk
Somerset
Bath Central Library
19 The Podium, Northgate Street, Bath, BA1 5AN Tel:
01225 428144 Fax: 01225 331839
Nailsea Library
Somerset Square, Nailsea, Somerset, BS19 2EX Tel: 01275
854583 Fax: 01275 858373
Bridgewater Reference Library
Binford Place, Bridgewater TA6 3LF Tel: 01278 450082
Fax: 01278 451027 Email: brwref@pobox.co.uk
WWW: www.somerset.gov.uk
Frome Reference Library
Justice Lane, Frome BA11 1BA Tel: 01373 471336
Fax: 01373 472003
Somerset Studies Taunton Library
Paul Street Taunton TA1 3XZ Tel: 01823 340300
Fax: 01823 340301
Weston Library
The Boulevard, Weston Super Mare, Somerset, BS23 1PL
Tel: 01934 636638 Fax: 01934 413046
Yeovil Library
King George Street, Yeovil, Somerset, BA20 1PY Tel: 01935
421910 Fax: 01935 431847

South Gloucestershire
Thornbury Library
St Mary Street, Thornbury, South Gloucestershire, BS35
2AA Tel: 01454 865655
South Yorkshire
Archives & Local Studies Central Library
Walker Place, Rotherham, South Yorkshire, S65 1JH Tel:
01709 823616 Fax: 01709 823650 Email:
archives@rotherham.gov.uk WWW:
www.rotherha.gov.uk/pages/living/learning/islib/callib.htm
South Yorkshire
Barnsley Archives and Local Studies Department,
Central Library
Shambles Street, Barnsley, South Yorkshire, S70 2JF Tel:
01226 773950 Tel: 01226 773938 Fax: 01226 773955 Email:
Archives@Barnsley.ac.uklibrarian@barnsley.ac.uk WWW:
http://www.barnsley.ac.uk/sites/library
Sheffield Central Library
Surrey Street, Sheffield, South Yorkshire, S1 1XZ Tel: 0114
273 4711 Fax: 0114 273 5009 Email:
sheffield.libraries@dial.pipex.com
Doncaster Local Studies Section, Central Library
Waterdale, Doncaster DN1 3JE Tel: 01302 734307 Fax:
01302 369749 Email: reference.library@doncaster.gov.uk
Staffordshire
Barton Library
Dunstall Road, Barton under Needwood DE13 8AX
Tel: 01283 713753
Biddulph Library
Tunstall Road, Biddulph, Stoke on Trent, Staffordshire, ST8
6HH Tel: 01782 512103
Brewood Library
Newport Street, Brewood ST19 9DT Tel: 01902 850087
Burton Library
Riverside, High Street, Burton on Trent, Staffordshire, DE14
1AH Tel: 01283 239556 Fax: 01283 239571 Email:
burton.library@staffordshire.gov.uk
Cannock Library
Manor Avenue, Cannock WS11 1AA Tel: 01543 502019
Fax: 01543 278509,
Email: cannock.library@staffordshire.gov.uk
Cheslyn Hay Library
Cheslyn Hay, Walsall WS56 7AE Tel: 01922 413956
Codsall Library
Histons Hill, Codsall WV8 1AA Tel: 01902 842764
Great Wyrley Library
John's Lane,Great Wyrley,Walsall WS6 6BY Tel: 01922 414632
Kinver Library
Vicarage Drive, Kinver, Stourbridge, Staffordshire, DY7 6HJ
Tel: 01384 872348
Leek Library
Nicholson Institute, Stockwell Street, Leek, Staffordshire,
ST13 6DW Tel: 01538 483207 Fax: 01538 483216
Email: leek.library@staffordshire.gov.uk
Lichfield Library (Local Studies Section)
The Friary, Lichfield, Staffordshire, WS13 6QG
Tel: 01543 510720 Fax: 01543 411138
Newcastle Library
Ironmarket, Newcastle under Lyme, Staffordshire, ST5 1AT
Tel: 01782 297310 Fax: 01782 297322 Email:
newcastle.library@staffordshire.gov.uk
Penkridge Library
Bellbrock, Penkridge ST19 9DL Tel: 01785 712916
Perton Library
Severn Drive, Perton, Staffordshire, WV6 7QU Tel: 01902
755794 Fax: 01902 756123 Email:
perton.library@staffordshire.gov.uk
Rugeley Library
Anson Street, Rugeley WS16 2BB Tel: 01889 583237

Hanley Library
Bethesda Street, Hanley, Stoke on Trent, Staffordshire, ST1
3RS Tel: 01782 238420 Fax: 01782 238499 Email:
stoke.archives@stoke.gov.uk
Tamworth Library
Corporation Street, Tamworth, Staffordshire, B79 7DN Tel:
01827 475645 Fax: 01827 475658 Email:
tamworth.library@staffordshire.gov.uk
Uttoxeter Library
High Street, Uttoxeter, Staffordshire, ST14 7JQ Tel: 01889
256371 Fax: 01889 256374
William Salt Library
Eastgate Street, Stafford, Staffordshire, ST16 2LZ Tel: 01785
278372 Fax: 01785 278414 Email:
william.salt.library@staffordshire.gov.uk WWW:
www.staffordshire.gov.uk/archives/saly.htm
Wombourne Library
Windmill Bank, Wombourne WV5 9JD Tel: 01902 892032
Surrey
L B of Merton Local Studies Centre
Merton Civic Centre, London Road, Morden, Surrey, SM4
5DX Tel: 0181 545 3239 Fax: 0181 545 4037 Email:
mertonlibs@compuserve.com
L B of Richmond upon Thames Local Studies Library
Old Town Hall, Whittaker Avenue, Richmond upon Thames,
Surrey, TW9 1TP Tel: 0181 332 6820 Fax: 0181 940 6899
Email: locstudies@richmond.gov.uk WWW:
http://www.richmond.gov.uk
L B of Richmond upon Thames Richmond Library
Old Town Hall, Whittaker Avenue, Richmond upon Thames,
Surrey, TW9 1TP Tel: 0181 940 5529 Ext 32 Fax: 0181 940
6899 Email: ref@richmond.gov.uk
Surrey History Service Library
Surrey History Centre, 130 Goldsworth Road, Woking,
Surrey, GU21 1ND Tel: 01483 594594 Fax: 01483 594595
Email: shc@surreycc.gov.uk
WWW: http://www.shs.surreycc.gov.uk
Sutton Central Library
St Nicholas Way, Sutton SM1 1EA Tel: 0181 7704745
Tyne and Wear
City Library
Princess Square, Newcastle upon Tyne NE99 1DX
Tel: 0191 261 0691 Fax: 0191 232 6885 Email: heritage@dial.pipex.com
City Library & Arts Centre
28 30 Fawcett Street, Sunderland, Tyne and Wear, BR1
1RE Tel: 0191 514235 Fax: 0191 514 8444
Gateshead Central Library
Prince Consort Road, Gateshead, Tyne and Wear, NE8 4LN
Tel: 0191 477 3478 Fax: 0191 477 7454 Email:
Local@gateslib.demon.co.uk WWW:
http://wamses.urn.ac.uk
South Tyneside Central Library
Library Building, Prince Georg Square, South Shields
NE33 2PE Tel: 0191 427 1818 Ext 2135 Fax: 0191 455 8085
Email: reference.library@s tyneside mbc.gov.uk WWW:
reference.library@s tyneside mbc.gov.uk
Central Library
Northumberland Square, North Shields, NE3O 1QU
Tel: 0191 200 5424 Fax: 0191 200 6118
Email: cen@ntlib.demon.co.uk
Warwickshire
Shakespeare Birthplace Trust Library
Shakespeare Centre Library, Henley Street, Stratford upon
Avon CV37 6QW Tel: 01789 204016 Tel: 01789 201813
Fax: 01789 296083 Email: library@shakespeare.org.uk
WWW: http://www.shakespeare.org.uk
Sutton Coldfield Library & Local Studies Centre
43 Lower Parade, Sutton Coldfield B72 1XX Tel: 0121 354
2274 Tel: 0121 464 0164 Fax: 0121 464 0173

University of Warwick Library
Coventry, Warwickshire, CV4 7AL Tel: 01203 524219
Warwick Library
Barrack Street, Warwick CV34 4TH Tel: 01926 412189 Fax:
01926 412784 Email: warcolib@dial.pipex.com
Leamington Library
Royal Pump Rooms,The Parade, Leamington Spa CV32 4AA
Tel: 01926 425873 Fax: 01926 330285,
Email: leamingtonlibrary@warwickshire.gov.uk
West Midlands
Dudley Archives & Local History Service
Mount Pleasant Street, Coseley, Dudley, West Midlands,
WV14 9JR Tel: 01384 812770 Fax: 01384 812770 Email:
archives.pls@mbc.dudley.gov.uk WWW:
http://dudleygov.uk/council/library/archives/archive1.htm
Local Studies Library Coventry Central Library
Smithford Way, Coventry CV1 1FY Tel: 012476 832336
Fax: 02476 832440 Email: covinfo@discover.co.uk
WWW: www.coventry.gov.uk/accent.htm
Sandwell Community History & Archives Service
Smethwick Library High Street, Smethwick, B66 1AB
Tel: 0121 558 2561 Fax: 0121 555 6064
West Bromwich Library
Town Hall, High Street, West Bromwich, West Midlands,
B70 8DX Tel: 0121 569 4909 Fax: 0121 569 4907 Email:
dm025@viscount.org.uk
Solihull Library
Homer Road, Solihull B91 3RG Tel: 0121 704 6977 Fax:
0121 704 6212 The library is NOT an archive repository,
sceondary sources only available for Solihull MBC area only
Walsall Local History Centre
Essex Street, Walsall WS2 7AS Tel: 01922 721305
Fax: 01922 634594 Email: ruthvyse@walsplsm.demon.uk
WWW:
http://www.walsall.gov.uk/culturalservices/library/welcome.
htm
Wolverhampton Archives & Local Studies
42 50 Snow Hill, Wolverhampton WV2 4AG Tel: 01902
552480 Fax: 01902 552481 Email:
wolvarch.and.ls@dial.pipex.com WWW:
http://www.wolverhampton.gov.uk/library/archives
West Sussex
Worthing Reference Library
Richmond Road, Worthing, BN11 1HD Tel: 01903 212060
Fax: 01903 821902 Email: mhayes@westsussex.gov.uk
West Yorkshire
Calderdale Central Library
Northgate House, Northgate, Halifax HX11 1UN
Tel: 01422392631 Fax: 01422 349458
WWW: www.calderdale.co.uk
Keighley Reference Library
North Street, Keighley, West Yorkshire, BD21 3SX
Tel: 01535 618215 Fax: 01535 618214
HuddersfieldLocal History Library
Huddersfield Library & Art Gallery, Princess Alexandra
Walk, Huddersfield, West Yorkshire, HD1 2SU Tel: 01484
221965 Fax: 01484 221952,
Email: reflibrary@geo2.poptel.org.uk WWW:
http://www.kirkleesmc.gov.uk
Local Studies Library Leeds Central Library
Calverley Street, Leeds LS1 3AB Tel: 0113 247 8290
Fax: 0113 247 8290 Email: local.studies@leeds.gov.uk
WWW: www.leeds.gov.uk/library/services/loc_reso.html
(Located in Leeds Town Hall 1st September 1999 to Spring 2000 whilst
essential repair work is carried out to the Central Library. Phone 0113 247
8290 for further details)
Bradford Central & Local Studies Reference Library
Prince's Way, Bradford, West Yorkshire, BD1 1NN Tel:
01274 753661 Fax: 01274 753660

Olicana Historical Society
54 Kings Road, Ilkley LS29 9AT Tel: 01943 609206
Pontefract Library & Local Studies Centre
Pontefract Library, Shoemarket, Pontefract, West Yorkshire,
WF8 1BD Tel: 01977 727692
Wakefield Library Local Studies Department
Balne Lane, Wakefield, West Yorkshire, WF2 0DQ Tel:
01924 302224 Fax: 01924 302245 Email:
localstudies@talk21.com WWW: www.wakefield.gov.uk
Castleford Library & Local Studies
Carlton Street, Castleford WF10 1BB Tel: 01977 722085
Yorkshire Archaeological Society
Claremont, 23 Clarendon Rd, Leeds, West Yorkshire, LS2
9NZ Tel: 0113 245 6342 Tel: 0113 245 7910 Fax: 0113 244
1979 Email: j.heron@shej.ac.uk
Wiltshire
Salisbury Local Studies Library
Market Place, Salisbury SP1 1BL Tel: 01722 410073
Swindon Local Studies Library
Swindon Central Library, Regent Circus, Swindon, Wiltshire,
SN11QG Tel: 01793 463240 Fax: 01793 541319 Email:
swindonref@swindon.gov.uk WWW:
http://www.swindon.gov.uk
Wiltshire Archaeological & Natural History Soc Library
WANHS Library 41 Long Street, Devizes SN10 1NS
Tel: 01380 727369 Fax: 01380 722150
Wiltshire Studies Library Trowbridge Reference Library
Bythesea Road, Trowbridge BA14 8BS Tel: 01225 713732
Tel: 01225 71372 Fax: 01225 713715
Email: trowref@compuserve.uk
Worcestershire
Bewdley Museum Research Library
Load Street, Bewdley DY12 2AE Tel: 01229 403573

Wales

National Library of Wales
Penglais, Aberystwyth, Ceredigion, SY23 3BU Tel: 01970
632800 Tel: 01970 623811 Fax: 01970 623852 and 01970
615709 Email: holi@llgc.org.uk WWW:
http://www.llgc.org.uk
Caerphilly
Bargoed Library
The Square, Bargoed, Caerphilly, CF8 8QQ Tel: 01443
875548 Fax: 01443 836057 Email: 9e465@dial.pipex.com
Caerphilly Library
Unit 7 Woodfieldside Business Park, Penmaen Road,
Pontllanfraith, Blackwood, Caerphilly, NP2 2DG Tel: 01495
235562
Cardiff
Cardiff Central Library (Local Studies Department)
St Davids Link, Frederick Street, Cardiff, CF1 4DT Tel:
01222 382116 Fax: 01222 871599 Email:
cardlib.demon.co.uk
Carmarthenshire
Carmarthen Library
St Peters Street, Carmarthen, Carmarthenshire, SA31 1LN
Tel: 01267 224822
Llanelli Public Library
Vaughan Street, Lanelli, Carmarthenshire, SA15 3AS Tel:
01554 773538
Ceredigion
Aberystwyth Reference Library
Corporation Street, Aberystwyth, Ceredigion, SY23 2DE Tel:
01970 617464
Flintshire
Flintshire Reference Library
County Hall, Mold, Flintshire, CH7 6NW Tel: 01352 704411
Fax: 01352 753662 Email: libraries@flintshire.gov.uk
WWW: www.flintshire.gov.uk

Bromsgrove Library
Stratford Road, Bromsgrove, Worcestershire, B60 1AP Tel:
01527 575855 Fax: 01527 575855
Evesham Library
Oat Street, Evesham, Worcestershire, WR11 4PJ Tel: 01386
442291 Fax: 01386 765855
Email: eveshamlib@worcestershire.gov.uk
WWW: www.worcestershire.gov.uk
Kidderminster Library
Market Street, Kidderminster, Worcestershire, DY10 1AD
Tel: 01562 824500 Fax: 01562 827303
Email: kidderminster@worcestershire.gov.uk
WWW: www.worcestershire.gov.uk
Malvern Library
Graham Road, Malvern, Worcestershire, WR14 2HU Tel:
01684 561223 Fax: 01684 892999
Redditch Library
15 Market Place, Redditch, B98 8AR Tel: 01527 63291 Fax:
01527 68571 Email: redditchlibrary@worcestershire.gov.uk
Worcester Library
Foregate Street, Worcester WR1 1DT Tel: 01905 765312
Fax: 01905 726664 Email:
worcesterlib@worcestershire.gov.uk WWW:
www.worcestershire.gov.uk/libraries
York
**City of York Libraries Local History & Reference
Collection**
York Central Library, Library Square, Museum Street, York,
YO1 7DS Tel: 01904 655631 Fax: 01904 611025 Email:
reference.library@york.gov.uk WWW:
http://www.york.gov.uk
York Minster Library
Dean's Park, York, YO1 2JD Tel: 01904 625308

Glamorgan
Barry Library
King Square, Holton Road, Barry, Glamorgan, CF63 4RW
Tel: 01446 735722
Bridgend Library & Information Service
Coed Parc, Park Street, Bridgend, Glamorgan, CF31 4BA
Tel: 01656 767451 Fax: 01656 645719 Email:
blis@bridgendlib.gov.uk
Dowlais Library
Church Street, Dowlais, Merthyr Tydfil, Glamorgan, CF48
3HS Tel: 01985 723051
Merthyr Tydfil Central Library (Local Studies Department)
Merthyr Library, High Street, Merthyr Tydfil, Glamorgan,
CF47 8AF Tel: 01685 723057 Fax: 01685 722146 Email:
library@merthyr.gov.btinternet.com
Neath Central Library (Local Studies Department)
29 Victoria Gardens, Neath, Glamorgan Tel: 01639 620139
Pontypridd Library
Library Road, Pontypridd, Glamorgan, CF37 2DY Tel:
01443 486850 Fax: 01443 493258
Port Talbot Library
1st Floor Aberafan Shopping Centre, Port Talbot,
Glamorgan, SA13 1PB Tel: 01639 763490
Swansea Reference Library
Alexandra Road, Swansea, SA1 5DX Tel: 01792 516753
Fax: 01792 516759 Extensive holdings of trade directories,
local census returns, newspapers (partially indexed)
Treorchy Library
Station Road, Treorchy, Glamorgan, CF42 6NN
Tel: 01443 773204 Fax: 01443 773204
Gwent
Abertillery Library
Station Hill, Abertillery, Gwent, NP13 1UJ Tel: 01495
212332 Fax: 01495 320995

Ebbw Vale Library
21 Bethcar Street, Ebbw Vale, Gwent, NP23 6HH Tel: 01495 303069 Fax: 01495 350547
Tredegar Library
The Circle, Tredegar, Gwent, NP2 3PS Tel: 01495 722687 Fax: 01495 717018
Gwynedd
Canolfan Dolgellau
FforddBala, Dolgellau, Gwynedd, LL40 2YF Tel: 01341 422771 Fax: 01341 423560 WWW:
http://www.gwynedd.gov.uk
Wales, Gwynedd, Llyfrgell Caernarfon, Lon Pafiliwn, Caernafon, Gwynedd, LL55 1AS Tel: 01286 679465 Fax: 01286 671137
Merthyr Tydfil
Merthyr Tydfil Central Library (Local Studies Department)
Merthyr Library, High Street, Merthyr Tydfil, Glamorgan, CF47 8AF Tel: 01685 723057 Fax: 01685 722146 Email: library@merthyr.gov.btinternet.com
Treharris Library
Perrott Street, Treharris, Merthyr Tydfil, CF46 5ET Tel: 01443 410517 Fax: 01443 410517
Monmoputhshire
Chepstow Library & Information Centre
Manor Way, Chepstow, Monmoputhshire, NP16 5HZ Tel: 01291 635730 Tel: 01291 635731 Fax: 01291 635736 Email: chepstowlibrary@monmouthshire.gov.uk WWW: www.monmouthshire.gov.uk/leisure/libraries
Pembrokeshire
Pembrokeshire Libraries
The County Library, Dew Street, Haverfordwest, Pembrokeshire, SA61 1SU Tel: 01437 762070 Fax: 01437 769218 Email: anita.thomas@pembrokeshire.gov.uk
(The Local Studies Library covers people, places and events realting to The County of Pembrokeshire past and present. The Library also houses The Francis Green Genealogical Collection consisting of over 800 pedigree sheets and 35 volumes of information relating to the prominent families of Pembraokeshire, Cardiganshire and Carmarthenshire)

Powys
Brecon Area Library
Ship Street, Brecon, Powys, LD3 9AE Tel: 01874 623346 Fax: 01874 622818 Email: breclib@mail.powys.gov.uk
Llandrindod Wells Library
Cefnllys Lane, Llandrindod Wells, Powys, LD1 5LD Tel: 01597 826870 Email: llandod.library@powys.gov.uk
Newtown Area Library
Park Lane, Newtown, Powys, SY16 1EJ Tel: 01686 626934 Fax: 01686 624935 Email: nlibrary@powys.gov.uk
Rhondda Cynon Taff
Aberdare Library
Green Street, Aberdare, Rhondda Cynon Taff, CF44 7AG Tel: 01685 885318 Fax: 01685 881181
Newport
Newport Library & Information Service
Newport Central Library, John Frost Square, Newport, South Wales, NP20 1PA Tel: 01633 211376 Fax: 01633 222615 Email: central.library@newport.gov.uk WWW: http://www.earl.org.uk/partners/newport/index.html
Newport
South Wales Miners' Library
University of Wales, Swansea, Hendrefoelan House, Gower Road, Swansea, SA2 7NB Tel: 01792 518603 Fax: 01792 518694 Email: miners@swansea.ac.uk WWW: http://www.swan.ac.uk/lis/swmi/
Neath Port Talbot
West Glamorgan Archive Service Port Talbot
Port Talbot Library Aberafan Centre, Port Talbot, West Glamorgan, SA13 1PJ Tel: 01639 763430 WWW: http://www.swansea.gov.uk/culture/laarindex.html
Wrexham
Wrexham Library and Arts Centre
Rhosddu Road, Wrexham, LL11 1AU Tel: 01978 292622 Fax: 01978 292611 Email: jthomas@wrexhamlib.u net.com WWW: www.wrexham.gov.uk

Scotland

National Library of Scotland
George IV Bridge, Edinburgh, EH1 1EW Tel: 0131 226 4531 Fax: 0131 622 4803 Email: enquiries@nls.uk WWW: http://www.nls.uk
National Museums of Scotland Library
Royal Museum, Chambers Street, Edinburgh, EH1 1JF Tel: 0131 247 4137 Fax: 0131 247 4311 Email: library@nms.ac.uk WWW: www.nms.ac.uk, Holds large collection of family histories, esp Scottish

Aberdeen
Reference and Local Studies Library
Central Library, Rosemount Viaduct, Aberdeen, AB25 1GW Tel: 01224 652511 Fax: 01224 624118 Email: refloc@arts rec.aberdeen.net.uk
Aberdeen Central Library Tel: 01224 652500
University of Aberdeen DISS: Heritage Division Special Collections & Archives
Kings College, Aberdeen, AB24 3SW Tel: 01224 272598 Fax: 01224 273891 Email: speclib@abdn.ac.uk WWW: http://www.abdn.ac.uk/diss/heritage
Aberdeenshire Library & Information Service
The Meadows Industrial Estate, Meldrum Meg Way, Oldmeldrum, Aberdeenshire, AB51 0GN Tel: 01651 872707 Tel: 01651 871219/871220 Fax: 01651 872142

Scottish United Services Museum Library
The Castle, Museum Square, Edinburgh, EH1 1 2NG Tel: 0131 225 7534 Ext 2O4 Fax: 0131 225 3848 Email: library@nms.ac.uk WWW: www.nms.ac.uk
Leadhills Miners's Library
Main Street, Leadhills Tel: 01659 74326
Scottish Genealogy Society Library
15 Victoria Terrace, Edinburgh, EH1 2JL Tel: 0131 220 3677 Fax: 0131 220 3677 Email: scotgensoc@sol.co.uk WWW: http://www.scotland.net/scotgensoc/
Angus
Angus Archives, Montrose Library
214 High Street, Montrose, Angus, DD10 8PH Tel: 01674 671415 Fax: 01674 671810 Email: anguscularch@sol.co.uk WWW: www.angus.gov.uk/history/history.htm
Tay Valley Family History Society & Family History Research Centre
Family History Research Centre 79–181 Princes Street, Dundee, DD4 6DQ Tel: 01382 461845 Email: tayvalleyfhs@sol.co.uk WWW: http://www.sol.co.uk/t/tayvalleyfhs/
Argyll
Argyll & Bute Council Archives & Library Service
Highland Avenue, Sandbank, Dunoon, Argyll, PA23 8PB Tel: 01369 703214

Ayrshire
East Ayrshire Libraries
Baird Institute
3 Lugar Street, Cumnock, Ayrshire, KA18 1AD Tel: 01290
421701 Fax: 01290 421701
Dick Institute
Elmbank Avenue, Kilmarnock, Ayrshire, KA1 3BU Tel:
01563 526401 Fax: 01563 529661 Email:
dick_institute@compuserve.co.
North Ayrshire Libraries
Library Headquarters
39   41 Princes Street, Ardrossan, Ayrshire, KA22 8BT Tel:
01294 469137 Fax: 01924 604236 Email:
reference@naclibhq.prestel.co.uk
South Ayrshire Carnegie Library
12 Main Street, Ayr, Ayrshire, KA8 8ED Tel: 01292 286385
Fax: 01292 611593 Email: carnegie@south ayrshire.gov.uk
Clackmannanshire
Alloa Library
26/28 Drysdale Street, Alloa, Clackmannanshire, FK10 1JL
Tel: 01259 722262 Fax: 01259 219469 Email:
clack.lib@mail.easynet.co.uk
Dumfries & Galloway
Ewart Library
Catherine Street, Dumfries, DG1 1JB Tel: 01387 260285 Tel:
01387 252070 Fax: 01387 260294 Email:
ruth_airley@dumgal.gov.uklibsxi@dumgal.gov.uk WWW:
www.dumgal.gov.ukf
Dunbartonshire
Dumbarton Public Library
Strathleven Place, Dumbarton G82 1BD Tel: 01389 733273
Fax: 01389 738324 Email: wdlibs@hotmail.com
Dundee
Dundee Central Library
The Wellgate, Dundee, DD1 1DB Tel: 01382 434377 Fax:
01382 434036 Email: local.studies@dundeecity.gov.uk
WWW:
http://www.dundeecity.gov.uk/dcchtml/nrd/loc_stud.htm
East Dunbartonshire
Local Record Offices &Reference Libraries
William Patrick Library 2 West High Street, Kirkintilloch,
East Dunbartonshire, G66 1AD Tel: 0141 776 8090 Fax:
0141 776 0408 Email: ref@edlib.freeserve.co.uk
East Renfrewshire
Giffnock Library
Station Road, Giffnock, Glasgow, East Renfrewshire, G46
6JF Tel: 0141 577 4976 Fax: 0141 577 4978
Edinburgh
Edinburgh Central Library
Edinburgh Room, George IV Bridge, Edinburgh, EH1 1EG
Tel: 0131 225 5584 Fax: 0131 225 8783
Falkirk
Falkirk Library
Hope Street, Falkirk, FK1 5AU Tel: Fax: Holds Local
Studies Collection
Falkirk Museum History Research Centre
Callendar House, Callendar Park, Falkirk, FK1 1YR Tel:
01324 503779 Fax: 01324 503771
Email: callandarhouse@falkirkmuseums.demon.co.uk
WWW: www.falkirkmuseums.demon.co.uk
Fife
Dunfermline Library   Local History Department
Abbot Street, Dunfermline, Fife, KY12 7NL Tel: 01383
312994 Fax: 01383 312608 Email: dunfermline@fife.ac.uk
Kirkcaldy Central Library
War Memorial Grounds, Kirkcaldy, Fife, KY1 1YG
Tel: 01592 412878 Fax: 01592 412750
Email: central@fifecouncil.demon.co.uk

St Andrews Library
Church Square, St Andrews, Fife, KY16 9NN Tel: 01334
412685 Fax: 01334 413029 Email: info@standres.fiflib.net
St Andrews University Library
North Street, St Andrews, Fife, KY16 9TR Tel: 01334
462281 Fax: 01334 462282 WWW: http://www.library.st
and.ac.uk
The Hay Fleming Reference Library
Church Square, St Andrews, Fife, KY16 9NN Tel: 01334
412685 Fax: 01334 413029
Glasgow
Brookwood Library
166 Drymen Road, Bearsden, Glasgow, G61 3RJ Tel: 0141
943 0121
Mitchell Library
North Street, Glasgow, G3 7DN Tel: 0141 287 2937 Fax:
0141 287 2912 Email: history_and_glasgow
@gcl.glasgow.gov.uk WWW:
wwww.glasgow.gov.uk/html/council/cindex.htm
Isle of Barra
Castlebay Community Library
Community School, Castlebay, Isle of Barra, HS95XD Tel:
01871 810471 Fax: 01871 810650
Isle of Benbecula
Community Library
Sgoil Lionacleit, Liniclate, Isle of Benbecula, HS7 5PJ Tel:
01870 602211 Fax: 01870 602817
Isle of Lewis
Stornoway Library
19 Cromwell Street, Stornoway, Isle of Lewis, HS1 2DA Tel:
01851 703064 Fax: 01851 705657/708676 Email: stornoway
library1@inesins.gov.uk
Lanarkshire
Airdrie Library
Wellwynd, Airdrie, Lanarkshire, ML6 0AG Tel: 01236
763221 Tel: 01236 760937 Fax: 01236 766027
Cumbernauld Central Library
8 Allander Walk, Cumbernauld, Lanarkshire, G67 1EE Tel:
01236 725664 Fax: 01236 458350
Midlothian
Midlothian Council Library Local Studies Collection
2 Clerk Street, Loanhead, Midlothian, EH20 9DR Tel: 0131
440 2210 Fax: 0131 440 4635 Email:
mc_libhq_blossoming@compuserve.com
Midlothian Libraries Local History Centre
2 Clerk Street, Loanhead, Midlothian, EH20 9DR Tel: 0131
440 2210 Fax: 0131 440 4635 Email:
local.studies@midlothian.gov.uk WWW:
http://www.earl.org.uk.partners/midlothian/index.html
Moray
Forres Library
Forres House, High Street, Forres, Moray, IV36 0BJ Tel:
01309 672834 Fax: 01309 675084
Local Heritage Centre
Local Heritage Centre, Grant Lodge, Cooper Park, Elgin,
Moray, IV30 1HS Tel: 01343 544475 Tel: 01343 563413
Fax: 01343 549050 Email:
graeme.wilson@techleis.moray.gov.uk
Buckie Library
Clunu Place, Buckie, Morayshire, AB56 1HB Tel: 01542
832121 Fax: 01542 835237 Email:
buckie.lib@techleis.moray.gov.uk
Keith Library
Union Street, Keith, Morayshire, AB55 5DP Tel: 01542
882225 Fax: 01542 882177
North Lanarkshire
Kilsyth Library
Burngreen, Kilsyth, North Lanarkshire, G65 0HT Tel: 01236
823147 Fax: 01236 823147

Motherwell Heritage Centre
High Road, Motherwell, North Lanarkshire, ML1 3HU Tel:
01698 251000 Fax: 01698 253433 Email:
heritage@mhc158.freeserve.co.uk
Shotts Library
Benhar Road, Shotts, North Lanarkshire, ML7 5EN Tel:
01501 821556
Orkney
Orkney Library
Laing Street, Kirkwall, Orkney, KWI5 1NW Tel: 01856
873166 Fax: 01856 875260 Email:
alison.fraser@orkney.gov.uk
Perthshire
Perth & Kinross Libraries, A K Bell Library
2 8 York Place, Perth, PH2 8EP Tel: 01738 477062 Fax:
01738 477010 Email: jaduncan@pkc.gov.uk
Renfrewshire
Paisley Central Library & Museum
High Street, Paisley, Renfrewshire, PA1 2BB Tel: 0141 889
2350 Fax: 0141 887 6468

Watt Library
9 Union Street, Greenock, PA16 8JH Tel: 01475 715628
Scottish Borders
Scottish Borders Archive & Local History Centre
Library Headquarters, St Mary's Mill, Selkirk, Scottish
Borders, TD7 5EW Tel: 01750 20842 Fax: 01750 22875
Email: Library1@netcomuk.co.uk
Shetland
Shetland Library
Lower Hillhead, Lerwick, Shetland, ZE1 0EL Tel: 01595
693868 Fax: 01595 694430 Email: info@shetland
library.gov.uk WWW: www.shetland library.gov.uk
West Lothian
West Lothian Council Libraries
Connolly House, Hopefield Road, Blackburn, West Lothian,
EH47 7HZ Tel: 01506 776331 Fax: 01506 776345 Email:
libhq@libhq.demon.co.uk WWW:
http://www.libhq.demon.co.uk

Northern Ireland

Antrim
North Eastern Library Board & Local Studies
Area Reference Library
Demesne Avenue, Ballymena, Antrim, BT43 7BG Tel:
01266 6641212 Fax: 01266 46680
Belfast
Belfast Central Library
Irish & Local Studies Dept, Royal Avenue, Belfast, BT1 1EA
Tel: 01232 243233 Fax: 01232 332819
Belfast Linen Hall Library
17 Donegall Square North, Belfast, BT1 5GD Tel: 01232
321707
Co Antrim, Local Studies Service, Area Library HQ,
Demesne Avenue, Ballymena, Co Antrim, BT43 7BG Tel:
01266 664121 Fax: 01266 46680 Email:
106004.1150@compuserve.com
Co Fermanagh
Enniskillen Library
Halls Lane, Enniskillen, Co Fermanagh, BT1 3HP Tel: 01365
322886 Fax: 01365 324685 Email:
librarian@eknlib.demon.co.uk

Co Londonderry
Central and Reference Library
35 Foyle Street, Londonderry, Co Londonderry, BT24 6AL
Tel: 01504 272300 Fax: 01504 269084 Email:
trishaw@online.rednet.co.uk
Irish Room
Coleraine County Hall, Castlerock Road, Coleraine, Co
Londonderry, BT1 3HP Tel: 01265 51026 Fax: 01265 51247
Co Tyrone
Omagh Library
1 Spillars Place, Omagh, Co Tyrone, BT78 1HL Tel: 01662
244821 Fax: 01662 246772 Email:
librarian@omahlib.demon.co.uk
County Down
South Eastern Library Board & Local Studies
Library HQ, Windmill Hill, Ballynahinch, County Down,
BT24 8DH Tel: 01238 562639 Fax: 01238 565072

Ireland

Dublin Public Libraries
Gilbert Library Dublin & Irish Collections
138 142 Pearse Street, Dublin, 2 Tel: 353 1 677 7662 Fax:
353 1 671 4354 Email: dubcoll@iol.ie WWW:
http:/www.iol.ie/ dublcilib/index.html
National Library of Ireland
Kildare Street, Dublin, 2 Tel: 661 8811 Fax: 676 6690
Society of Friends (Quakers) Historical Library
Swanbrook House Morehampton R d Dublin 4 Tel: 668 7157
Co Clare
Clare County Library
The Manse, Harmony Row, Ennis, Co Clare Tel: 065
6821616 Fax: 065 6842462 Email: clarelib@iol.ie WWW:
www.iol.ie/~clarelib
Co Cork
Cork City Library
Grand Parade, Cork, Co Cork Tel: 021 277110 Fax: 021
275684 Email: cork.city.library@indigo.ie
Mallow Heritage Centre
27/28 Bank Place, Mallow, Co Cork Tel: 022 50302
Co Kerry
Kerry County Library Genealogical Centre
Cathedral Walk, Killarney, Co Kerry Tel: 353 0 64 359946

Co Kildare
Kildare Hertiage & Genealogy, Kildare County Library
Newbridge, Co Kildare Tel: 045 431109 Tel: 045 433602
Fax: 045 432490 Email: capinfo@iol.ie WWW:
www.kildare.ie
Co Mayo
Central Library
Castlebar, Co Mayo Tel: 094 24444 Fax: 094 24774 Email:
cbarlib@iol.ie
Co Sligo
Sligo County Library
Westward Town Centre, Bridge Street, Sligo, Co Sligo Tel:
00 353 71 47190 Fax: 00 353 71 46798 Email:
sligolib@iol.ie
Co Tipperary
Tipperary County Libary Local Studies Department
Castle Avenue, Thurles, Co Tipperary Tel: 0504 21555 Fax:
0504 23442 Email: studies@tipplibs.iol.ie WWW:
www.iol.ie/~TIPPLIBS
Co Waterford
Waterford County Library
Central Library, Davitt's Quay, Dungarvan, Co Waterford
Tel: 058 41231 Fax: 058 54877

Co Wexford
Enniscorthy Branch Library
Lymington Road, Enniscorthy, Co Wexford Tel: 054 36055
New Ross Branch Library
Barrack Lane, New Ross, Co Wexford Tel: 051 21877
Wexford Branch Library
Teach Shionoid, Abbey Street, Wexford, Co Wexford Tel:
053 42211 Fax: 053 21097
County Donegal
Donegal Local Studies Centre
Central Library & Arts Centre Oliver Plunkett Road,
Letterkenny, County Donegal Tel: 00353 74 24950 Fax:

Isle of Man
Manx National Heritage Library
Douglas, Isle of Man, IM1 3LY Tel: 01624 648000 Fax:
01624 648001

Australia

Capital Territory
National Library of Australia
Canberra, ACT, 2600 Tel: 02 6262 1111 Email:
http://www.nla.gov.au
New South Wales
Mitchell Library
Macquarie Street, Sydney, New South Wales, 2000 Tel: 02
9230 1693 Fax: 02 9235 1687 Email: slinfo@slsw.gov.au
State Library of New South Wales
Macquarie Street, Sydncy, New South Wales, 2000 Tel: 02
9230 1414 Fax: 02 9223 3369 Email: slinfo@slsw.gov.au
Queensland
State Library of Queensland
PO Box 3488, Cnr Peel and Stanley Streets, South Brisbane,
Brisbane, Queensland, 4101 Tel: 07 3840 7775 Fax: 07 3840
7840 Email: genie@slq.qld.gov.au WWW:
http://www.slq.qld.gov.au/subgenie/htm

New Zealand

Alexander Turnbull Library
PO Box 12 349, Wellington, 6038 Tel: 04 474 3050 Fax: 04
474 3063
Auckland Research Centre, Auckland City Libraries
PO Box 4138, 44 46 Lorne Street, Auckland Tel: 64 9 377
0209 Fax: 64 9 307 7741 Email: heritage@auckland
library.govt.nz
Canterbury Public Library
PO Box 1466, Christchurch Tel: 03 379 6914 Fax: 03 365
1751
Dunedin Public Libraries
PO Box 5542, Moray Place, Dunedin Tel: 03 474 3651 Fax:
03 474 3660 Email: library@dcc.govt.nz
Fielding Public Library
PO Box 264, Fielding, 5600 Tel: 06 323 5373
Hamilton Public Library
PO Box 933, Garden Place, Hamilton, 2015 Tel: 07 838 6827
Fax: 07 838 6858

South Africa

Cory Library for Historical Research
Rhodes University, Grahamstown, 6140 Tel: 0461 318438
Fax: 0461 23487 Email: lbsr@giraffe.ru.ac.za
South African Library
PO Box 496, Cape Town, 8000 Tel: 021 246320 Fax: 021
244848

00353 74 24950 Email: dgcolib@iol.ie WWW: donegal.ie
Co Dublin
Dun Laoghaire Library
George's Street, Dun Laoghaire, Co Dublin Tel: 2801254
Fax: 2846141
Ballyfermot Public Library
Ballyfermot, Dublin, 10
County Limerick
Limerick City Library
The Granary, Michael Street, Limerick, County Limerick
Tel: 061 314668

South Australia
South Australia State Library
PO Box 419, Adelaide, South Australia, 5001 Tel: (08) 8207
7235 Fax: (08) 8207 7247 Email: famhist@slsa.sa.gov.au
WWW: http://www.slsa.sa.gov.au/library/collres/famhist/
Victoria
State Library of Victoria
328 Swanston Street Walk, Melbourne, Victoria, 3000 Tel:
03 9669 9080 Email: granth@newvenus.slv.vic.gov.au
WWW: http://www.slv.vic.gov.au/slv/genealogy/index
Western Australia
State Library
Alexander Library, Perth Cultural Centre, Perth, Western
Australia, 6000 Tel: 09 427 3111 Fax: 09 427 3256

Hocken Library
PO Box 56, Dunedin Tel: 03 479 8873 Fax: 03 479 5078
National Library of New Zealand
PO Box 1467, Thorndon, Wellington Tel: (0064)4 474 3030
Fax: (0064)4 474 3063 WWW: http://www.natlib.govt.nz
Porirua Public Library
PO Box 50218, Porirua, 6215 Tel: 04 237 1541 Fax: 04 237
7320
Takapuna Public Library
Private Bag 93508, Takapuna, 1309 Tel: 09 486 8466 Fax:
09 486 8519
Wanganui District Library
Private Bag 3005, Alexander Building, Queens Park,
Wanganui, 5001 Tel: 06 345 8195 Fax: 06 345 5516 Email:
wap@wdl.govt.nz

South African Library National Reference &
Preservation
P O Box 496, Cape Town, 8000 Tel: 021 246320 Fax: 021
244848 Email: postmaster@salib.ac.za
Eastern Cape Province
Cory Library for Historical Research
Rhodes University, PO Box 184, Grahamstown, Eastern
Cape Province, 6140 Tel: +27 46 6038438 Fax: +27 46
6223487 Email: s.poole@ru.ac.za also e.dewet@ru.ac.za
WWW: http://www.ru.ac.za/library/coru.html

Canada

Alberta
Calgary Public Library
616 MacLeod Tr SE, Calgary, Alberta, T2G 2M2 Tel: 260 2785
Glenbow Library & Archives
130 9th Avenue SE, Calgary, Alberta, T2G 0P3 Tel: 403 268 4197 Fax: 403 232 6569
British Columbia
British Columbia Archives
865 Yates Street, Victoria, British Columbia, V8V 1X4 Tel: 604 387 1952 Fax: 604 387 2072 Email: rfrogner@maynard.bcars.gs.gov.bc.ca
Cloverdale Library
5642 176a Street, Surrey, British Columbia, V3S 4G9 Tel: 604 576 1384 Fax: 604 576 0120 Email: GenealogyResearch@city.surrey.bc.ca WWW: http://www.city.surrey.bc.ca/spl/
New Brunswick
Harriet Irving Library
PO Box 7500, Fredericton, New Brunswick, E3B 5H5 Tel: 506 453 4748 Fax: 506 453 4595
Loyalist Collection & Reference Library
PO Box 7500, Fredericton, New Brunswick, E3B 5H5 Tel: 506 453 4749 Fax: 506 453 4596
Newfoundland
Newfoundland Provincial Resource Library
Arts and Cultural Centre, Allandale Road, St Johns, Newfoundland, A1B 3A3 Tel: 709 737 3955 Fax: 709 737 2660 Email: genealog@publib.nf.ca WWW: http://www.publib.nf.ca
Ontario
James Gibson Reference Library
500 Glenridge Avenue, St Catherines, Ontario, L2S 3A1 Tel: 905 688 5550 Fax: 905 988 5490
National Library
395 Wellington Street, Ottawa, Ontario, K1A 0N4 Tel: 613 995 9481 Fax: 613 943 1112 Email: http://www.nlc bnc.careference@nlc bnc.ca
Hamilton Public Library
PO Box 2700, Station LCD 1, Hamilton, Ontario, L8N 4E4 Tel: 546 3408 Fax: 546 3202 Email: speccol@hpl.hamilton.on.ca

Kitchener Public Library
85 Queen Street North, Kitchener, Ontario, N2H 2H1 Tel: 519 743 0271 Fax: 519 570 1360
London Public Library
305 Queens Avenue, London, Ontario, N6B 3L7 Tel: 519 661 4600 Fax: 519 663 5396
Mississauga Public Library
301 Burnhamthorpe Road West, Mississauga, Ontario, L5B 3Y3 Tel: 905 615 3500 Fax: 905 615 3696 Email: library.info@city.mississauga.on.cahttp://www.city.mississauga.on.ca/library
Sudbury Public Library
74 Mackenzie Street, Sudbury, Ontario, P3C 4X8 Tel: 673 1155 Fax: 673 9603
St Catharines Public Library
54 Church Street, St Catharines, Ontario, L2R 7K2 Tel: 905 688 6103 Fax: 905 688 2811 Email: scpublib@stcatharines.library.on.ca WWW: http://www.stcatharines.library.on.ca
Toronto Public Library
North York (Entral Library) Canadiana Department, 5120 Yonge Street, North York, Ontario, M2N 5N9 Tel: 416 395 5623 Fax: WWW: http://www.tpl.tor.on.ca
Toronto Reference Library
789 Yonge Street, Toronto, Ontario, M4W 2G8 Tel: 416 393 7155 Fax: 416 393 7229
Quebec
Bibliotheque De Montreal
1210, Rue Sherbrooke East Street, Montreal, Quebec, H2L 1L9 Tel: 514 872 1616 Fax: 514 872 4654 Email: daniel_olivier@ville.montreal.qc.ca WWW: http://www.ville.montreal.qc.ca/biblio/pageacc.htm
Saskatchewan
Regina Public Library
PO Box 2311, Regina, Saskatchewan, S4P 3Z5 Tel: 306 777 6011 Fax: 306 352 5550 Email: kaitken@rpl.sk.ca
Saskatoon Public Library
311 23rd Street East, Saskatoon, Saskatchewan, S7K 0J6 Tel: 306 975 7555 Fax: 306 975 7542

United States of America

Alabama
Birmingham Public Library
2100 Park Place, Birmingham, Alabama, 325203 2794 Tel: 205 226 3665 Email: sou@bham.lib.al.us
Arizona
Arizona Historical Foundation Library
Hayden Library, Arizona State Univeristy, Tempe, Arizona, 85287 Tel: 602 966 8331
Flagstaff Public Library
300 West Aspen, Flagstaff, Arizona, 86001 Tel: 602 779 7670
Phoenix Public Library
12 East McDowell, Phoenix, Arizona, 85004 Tel: 602 262 4636
California
State Library
PO Box 942837, 914 Capitol Mall, Sacramento, California, 94237 0001 Tel: 916 654 0176
State Library
480 Winston Drive, San Francisco, California, 94132 Tel: 415 557 0421
State Library
630 West Fifth Street, Los Angeles, California, 90071 2002 Tel: 213 228 7400 Fax: 213 228 7409
Connecticut
Connecticut State Library
231 Capitol Avenue, Hartford, Connecticut, 6106 Tel: 203 566 3690
District of Colombia
Library of Congress
L H & Genealogy Reading Room, 101 Independence Avenue SE, Washington, District of Colombia, 20540 4660 Tel: 202 707 5537 Fax: 202 707 1957 Email: lcinfo@loc.gov WWW: http://www.lcweb.loc.gov//nn/genealogy

Daughters of the American Revolution Library
1776 D Street N W, Washington, District of Columbia, 20006 5392 Tel: 202 879 3229
Hawaii
Hawaii State Library
478 South King Street, Honolulu, Hawaii, 96813 Tel:
Illinois
Newberry Library
60 West Walton Street, Chicago, Illinois, 60610 3380 Tel: 312 943 9090
Indiana
Allen County Public Library
PO Box 2270, Fort Wayne, Indiana, 46801 2270 Tel: 219 424 7241 Fax: 219 4229688
Iowa
Iowa State Library
402 Iowa Avenue, Iowa City, Iowa, 52240 1806 Tel: 319 335 3916
Kansas
Kansas State Historical Society Library
6425 SW Sixth Street, Topeka, Kansas, 66615 1099 Tel: 913 272 8681 Fax: 913 272 8682 Email: reference@hspo.wpo.state.ks.us WWW: http://www.kshs.org
Kentucky
Alice Lloyd College Library
Appalachian Oral History Project, Pippa Passes, Kentucky, 414844 Tel: 606 368 2101
Louisiana
Louisiana State Archives
PO Box 94125, Baton Rouge, Louisiana, 70804 9125 Tel: 504 922 1209

Vernon Parish Library
1401 Nolan Trace, Leesville, Louisiana, 71446 Tel: 318 239 2027 Tel: 1 800 737 2231 Fax: 318 238 0666 Email: vernon@alpha.nsula.edu
Maryland
Maryland State Law Library
Courts of Appeal Building, 361 Rowe Boulevard, Annapolis, Maryland, 21401 1697 Tel: (410) 260 1430 Fax: (410) 974 2063 Email: mike.miller@courts.state.md.us WWW: http://www.lawlib.state.md.us
Michigan
Detroit Public Library
5201 Woodward Avenue, Detroit, Michigan, 48202 Tel: 313 833 1480
Dickinson County Public Library
401 Iron Mountain Street, Iron Mountain, Michigan, 49801 Tel: 313 833 1480
Farmington Community Public Library
23500 Liberty Street, Farmington, Michigan, 48335 Tel: 313 474 7770
Herrick District Public Library
300 River Avenue, Holland, Michigan, 49423 Tel: 616 355 1427 Email: holrh@lakeland.lib.mi.us
Jackson Public Library
244 West Michigan Avenue, Jackson, Michigan, 49201
Marguerite DeAngeli Branch Library
921 West Nepessing Street, Lapeer, Michigan, 48446 Tel: 313 664 6971
Mitchell Public Library
22 North Manning Street, Hillsdale, Michigan, 49242 Tel: 517 437 2581
Missouri
Missouri State Library
PO Box 387, 301 West High Street, Jefferson City 65102 Tel: 314 751 3615
Public Library
15616 East Highway 24, Independence 64050 Tel: 816 252 0950
Montana
Mansfield Library
University of Montana, Missoula, Montana, 59812 1195 Tel: 406 243 6860
Nebraska
Beatrice Public Library
100 North 16th Street, Beatrice, Nebraska, 68310
Nebraska State Historical Society Library/Archives
PO Box 82554, 1500 R Street, Lincoln, Nebraska, 68501 2554 Tel: 402 471 4751 Fax: 402 471 8922 WWW: http://www.nebraskahistory.org
Nevada State Library
Division of Archives & Records, 100 Stewart Street, Carson City, Nevada, 89710 Tel: 702 687 5210
New Hampshire
New Hampshire State Library
20 Park Street, Concord, New Hampshire, 3301 Tel: 603 271 6823 Fax: 603 271 2205
New Jersey
Morris County Library
30 East Hanover Avenue, Whippany, New Jersey, 07981 1825 Tel: 973 285 6974 Email: heagney@main.morris.org
New Jersey State Library
185 West State Street, Trenton, New Jersey, 08625 0520 Tel: 609 292 6274
New Mexico
New Mexico State Library
325 Don Gaspar Avenue, Sante Fe, New Mexico, 87503 Tel: 505 827 3805
Alberquerque Public Library
423 Central Avenue NE, Alberquerque, New Mexico, 87102 3517
New York
New York Public Library Center for Humanities
US Local History & Genealogy Division, Fifth Avenue & 42nd Street, New York, New York, 10018 Tel: 212 930 0828

Ohio
Ohio State Library
65 South Front Street, Columbus, Ohio, 43266 0334 Tel: 614 644 6966
Pennsylvania
Pennsylvania State Library
Forum Building, Walnut Street & Commonwealth Avenue, Harrisburg, Pennsylvania, 17105 Tel: 717 787 4440
South Carolina
South Carolina State Library
PO Box 11469, 1500 Senate Street, Columbia, South Carolina, 29211 Tel: 803 734 8666
South Dakota
South Dakota State Library
Memorial Building Branch, 800 Governors Drive, Pierre, South Dakota, 57501 2294 Tel: 605 773 3131
Tennessee
Tennessee State Library
403 7th Avenue North, Nashville, Tennessee, 37243 0312 Tel: 615 741 2764
Texas
Amarillo Public Library
413 East Fourth Street, Amarillo, Texas, 79189 2171 Tel: 806 378 3054
Dallas Public Library
1515 Young Street, Dallas, Texas, 75201 5417 Tel: 214 670 1433
Houston Public Library
5300 Caroline, Houston, Texas, 77004 6896 Tel: 713 524 0101
Midland County Public Library
310 West Missouri, Midland, Texas, 79701 Tel: 915 688 8991
Texas State Library
PO Box 12927, Austin, Texas, 78711 2927 Tel: 512 463 5463
Utah
Church of Jesus Christ of Latter Day Saints, Family History Library
35 North West Temple Street, Salt Lake City, Utah, 84150 Tel: 801 240 2331 Fax: 801 240 5551 Email: fhl@ldschurch.org
Vermont
Vermont Department of Libraries, Pavilion Office Building, 109 State Street, Montpelier, Vermont, 05609 0601 Tel: 802 828 3268
Virginia
Library of Virginia
800 East Broad Street, Richmond, Virginia, 23219 3491 Tel: 804 692 3777
Alexandria Public Library
220 North Washington Avenue, Alexandria, Virginia, 23219 Tel: 703 838 4577 Fax: 703 706 3912
Fredericksburg Public Library
1201 Caroline Street, Fredericksburg, Virginia, 22401 Tel: 540 372 1144
Virginia State Library
11th Street at Capitol Square, Richmond, Virginia, 23219 3491 Tel: 804 786 8929
West Virginia
West Virginia State Library
The Cultural Center, 1900 Kanawha Boulevard East, Charleston, West Virginia, 25305 0300 Tel: 304 558 0230
Wisconsin
Wisconsin State Library
816 State Street, Madison, Wisconsin, 53706 Tel: 608 264 6535
Wyoming
Laramie County Library Service
2800 Central Avenue, Cheyenne, Wyoming, 82001 2799 Tel: 307 634 3561
Wyoming State Library
Supreme Court Building, 2301 Capitol Avenue, Cheyenne, Wyoming, 82002 Tel: 307 777 7281

PROBATE RECORDS AT THE BORTHWICK INSTITUTE
Professor D M Smith, MA, PhD, FSA Director

The Borthwick Institute of the University of York houses the probate records of the Archbishop of York both as diocesan and as head of the northern province, so as such is a really valuable source for family history. The diocesan probate court was known as the Exchequer; that of the province as the Prerogative Court. Since the Church authorities were chiefly responsible for the administration of the probate jurisdiction before 1858 then it follows that the location of a particular will depends upon a familiarity with the jurisdictional structure of the Church - A from province through diocese, archdeaconry, rural deanery, to parish.

The Exchequer Court exercised probate jurisdiction in respect of the laity and (after the middle ages) unbeneficed clergy having goods solely in the diocese of York. The post Reformation diocese covered the whole of Yorkshire (except for the north western part of the county which formed part of the Richmond archdeaconry in Chester diocese) and Nottinghamshire and the Archbishop also possessed the liberties of Ripon and Hexhamshire (the latter being in Northumberland). The original wills are arranged chronologically by month of probate in rural deanery bundles. The series of original probate material begins in 1427 but before 1591 there are only one or two items for the years when wills survive. From 1591 there are some wills extant for most years but the series is not generally complete until the 1630s onwards. Between 1653 and 1660 when the Commonwealth authorities established their own central probate court system, probate records of Yorkshire and the north of England are at the Public Record Office, London. From about 1688 the bundles generally include inventories, probate and administration bonds, declarations, renunciations etc. The inventories do not survive much after the mid 18th century and are replaced by simple declarations of the value of the estate. The original probate records of the Exchequer Court from the Nottinghamshire rural deaneries of the diocese have been transferred to the Nottingham County Record Office. As well as the original records (which are contained in some 3,000 archive boxes, in itself an indication of the size of the collection), there is a more complete series of probate registers running from 1389 to January 1858, when the Church authorities ceased to exercise probate jurisdiction. These registers contain contemporaneous registered copies of wills proved in both the Exchequer and the Prerogative Courts. From 1502 grants of probate and administration of intestates were entered into act books arranged by individual rural deanery.

The Prerogative Court of the Archbishop has its origin in the late 16th century and exercised jurisdiction in respect of probate or administration of persons with bona notabilia that is, goods etc. to the value of £5 and over either in more than one jurisdiction within the diocesan boundaries of York, or in more than one diocese in the northern province (until the 19th century the dioceses of York, Carlisle, Chester and Durham, covering the counties of Cheshire, Cumberland, Durham, Lancashire, Northumberland, Nottinghamshire, Westmorland and Yorkshire), or in both northern and southern provinces. In such as the last case, the Prerogative Court of Canterbury was also usually resorted to in the first instance (its records are at the Public Record Office, London). The original records of the Prerogative Court of York are also arranged chronologically by month of probate and are stored with the Exchequer material. The registered copies of wills proved in the Prerogative Court are entered in the same series of volumes as described above for the Exchequer Court. A separate series of act books for the Prerogative Court (containing probate acts and grants of administration) survive from 1587.

A third York probate court is found from the middle ages onwards the **Chancery Court of the Archbishop**. Originally used for wills proved before the Archbishop in person rather than before his probate officials in the Exchequer, the Chancery came to have jurisdiction over the probate and administration of the goods of beneficed clergy in the York diocese and probate by reason of the Archbishop's periodic visitations of an inferior ecclesiastical jurisdiction. The original records survive from 1535 onwards (although rather sparsely until the late 16th century) but copies of wills have been registered in the Archbishops' registers from 1316 to 1857.

In addition to the diocesan and provincial probate jurisdictions there were a whole series of what were known as **peculiar jurisdictions** small ecclesiastical enclaves comprising several parishes or perhaps just one, linked to an ecclesiastical corporation such as a cathedral or monastery, or to a manor which exercised probate jurisdiction over laity h aving goods just in these enclaves. The Institute houses an extensive collection of the probate records of some 53 Yorkshire peculiars.

Most of the categories of probate jurisdictions described above have some kind of name index, whether printed, typescript, or manuscript. The indexes to the Exchequer and Prerogative Courts records have been published from 1359 to 1688 by the Yorkshire Archaeological Society Record Series (vols. 4, 6, 11, 14, 19, 22, 24, 26, 28, 32, 35, 49, 60, 68, 78, 89). Between 1688 and 1731 there are typescript indexes and from 1731 to 1858 there are 29 contemporaneous manuscript volumes of indexes arranged within short chronological probate periods by person. In respect of the Chancery Court there are two printed indexes published in the Yorkshire Archaeological Society Record Series under the erroneous title of Consistory Wills (vols. 73, 93). Details of these indexes are given in the *Guide to the Archive Collections in the Borthwick Institute of Historical Research* (1973), pp.155 - 180. A typescript Parish Index at the Borthwick Institute details which parishes were in which ecclesiastical jurisdiction.

(This article first appeared in the 1998 Edition)

PROBATE RECORDS AND FAMILY HISTORIANS

Information from Probate records can provide vital pieces of the genealogical puzzle. Although often not as useful as records of births, marriages and deaths, which can evidence crucial links to previous generations, they can provide evidence of relatedness within generations, and often contain fascinating insights into the financial affairs of people in times past.

Probate is a process whereby some person or persons, usually the executor(s) of a Will if there was one, or one or more of the next-of-kin if there was no Will, are appointed in law to administer the estate of someone who has died. This is usually only necessary if the deceased person left fairly substantial assets, so don't expect to find any Probate record relating to the estate of a person who had little or no estate of their own. The Probate concept of 'estate' refers just to assets held in the sole name of the person who has died, and so Probate isn't necessary for the release of assets held jointly with another person. When an application for Probate is made, any Will that the deceased person left must be submitted to the Probate Registry. The Will, if judged to be valid, is thereafter kept on file, and it is normally possible for anyone to obtain a copy of it. There are exceptions, however, such as the Wills of members of the Royal family. The important point is that Wills are available from the Probate Registries only as a by-product of the Probate process: if Probate wasn't needed, then the Probate Registries have no record of the estate at all.

You should bear in mind that the Probate record, if any, will be dated some time after the date of death of the person concerned, so start searching from the year of death, or the year in which think the person died. You should normally expect to find the Probate record within the first year or two after the date of death, and, if you have not found it within three, you can usually assume that Probate wasn't necessary. However, in a very small number of cases, Probate is granted many years after the person in question died. Take a tip from the professionals: if you don't find a probate record within three years, the next most likely time to search is the year in which their heir(s) died. This is because unadministered estate is most likely to come to light at that time. How far you want to go with the search will probably depend on how crucial the person in question is to your research, but there is as yet no shortcut: you will have to search the index for each year separately.

Control of Probate record-keeping passed from the Church to the state in 1858, at which point the records were unified into one Calendar index. These indexes, which summarise all Probate grants for England and Wales during a given year, act as a table of contents for the vast store of records held by the Probate Registries. If the subject of your research died before 1858, it will be more difficult to trace their Will. However, if they were very wealthy or owned a lot of land, consult the indexes of the Prerogative Court of Canterbury (PCC) first, and then those of the lesser ecclesiastical courts of the region in which they lived. PCC records are held by the Family Records Centre in London (Tel: (020) 8392 5300), but records of the lesser ecclesiastical Probate courts are highly dispersed. Try the local authority archives, such as public libraries and County Record Offices of the appropriate region, and also any local historical research institutes. Major ecclesiastical centres are also likely to have their own archives.

The table below lists the Calendar indexes held by the various Probate Registries in England and Wales. You can usually call in to consult the indexes, but check with the Registry concerned first, especially if you intend to travel any distance. Probate grants for each year are listed alphabetically by surname. The crucial parts of the Probate record are the Grant type, which is usually 'Probate', 'Administration' or 'Administration with Will', the issuing Registry, and the grant issue date. They are normally written in sequence towards the end of the index entry, but the older books give the grant date first and highlight the issuing Registry in the text of the entry. The grant type can be inferred from the text, but note that the indexes prior to 1871 listed the 'Administration' grants in a separate part of the book from the 'Probate' and 'Administration with Will' grants, so be sure to search in both places for years prior to this. In addition, there may be a handwritten number next to entries for Wills proved in the Principal Probate Registry (London) between 1858 and 1930. This is the Folio number, which is used by the Probate Registries when obtaining copies of the Will. Always make a note of this if applicable.

If the grant type is 'Administration', this tells you that the person in question did not leave a valid Will. However, the Probate Registries can still supply a copy of the grant, which is the document naming the person appointed in law as the administrator of the estate. This can provide genealogical information, especially in older grants where the relationship of the applicant to the deceased was stated. It also gives the value of the estate, although in most cases this is stated as 'not exceeding' a certain figure rather than quoting an exact amount. In fact, the Probate record contains very little information about the estate at all, and no information about its composition. Don't expect to find inventories on file for records after 1858, although they sometimes form part of the Probate record prior to this.

In many cases you can save a lot of time and money by making the search yourself, but there is a postal service by which a search is made on your behalf for a period of four years. There is a fee of £5 for this, but this includes copies of the Will and/or grant if a record is found. It also gives you the benefit of the experience of Probate staff, for instance in knowing when to search and judging under which name the record is likely to be listed. If you want the Probate Registry to conduct a search for a period longer than the standard four years, there is an additional fee of £3 for each 4-year period after the first four. Thus, an 8-year search will cost £8, a 12-year search £11, and so on.

If you want to make a postal search, contact The Postal Searches and Copies Department, The Probate Registry, Duncombe Place, York YO1 7EA, United Kingdom Tel: +44 (1904) 624210 Fax: +44 (1904) 671782.

Applications for searches must be made in writing, and give the full name, last known address and date of death of the person concerned. A search can normally be made using less detail, but if the date of death is not known, you must state the year from which you want the search to be made, or give some other evidence that might indicate when the person died. If you have information about legal actions related to Probate or the disposition of assets, include that on your application. Many people find it convenient to order copies in this way even if they have already made a search of the Probate indexes and located a record relating to the subject of their research, but if this is the case, please include the grant type, issuing Registry and grant issue date on your application, as well as the Folio number if applicable (see above) as this can speed up the supply of copies considerably. The fee should be payable to "H.M.Paymaster General", and if it is paid from abroad, must be made by International Money Order or bank draft, payable through a United Kingdom bank and made out in £ sterling. If you are applying for a search as well, you can request a search of any length, and fees for this are outlined above.

The records referred to here relate only to estates held in England and Wales. If the subject of your research lived in Scotland, contact the Scottish Record Office (Tel: (0131) 535 1337), for Northern Ireland contact the Public Record Office of Northern Ireland (Tel: (028) 9025 1318), and for the Republic of Ireland contact the Principal Probate Registry in Dublin (Tel: Dublin 725555). The Channel Islands and the Isle of Man also have independent Probate courts.

The list below shows what indexes the various Probate Registries hold. Most Registries will have had indexes dating back to 1858, but are not required to keep them for more than fifty years. Usually, the older indexes will have been donated to local authority archives. Contact your local public library or County/City Record Office to see what Probate records they have. If you know of any historical research institute in your area, find out if they have any Probate records. Please note that, since the York Probate Registry serves as a national centre for postal requests for searches and copies, it is not possible to inspect the Probate indexes in person there.

REGISTRY	RECORDS	TELEPHONE
Bangor Probate Sub-Registry	1946 to 1966 and 1973 to 1998	(01248) 362410
Council Offices, FFord, Bangor LL57 1DT		
Birmingham District Probate Registry	1948 to date	(0121) 681 3400
The Priory Courts, 33 Bull Street, Birmingham B4 6DU		
Bodmin Probate Sub-Registry	1858 to 1966 and 1973 to 1998	(01208) 72279
Market Street, Bodmin PL31 2JW		
Brighton District Probate Registry	1935 to date	(01273) 684071
William Street Brighton BN2 2LG		
Bristol District Probate Registry	1901 to date	(0117) 927 3915
Ground Floor, The Crescent Centre, Temple Back, Bristol BS1 6EP		
Carmarthen Probate Sub-Registry	1973 to 1998	(01267) 236238
14 King Street, Carmarthen SA31 1BL		
Chester Probate Sub-Registry	1948 to 1966	(01244) 345082
5th Floor, Hamilton House, Hamilton Place, Chester CH1 2DA		
Exeter Probate Sub-Registry	1858 to 1966 and 1973 to 1998	(01392) 274515
Finance House, Barnfield Road, Exeter EX1 1QR		
Gloucester Probate Sub-Registry	1947 to 1966	(01452) 522585
2nd Floor, Combined Court Building, Kimbrose Way, Gloucester GL1 2DG		
Ipswich District Probate Registry	1936 to date	(01473) 253724
Level 3, Haven House, 17 Lower Brook Street, Ipswich IP4 1DN		
Leeds District Probate Registry	1949 to date	(0113) 243 1505
3rd Floor, Coronet House, Queen Street, Leeds LS1 2BA		
Leicester Probate Sub-Registry	1890 to 1966 and 1973 to date	(0116) 253 8558
5th Floor, Leicester House, Lee Circle, Leicester LE1 3RE		
Lincoln Probate Sub-Registry	1936 to 1966 and 1973 to 1998	(01522) 523648
Mill House, Brayford Side North, Lincoln LN1 1YW		
Liverpool District Probate Registry	1946 to date	(0151) 236 8264

Queen Elizabeth II Law Courts, Derby Square, Liverpool L2 1XA

Manchester District Probate Registry   1947 to date   (0161) 834 4319
9th Floor, Astley House, 23 Quay Street, Manchester M3 4AT

Middlesbrough Probate Sub-Registry   1973 to 1998   (01642) 340001
Teesside Combined Court Centre, Russell Street, Middlesbrough TS1 2AE

Newcastle-upon-Tyne District Probate Registry   1929 to date   (0191) 261 8383
2nd Floor, Plummer House, Croft Street, Newcastle-upon-Tyne NE1 6NP

Nottingham Probate Sub-Registry   1973 to 1998   (0115) 941 4288
Butt Dyke House, Park Row, Nottingham NG1 6GR

Oxford District Probate Registry   1940 to date   (01865) 241163
10a New Street, Oxford OX1 1LY

Sheffield Probate Sub-Registry   1935 to 1966 and 1973 to 1998   (0114) 281 2596
PO Box 832, The Law Courts, 50 West Bar, Sheffield S3 8YR

Stoke-on-Trent Probate Sub-Registry   1973 to 1998   (01782) 854065
Combined Court Centre, Bethesda Street, Hanley, Stoke-on-Trent ST1 3BP

Winchester District Probate Registry   1944 to date   (01962) 863771
4th Floor, Cromwell House, Andover Road, Winchester SO23 7EW

Probate Registry of Wales   1951 to date   (029) 2037 6479
PO Box 474, 2 Park Street, Cardiff CF1 1ET

Principal Probate Registry   1858 to date   (020) 7936 7000
First Avenue House, 42-49 High Holborn, London WC1

The Service has undergone a process of computerisation, but as yet this covers only recently-issued grants, which will be of limited interest to genealogists. However, anyone who is interested in checking up on grants since 1996 can search the Probate Service database themselves. To date, workstations for public use have been installed at the Principal Probate Registry and Manchester District Probate Registry. The Postal Searches and Copies Department at York is also completing a long period of computerisation, which should see a much-improved service to family history researchers, with clearer and more comprehensive information and quicker supply of documents.

1999 has also seen the establishment of a central repository for all Wills proved in England and Wales since 1858. All the considerable problems associated with the removal of records from the various Registries to the central repository should have been resolved by March 2000, although a small number of applications for copies may still be subject to an unavoidable delay. Applications for copies will be by post or in person at a Probate Registry as now, but copy supply should in most cases be much quicker than at present. Because Registries will no longer keep records for more than a year, bear in mind that you won't be able to get copies 'locally' in future.

This information is based on details supplied by the Probate Service. The details are liable to change without notice. Always telephone the Registry before visiting, to check opening times and the availability of records. While every effort is made to ensure the accuracy of these details, the Probate Service cannot be held responsible for any consequence of errors.

Editors' Note:

We are aware of the uproar caused by the increase in fees in April 1999. Although the Probate Service was not able to provide an official statement, we know that staff feel that the price still compares favourably with copies of similar documents such as death certificates, and that copies of Probate documents have remained very cheap for a long time. This has hindered investment, which was apparently needed in order to reduce waiting times and rationalise the storage of Probate records, and staff are confident that, in the future, they will be able to provide an improved service. We also know that Probate staff accept that it is unfair for the fee to be the same regardless of whether a search has been made, and this is something which may be rectified in the future.

These details are liable to change without notice. Always telephone the Registry before visiting, to check opening times and the availability of records. While every effort is made to ensure the accuracy of these details, the Probate Service cannot be held responsible for any consequence of errors.

The information contained in this article and the addresses provided were kindly supplied for
The Genealogical Services Directory
by the Postal Searches and Copies Department of the Probate Sub-Registry, York
for which we offer our sincere appreciation.
December 1999

Probate Records for Scotland

Persons wishing to have information concerning probate records for deaths prior to the last 15 years for Scotland should contact the Scottish Record Office at HM General Register House, Edinburgh, EH1 3YY Tel: 0131-535-1352 Fax: 0131-535-1345

Probate Records for The Channel Islands

Probate records are held at Judicial Greffe, Probate Registry, Westaway Cambers, Don Street, St Helier, Jersey JE2 4TR Tel: 01534-502300 Fax: 01534-502399 This Registry contains wills of personalty and realty. The Registers run from approximately 1660 to the present day and grants of letters of administration from 1848 to 1964, when they were integrated with the record of wills. The Registry is not open to the general public but searches can be carried out by the Department time permitting) and in most cases copies issued. However, some of the earlier documents are in such a condition that copying is not permitted. The search fee is £10.00 per 1/2 hour plus 25p per copied sheet. (1997) It is essential to provide as much information as possible ie full name of deceased, including maiden name where applicable, and date of death alternatively, a reasonable time span over which to search.

Public Registry(Jersey)

The "Loi sur les Testaments d'Immeubles" passed in 1851 gave persons the right to dispose of their real estate by will, subject to certain conditions. There are a few wills of an earlier date. The index is integrated with the index of Deeds of Sale and hypothecation of real estate. Again full details are required when requesting a search for which fees are £5.00 per 1/2 hour plus 50p per photocopies sheet.

Probate Records for Northern Ireland

Probate records for Northern Ireland for deaths more than 7 years ago are held at The Public Record Office of Northern Ireland, 66 Balmoral Street, Belfast, BT7 6NY, Tel: 012321-661621

Probate Records for the Republic of Ireland

Probate records for the Republic of Ireland for records more than 20 years old are retained at The Probate Section, National Archives, Bishop Street, Dublin 8 Tel Dublin 407 2300

MAKIN' WHOOPEE	WE SEEK THEM EVERYWHERE
Another genealogical song parody in the vein of Makin' Whoopee	*Another poem about our never-ending search for ancestor*

MAKIN' WHOOPEE

Another genealogical song parody in the vein of Makin' Whoopee

Another record,
Another file,
Another forebear,
That brings a smile;
Whate'er the season,
There's always reason
For gen-e-alogy.

We're hunting births
And weddings, too'
We all make faults We learn to rue;
But don't forget, folks,
That's what you get, folks
For gen-e-alogy.

You find a date, It doesn't fit,
You tear your hair out
And want to quit;
But that's the fun, guys,
You're never done, guys,
With gen-e-alogy.

Picture the same old records,
Somehow, they just don't zing,
Study those same old records,
See what luck can bring.

You're finding forebears,
Ancestors fine,
Not just your own,
But maybe mine;
And where's the harm, folks?
For that's the charm, folks
Of gen-e-alogy!

WE SEEK THEM EVERYWHERE

Another poem about our never-ending search for ancestor

We seek them here, we seek them there,
We seek our forebears everywhere.
From the Isle of Skye to County Down,
We seek them in parish, village and town.

We seek them in Yorkshire, we seek them in Lancs,
We seek out their names in neat, serried ranks.
We comb ancient records for ancestors afar,
Now what was that birth-date for great-grandma?

We pore with delight over musty old wills,
And thrill to the charm of names written with quills.
We haunt old graveyards a-tumbling with stones,
Are we now treading on great-grandpa's bones?.

Who were they, we wonder, these forebears of ours,
Did they live in bleak hovels or great regal towers?
How rich or how humble, there's one thing that's sure,
We all have a right to our pedigree pure.

Who were they, we wonder, peasants or peers,
Could they have been Roundheads or Cavaliers?
Are we descended in some noble way,
Or from a felon transported to Botany Bay?

As we scour the pages of times long gone by,
Let's drink a toast to our ancestors nigh,
For one truth be known and let's make it clear,
Without any of them, none of us would be here!

from *Rhyming Relations* Genealogy in Verse
by Roy Stockdill
Obtainable from the Author 6 First Avenue, Garston, Watford, Hertfordshire WD2 6PZ
Email: roystock@compuserve.com

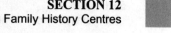
Family History Centres of The Church of Jesus Christ of Latter Day Saints

The Church has established Family History Centres. They usually hold many local records on film and microfiche. These centres are open to the public at certain times each week. Appointments may be necessary and should always be booked in advance. Where telephone numbers are known they have been provided. The Centres are run on a voluntary basis and whilst donations are not sought by the Church they are usually appreciated to assist with the maintenance of the Centre.

England

Bristol
Bristol Family History Centre
721 Wells Road, Whitchurch, Bristol, BS14 9HU
Tel: 01275-838326 Correspondence to: The Director18 Grovemead, Frome. BA11 4BU
Avon
Yate Family History Centre
Wellington Rd, Yate, Avon, BS37 5UY, Tel: 01454-323004
Bedfordshire
St Albans Family History Centre
London Road/Cutenhoe Road, Luton LU1 3NQ
Tel: 01582-482234 Please telephone for appointment
Berkshire
Reading Family History Centre
280 The Meadway, Tilehurst, Reading RG3 4PF, Tel: 0118-942-7524
Cambridgeshire
Cambridgeshire Family History Centre
670 Cherry Hinton Road, Cambridge, Cambridgeshire, CB1 4DR, Tel: 01223-247010 Correspondence to: Ms S Mitchel-King, 6 Hawthorn Way, Burwell. Cambs. CB5 0DQ
Peterborough Family History Centre
Cottesmore Close off Atherstone Av, Netherton Estate, Peterborough, Cambridgeshire, PE3 9TP, Tel: 01733-263374
Cheshire
Chester Family History Centre
Clifton Drive, Blacon, Chester CH1 5LT Tel: 01244-390796
Cleveland
Billingham Family Historey Centre
The Linkway, Billingham TS23 3HG Tel: 01642-563162
Cornwall
Helston Family History Centre
Clodgey Lane, Helston, Cornwall, Tel: 01326-564503
Correspondence to M E Topham, 5 Elizabeth Terrace St Michael's Mount, Maraslow. TR17 0HT
Cumbria
Carlisle Family History Centre
Langrigg Rd, Morton Park, Carlisle CA2 5HT, Tel: 01228-26767
Devon
Exeter Family History Centre
Wonford Road, Exeter, Devon, Tel: 01392-250723
Plymouth Family History Centre
Mannamead Rd, Plymouth PL3 5QJ, Tel: 01752-668666
Dorset
Poole Family History Centre
8 Mount Rd, Parkstone, Poole BH14 0QW
Tel: 01202 730646
East Sussex
Crawley Family History Centre
Old Horsham Road, Crawley RH11 8PD, Tel: 01293-516151
Essex
Romford Family History Centre
64 Butts Green Rd, Hornshurch RM11 2JJ
Tel: 01708-620727
Gloucestershire
Cheltenham Family History Centre
Thirlestaine Rd, Cheltenham GL53 7AS, Tel: 01242-523433
Gloucestershire
Forest of Dean Family History Centre
Wynol's Hill, Queensway, Coleford Tel: 01594-542480
Greater Manchester
Manchester Family History Centre
Altrincham Road, Wythenshawe Road, Manchester M22 4BJ, Tel: 0161-902-9279

Hampshire
Portsmouth Family History Centre
82 Kingston Cres, Portsmouth PO2 8AQ, Tel: 01705-696243
Hull
Hull Family History Centre
725 Holderness Road, Kingston upon Hull HU4 7RT
Tel: 01482-701439
Isle of Wight
Newport Family History Centre
Chestnut Cl, Shide Rd, Newport PO30 1YE Tel: 01983-529643
Kent
Maidstone Family History Centre
76b London Rd, Maidstone ME16 0DR, Tel: 01622-757811
Lancashire
Ashton Family History Centre
Patterdale Road, Ashton-under-Lyne OL7 Tel: 0161-330-1270
Blackpool Family History Centre
Warren Drive, Cleveleys, Blackpool, Lancashire, FY5 3TG, Tel: 01253-858218 Correspondence to Mrs Grady. Apt 8, 1 Beach Road, St Annes. Lancs FY8 2NR
Chorley Family History Centre
33 - 41 Water Street, Chorley PR7 1EE Tel: 01257-233687
Lancaster Family History Centre
Ovangle Road, Lancaster LA1 5HZ Tel: 01254-33571
Rawtenstall Family History Centre
Haslingden Road, Rawtenstall, Rossendale BB4 0QX
Tel: 01706-213460
Leicestershire
Leicestershire Family History Centre
Wakerley Rd, Leicester LE5 4WD Tel: 0116-233-5544
Lincolnshire
Lincoln Family History Centre
Skellingthorpe Road, Lincoln LN6 0PB Tel: 01522-680117
London
Hyde Park Family History Centre
64 - 68 Exhibition Road, South Kensington, London SW7 2PA, Tel: 0171-589-8561
Wandsworth Family History Centre
149 Nightingale Lane, Balham, London, SW12 Tel: 0181-673-6741
Merseyside
Liverpool Family History Centre
4 Mill Bank, Liverpool L13 0BW Tel: 0151-228-0433
Middlesex
Staines Family History Centre
41 Kingston Road, Staines TW14 0ND Tel: 01784-462627
Norfolk
Kings Lynn Family History Centre
Reffley Lane, Kings Lynn, PE30 3EQ, Tel: 01553-67000
Norwich Family History Centre
19 Greenways, Eaton, Norwich NR4 6PA
Tel: 01603-452440
North East Lincolnshire
Grimsby Family History Centre
Linwood Avenue, Scartho, Grimsby DN33 2NL
Tel: 01472-828876 Correspondence to Mr B Collier, 12 Southfield Avenue, Scartho, Grimsby DN33 2PA
North Yorkshire
Scarborough Family History Centre
Stepney Drive/Whitby Road, Scarborough, North Yorkshire,
Northamptonshire
Northampton Family History Centre
137 Harlestone Road, Duston, Northampton, NN5 6AA Tel: 01604-587630

Nottinghamshire
Mansfield Family History Centre
Southridge Drive, Mansfield NG18 4RJ, Tel: 01623-26729
Nottingham Family History Centre
Hempshill Lane, Bulwell, Nottingham NG6 8PA Tel: 0115-927-4194
Shropshire
Telford Family History Centre
72 Glebe Street, Wellington, Shropshire
Somerset
Yeovil Family History Centre
Forest Hill, Yeovil, Somerset, BA20 2PH, Tel: 01935-26817
South Yorkshire
Sheffield Family History Centre
Wheel Lane, Grenoside, Sheffield S30 3RL Tel: 0114-245-3124
Staffordshire
Lichfield Family History Centre
Purcell Avenue, Lichfield WS14 9XA, Tel: 01543-414843
Newcastle under Lyme Family History Centre
PO Box 457, Newcastle under Lyme ST5 0TD Tel: 01782-620653
Suffolk
Ipswich Family History Centre
42 Sidegate Lane West, Ipswich IP4 3DB Tel: 01473-723182 Correspondence: Mr Jack Jacobs, 22 Blackdown Avenue, Rushmere. St Andrews. IP5 1AZ
Lowestoft Family History Centre
165 Yarmouth Road, Lowestoft, Suffolk, Tel: 01502-573851
Tyne and Wear
Sunderland Family History Centre
Linden Road off Queen Alexandra Road, Sunderland SR2 9BT, Tel: 0191-528-5787

Isle of Man
Douglas Family History Centre
Woodbourne Road, Douglas IM2 3AP Tel: 01624-675834

Wales
Denbighshire
Rhyl Family History Centre
Rhuddlan Road, Rhyl, Denbighshire
Glamorgan
Merthyr Tydfil Family History Centre
Swansea Road, Merthyr Tydfil CF 48 1NR, Tel: 01685-722455

Scotland
Edinburgh Family History Centre
30a Colinton Rd, Edinburgh, EH4 3SN, Tel: 0130-337-3049
Glasgow Family History Centre
35 Julian Avenue, Glasgow, G12 0RB, Tel: 0141-357-1024
Ayrshire
Kilmarnock Family History Centre
Wahtriggs Road, Kilmarnock KA1 3QY, Tel: 01563-26560
Dumfrieshire
Dumfries Family History Centre
36 Edinburgh Road, Albanybank, Dumfries, Dumfrieshire, DG1 1JQ, Tel: 01387-254865 Contact: Brian Harkness, 17 Mossgiel Avenue, Dumfries, DG2 9EA Tel: 01387-254342
Fife
Kirkcaldy Family History Centre
Winifred Crescent, Forth Park, Kirkcaldy, Fife, KY2 5SX, Tel: 01592-640041

Northern Ireland
Belfast Family History Centre
401 Holywood Road, Belfast, BT4 2GU, Tel: 01232-768250

Ireland
Co Dublin
Dublin Family History Centre
The Willows, Finglas, Dublin 11, Tel: ++-353-4625609

West Midlands
Coventry Family History Centre
Riverside Close, Whitley, Coventry Tel: 01203-301420
Harborne Family History Centre
38 Lordswood Road, Harborne, Birmingham, West Midlands, B17 9QS, Tel: 0121-427-9291
Sutton Coldfield Family History Centre
185 Penns Lane, Sutton Coldfield, Birmingham, West Midlands, B76 1JU, Tel: 0121-386-1690
Wednesfield Family History Centre
Linthouse Lane, Wednesfield, Wolverhampton Tel: 01902-724097
West Sussex
Worthing Family History Centre
Goring Street, Worthing, West Sussex, BN12 5AR
West Yorkshire
Huddersfield Family History Centre
12 Halifax Road, Birchencliffe, Huddersfield, West Yorkshire, HD3 3BS, Tel: 01484-454573
Leeds Family History Centre
Vesper Road, Leeds LS5 3QT, Tel: 0113-258-5297
Worcestershire
Redditch Family History Centre
321 Evesham Road, Crabbs Cross, Redditch, B97 5JA, Tel: 01527-550657
York
York Family History Centre
West Bank, Acomb, York, Tel: 01904-785128

Channel Islands
Jersey
St Helier Family History Centre La Rue de la Vallee, St Mary, Jersey, JE3 3DL Tel: 01534-82171

Swansea Family History Centre
Cockett Road, Swansea, Glamorgan, SA2 0FH, Tel: 01792-419520 Ms Ruth Thomas, 12 Ffordd y Brain, Ravenhill, Swansea. SA5 5DY
South Glamorgan
Cardiff Family History Centre
Heol y Deri, Rhiwbina, Cardiff, South Glamorgan, CF4 6UH, Tel: 01222-620205

Grampian
Aberdeen Family History Centre
North Anderson Drive, Aberdeen AB2 6DD, Tel: 01224-692206
Invernesshire
Inverness Family History Centre
13 Ness Walk, Inverness IV3 5SQ Tel: 01463-231220
Renfrewshire
Paisley Family History Centre
Campbell Street, Paisley, Johnstone, PA5 8LD, Tel: 01505-20886
Shetland
Lerwick Family History Centre
Baila Croft, Lerwick, Shetland, ZE1 0EY, Tel: 01595-695732, Tel: 01950-431469
Tayside
Dundee Family History Centre
22 - 26 Bingham Terrace, Dundee, Tayside, DD4 7HH, Tel: 01382-451247
Londonderry Family History Centre
Racecourse Road, Belmont Estate, Londonderry, Tel: Sun-only-01504-350179 NB: 1st Jan to 1st July FHC at Londerry and 1st July to Jan 1st located at Church Buildings in Coleraine

Cemeteries & Crematoria

In order to provide additional useful listings the next pages contain a list of Cemeteries and Crematoria. The list is not exhaustive and we would be pleased to receive details of other cemeteries & crematoria to add to our future lists.

England

Avon

Bristol General Cemetery Co
East Lodge, Bath Rd, Arnos Vale, Bristol, Avon, BS4 3EW Tel:0117 971 3294
Canford Crematorium & Cemetery
Canford Lane, Westbury On Trym, Bristol, Avon, BS9 3PQ Tel:0117 950 3535
Cemetery of Holy Souls
Bath Rd, Bristol, Avon, BS4 3EW Tel:0117 977 2386
Haycombe Crematorium & Cemetery
Whiteway Rd, Bath, Avon, BA2 2RQ Tel:01225 423682
South Bristol Crematorium & Cemetery
Bridgwater Rd, Bristol, Avon, BS13 7AS Tel:0117 963 4141
Westerleigh Crematorium
Westerleigh Rd, Westerleigh, Bristol, Avon, BS37 8QP Tel:0117 937 4619
Weston Super Mare Crematorium
Ebdon Rd, Worle, Weston-Super-Mare, Avon, BS22 9NY Tel:01934 511717
Bedfordshire
Norse Rd Crematorium
104 Norse Rd, Bedford, Bedfordshire, MK41 0RL Tel:01234 353701
Church Burial Ground
26 Crawley Green Rd, Luton, Bedfordshire, LU2 0QX Tel:01582 722874
Dunstable Cemetery
West St, Dunstable, Bedfordshire, LU6 1PB Tel:01582 662772
Kempston Cemetery
2 Green End Rd, Kempston, Bedford MK43 8RJ Tel:01234 851823
Luton Crematorium
The Vale, Butterfield Green, Stopsley, Luton LU2 8DD Tel:01582 723700
Luton General Cemetery
Rothesay Rd, Luton, Bedfordshire, LU1 1QX Tel:01582 727480
Berkshire
Easthampstead Park Cemetry & Crematorium
Nine Mile Ride, Wokingham, Berkshire, RG40 3DW Tel:01344 420314
Henley Road Cemetery & Reading Crematorium
All Hallows Rd, Henley Rd, Caversham, Reading, RG4 5LP Tel:0118 947 2433
Larges Lane Cemetery
Larges Lane, Bracknell, Berkshire, RG12 9AL Tel:01344 450665
Newbury Cemetery
Shaw Hill, Shaw Fields, Shaw, Newbury, Berkshire, RG14 2EQ Tel:01635 40096
Slough Cemetery & Crematorium
Stoke Rd, Slough, Berkshire, SL2 5AX Tel:01753 523127 (Cemetery)
Tel:01753 520702 (Crematorium)
Buckinghamshire
Chilterns Crematorium
Whielden Lane, Winchmore Hill, Amersham HP7 0ND Tel:01494 724263
Cambridgeshire
American Military Cemetery
Madingley Rd, Coton, Cambridge, CB3 7PH Tel:01954 210350
Cambridge City Crematorium
Huntingdon Rd, Girton, Cambridge, CB3 0JJ Tel:01954 780681
Ely Cemetary
Beech Lane, Ely, CB7 4QZ Tel:01353 669659
Marholm Crematorium
Mowbray Rd, Peterborough, PE6 7JE Tel:01733 262639
Cheshire
Altrincham Cemetery
Hale Rd, Altrincham, Cheshire, WA14 2EW Tel:0161 980 4441
Altrincham Crematorium
White House Lane, Dunham Massey, Altrincham WA14 5RH Tel:0161 928 7771
Cemetery Management Ltd
Church Walk, Nantwich, Cheshire, CW5 5RG Tel:01270 626037
Chester Cemeteries & Crematorium
Blacon Avenue, Blacon, Chester, Cheshire, CH1 5BB Tel:01244 372428
Dukinfield Crematorium
Hall Green Rd, Dukinfield, Cheshire, SK16 4EP Tel:0161 330 1901
Macclesfield Cemetery
87 Prestbury Rd, Macclesfield SK10 3BU Tel:01625 422330

Middlewich Cemetery
12 Chester Rd, Middlewich, Cheshire, CW10 9ET Tel:01606 737101
Overleigh Rd Cemetery
The Lodge, Overleigh Rd, Chester, Cheshire, CH4 7HW Tel:01244 682529
Walton Lea Crematorium
Chester Rd, Higher Walton, Warrington, Cheshire, WA4 6TB Tel:01925 267731
Widnes Cemetery & Crematorium
Birchfield Rd, Widnes, Cheshire, WA8 9EE Tel:0151 471 7332
Cleveland
Teesside Crematorium
Acklam Rd, Middlesbrough, Cleveland, TS5 7HD Tel:01642 817725
Cornwall
Glynn Valley Crematorium
Turfdown Rd, Fletchers Bridge, Bodmin, Cornwall, PL30 4AU Tel:01208 73858
Penmount Crematorium
Penmount, Truro, Cornwall, TR4 9AA Tel:01872 272871
County Durham
Birtley Cemetery & Crematorium
Windsor Rd, Birtley, Chester Le Street DH3 1PQ Tel:0191 4102381
Chester Le Street Cemetery
Chester Le Street District Council Civic Centre, Newcastle Rd, Chester Le Street, County Durham, DH3 3UT Tel:0191 3872117
Horden Cemetery
Lodge, Thorpe Rd, Horden, Peterlee, County Durham, SR8 4TP Tel:0191 5863870
Mountsett Crematorium
Ewehurst Rd, Dipton, Stanley DH9 0HN Tel:01207 570255
Murton Cemetery
Lodge, Church Lane, Murton, Seaham, County Durham, SR7 9RD
Tel:0191 5263973
Newton Aycliffe Cemetery
Stephenson Way, Newton Aycliffe, County Durham, DL5 7DF Tel:01325 312861
Princess Road Cemetery
Princess Rd, Seaham, County Durham, SR7 7TD Tel:0191 5812943
Trimdon Foundry Cemetary
Lodge, Thornley Rd, Trimdon Station, County Durham, TS29 6NX
Tel:01429 880592
Trimdon Parish Council Cemetery
Lodge, Northside, Trimdon Grange, Trimdon Station TS29 6HN Tel:01429 880538
Wear Valley Cemetery
Lodge, South Church Rd, Bishop Auckland DL14 7NA Tel:01388 603396
Cumbria
Carlisle Cemetery
Richardson St, Carlisle CA2 6AL Tel:01228 625310
Penrith Cemetery
Beacon Edge, Penrith CA11 7RZ Tel:01768 862152
Wigton Burial Joint Committee
Cemetery, Station Hill, Wigton CA7 9BN Tel:016973 42442
Derbyshire
Castle Donington Parish Council
Cemetery House, The Barroon, Castle Donington, Derby, Derbyshire, DE74 2PF
Tel:01332 810202
Chesterfield & District Joint Crematorium
Chesterfield Rd, Brimington S43 1AU Tel:01246 345888
Clay Cross Cemetery
Cemetery Rd, Danesmoor S45 9RL Tel:01246 863225
Glossop Cemetery
Arundel House, Cemetery Rd, Glossop, Derbyshire, SK13 7QG Tel:01457 852269
Markeaton Crematorium
Markeaton Lane, Derby DE22 4NH Tel:01332 341012
Melbourne Cemetery
Pack Horse Rd, Melbourne, Derby DE73 1BZ Tel:01332 863369
Devon
Drake Memorial Park Ltd
Haye Rd, Plympton, Plymouth, Devon, PL7 1UQ Tel:01752 337937
Exeter & Devon Crematorium
Topsham Rd, Exeter, Devon, EX2 6EU Tel:01392 496333

Littleham Church Yard
Littleham Village, Littleham, Exmouth, Devon, EX8 2RQ Tel:01395 225579
Mole Valley Green Burial Ground
Woodhouse Farm, Queens Nympton, South Molton, Devon, EX36 4JH
Tel:01769 574512
North Devon Crematorium
Old Torrington Rd, Barnstaple, Devon, EX31 3NW Tel:01271 345431
Plymouth Devonport & Stonehouse Cemetery Co
Ford Park Rd, Plymouth, Devon, PL4 6NT Tel:01752 665442
Tavistock Cemetery
Cemetery Lodge, Plymouth Rd, Tavistock, Devon, PL19 8BY Tel:01822 612799
Torquay Crematorium & Cemetery
Hele Rd, Torquay, Devon, TQ2 7QG Tel:01803 327768
Dorset
Dorchester Cemetery Office
31a Weymouth Avenue, Dorchester, Dorset, DT1 2EN Tel:01305 263900
Parkstone Cemetery
134 Pottery Rd, Parkstone, Poole, Dorset, BH14 8RD Tel:01202 741104
Poole Cemetery
Dorchester Rd, Oakdale, Poole, Dorset, BH15 3RZ Tel:01202 741106
Poole Crematorium
Gravel Hill, Poole, Dorset, BH17 9BQ Tel:01202 602582
Sherborne Cemetery
Lenthey Rd, Sherborne, Dorset, DT9 3 Tel:01935 812909
Weymouth Crematorium
Quibo Lane, Weymouth, Dorset, DT4 0RR Tel:01305 786984
East Sussex
Brighton Borough Mortuary
Lewes Rd, Brighton, East Sussex, BN2 3QB Tel:01273 602345
Downs Crematorium
Bear Rd, Brighton, East Sussex, BN2 3PL Tel:01273 601601
Eastbourne Cemeteries & Crematorium
Hide Hollow, Langney, Eastbourne, East Sussex, BN23 8AE
Tel:01323 766536(Cemetery)Tel:01323 761093(Crematorium)
Woodvale Crematorium
Lewes Rd, Brighton, BN2 3QB Tel:01273 604020
Essex
Basildon & District Crematorium
Church Rd, Bowers Gifford, Basildon, Essex, SS13 2HG Tel:01268 584411
Chadwell Heath Cemetery
Whalebone Lane, North Chadwell Heath, Romford, Essex, RM6 5QX Tel:0181
590 3280
Chelmsford Crematorium
Writtle Rd, Chelmsford, Essex, CM1 3BL Tel:01245 256946
Chigwell Cemetery
Frog Hall Lane, Manor Rd, Chigwell, Essex, IG7 4JX Tel:0181 501 0419
Colchester Cemetery & Crematorium
Mersea Rd, Colchester, Essex, CO2 8RU Tel:01206 282950
Eastbrookend Cemetery
Dagenham Rd, Dagenham, Essex, RM10 7DR Tel:01708 447451
Federation of Synagogues Burial Society
416 Upminster Rd North, Rainham RM13 9SB Tel:01708 552825
Great Burstead Cemetery
Church St, Great Burstead, Billericay CM11 2TR Tel:01277 654334
Harlow Crematorium
Parndon Wood Rd, Harlow CM19 4SF Tel:01279 423800
Pitsea Cemetery
Church Rd, Pitsea, Basildon, Essex, SS13 2EZ Tel:01268 552132
Romford Cemetery
Crow Lane, Romford, Essex, RM7 0EP Tel:01708 740791
Sewardstone Road Cemetery
Sewardstone Rd, Waltham Abbey, Essex, EN9 1NX Tel:01992 712525
South Essex Crematorium
Ockendon Rd, Corbets Tey, Upminster, Essex, RM14 2UY Tel:01708 222188
Sutton Road Cemetary
The Lodge, Sutton Rd, Southend-On-Sea, Essex, SS2 5PX Tel:01702 355015
Weeley Crematorium
Colchester Rd, Weeley, Clacton-On-Sea, Essex, CO16 9JP Tel:01255 831108
Wickford Cemetery
Park Drive, Wickford, Essex, SS12 9DH Tel:01268 733335

Gloucestershire
Cheltenham Cemetery & Crematorium
Bouncers Lane, Cheltenham, Gloucestershire, GL52 5JT Tel:01242 244245
Coney Hill Crematorium
Coney Hill Rd, Gloucester GL4 4PA Tel:01452 523902
Forest of Dean Crematorium
Yew Tree Brake, Speech House Rd, Cinderford GL14 3HU Tel:01594 826624
Mile End Cemetery
Mile End, Coleford GL16 7DB Tel:01594 832848
Hampshire
Aldershot Crematorium
48 Guildford Rd, Aldershot GU12 4BP Tel:01252 321653
Anns Hill Rd Cemetery
Anns Hill Rd, Gosport, Hampshire, PO12 3JX Tel:01705 580181
Basingstoke Crematorium
Manor Farm, Stockbridge Rd, North Waltham, Basingstoke, Hampshire,
RG25 2BA Tel:01256 398784
Magdalen Hill Cematary
Magdalen Hill, Arlesesford Rd, Winchester SO21 1HE Tel:01962 854135
Portchester Crematorium
Upper Cornaway Lane, Portchester, Fareham PO16 8NE Tel:01329 822533
Portsmouth Cemeteries Office
Milton Rd, Southsea, Hampshire, PO4 8 Tel:01705 732559
Southampton City Council
6 Bugle St, Southampton, Hampshire, SO14 2AJ Tel:01703 228609
Warblington Cemetery
Church Lane, Warblington, Havant, Hampshire, PO9 2TU Tel:01705 452540
Worting Rd Cemetery
105 Worting Rd, Basingstoke, Hampshire, RG21 8YZ Tel:01256 321737
Herefordshire
Hereford Cemetery & Crematorium
Westfaling St, Hereford, Herefordshire, HR4 0JE Tel:01432 272024
Hertfordshire
Almonds Lane Cemetery
Almonds Lane, Stevenage, Hertfordshire, SG1 3RR Tel:01438 350902
Bushey Jewish Cemetery
Little Bushey Lane, Bushey, Watford, Hertfordshire, WD2 3TP Tel:0181 950 6299
Chorleywood Road Cemetery
Chorleywood Rd, Rickmansworth, Hertfordshire, WD3 4EH Tel:01923 772646
Woodwells Cemetery
Buncefield Lane, Hemel Hempstead, Hertfordshire, HP2 7HY Tel:01442 252856
Harwood Park Crematorium Ltd,
Watton Rd, Stevenage, Hertfordshire, SG2 8XT Tel:01438 815555
Hatfield Road Cemetery
Hatfield Rd, St. Albans, Hertfordshire, AL1 3LA Tel:01727 819362
North Watford Cemetery
North Western Avenue, Watford, Hertfordshire, WD2 6AW Tel:01923 672157
Tring Cemetery
Aylesbury Rd, Aylesbury, Tring, Hertfordshire, HP23 4DH Tel:01442 822248
Vicarage Road Cemetery
Vicarage Rd, Watford, Hertfordshire, WD1 8EJ Tel:01923 225147
Watton Rd Cemetery
Watton Rd, Ware, Hertfordshire, SG12 0AX Tel:01920 463261
West Herts Crematorium
High Elms Lane, Watford, Hertfordshire, WD2 7JS Tel:01923 673285
Western Synagogue Cemetery
Cheshunt Cemetery
Bulls Cross Ride, Waltham Cross, Hertfordshire, EN7 5HT Tel:01992 717820
Weston Road Cemetery
Weston Rd, Stevenage, Hertfordshire, SG1 4DE Tel:01438 367109
Woodcock Hill Cemetery
Lodge, Woodcock Hill, Harefield Rd, Rickmansworth, Hertfordshire, WD3 1PT
Tel:01923 775188
Isle Of Wight
Shanklin Cemetery
1 Cemetery Rd, Lake Sandown, Sandown PO36 9NN Tel:01983 403743
Kent
Barham Crematorium
Canterbury Rd, Barham, Canterbury, Kent, CT4 6QU Tel:01227 831351

Beckenham Crematorium & Cemetery
Elmers End Rd, Beckenham, Kent, BR3 4TD Tel:0208650 0322
Chartham Cemetery Lodge
Ashford Rd, Chartham, Canterbury, Kent, CT4 7NY Tel:01227 738211
Gravesham Borough Council,
Old Rd West, Gravesend, Kent, DA11 0LS Tel:01474 337491
Hawkinge Cemetery & Crematorium
Aerodrome Rd, Hawkinge, Folkestone, Kent, CT18 7AG Tel:01303 892215
Kent & Sussex Crematorium
Benhall Mill Rd., Tunbridge Wells, Kent, TN2 5JH Tel:01892 523894
Kent County Crematorium plc
Newcourt Wood, Charing, Ashford, Kent, TN27 0EB Tel:01233 712443
Medway Crematorium
Robin Hood Lane, Blue Bell Hill, Chatham, Kent, ME5 9QU Tel:01634 861639
Northfleet Cemetery
Springhead Rd, Northfleet, Gravesend, Kent, DA11 8HW Tel:01474 533260
Snodland Cemetery
Cemetery Cottage, Cemetery Rd, Snodland, Kent, ME6 5DN Tel:01634 240764
Thanet Crematorium
Manston Rd, Margate, Kent, CT9 4LY Tel:01843 224492
The Cremation Society
Brecon House, 16 Albion Place, Maidstone, Kent, ME14 5DZ Tel:01622 688292
Vinters Park Crematorium
Bearstead Rd, Weavering, Maidstone, Kent, ME14 5LG Tel:01622 738172
Lancashire
Accrington Cemetry & Crematorium
Burnley Rd, Accrington, Lancashire, BB5 6HA Tel:01254 232933
Audenshaw Cemetery
Cemetery Rd, Audenshaw, Manchester, Lancashire, M34 5AII Tel:0161 336 2675
Blackley Cemetery & Crematorium
Victoria Avenue, Manchester, M9 8 Tel:0161 740 5359
Burnley Cemetery
Rossendale Rd, Burnley BB11 5DD Tel:01282 435411
Carleton Crematorium
Stocks Lane, Carleton, Poulton-Le-Fylde, Lancashire, FY6 7QS Tel:01253 882541
Central & North Manchester Synagogue Jewish Cemetery
Rainsough Brow, Prestwich, Manchester M25 9XW Tel:0161 773 2641
Central & North Manchester Synagogue Jewish Cemetery
Rochdale Rd, Manchester M9 6FQ Tel:0161 740 2317
Chadderton Cemetery
Cemetery Lodge, Middleton Rd, Oldham OL9 7el:0161 624 2301
Gidlow Cemetery
Gidlow Lane, Standish, Wigan, Lancashire, WN6 8RT Tel:01257 424127
Greenacres Cemetery
Greenacres Rd, Oldham, Lancashire, OL4 3HT Tel:0161 624 2294
Hollinwood Cemetery
Roman Rd, Hollinwood, Oldham, Lancashire, OL8 3LU Tel:0161 681 1312
Howe Bridge Crematorium
Lovers Lane, Atherton, Manchester, Lancashire, M46 0PZ Tel:01942 870811
Leigh Cemetery
Manchester Rd, Leigh WN7 2 Tel:01942 671560

London
Brockley Ladywell Hithergreen & Grove Park Cemeteries
Verdant Lane, Catford, London , SE6 1TP Tel:0181 697 2555
Brompton Cemetery
Fulham Rd, London, SW10 9UG Tel:0171 352 1201
Cemetery Management Ltd
38 Uxbridge Rd, London, W7 3PP Tel:0181 567 0913
Charlton Cemetery
Cemetery Lane, London, SE7 8DZ Tel:0181 854 0235
City of London Cemetery & Crematorium
Aldersbrook Rd, London, E12 5DQ Tel:0181 530 2151
Coroners Court
8 Ladywell Rd, Lewisham, London, SE13 7UW Tel:0208690 5138
East London Cemetery Co.Ltd
Grange Rd, London, E13 0HB Tel:0171 476 5109
Edmonton Cemetery
Church St, Edmonton, London, N9 9HP Tel:0208360 2157

Lower Ince Crematorium
Warrington Rd, Lower Ince, Wigan, Lancashire, WN3 4NH Tel:01942 866455
Lytham Park Cemetery & Cremarotium
Regent Avenue, Lytham St. Annes, Lancashire, FY8 4AB Tel:01253 735429
Manchester Crematorium Ltd
Barlow Moor Rd, Manchester, Lancashire, M21 7GZ Tel:0161 881 5269
Middleton New Cemetery
Boarshaw Rd, Middleton, Manchester, Lancashire, M24 6 Tel:0161 655 3765
New Manchester Woodland Cemetery
City Rd, Ellenbrook, Worsley, Manchester M28 1BD Tel:0161 790 1300
Overdale Crematorium
Overdale Drive, Chorley New Rd, Heaton, Bolton BL1 5BU Tel:01204 840214
Padiham Public Cemetery
St. Johns Rd, Padiham, Burnley, Lancashire, BB12 7BN Tel:01282 778139
Preston Cemetery
New Hall Lane, Preston, Lancashire, PR1 4SY Tel:01772 794585
Preston Crematorium
Longridge Rd, Ribbleton, Preston, Lancashire, PR2 6RL Tel:01772 792391
Rochdale Cemetery
Bury Rd, Rochdale, Lancashire, OL11 4DG Tel:01706 645219
Southern Cemetery
Barlow Moor Rd, Manchester, Lancashire, M21 7GL Tel:0161 881 2208
St. Mary's Catholic Cemetery
Manchester Rd, Wardley, Manchester, Lancashire, M28 2UJ Tel:0161 794 2194
St.Joseph's Cemetery
Moston Lane, Manchester, Lancashire, M40 9QL Tel:0161 681 1582
United Synagogue Burial Ground
Worsley Hill Farm Whitefield, Manchester, M45 7ED Tel:0161 766 2065
Whitworth Cemetery
Edward St, Whitworth, Rochdale, Lancashire, OL16 2EJ Tel:01706 852352
Leicestershire
Melton Mowbray Cemetery
Cemetery Lodge, Thorpe Rd, Melton Mowbray LE13 1SH Tel:01664 562223
Loughborough Crematorium
Leicester Rd, Loughborough, Leicestershire, LE11 2AF Tel:01743 353046
Saffron Hill Cemetery
Stonesby Avenue, Leicester, Leicestershire, LE2 6TY Tel:0116 222 1049
Lincolnshire
Boston Crematorium
Marian Rd, Boston, Lincolnshire, PE21 9HA Tel:01205 364612
Bourne Town Cemetery
South Rd, Bourne, Lincolnshire, PE10 9JB Tel:01778 422796
Grantham Cemetery & Crematorium
Harrowby Rd, Grantham, Lincolnshire, NG31 9DT Tel:01476 563083
Horncastle Cemetery
Boston Rd, Horncastle, Lincolnshire, LN9 6NF Tel:01507 527118
Stamford Cemetery
Wichendom, Little Casterton Rd, Stamford, Lincolnshire, PE9 1BB Tel:01780 762316
Tyler Landscapes, Newport Cemetery
Manor Rd, Newport, Lincoln, Lincolnshire, LN4 1RT Tel:01522 525195

Eltham Cemetery & Crematorium
Crown Woods Way, Eltham, London, SE9 2RF Tel:0181 850 2921 (Cemetery)
Tel:0181 850 7046 (Crematorium)
Gap Road Cemetery
Gap Rd, London, SW19 8JF Tel:0208879 0701
Golders Green Crematorium
62 Hoop Lane, London, NW11 7NL Tel:0208455 2374
Greenwich Cemetery
Well Hall Rd, London, SE9 6TZ Tel:0181 856 8666
London Borough of Hackney Mortuary
Lower Clapton Rd, London, E5 8EQ Tel:0181 985 2808
Abney Park Cemetery
High St, Stoke Newington, London, N16 0LH Tel:0171 275 7557
Hendon Cemetery & Crematorium
Holders Hill Rd, London, NW7 1NB Tel:0181 346 0657
Highgate Cemetery
Swains Lane, London, N6 6PJ Tel:0181 340 1834

Honor Oak Crematorium
Brenchley Gardens, London, SE23 3RB Tel:0171 639 7499
Islington Cemetery & Crematorium
High Rd, East Finchley, London, N2 9AG Tel:0208883 1230
Kensal Green Cemetery
Harrow Rd, London, W10 4RA Tel:0181 969 0152
L.B.S Cemeteries
Brenchley Gardens, London, SE23 3RD Tel:0171 639 3121
Lambeth Cemetery and Crematorium
Cemetary Lodge, Blackshaw Rd, Tooting, London, SW17 0BY Tel:0181 672 1390
Lewisham Crematorium
Verdant Lane, London, SE6 1TP Tel:0208698 4955
Liberal Jewish Cemetery
The Lodge, Pound Lane, London, NW10 2HG Tel:0181 459 1635
Manor Park Cemetery Co.Ltd
Sebert Rd, Forest Gate, London, E7 0NP Tel:0181 534 1486
New Southgate Cemetery & Crematorium Ltd
98 Brunswick Park Rd, London, N11 1JJ Tel:0181 361 1713
London Borough of Newham Cemeteries
High St South, London, E6 6ET Tel:0181 472 9111
Plumstead Cemetery
Wickham Lane, London, SE2 0NS Tel:0181 854 0785
Putney Vale Cemetery & Crematorium
Kingston Rd, London, SW15 3SB Tel:0181 788 2113
South London Crematorium & Streatham Park Cemetery
Rowan Rd, London, SW16 5JG Tel:0181 764 2255

Merseyside
Anfield Crematorium
Priory Rd, Anfield, Liverpool, Merseyside, L4 2SL Tel:0151 263 3267
Southport Cemeteries & Crematoria
Southport Rd, Scarisbrick, Southport, Merseyside, PR8 5JQ Tel:01704 533443
St.Helens Cemetery & Crematorium
Rainford Rd, Windle, St. Helens, Merseyside, WA10 6DF Tel:01744 26567
Thornton Garden Of Rest
Lydiate Lane, Thornton, Liverpool, Merseyside, L23 1TP Tel:0151 924 5143
Middlesex
Adath Yisroel Synagogue & Burial Society
Carterhatch Lane, Enfield, Middlesex, EN1 4BG Tel:0181 363 3384
Breakspear Crematorium
Breakspear Rd, Ruislip, Middlesex, HA4 7SJ Tel:01895 632843
Enfield Crematorium
Great Cambridge Rd, Enfield, Middlesex, EN1 4DS Tel:0181 363 8324
Heston & Isleworth Borough Cemetry
190 Powder Mill Lane, Twickenham, Middlesex, TW2 6EJ Tel:0181 894 3830
South West Middlesex Crematorium
Hounslow Rd, Hanworth, Feltham, Middlesex, TW13 5JH Tel:0208894 9001
Spelthorne Borough Council
Green Way, Sunbury-On-Thames, Middlesex, TW16 6NW Tel:01932 780244
Norfolk
Colney Wood Memorial Park
Colney Hall, Watton Rd, Norwich, Norfolk, NR4 7TY Tel:01603 811556
Mintlyn Crematorium
Lynn Rd, Bawsey, King's Lynn, Norfolk, PE32 1HB Tel:01553 630533
Norwich & Norfolk Crematoria - St. Faiths & Earlham
75 Manor Rd, Horsham St. Faith, Norwich, Norfolk, NR10 3LF Tel:01603 898264
Sprowston Cemetery
Church Lane, Sprowston, Norwich, Norfolk, NR7 8AU Tel:01603 425354
East Yorkshire
East Riding Crematorium Ltd
Octon Cross Rd, Langtoft, Driffield, East Yorkshire YO25 3BL Tel:01377 267604
East Yorkshire Council
Cemetery Lodge, Sewerby Rd, Bridlington, East Yorkshire YO16 7DS
Tel:01262 672138
Goole Cemetery
Hook Rd, Goole DN14 5LU Tel:01405 762725
North Yorkshire
Fulford New Cemetery
Cemetery Lodge, Fordlands Rd, Fulford, York YO19 4QG Tel:01904 633151

St. Marylebone Crematorium
East End Rd, Finchley, London, N2 0RZ Tel:0208343 2233
St. Pancras Cemetery (London Borough Of Camden)
High Rd, East Finchley, London, N2 9AG Tel:0181 883 1231
St. Patrick's Catholic Cemetery
Langthorne Rd, London, E11 4HL Tel:0181 539 2451
St.Mary's Catholic Cemetery
Harrow Rd, London, NW10 5NU Tel:0181 969 1145
Tottenham Park Cemetery
Montagu Rd, Edmonton, London, N18 2NF Tel:0181 807 1617
United Synagogue
Beaconsfield Rd, Willesden, London, NW10 2JE Tel:0208459 0394
Chingford Mount Cemetery
Old Church Rd, London, E4 6ST Tel:0181 524 5030
West End Chesed V'Ameth Burial Society
3 Rowan Rd, London, SW16 5JF Tel:0181 764 1566
West Ham Cemetery
Cemetery Rd, London, E7 9DG Tel:0208534 1566
West London Synagogue
Hoop Lane, London, NW11 7NJ Tel:0208455 2569
West Norwood Cemetery & Crematorium
Norwood Rd, London, SE27 9AJ Tel:0207926 7900
Woodgrange Park Cemetery
Romford Rd, London, E7 8AF Tel:0181 472 3433
Woolwich Cemetery
Kings Highway, London, SE18 2BJ Tel:0181 854 0740

Mowthorpe Garden of Rest
Southwood Farm, Terrington, York YO60 6QB Tel:01653 648459
Stonefall Cemetery & Cremetoria
Wetherby Rd, Harrogate, North Yorkshire, HG3 1DE Tel:01423 883523
Waltonwrays Cemetery
The Gatehouse, Carlton Rd, Skipton, North Yorkshire, BD23 3BT Tel:01756 793168
York Cemetery
Gate House, Cemetery Rd, York YO10 5AF Tel:01904 610578
Northamptonshire
Counties Crematorium
Towcester Rd, Milton Malsor, Northampton NN4 9RN Tel:01604 858280
Dallington Cemetery
Harlstone Rd, Dallington, Northampton NN5 Tel:01604 751589
Northumberland
Alnwick Cemetary, Cemetary Lodge, South Rd, Alnwick, Northumberland,
NE66 2PH Tel:01665 602598
Blyth Cemetery
Links Rd, Blyth NE24 3PJ Tel:01670 369623
Cowpen Cemetery
Cowpen Rd, Blyth NE24 5SZ Tel:01670 352107
Embleton Joint Burial Committee
Spitalford, Embleton, Alnwick, Northumberland, NE66 3DW Tel:01665 576632
Haltwhistle & District Joint Burial Committee
Cemetery Lodge, Haltwhistle NE49 0LF Tel:01434 320266
Rothbury Cemetery
Cemetery Lodge, Whitton Rd , Rothbury, Morpeth, Northumberland, NE65 7RX
Tel:01669 620451
Nottinghamshire
Bramcote Crematorium
Coventry Lane, Beeston, Nottingham, Nottinghamshire, NG9 3GJ
Tel:0115 922 1837
Mansfield & District Crematorium
Derby Rd, Mansfield NG18 5BJ Tel:01623 621811
Northern Cemetery
Hempshill Lane, Bulwell NG6 8PF Tel:0115 915 3245
Shirebrook Town Council
Common Lane, Shirebrook, Mansfield,NG20 8PA Tel:01623 742509
Southern Cemetery & Crematoria
Wilford Hill, West Bridgford, Nottingham, Nottinghamshire, NG2 7FE
Tel:0115 915 2340
Tithe Green Woodland Burial Ground
Salterford Lane, Calverton, Nottingham NG14 6NZ Tel:01623 882210

Oxfordshire
Oxford Crematorium Ltd
Bayswater Rd, Headington OX3 9RZ Tel:01865 351255
Shropshire
Bridgnorth Cemetery
Mill St, Bridgnorth WV15 5NG Tel:01746 762386
Emstrey Crematorium
London Rd, Shrewsbury SY2 6PS Tel:01743 359883
Hadley Cemetery
85 Hadley Park Rd, Hadley, Telford, Shropshire, TF1 4PY Tel:01952 223418
Longden Road Cemetery
Longden Rd, Shrewsbury SY3 7HS Tel:01743 353046
Market Drayton Burial Committee
Cemetery Lodge, Cemetery Rd, Market Drayton, TF9 3BD Tel:01630 652833
Oswestry Cemetery
Cemetery Lodge
Victoria Rd, Oswestry SY11 2HU Tel:01691 652013
Whitchurch Joint Cemetery Board
The Cemetery Lodge, Mile Bank Rd, Whitchurch SY13 4JY Tel:01948 665477
Somerset
Burnham Area Burial Board
The Old Courthouse, Jaycroft Rd, Burnham-On-Sea TA8 1LE Tel:01278 795111
Chard Burial Joint Committee
The Chapel, Combe St, Chard TA20 1JH Tel:01460 62170
Minehead Cemetery
Porlock Rd, Woodcombe, Minehead, Somerset, TA24 8RY Tel:01643 705243
Sedgemoor District Council Cemetery
Quantock Rd, Bridgwater, Somerset, TA6 7EJ Tel:01278 423993
Taunton Deane Cemeteries & Crematorium
Wellington New Rd, Taunton TA1 5NE Tel:01823 284811
Wells Burial Joint Committee
127 Portway, Wells, Somerset, BA5 1LY Tel:01749 672049
Yeovil Cemetery
Preston Rd, Yeovil, Somerset, BA21 3AG Tel:01935 423742
Yeovil Crematorium
Bunford Lane, Yeovil BA20 2EJ Tel:01935 476718
Lincolnshire
Cleethorpes Cemetery
Trinity Rd, Cleethorpes DN35 8 Tel:01472 691685
Grimsby Crematorium
Weelsby Avenue, Grimsby DN32 0BB Tel:01472 324869
Woodlands Crematorium
Brumby Wood Lane, Scunthorpe DN17 1SP Tel:01724 280289
South Yorkshire
Barnsley Crematorium & Cemetery
Doncaster Rd, Ardsley, Barnsley, South Yorkshire, S71 5EH Tel:01226 206053
City Road Cemetery
City Rd, Sheffield, South Yorkshire, S2 1GD Tel:0114 239 6068
Dronfield Cemetery
Cemetery Lodge, 42 Cemetery Rd, Dronfield S18 1XY Tel:01246 412373
Ecclesfield Cemetery
Priory Lane, Ecclesfield, Sheffield, South Yorkshire, S35 9XZ Tel:0114 256 0583
Eckington Cemetery
Sheffield Rd, Eckington, Sheffield, South Yorkshire, S21 4FP Tel:01246 432197
Grenoside Crematorium
5 Skew Hill Lane, Grenoside, Sheffield S35 8RZ Tel:0114 245 3999
Handsworth Cemetery
51 Orgreave Lane, Handsworth, Sheffield S13 9NE Tel:0114 254 0832
Hatfield Cemetery
Cemetery Rd, Hatfield, Doncaster, South Yorkshire, DN7 6LX Tel:01302 840242
Mexborough Cemetery
Cemetery Rd, Mexborough, South Yorkshire, S64 9PN Tel:01709 585184
Rose Hill Crematorium
Cantley Lane, Doncaster, South Yorkshire , DN4 6NE Tel:01302 535191
Rotherham Cemeteries & Crematorium
Ridgeway East, Herringthorpe, Rotherham S65 3NN Tel:01709 850344
Sheffield Cemeteries
City Rd, Sheffield, South Yorkshire, S2 1GD Tel:0114 253 0614
Stainforth Town Council Cemetery
Office, Church Rd, Stainforth, Doncaster DN7 5AA Tel:01302 845158

Staffordshire
Bretby Crematorium
Geary Lane, Bretby, Burton-On-Trent, Staffordshire, DE15 0QE Tel:01283 221505
Cannock Cemetery
Cemetery Lodge, 160 Pye Green Rd, Cannock WS11 2SJ Tel:01543 503176
Carmountside Crematorium
Leek Rd, Milton, Stoke-On-Trent ST2 7AB Tel:01782 235050
Leek Cemetery
Condlyffe Rd, Leek ST13 5PP Tel:01538 382616
Newcastle Cemetery
Lymewood Grove, Newcastle ST5 2EH Tel:01782 616379
Newcastle Crematorium
Chatterley Close, Bradwell, Newcastle, Staffordshire, ST5 8LE Tel:01782 635498
Stafford Crematorium
Tixall Rd, Stafford ST18 0XZ Tel:01785 242594
Stapenhill Cemetery
38 Stapenhill Rd, Burton-On-Trent DE15 9AE Tel:01283 508572
Stilecop Cematary
Stilecop Rd, Rugeley WS15 1ND Tel:01889 577739
Uttoxeter Town Council, Cemetery
Lodge, Stafford Rd, Uttoxeter ST14 8DS Tel:01889 563374
Suffolk
Brinkley Woodland Cemetery
147 All Saints Rd, Newmarket CB8 8HH Tel:01638 600693
Bury St. Edmunds Cemetery
91 Kings Rd, Bury St. Edmunds, Suffolk, IP33 3DT Tel:01284 754447
Hadleigh Town Council
Friars Rd, Hadleigh, Ipswich IP7 6DF Tel:01473 822034
Haverhill Cemetery
Withersfield Rd, Haverhill CB9 9HF Tel:01440 703810
Ipswich Cemetery & Crematorium
Cemetery Rd, Ipswich, Suffolk, IP4 2HN Tel:01473 252931
Leiston Cemetery
Waterloo Avenue, Leiston IP16 4EH Tel:01728 831043
West Suffolk Crematorium
Risby, Bury St. Edmunds IP28 6RR Tel:01284 755118
Surrey
American Cemetery
Cemetery Pales, Brookwood, Woking, Surrey, GU24 0BL Tel:01483 473237
Bandon Hill Cemetery
Plough Lane, Wallington SM6 8JQ Tel:0181 647 1024
Brookwood Cemetery
Cemetery Pales, Brookwood, Woking, Surrey, GU24 0BL Tel:01483 472222
Confederation of Burial Authorities
The Gate House, Kew Meadow Path, Richmond TW9 4EN Tel:0181 392 9487
Guildford Crematorium & Cemetaries
Broadwater, New Pond Rd, Godalming, Godalming GU7 3DB Tel:01483 444711
Kingston Cemetary & Crematorium
Bonner Hill Rd, Kingston Upon Thames, Surrey, KT1 3EZ Tel:0208546 4462
London Road Cemetery
Figs Marsh, London Rd, Mitcham CR4 3 Tel:0208648 4115
Merton & Sutton Joint Cemetery
Garth Rd, Morden, Surrey, SM4 4LL Tel:0208337 4420
Mortlake Crematorium Board
Kew Meadow Path, Town Mead Rd, Richmond TW9 4EN Tel:0181 876 8056
Mount Cemetery
Weyside Rd, Guildford GU1 1HZ Tel:01483 561927
North East Surrey Crematorium
Lower Morden Lane, Morden, Surrey, SM4 4NU Tel:0181 337 4835
Randalls Park Crematorium
Randalls Rd, Leatherhead KT22 0AG Tel:01372 373813
Red Stone Cemetery
Philanthropic Rd, Redhill RH1 4DN Tel:01737 761592
Reigate Road Cemetery
Reigate Rd, Dorking, Surrey, RH4 1QF Tel:01306 883769
London Borough of Richmond Cemeteries
Sheen Rd, Richmond, Surrey, TW10 5BJ Tel:0208876 4511
Surbiton Cemetery
Lower Marsh Lane, Kingston Upon Thames, Surrey, KT1 3BN Tel:0208546 4463

Sutton & Cuddington Cemetery
Alcom Close, Sutton Common Rd, Sutton, Surrey, SM3 9PX Tel:0181 644 9437
The Godalming Joint Burial Committee
New Cemetery Lodge, Ockford Ridge, Godalming GU7 2NP Tel:01483 421559
Woking Crematorium
Hermitage Rd, Woking, Surrey, GU21 1TJ Tel:01483 472197
Tyne And Wear
Byker & Heaton Cemetery
18 Benton Rd, Heaton, Newcastle Upon Tyne NE7 7DS Tel:0191 2662017
Gateshead East Cemetery
Cemetery Rd, Gateshead, Tyne And Wear, NE8 4HJ Tel:0191 4771819
Heworth Cemetery
Sunderland Rd, Felling, Gateshead, Tyne And Wear, NE10 0NT Tel:0191 4697851
Longbenton Cemetery
Longbenton, Newcastle Upon Tyne NE12 8EY Tel:0191 2661261
Whitley Bay Cemetery
Blyth Rd, Whitley Bay, NE26 4NH Tel:0191 2533664
Earsdon Cemetery
Earsdon, Whitley Bay NE25 9LR Tel:0191 2529455
Preston Cemetery & Tynemouth Crematorium
Walton Avenue, North Shields NE29 9NJ Tel:0191 2005861
Saltwell Crematorium
Saltwell Rd South, Gateshead NE8 4TQ Tel:0191 4910553
St. Andrews Cemetery
1-2, Great North Rd, Jesmond, Newcastle -U- Tyne r,NE2 3BU Tel:0191 2810953
St. Johns & Elswick Cemetery
Elswick Rd, Newcastle Upon Tyne NE4 8DL Tel:0191 2734127
St. Nicholas Cemetery
Wingrove Avenue Back, Newcastle Upon Tyne, NE4 9AP Tel:0191 2735112
Union Hall Cemetery
Union Hall Rd, Newcastle Upon Tyne NE15 7JS Tel:0191 2674398
West Road Cemetery
West Rd, Newcastle Upon Tyne NE5 2JL Tel:0191 2744737
Warwickshire
Mid-Warwickshire Crematorium & Cemeteries
Oakley Wood, Bishops Tachbrook, Leamington Spa CV33 9QP Tel:01926 651418
Nuneaton Cemetery & Crematorium
Oaston Rd, Nuneaton, Warwickshire, CV11 6JZ Tel:01203 376120
Stratford-on-Avon Cemetery
Evesham Rd, Stratford-Upon-Avon, Warwickshire, CV37 9AA Tel:01789 292676
West Midlands
Birmingham Crematorium
389 Walsall Rd, Perry Barr, Birmingham B42 2LR Tel:0121 356 9476
Birmingham Hebrew Congregation Cemetery
The Ridgeway, Erdington, Birmingham B23 7TD Tel:0121 356 4615
Brandwood End Cemetery
Woodthorpe Rd, Kings Heath, Birmingham B14 6EQ Tel:0121 444 1328
Coventry Bereavement Services
The Cemeteries & Crematorium Office, Cannon Hill Rd, Canley, Coventry, West Midlands, CV4 7DF Tel:01203 418055
Grave Care
5 Ennersdale Close, Coleshill, Birmingham B46 1HA Tel:01675 463385
Handsworth Cemetery
Oxhill Rd, Birmingham, West Midlands, B21 8JT Tel:0121 554 0096
Lodge Hill Cemetery & Cremetorium
Weoley Park Rd, Birmingham, West Midlands, B29 5AA Tel:0121 472 1575
Quinton Cemetery
Halesowen Rd, Halesowen B62 9AF Tel:0121 422 2023
Stourbridge Cemetery & Crematorium
South Rd, Stourbridge, West Midlands, DY8 3RQ Tel:01384 813985
Streetly Cemetery & Crematorium
Little Hardwick Rd, Aldridge, Walsall, West Midlands, WS9 0SG Tel:0121 353 7228
Sutton Coldfield Cemetery
Rectory Rd, Sutton Coldfield, West Midlands, B75 7RP Tel:0121 378 0224
Sutton Coldfield Cremetorium
Tamworth Rd, Four Oaks, Sutton Coldfield B75 6LG Tel:0121 308 3812
West Bromwich Crematorium
Forge Lane, West Bromwich, West Midlands, B71 3SX Tel:0121 588 2160
Willenhall Lawn Cemetery
Bentley Lane, Willenhall, West Midlands, WV12 4AE Tel:01902 368621

Witton Cemetery
Moor Lane Witton, Birmingham, West Midlands, B6 7AE Tel:0121 356 4363
Woodlands Cemetery
Birmingham Rd, Coleshill, Birmingham, West Midlands, B46 2ET Tel:01675 464835
West Sussex
Chichester Crematorium
Westhampnett Rd, Chichester, West Sussex, PO19 4UH Tel:01243 787755
Midhurst Burial Authority
Cemetery Lodge, Carron Lane, Midhurst, West Sussex, GU29 9LF
Tel:01730 812758
Surrey & Sussex Crematorium
Balcombe Rd, Crawley, West Sussex, RH10 3NQ Tel:01293 888930
Worthing Crematorium & Cemeteries
Horsham Rd, Findon, Worthing, West Sussex, BN14 0RG Tel:01903 872678
West Yorkshire
Brighouse Cemetery
Cemetery Lodge, 132 Lightcliffe Rd, Brighouse HD6 2HY Tel:01484 715183
Cottingly Hall
Elland Rd, Leeds, West Yorkshire, LS11 0 Tel:0113 271 6101
Dewsbury Moor Crematorium
Heckmondwike Rd, Dewsbury, West Yorkshire, WF13 3PL Tel:01924 325180
Exley Lane Cemetery
Exley Lane, Elland, West Yorkshire, HX5 0SW Tel:01422 372449
Killingbeck Cemetery
York Rd, Killingbeck, Leeds, West Yorkshire, LS14 6AB Tel:0113 264 5247
Lawnswood Cemetery & Crematorium
Otley Rd, Adel, Leeds, West Yorkshire, LS16 6AH Tel:0113 267 3188
Leeds Jewish Workers Co-Op Society
717 Whitehall Rd, New Farnley, Leeds LS12 6JL Tel:0113 285 2521
Moorthorpe Cemetery
Barnsley Rd, Moorthorpe, Pontefract, West Yorkshire, WF9 2BP Tel:01977 642433
Nab Wood Crematorium
Bingley Rd, Shipley, West Yorkshire, BD18 4DB Tel:01274 584109
Oakworth Crematorium
Wide Lane, Oakworth, Keighley, West Yorkshire, BD22 0RJ Tel:01535 603162
Park Wood Crematorium
Park Rd, Elland, West Yorkshire, HX5 9HZ Tel:01422 372293
Pontefract Crematorium
Wakefield Rd, Pontefract, West Yorkshire, WF8 4HA Tel:01977 723455
Rawdon Crematorium
Leeds Rd, Rawdon, Leeds, West Yorkshire, LS19 6JP Tel:0113 250 2904
Scholemoor Cemetery & Crematorium
Necropolis Rd, Bradford, West Yorkshire, BD7 2PS Tel:01274 571313
Sowerby Bridge Cemetery
Sowerby New Rd, Sowerby Bridge HX6 1LQ Tel:01422 831193
United Hebrew Congregation Leeds, Jewish Cemetery
Gelderd Rd, Leeds, West Yorkshire, LS7 4BU Tel:0113 263 8684
Wakefield Crematorium
Standbridge Lane, Crigglestone, Wakefield WF4 3JA Tel:01924 303380
Wetherby Cemetery
Sexton House, Hallfield Lane, Wetherby LS22 6JQ Tel:01937 582451
Wiltshire
Box Cemetery
Bath Rd, Box, Corsham, Wiltshire, SN13 8AA Tel:01225 742476
Devizes & Roundway Joint Burial Committee
Cemetry Lodge, Rotherstone, Devizes SN10 2DE Tel:01380 722821
Salisbury Crematorium
Barrington Rd, Salisbury, Wiltshire, SP1 3JB Tel:01722 333632
Chippenham Cemetery
London Road, Chippenham, Wiltshire, SN15 3RD Tel:01249 652728
West Wiltshire Crematorium
Devizes Rd, Semington, Trowbridge BA14 7QH Tel:01380 871101
Wirral
Landican Cemetery
Arrowe Park Rd, Birkenhead, Wirral, CH49 5LW Tel:0151 677 2361
Worcestershire
Pershore Cemetery
Defford Rd, Pershore, Worcestershire, WR10 3BX Tel:01386 552043
Redith Crematorium & Abbey Cemetary
Bordesley Lane, Redditch, Worcestershire, B97 6RR Tel:01527 62174

Westall Park Woodland Burial
Holberrow Green, Redditch, Worcestershire, B96 6JY Tel:01386 792806

Wales
Clwyd
Bron-y-Nant Crematorium
Dinerth Rd, Colwyn Bay, LL28 4YN Tel:01492 544677
Mold Town Cemetery
Cemetery Lodge, Alexandra Rd, Mold, Clwyd, CH7 1HJ Tel:01352 753820
Wrexham Cemeteries & Crematorium
Pentre Bychan, Wrexham, Clwyd, LL14 4EP Tel:01978 840068
Wrexham Cemetery Lodge
Ruabon Rd, Wrexham LL13 7NY Tel:01978 263159
Aberystwyth Crematorium
Clarach Rd, Aberystwyth, Dyfed, SY23 3DG Tel:01970 626942
Dyfed
Carmarthen Cemetery
Elim Rd, Carmarthen, Dyfed, SA31 1TX Tel:01267 234134
Llanelli District Cemetery
Swansea Rd, Llanelli, Dyfed, SA15 3EX Tel:01554 773710
Milford Haven Cemetery
The Cemetery, Milford Haven, Dyfed, SA73 2RP Tel:01646 693324
Gwent
Ebbw Vale Cemetery
Waun-y-Pound Rd, Ebbw Vale, Gwent, NP23 6LE Tel:01495 302187
Grave Tending Service
14 Kelly Rd, Newport, Gwent, NP19 7RF Tel:01633 667510
Christchurch Cemetry
Christchurch, Newport, Gwent, NP18 1JJ Tel:01633 277566
Gwent Crematorium
Treherbert Rd, Croesyceliog, Cwmbran, Gwent, NP44 2BZ Tel:01633 482784
Gwynedd
Bangor Crematorium
Llandygai Rd, Bangor, Gwynedd, LL57 4HP Tel:01248 370500
Mid Glamorgan
Cemetery Section, Monks St, Aberdare, Mid Glamorgan, CF44 7PA
Tel:01685 885345

Scotland
Aberdeenshire
Springbank Cemetery
Countesswells Rd, Springbank, Aberdeen, Aberdeenshire, AB15 7YH
Tel:01224 317323
St. Peter's Cemetery
King St, Aberdeen AB24 3BX Tel:01224 638490
Trinity Cemetery
Erroll St, Aberdeen AB24 5PP Tel:01224 633747
Angus
Barnhill Cemetery
27 Strathmore St, Broughty Ferry, Dundee, Angus, DD5 2NY Tel:01382 477139
Dundee Crematorium
Macalpine Rd, Dundee, Angus, DD3 8 Tel:01382 825601
Park Grove Crematorium
Douglasmuir, Friocheim, Arbroath, Angus, DD11 4UN Tel:01241 828959
Ayrshire
Ardrossan Cemetery
Sorbie Rd, Ardrossan KA22 8AQ Tel:01294 463133
Dreghorn Cemetery
Station Rd, Dreghorn, Irvine KA11 4AJ Tel:01294 211101
Hawkhill Cemetery
Kilwinning Rd, Saltcoats, Stevenston KA20 3DE Tel:01294 465241
Holmsford Bridge Crematorium
Dreghorn, Irvine, Ayrshire, KA11 4EF Tel:01294 214720
Kilwinning Cemetery
Bridgend, Kilwinning KA13 7LY Tel:01294 552102
Largs Cemetery
Greenock Rd, Largs KA30 8NG Tel:01475 673149
Maybole Cemetery
Crosshill Rd, Maybole, Ayrshire, KA19 7BN Tel:01655 882217

Worcester Crematorium
Astwood Rd, Tintern Avenue, Worcester, Worcestershire, WR3 8HA
Tel:01905 22633

Coychurch Crematorium
Coychurch, Bridgend, Mid Glamorgan, CF35 6AB Tel:01656 656605
Ferndale Cemetery
Cemetery Lodge, Highfield, Ferndale, Mid Glamorgan, CF43 4TD
Tel:01443 730321
Llwydcoed Crematorium
Llwydcoed, Aberdare, Mid Glamorgan, CF44 0DJ Tel:01685 874115
Fax:01685 874115
Maesteg Cemetery
Cemetery Rd, Maesteg, Mid Glamorgan, CF34 0DN Tel:01656 735485
Penrhys Cemetery
Cemetery Lodge, Penrhys, Tylorstown, Ferndale CF43 3PN Tel:01443 730465
Trane Cemetery
Gilfach Rd, Tonyrefail, Porth, Mid Glamorgan, CF39 8HL Tel:01443 670280
Treorchy Cemetery
The Lodge, Cemetery Rd, Treorchy CF42 6TB Tel:01443 772336
Ynysybwl Cemetery
Heol Y Plwyf, Ynysybwl, Pontypridd, CF37 3HU Tel:01443 790159
South Glamorgan
Bereavement Services, Thornhill Rd, Cardiff CF14 9UA Tel:01222 623294
Cathays Cemetery
Fairoak Rd, Cathays, Cardiff, South Glamorgan, CF24 4PY Tel:01222 750433
Western Cemetery
Cowbridge Rd West, Cardiff, South Glamorgan, CF5 5TF Tel:01222 593231
West Glamorgan
Goytre Cemetery
Goytre Rd, Port Talbot, West Glamorgan, SA13 2YN Tel:01639 883378
Margam Crematorium
Longland Lane, Margam, Port Talbot SA13 2NR Tel:01639 883570
Oystermouth Cemetery
Oystermouth Rd, Swansea, West Glamorgan, SA1 3SW Tel:01792 366302
Wrexham
Coedpoeth Cemetery
The Lodge, Cemetery Rd, Coedpoeth, Wrexham, LL11 3SP Tel:01978 755617

Newmilns Cemetery
Dalwhatswood Rd, Newmilns, Ayrshire, KA16 9LT Tel:01560 320191
Prestwick Cemetery
Shaw Rd, Prestwick, Ayrshire, KA9 2LP Tel:01292 477759
Stewarton Cemetery
Dalry Rd, Stewarton, Kilmarnock, Ayrshire, KA3 3DY Tel:01560 482888
West Kilbride Cemetery
Hunterston Rd, West Kilbride, Ayrshire, KA23 9EX Tel:01294 822818
Banffshire
Moray Crematorium
Clochan, Buckie, Banffshire, AB56 5HQ Tel:01542 850488
Clackmannanshire
Alva Cemetery
The Glebe, Alva, Clackmannanshire, FK12 5HR Tel:01259 760354
Sunnyside Cemetery
Sunnyside Rd, Alloa, Clackmannanshire, FK10 2AP Tel:01259 723575
Tillicoultry Cemetery
Dollar Rd, Tillicoultry, Clackmannanshire, FK13 6PF Tel:01259 750216
Dunbartonshire
Cardross Crematorium
Main Rd, Cardross, Dumbarton, Dunbartonshire, G82 5HD Tel:01389 841313
Dumbarton Cemetery
Stirling Rd, Dumbarton, Dunbartonshire, G82 2PF Tel:01389 762033
Vale Of Leven Cemetery
Overton Rd, Alexandria , Dunbartonshire, G83 0LJ Tel:01389 752266
West Dumbartonshire Crematorium
North Dalnottar, Clydebank, Dunbartonshire, G81 4SL Tel:01389 874318
West Dunbartonshire Crematorium
Roseberry Place, Clydebank, Dunbartonshire, G81 1TG Tel:01389 738709

Fife
Dunfermline Cemetery
Halbeath Rd, Dunfermline, Fife, KY12 7RA Tel:01383 724899
Dunfermline Crematorium
Masterton Rd, Dunfermline, Fife, KY11 8QR Tel:01383 724653
Kirkcaldy Crematorium
Dunnikier Way, Kirkcaldy, Fife, KY1 3PL Tel:01592 260277
Inverness-Shire
Inverness Crematorium
Kilvean Rd, Kilvean, Inverness, Inverness-Shire, IV3 8JN Tel:01463 717849
Isle Of Cumbrae
Millport Cemetery
Golf Rd, Millport, Isle Of Cumbrae, KA28 0HB Tel:01475 530442
Lanarkshire
Airbles Cemetery
Airbles Rd, Motherwell, Lanarkshire, ML1 3AW Tel:01698 263986
Bedlay Cemetery
Bedlay Walk, Moodiesburn, Glasgow, Lanarkshire, G69 0QG Tel:01236 872446
Bothwellpark Cemetery
New Edinburgh Rd, Bellshill, Lanarkshire, ML4 3HH Tel:01698 748146
Cadder Cemetery
Kirkintilloch Rd, Bishopbriggs, Glasgow, Lanarkshire, G64 2QG Tel:0141 772 1977
Cambusnethan Cemetery
Kirk Rd, Wishaw, Lanarkshire, ML2 8NP Tel:01698 384481
Campsie Cemetery
High Church of Scotland, Main St, Lennoxtown, Glasgow, Lanarkshire, G66 7DA Tel:01360 311127
Cardonald Cemetery
547 Mosspark Boulevard, Glasgow, Lanarkshire, G52 1SB Tel:0141 882 1059
Daldowie Crematorium
Daldowie Estate, Uddingston, Glasgow, Lanarkshire, G71 7RU Tel:0141 771 1004
Glasgow Crematorium
Western Necropolis, Tresta Rd, Glasgow G23 5AA Tel:0141 946 2895
Glebe Cemetery
Vicars Rd, Stonehouse, Larkhall, Lanarkshire, ML9 3EB Tel:01698 793674
Glenduffhill Cemetery
278 Hallhill Rd, Glasgow, Lanarkshire, G33 4RU Tel:0141 771 2446

Kilsyth Parish Cemetery
Howe Rd, Kirklands, Glasgow, Lanarkshire, G65 0LA Tel:01236 822144
Larkhall Cemetery
The Cemetery Lodge, Duke St, Larkhall, Lanarkshire, ML9 2AL
Tel:01698 883049
Old Aisle Cemetery
Old Aisle Rd, Kirkintilloch, Glasgow, Lanarkshire, G66 3HH Tel:0141 776 2330
St. Conval's Cemetery
Glasgow Rd, Barrhead, Glasgow, Lanarkshire, G78 1TH Tel:0141 881 1058
St. Patrick's Cemetery
Kings Drive, New Stevenston, Motherwell, Lanarkshire, ML1 4HY
Tel:01698 732938
St. Peters Cemetery
1900 London Rd, Glasgow, Lanarkshire, G32 8RD Tel:0141 778 1183
The Necropolis
50 Cathedral Square, Glasgow, Lanarkshire, G4 0UZ Tel:0141 552 3145
Midlothian
Dean Cemetery
Dean Path, Edinburgh, Midlothian, EH4 3AT Tel:0131 332 1496
Edinburgh Crematorium Ltd
3 Walker St, Edinburgh, Midlothian, EH3 7JY Tel:0131 225 7227
Seafield Cemetery & Crematorium
Seafield Rd, Edinburgh, Midlothian, EH6 7LQ Tel:0131 554 3496
Warriston Crematorium
36 Warriston Rd, Edinburgh, Midlothian, EH7 4HW Tel:0131 552 3020
Perthshire
Perth Crematorium
Crieff Rd, Perth, Perthshire, PH1 2PE Tel:01738 625068
Hawkhead Cemetery
133 Hawkhead Rd, Paisley, Renfrewshire, PA2 7BE Tel:0141 889 3472
Renfrewshire
Paisley Cemetery Co.Ltd
46 Broomlands St, Paisley, Renfrewshire, PA1 2NP Tel:0141 889 2260
Stirlingshire
Larbert Cemetery
25 Muirhead Rd, Larbert, Stirlingshire, FK5 4HZ Tel:01324 557867

Northern Ireland
County Antrim
Ballymena Cemetery
Cushendall Rd, Ballymena BT43 6QE Tel:01266 656026
Ballymoney Cemetery
44 Knock Rd, Ballymoney BT53 6LX Tel:012656 66364
Blaris New Cemetery
25 Blaris Rd, Lisburn, County Antrim, BT27 5RA Tel:01846 607143
Carnmoney Cemetery
10 Prince Charles Way, Newtownabbey BT36 7LG Tel:01232 832428
City Cemetery
511 Falls Rd, Belfast BT12 6DE Tel:028 90323112
City of Belfast Crematorium
Roselawn Cemetery
Ballygowan Rd, Crossnacreevy, Belfast, County Antrim, BT5 7TZ
Tel:01232 448342
Greenland Cemetery
Upper Cairncastle Rd, Larne, County Antrim, BT40 2EG Tel:01574 272543
Milltown Cemetery Office
546 Falls Rd, Belfast, County Antrim, BT12 6EQ Tel:01232 613972
Roselawn Cemetery
127 Ballygowan Rd, Crossnacreevy, Belfast, County Antrim, BT5 7TZ
Tel:01232 448288
County Armagh
Kernan Cemetery
Kernan Hill Rd, Portadown, Craigavon BT63 5YB Tel:028 38339059
Lurgan Cemetery
57 Tandragee Rd, Lurgan, Craigavon BT66 8TL Tel:028 38342853
County Down
Ballyvestry Cemetery
6 Edgewater Millisle, Newtownards, County Down, BT23 5 Tel:01247 882657

Banbridge Public Cemetery
Newry Rd, Banbridge, County Down, BT32 3NB Tel:018206 62623
Bangor Cemetery
62 Newtownards Rd, Bangor, County Down, BT20 4DN Tel:028 91271909
Clandeboye Cemetery
300 Old Belfast Rd, Bangor, County Down, BT19 1RH Tel:028 91853246
Comber Cemetery
31 Newtownards Rd, Comber, Newtownards BT23 5AZ Tel:01247 872529
Struell Cemetery
Old Course Rd, Downpatrick, County Down, BT30 8AQ Tel:01396 613086
Lough Inch Cemetery
Riverside Rd, Ballynahinch, County Down, BT24 8JB Tel:01238 562987
Kirkistown Cemetary
Main Rd, Portavogie, Newtownards, County Down, BT22 1EL Tel:012477 71773
Movilla Cemetary
Movilla Rd, Newtownards, County Down, BT23 8EY Tel:01247 812276
Redburn Cemetery
Old Holywood Rd, Holywood, County Down, BT18 9QH Tel:01232 425547
Whitechurch Cemetary
19 Dunover Rd, Newtownards, County Down, BT22 2LE Tel:012477 58659
County Londonderry
Altnagelvin Cemetery
Church Brae, Altnagelvin, Londonderry, County Londonderry, BT47 3QG
Tel:01504 343351
City Cemetery
Lone Moor Rd, Londonderry, County Londonderry, BT48 9LA Tel:01504 362615
County Tyrone
Greenhill Cemetery
Mountjoy Rd, Omagh, County Tyrone, BT79 7BL Tel:01662 244918
Westland Road Cemetery
Westland Rd, Cookstown, County Tyrone, BT80 8BX Tel:016487 66087

About the Editors

Robert Blatchford
has been involved in genealogy for several years. He is Chairman of The City of York & District Family History Society, a member of Cleveland, Devon, Dyfed, Glamorgan and Gwent Family History Societies. He is also Vice Chairman of the North East Group of Family History Societies. He has undertaken research in the United Kingdom & Australia.

Geoffrey Heslop
has also been involved in Genealogy for many years. He is a member of The City of York & District Family History Society, Cumbria Family History Society as well as several other Societies. He is an experienced researcher and has undertaken research in the United Kingdom and Canada.

YORKSHIRE

FAMILY HISTORY FAIR

YORK RACECOURSE
KNAVESMIRE STAND
(UNDERCOVER)

SATURDAY 24TH JUNE 2000

10.00.A.M. TO 4.30.P.M.

Many Stalls including:

Society of Genealogists, Federation Publications
Family Tree Magazine, Local Archives,
Family History Societies from all over Great Britain
Maps, Postcards, Printouts,
New and Second-hand Microfiche Readers
Advice Table

FREE CAR PARKING

ADMISSION £2.00

Further Details from:
Mr A Sampson
1 Oxgang Close
Redcar
TS10 4ND
Tel: 01642 486615

NOTE FOR YOUR DIARY:

YEAR 2001 - YORKSHIRE FAMILY HISTORY FAIR
SATURDAY 23RD JUNE 2001

North West Group of Family History Societies

Family History Fair

Saturday 28th October 2000
10.00.a.m. to 4.30.p.m.

The Guild Hall
Preston, Lancashire

**Lectures
Throughout
The Day**

Details from:
Mr E W Gullick
4 Lawrence Avenue
Simonstone
Burnley
Lancashire
BB12 7HX
(Please Enclose S.A.E.)

Admission £1.50

On site Car Park
Refreshments Licensed Bar

Exhibitors:
Family History Societies
Local History Societies
Local Studies Libraries

Record Offices
Booksellers
Computeres
Recording Aids
Fiche Readers
Open University
Preservation

Keighley & District Family History Society

Family History Fair

Saturday 13th May 2000
10.00.a.m. to 4.00.p.m.
at

Details from:
Mrs S Daynes, 2 The Hallows
Shann Park, Keighley
West Yorkshire BD20 6HY

St Andrew's Church Hall
Newmarket Street
Skipton, West Yorkshire

Free Admission
Family History Societies
Bookstalls   Displays
Refreshments

Disclaimer

The Editors and Publishers of The Genealogical Services Directory make every effort to verify all information published. We cannot accept responsibilty for any errors or omissions or for any losses that may arise.

Advertisers are expected to provide a high standard of service to our readers. If there is a failure to provide such a service the Editors and Publishers reserve the right to refuse to accept advertising in future editions.

The Editors and Publishers cannot be held responsible for the errors, omissions or non performance by advertisers. Where an advertisers performance falls below an acceptable level readers are asked to notify The Genealogical Services Directory in writing.

The views and opinions expressed in each of the articles are those of the author and do not necessarily reflect the opinions of the Editors.

The Genealogist's & Family Historians Events Diary

2000

Date	Event	Location / Details
Sun, Mar 5, 2000	Family History Fairs	Royal Spa Centre, Royal Leamington Spa Tel: 01344 451479
Fri, Mar 10, 2000	The Commonwealth Gap 3 day Residential Course	Institute of Heraldic & Genealogical Studies at LSE
Sat, Mar 18, 2000	City of York & District FHS Silver Jubilee Day	The Priory Centre, Priory St, York
Sat, Mar 25, 2000	Dorset Family History Society Open Day	Details Brian Galpin, 72 Tatnam Road, Poole BH15 2DS
Sun, Mar 26, 2000	Family History Fairs	Hulme Hall, Port Sunlight, Wirral Details 01344 451479
Sat, Apr 1, 2000	Herefordshire FHS Family History Fair	Shire Hall, Hereford 10.00.a.m.
Sat, Apr 1, 2000	Cumbria FHS Family & Local History Fair	Trinity School, Carlisle 10.00.a.m. to 4.00.p.m. Details from Mrs J Arnison, Jack Dike, Cliburn,Penrith,Cumbria CA11 3AL
Sat, Apr 8, 2000	Computers in Genealogy & Family History Conference N E Group of FH Socs & The Society of Genealogists	Details: Mr J Le Seelleur, Bern Fold, 45b Ashgap Lane Normanton WF6 2DT
Sat, Apr 8, 2000	Codicote Local History Society - Family History Day	Details from: A E Jones, 34 Harkness Way, Hitchin, SG4 0QL
Apr 12 - 16, 2000	Millennium British F H Conference Wiltshire FHS	Bath University
Apr 14 - 16, 2000	GOONS 21st Anniversary AGM & Conference	
Sat, May 13, 2000	South Ayrshire History Fair Walker Hall, South Beach, Troon,	Details: Tel: 01292 288820
Sat, May 13, 2000	Keighley & District Family History Fair 10.00.a.m. to 4.00.p.m.	St Andrew's Church Hall, Newmarket Street, Skipton
Sat, June 3, 2000	2000 Phillimore Lecture The Scope of Local History Professor Margaret Spufford FBA	Stationers Hall, London at 1.30.p.m. Tickets & Details from BALH(GSD) PO Box 1576, Salisbury SP2 8SY
Jun 22 to 22 July 2000	York Millenium Mystery Plays York Minister 2000	Details: +44 (0) 1904 635444
Sat, Jun 24, 2000 to	Pomeroy Family Gathering	Infomation from 3 Stokehouse Street, Poundbury, Dorchester DT1 3GP
Sat, Jun 24, 2000	Yorkshire Family History Fair	The Racecourse, Knavesmire, York
Sat, Jul 1, 2000	East Anglian Group of FHS FH Fair & Conference	Swavesey Village College,Cambs
Sat, Jul 22, 2000	Buckinghamshire Family History Society Open Day	Aylesbury Grammar School, Walton Road, Aylesbury 10.00.am - 4.00.pm
Sat, Jul 22, 2000	Local & Family History Day Alsager Civic Centre	Details from 9 Woodgate Avenue Church Lawton ST7 3EF
Fri, Jul 28, 2000 to Thu, Aug 3, 2000	Stockton Society Millenium Renion	Details from The Secretary, 101 Woodthorpe Dr, Bewdley,DY12 2RL
Sat, Aug 5, 2000	East Midlands Family History Conference	Pears School, Repton, Derbyshire
Sun, Aug 6, 2000	Hillingdon Family History Fair 10.00.a.m. to 4.00.p.m.	The Great Barn, Ruislip, Middlesex Details from 20 Moreland Drive, Gerrards Cross, Buckis SL9 8BB
Wed, Sep 27, 2000 to Sun, Oct 1, 2000	9th Australian Congress on Genealogy & Heraldry	Perth, Western Australia, Keynote Conferences, PO BOx 1126, West Leederville, Western Australia 6901 Keynote@ca.com.au
Sat, Sep 30, 2000	West Yorkshire Archives Service Millennium Event	Leeds Town Hall, West Yorkshire http://www.archives.wyjs.org.uk
Sat, Oct 28, 2000	Millennium Family History Day Doncaster & District FHS	Details from Mrs June Staniforth, 125 The Grove, Wheatley Hills Doncaster DN2 5SN
Sat, Oct 28, 2000	North West Family History Fair The Guildhall, Preston Lancashire	10.00.am to 4.30.pm Admission £1.50 SAE to:Mr E Gullick,4 Lawrence Ave, Simonstone, Burnley, BB12 7HX

2001

Date	Event	Location / Details
Apr 6 to 8 Apr 2001	GOONS AGM & Conference	
Sat, Apr 14, 2001	Yesterday Belongs to You 5 Family & Local History Day	Durham Record Office, County Hall Durham, DH1 5UL
Sat, June 2, 2001	2001 Phillimore Lecture	Stationers Hall, London at 1.30.p.m. Tickets & Details from BALH(GSD) PO Box 1576, Salisbury SP2 8SY
Sat, Jun 23, 2001	Yorkshire Family History Fair	The Racecourse, Knavesmire, York
Sat, Jul 7, 2001	South West Family History Fair	Details: Miss Kerry James, 55 Osborne Rd, Weston S Mare,BS23 3EJ

2002

Date	Event	Location / Details
Sat, Jun 22, 2002	Yorkshire Family History Fair	The Racecourse, Knavesmire, York

Published by

G R Specialist Information Services

33 Nursery Road
Nether Poppleton
YORK
YO26 6NN
England

E Mail: publishers@genealogical.co.uk

WWW: http://www.genealogical.co.uk

First Edition Published 1997

Second Edition Published January 1998
Revised and Reprinted April 1998

Third Edition Published January 1999
Fourth Edition Published January 2000

ISSN 1368-9150
ISBN 0 9530297 3 5

Printed by
AWP
718 Ripponden Road
Oldham
OL4 2LP

A B M Publishing, 30, 78
Aberdeen & North East Scotland Family History Society, 134
Achievements (Established 1961), 60
Alan Godfrey Maps, 40
Ancestor Detective, 72
Ancestors in Nottinghamshire, 96
Ancestors of Dover Ltd, 60
Ancestral Locations, 60
Ancestral Research by Paul Lister, 72
Ancestral Trails, 88
AGRA, 18

Back to Roots, 198/199
Bayard Plastics Ltd, 210
BBC History 2000, 242
Beamish Museum, 70
Birmingham & Midland Society for Genealogy & Heraldry, 80
Bob Dobson Books, 94
Border Regiment Regt Museum, 176
Bradford Family History Society, 106
Brewster International, Inside Front cover
Brian Walker, 76
British Association Local History, 235, 236
British Directories on Microfiche, 44
British Records Association, 26
Broderbund Software Ltd, 50/51, 200/201
Buckinghamshire FHS, 83

Canterbury Research Services, 72
Caroline Gerard, 126
Carolynn Boucher, 72
CARW, 116
Centre for Kentish Studies Service, 92
Chapel Books, 118
Chess Valley A & Historical Society, 90
Chris E Makepeace, 92
Christine Foley Secretarial Services, 211
City of York FHS, 110
Cleveland Family History Society, 82
CO LEIS THU? Research Centre, 122
Colin Dale Researches (GSD), 160
Colin Davison Research, 80
Cornwall Family History Society, 54
Cottage Books, 160
Creative Digital Imaging, 28
Cumbria Family History Society, 84
Current Archaeology,
Currer Briggs Genealogical Index, 14
CW & S Parkinson (GSD), 26

David G C Burns Researcher, 126
David J Barnes (Military Research), 165
David Walker Photography, 207
Debrett Ancestry Research, 46, 76, 90
Don Steel: Family History Enterprises, 42
Doncaster & District FHS, 107
Donegal Ancestry, 144
Dundee City Genealogy Unit, 134
Dyfed Family History Society, 120

East Anglian Village Research, 86
East Midlands Ancestor, 52
Elizabeth Mortimer, 128
Embla AS (Family Treasurer), 194/195
Essex Record Office, 86

Family Chronicle Magazine, 155
Family History Fairs, 202
Family History Indexes, 22
Family History Monthly, 12
Family History Shop & Library, 94
Family Tree Services, 20, 52
Federation of FH Societies, 4, 71
Fine Detail Art, 186
Flyleaf Press, 144
Foreign Missions Club, 66
Friends of Historic Essex, 86

Gendocs, 74
GRD, Inside Back Cover
Genealogical Society of Victoria, 150
genealogyPro, 203
GENfair, 193

Geoff Nicholson, 102
Gill Blanchard, 94
Glamorgan Family History Society, 112
Glasgow Family History Society, 130
Gloucestershire FHS, 88
Gould Books, 148
GR Specialist Information Services, 11, 52
Grandpa Staten's Family History, 46
Gwen Kingsley, BA(Hons), 16

Herefordshire Family History Research, 16
Heritage World F. History Services, 145
Hertfordshire Archives, 91
Hertfordshire Family & P H Society, 90
Hidden Heritage, 87
Hilary Clare, 96
Hillingdon Family History Society, 212
Historical Research Associates, 144
Historical Research Ireland, 145
History Today Magazine,
Holts Tours Ltd, 164
Hull Family History Unit, 91

Ian J Hilder, BA(Hons), 76
Inst of Heraldic & Genealogical Studies, 39
Interlink Bookshop & Services, 156
Internet History Resources, 151
Irish Roots, 145
Isle of Man Family History Society, 90

Jane Hamby, 94
Janet & Bruce Bishop, 139
Janice O'Brien 74
Jayne Shrimpton, 161
Jennifer Day, 98
Joanne H Harvey, 156
John Adams, 126
John Dagger, 66
John S Griffiths, 96

Kathleen Wilshaw, BA, 96
Keighley Family History Society, 108, 356
Kin in Kent, 93
Kingfisher Booksearch, 26, 187
Kingpin (North Easterner Magazine), 102
Kinship Genealogical Research, 162

Lancashire Record Office, 273
Learning Company (UK) Ltd, 188, 192
Leicester Microdata Bureau Ltd, 28
Leicestershire Record Office, 95
Leitrim Genealogy Centre, 144
Len Barnett Research, 162
Leopard Magazine, 122
Leslie Hodgson, 126
Lincolnshire Family History Society, 94
Link Investigations, 160
Link Line Ancestral Research, 72
Linklines Genealogy, 105
Local History Press Limited, 34
Local History Publications, 44
Lochin Publishing, 32
London Bed & Breakfast, 187
Looking Back, 96
Loreley A Morling, 151
Lost Ancestors - Monumental Inscriptions, 44

Maggi Young, 92
Marathon Microfilming Ltd, 205
Marcorrie Hotel, 48
Marie Lynskey, 40
MC Research Service, 144
Merthyr Tydfil Historical Society, 114
Microfilm Shop, 204
MM Publications, 22
Montgomeryshire Gen Society, 114
Murder Files, 46

Name Shop, 18
National Library of Scotland, 130
National Library of Wales, 111
Naval & Military Press, 170
Neil Richardson, 102
New Zealand Genealogical Research, 152
Newport Reference Library, 118

Nicholas J Davey, 116
North Cheshire Family History Society, 84
North West Group Fam History Fairs, 356
Northern Writers Advisory Services, 84

Open University History Society, 14
Original Indexes, 102

P A & S Smith (Custodian), 197
Paperchase Research Services, 98
Parchment Oxford Limited, 206, 208
Patrick Yarnold Research, 72
Paul Blake, 64
People Search Tracing Services, 62
Peter F Gardner, 64
Picture Past, 14
Pinhorns, 62
Pomerology, 14
Powys Family History Society, 112
Printability Publishing Ltd, 102
Public Record Office of Northern Ireland,

R-CRAFT Bookbinding and Restoration/Conservation, 29
Real Life Recordings, 209
Red Cat Research, 74
Ripon Historical Soc & FHS Group, 109
Robert J Haines, BSc, 89
Root-Finder, 136
Roots Family History Service, 94
Rosemary Philip, 128
Rosie Taylor, 66

S & N Genealogy Supplies, 2
S A & M J Raymond, 44
Scots Ancestry Research Society, 130
Scots-Heritage of Auchterarder, 128
Scottish Genealogy Society, 121
Simon Neal, 98
Society of Genealogists, 56, 69, 70
Society of Indexers, 49
South African War 1899 - 1902, 165
Southern Counties Ancestry, 88
Staffs & Stoke Archive Service, 98
Staffordshire Knot Research, 98
Stepping Stones, 109
Stockdill Family History Society, 70
Sue Cleaves 98
Sue Comont Research Services, 96
Suffolk Record Office, 100
Sunset Militaria, 176
Susan Miller, 130
Sussex Family History Group, 212
Sutton Publishing, 360
Sydney G Smith, 66
Sylvia Hunt-Whitaker Research, 86

Tony Shopland Research, 84
Tree of Discovery, 74
Tree Tops, 14, 54, 57
Trueflare Ltd, 75

U.K. Searches, 62
UK Tracing Services, 74
Upper Carr Chalet & Touring Park, 354

Vanessa Morgan, 88
Victor Longhorn, 80
Victoria Walker, 84

War Research Society, 166
Welsh Ancestors, 116
Wendy Baker, 151
West Yorkshire Archive Service, 104
Wharfedale Family History Group, 108
Wiltshire Archaeological Society, 104
Wiltshire Index Service, 104
Windsor Ancestry Research, 58

York Accommodation, 187
York Minster Library Databank, 104
Yorkshire Archaeological Society, 109
Yorkshire Family History Fair, 355

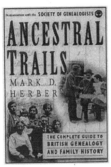
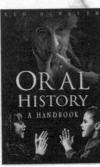